Blackstone's Statutes on

Evidence

18th edition

edited by

Amelia Shooter

LLB, LLM, PhD

Assistant Professor in Law, University of Nottingham

OXFORD
UNIVERSITY PRESS

OXFORD
UNIVERSITY PRESS

Great Clarendon Street, Oxford, OX2 6DP,
United Kingdom

Oxford University Press is a department of the University of Oxford.
It furthers the University's objective of excellence in research, scholarship,
and education by publishing worldwide. Oxford is a registered trade mark of
Oxford University Press in the UK and in certain other countries

First published by Blackstone Press 1991

Fifteenth edition 2018
Sixteenth edition 2020
Seventeenth edition 2023
Eighteenth edition 2026

Published in the United States of America by Oxford University Press
198 Madison Avenue, New York, NY 10016, United States of America

British Library Cataloguing in Publication Data
Data available

ISBN 978–0–19–897128–3

Printed in the UK by
Bell & Bain Ltd., Glasgow

Contents

Alphabetical contents

Chronological contents

Editor's preface

In the three years since the previous edition was published, the law of evidence has been subject to a steady but important tidying exercise. There are new editions of the Criminal Procedure Rules, PACE Codes C and D, and Disclosure Guidelines. As ever, there are minor updates to the Police and Criminal Evidence Act 1984, largely to reflect the creation of the National Security Act 2023. No legislation has been removed from this edition of the text, and there are no major additions—at the time of writing, the Courts and Tribunals Bill remains in parliamentary scrutiny. All materials within the edition have been revised and updated. Most of these materials have been reproduced in full, with omissions indicated by ellipses.

As a new editor, I would like to thank Kelly Lewars and Helen Swann at OUP for welcoming me, and for their patience and assistance in preparing this edition.

The law is as stated on 15 April 2026.

Amelia Shooter

New to this edition

The 18th edition of *Blackstone's Statutes on Evidence* has been fully revised and updated with all relevant legislation through to 15 April 2026 including:

- Updated Police and Criminal Evidence Act 1984
- PACE Code C (2023)
- PACE Code D (2023)
- Criminal Procedure Rules 2025
- Attorney General's Guidelines on Disclosure for investigators, prosecutors and defence practitioners 2024

Blackstone's Statutes
Unsurpassed in authority, reliability, and accuracy

The titles in the Blackstone's Statutes series are a collection of carefully reviewed and selected unannotated legislative material and official documents.

We make every effort to ensure titles in the series meet the needs of their target market. They are reviewed by lecturers to match university courses closely and are expertly edited to be manageable in size, whilst retaining their comprehensive coverage.

The editors only include material from legislation that will be valuable to students and lecturers and it is therefore abridged where necessary.

Conventions used in *Blackstone's Statutes on Evidence*

An ellipsis symbol . . . indicates text that has not been included in this edition.

The material in this book is reproduced in its most up-to-date form. Supplementary notes and details of amending provisions are generally not included.

All statutes have been enacted but some very recent legislation may not yet be in force.

Part I

Criminal Proceedings—Statutes

Criminal Procedure Act 1865

(1865, c. 18)

3 How far witnesses may be discredited by the party producing

A party producing a witness shall not be allowed to impeach his credit by general evidence of bad character; but he may, in case the witness shall in the opinion of the judge prove adverse, contradict him by other evidence, or, by leave of the judge, prove that he has made at other times a statement inconsistent with his present testimony; but before such last-mentioned proof can be given the circumstances of the supposed statement, sufficient to designate the particular occasion, must be mentioned to the witness, and he must be asked whether or not he has made such statement.

4 As to proof of contradictory statements of adverse witness

If a witness, upon cross-examination as to a former statement made by him relative to the subject matter of the indictment or proceeding, and inconsistent with his present testimony, does not distinctly admit that he has made such statement, proof may be given that he did in fact make it; but before such proof can be given the circumstances of the supposed statement, sufficient to designate the particular occasion, must be mentioned to the witness, and he must be asked whether or not he has made such statement.

5 Cross-examinations as to previous statements in writing

A witness may be cross-examined as to previous statements made by him in writing, or reduced into writing, relative to the subject matter of the indictment or proceeding, without such writing being shown to him; but if it is intended to contradict such witness by the writing, his attention must, before such contradictory proof can be given, be called to those parts of the writing which are to be used for the purpose of so contradicting him: Provided always, that it shall be competent for the judge, at any time during the trial, to require the production of the writing for his inspection, and he may thereupon make such use of it for the purposes of the trial as he may think fit.

6 Proof of conviction of witness may be given

(1) If upon a witness being lawfully questioned as to whether he has been convicted of any felony or misdemeanour, he either denies or does not admit the fact, or refuses to answer, it shall be lawful for the cross examining party to prove such conviction; and a certificate containing the substance and effect only (omitting the formal part) of the indictment and conviction for such offence, purporting to be signed by the proper officer of the court where the offender was convicted having the custody of the records of the court where the offender was convicted, or by the deputy of such clerk of officer, (for which certificate a fee of (25p) and no more shall be demanded or taken), shall upon proof of the identity of the person, be sufficient evidence of the said conviction, without proof of the signature or official character of the person appearing to have signed the same.

(2) In subsection (1) 'proper officer' means—

(a) in relation to a magistrates' court in England and Wales, the designated officer for the court; and

(b) in relation to any other court, the clerk of the court or other officer having the custody of the records of the court, or the deputy of such clerk or other officer.

Criminal Evidence Act 1898

(1898, c. 36)

1 Competency of witnesses in criminal cases

(1) A person charged in criminal proceedings shall not be called as a witness in the proceedings except upon his own application.

(2) Subject to section 101 of the Criminal Justice Act 2003 (admissibility of evidence of defendant's bad character), a person charged in criminal proceedings who is called as a witness in the proceedings may be asked any question in cross-examination notwithstanding that it would tend to criminate him as to any offence with which he is charged in the proceedings.

(4) Every person charged in criminal proceedings who is called as a witness in the proceedings shall, unless otherwise ordered by the court, give his evidence from the witness box or other place from which the other witnesses give their evidence.

2 Evidence of person charged

Where the only witness to the facts of the case called by the defence is the person charged, he shall be called as a witness immediately after the close of the evidence for the prosecution.

3 Right of reply

The fact that the person charged has been called as a witness shall not of itself confer on the prosecution the right of reply.

Perjury Act 1911

(1911, c. 6)

13 Corroboration

A person shall not be liable to be convicted of any offence against this Act, or of any offence declared by any other Act to be perjury or subornation of perjury, or to be punishable as perjury or subornation of perjury, solely upon the evidence of one witness as to the falsity of any statement alleged to be false.

14 Proof of certain proceedings on which perjury is assigned

On a prosecution—

(a) for perjury alleged to have been committed on the trial of an indictment for misdemeanour; or

(b) for procuring or suborning the commission of perjury on any such trial,

the fact of the former trial shall be sufficiently proved by the production of a certificate containing the substance and effect (omitting the formal parts) of the indictment and trial purporting to be signed by the clerk of the court, or other person having the custody of the records of the court where the indictment was tried, or by the deputy of that clerk or other person, without proof of the signature or official character of the clerk or person appearing to have signed the certificate.

Prevention of Crime Act 1953

(1953, c. 14)

1 Prohibition of the carrying of offensive weapons without lawful authority or reasonable excuse

(1) Any person who without lawful authority or reasonable excuse, the proof whereof shall lie on him, has with him in any public place any offensive weapon shall be guilty of an offence, and shall be liable—

- (a) on summary conviction, to imprisonment for a term not exceeding six months or a fine not exceeding £200 or both;
- (b) on conviction on indictment, to imprisonment for a term not exceeding four years or a fine . . . or both.

(2) Where any person is convicted of an offence under subsection (1) of this section the court may make an order for the forfeiture or disposal of any weapon in respect of which the offence was committed.

(2ZA) See section 315 of the Sentencing Code for provision about the sentence which the court may be required to impose where a person aged 16 or over who has a previous relevant conviction (within the meaning of that section) is convicted of an offence under this section.

(4) In this section 'public place' includes any highway . . . and any other premises or place to which at the material time the public have or are permitted to have access, whether on payment or otherwise; and 'offensive weapon' means any article made or adapted for use for causing injury to the person, or intended by the person having it with him for such use by him or by some other person.

Homicide Act 1957

(1957, c. 11)

2 Persons suffering from diminished responsibility

(1) A person ('D') who kills or is a party to the killing of another is not to be convicted of murder if D was suffering from an abnormality of mental functioning which—

- (a) arose from a recognised medical condition,
- (b) substantially impaired D's ability to do one or more of the things mentioned in subsection (1A), and
- (c) provides an explanation for D's acts and omissions in doing or being a party to the killing.

(1A) Those things are—

- (a) to understand the nature of D's conduct;
- (b) to form a rational judgment;
- (c) to exercise self-control.

(1B) For the purposes of subsection (1)(c), an abnormality of mental functioning provides an explanation for D's conduct if it causes, or is a significant contributory factor in causing, D to carry out that conduct.

(2) On a charge of murder, it shall be for the defence to prove that the person charged is by virtue of this section not liable to be convicted of murder.

(3) A person who but for this section would be liable, whether as principal or as accessory, to be convicted of murder shall be liable instead to be convicted of manslaughter.

(4) The fact that one party to a killing is by virtue of this section not liable to be convicted of murder shall not affect the question whether the killing amounted to murder in the case of any other party to it.

Criminal Justice Act 1967

(1967, c. 80)

9 Proof by written statement

(1) In any criminal proceedings, a written statement by any person shall, if such of the conditions mentioned in the next following subsection as are applicable are satisfied, be admissible as evidence to the like extent as oral evidence to the like effect by that person.

(2) The said conditions are—

(a) the statement purports to be signed by the person who made it;

(b) the statement contains a declaration by the person to the effect that it is true to the best of his knowledge and belief and that he made the statement knowing that, if it were tendered in evidence, he would be liable to prosecution if he wilfully stated in it anything which he knew to be false or did not believe to be true;

(c) before the hearing at which the statement is tendered in evidence, a copy of the statement is served, by or on behalf of the party proposing to tender it, on each of the other parties to the proceedings; and

(d) none of the other parties or their solicitors, within the relevant period serves a notice on the party so proposing objecting to the statement being tendered in evidence under this section:

Provided that the conditions mentioned in paragraphs (c) and (d) of this subsection shall not apply if the parties agree before or during the hearing that the statement shall be so tendered.

(2A) For the purposes of subsection (2)(d), 'the relevant period' is—

(a) such number of days, which may not be less than seven, from the service of the copy of the statement as may be prescribed by Criminal Procedure Rules, or

(b) if no such number is prescribed, seven days from the service of the copy of the statement.

(4) Notwithstanding that a written statement made by any person may be admissible as evidence by virtue of this section—

(a) the party by whom or on whose behalf a copy of the statement was served may call that person to give evidence; and

(b) the court may, of its own motion or on the application of any party to the proceedings, require that person to attend before the court and give evidence.

(5) An application under paragraph (b) of the last foregoing subsection to a court other than a magistrates' court may be made before the hearing and on any such application the powers of the court shall be exercisable

(a) by a puisne judge of the High Court, a Circuit judge or Recorder sitting alone; or

(b) subject to subsection (5A), by a qualifying judge advocate (within the meaning of the Senior Courts Act 1981) sitting alone.

(5A) Subsection (5)(b) applies only where the application in question is to the Crown Court.

(7) Any document or object referred to as an exhibit and identified in a written statement tendered in evidence under this section shall be treated as if it had been produced as an exhibit and identified in court by the maker of the statement.

10 Proof by formal admission

(1) Subject to the provisions of this section, any fact of which oral evidence may be given in any criminal proceedings may be admitted for the purpose of those proceedings by or on behalf of the prosecutor or defendant, and the admission by any party of any such fact under this section shall as against that party be conclusive evidence in those proceedings of the fact admitted.

(2) An admission under this section—

(a) may be made before or at the proceedings;

(b) if made otherwise than in court, shall be in writing;

(c) if made in writing by an individual, shall purport to be signed by the person making it and, if so made by a body corporate, shall purport to be signed by a director or manager, or the secretary or clerk, or some other similar officer of the body corporate;

(d) if made on behalf of a defendant who is an individual, shall be made by his counsel or solicitor;

(e) if made at any stage before the trial by a defendant who is an individual, must be approved by his counsel or solicitor (whether at the time it was made or subsequently) before or at the proceedings in question.

(3) An admission under this section for the purpose of proceedings relating to any matter shall be treated as an admission for the purpose of any subsequent criminal proceedings relating to that matter (including any appeal or retrial).

(4) An admission under this section may with the leave of the court be withdrawn in the proceedings for the purpose of which it is made or any subsequent criminal proceedings relating to the same matter.

Criminal Appeal Act 1968

(1968, c. 19)

PART I APPEAL TO COURT OF APPEAL IN CRIMINAL CASES

Appeal against conviction on indictment

1 Right of appeal

(1) Subject to subsection (3) below a person convicted of an offence on indictment may appeal to the Court of Appeal against his conviction.

(2) An appeal under this section lies only—

(a) with the leave of the Court of Appeal; or

(b) if, within 28 days of the date of conviction, the judge of the court of trial grants a certificate that the case is fit for appeal.

(3) Where a person is convicted before the Crown Court of a scheduled offence it shall not be open to him to appeal to the Court of Appeal against the conviction on the ground that the decision of the court which sent him to the Crown Court for trial as to the value involved was mistaken.

(4) In subsection (3) above 'scheduled offence' and 'the value involved' have the same meanings as they have in section 22 of the Magistrates' Courts Act 1980 (certain offences against property to be tried summarily if value of property or damage is small).

23 Evidence

(1) For the purposes of an appeal, or on an application for leave to appeal, under this Part of this Act the Court of Appeal may, if they think it necessary or expedient in the interests of justice—

(a) order the production of any document, exhibit or other thing connected with the proceedings, the production of which appears to them necessary for the determination of the case;

(b) order any witness to attend for examination and be examined before the Court (whether or not he was called in the proceedings from which the appeal lies); and

(c) receive any evidence which was not adduced in the proceedings from which the appeal lies.

(1A) The power conferred by subsection (1)(a) may be exercised so as to require the production of any document, exhibit or other thing mentioned in that subsection to—

(a) the Court;

(b) the appellant;

(c) the respondent.

(2) The Court of Appeal shall, in considering whether to receive any evidence, have regard in particular to—

(a) whether the evidence appears to the Court to be capable of belief;

(b) whether it appears to the Court that the evidence may afford any ground for allowing the appeal;

(c) whether the evidence would have been admissible in the proceedings from which the appeal lies on an issue which is the subject of the appeal; and

(d) whether there is a reasonable explanation for the failure to adduce the evidence in those proceedings.

(3) Subsection (1)(c) above applies to evidence of a witness (including the appellant) who is competent but not compellable.

(4) For the purposes of an appeal, or an application for leave to appeal, under this Part of this Act, the Court of Appeal may, if they think it necessary or expedient in the interests of justice, order the examination of any witness whose attendance might be required under subsection (1)(b) above to be conducted, in manner provided by rules of court, before any judge or officer of the Court or other person appointed by the Court for the purpose, and allow the admission of any depositions so taken as evidence before the Court.

(6) In this section, 'respondent' includes a person who will be a respondent if leave to appeal is granted.

Theft Act 1968

(1968, c. 60)

22 Handling stolen goods

(1) A person handles stolen goods if (otherwise than in the course of the stealing) knowing or believing them to be stolen goods he dishonestly receives the goods, or dishonestly undertakes or assists in their retention, removal, disposal or realisation by or for the benefit of another person, or if he arranges to do so.

(2) A person guilty of handling stolen goods shall on conviction on indictment be liable to imprisonment for a term not exceeding fourteen years.

25 Going equipped for stealing, etc.

(1) A person shall be guilty of an offence if, when not at his place of abode, he has with him any article for use in the course of or in connection with any burglary or theft.

(2) A person guilty of an offence under this section shall on conviction on indictment be liable to imprisonment for a term not exceeding three years.

(3) Where a person is charged with an offence under this section, proof that he had with him any article made or adapted for use in committing a burglary or theft shall be evidence that he had it with him for such use.

(5) For purposes of this section an offence under section 12(1) of this Act of taking a conveyance shall be treated as theft.

27 Evidence and procedure on charge of theft or handling stolen goods

(1) Any number of persons may be charged in one indictment, with reference to the same theft, with having at different times or at the same time handled all or any of the stolen goods, and the persons so charged may be tried together.

(2) On the trial of two or more persons indicted for jointly handling any stolen goods the jury may find any of the accused guilty if the jury are satisfied that he handled all or any of the stolen goods, whether or not he did so jointly with the other accused or any of them.

(3) Where a person is being proceeded against for handling stolen goods (but not for any offence other than handling stolen goods), then at any stage of the proceedings, if evidence has been given of his having or arranging to have in his possession the goods the subject of the charge, or of his undertaking or assisting in, or arranging to undertake or assist in, their retention, removal, disposal or realisation, the following evidence shall be admissible for the purpose of proving that he knew or believed the goods to be stolen goods:—

(a) evidence that he has had in his possession, or has undertaken or assisted in the retention, removal, disposal or realisation of, stolen goods from any theft taking place not earlier than twelve months before the offence charged; and

(b) (provided that seven days' notice in writing has been given to him of the intention to prove the conviction) evidence that he has within the five years preceding the date of the offence charged been convicted of theft or of handling stolen goods.

(4) In any proceedings for the theft of anything in the course of transmission (whether by post or otherwise), or for handling stolen goods from such a theft, a statutory declaration made by any person that he despatched or received or failed to receive any goods or postal packet, or that any goods or postal packet when despatched or received by him were in a particular state or condition, shall be admissible as evidence of the facts stated in the declaration, subject to the following conditions:—

(a) a statutory declaration shall only be admissible where and to the extent to which oral evidence to the like effect would have been admissible in the proceedings; and

(b) a statutory declaration shall only be admissible if at least seven days before the hearing or trial a copy of it has been given to the person charged, and he has not, at least three days before the hearing or trial or within such further time as the court may in special circumstances allow, given the prosecutor written notice requiring the attendance at the hearing or trial of the person making the declaration.

(5) This section is to be construed in accordance with section 24 of this Act; and in subsection (3)(b) above the reference to handling stolen goods shall include any corresponding offence committed before the commencement of this Act.

30 Spouses and civil partners

(1) This Act shall apply in relation to the parties to a marriage, and to property belonging to the wife or husband whether or not by reason of an interest derived from the marriage, as it would apply if they were not married and any such interest subsisted independently of the marriage.

(2) Subject to subsection (4) below, a person shall have the same right to bring proceedings against that person's wife or husband for any offence (whether under this Act or otherwise), as if they were not married and a person bringing any such proceedings shall be competent to give evidence for the prosecution at every stage of the proceedings.

(4) Proceedings shall not be instituted against a person for any offence of stealing or doing unlawful damage to property which at the time of the offence belongs to that person's wife or husband or civil partner, or for any attempt, incitement or conspiracy to commit such an offence, unless the proceedings are instituted by or with the consent of the Director of Public Prosecutions:

Provided that—

(a) this subsection shall not apply to proceedings against a person for an offence—

(i) if that person is charged with committing the offence jointly with the wife or husband or civil partner;

(ii) if by virtue of any judicial decree or order (wherever made) that person and the wife or husband are at the time of the offence under no obligation to cohabit; or

(iii) an order (wherever made) is in force providing for the separation of that person and his or her civil partner.

(5) Notwithstanding section 6 of the Prosecution of Offences Act 1979 subsection (4) of this section shall apply—

(a) to an arrest (if without warrant) made by the wife or husband or civil partner, and

(b) to a warrant of arrest issued on an information laid by the wife or husband or civil partner.

31 Effect on civil proceedings and rights

(1) A person shall not be excused, by reason that to do so may incriminate that person or the spouse or civil partner of that person of an offence under this Act—

(a) from answering any question put to that person in proceedings for the recovery or administration of any property, for the execution of any trust or for an account of any property or dealings with property; or

(b) from complying with any order made in any such proceedings;

but no statement or admission made by a person in answering a question put or complying with an order made as aforesaid shall, in proceedings for an offence under this Act, be admissible in evidence against that person or (unless they married or became civil partners after the making of the statement of admission) against the spouse or civil partner of that person.

(2) Notwithstanding any enactment to the contrary, where property has been stolen or obtained by fraud or other wrongful means, the title to that or any other property shall not be affected by reason only of the conviction of the offender.

Misuse of Drugs Act 1971

(1971, c. 38)

5 Restriction of possession of controlled drugs

(1) Subject to any regulations under section 7 of this Act for the time being in force, it shall not be lawful for a person to have a controlled drug in his possession.

(2) Subject to section 28 of this Act and to subsection (4) below, it is an offence for a person to have a controlled drug in his possession in contravention of subsection (1) above.

(2A) Subsections (1) and (2) do not apply in relation to a temporary class drug.

(3) Subject to section 28 of this Act, it is an offence for a person to have a controlled drug in his possession, whether lawfully or not, with intent to supply it to another in contravention of section 4(1) of this Act.

(4) In any proceedings for an offence under subsection (2) above in which it is proved that the accused had a controlled drug in his possession, it shall be a defence for him to prove—

(a) that, knowing or suspecting it to be a controlled drug, he took possession of it for the purpose of preventing another from committing or continuing to commit an offence in connection with that drug and that as soon as possible after taking possession of it he took all such steps as were reasonably open to him to destroy the drug or to deliver it into the custody of a person lawfully entitled to take custody of it; or

(b) that, knowing or suspecting it to be a controlled drug, he took possession of it for the purpose of delivering it into the custody of a person lawfully entitled to take custody of it and that as soon as possible after taking possession of it he took all such steps as were reasonably open to him to deliver it into the custody of such a person.

(6) Nothing in subsection (4) above shall prejudice any defence which it is open to a person charged with an offence under this section to raise apart from that subsection.

28 Proof of lack of knowledge etc. to be a defence in proceedings for certain offences

(1) This section applies to offences under any of the following provisions of this Act, that is to say section 4(2) and (3), section 5(2) and (3), section 6(2) and section 9.

(2) Subject to subsection (3) below, in any proceedings for an offence to which this section applies it shall be a defence for the accused to prove that he neither knew of nor suspected nor had reason to suspect the existence of some fact alleged by the prosecution which it is necessary for the prosecution to prove if he is to be convicted of the offence charged.

(3) Where in any proceedings for an offence to which this section applies it is necessary, if the accused is to be convicted of the offence charged, for the prosecution to prove that some substance or product involved in the alleged offence was the controlled drug which the prosecution alleges it to have been, and it is proved that the substance or product in question was that controlled drug, the accused—

(a) shall not be acquitted of the offence charged by reason only of proving that he neither knew nor suspected nor had reason to suspect that the substance or product in question was the particular controlled drug alleged; but

(b) shall be acquitted thereof—

(i) if he proves that he neither believed nor suspected nor had reason to suspect that the substance or product in question was a controlled drug; or

(ii) if he proves that he believed the substance or product in question to be a controlled drug, or a controlled drug of a description, such that, if it had in fact been that controlled drug or a controlled drug of that description, he would not at the material time have been committing any offence to which this section applies.

(4) Nothing in this section shall prejudice any defence which it is open to a person charged with an offence to which this section applies to raise apart from this section.

Magistrates' Courts Act 1980

(1980, c. 43)

98 Evidence on oath

Subject to the provisions of any enactment or rule of law authorising the reception of unsworn evidence, evidence given before a magistrates' court shall be given on oath.

101 Onus of proving exceptions, etc.

Where the defendant to an information or complaint relies for his defence on any exception, exemption, proviso, excuse or qualification, whether or not it accompanies the description of the offence or matter of complaint in the enactment creating the offence or on which the complaint is founded, the burden of proving the exception, exemption, proviso, excuse or qualification shall be on him; and this notwithstanding that the information or complaint contains an allegation negativing the exception, exemption, proviso, excuse or qualification.

104 Proof of previous convictions

Where a person is convicted of a summary offence by a magistrates' court, other than a youth court, and—

(a) it is proved to the satisfaction of the court, on oath or in such other manner as may be prescribed, that not less than 7 days previously a notice was served on the accused in the prescribed form and manner specifying any alleged previous conviction of the accused of a summary offence proposed to be brought to the notice of the court in the event of his conviction of the offence charged; and

(b) the accused is not present in person before the court,

the court may take account of any such previous conviction so specified as if the accused had appeared and admitted it.

107 False statements in declaration proving service, etc.

If, in any solemn declaration, certificate or other writing made or given for the purpose of its being used in pursuance of rules of court as evidence of the service of any document or the handwriting or seal of any person, a person makes a statement that he knows to be false in a material particular, or recklessly makes any statement that is false in a material particular, he shall be liable on summary conviction to imprisonment for a term not exceeding 6 months or a fine not exceeding level 3 on the standard scale or both.

Criminal Justice Act 1982

(1982, c. 48)

Unsworn statements

72 Abolition of right of accused to make unsworn statement

(1) Subject to subsections (2) and (3) below, in any criminal proceedings the accused shall not be entitled to make a statement without being sworn, and accordingly, if he gives evidence, he shall do so (subject to sections 55 and 56 of the Youth Justice and Criminal Evidence Act 1999) on oath and be liable to cross-examination; but this section shall not affect the right of the accused, if not represented by counsel or a solicitor, to address the court or jury otherwise than on oath on any matter on which, if he were so represented, counsel or a solicitor could address the court or jury on his behalf.

(2) Nothing in subsection (1) above shall prevent the accused making a statement without being sworn—

(a) if it is one which he is required by law to make personally; or

(b) if he makes it by way of mitigation before the court passes sentence upon him.

Police and Criminal Evidence Act 1984

(1984, c. 60)

PART II POWERS OF ENTRY, SEARCH AND SEIZURE

Search warrants

8 Power of justice of the peace to authorise entry and search of premises*

(1) If on an application made by a constable a justice of the peace is satisfied that there are reasonable grounds for believing—

(a) that an indictable offence has been committed; and

(b) that there is material on premises mentioned in subsection (1A) below which is likely to be of substantial value (whether by itself or together with other material) to the investigation of the offence; and

(c) that the material is likely to be relevant evidence; and

(d) that it does not consist of or include items subject to legal privilege, excluded material or special procedure material; and

(e) that any of the conditions specified in subsection (3) below applies,

he may issue a warrant authorising a constable to enter and search the premises in relation to each set of premises specified in the application.

(1A) The premises referred to in subsection (1)(b) above are—

(a) one or more sets of premises specified in the application (in which case the application is for a 'specific premises warrant'); or

(b) any premises occupied or controlled by a person specified in the application, including such sets of premises as are so specified (in which case the application is for an 'all premises warrant').

(1B) If the application is for an all premises warrant, the justice of the peace must also be satisfied—

(a) that because of the particulars of the offence referred to in paragraph (a) of subsection (1) above, there are reasonable grounds for believing that it is necessary to search premises occupied or controlled by the person in question which are not specified in the application in order to find the material referred to in paragraph (b) of that subsection; and

(b) that it is not reasonably practicable to specify in the application all the premises which he occupies or controls and which might need to be searched.

(1C) The warrant may authorise entry to and search of premises on more than one occasion if, on the application, the justice of the peace is satisfied that it is necessary to authorise multiple entries in order to achieve the purpose for which he issues the warrant.

(1D) If it authorises multiple entries, the number of entries authorised may be unlimited, or limited to a maximum.

(2) A constable may seize and retain anything for which a search has been authorised under subsection (1) above.

(3) The conditions mentioned in subsection (1)(e) above are—

(a) that it is not practicable to communicate with any person entitled to grant entry to the premises;

(b) that it is practicable to communicate with a person entitled to grant entry to the premises but it is not practicable to communicate with any person entitled to grant access to the evidence;

(c) that entry to the premises will not be granted unless a warrant is produced;

(d) that the purpose of a search may be frustrated or seriously prejudiced unless a constable arriving at the premises can secure immediate entry to them.

* **Editor's Note:** This section has effect in relation to powers of entry for the enforcement of social security offences, under the Social Security Administration Act 1992, section 109D and the Public Authorities (Fraud, Error and Recovery) Act 2025, section 7.

(4) In this Act 'relevant evidence', in relation to an offence, means anything that would be admissible in evidence at a trial for the offence.

(5) The power to issue a warrant conferred by this section is in addition to any such power otherwise conferred.

(6) This section applies in relation to a relevant offence (as defined in section 28D(4) of the Immigration Act 1971) as it applies in relation to an indictable offence.

(7) . . .*

9 Special provisions as to access**

(1) A constable may obtain access to excluded material or special procedure material for the purposes of a criminal investigation by making an application under Schedule 1 below and in accordance with that Schedule.

(2) Any Act (including a local Act) passed before this Act under which a search of premises for the purposes of a criminal investigation could be authorised by the issue of a warrant to a constable shall cease to have effect so far as it relates to the authorisation of searches—

(a) for items subject to legal privilege; or
(b) for excluded material; or
(c) for special procedure material consisting of documents or records other than documents.

(2A) . . .***

10 Meaning of 'items subject to legal privilege'****

(1) Subject to subsection (2) below, in this Act 'items subject to legal privilege' means—

(a) communications between a professional legal adviser and his client or any person representing his client made in connection with the giving of legal advice to the client;
(b) communications between a professional legal adviser and his client or any person representing his client or between such an adviser or his client or any such representative and any other person made in connection with or in contemplation of legal proceedings and for the purposes of such proceedings; and
(c) items enclosed with or referred to in such communications and made—
  (i) in connection with the giving of legal advice; or
  (ii) in connection with or in contemplation of legal proceedings and for the purposes of such proceedings,

when they are in the possession of a person who is entitled to possession of them.

(2) Items held with the intention of furthering a criminal purpose are not items subject to legal privilege.

11 Meaning of 'excluded material'*****

(1) Subject to the following provisions of this section, in this Act 'excluded material' means—

(a) personal records which a person has acquired or created in the course of any trade, business, profession or other occupation or for the purposes of any paid or unpaid office and which he holds in confidence;
(b) human tissue or tissue fluid which has been taken for the purposes of diagnosis or medical treatment and which a person holds in confidence;
(c) journalistic material which a person holds in confidence and which consists—
  (i) of documents; or
  (ii) of records other than documents.

(2) A person holds material other than journalistic material in confidence for the purposes of this section if he holds it subject—

* **Editor's Note:** Execution of process of English courts in Scotland.

** **Editor's Note:** This section has effect in relation to powers of entry for the enforcement of social security offences, under the Social Security Administration Act 1992, section 109D and the Public Authorities (Fraud, Error and Recovery) Act 2025, section 7.

*** **Editor's Note:** Execution of process of English courts in Scotland and Northern Ireland.

**** **Editor's Note:** This section has effect in relation to powers of entry for the enforcement of social security offences, under the Social Security Administration Act 1992, section 109D and the Public Authorities (Fraud, Error and Recovery) Act 2025, section 7.

***** **Editor's Note:** This section has effect in relation to powers of entry for the enforcement of social security offences, under the Social Security Administration Act 1992, section 109D and the Public Authorities (Fraud, Error and Recovery) Act 2025, section 7.

(a) to an express or implied undertaking to hold it in confidence; or

(b) to a restriction on disclosure or an obligation of secrecy contained in any enactment, including an enactment contained in an Act passed after this Act.

(3) A person holds journalistic material in confidence for the purposes of this section if—

(a) he holds it subject to such an undertaking, restriction or obligation; and

(b) it has been continuously held (by one or more persons) subject to such an undertaking, restriction or obligation since it was first acquired or created for the purposes of journalism.

12 Meaning of 'personal records'*

In this Part of this Act 'personal records' means documentary and other records concerning an individual (whether living or dead) who can be identified from them and relating—

(a) to his physical or mental health;

(b) to spiritual counselling or assistance given or to be given to him; or

(c) to counselling or assistance given or to be given to him, for the purposes of his personal welfare, by any voluntary organisation or by any individual who—

(i) by reason of his office or occupation has responsibilities for his personal welfare; or

(ii) by reason of an order of a court has responsibilities for his supervision.

13 Meaning of 'journalistic material'**

(1) Subject to subsection (2) below, in this Act 'journalistic material' means material acquired or created for the purposes of journalism.

(2) Material is only journalistic material for the purposes of this Act if it is in the possession of a person who acquired or created it for the purposes of journalism.

(3) A person who receives material from someone who intends that the recipient shall use it for the purposes of journalism is to be taken to have acquired it for those purposes.

14 Meaning of 'special procedure material'***

(1) In this Act 'special procedure material' means—

(a) material to which subsection (2) below applies; and

(b) journalistic material, other than excluded material.

(2) Subject to the following provisions of this section, this subsection applies to material, other than items subject to legal privilege and excluded material, in the possession of a person who—

(a) acquired or created it in the course of any trade, business, profession or other occupation or for the purpose of any paid or unpaid office; and

(b) holds it subject—

(i) to an express or implied undertaking to hold it in confidence; or

(ii) to a restriction or obligation such as is mentioned in section 11(2)(b) above.

(3) Where material is acquired—

(a) by an employee from his employer and in the course of his employment; or

(b) by a company from an associated company,

it is only special procedure material if it was special procedure material immediately before the acquisition.

(4) Where material is created by an employee in the course of his employment, it is only special procedure material if it would have been special procedure material had his employer created it.

(5) Where material is created by a company on behalf of an associated company, it is only special procedure material if it would have been special procedure material had the associated company created it.

(6) A company is to be treated as another's associated company for the purposes of this section if it would be so treated under section 449 of the Corporation Tax Act 2010.

* **Editor's Note:** This section has effect in relation to powers of entry for the enforcement of social security offences, under the Social Security Administration Act 1992, section 109D and the Public Authorities (Fraud, Error and Recovery) Act 2025, section 7.

** **Editor's Note:** This section has effect in relation to powers of entry for the enforcement of social security offences, under the Social Security Administration Act 1992, section 109D and the Public Authorities (Fraud, Error and Recovery) Act 2025, section 7.

*** **Editor's Note:** This section has effect in relation to powers of entry for the enforcement of social security offences, under the Social Security Administration Act 1992, section 109D and the Public Authorities (Fraud, Error and Recovery) Act 2025, section 7.

15 Search warrants—safeguards*

(1) This section and section 16 below have effect in relation to the issue to constables under any enactment, including an enactment contained in an Act passed after this Act, of warrants to enter and search premises; and an entry on or search of premises under a warrant is unlawful unless it complies with this section and section 16 below.

(2) Where a constable applies for any such warrant, it shall be his duty—

(a) to state—

(i) the ground on which he makes the application;

(ii) the enactment under which the warrant would be issued; and

(iii) if the application is for a warrant authorising entry and search on more than one occasion, the ground on which he applies for such a warrant, and whether he seeks a warrant authorising an unlimited number of entries, or (if not) the maximum number of entries desired;

(b) to specify the matters set out in subsection (2A) below; and

(c) to identify, so far as is practicable, the articles or persons to be sought.

(2A) The matters which must be specified pursuant to subsection (2)(b) above are—

(a) if the application relates to one or more sets of premises specified in the application, each set of premises which it is desired to enter and search;

(b) if the application relates to any premises occupied or controlled by a person specified in the application—

(i) as many sets of premises which it is desired to enter and search as it is reasonably practicable to specify;

(ii) the person who is in occupation or control of those premises and any others which it is desired to enter and search;

(iii) why it is necessary to search more premises than those specified under sub-paragraph (i); and

(iv) why it is not reasonably practicable to specify all the premises which it is desired to enter and search.

(3) An application for such a warrant shall be made ex parte and supported by an information in writing.

(4) The constable shall answer on oath any question that the justice of the peace or judge hearing the application asks him.

(5) A warrant shall authorise an entry on one occasion only unless it specifies that it authorises multiple entries.

(5A) If it specifies that it authorises multiple entries, it must also specify whether the number of entries authorised is unlimited, or limited to a specified maximum.

(6) A warrant—

(a) shall specify—

(i) the name of the person who applies for it;

(ii) the date on which it is issued;

(iii) the enactment under which it is issued; and

(iv) each set of premises to be searched, or (in the case of an all premises warrant) the person who is in occupation or control of premises to be searched, together with any premises under his occupation or control which can be specified and which are to be searched; and

(b) shall identify, so far as is practicable, the articles or persons to be sought.

(7) Two copies shall be made of a warrant which specifies only one set of premises and does not authorise multiple entries; and as many copies as are reasonably required may be made of any other kind of warrant.

(8) The copies shall be clearly certified as copies.

* **Editor's Note:** This section has effect in relation to powers of entry for the enforcement of social security offences, under the Social Security Administration Act 1992, section 109D and the Public Authorities (Fraud, Error and Recovery) Act 2025, section 7.

16 Execution of warrants*

(1) A warrant to enter and search premises may be executed by any constable.

(2) Such a warrant may authorise persons to accompany any constable who is executing it.

(2A) A person so authorised has the same powers as the constable whom he accompanies in respect of—

(a) the execution of the warrant, and

(b) the seizure of anything to which the warrant relates.

(2B) But he may exercise those powers only in the company, and under the supervision, of a constable.

(3) Entry and search under a warrant must be within three months from the date of its issue.

(3A) If the warrant is an all premises warrant, no premises which are not specified in it may be entered or searched unless a police officer of at least the rank of inspector has in writing authorised them to be entered.

(3B) No premises may be entered or searched for the second or any subsequent time under a warrant which authorises multiple entries unless a police officer of at least the rank of inspector has in writing authorised that entry to those premises.

(4) Entry and search under a warrant must be at a reasonable hour unless it appears to the constable executing it that the purpose of a search may be frustrated on an entry at a reasonable hour.

(5) Where the occupier of premises which are to be entered and searched is present at the time when a constable seeks to execute a warrant to enter and search them, the constable—

(a) shall identify himself to the occupier and, if not in uniform, shall produce to him documentary evidence that he is a constable;

(b) shall produce the warrant to him; and

(c) shall supply him with a copy of it.

(6) Where—

(a) the occupier of such premises is not present at the time when a constable seeks to execute such a warrant; but

(b) some other person who appears to the constable to be in charge of the premises is present,

subsection (5) above shall have effect as if any reference to the occupier were a reference to that other person.

(7) If there is no person who appears to the constable to be in charge of the premises, he shall leave a copy of the warrant in a prominent place on the premises.

(8) A search under a warrant may only be a search to the extent required for the purpose for which the warrant was issued.

(9) A constable executing a warrant shall make an endorsement on it stating—

(a) whether the articles or persons sought were found; and

(b) whether any articles were seized, other than articles which were sought

and, unless the warrant is a warrant specifying one set of premises only, he shall do so separately in respect of each set of premises entered and searched, which he shall in each case state in the endorsement.

(10) A warrant shall be returned to the appropriate person mentioned in subsection (10A) below—

(a) when it has been executed; or

(b) in the case of a specific premises warrant which has not been executed, or an all premises warrant, or any warrant authorising multiple entries, upon the expiry of the period of three months referred to in subsection (3) above or sooner.

(10A) The appropriate person is—

(a) if the warrant was issued by a justice of the peace, the designated officer for the local justice area in which the justice was acting when he issued the warrant;

* **Editor's Note:** This section has effect in relation to powers of entry for the enforcement of social security offences, under the Social Security Administration Act 1992, section 109D and the Public Authorities (Fraud, Error and Recovery) Act 2025, section 7.

(b) if it was issued by a judge, the appropriate officer of the court from which he issued it.

(11) A warrant which is returned under subsection (10) above shall be retained for 12 months from its return—

(a) by the designated officer for the local justice area, if it was returned under paragraph (i) of that subsection; and

(b) by the appropriate officer, if it was returned under paragraph (ii).

(12) If during the period for which a warrant is to be retained the occupier of premises to which it relates asks to inspect it, he shall be allowed to do so.

Entry and search without search warrant

17 Entry for purpose of arrest etc.

(1) Subject to the following provisions of this section, and without prejudice to any other enactment, a constable may enter and search any premises for the purpose—

(a) of executing—

(i) a warrant of arrest issued in connection with or arising out of criminal proceedings; or

(ii) a warrant of commitment issued under section 76 of the Magistrates' Courts Act 1980;

(b) of arresting a person for an indictable offence;

(c) of arresting a person for an offence under—

(i) section 1 (prohibition of uniforms in connection with political objects), of the Public Order Act 1936;

(ii) any enactment contained in sections 6 to 8 or 10 of the Criminal Law Act 1977 (offences relating to entering and remaining on property);

(iii) section 4 of the Public Order Act 1986 (fear or provocation of violence);

(iiia) section 4 (driving etc. when under influence of drink or drugs) or 163 (failure to stop when required to do so by constable in uniform) of the Road Traffic Act 1988;

(iiib) section 27 of the Transport and Works Act 1992 (which relates to offences involving drink or drugs);

(iv) section 76 of the Criminal Justice and Public Order Act 1994 (failure to comply with interim possession order);

(v) any of the sections 4, 5, 6(1) and (2), 7 and 8(1) and (2) of the Animal Welfare Act 2006 (offences relating to the prevention of harm to animals);

(vi) section 144 of the Legal Aid, Sentencing and Punishment of Offenders Act 2012 (squatting in a residential building);

(cza) of arresting a person who the constable has reasonable grounds for believing is in breach of a domestic abuse protection notice given under section 22 of the Domestic Abuse Act 2021.

(ca) of arresting, in pursuance of section 32(1A) of the Children and Young Persons Act 1969, any child or young person who has been remanded to local authority accommodation or youth detention accommodation under section 91 of the Legal Aid, Sentencing and Punishment of Offenders Act 2012;

(caa) of arresting a person for an offence to which section 61 of the Animal Health Act 1981 applies;

(cab) of arresting a person under any of the following provisions—

(i) section 30D(1) or (2A);

(ii) section 46A(1) or (1A);

(iii) section 5B(7) of the Bail Act 1976 (arrest where a person fails to surrender to custody in accordance with a court order);

(iv) section 7(3) of the Bail Act 1976 (arrest where a person is not likely to surrender to custody etc);

(v) section 97(1) of the Legal Aid, Sentencing and Punishment of Offenders Act 2012 (arrest where a child is suspected of breaking conditions of remand);

(cb) of recapturing any person who is, or is deemed for any purpose to be, unlawfully at large while liable to be detained—

(i) in a prison, young offender institution, secure training centre or secure college, or

(ii) in pursuance of section 92 of the Powers of Criminal Courts (Sentencing) Act 2000 or section 260 of the Sentencing Code (dealing with children and young persons guilty of grave crimes), in any other place.

(d) of recapturing any person whatever who is unlawfully at large and whom he is pursuing; or

(e) of saving life or limb or preventing serious damage to property.

(2) Except for the purpose specified in paragraph (e) of subsection (1) above, the powers of entry and search conferred by this section—

(a) are only exercisable if the constable has reasonable grounds for believing that the person whom he is seeking is on the premises; and

(b) are limited, in relation to premises consisting of two or more separate dwellings, to powers to enter and search—

(i) any parts of the premises which the occupiers of any dwelling comprised in the premises use in common with the occupiers of any other such dwelling; and

(ii) any such dwelling in which the constable has reasonable grounds for believing that the person whom he is seeking may be.

(3) The powers of entry and search conferred by this section are only exercisable for the purposes specified in subsection (1)(c)(ii) (iv) or (vi) above by a constable in uniform.

(4) The power of search conferred by this section is only a power to search to the extent that is reasonably required for the purpose for which the power of entry is exercised.

(5) Subject to subsection (6) below, all the rules of common law under which a constable has power to enter premises without a warrant are hereby abolished.

(6) Nothing in subsection (5) above affects any power of entry to deal with or prevent a breach of the peace.

18 Entry and search after arrest

(1) Subject to the following provisions of this section, a constable may enter and search any premises occupied or controlled by a person who is under arrest for an indictable offence, if he has reasonable grounds for suspecting that there is on the premises evidence, other than items subject to legal privilege, that relates—

(a) to that offence; or

(b) to some other indictable offence which is connected with or similar to that offence.

(2) A constable may seize and retain anything for which he may search under subsection (1) above.

(3) The power to search conferred by subsection (1) above is only a power to search to the extent that is reasonably required for the purpose of discovering such evidence.

(4) Subject to subsection (5) below, the powers conferred by this section may not be exercised unless an officer of the rank of inspector or above has authorised them in writing.

(5) A constable may conduct a search under subsection (1)—

(a) before the person is taken to a police station or released under section 30A, and

(b) without obtaining an authorisation under subsection (4),

if the condition in subsection (5A) is satisfied.

(5A) The condition is that the presence of the person at a place (other than a police station) is necessary for the effective investigation of the offence.

(6) If a constable conducts a search by virtue of subsection (5) above, he shall inform an officer of the rank of inspector or above that he has made the search as soon as practicable after he has made it.

(7) An officer who—

(a) authorises a search; or

(b) is informed of a search under subsection (6) above,

shall make a record in writing—

(i) of the grounds for the search; and

(ii) of the nature of the evidence that was sought.

(8) If the person who was in occupation or control of the premises at the time of the search is in police detention at the time the record is to be made, the officer shall make the record as part of his custody record.

Seizure etc.

19 General power of seizure etc.*

(1) The powers conferred by subsections (2), (3) and (4) below are exercisable by a constable who is lawfully on any premises.

(2) The constable may seize anything which is on the premises if he has reasonable grounds for believing—

(a) that it has been obtained in consequence of the commission of an offence; and

(b) that it is necessary to seize it in order to prevent it being concealed, lost, damaged, altered or destroyed.

(3) The constable may seize anything which is on the premises if he has reasonable grounds for believing—

(a) that it is evidence in relation to an offence which he is investigating or any other offence; and

(b) that it is necessary to seize it in order to prevent the evidence being concealed, lost, altered or destroyed.

(4) The constable may require any information which is stored in any electronic form and is accessible from the premises to be produced in a form in which it can be taken away and in which it is visible and legible or from which it can readily be produced in a visible and legible form if he has reasonable grounds for believing—

(a) that—

(i) it is evidence in relation to an offence which he is investigating or any other offence; or

(ii) it has been obtained in consequence of the commission of an offence; and

(b) that it is necessary to do so in order to prevent it being concealed, lost, tampered with or destroyed.

(5) The powers conferred by this section are in addition to any power otherwise conferred.

(6) No power of seizure conferred on a constable under any enactment (including an enactment contained in an Act passed after this Act) is to be taken to authorise the seizure of an item which the constable exercising the power has reasonable grounds for believing to be subject to legal privilege.

20 Extension of powers of seizure to computerised information**

(1) Every power of seizure which is conferred by an enactment to which this section applies on a constable who has entered premises in the exercise of a power conferred by an enactment shall be construed as including a power to require any information stored in any electronic form and accessible from the premises to be produced in a form in which it can be taken away and in which it is visible and legible or from which it can readily be produced in a visible and legible form.

(2) This section applies—

(a) to any enactment contained in an Act passed before this Act;

(b) to sections 8 and 18 above;

* **Editor's Note:** This section has effect in relation to powers of entry for the enforcement of social security offences, under the Social Security Administration Act 1992, section 109D and the Public Authorities (Fraud, Error and Recovery) Act 2025, section 7.

** **Editor's Note:** This section has effect in relation to powers of entry for the enforcement of social security offences, under the Social Security Administration Act 1992, section 109D and the Public Authorities (Fraud, Error and Recovery) Act 2025, section 7.

(c) to paragraph 13 of Schedule 1 to this Act; and
(d) to any enactment contained in an Act passed after this Act.

21 Access and copying*

(1) A constable who seizes anything in the exercise of a power conferred by any enactment, including an enactment contained in an Act passed after this Act, shall, if so requested by a person showing himself—

(a) to be the occupier of premises on which it was seized; or
(b) to have had custody or control of it immediately before the seizure,

provide that person with a record of what he seized.

(2) The officer shall provide the record within a reasonable time from the making of the request for it.

(3) Subject to subsection (8) below, if a request for permission to be granted access to anything which—

(a) has been seized by a constable; and
(b) is retained by the police for the purpose of investigating an offence,

is made to the officer in charge of the investigation by a person who had custody or control of the thing immediately before it was so seized or by someone acting on behalf of such a person, the officer shall allow the person who made the request access to it under the supervision of a constable.

(4) Subject to subsection (8) below, if a request for a photograph or copy of any such thing is made to the officer in charge of the investigation by a person who had custody or control of the thing immediately before it was so seized, or by someone acting on behalf of such a person, the officer shall—

(a) allow the person who made the request access to it under the supervision of a constable for the purpose of photographing or copying it; or
(b) photograph or copy it, or cause it to be photographed or copied.

(5) A constable may also photograph or copy, or have photographed or copied, anything which he has power to seize, without a request being made under subsection (4) above.

(6) Where anything is photographed or copied under subsection (4)(b) above, the photograph or copy shall be supplied to the person who made the request.

(7) The photograph or copy shall be so supplied within a reasonable time from the making of the request.

(8) There is no duty under this section to grant access to, or to supply a photograph or copy of, anything if the officer in charge of the investigation for the purposes of which it was seized has reasonable grounds for believing that to do so would prejudice—

(a) that investigation;
(b) the investigation of an offence other than the offence for the purposes of investigating which the thing was seized; or
(c) any criminal proceedings which may be brought as a result of—
 (i) the investigation of which he is in charge; or
 (ii) any such investigation as is mentioned in paragraph (b) above.

(9) The references to a constable in subsections (1), (2), (3)(a) and (5) include a person authorised under section 16(2) to accompany a constable executing a warrant.

(10) The references to a constable in subsections (1) and (2) do not include a constable who has seized a thing under paragraph 19ZE of Schedule 3 to the Police Reform Act 2002.

22 Retention**

(1) Subject to subsection (4) below, anything which has been seized by a constable or taken away by a constable following a requirement made by virtue of section 19 or 20 above may be retained so long as is necessary in all the circumstances.

* **Editor's Note:** This section has effect in relation to powers of entry for the enforcement of social security offences, under the Social Security Administration Act 1992, section 109D and the Public Authorities (Fraud, Error and Recovery) Act 2025, section 7.

** **Editor's Note:** This section has effect in relation to powers of entry for the enforcement of social security offences, under the Social Security Administration Act 1992, section 109D and the Public Authorities (Fraud, Error and Recovery) Act 2025, section 7.

(2) Without prejudice to the generality of subsection (1) above—

(a) anything seized for the purposes of a criminal investigation may be retained, except as provided by subsection (4) below,—

(i) for use as evidence at a trial for an offence; or

(ii) for forensic examination or for investigation in connection with an offence; and

(b) anything may be retained in order to establish its lawful owner, where there are reasonable grounds for believing that it has been obtained in consequence of the commission of an offence.

(3) Nothing seized on the ground that it may be used—

(a) to cause physical injury to any person;

(b) to damage property;

(c) to interfere with evidence; or

(d) to assist in escape from police detention or lawful custody,

may be retained when the person from whom it was seized is no longer in police detention or the custody of a court or is in the custody of a court but has been released on bail.

(4) Nothing may be retained for either of the purposes mentioned in subsection (2)(a) above if a photograph or copy would be sufficient for that purpose.

(5) Nothing in this section affects any power of a court to make an order under section 1 of the Police (Property) Act 1897.

(6) This section also applies to anything retained by the police under section 28H(5) of the Immigration Act 1971.

(7) The reference in subsection (1) to anything seized by a constable includes anything seized by a person authorised under section 16(2) to accompany a constable executing a warrant.

Supplementary

23 Meaning of 'premises' etc.*

In this Act—

'premises' includes any place and, in particular, includes—

(a) any vehicle, vessel, aircraft or hovercraft;

(b) any offshore installation;

(ba) any renewable energy installation;

(c) any tent or movable structure.

'offshore installation' has the meaning given to it by section 1 of the Mineral Workings (Offshore Installations) Act 1971.

'renewable energy installation' has the same meaning as in Chapter 2 of Part 2 of the Energy Act 2004.

PART III ARREST

24 Arrest without warrant: constables

(1) A constable may arrest without a warrant—

(a) anyone who is about to commit an offence;

(b) anyone who is in the act of committing an offence;

(c) anyone whom he has reasonable grounds for suspecting to be about to commit an offence;

(d) anyone whom he has reasonable grounds for suspecting to be committing an offence.

* **Editor's Note:** This section has effect in relation to powers of entry for the enforcement of social security offences, under the Social Security Administration Act 1992, section 109D and the Public Authorities (Fraud, Error and Recovery) Act 2025, section 7.

(2) If a constable has reasonable grounds for suspecting that an offence has been committed, he may arrest without a warrant anyone whom he has reasonable grounds to suspect of being guilty of it.

(3) If an offence has been committed, a constable may arrest without a warrant—

(a) anyone who is guilty of the offence;

(b) anyone whom he has reasonable grounds for suspecting to be guilty of it.

(4) But the power of summary arrest conferred by subsection (1), (2) or (3) is exercisable only if the constable has reasonable grounds for believing that for any of the reasons mentioned in subsection (5) it is necessary to arrest the person in question.

(5) The reasons are—

(a) to enable the name of the person in question to be ascertained (in the case where the constable does not know, and cannot readily ascertain, the person's name, or has reasonable grounds for doubting whether a name given by the person as his name is his real name);

(b) correspondingly as regards the person's address;

(c) to prevent the person in question—

(i) causing physical injury to himself or any other person;

(ii) suffering physical injury;

(iii) causing loss of or damage to property;

(iv) committing an offence against public decency (subject to subsection (6)); or

(v) causing an unlawful obstruction of the highway;

(d) to protect a child or other vulnerable person from the person in question;

(e) to allow the prompt and effective investigation of the offence or of the conduct of the person in question;

(f) to prevent any prosecution for the offence from being hindered by the disappearance of the person in question.

(6) Subsection (5)(c)(iv) applies only where members of the public going about their normal business cannot reasonably be expected to avoid the person in question.

24A Arrest without warrant: other persons*

(1) A person other than a constable may arrest without a warrant—

(a) anyone who is in the act of committing an indictable offence;

(b) anyone whom he has reasonable grounds for suspecting to be committing an indictable offence.

(2) Where an indictable offence has been committed, a person other than a constable may arrest without a warrant—

(a) anyone who is guilty of the offence;

(b) anyone whom he has reasonable grounds for suspecting to be guilty of it.

(3) But the power of summary arrest conferred by subsection (1) or (2) is exercisable only if—

(a) the person making the arrest has reasonable grounds for believing that for any of the reasons mentioned in subsection (4) it is necessary to arrest the person in question; and

(b) it appears to the person making the arrest that it is not reasonably practicable for a constable to make it instead.

(4) The reasons are to prevent the person in question—

(a) causing physical injury to himself or any other person;

(b) suffering physical injury;

(c) causing loss of or damage to property; or

(d) making off before a constable can assume responsibility for him.

(5) This section does not apply in relation to an offence under Part 3 or 3A of the Public Order Act 1986.

* **Editor's Note:** The operation of this section is restricted by the provisions of SI 2012/1917.

26 Repeal of statutory powers of arrest without warrant or order

(1) Subject to subsection (2) below, so much of any Act (including a local Act) passed before this Act as enables a constable—

(a) to arrest a person for an offence without a warrant; or

(b) to arrest a person otherwise than for an offence without a warrant or an order of a court,

shall cease to have effect.

(2) Nothing in subsection (1) above affects the enactments specified in Schedule 2 to this Act.

27 Fingerprinting of certain offenders

(4) The Secretary of State may by regulations make provision for recording in national police records convictions for such offences as are specified in the regulations.

(4A) In subsection (4) 'conviction' includes—

(a) a caution within the meaning of Part 5 of the Police Act 1997; and

(b) a reprimand or warning given under section 65 of the Crime and Disorder Act 1998.

(5) Regulations under this section shall be made by statutory instrument and shall be subject to annulment in pursuance of a resolution of either House of Parliament.

28 Information to be given on arrest

(1) Subject to subsection (5) below, where a person is arrested, otherwise than by being informed that he is under arrest, the arrest is not lawful unless the person arrested is informed that he is under arrest as soon as is practicable after his arrest.

(2) Where a person is arrested by a constable, subsection (1) above applies regardless of whether the fact of the arrest is obvious.

(3) Subject to subsection (5) below, no arrest is lawful unless the person arrested is informed of the ground for the arrest at the time of, or as soon as is practicable after, the arrest.

(4) Where a person is arrested by a constable, subsection (3) above applies regardless of whether the ground for the arrest is obvious.

(5) Nothing in this section is to be taken to require a person to be informed—

(a) that he is under arrest; or

(b) of the ground for the arrest,

if it was not reasonably practicable for him to be so informed by reason of his having escaped from arrest before the information could be given.

29 Voluntary attendance at police station etc.

Where for the purpose of assisting with an investigation a person attends voluntarily at a police station or at any other place where a constable is present or accompanies a constable to a police station or any such other place without having been arrested—

(a) he shall be entitled to leave at will unless he is placed under arrest;

(b) he shall be informed at once that he is under arrest if a decision is taken by a constable to prevent him from leaving at will.

30 Arrest elsewhere than at police station

(1) Subsection (1A) applies where a person is, at any place other than a police station—

(a) arrested by a constable for an offence, or

(b) taken into custody by a constable after being arrested for an offence by a person other than a constable.

(1A) The person must be taken by a constable to a police station as soon as practicable after the arrest.

(1B) Subsection (1A) has effect subject to section 30A (release of a person arrested elsewhere than at police station) and subsection (7) (release without bail).

(2) Subject to subsections (3) and (5) below, the police station to which an arrested person is taken under subsection (1A) above shall be a designated police station.

(3) A constable to whom this subsection applies may take an arrested person to any police station unless it appears to the constable that it may be necessary to keep the arrested person in police detention for more than six hours.

(4) Subsection (3) above applies—

(a) to a constable who is working in a locality covered by a police station which is not a designated police station; and

(b) to a constable belonging to a body of constables maintained by an authority other than a local policing body.

(5) Any constable may take an arrested person to any police station if—

(a) either of the following conditions is satisfied—

(i) the constable has arrested him without the assistance of any other constable and no other constable is available to assist him;

(ii) the constable has taken him into custody from a person other than a constable without the assistance of any other constable and no other constable is available to assist him; and

(b) it appears to the constable that he will be unable to take the arrested person to a designated police station without the arrested person injuring himself, the constable or some other person.

(6) If the first police station to which an arrested person is taken after his arrest is not a designated police station, he shall be taken to a designated police station not more than six hours after his arrival at the first police station unless he is released previously.

(7) A person arrested by a constable at any place other than a police station must be released without bail if the condition in subsection (7A) is satisfied.

(7A) The condition is that, at any time before the person arrested reaches a police station, a constable is satisfied that there are no grounds for keeping him under arrest.

(8) A constable who releases a person under subsection (7) above shall record the fact that he has done so.

(9) The constable shall make the record as soon as is practicable after the release.

(10) Nothing in subsection (1A) or in section 30A prevents a constable delaying taking a person to a police station or releasing him under section 30A if the condition in subsection (10A) is satisfied.

(10A) The condition is that the presence of the person at a place (other than a police station) is necessary in order to carry out such investigations as it is reasonable to carry out immediately.

(11) Where there is any such delay the reasons for the delay must be recorded when the person first arrives at the police station or (as the case may be) is released under section 30A.

(12) Nothing in subsection (1A) or section 30A above shall be taken to affect—

(a) paragraphs 16(3) or 18(1) of Schedule 2 to the Immigration Act 1971;

(b) section 34(1) of the Criminal Justice Act 1972;

(c) any provision of the Terrorism Act 2000; or

(d) section 27 of and Schedule 6 to the National Security Act 2023.

(13) Nothing in subsection (10) above shall be taken to affect paragraph 18(3) of Schedule 2 to the Immigration Act 1971.

30A Release of a person arrested elsewhere than at police station

(1) If subsection (1A) applies, a constable may release on bail a person who is arrested or taken into custody in the circumstances mentioned in section 30(1).

(1A) This subsection applies if—

(a) the constable is satisfied that releasing the person on bail is necessary and proportionate in all the circumstances (having regard, in particular, to any conditions of bail which would be imposed), and

(b) a custody officer authorises the release on bail (having considered any representations made by the person).

(1B) In determining whether releasing the person on bail is necessary and proportionate in all the circumstances, the constable must have regard in particular to—

(a) the need to secure that the person surrenders to custody,

(b) the need to prevent offending by the person,

(c) the need to safeguard victims of crime and witnesses, taking into account any vulnerabilities of any alleged victim of, or alleged witness to, the offence for which the person was arrested where these vulnerabilities have been identified by the constable,

(d) the need to safeguard the person, taking into account any vulnerabilities of the person where these vulnerabilities have been identified by the constable, and

(e) the need to manage risks to the public.

(1C) If subsection (1A) does not apply, a constable may release without bail a person who is arrested or taken into custody in the circumstances mentioned in section 30(1).

(2) A person may be released under subsection (1) or (1C) at any time before he arrives at a police station.

(3) A person released on bail under subsection (1) must be required to attend a police station.

(3A) Where a constable releases a person on bail under subsection (1)—

(a) no recognizance for the person's surrender to custody shall be taken from the person,

(b) no security for the person's surrender to custody shall be taken from the person or from anyone else on the person's behalf,

(c) the person shall not be required to provide a surety or sureties for his surrender to custody, and

(d) no requirement to reside in a bail hostel may be imposed as a condition of bail.

(3B) Subject to subsection (3A), where a constable releases a person on bail under subsection (1) the constable may impose, as conditions of the bail, such requirements as appear to the constable to be necessary—

(a) to secure that the person surrenders to custody,

(b) to secure that the person does not commit an offence while on bail,

(c) to secure that the person does not interfere with witnesses or otherwise obstruct the course of justice, whether in relation to himself or any other person, or

(d) for the person's own protection or, if the person is under the age of 18, for the person's own welfare or in the person's own interests.

(4) Where a person is released on bail under subsection (1), a requirement may be imposed on the person as a condition of bail only under the preceding provisions of this section.

(5) The police station which the person is required to attend may be any police station.

30B Section 30A: notices

(1) Where a constable releases a person under section 30A, he must give that person a notice in writing before he is released.

(2) The notice must state—

(a) the offence for which he was arrested,

(b) the ground on which he was arrested, and

(c) whether the person is being released without bail or on bail.

(3) A notice given to a person who is released on bail must inform him that he is required to attend a police station.

(4) The notice must also specify—

(a) the police station which the person is required to attend, and

(b) the time on the bail end date when the person is required to attend the police station.

(4A) If the person is granted bail subject to conditions under section 30A(3B), the notice also—

(a) must specify the requirements imposed by those conditions,

(b) must explain the opportunities under sections 30CA(1) and 30CB(1) for variation of those conditions,

(6) The person may be required to attend a different police station from that specified in the notice under subsection (1) or (5) or to attend at a different time or an additional time.

(6A) A person may not be required under subsection 6 to attend a police station at a time which is after the bail end date in relation to the person.

(7) He must be given notice in writing of any such change as is mentioned in subsection (6) but more than one such notice may be given to him.

(8) In this section 'bail end date', in relation to a person, means the last day of the period of 3 months beginning with the day after the day on which the person was arrested for the offence in relation to which bail is granted under section 30A.

30C Section 30A: supplemental

(1) A person who has been required to attend a police station is not required to do so if he is given notice in writing that his attendance is no longer required.

(2) If a person is required to attend a police station which is not a designated police station he must be—

(a) released, or

(b) taken to a designated police station,

not more than six hours after his arrival.

(3) Nothing in the Bail Act 1976 applies in relation to bail under section 30A.

(4) Nothing in section 30A or 30B or in this section prevents the re-arrest without a warrant of a person released under section 30A if, since the person's release, new evidence has come to light or an examination or analysis of existing evidence has been made which could not reasonably have been made before the person's release.

30CA Bail under section 30A: variation of conditions by police

(1) Where a person released on bail under section 30A(1) is on bail subject to conditions—

(a) a relevant officer at the police station at which the person is required to attend,

may, at the request of the person but subject to subsection (2), vary the conditions.

(2) On any subsequent request made in respect of the same grant of bail, subsection (1) confers power to vary the conditions of the bail only if the request is based on information that, in the case of the previous request or each previous request, was not available to the relevant officer considering that previous request when he was considering it.

(3) Where conditions of bail granted to a person under section 30A(1) are varied under subsection (1)—

(a) paragraphs (a) to (d) of section 30A(3A) apply,

(b) requirements imposed by the conditions as so varied must be requirements that appear to the relevant officer varying the conditions to be necessary for any of the purposes mentioned in paragraphs (a) to (d) of section 30A(3B), and

(c) the relevant officer who varies the conditions must give the person notice in writing of the variation.

(4) Power under subsection (1) to vary conditions is, subject to subsection (3)(a) and (b), power—

(a) to vary or rescind any of the conditions, and

(b) to impose further conditions.

(4A) If it is reasonably practicable to do so, the investigating officer must seek the views of the alleged victim (if any) of the relevant offence on—

(a) whether any of the conditions that are relevant conditions should be varied under subsection (1), and

(b) if so, what variations should be made to those conditions.

(4B) The investigating officer must inform the relevant officer of any views obtained under subsection (4A).

(4C) If any of the conditions which are relevant conditions are varied under subsection (1), the investigating officer must, if it is reasonably practicable to do so, notify the alleged victim of the variations.

(4D) If the alleged victim of the relvant offence appears to the investigating officer to be vulnerable, subsections (4A|) and (4C) apply as if references to the alleged victim of the offence were to a person appearing to the officer to represent the alleged victim.

(5) In this section—

'investigating officer', in relation to the relevant offence, means the constable or other person in charge of the investigation of the offence;

'relevant condition', in relation to the relevant offence and an alleged victim of that offence, means a condition that relates to the safeguarding of the alleged victim;

'relevant offence' means the offence for which the person making the request under subsection (1) was under arrest when granted bail under section 30A(1);

'relevant officer', in relation to a designated police station, means a custody officer but, in relation to any other police station—

- (a) means a constable who is not involved in the investigation of the relevant offence, if such a constable is readily available, and
- (b) if no such constable is readily available—
  - (i) means a constable other than the one who granted bail to the person, if such a constable is readily available, and
  - (ii) if no such constable is readily available, means the constable who granted bail.

(6) For the purposes of this section a person ('P') is an alleged victim of an offence if—

- (a) an allegation has been made to a constable or other person involved in the investigation of the offence that P has suffered physical, mental or emotional harm, or economic loss, which was directly caused by the offence, and
- (b) P is an individual.

(7) For the purpose of this section an alleged victim of an offence is vulnerable if the alleged victim—

- (a) was aged under 18 at the time of the offence, or
- (b) may have difficulty understanding a communication from an investigating officer under this section, or communicating effectively in response to it, by reason of—
  - (i) a physical or mental disorder,
  - (ii) a mental disorder within the meaning of the Mental Health Act 1983, or
  - (iii) a significant impairment of intelligence and social functioning.

30CB Bail under section 30A: variation of conditions by court

(1) Where a person released on bail under section 30A(1) is on bail subject to conditions, a magistrates' court may, on an application by or on behalf of the person, vary the conditions if—

- (a) the conditions have been varied under section 30CA(1) since being imposed under section 30A(3B),
- (b) a request for variation under section 30CA(1) of the conditions has been made and refused, or
- (c) a request for variation under section 30CA(1) of the conditions has been made and the period of 48 hours beginning with the day when the request was made has expired without the request having been withdrawn or the conditions having been varied in response to the request.

(2) In proceedings on an application for a variation under subsection (1), a ground may not be relied upon unless—

- (a) in a case falling within subsection (1)(a), the ground was relied upon in the request in response to which the conditions were varied under section 30CA(1), or
- (b) in a case falling within paragraph (b) or (c) of subsection (1), the ground was relied upon in the request mentioned in that paragraph,

but this does not prevent the court, when deciding the application, from considering different grounds arising out of a change in circumstances that has occurred since the making of the application.

(3) Where conditions of bail granted to a person under section 30A(1) are varied under subsection (1)—

(a) paragraphs (a) to (d) of section 30A(3A) apply,
(b) requirements imposed by the conditions as so varied must be requirements that appear to the court varying the conditions to be necessary for any of the purposes mentioned in paragraphs (a) to (d) of section 30A(3B), and
(c) that bail shall not lapse but shall continue subject to the conditions as so varied.

(4) Power under subsection (1) to vary conditions is, subject to subsection (3)(a) and (b), power—
(a) to vary or rescind any of the conditions, and
(b) to impose further conditions.

30D Failure to answer to bail under section 30A

(1) A constable may arrest without a warrant a person who—
(a) has been released on bail under section 30A subject to a requirement to attend a specified police station, but
(b) fails to attend the police station at the specified time.

(2) A person arrested under subsection (1) must be taken to a police station (which may be the specified police station or any other police station) as soon as practicable after the arrest.

(2A) A person who has been released on bail under section 30A may be arrested without a warrant by a constable if the constable has reasonable grounds for suspecting that the person has broken any of the conditions of bail.

(2B) A person arrested under subsection (2A) must be taken to a police station (which may be the specified police station mentioned in subsection (1) or any other police station) as soon as practicable after the arrest.

(3) In subsection (1), 'specified' means specified in a notice under subsection (1) of section 30B or, if notice of change has been given under subsection (7) of that section, in that notice.

(4) For the purposes of—
(a) section 30 (subject to the obligations in subsections (2) and (2B)), and
(b) section 31,

an arrest under this section is to be treated as an arrest for an offence.

31 Arrest for further offence

Where—
(a) a person—
(i) has been arrested for an offence; and
(ii) is at a police station in consequence of that arrest; and
(b) it appears to a constable that, if he were released from that arrest, he would be liable to arrest for some other offence,

he shall be arrested for that other offence.

32 Search upon arrest

(1) A constable may search an arrested person, in any case where the person to be searched has been arrested at a place other than a police station, if the constable has reasonable grounds for believing that the arrested person may present a danger to himself or others.

(2) Subject to subsections (3) to (5) below, a constable shall also have power in any such case—
(a) to search the arrested person for anything—
(i) which he might use to assist him to escape from lawful custody; or
(ii) which might be evidence relating to an offence; and
(b) if the offence for which he has been arrested is an indictable offence, to enter and search any premises in which he was when arrested or immediately before he was arrested for evidence relating to the offence.

(3) The power to search conferred by subsection (2) above is only a power to search to the extent that is reasonably required for the purpose of discovering any such thing or any such evidence.

(4) The powers conferred by this section to search a person are not to be construed as authorising a constable to require a person to remove any of his clothing in public other than an outer coat, jacket or gloves but they do authorise a search of a person's mouth.

(5) A constable may not search a person in the exercise of the power conferred by subsection (2)(a) above unless he has reasonable grounds for believing that the person to be searched may have concealed on him anything for which a search is permitted under that paragraph.

(6) A constable may not search premises in the exercise of the power conferred by subsection (2)(b) above unless he has reasonable grounds for believing that there is evidence for which a search is permitted under that paragraph on the premises.

(7) In so far as the power of search conferred by subsection (2)(b) above relates to premises consisting of two or more separate dwellings, it is limited to a power to search—

(a) any dwelling in which the arrest took place or in which the person arrested was immediately before his arrest; and

(b) any parts of the premises which the occupier of any such dwelling uses in common with the occupiers of any other dwellings comprised in the premises.

(8) A constable searching a person in the exercise of the power conferred by subsection (1) above may seize and retain anything he finds, if he has reasonable grounds for believing that the person searched might use it to cause physical injury to himself or to any other person.

(9) A constable searching a person in the exercise of the power conferred by subsection (2)(a) above may seize and retain anything he finds, other than an item subject to legal privilege, if he has reasonable grounds for believing—

(a) that he might use it to assist him to escape from lawful custody; or

(b) that it is evidence of an offence or has been obtained in consequence of the commission of an offence.

(10) Nothing in this section shall be taken to affect the power conferred by section 43 of the Terrorism Act 2000.

. . .

PART IV DETENTION

Detention—conditions and duration

34 Limitations on police detention

(1) A person arrested for an offence shall not be kept in police detention except in accordance with the provisions of this Part of this Act.

(2) Subject to subsection (3) below, if at any time a custody officer—

(a) becomes aware, in relation to any person in police detention, that the grounds for the detention of that person have ceased to apply and

(b) is not aware of any other grounds on which the continued detention of that person could be justified under the provisions of this part of this Act,

it shall be the duty of the custody officer, subject to subsection (4) below, to order his immediate release from custody.

(3) No person in police detention shall be released except on the authority of a custody officer at the police station where his detention was authorised, or if it was authorised at more than one station, a custody officer at the station where it was last authorised.

(4) A person who appears to the custody officer to have been unlawfully at large when he was arrested is not to be released under subsection (2) above.

(5) A person whose release is ordered under subsection (2) must be released on bail if subsection (5A) applies.

(5A) This subsection applies if—

(a) it appears to the custody officer—

(i) that there is need for further investigation of any matter in connection with which the person was detained at any time during the period of the person's detention, or

(ii) that, in respect of any such matter, proceedings may be taken against the person or the person may be given a youth caution under section 66ZA of the Crime and Disorder Act 1998, and

(b) the pre-conditions for bail are satisfied.

(5AA) A person whose release is ordered under subsection (2) must be released without bail if subsection (5A) does not apply.

(5B) Subsection (5C) applies where—

(a) a person is released under subsection (5) or (5AA), and

(b) the custody officer determines that—

(i) there is not sufficient evidence to charge the person with an offence, or

(ii) there is sufficient evidence to charge the person with an offence but the person should not be charged with an offence or given a caution in respect of an offence.

(5C) The custody officer must give the person notice in writing that the person is not to be prosecuted.

(5D) Subsection (5C) does not prevent the prosecution of the person for an offence if new evidence comes to light after the notice was given.

(5E) In this Part 'caution' means—

(a) a diversionary or community caution under Part 6 of the Police, Crime, Sentencing and Courts Act 2022;

(b) a youth conditional caution within the meaning of Chapter 1 of Part 4 of the Crime and Disorder Act 1998;

(c) a youth caution under section 66ZA of that Act.

(6) For the purposes of this Part of this Act a person arrested under section 6D of the Road Traffic Act 1988 or section 30(2) of the Transport and Works Act 1992 is arrested for an offence.

(7) For the purposes of this Part a person who—

(a) attends a police station to answer to bail granted under section 30A,

(b) returns to a police station to answer to bail granted under this Part, or

(c) is arrested under section 30D or 46A,

is to be treated as arrested for an offence and that offence is the offence in connection with which he was granted bail. But this subsection is subject to section 47(6) (which provides for the calculation of certain periods, where a person has been granted bail under this Part, by reference to time when the person is in police detention only).

(8) Subsection (7) does not apply in relation to a person who is granted bail subject to the duty mentioned in section 47(3)(b) and who either—

(a) attends a police station to answer to such bail, or

(b) is arrested under section 46A for failing to do so,

(provision as to the treatment of such persons for the purposes of this Part being made by section 46ZA).

35 Designated police stations

(1) The chief officer of police for each police area shall designate the police stations in his area which, subject to sections 30(3) and (5), 30A(5) and 30D(2) above, are to be the stations in that area to be used for the purpose of detaining arrested persons.

(2) A chief officer's duty under subsection (1) above is to designate police stations appearing to him to provide enough accommodation for that purpose.

(2A) The Chief Constable of the British Transport Police Force may designate police stations which (in addition to those designated under subsection (1) above) may be used for the purpose of detaining arrested persons.

(3) Without prejudice to section 12 of the Interpretation Act 1978 (continuity of duties) a chief officer—

(a) may designate a station which was not previously designated; and

(b) may direct that a designation of a station previously made shall cease to operate.

(4) In this Act 'designated police station' means a police station for the time being designated under this section.

36 Custody officers at police stations

(1) One or more custody officers shall be appointed for each designated police station.

(2) A custody officer for a police station designated under section 35(1) above shall be appointed—

(a) by the chief officer of police for the area in which the designated police station is situated; or

(b) by such other police officer as the chief officer of police for that area may direct.

(2A) A custody officer for a police station designated under section 35(2A) above shall be appointed—

(a) by the Chief Constable of the British Police Transport Force; or

(b) by such other member of that Force as that Chief Constable may direct.

(3) No officer may be appointed a custody officer unless the officer is of at least the rank of sergeant.

(4) An officer of any rank may perform the functions of a custody officer at a designated police station if a custody officer is not readily available to perform them.

(5) Subject to the following provisions of this section and to section 39(2) below, none of the functions of a custody officer in relation to a person shall be performed by an officer who at the time when the function falls to be performed is involved in the investigation of an offence for which that person is in police detention at that time.

(6) Nothing in subsection (5) above is to be taken to prevent a custody officer—

(a) performing any function assigned to custody officers—

(i) by this Act; or

(ii) by a code of practice issued under this Act;

(b) carrying out the duty imposed on custody officers by section 39 below;

(c) doing anything in connection with the identification of a suspect; or

(d) doing anything under sections 7 and 8 of the Road Traffic Act 1988.

(7) Where an arrested person is taken to a police station which is not a designated police station, the functions in relation to him which at a designated police station would be the functions of a custody officer shall be performed—

(a) by an officer who is not involved in the investigation of an offence for which he is in police detention, if such an officer is readily available; and

(b) if no such officer is readily available, by the officer who took him to the station or any other officer.

(7A) Subject to subsection (7B), subsection (7) applies where a person attends a police station which is not a designated station to answer to bail granted under section 30A as it applies where a person is taken to such a station.

(7B) Where subsection (7) applies because of subsection (7A), the reference in subsection (7)(b) to the officer who took him to the station is to be read as a reference to the officer who granted him bail.

(7C) The reference to a custody officer in section 30A(1A)(b) includes a reference to an officer other than a custody officer who is performing the functions of a custody officer by virtue of subsection (4) above.

(8) References to a custody officer in section 34 above or in the following provisions of this Act include references to an officer other than a custody officer who is performing the functions of a custody officer by virtue of subsection (4) or (7) above.

(9) Where by virtue of subsection (7) above an officer of a force maintained by a local policing body who took an arrested person to a police station is to perform the functions of a custody officer in relation to him, the officer shall inform an officer who—

(a) is attached to a designated police station; and

(b) is of at least the rank of inspector,

that he is to do so.

(10) The duty imposed by subsection (9) above shall be performed as soon as it is practicable to perform it.

37 Duties of custody officer before charge

(1) Where—

(a) a person is arrested for an offence—

(i) without a warrant; or

(ii) under a warrant not endorsed for bail,

the custody officer at each police station where he is detained after his arrest shall determine whether he has before him sufficient evidence to charge that person with the offence for which he was arrested and may detain him at the police station for such period as is necessary to enable him to do so.

(2) If—

(a) the custody officer ('C') determines that C does not have such evidence before C, and

(b) the pre-conditions for bail are satisfied,

the person arrested must be released on bail (subject to subsection (3)).

(2A) If—

(a) the custody officer ('C') determines that C does not have such evidence before C, and

(b) the pre-conditions for bail are not satisfied,

the person must be released without bail (subject to subsection (3)).

(3) If the custody officer has reasonable grounds for believing that the person's detention without being charged is necessary to secure or preserve evidence relating to an offence for which the person is under arrest or to obtain such evidence by questioning the person, he may authorise the person arrested to be kept in police detention.

(4) Where a custody officer authorises a person who has not been charged to be kept in police detention, he shall, as soon as is practicable, make a written record of the grounds for the detention.

(5) Subject to subsection (6) below, the written record shall be made in the presence of the person arrested who shall at that time be informed by the custody officer of the grounds for his detention.

(6) Subsection (5) above shall not apply where the person arrested is, at the time when the written record is made—

(a) incapable of understanding what is said to him;

(b) violent or likely to become violent; or

(c) in urgent need of medical attention.

(6A) Subsection (6B) applies where

(a) a person is released under subsection (2) of (2A), and

(b) the custody officer determines that—

(i) there is not sufficient evidence to charge the person with an offence, or

(ii) there is sufficient evidence to charge the person with an offence but the person should not be charged with an offence or given a caution in respect of an offence.

(6B) The custody officer must give the person notice in writing that the person is not to be prosecuted.

(6C) Subsection (6B) does not prevent the prosecution of the person for an offence if new evidence comes to light after the notice was given.

(7) Subject to section 41(7) below, if the custody officer determines that he has before him sufficient evidence to charge the person arrested with the offence for which he was arrested, the person arrested—

(a) shall be—

(i) released without charge and on bail, or

(ii) kept in police detention,

for the purpose of enabling the Director of Public Prosecutions to make a decision under section 37B below,

(b) shall be released—
(i) without charge, and
(ii) if the pre-conditions for bail are satisfied, on bail
but not for the purpose mentioned in paragraph (a),
(c) shall be released—
(i) without charge, and
(ii) if the pre-conditions for bail are not satisfied, without bail, or
(d) shall be charged.

(7A) The decision as to how a person is to be dealt with under subsection (7) above shall be that of the custody officer.

(7B) Where a person is dealt with under subsection (7)(a) above, it shall be the duty of the custody officer to inform him that he is being released, or (as the case may be) detained, to enable the Director of Public Prosecutions to make a decision under section 37B below.

(8) Where—
(a) a person is released under subsection (7)(b) or (c) above; and
(b) at the time of his release a decision whether he should be prosecuted for the offence for which he was arrested has not been taken,
it shall be the duty of the custody officer so to inform him.

(8ZA) Where—
(a) a person is released under subsection (7)(b) or (c), and
(b) the custody officer makes a determination as mentioned in subsection (6A)(b), subsections (6B) and (6C) apply.

(8A) Subsection (8B) applies if the offence for which the person is arrested is one in relation to which a sample could be taken under section 63B below and the custody officer—
(a) is required in pursuance of subsection (2) above to release the person arrested and decides to release him on bail, or
(b) decides in pursuance of subsection (7)(a) or (b) above to release the person without charge and on bail.

(8B) The detention of the person may be continued to enable a sample to be taken under section 63B, but this subsection does not permit a person to be detained for a period of more than 24 hours after the relevant time.

(9) If the person arrested is not in a fit state to be dealt with under subsection (7) above, he may be kept in police detention until he is.

(10) The duty imposed on the custody officer under subsection (1) above shall be carried out by him as soon as practicable after the person arrested arrives at the police station or, in the case of a person arrested at the police station, as soon as practicable after the arrest.

(15) In this Part of this Act—

'arrested juvenile' means a person arrested with or without a warrant who appears to be under the age of 18;

'endorsed for bail' means endorsed with a direction for bail in accordance with section 117(2) of the Magistrates' Courts Act 1980.

37A Guidance

(1) The Director of Public Prosecutions may issue guidance—
(a) for the purpose of enabling custody officers to decide how persons should be dealt with under section 37(7) above or 37C(2) or 37CA(2) below, and
(b) as to the information to be sent to the Director of Public Prosecutions under section 37B(1) below.

(2) The Director of Public Prosecutions may from time to time revise guidance issued under this section.

(3) Custody officers are to have regard to guidance under this section in deciding how persons should be dealt with under section 37(7) above or 37C(2) or 37CA(2) below.

(4) A report under section 9 of the Prosecution of Offences Act 1985 (report by DPP to Attorney General) must set out the provisions of any guidance issued, and any revisions to guidance made, in the year to which the report relates.

(5) The Director of Public Prosecutions must publish in such manner as he thinks fit—

(a) any guidance issued under this section, and

(b) any revisions made to such guidance.

(6) Guidance under this section may make different provision for different cases, circumstances or areas.

37B Consultation with the Director of Public Prosecutions

(1) Where a person is dealt with under section 37(7)(a) above, an officer involved in the investigation of the offence shall, as soon as is practicable, send to the Director of Public Prosecutions such information as may be specified in guidance under section 37A above.

(2) The Director of Public Prosecutions shall decide whether there is sufficient evidence to charge the person with an offence.

(3) If he decides that there is sufficient evidence to charge the person with an offence, he shall decide—

(a) whether or not the person should be charged and, if so, the offence with which he should be charged, and

(b) whether or not the person should be given a caution and, if so, the offence in respect of which he should be given a caution.

(4) The Director of Public Prosecutions shall give notice of his decision to an officer involved in the investigation of the offence.

(4A) Notice under subsection (4) above shall be in writing, but in the case of a person kept in police detention under section 37(7)(a) above it may be given orally in the first instance and confirmed in writing subsequently.

(5) If his decision is—

(a) that there is not sufficient evidence to charge the person with an offence, or

(b) that there is sufficient evidence to charge the person with an offence but that the person should not be charged with an offence or given a caution in respect of an offence,

a custody officer shall give the person notice in writing that he is not to be prosecuted.

(5A) Subsection (5) does not prevent the prosecution of the person for an offence if new evidence comes to light after the notice was given.

(6) If the decision of the Director of Public Prosecutions is that the person should be charged with an offence, or given a caution in respect of an offence, the person shall be charged or cautioned accordingly.

(7) But if his decision is that the person should be given a caution in respect of the offence and it proves not to be possible to give the person such a caution (whether because of any restriction on the giving of the caution under Part 6 of the Police, Crime, Sentencing and Courts Act 2022 or for any other reason), he shall instead be charged with the offence.

(8) For the purposes of this section, a person is to be charged with an offence either—

(a) when he is in police detention at a police station (whether because he has returned to answer bail, because he is detained under section 37(7)(a) above or for some other reason), or

(b) in accordance with section 29 of the Criminal Justice Act 2003.

37C Breach of bail following release under section 37(7)(a)

(1) This section applies where—

(a) a person released on bail under section 37(7)(a) above or subsection (2)(b) below is arrested under section 46A below in respect of that bail, and

(b) at the time of his detention following that arrest at the police station mentioned in section 46A(2) below, notice under section 37B(4) above has not been given.

(2) The person arrested—

(a) shall be charged, or

(b) shall be released without charge, either on bail or without bail.

(3) The decision as to how a person is to be dealt with under subsection (2) above shall be that of a custody officer.

(4) A person released on bail under subsection (2)(b) above shall be released on bail subject to the same conditions (if any) which applied immediately before his arrest.

37CA Breach of bail following release under section 37(7)(b)

(1) This section applies where a person released on bail under section 37(7)(b) above or subsection (2)(b) below—

(a) is arrested under section 46A below in respect of that bail, and

(b) is being detained following that arrest at the police station mentioned in section 46A(2) below.

(2) The person arrested—

(a) shall be charged, or

(b) shall be released—

(i) without charge, and

(ii) if the pre-conditions for bail are satisfied, on bail or

(c) shall be released—

(i) without charge, and

(ii) if the pre-conditions for bail are not satisfied, without bail.

(3) The decision as to how a person is to be dealt with under subsection (2) above shall be that of a custody officer.

(4) A person released on bail under subsection (2)(b) above shall be released on bail subject to the same conditions (if any) which applied immediately before his arrest (and the reference in section 50A to any conditions of bail which would be imposed is to be read accordingly).

(5) Subsection (6) applies where—

(a) a person is released under subsection (2), and

(b) a custody officer determines that—

(i) there is not sufficient evidence to charge the person with an offence, or

(ii) there is sufficient evidence to charge the person with an offence but the person should not be charged with an offence or given a caution in respect of an offence.

(6) The custody officer must give the person notice in writing that the person is not to be prosecuted.

(7) Subsection (6) does not prevent the prosecution of the person for an offence if new evidence comes to light after the notice was given.

37D Release on bail under section 37(7): further provision

(4) Where a person released on bail under section 37(7)(a) or 37C(2)(b) above returns to a police station to answer bail or is otherwise in police detention at a police station, he may be kept in police detention to enable him to be dealt with in accordance with section 37B or 37C above or to enable the power under section 47(4A) to be exercised.

(4A) Where a person released on bail under section 37(7)(b) or 37CA(2)(b) above returns to a police station to answer bail or is otherwise in police detention at a police station, he may be kept in police detention to enable him to be dealt with in accordance with section 37CA above or to enable the power under section 47(4A) to be exercised.

(5) If the person mentioned in subsection (4) or (4A) above is not in a fit state to enable him to be dealt with as mentioned in that subsection or to enable the power under section 47(4A) to be exercised, he may be kept in police detention until he is.

(6) Where a person is kept in police detention by virtue of subsection (4), (4A) or (5) above, section 37(1) to (3) and (7) above (and section 40(8) below so far as it relates to section 37(1) to (3)) shall not apply to the offence in connection with which he was released on bail under section 37(7), 37C(2)(b) or 37CA(2)(b) above.

38 Duties of custody officer after charge

(1) Where a person arrested for an offence otherwise than under a warrant endorsed for bail is charged with an offence, the custody officer shall, subject to section 25 of the Criminal Justice and Public Order Act 1994, order his release from police detention, either on bail or without bail, unless—

- (a) if the person arrested is not an arrested juvenile—
  - (i) his name or address cannot be ascertained or the custody officer has reasonable grounds for doubting whether a name or address furnished by him as his name or address is his real name or address;
  - (ii) the custody officer has reasonable grounds for believing that the person arrested will fail to appear in court to answer to bail;
  - (iii) in the case of a person arrested for an imprisonable offence, the custody officer has reasonable grounds for believing that the detention of the person arrested is necessary to prevent him from committing an offence;
  - (iiia) in a case where a sample may be taken from the person under section 63B below, the custody officer has reasonable grounds for believing that the detention of the person is necessary to enable the sample to be taken from him;
  - (iv) in the case of a person arrested for an offence which is not an imprisonable offence, the custody officer has reasonable grounds for believing that the detention of the person arrested is necessary to prevent him from causing physical injury to any other person or from causing loss of or damage to property;
  - (v) the custody officer has reasonable grounds for believing that the detention of the person arrested is necessary to prevent him from interfering with the administration of justice or with the investigation of offences or of a particular offence; or
  - (vi) the custody officer has reasonable grounds for believing that the detention of the person arrested is necessary for his own protection;
- (b) if he is an arrested juvenile—
  - (i) any of the requirements of paragraph (a) above is satisfied (but, in the case of paragraph (a)(iiia) above, only if the arrested juvenile has attained the minimum age); or
  - (ii) the custody officer has reasonable grounds for believing that he ought to be detained in his own interests;
- (c) the offence with which the person is charged is murder.

(2) If the release of a person arrested is not required by subsection (1) above, the custody officer may authorise him to be kept in police detention but may not authorise a person to be kept in police detention by virtue of subsection (1)(a)(iiia) after the end of the period of six hours beginning with when he was charged with the offence.

(2A) The custody officer, in taking the decisions required by subsection (1)(a) and (b) above (except (a)(i) and (vi) and (b)(ii), shall have regard to the same considerations as those which a court is required to have regard to in taking the corresponding decisions under paragraph 2(1) of Part I of Schedule 1 to the Bail Act 1976 disregarding paragraphs 1A and 2(2) of that Part.

(3) Where a custody officer authorises a person who has been charged to be kept in police detention, he shall, as soon as practicable, make a written record of the grounds for the detention.

(4) Subject to subsection (5) below, the written record shall be made in the presence of the person charged who shall at that time be informed by the custody officer of the grounds for his detention.

(5) Subsection (4) above shall not apply where the person charged is, at the time when the written record is made—

(a) incapable of understanding what is said to him;

(b) violent or likely to become violent; or

(c) in urgent need of medical attention.

(6) Where a custody officer authorises an arrested juvenile to be kept in police detention under subsection (1) above, the custody officer shall, unless he certifies—

(a) that, by reason of such circumstances as are specified in the certificate, it is impracticable for him to do so; or

(b) in the case of an arrested juvenile who has attained the age of 12 years, that no secure accommodation is available and that keeping him in other local authority accommodation would not be adequate to protect the public from serious harm from him,

secure that the arrested juvenile is moved to local authority accommodation.

(6A) In this section—

'local authority accommodation' means accommodation provided by or on behalf of a local authority (within the meaning of the Children Act 1989);

'minimum age' means the age specified in section 63B(3)(b) below;

'secure accommodation' means accommodation provided for the purpose of restricting liberty;

'sexual offence' means an offence specified in Part 2 of Schedule 18 to the Sentencing Code;

'terrorism offence' means an offence specified in Part 3 of that Schedule;

'violent offence' means murder or an offence specified in Part 1 of that Schedule;

and any reference, in relation to an arrested juvenile charged with a violent, sexual or terrorism offence, to protecting the public from serious harm from him shall be construed as a reference to protecting members of the public from death or serious personal injury, whether physical or psychological, occasioned by further such offences committed by him.

(6B) Where an arrested juvenile is moved to local authority accommodation under subsection (6) above, it shall be lawful for any person acting on behalf of the authority to detain him.

(7) A certificate made under subsection (6) above in respect of an arrested juvenile shall be produced to the court before which he is first brought thereafter.

(7A) In this section 'imprisonable offence' has the same meaning as in Schedule 1 to the Bail Act 1976.

(8) In this Part of this Act 'local authority' has the same meaning as in the Children Act 1989.

39 Responsibilities in relation to persons detained

(1) Subject to subsections (2) and (4) below, it shall be the duty of the custody officer at a police station to ensure—

(a) that all persons in police detention at that station are treated in accordance with this Act and any code of practice issued under it and relating to the treatment of persons in police detention; and

(b) that all matters relating to such persons which are required by this Act or by such codes of practice to be recorded are recorded in the custody records relating to such persons.

(2) If the custody officer, in accordance with any code of practice issued under this Act, transfers or permits the transfer of a person in police detention—

(a) to the custody of another police officer at the police station where the person is in police detention, for the purpose of an interview that is part of the investigation of an offence for which the person is in police detention or otherwise in connection with the investigation of such an offence; or

(b) to the custody of an officer who has charge of that person outside the police station,

the custody officer shall cease in relation to that person to be subject to the duty imposed on him by subsection (1)(a) above; and it shall be the duty of the officer to whom the transfer is made to ensure that he is treated in accordance with the provisions of this Act and of any such codes of practice as are mentioned in subsection (1) above.

(3) If the person detained is subsequently returned to the custody of the custody officer, it shall be the duty of the officer investigating the offence to report to the custody officer as to the manner in which this section and the codes of practice have been complied with while that person was in his custody.

(3A) Subsections (3B) and (3C) apply if the custody officer, in accordance with any code of practice issued under this Act, transfers or permits the transfer of a person in police detention to an officer mentioned in subsection (2)(a) for the purpose of an interview that is to be conducted to any extent by means of a live link by another police officer who is investigating the offence but is not at the police station where the person in police detention is held at the time of the interview.

(3B) The officer who is not at the police station has the same duty as the officer mentioned in subsection (2)(a) to ensure that the person is treated in accordance with the provisions of this Act and of any such codes of practice as are mentioned in subsection (1).

(3C) If the person detained is subsequently returned to the custody of the custody officer, the officer who is not at the police station also has the same duty under subsection (3) as the officer mentioned in subsection (2)(a).

(3D) For the purpose of subsection (3C), subsection (3) applies as if the reference to 'in his custody' were a reference to 'being interviewed'.

(3E) In subsection (3A), 'live link' means an arrangement by which the officer who is not at the police station is able to see and hear, and to be seen and heard by, the person in police detention, any legal representative of that person and the officer who has custody of that person at the police station (and for this purpose any impairment of eyesight or hearing is to be disregarded).

(4) If an arrested juvenile is moved to local authority accommodation under section 38(6) above, the custody officer shall cease in relation to that person to be subject to the duty imposed on him by subsection (1) above.

(6) Where—

- (a) an officer of higher rank than the custody officer gives directions relating to a person in police detention; and
- (b) the directions are at variance—
  - (i) with any decision made or action taken by the custody officer in the performance of a duty imposed on him under this Part of this Act; or
  - (ii) with any decision or action which would but for the directions have been made or taken by him in the performance of such a duty,

the custody officer shall refer the matter at once to an officer of the rank of superintendent or above who is responsible for the police station for which the custody officer is acting as custody officer.

40 Review of police detention

(1) Reviews of the detention of each person in police detention in connection with the investigation of an offence shall be carried out periodically in accordance with the following provisions of this section—

- (a) in the case of a person who has been arrested and charged, by the custody officer; and
- (b) in the case of a person who has been arrested but not charged, by an officer of at least the rank of inspector who has not been directly involved in the investigation.

(2) The officer to whom it falls to carry out a review is referred to in this section as a 'review officer'.

(3) Subject to subsection (4) below—

- (a) the first review shall be not later than six hours after the detention was first authorised;
- (b) the second review shall be not later than nine hours after the first;
- (c) subsequent reviews shall be at intervals of not more than nine hours.

(4) A review may be postponed—

- (a) if, having regard to all the circumstances prevailing at the latest time for it specified in subsection (3) above, it is not practicable to carry out the review at that time;
- (b) without prejudice to the generality of paragraph (a) above—

(i) if at that time the person in detention is being questioned by a police officer and the review officer is satisfied that an interruption of the questioning for the purpose of carrying out the review would prejudice the investigation in connection with which he is being questioned; or

(ii) if at that time no review officer is readily available.

(5) If a review is postponed under subsection (4) above it shall be carried out as soon as practicable after the latest time specified for it in subsection (3) above.

(6) If a review is carried out after postponement under subsection (4) above, the fact that it was so carried out shall not affect any requirement of this section as to the time at which any subsequent review is to be carried out.

(7) The review officer shall record the reasons for any postponement of a review in the custody record.

(8) Subject to subsection (9) below, where the person whose detention is under review has not been charged before the time of the review, section 37(1) to (6) above shall have effect in relation to him, but with the modifications specified in subsection (8A).

(8A) The modifications are—

(a) the substitution of references to the person whose detention is under review for references to the person arrested;

(b) the substitution of references to the review officer for references to the custody officer; and

(c) in subsection (6), the insertion of the following paragraph after paragraph (a)—
'(aa) "asleep;".'

(9) Where a person has been kept in police detention by virtue of section 37(9) or 37D(5) above, section 37(1) to (6) shall not have effect in relation to him but it shall be the duty of the review officer to determine whether he is yet in a fit state.

(10) Where the person whose detention is under review has been charged before the time of the review, section 38(1) to (6B) above shall have effect in relation to him, but with the modifications specified in subsection (10A).

(10A) The modifications are—

(a) the substitution of a reference to the person whose detention is under review for any reference to the person arrested or to the person charged; and

(b) in subsection (5), the insertion of the following paragraph after paragraph (a)—
'(aa) "asleep;".'

(11) Where—

(a) an officer of higher rank than the review officer gives directions relating to a person in police detention; and

(b) the directions are at variance—

(i) with any decision made or action taken by the review officer in the performance of a duty imposed on him under this Part of this Act; or

(ii) with any decision or action which would but for the directions have been made or taken by him in the performance of such a duty,

the review officer shall refer the matter at once to an officer of the rank of superintendent or above who is responsible for the police station for which the review officer is acting as review officer in connection with the detention.

(12) Before determining whether to authorise a person's continued detention the review officer shall give—

(a) that person (unless he is asleep); or

(b) any solicitor representing him who is available at the time of the review,

an opportunity to make representations to him about the detention.

(13) Subject to subsection (14) below, the person whose detention is under review or his solicitor may make representations under subsection (12) above either orally or in writing.

(14) The review officer may refuse to hear oral representations from the person whose detention is under review if he considers that he is unfit to make such representations by reason of his condition or behaviour.

40A Use of telephone for review under s. 40

(1) A review under section 40(1)(b) may be carried out by means of a discussion, conducted by telephone, with one or more persons at the police station where the arrested person is held.

(2) But subsection (1) does not apply if—

(a) the review is of a kind authorised by regulations under section 45A to be carried out using a live link; and

(b) it is reasonably practicable to carry it out in accordance with those regulations.

(3) Where any review is carried out under this section by an officer who is not present at the station where the arrested person is held—

(a) any obligation of that officer to make a record in connection with the carrying out of the review shall have effect as an obligation to cause another officer to make the record;

(b) any requirement for the record to be made in the presence of the arrested person shall apply to the making of that record by that other officer; and

(c) the requirements under section 40(12) and (13) above for—

(i) the arrested person, or

(ii) solicitor representing him,

to be given any opportunity to make representations (whether in writing or orally) to that officer shall have effect as a requirement for that person, or such a solicitor, to be given an opportunity to make representations in a manner authorised by subsection (4) below.

(4) Representations are made in a manner authorised by this subsection—

(a) in a case where facilities exist for the immediate transmission of written representations to the officer carrying out the review, if they are made either—

(i) orally by telephone to that officer; or

(ii) in writing to that officer by means of those facilities;

and

(b) in any other case, if they are made orally by telephone to that officer.

(5) In this section 'a live link' has the same meaning as in section 45A below.

41 Limits on period of detention without charge

(1) Subject to the following provisions of this section and to sections 42 and 43 below, a person shall not be kept in police detention for more than 24 hours without being charged.

(2) The time from which the period of detention of a person is to be calculated (in this Act referred to as 'the relevant time')—

(a) in the case of a person to whom this paragraph applies, shall be—

(i) the time at which that person arrives at the relevant police station; or

(ii) the time 24 hours after the time of that person's arrest,

whichever is the earlier;

(b) in the case of a person arrested outside England and Wales, shall be—

(i) the time at which that person arrives at the first police station to which he is taken in the police area in England or Wales in which the offence for which he was arrested is being investigated; or

(ii) the time 24 hours after the time of that person's entry into England and Wales,

whichever is the earlier;

(c) in the case of a person who—

(i) attends voluntarily at a police station; or

(ii) accompanies a constable to a police station without having been arrested, and is arrested at the police station,

the time of his arrest;

(ca) in the case of a person who attends a police station to answer to bail granted under section 30A, the time when he arrives at the police station;

(d) in any other case, except where subsection (5) below applies, shall be the time at which the person arrested arrives at the first police station to which he is taken after his arrest.

(3) Subsection (2)(a) above applies to a person if—

(a) his arrest is sought in one police area in England and Wales;

(b) he is arrested in another police area; and

(c) he is not questioned in the area in which he is arrested in order to obtain evidence in relation to an offence for which he is arrested;

and in sub-paragraph (i) of that paragraph 'the relevant police station' means the first police station to which he is taken in the police area in which his arrest was sought.

(4) Subsection (2) above shall have effect in relation to a person arrested under section 31 above as if every reference in it to his arrest or his being arrested were a reference to his arrest or his being arrested for the offence for which he was originally arrested.

(5) If—

(a) a person is in police detention in a police area in England and Wales ('the first area'); and

(b) his arrest for an offence is sought in some other police area in England and Wales ('the second area'); and

(c) he is taken to the second area for the purposes of investigating that offence, without being questioned in the first area in order to obtain evidence in relation to it,

the relevant time shall be—

(i) the time 24 hours after he leaves the place where he is detained in the first area; or

(ii) the time at which he arrives at the first police station to which he is taken in the second area,

whichever is the earlier.

(6) When a person who is in police detention is removed to hospital because he is in need of medical treatment, any time during which he is being questioned in hospital or on the way there or back by a police officer for the purpose of obtaining evidence relating to an offence shall be included in any period which falls to be calculated for the purposes of this Part of this Act, but any other time while he is in hospital or on his way there or back shall not be so included.

(7) Subject to subsection (8) below, a person who at the expiry of 24 hours after the relevant time is in police detention and has not been charged shall be released at that time

(a) on bail, if the pre-conditions for bail are satisfied, or

(b) without bail, if those pre-conditions are not satisfied.

(8) Subsection (7) above does not apply to a person whose detention for more than 24 hours after the relevant time has been authorised or is otherwise permitted in accordance with section 42 or 43 below.

(9) A person released under subsection (7) above shall not be re-arrested without a warrant for the offence for which he was previously arrested unless, since the person's release, new evidence has come to light or an examination or analysis of existing evidence has been made which could not reasonably have been made before his release; but this subsection does not prevent an arrest under section 46A below.

(10) Subsection (11) applies where—

(a) a person is released under subsection (7), and

(b) a custody officer determines that—

(i) there is not sufficient evidence to charge the person with an offence, or

(ii) there is sufficient evidence to charge the person with an offence but the person should not be charged with an offence or given a caution in respect of an offence.

(11) The custody officer must give the person notice in writing that the person is not to be prosecuted.

(12) Subsection (11) does not prevent the prosecution of the person for an offence if new evidence comes to light after the notice was given.

(13) Section 47(6) and (6A) makes further provision about the calculation of a period of police detention for the purposes of this Part.

42 Authorisation of continued detention

(1) Where a police officer of the rank of superintendent or above who s is responsible for the police station at which a person is detained has reasonable grounds for believing that—

(a) the detention of that person without charge is necessary to secure or preserve evidence relating to an offence for which he is under arrest or to obtain such evidence by questioning him;

(b) an offence for which he is under arrest is an indictable offence; and

(c) the investigation is being conducted diligently and expeditiously,

he may authorise the keeping of that person in police detention for a period expiring at or before 36 hours after the relevant time.

(2) Where an officer such as is mentioned in subsection (1) above has authorised the keeping of a person in police detention for a period expiring less than 36 hours after the relevant time, such an officer may authorise the keeping of that person in police detention for a further period expiring not more than 36 hours after that time if the conditions specified in subsection (1) above are still satisfied when he gives the authorisation.

(3) If it is proposed to transfer a person in police detention to another police area, the officer determining whether or not to authorise keeping him in detention under subsection (1) above shall have regard to the distance and the time the journey would take.

(4) No authorisation under subsection (1) above shall be given in respect of any person—

(a) more than 24 hours after the relevant time; or

(b) before the second review of his detention under section 40 above has been carried out.

(5) Where an officer authorises the keeping of a person in police detention under subsection (1) above, it shall be his duty—

(a) to inform that person of the grounds for his continued detention; and

(b) to record the grounds in that person's custody record.

(6) Before determining whether to authorise the keeping of a person in detention under subsection (1) or (2) above, an officer shall give—

(a) that person; or

(b) any solicitor representing him who is available at the time when it falls to the officer to determine whether to give the authorisation,

an opportunity to make representations to him about the detention.

(7) Subject to subsection (8) below, the person in detention or his solicitor may make representations under subsection (6) above either orally or in writing.

(8) The officer to whom it falls to determine whether to give the authorisation may refuse to hear oral representations from the person in detention if he considers that he is unfit to make such representations by reason of his condition or behaviour.

(9) Where—

(a) an officer authorises the keeping of a person in detention under subsection (1) above; and

(b) at the time of the authorisation he has not yet exercised a right conferred on him by section 56 or 58 below,

the officer—

(i) shall inform him of that right;

(ii) shall decide whether he should be permitted to exercise it;

(iii) shall record the decision in his custody record; and

(iv) if the decision is to refuse to permit the exercise of the right, shall also record the grounds for the decision in that record.

(10) Where an officer has authorised the keeping of a person who has not been charged in detention under subsection (1) or (2) above, he shall be released from detention not later than 36 hours after the relevant time

(a) on bail, if the pre-conditions for bail are satisfied, or

(b) without bail, if those pre-conditions are not satisfied, (subject to subsection (10A)).

(10A) Subsection (10) does not apply if—

(a) the person has been charged with an offence, or

(b) the person's continued detention is authorised or otherwise permitted in accordance with section 43.

(11) A person released under subsection (10) above shall not be re-arrested without a warrant for the offence for which he was previously arrested unless, since the person's release, new evidence has come to light or an examination or analysis of existing evidence has been made which could not reasonably have been made before his release but this subsection does not prevent an arrest under section 46A below.

(12) Subsection (13) applies where—

(a) a person is released under subsection (10), and

(b) a custody officer determines that—

(i) there is not sufficient evidence to charge the person with an offence, or

(ii) there is sufficient evidence to charge the person with an offence but the person should not be charged with an offence or given a caution in respect of an offence.

(13) The custody officer must give the person notice in writing that the person is not to be prosecuted.

(14) Subsection (13) does not prevent the prosecution of the person for an offence if new evidence comes to light after the notice was given.

43 Warrants of further detention

(1) Where, on an application on oath made by a constable and supported by an information, a magistrates' court is satisfied that there are reasonable grounds for believing that the further detention of the person to whom the application relates is justified, it may issue a warrant of further detention authorising the keeping of that person in police detention.

(2) A court may not hear an application for a warrant of further detention unless the person to whom the application relates—

(a) has been furnished with a copy of the information; and

(b) has been brought before the court for the hearing.

(3) The person to whom the application relates shall be entitled to be legally represented at the hearing and, if he is not so represented but wishes to be so represented—

(a) the court shall adjourn the hearing to enable him to obtain representation; and

(b) he may be kept in police detention during the adjournment.

(4) A person's further detention is only justified for the purposes of this section or section 44 below if—

(a) his detention without charge is necessary to secure or preserve evidence relating to an offence for which he is under arrest or to obtain such evidence by questioning him;

(b) an offence for which he is under arrest is an indictable offence; and

(c) the investigation is being conducted diligently and expeditiously.

(5) Subject to subsection (7) below, an application for a warrant of further detention may be made—

(a) at any time before the expiry of 36 hours after the relevant time; or

(b) in a case where—

(i) it is not practicable for the magistrates' court to which the application will be made to sit at the expiry of 36 hours after the relevant time; but

(ii) the court will sit during the 6 hours following the end of that period, at any time before the expiry of the said 6 hours.

(6) In a case to which subsection (5)(b) above applies—

(a) the person to whom the application relates may be kept in police detention until the application is heard; and

(b) the custody officer shall make a note in that person's custody record—

(i) of the fact that he was kept in police detention for more than 36 hours after the relevant time; and

(ii) of the reason why he was so kept.

(7) If—

(a) an application for a warrant of further detention is made after the expiry of 36 hours after the relevant time; and

(b) it appears to the magistrates' court that it would have been reasonable for the police to make it before the expiry of that period,

the court shall dismiss the application.

(8) Where on an application such as is mentioned in subsection (1) above a magistrates' court is not satisfied that there are reasonable grounds for believing that the further detention of the person to whom the application relates is justified, it shall be its duty—

(a) to refuse the application; or

(b) to adjourn the hearing of it until a time not later than 36 hours after the relevant time.

(9) The person to whom the application relates may be kept in police detention during the adjournment.

(10) A warrant of further detention shall—

(a) state the time at which it is issued;

(b) authorise the keeping in police detention of the person to whom it relates for the period stated in it.

(11) Subject to subsection (12) below, the period stated in a warrant of further detention shall be such period as the magistrates' court thinks fit, having regard to the evidence before it.

(12) The period shall not be longer than 36 hours.

(13) If it is proposed to transfer a person in police detention to a police area other than that in which he is detained when the application for a warrant of further detention is made, the court hearing the application shall have regard to the distance and the time the journey would take.

(14) Any information submitted in support of an application under this section shall state—

(a) the nature of the offence for which the person to whom the application relates has been arrested;

(b) the general nature of the evidence on which that person was arrested;

(c) what inquiries relating to the offence have been made by the police and what further inquiries are proposed by them;

(d) the reasons for believing the continued detention of that person to be necessary for the purposes of such further inquiries.

(15) Where an application under this section is refused, the person to whom the application relates shall forthwith be charged or, subject to subsection (16) below, released—

(a) on bail, if the pre-conditions for bail are satisfied, or

(b) without bail, if those pre-conditions are not satisfied.

(16) A person need not be released under subsection (15) above—

(a) before the expiry of 24 hours after the relevant time; or

(b) before the expiry of any longer period for which his continued detention is or has been authorised under section 42 above.

(17) Where an application under this section is refused, no further application shall be made under this section in respect of the person to whom the refusal relates, unless supported by evidence which has come to light since the refusal.

(18) Where a warrant of further detention is issued, the person to whom it relates shall, unless the person is charged, be released from police detention upon or before the expiry of the warrant—

(a) on bail, if the pre-conditions for bail are satisfied, or

(b) without bail, if those pre-conditions are not satisfied.

(19) A person released under subsection (18) above shall not be re-arrested without a warrant for the offence for which he was previously arrested unless, since the person's release, new evidence has come to light or an examination or analysis of existing evidence has been made which could not reasonably have been made before his release; but this subsection does not prevent an arrest under section 46A below.

(20) Subsection (21) applies where—

(a) a person is released under subsection (15) or (18), and

(b) a custody officer determines that—

(i) there is not sufficient evidence to charge the person with an offence, or

(ii) there is sufficient evidence to charge the person with an offence but the person should not be charged with an offence or given a caution in respect of an offence.

(21) The custody officer must give the person notice in writing that the person is not to be prosecuted.

(22) Subsection (21) does not prevent the prosecution of the person for an offence if new evidence comes to light after the notice was given.

44 Extension of warrants of further detention

(1) On an application on oath made by a constable and supported by an information a magistrates' court may extend a warrant of further detention issued under section 43 above if it is satisfied that there are reasonable grounds for believing that the further detention of the person to whom the application relates is justified.

(2) Subject to subsection (3) below, the period for which a warrant of further detention may be extended shall be such period as the court thinks fit, having regard to the evidence before it.

(3) The period shall not—

(a) be longer than 36 hours; or

(b) end later than 96 hours after the relevant time.

(4) Where a warrant of further detention has been extended under subsection (1) above, or further extended under this subsection, for a period ending before 96 hours after the relevant time, on an application such as is mentioned in that subsection a magistrates' court may further extend the warrant if it is satisfied as there mentioned; and subsections (2) and (3) above apply to such further extensions as they apply to extensions under subsection (1) above.

(5) A warrant of further detention shall, if extended or further extended under this section, be endorsed with a note of the period of the extension.

(6) Subsections (2), (3) and (14) of section 43 above shall apply to an application made under this section as they apply to an application made under that section.

(7) Where an application under this section is refused, the person to whom the application relates shall forthwith be charged or, subject to subsection (8) below, released—

(a) on bail, if the pre-conditions for bail are satisfied, or

(b) without bail, if those pre-conditions are not satisfied.

(8) A person need not be released under subsection (7) above before the expiry of any period for which a warrant of further detention issued in relation to him has been extended or further extended on an earlier application made under this section.

(9) Subsection (10) applies where—

(a) a person is released under subsection (7), and

(b) a custody officer determines that—

(i) there is not sufficient evidence to charge the person with an offence, or

(ii) there is sufficient evidence to charge the person with an offence but the person should not be charged with an offence or given a caution in respect of an offence.

(10) The custody officer must give the person notice in writing that the person is not to be prosecuted.

(11) Subsection (10) does not prevent the prosecution of the person for an offence if new evidence comes to light after the notice was given.

45 Detention before charge—supplementary

(1) In sections 43, 44 and 45ZB of this Act 'magistrates' court' means a court consisting of two or more justices of the peace sitting otherwise than in open court.

(2) Any reference in this Part of this Act to a period of time or a time of day is to be treated as approximate only.

45ZA Functions of extending detention: use of live links

(1) The functions of a police officer under section 42(1) or (2) may be performed, in relation to an arrested person who is held at a police station, by an officer who is not present at the police station but has access to the use of a live link if—

(a) a custody officer considers that the use of the live link is appropriate,

(b) the arrested person has had advice from a solicitor on the use of the live link, and

(c) the appropriate consent to the use of the live link has been given.

(2) In subsection (1)(c), 'the appropriate consent' means—

(a) in relation to a person who has attained the age of 18, the consent of that person;

(b) in relation to a person who has not attained that age but has attained the age of 14, the consent of that person and of his or her parent or guardian;

(c) in relation to a person who has not attained the age of 14, the consent of his or her parent or guardian.

(3) The consent of a person who has not attained the age of 18 (but has attained the age of 14), or who is a vulnerable adult, may only be given in the presence of an appropriate adult.

(4) Section 42 applies with the modifications set out in subsections (5) to (7) below in any case where the functions of a police officer under that section are, by virtue of subsection (1), performed by an officer who is not at the police station where the arrested person is held.

(5) Subsections (5)(b) and (9)(iii) and (iv) of that section are each to be read as if, instead of requiring the officer to make a record, they required the officer to cause another police officer to make a record.

(6) Subsection (6) of that section is to be read as if it required the officer to give the persons mentioned in that subsection an opportunity to make representations—

(a) if facilities exist for the immediate transmission of written representations to the officer, either in writing by means of those facilities or orally by means of the live link, or

(b) in any other case, orally by means of the live link.

(7) Subsection (9) of that section is to be read as if the reference in paragraph (b) to the right conferred by section 58 were omitted.

(8) In this section—

'live link' means an arrangement by which an officer who is not present at the police station where an arrested person is held is able to see and hear, and to be seen and heard by, the arrested person and the arrested person's solicitor (and for this purpose any impairment of eyesight or hearing is to be disregarded);

'vulnerable adult' means a person aged 18 or over who may have difficulty understanding the purpose of an authorisation under section 42(1) or (2) or anything that occurs in connection with a decision whether to give such an authorisation (whether because of a mental disorder or for any other reason);

'appropriate adult', in relation to a person who has not attained the age of 18, means—

(a) the person's parent or guardian or, if the person is in the care of a local authority or voluntary organisation, a person representing that authority or organisation,

(b) a social worker of a local authority, or

(c) if no person falling within paragraph (a) or (b) is available, any responsible person aged 18 or over who is not a police officer or a person employed for, or engaged on, police purposes;

'appropriate adult', in relation to a vulnerable adult, means—

(a) a relative, guardian or other person responsible for the vulnerable adult's care,

(b) a person who is experienced in dealing with vulnerable adults but who is not a police officer or a person employed for, or engaged on, police purposes, or

(c) if no person falling within paragraph (a) or (b) is available, any responsible person aged 18 or over who is not a police officer or a person employed for, or engaged on, police purposes.

(9) In subsection (8), in both definitions of 'appropriate adult', 'police purposes' has the meaning given by section 101(2) of the Police Act 1996.

45ZB Warrants for further detention: use of live links

(1) A magistrates' court may give a live link direction for the purpose of the hearing of an application under section 43 for a warrant authorising further detention of a person, or the hearing of an application under section 44 for an extension of such a warrant, if—

(a) a custody officer considers that the use of a live link for that purpose is appropriate,

(b) the person to whom the application relates has had legal advice on the use of the live link,

(c) the appropriate consent to the use of the live link has been given, and

(d) it is not contrary to the interests of justice to give the direction.

(2) In subsection (1)(c), 'the appropriate consent' means—

(a) in relation to a person who has attained the age of 18, the consent of that person;

(b) in relation to a person who has not attained that age but has attained the age of 14, the consent of that person and of his or her parent or guardian;

(c) in relation to a person who has not attained the age of 14, the consent of his or her parent or guardian.

(3) Where a live link direction is given, the requirement under section 43(2)(b) for the person to whom the application relates to be brought before the court for the hearing does not apply.

(4) In this section—

'live link direction' means a direction that a live link be used for the purposes of the hearing;

'live link' means an arrangement by which a person (when not in the place where the hearing is being held) is able to see and hear, and to be seen and heard by, the court during a hearing (and for this purpose any impairment of eyesight or hearing is to be disregarded);

'vulnerable adult' means a person aged 18 or over who may have difficulty understanding the purpose of the hearing or what occurs at it (whether because of a mental disorder or for any other reason);

'appropriate adult', in relation to a person aged under 18, means—

(a) the person's parent or guardian or, if the person is in the care of a local authority or voluntary organisation, a person representing that authority or organisation,

(b) a social worker of a local authority, or

(c) if no person falling within paragraph (a) or (b) is available, any responsible person aged 18 or over who is not a police officer or a person employed for, or engaged on, police purposes;

'appropriate adult', in relation to a vulnerable adult, means—

(a) a relative, guardian or other person responsible for the appropriate adult's care,

(b) a person who is experienced in dealing with vulnerable adults but who is not a police officer or a person employed for, or engaged on, police purposes, or

(c) if no person falling within paragraph (a) or (b) is available, any responsible person aged 18 or over who is not a police officer or a person employed for, or engaged on, police purposes.

(5) In subsection (4), in both definitions of 'appropriate adult', 'police purposes' has the meaning given by section 101(2) of the Police Act 1996.

45A Use of live links for other decisions about detention

(1) Subject to the following provisions of this section, the Secretary of State may by regulations provide that, in the case of an arrested person who is held in a police station, some or all of the functions mentioned in subsection (2) may be performed (notwithstanding anything in the preceding provisions of this Part) by an officer who—

(a) is not present in that police station; but

(b) has access to the use of a live link.

(2) Those functions are—

(a) the functions in relation to an arrested person taken to, or answering to bail at, a police station that is not a designated police station which, in the case of an arrested person taken to a station that is a designated police station, are functions of a custody officer under section 37, 38 or 40 above; and

(b) the function of carrying out a review under section 40(1)(b) above (review, by an officer of at least the rank of inspector, of the detention of person arrested but not charged).

(3) Regulations under this section shall specify the use to be made in the performance of the functions mentioned in subsection (2) above of a live link.

(4) Regulations under this section shall not authorise the performance of any of the functions mentioned in subsection (2)(a) above by such an officer as is mentioned in subsection (1) above unless he is a custody officer for a designated police station.

(5) Where any functions mentioned in subsection (2) above are performed in a manner authorised by regulations under this section—

(a) any obligation of the officer performing those functions to make a record in connection with the performance of those functions shall have effect as an obligation to cause another officer to make the record; and

(b) any requirement for the record to be made in the presence of the arrested person shall apply to the making of that record by that other officer.

(6) Where the functions mentioned in subsection (2)(b) are performed in a manner authorised by regulations under this section, the requirements under section 40(12) and (13) above for—

(a) the arrested person, or

(b) a solicitor representing him,

to be given any opportunity to make representations (whether in writing or orally) to the person performing those functions shall have effect as a requirement for that person, or such a solicitor, to be given an opportunity to make representations in a manner authorised by subsection (7) below.

(7) Representations are made in a manner authorised by this subsection—

(a) in a case where facilities exist for the immediate transmission of written representations to the officer performing the functions, if they are made either—

(i) orally to that officer by means of the live link used by him for performing those functions; or

(ii) in writing to that officer by means of the facilities available for the immediate transmission of the representations; and

(b) in any other case if they are made orally to that officer by means of the live link used by him for performing the functions.

(8) Regulations under this section may make different provision for different cases and may be made so as to have effect in relation only to the police stations specified or described in the regulations.

(9) Regulations under this section shall be made by statutory instrument and shall be subject to annulment in pursuance of a resolution of either House of Parliament.

(10) In this section, 'live link', in relation to any functions, means an arrangement by which the functions may be performed by an officer who is not present at the police station where an arrested person is held but who is able (for the purpose of the functions) to see and hear, and to be seen and heard by, the arrested person and any legal representative of that person (and for this purpose any impairment of eyesight or hearing is to be disregarded).

Detention—miscellaneous

46 Detention after charge

(1) Where a person—

(a) is charged with an offence; and

(b) after being charged—

(i) is kept in police detention; or

(ii) is detained by a local authority in pursuance of arrangements made under section 38(6) above,

he shall be brought before a magistrates' court in accordance with the provisions of this section.

(2) If he is to be brought before a magistrates' court in the local justice area in which the police station at which he was charged is situated, he shall be brought before such a court as soon as is practicable and in any event not later than the first sitting after he is charged with the offence.

(3) If no magistrates' court in that area is due to sit either on the day on which he is charged or on the next day, the custody officer for the police station at which he was charged shall inform the designated officer for the area that there is a person in the area to whom subsection (2) above applies.

(4) If the person charged is to be brought before a magistrates' court in a local justice area other than that in which the police station at which he was charged is situated, he shall be removed to that area as soon as is practicable and brought before such a court as soon as is practicable after his arrival in the area and in any event not later than the first sitting of a magistrates' court in that area after his arrival in the area.

(5) If no magistrates' court in that area is due to sit either on the day on which he arrives in the area or on the next day—

(a) he shall be taken to a police station in the area; and

(b) the custody officer at that station shall inform the designated officer for the area that there is a person in the area to whom subsection (4) applies.

(6) Subject to subsection (8) below, where the designated officer for a local justice area has been informed—

(a) under subsection (3) above that there is a person in the area to whom subsection (2) above applies; or

(b) under subsection (5) above that there is a person in the area to whom subsection (4) above applies,

the designated officer shall arrange for a magistrates' court to sit not later than the day next following the relevant day.

(7) In this section 'the relevant day'—

(a) in relation to a person who is to be brought before a magistrates' court in the local justice area in which the police station at which he was charged is situated, means the day on which he was charged; and

(b) in relation to a person who is to be brought before a magistrates' court in any other local justice area, means the day on which he arrives in the area.

(8) Where the day next following the relevant day is Christmas Day, Good Friday or a Sunday, the duty of the designated officer under subsection (6) above is a duty to arrange for a magistrates' court to sit not later than the first day after the relevant day which is not one of those days.

(9) Nothing in this section requires a person who is in hospital to be brought before a court if he is not well enough.

46ZA Persons granted live link bail

(1) This section applies in relation to bail granted under this Part subject to the duty mentioned in section 47(3)(b) ('live link bail').

(2) An accused person who attends a police station to answer to live link bail is not to be treated as in police detention for the purposes of this Act.

(3) Subsection (2) does not apply in relation to an accused person if—

(b) at any time before the beginning of the proceedings referred to in section 47(3)(b)(i), a constable informs him that a live link will not be available for his use for the purposes of those proceedings; or

(d) the court determines for any reason not to give a direction of the sort referred to in section 47(3)(b)(ii).

(4) If paragraph (b) or (d) of subsection (3) applies in relation to a person, he is to be treated for the purposes of this Part—

(a) as if he had been arrested for and charged with the offence in connection with which he was granted bail, and

(b) as if he had been so charged at the time when that paragraph first applied in relation to him.

(5) An accused person who is arrested under section 46A for failing to attend at a police station to answer to live link bail, and who is brought to a police station in accordance with that section, is to be treated for the purposes of this Part—

(a) as if he had been arrested for and charged with the offence in connection with which he was granted bail, and

(b) as if he had been so charged at the time when he is brought to the station.

(6) Nothing in subsection (4) or (5) affects the operation of section 47(6).

46A Power of arrest for failure to answer to police bail

(1) A constable may arrest without a warrant any person who, having been released on bail under this Part of this Act subject to a duty to attend at a police station, fails to attend at that police station at the time appointed for him to do so.

(1ZA) The reference in subsection (1) to a person who fails to attend at a police station at the time appointed for him to do so includes a reference to a person who—

(a) attends at a police station to answer to bail granted subject to the duty mentioned in section 47(3)(b), but

(b) leaves the police station at any time before the beginning of the proceedings referred to in sub-paragraph (i) of that provision.

(1ZB) The reference in subsection (1) to a person who fails to attend at a police station at the time appointed for the person to do so includes a reference to a person who—

(a) attends at a police station to answer to bail granted subject to the duty mentioned in section 47(3)(b), but

(b) refuses to be searched under section 54B.

(1A) A person who has been released on bail under this Part may be arrested without warrant by a constable if the constable has reasonable grounds for suspecting that the person has broken any of the conditions of bail.

(2) A person who is arrested under this section shall be taken to the police station appointed as the place at which he is to surrender to custody as soon as practicable after the arrest.

(3) For the purposes of—

(a) section 30 above (subject to the obligation in subsection (2) above), and

(b) section 31 above,

an arrest under this section shall be treated as an arrest for an offence.

47 Bail after arrest

(1) Subject to the following provisions of this section, a release on bail of a person under this Part of this Act shall be a release on bail granted in accordance with sections 3, 3A, 5 and 5A of the Bail Act 1976 as they apply to bail granted by a constable.

(1A) The normal powers to impose conditions of bail shall be available to him where a custody officer releases a person on bail under this Part (except sections 37C(2)(b) and 37CA(2)(b)). In this subsection, 'the normal powers to impose conditions of bail' has the meaning given in section 3(6) of the Bail Act 1976.

(1B) No application may be made under section 5B of the Bail Act 1976 if a person is released on bail under section 37C(2)(b) or 37CA(2)(b) above.

(1C) Subsections (1D) to (1F) below apply where a person released on bail under section 37C(2)(b) or 37CA(2)(b) above is on bail subject to conditions.

(1D) The person shall not be entitled to make an application under section 43B of the Magistrates' Courts Act 1980.

(1E) A magistrates' court may, on an application by or on behalf of the person, vary the conditions of bail; and in this subsection 'vary' has the same meaning as in the Bail Act 1976.

(1F) Where a magistrates' court varies the conditions of bail under subsection (1E) above, that bail shall not lapse but shall continue subject to the conditions as so varied.

(2) Nothing in the Bail Act 1976 shall prevent the re-arrest without warrant of a person released on bail subject to a duty to attend at a police station if, since the person's release, new evidence has come to light or an examination or analysis of existing evidence has been made which could not reasonably have been made before the person's release.

(3) Subject to subsections (3A) and (4) below, in this Part of this Act references to 'bail' are references to bail subject to a duty—

- (a) to appear before a magistrates' court at such time and such place as the custody officer may appoint;
- (b) to attend at such police station as the custody officer may appoint at such time as he may appoint for the purposes of—
  - (i) proceedings held for the purposes of section 51 of the Criminal Justice Act 2003 (directions for live links in criminal proceedings) so far as that section applies to preliminary hearings (within the meaning of that section), and
  - (ii) any such hearing in relation to which a direction under that section is given requiring or permitting the person on bail to take part through a live audio link or a live video link (within the meaning of that section);
- (c) to attend at such police station as the custody officer may appoint at such time as he may appoint for purposes other than those mentioned in paragraph (b) (subject to section 47ZA)

(3A) Where a custody officer grants bail to a person subject to a duty to appear before a magistrates' court, he shall appoint for the appearance—

- (a) a date which is not later than the first sitting of the court after the person is charged with the offence; or
- (b) where he is informed by the designated officer for the relevant local justice area that the appearance cannot be accommodated until a later date, that later date.

(4) Where a custody officer has granted bail to a person subject to a duty to appear at a police station, the custody officer may give notice in writing to that person that his attendance at the police station is not required.

(4A) Where a person has been granted bail under this Part subject to a duty to attend at a police station, a custody officer may subsequently appoint a different time, or an additional time, at which the person is to attend at the police station to answer bail.

(4B) The custody officer must give the person notice in writing of the exercise of the power under subsection (4A).

(4C) The exercise of the power under subsection (4A) does not affect the conditions of bail (if any).

(4D) A custody officer may not appoint a time for a person's attendance under subsection (4A) which is after the end of the applicable bail period in relation to the person.

(4E) Subsection (4D) is subject to section 47ZL.

(6) Where a person who has been granted bail under this Part and has either attended at the police station in accordance with the grant of bail or has been arrested under section 46A above is detained at a police station, any time during which he was in police detention prior to being

granted bail shall be included as part of any period which falls to be calculated under this Part of this Act and any time during which he was on bail shall not be so included.

(6A) Where a person has been arrested under section 46A above (other than in a case within subsection (1ZA) or (1ZB) of that section) the period of 3 hours beginning with the time at which the person arrives at a police station following the arrest is not to be included as part of any period of police detention which falls to be calculated in relation to the person under this Part of this Act.

(7) Where a person who was released on bail under this Part subject to a duty to attend at a police station is re-arrested, the provisions of this Part of this Act shall apply to him as they apply to a person arrested for the first time, but this subsection does not apply to a person who is arrested under section 46A above or has attended a police station in accordance with the grant of bail (and who accordingly is deemed by section 34(7) above to have been arrested for an offence) or to a person to whom section 46ZA(4) or (5) applies.

(8) ...*

47ZZA Duty to seek views of alleged victims on conditions of pre-charge bail

(1) Subsections (2) to (5) apply if—

(a) a person has been arrested for an offence, and

(b) a custody officer proposes to release the person on bail under this Part (except section 37C(2)(b) or 37CA(2)(b)).

(2) If it is reasonably practicable to do so, the investigating officer must seek the views of the alleged victim (if any) of the offence on—

(a) whether relevant conditions should be imposed on the person's bail, and

(b) if so, what relevant conditions should be imposed.

(3) In this section 'relevant condition', in relation to an offence and an alleged victim of that offence, means a condition that relates to the safeguarding of the alleged victim.

(4) The investigating officer must inform the custody officer of any views obtained under subsection (2).

(5) If the person is granted bail subject to relevant conditions, the investigating officer must, if it is reasonably practicable to do so, notify the alleged victim of the offence of those conditions.

(6) If the alleged victim of the offence appears to the investigating officer to be vulnerable, subsections (2) and (5) apply as if references to the alleged victim of the offence were to a person appearing to the officer to represent the alleged victim.

(7) Subsections (8) to (11) apply if—

(a) a person has been arrested for an offence,

(b the person has been released on bail under this Part subject to conditions, and

(c) the person requests a custody officer to vary the conditions under section 3A(8) of the Bail Act 1976.

(8) If it is reasonably practicable to do so, the investigating officer must seek the views of the alleged victim (if any) of the offence on—

(a) whether any of the conditions that are relevant conditions should be varied, and

(b) if so, what variations should be made to those conditions.

(9) The investigating officer must inform the custody officer of any views obtained under subsection (8).

(10) If any of the conditions which are relevant conditions are varied, the investigating officer must, if it is reasonably practicable to do so, notify the alleged victim of the variations.

(11) If the alleged victim of the offence appears to the investigating officer to be vulnerable, subsections (8) and (10) apply as if references to the alleged victim of the offence were to a person appearing to the officer to represent the alleged victim.

(12) In this section 'investigating officer' in relation to an offence, means the constable or other person in charge of the investigation of the offence.

(13) For the purposes of this section a person ('P') is an alleged victim of an offence if—

* **Editor's Note:** Makes changes to the Magistrates' Courts Act 1980, sections 43 and 117(3).

(a) an allegation has been made to a constable or other person involved in the investigation of the offence that P has suffered physical, mental or emotional harm, or economic loss, which was directly caused by the offence, and
(b) P is an individual.

(14) For the purposes of this section an alleged victim of an offence is vulnerable if the alleged victim—
(a) was aged under 18 at the time of the offence, or
(b) may have difficulty understanding a communication from an investigating officer under this section, or communicating effectively in response to it, by reason of—
(i) a physical disability or disorder,
(ii) a mental disorder within the meaning of the Mental Health Act 1983, or
(iii) a significant impairment of intelligence and social functioning.

47ZA Limits on period of bail without charge

(1) This section applies in relation to the power conferred on a custody officer, when releasing a person on bail under this Part, to appoint a time for the person to attend at a police station in accordance with section 47(3)(c).

(2) The power must be exercised so as to appoint a time on the day on which the applicable bail period in relation to the person ends, unless subsection (3) or (4) applies.

(3) This subsection applies where—
(a) at the time of the exercise of the power the person is on bail under this Part in relation to one or more offences other than the relevant offence, and
(b) the custody officer believes that it is appropriate to align the person's attendance in relation to the relevant offence with the person's attendance in relation to the one or more other offences.

(4) This subsection applies where the custody officer believes that a decision as to whether to charge the person with the relevant offence would be made before the end of the applicable bail period in relation to the person.

(5) Where subsection (3) or (4) applies, the power may be exercised so as to appoint a time on a day falling before the end of the applicable bail period in relation to the person.

(6) This section is subject to section 47ZL.

(7) In this section references to attendance are to attendance at a police station in accordance with section 47(3)(c).

(8) In this Part the 'relevant offence', in relation to a person, means the offence in respect of which the power mentioned in subsection (1) is exercised in relation to the person.

47ZB Applicable bail period: initial limit

(1) In this Part the 'applicable bail period', in relation to a person, means—
(a) in an FCA case, HMRC case, NCA case or SFO case, the period of 6 months beginning with the person's bail start date, or
(b) in any other case, the period of 3 months beginning with the person's bail start date.

(2) The applicable bail period in relation to a person may be extended under sections 47ZD to 47ZG or treated as extended under section 47ZJ(3).

(3) Subsection (1) and sections 47ZD to 47ZG are subject to sections 47ZL and 47ZM.

(4) For the purposes of this Part—
(a) a person's bail start date is the day after the day on which the person was arrested for the relevant offence,
(b) an 'FCA case' is a case in which—
(i) the relevant offence in relation to the person is being investigated by the Financial Conduct Authority, and
(ii) a member of staff of that Authority who is of the description designated for the purposes of this sub-paragraph by the Chief Executive of that Authority confirms that sub-paragraph (i) applies,

(ba) an 'HMRC case' is a case in which—
(i) the relevant offence in relation to the person is being investigated by an officer of Revenue and Customs, and
(ii) an officer of Revenue and Customs confirms that sub-paragraph (i) applies,
(bb) an 'NCA case' is a case in which—
(i) the relevant offence in relation to the person is being investigated by the National Crime Agency, and
(ii) a National Crime Agency officer confirms that sub-paragraph (i) applies,
(c) an 'SFO case' is a case in which—
(i) the relevant offence in relation to the person is being investigated by the Director of the Serious Fraud Office, and
(ii) a member of the Serious Fraud Office confirms that sub-paragraph (i) applies.

47ZC Applicable bail period: conditions A to D in sections 47ZD to 47ZG

(1) This section applies for the purposes of sections 47ZD to 47ZG.

(2) Condition A is that the decision-maker has reasonable grounds for suspecting the person in question to be guilty of the relevant offence.

(3) Condition B is that the decision-maker has reasonable grounds for believing—
(a) in a case where the person in question is or is to be released on bail under section 37(7)(b) or 37CA(2)(b), that further time is needed for making a decision as to whether to charge the person with the relevant offence, or
(b) otherwise, that further investigation is needed of any matter in connection with the relevant offence.

(4) Condition C is that the decision-maker has reasonable grounds for believing—
(a) in a case where the person in question is or is to be released on bail under section 37(7)(b) or 37CA(2)(b), that the decision as to whether to charge the person with the relevant offence is being made diligently and expeditiously, or
(b) otherwise, that the investigation is being conducted diligently and expeditiously.

(5) Condition D is that the decision-maker has reasonable grounds for believing that the release on bail of the person in question is necessary and proportionate in all the circumstances (having regard, in particular, to any conditions of bail which are, or are to be, imposed).

(6) In this section 'decision-maker' means—
(a) in relation to a condition which falls to be considered by virtue of section 47ZD, the relevant officer in question;
(aa) in relation to a condition which falls to be considered by virtue of section 47ZDA, the senior officer in question,
(ab) in relation to a condition which falls to be considered by virtue of section 47ZDB, the appropriate decision-maker in question,
(b) in relation to a condition which falls to be considered by virtue of section 47ZE, the qualifying police officer in question;
(c) in relation to a condition which falls to be considered by virtue of section 47ZF or 47ZG, the court in question.

47ZD Applicable bail period: extension of initial limit in standard cases

(1) This section applies in relation to a person if—
(a) the applicable bail period in relation to the person is the period mentioned in section 47ZB(1)(b),
(b) that period has not ended, and
(c) a relevant officer is satisfied that conditions A to D are met in relation to the person.

(2) The relevant officer may authorise the applicable bail period in relation to the person to be extended so that it ends at the end of the period of 6 months beginning with the person's bail start date.

(3) Before determining whether to give an authorisation under subsection (2) in relation to a person, the relevant officer must arrange for the person or the person's legal representative to be informed that a determination is to be made.

(4) In determining whether to give an authorisation under subsection (2) in relation to a person, the relevant officer must consider any representations made by the person or the person's legal representative.

(5) The relevant officer must arrange for the person or the person's legal representative to be informed whether an authorisation under subsection (2) has been given in relation to the person.

(6) For the purposes of this Part 'relevant officer' means a police officer of the rank of inspector or above.

47ZDA Applicable bail period: further extension of limit in standard cases

(1) This section applies in relation to a person if—

(a) a relevantofficer has authorised an extension of the applicable bail period in relation to the person under section 47ZD,

(b) that period has not ended, and

(c) a senior officer is satisfied that conditions A to D are met in relation to the person.

(2) The senior officer may authorise the applicable bail period in relation to the person to be extended so that it ends at the end of the period of 9 months beginning with the person's bail start date.

(3) Before determining whether to give an authorisation under subsection (2) in relation to a person, the senior officer must arrange for the person or the person's legal representative to be informed that a determination is to be made.

(4) In determining whether to give an authorisation under subsection (2) in relation to a person, the senior officer must consider any representations made by the person or the person's legal representative.

(5) The senior officer must arrange for the person or the person's legal representative to be informed whether an authorisation under subsection (2) has been given in relation to the person.

(6) For the purposes of this Part 'senior officer' means a police officer of the rank of superintendent or above.

47ZDB Applicable bail period: extension of limit in non-standard cases

(1) This section applies in relation to a person if—

(a) the applicable bail period in relation to a person is the period mentioned in section 47ZB(1)(a),

(b) that period has not ended, and

(c) an appropriate decision-maker is satisfied that conditions A to D are met in relation to the person.

(2) The appropriate decision-maker may authorise the applicable bail period in relation to the person to be extended so that it ends at the end of the period of 12 months beginning with the person's bail start date.

(3) Before determining whether to give an authorisation under subsection (2) in relation to a person, the appropriate decision-maker must arrange for the person or the person's legal representative to be informed that a determination is to be made.

(4) In determining whether to give an authorisation under subsection (2) in relation to a person, the appropriate decision-maker must consider any representations made by the person or the person's legal representative.

(5) The appropriate decision-maker must arrange for the person or the person's legal representative to be informed whether an authorisation under subsection (2) has been given in relation to the person.

(6) For the purposes of this Part 'appropriate decision-maker' means—

(a) in an FCA case, a member of staff of the Financial Conduct Authority who is of the description designated for the purposes of this section by the Chief Executive of that Authority,

(b) in an HMRC case, an officer of Revenue and Customs of a grade that is equivalent to the rank of superintendent or above,

(c) in an NCA case, a National Crime Agency officer of a grade that is equivalent to the rank of superintendent or above, and

(d) in an SFO case, a member of the Serious Fraud Office who is of the Senior Civil Service.

47ZE Applicable bail period: extension of limit in designated cases

(1) This section applies in relation to a person if a senior officer has authorised an extension of the applicable bail period in relation to the person under section 47ZDA.

(2) The Director of Public Prosecutions may designate the person's case as being an exceptionally complex case (a 'designated case').

(3) If a qualifying police officer is satisfied that conditions A to D are met in relation to the person in a designated case, the officer may authorise the applicable bail period in relation to the person to be extended so that it ends at the end of the period of 12 months beginning with the person's bail start date.

(5) Before determining whether to give an authorisation under subsection (3) in relation to a person—

(a) the qualifying police officer must arrange for the person or the person's legal representative to be informed that a determination is to be made, and

(b) the qualifying police officer must consult the Director of Public Prosecutions.

(6) In determining whether to give an authorisation under subsection (3) in relation to a person, the qualifying police officer must consider any representations made by the person or the person's legal representative.

(7) The qualifying police officer must arrange for the person or the person's legal representative to be informed whether an authorisation under subsection (3) has been given in relation to the person.

(8) Any designation under subsection (2) must be made, and any authorisation under subsection (3) must be given, before the applicable bail period in relation to the person has ended.

(9) In this section—

'qualifying police officer' means a police officer of the rank of commander or assistant chief constable or above.

47ZF Applicable bail period: first extension of limit by court

(1) This section applies in relation to a person if—

(b) a senior officer has authorised an extension of the applicable bail period in relation to the person under section 47ZDA, or

(ba) an appropriate decision-maker has authorised an extension of the applicable bail period in relation to the person under section 47ZDB, or

(c) a qualifying police officer has authorised an extension of the applicable bail period in relation to the person under section 47ZE.

(2) Before the applicable bail period in relation to the person ends a qualifying applicant may apply to a magistrates' court for it to authorise an extension of the applicable bail period in relation to the person under this section.

(3) If the court is satisfied that—

(a) conditions B to D are met in relation to the person, and

(b) the case does not fall within subsection (7),

it may authorise the applicable bail period to be extended as specified in subsection (4).

(4) The applicable bail period is to end—

(a) in a case falling within subsection (1) (b), at the end of the period of 12 months beginning with the person's bail start date;

(b) in a case falling within subsection (1)(ba) or (c), at the end of the period of 18 months beginning with the person's bail start date.

(5) If the court is satisfied that—

(a) conditions B to D are met in relation to the person, and

(b) the case falls within subsection (7),

it may authorise the applicable bail period to be extended as specified in subsection (6).

(6) The applicable bail period is to end—

(a) in a case falling within subsection (1) (b), at the end of the period of 18 months beginning with the person's bail start date;

(b) in a case falling within subsection (1)(ba) or (c), at the end of the period of 24 months beginning with the person's bail start date.

(7) A case falls within this subsection if the nature of the decision or further investigations mentioned in condition B means that that decision is unlikely to be made or those investigations completed if the applicable bail period in relation to the person is not extended as specified in subsection (6).

(8) In this section 'qualifying applicant' means—

(a) a constable,

(b) a member of staff of the Financial Conduct Authority who is of the description designated for the purposes of this subsection by the Chief Executive of the Authority,

(ba) an officer of Revenue and Customs,

(bb) a National Crime Agency officer,

(c) a member of the Serious Fraud Office, or

(d) a Crown Prosecutor.

47ZG Applicable bail period: subsequent extensions of limit by court

(1) Subsections (2) to (6) apply where a court has authorised an extension of the applicable bail period in relation to a person under section 47ZF.

(2) Before the applicable bail period in relation to the person ends a qualifying applicant may apply to a magistrates' court for it to authorise an extension of the applicable bail period in relation to the person under this section.

(3) If the court is satisfied that—

(a) conditions B to D are met in relation to the person, and

(b) the case does not fall within subsection (8),

it may authorise the applicable bail period to be extended as specified in subsection (4).

(4) The applicable bail period is to end at the end of the period of 3 months beginning with the end of the current applicable bail period in relation to the person.

(5) If the court is satisfied that—

(a) conditions B to D are met in relation to the person, and

(b) the case falls within subsection (8),

it may authorise the applicable bail period to be extended as specified in subsection (6).

(6) The applicable bail period is to end at the end of the period of 6 months beginning with the end of the current applicable bail period in relation to the person.

(7) Where a court has authorised an extension of the applicable bail period in relation to a person under subsection (3) or (5), a qualifying applicant may make further applications under subsection (2) (and subsections (3) to (6) apply accordingly).

(8) A case falls within this subsection if the nature of the decision or further investigations mentioned in condition B means that that decision is unlikely to be made or those investigations completed if the current applicable bail period in relation to the person is not extended as specified in subsection (6).

(9) For the purposes of this section—

(a) references to the current applicable bail period in relation to a person are to the applicable bail period applying to the person when the application under this section is made (subject to section 47ZJ(3)), and

(b) 'qualifying applicant' has the same meaning as in section 47ZF.

47ZH Sections 47ZF and 47ZG: withholding sensitive information

(1) This section applies where a qualifying applicant makes an application to a magistrates' court under section 47ZF or 47ZG in relation to a person.

(2) The qualifying applicant may apply to the court for it to authorise the specified information to be withheld from the person and any legal representative of the person.

(3) The court may grant an application under subsection (2) only if satisfied that there are reasonable grounds for believing that the specified information is sensitive information.

(4) For the purposes of this section information is sensitive information if its disclosure would have one or more of the following results—

(a) evidence connected with an indictable offence would be interfered with or harmed;
(b) a person would be interfered with or physically injured;
(c) a person suspected of having committed an indictable offence but not yet arrested for the offence would be alerted;
(d) the recovery of property obtained as a result of an indictable offence would be hindered.

(5) In this section 'specified information' means the information specified in the application under subsection (2).

47ZI Sections 47ZF to 47ZH: proceedings in magistrates' court

(1) An application made to a magistrates' court under section 47ZF or 47ZG in relation to a person is to be determined by a single justice of the peace on written evidence unless subsection (2) or (3) applies.

(2) This subsection applies if—
(a) the effect of the application would be to extend the applicable bail period in relation to the person so that it ends at or before the end of the period of 24 months beginning with the person's bail start date, and
(b) a single justice of the peace considers that the interests of justice require an oral hearing.

(3) This subsection applies if—
(a) the effect of the application would be to extend the applicable bail period in relation to the person so that it ends after the end of the period of 24 months beginning with the person's bail start date, and
(b) the person, or the person who made the application, requests an oral hearing.

(4) If subsection (2) or (3) applies, the application is to be determined by two or more justices of the peace sitting otherwise than in open court.

(5) Where an application under section 47ZF or 47ZG in relation to a person is to be determined as mentioned in subsection (4), the justices may direct that the person and any legal representative of the person be excluded from any part of the hearing.

(6) The justices may give a direction under subsection (5) only if satisfied that there are reasonable grounds for believing that sensitive information would be disclosed at the part of the hearing in question.

(7) An application under section 47ZH is to be determined by a single justice of the peace on written evidence unless the justice determines that the interests of justice require an oral hearing.

(8) If the justice makes a determination under subsection (7)—
(a) the application is to be determined by two or more justices of the peace sitting otherwise than in open court, and
(b) the justices hearing the application must direct that the person to whom the application relates and any legal representative of the person be excluded from the hearing.

(9) In this section 'sensitive information' has the meaning given in section 47ZH(4).

47ZJ Sections 47ZF and 47ZG: late applications to magistrates' court

(1) This section applies where—
(a) an application under section 47ZF or 47ZG is made to a magistrates' court before the end of the applicable bail period in relation to a person, but
(b) it is not practicable for the court to determine the application before the end of that period.

(2) The court must determine the application as soon as is practicable.

(3) The applicable bail period in relation to the person is to be treated as extended until the application is determined.

(4) If it appears to the court that it would have been reasonable for the application to have been made in time for it to have been determined by the court before the end of the applicable bail period in relation to the person, it may refuse the application.

47ZK Rules

Criminal Procedure Rules may make provision in connection with applications under sections 47ZF, 47ZG and 47ZH and the proceedings for determining such applications.

47ZL Applicable bail period and bail return date: special case of release on bail under section 37(7)(a) or 37C(2)(b)

(1) This section applies where a person is released on bail under section 37(7)(a) or 37C(2)(b).

(2) The running of the applicable bail period in relation to the person—

(a) does not begin (in the case of a first release on bail), or

(b) is suspended (in any other case),

(subject to subsection (6)).

(3) Accordingly section 47ZA does not apply to the exercise of the power mentioned in section 47ZA(1) when releasing the person on bail.

(4) Subsections (5) and (6) apply if a DPP request is made in relation to the person.

(5) A custody officer must exercise the power mentioned in section 47(4A) to appoint a different time for the person to attend at the police station (and section 47(4B) to (4D) applies accordingly).

(6) The applicable bail period in relation to the person—

(a) begins to run on the day on which the DPP request is made (in the case of a first release on bail), or

(b) resumes running on that day (in any other case).

(7) Subsection (8) applies where—

(a) a DPP request has been made in relation to the person, and

(b) the applicable bail period in relation to the person would end before the end of the period of 7 days beginning with the day on which the DPP request was made.

(8) The running of the applicable bail period in relation to the person is suspended for the number of days necessary to secure that the applicable bail period ends at the end of the period of 7 days beginning with the day on which the DPP request was made.

(9) Subsections (10) and (11) apply if the DPP request made in relation to the person is met.

(10) The running of the applicable bail period in relation to the person is suspended.

(11) Accordingly section 47(4D) does not apply to any exercise of the power under section 47(4A).

(12) For the purposes of this section—

(a) a 'DPP request', in relation to a person, means a request by the Director of Public Prosecutions for the further information specified in the request to be provided before the Director decides under section 37B(2) whether there is sufficient evidence to charge the person with the relevant offence,

(b) a DPP request is met when the further information specified in the request is provided, and

(c) references to the case of a first release on bail are to a case where the person has not been released on bail in relation to the relevant offence under any other provision of this Part or under section 30A.

47ZM Applicable bail period: special cases of release on bail under section 30A and periods in hospital

(1) Subsections (2) and (3) apply where a person was released on bail under section 30A.

(2) The period of 3 months mentioned in section 30B(8) in relation to the person is to be treated as being the period of 3 months mentioned in section 47ZB(1)(b) in relation to the person.

(3) Any reference to the relevant offence, in relation to the person, is to be read as a reference to the offence in respect of which the power in section 30A(1) was exercised.

(4) Subsection (5) applies if, at any time on the day on which the applicable bail period in relation to a person would end, the person is in hospital as an in-patient.

(5) The running of the applicable bail period in relation to the person is to be treated as having been suspended for any day on which the patient was in hospital as an in-patient.

48 Remands to police detention

...*

* **Editor's Note:** Makes changes to the Magistrates' Court Act 1980, section 128.

49 Police detention to count towards custodial sentence

...*

50 Records of detention

(1) Each police force shall keep written records showing on an annual basis—

(a) the number of persons kept in police detention for more than 24 hours and subsequently released without charge;

(b) the number of applications for warrants of further detention and the results of the applications; and

(c) in relation to each warrant of further detention—

(i) the period of further detention authorised by it;

(ii) the period which the person named in it spent in police detention on its authority; and

(iii) whether he was charged or released without charge.

(2) Every annual report

(a) under section 22 of the Police Act 1996; or

(b) made by the Commissioner of Police of the Metropolis,

shall contain information about the matters mentioned in subsection (1) above in respect of the period to which the report relates.

50A Interpretation of references to pre-conditions for bail

(1) For the purposes of this Part the following are the pre-conditions for bail in relation to the release of a person by a custody officer—

(a) that the custody officer is satisfied that releasing the person on bail is necessary and proportionate in all the circumstances (having regard, in particular, to any conditions of bail which would be imposed), and

(b) that the custody officer has considered any representations made by the person or the person's legal representative.

(2) In determining whether releasing the person on bail is necessary and proportionate in all the circumstances, the custody officer must have regard in particular to—

(a) the need to secure that the person surrenders to custody,

(b) the need to prevent offending by the person,

(c) the need to safeguard victims of crime and witnesses, taking into account any vulnerabilities of any alleged victim of, or alleged witness to, the offence for which the person was arrested where these vulnerabilities have been identified by the custody officer,

(d) the need to safeguard the person, taking into account any vulnerabilities of the person where these vulnerabilities have been identified by the custody officer, and

(e) the need to manage risks to the public.

50B Guidance from the College of Policing on pre-charge bail

(1) The College of Policing may, with the approval of the Secretary of State, issue guidance on bail that is granted to a person under Part 3 or this Part ('pre-charge bail').

(2) Guidance on pre-charge bail may in particular cover—

(a) the exercise of powers to release a person on pre-charge bail;

(b) the exercise of powers to impose or vary conditions of pre-charge bail;

(c) the exercise of powers to arrest a person—

(i) for failing to answer pre-charge bail, or

(ii) for breaching any conditions of pre-charge bail;

(d) the exercise of powers to extend the period of pre-charge bail;

(e) the duty to seek the views of alleged victims about conditions of pre-charge bail.

(3) The College of Policing may, with the approval of the Secretary of State, from time to time revise the whole or any part of its guidance on pre-charge bail.

* **Editor's Note:** Makes changes to the Criminal Justice Act 1967, section 67.

(4) Before issuing or revising guidance on pre-charge bail, the College of Policing must consult—

(a) the National Police Chiefs' Council,

(b) such persons as appear to the College to represent the views of local policing bodies, and

(c) such other persons as the College thinks fit.

(5) The Secretary of State must lay before Parliament any guidance on pre-charge bail issued by the College of Policing, and any revision of such guidance.

(6) The Secretary of State is not required by subsection (5) to lay before Parliament, or may exclude from what is laid, anything the publication of which, in the opinion of the Secretary of State—

(a) could prejudice the prevention or detection of crime or the apprehension or prosecution of offenders, or

(b) could jeopardise the safety of any person.

(7) A person who exercises functions relating to pre-charge bail must have regard to the guidance.

(8) But subsection (7) does not apply to—

(a) a member of the Serious Fraud Office,

(b) a member of staff of the Financial Conduct Authority,

(c) an officer of Revenue and Customs, or

(d) a National Crime Agency officer.

(9) A failure on the part of a person to whom subsection (7) applies to comply with the guidance does not of itself render the person liable to any criminal or civil proceedings.

(10) But guidance on pre-charge bail is admissible in evidence in criminal or civil proceedings and a court may take into account a failure to comply with it in determining a question in the proceedings.

51 Savings

Nothing in this Part of this Act shall affect—

(a) the powers conferred on immigration officers by section 4 of and Schedule 2 to the Immigration Act 1971 (administrative provisions as to control on entry etc.);

(b) the powers conferred by or by virtue of section 41 or 43B of, or Schedule 7 to, the Terrorism Act 2000 (powers of arrest and detention);

(ba) the powers conferred by virtue of Part 1 of Schedule 3 to the Counter-Terrorism and Border Security Act 2019 (powers of detention);

(bb) the powers conferred by virtue of section 27 of and Schedule 6 to the National Security Act 2023;

(d) any right of a person in police detention to apply for a writ of habeas corpus or other prerogative remedy.

PART V QUESTIONING AND TREATMENT OF PERSONS BY POLICE

53 Abolition of certain powers of constables to search persons

(1) Subject to subsection (2) below, there shall cease to have effect any Act (including a local Act) passed before this Act in so far as it authorises—

(a) any search by a constable of a person in police detention at a police station; or

(b) an intimate search of a person by a constable;

and any rule of common law which authorises a search such as is mentioned in paragraph (a) or (b) above is abolished.

54 Searches of detained persons

(1) The custody officer at a police station shall ascertain everything which a person has with him when he is—

(a) brought to the station after being arrested elsewhere or after being committed to custody by an order or sentence of a court; or

(b) arrested at the station or detained there, as a person falling within section 34(7), under section 37 above or as a person to whom section 46ZA(4) or (5) applies.

(2) The custody officer may record or cause to be recorded all or any of the things which he ascertains under subsection (1).

(2A) In the case of an arrested person, any such record may be made as part of his custody record.

(3) Subject to subsection (4) below, a custody officer may seize and retain any such thing or cause any such thing to be seized and retained.

(4) Clothes and personal effects may only be seized if the custody officer—

(a) believes that the person from whom they are seized may use them—

(i) to cause physical injury to himself or any other person;

(ii) to damage property;

(iii) to interfere with evidence; or

(iv) to assist him to escape; or

(b) has reasonable grounds for believing that they may be evidence relating to an offence.

(5) Where anything is seized, the person from whom it is seized shall be told the reason for the seizure unless he is—

(a) violent or likely to become violent; or

(b) incapable of understanding what is said to him.

(6) Subject to subsection (7) below, a person may be searched if the custody officer considers it necessary to enable him to carry out his duty under subsection (1) above and to the extent that the custody officer considers necessary for that purpose.

(6A) A person who is in custody at a police station or is in police detention otherwise than at a police station may at any time be searched in order to ascertain whether he has with him anything which he could use for any of the purposes specified in subsection (4)(a) above.

(6B) Subject to subsection (6C) below, a constable may seize and retain, or cause to be seized and retained, anything found on such a search.

(6C) A constable may only seize clothes and personal effects in the circumstances specified in subsection (4) above.

(7) An intimate search may not be conducted under this section.

(8) A search under this section shall be carried out by a constable.

(9) The constable carrying out a search shall be of the same sex as the person searched.

54A Searches and examination to ascertain identity

(1) If an officer of at least the rank of inspector authorises it, a person who is detained in a police station may be searched or examined, or both—

(a) for the purpose of ascertaining whether he has any mark that would tend to identify him as a person involved in the commission of an offence; or

(b) for the purpose of facilitating the ascertainment of his identity.

(2) An officer may only give an authorisation under subsection (1) for the purpose mentioned in paragraph (a) of that subsection if—

(a) the appropriate consent to a search or examination that would reveal whether the mark in question exists has been withheld; or

(b) it is not practicable to obtain such consent.

(3) An officer may only give an authorisation under subsection (1) in a case in which subsection (2) does not apply if—

(a) the person in question has refused to identify himself; or

(b) the officer has reasonable grounds for suspecting that that person is not who he claims to be.

(4) An officer may give an authorisation under subsection (1) orally or in writing but, if he gives it orally, he shall confirm it in writing as soon as is practicable.

(5) Any identifying mark found on a search or examination under this section may be photographed—

(a) with the appropriate consent; or

(b) if the appropriate consent is withheld or it is not practicable to obtain it, without it.

(6) Where a search or examination may be carried out under this section, or a photograph may be taken under this section, the only persons entitled to carry out the search or examination, or to take the photograph, are constables.

(7) A person may not under this section carry out a search or examination of a person of the opposite sex or take a photograph of any part of the body of a person of the opposite sex.

(8) An intimate search may not be carried out under this section.

(9) A photograph taken under this section—

(a) may be used by, or disclosed to, any person for any purpose related to the prevention or detection of crime, the investigation of an offence or the conduct of a prosecution; and

(b) after being so used or disclosed, may be retained but may not be used or disclosed except for a purpose so related.

(10) In subsection (9)—

(a) the reference to crime includes a reference to any conduct which—

(i) constitutes one or more criminal offences (whether under the law of a part of the United Kingdom or of a country or territory outside the United Kingdom); or

(ii) is, or corresponds to, any conduct which, if it all took place in any one part of the United Kingdom, would constitute one or more criminal offences;

and

(b) the references to an investigation and to a prosecution include references, respectively, to any investigation outside the United Kingdom of any crime or suspected crime and to a prosecution brought in respect of any crime in a country or territory outside the United Kingdom.

(11) In this section—

(a) references to ascertaining a person's identity include references to showing that he is not a particular person; and

(b) references to taking a photograph include references to using any process by means of which a visual image may be produced, and references to photographing a person shall be construed accordingly.

(12) In this section 'mark' includes features and injuries; and a mark is an identifying mark for the purposes of this section if its existence in any person's case facilitates the ascertainment of his identity or his identification as a person involved in the commission of an offence.

(13) Nothing in this section applies to a person arrested under an extradition arrest power.

54B Searches of persons answering to live link bail

(1) A constable may search at any time—

(a) any person who is at a police station to answer to live link bail; and

(b) any article in the possession of such a person.

(2) If the constable reasonably believes a thing in the possession of the person ought to be seized on any of the grounds mentioned in subsection (3), the constable may seize and retain it or cause it to be seized and retained.

(3) The grounds are that the thing—

(a) may jeopardise the maintenance of order in the police station;

(b) may put the safety of any person in the police station at risk; or

(c) may be evidence of, or in relation to, an offence.

(4) The constable may record or cause to be recorded all or any of the things seized and retained pursuant to subsection (2).

(5) An intimate search may not be carried out under this section.

(6) The constable carrying out a search under subsection (1) must be of the same sex as the person being searched.

(7) In this section 'live link bail' means bail granted under Part 4 of this Act subject to the duty mentioned in section 47(3)(b).

54C Power to retain articles seized

(1) Except as provided by subsections (2) and (3), a constable may retain a thing seized under section 54B until the time when the person from whom it was seized leaves the police station.

(2) A constable may retain a thing seized under section 54B in order to establish its lawful owner, where there are reasonable grounds for believing that it has been obtained in consequence of the commission of an offence.

(3) If a thing seized under section 54B may be evidence of, or in relation to, an offence, a constable may retain it—

(a) for use as evidence at a trial for an offence; or

(b) for forensic examination or for investigation in connection with an offence.

(4) Nothing may be retained for either of the purposes mentioned in subsection (3) if a photograph or copy would be sufficient for that purpose.

(5) Nothing in this section affects any power of a court to make an order under section 1 of the Police (Property) Act 1897.

(6) The references in this section to anything seized under section 54B include anything seized by a person to whom paragraph 27A of Schedule 4 to the Police Reform Act 2002 applies.

55 Intimate searches

(1) Subject to the following provisions of this section, if an officer of at least the rank of inspector has reasonable grounds for believing—

(a) that a person who has been arrested and is in police detention may have concealed on him anything which—

(i) he could use to cause physical injury to himself or others; and

(ii) he might so use while he is in police detention or in the custody of a court; or

(b) that such a person—

(i) may have a Class A drug concealed on him; and

(ii) was in possession of it with the appropriate criminal intent before his arrest,

he may authorise an intimate search of that person.

(2) An officer may not authorise an intimate search of a person for anything unless he has reasonable grounds for believing that it cannot be found without his being intimately searched.

(3) An officer may give an authorisation under subsection (1) above orally or in writing but, if he gives it orally, he shall confirm it in writing as soon as is practicable.

(3A) A drug offence search shall not be carried out unless the appropriate consent has been given in writing.

(3B) Where it is proposed that a drug offence search be carried out, an appropriate officer shall inform the person who is to be subject to it—

(a) of the giving of the authorisation for it; and

(b) of the grounds for giving the authorisation.

(4) An intimate search which is only a drug offence search shall be by way of examination by a suitably qualified person.

(5) Except as provided by subsection (4) above, an intimate search shall be by way of examination by a suitably qualified person unless an officer of at least the rank of inspector considers that this is not practicable.

(6) An intimate search which is not carried out as mentioned in subsection (5) above shall be carried out by a constable.

(7) A constable may not carry out an intimate search of a person of the opposite sex.

(8) No intimate search may be carried out except—

(a) at a police station;

(b) at a hospital;

(c) at a registered medical practitioner's surgery; or

(d) at some other place used for medical purposes.

(9) An intimate search which is only a drug offence search may not be carried out at a police station.

(10) If an intimate search of a person is carried out, the custody record relating to him shall state—

(a) which parts of his body were searched; and

(b) why they were searched.

(10A) If the intimate search is a drug offence search, the custody record relating to that person shall also state—

(a) the authorisation by virtue of which the search was carried out;

(b) the grounds for giving the authorisation; and

(c) the fact that the appropriate consent was given

(11) The information required to be recorded by subsections (10) and (10A) above shall be recorded as soon as practicable after the completion of the search.

(12) The custody officer at a police station may seize and retain anything which is found on an intimate search of a person, or cause any such thing to be seized and retained—

(a) if he believes that the person from whom it is seized may use it—

(i) to cause physical injury to himself or any other person;

(ii) to damage property;

(iii) to interfere with evidence; or

(iv) to assist him to escape; or

(b) if he has reasonable grounds for believing that it may be evidence relating to an offence.

(13) Where anything is seized under this section, the person from whom it is seized shall be told the reason for the seizure unless he is—

(a) violent or likely to become violent; or

(b) incapable of understanding what is said to him.

(13A) Where the appropriate consent to a drug offence search of any person was refused without good cause, in any proceedings against that person for an offence—

(a) the court, in determining whether there is a case to answer;

(b) a judge, in deciding whether to grant an application made by the accused under paragraph 2 of Schedule 3 to the Crime and Disorder Act 1998 (applications for dismissal); and

(c) the court or jury, in determining whether that person is guilty of the offence charged,

may draw such inferences from the refusal as appear proper.

(14)–(16) …*

(17) In this section—

'the appropriate criminal intent' means an intent to commit an offence under—

(a) section 5(3) of the Misuse of Drugs Act 1971 (possession of controlled drug with intent to supply to another); or

(b) section 68(2) of the Customs and Excise Management Act 1979 (exportation etc., with intent to evade a prohibition or restriction);

'appropriate officer' means—

(a) a constable,

'Class A drug' has the meaning assigned to it by section 2(1)(b) of the Misuse of Drugs Act 1971;

'drug offence search' means an intimate search for a Class A drug which an officer has authorised by virtue of subsection (1)(b) above; and

'suitably qualified person' means—

(a) a registered medical practitioner; or

(b) a registered nurse.

55A X-rays and ultrasound scans

(1) If an officer of at least the rank of inspector has reasonable grounds for believing that a person who has been arrested for an offence and is in police detention—

(a) may have swallowed a Class A drug, and

(b) was in possession of it with the appropriate criminal intent before his arrest,

the officer may authorise that an x-ray is taken of the person or an ultrasound scan is carried out on the person (or both).

(2) An x-ray must not be taken of a person and an ultrasound scan must not be carried out on him unless the appropriate consent has been given in writing.

* **Editor's Note:** Information to be contained in annual reports.

(3) If it is proposed that an x-ray is taken or an ultrasound scan is carried out, an appropriate officer must inform the person who is to be subject to it—

(a) of the giving of the authorisation for it, and

(b) of the grounds for giving the authorisation.

(4) An x-ray may be taken or an ultrasound scan carried out only by a suitably qualified person and only at—

(a) a hospital,

(b) a registered medical practitioner's surgery, or

(c) some other place used for medical purposes.

(5) The custody record of the person must also state—

(a) the authorisation by virtue of which the x-ray was taken or the ultrasound scan was carried out,

(b) the grounds for giving the authorisation, and

(c) the fact that the appropriate consent was given.

(6) The information required to be recorded by subsection (5) must be recorded as soon as practicable after the x-ray has been taken or ultrasound scan carried out (as the case may be).

(7), (8) ...*

(9) If the appropriate consent to an x-ray or ultrasound scan of any person is refused without good cause, in any proceedings against that person for an offence—

(a) the court, in determining whether there is a case to answer,

(b) a judge, in deciding whether to grant an application made by the accused under paragraph 2 of Schedule 3 to the Crime and Disorder Act 1998 (applications for dismissal), and

(c) the court or jury, in determining whether that person is guilty of the offence charged,

may draw such inferences from the refusal as appear proper.

(10) In this section 'the appropriate criminal intent', 'appropriate officer', 'Class A drug' and 'suitably qualified person' have the same meanings as in section 55 above.

56 Right to have someone informed when arrested

(1) Where a person has been arrested and is being held in custody in a police station or other premises, he shall be entitled, if he so requests, to have one friend or relative or other person who is known to him or who is likely to take an interest in his welfare told, as soon as is practicable except to the extent that delay is permitted by this section, that he has been arrested and is being detained there.

(2) Delay is only permitted—

(a) in the case of a person who is in police detention for an indictable offence; and

(b) if an officer of at least the rank of inspector authorises it.

(3) In any case the person in custody must be permitted to exercise the right conferred by subsection (1) above within 36 hours from the relevant time, as defined in section 41(2) above.

(4) An officer may give an authorisation under subsection (2) above orally or in writing but, if he gives it orally, he shall confirm it in writing as soon as is practicable.

(5) Subject to subsection (5A) below an officer may only authorise delay where he has reasonable grounds for believing that telling the named person of the arrest—

(a) will lead to interference with or harm to evidence connected with an indictable offence or interference with or physical injury to other persons; or

(b) will lead to the alerting of other persons suspected of having committed such an offence but not yet arrested for it; or

(c) will hinder the recovery of any property obtained as a result of such an offence.

(5A) An officer may also authorise delay where he has reasonable grounds for believing that—

(a) the person detained for the indictable offence has benefited from his criminal conduct, and

(b) the recovery of the value of the property constituting the benefit will be hindered by telling the named person of the arrest.

* **Editor's Note:** Annual reports.

(5B) For the purposes of subsection (5A) above the question whether a person has benefited from his criminal conduct is to be decided in accordance with Part 2 of the Proceeds of Crime Act 2002.

(6) If a delay is authorised—

(a) the detained person shall be told the reason for it, and

(b) the reason shall be noted on his custody record.

(7) The duties imposed by subsection (6) above shall be performed as soon as is practicable.

(8) The rights conferred by this section on a person detained at a police station or other premises are exercisable whenever he is transferred from one place to another; and this section applies to each subsequent occasion on which they are exercisable as it applies to the first such occasion.

(9) There may be no further delay in permitting the exercise of the right conferred by subsection (1) above once the reason for authorising delay ceases to subsist.

(10) Nothing in this section applies to a person arrested or detained under the terrorism provisions or under section 27 of the National Security Act 2023, or detained under Part 1 of Schedule 3 to the Counter-Terrorism and Border Security Act 2019.

57 Additional rights of children and young persons

. . .*

58 Access to legal advice

(1) A person arrested and held in custody in a police station or other premises shall be entitled, if he so requests, to consult a solicitor privately at any time.

(2) Subject to subsection (3) below, a request under subsection (1) above and the time at which it was made shall be recorded in the custody record.

(3) Such a request need not be recorded in the custody record of a person who makes it at a time while he is at a court after being charged with an offence.

(4) If a person makes such a request, he must be permitted to consult a solicitor as soon as is practicable except to the extent that delay is permitted by this section.

(5) In any case he must be permitted to consult a solicitor within 36 hours from the relevant time, as defined in section 41(2) above.

(6) Delay in compliance with a request is only permitted—

(a) in the case of a person who is in police detention for an indictable offence; and

(b) if an officer of at least the rank of superintendent authorises it.

(7) An officer may give an authorisation under subsection (6) above orally or in writing but, if he gives it orally, he shall confirm it in writing as soon as is practicable.

(8) Subject to subsection (8A) below an officer may only authorise delay where he has reasonable grounds for believing that the exercise of the right conferred by subsection (1) above at the time when the person detained desires to exercise it—

(a) will lead to interference with or harm to evidence connected with an indictable offence or interference with or physical injury to other persons; or

(b) will lead to the alerting of other persons suspected of having committed such an offence but not yet arrested for it; or

(c) will hinder the recovery of any property obtained as a result of such an offence.

(8A) An officer may also authorise delay where he has reasonable grounds for believing that—

(a) the person detained for the indictable offence has benefited from his criminal conduct, and

(b) the recovery of the value of the property constituting the benefit will be hindered by the exercise of the right conferred by subsection (1) above.

(8B) For the purposes of subsection (8A) above the question whether a person has benefited from his criminal conduct is to be decided in accordance with Part 2 of the Proceeds of Crime Act 2002.

(9) If delay is authorised—

(a) the detained person shall be told the reason for it; and

(b) the reason shall be noted on his custody record.

(10) The duties imposed by subsection (9) above shall be performed as soon as is practicable.

* **Editor's Note:** Amends the Children and Young Persons Act 1933, section 34(2).

(11) There may be no further delay in permitting the exercise of the right conferred by subsection (1) above once the reason for authorising delay ceases to subsist.

(12) Nothing in this section applies to a person arrested or detained under the terrorism provisions or under section 27 of the National Security Act 2023, or detained under Part 1 of Schedule 3 to the Counter-Terrorism and Border Security Act 2019.

60 Audio recording of interviews

(1) It shall be the duty of the Secretary of State—

(a) to issue a code of practice in connection with the audio recording of interviews of persons suspected of the commission of criminal offences which are held by police officers at police stations; and

(b) to make an order requiring the audio recording of interviews of persons suspected of the commission of criminal offences, or of such descriptions of criminal offences as may be specified in the order, which are so held, in accordance with the code as it has effect for the time being.

(2) An order under subsection (1) above shall be made by statutory instrument and shall be subject to annulment in pursuance of a resolution of either House of Parliament.

60A Visual recording of interviews

(1) The Secretary of State shall have power—

(a) to issue a code of practice for the visual recording of interviews held by police officers at police stations; and

(b) to make an order requiring the visual recording of interviews so held, and requiring the visual recording to be in accordance with the code for the time being in force under this section.

(2) A requirement imposed by an order under this section may be imposed in relation to such cases or police stations in such areas, or both, as may be specified or described in the order.

(3) An order under subsection (1) above shall be made by statutory instrument and shall be subject to annulment in pursuance of a resolution of either House of Parliament.

(4) In this section—

(a) references to any interview are references to an interview of a person suspected of a criminal offence; and

(b) references to a visual recording include references to a visual recording in which an audio recording is comprised.

60B Notification of decision not to prosecute person interviewed

(1) This section applies where—

(a) a person suspected of the commission of a criminal offence is interviewed by a police officer but is not arrested for the offence, and

(b) the police officer in charge of investigating the offence determines that—

(i) there is not sufficient evidence to charge the person with an offence, or

(ii) there is sufficient evidence to charge the person with an offence but the person should not be charged with an offence or given a caution in respect of an offence.

(2) A police officer must give the person notice in writing that the person is not to be prosecuted.

(3) Subsection (2) does not prevent the prosecution of the person for an offence if new evidence comes to light after the notice was given.

(4) In this section 'caution' means—

(a) a diversionary or community caution under Part 6 of the Police, Crime, Sentencing and Courts Act 2022;

(b) a youth conditional caution within the meaning of Chapter 1 of Part 4 of the Crime and Disorder Act 1998;

(c) a youth caution under section 66ZA of that Act.

61 Finger-printing

(1) Except as provided by this section no person's fingerprints may be taken without the appropriate consent.

(2) Consent to the taking of a person's fingerprints must be in writing if it is given at a time when he is at a police station.

(3) The fingerprints of a person detained at a police station may be taken without the appropriate consent if—

(a) he is detained in consequence of his arrest for a recordable offence; and

(b) he has not had his fingerprints taken in the course of the investigation of the offence by the police.

(3A) Where a person mentioned in paragraph (a) of subsection (3) or (4) has already had his fingerprints taken in the course of the investigation of the offence by the police, that fact shall be disregarded for the purposes of that subsection if—

(a) the fingerprints taken on the previous occasion do not constitute a complete set of his fingerprints; or

(b) some or all of the fingerprints taken on the previous occasion are not of sufficient quality to allow satisfactory analysis, comparison or matching (whether in the case in question or generally).

(4) The fingerprints of a person detained at a police station may be taken without the appropriate consent if—

(a) he has been charged with a recordable offence or informed that he will be reported for such an offence; and

(b) he has not had his fingerprints taken in the course of the investigation of the offence by the police.

(4A) The fingerprints of a person who has answered to bail at a court or police station may be taken without the appropriate consent at the court or station if—

(a) the court, or

(b) an officer of at least the rank of inspector,

authorises them to be taken.

(4B) A court or officer may only give an authorisation under subsection (4A) if—

(a) the person who has answered to bail has answered to it for a person whose fingerprints were taken on a previous occasion and there are reasonable grounds for believing that he is not the same person; or

(b) the person who has answered to bail claims to be a different person from a person whose fingerprints were taken on a previous occasion.

(5) An officer may give an authorisation under subsection (4A) above orally or in writing but, if he gives it orally, he shall confirm it in writing as soon as is practicable.

(5A) The fingerprints of a person may be taken without the appropriate consent if (before or after the coming into force of this subsection) he has been arrested for a recordable offence and released and—

(a) he has not had his fingerprints taken in the course of the investigation of the offence by the police; or

(b) he has had his fingerprints taken in the course of that investigation but

(i) subsection (3A)(a) or (b) above applies, or

(ii) subsection (5C) below applies.

(5B) The fingerprints of a person not detained at a police station may be taken without the appropriate consent if (before or after the coming into force of this subsection) he has been charged with a recordable offence or informed that he will be reported for such an offence and—

(a) he has not had his fingerprints taken in the course of the investigation of the offence by the police; or

(b) he has had his fingerprints taken in the course of that investigation but

(i) subsection (3A)(a) or (b) above applies, or

(ii) subsection (5C) below applies.

(5C) This subsection applies where—

(a) the investigation was discontinued but subsequently resumed, and

(b) before the resumption of the investigation the fingerprints were destroyed pursuant to section 63D(3) below.

(6) Subject to this section, the fingerprints of a person may be taken without the appropriate consent if (before or after the coming into force of this subsection)—

(a) he has been convicted of a recordable offence, or

(b) he has been given a caution in respect of a recordable offence which, at the time of the caution, he has admitted, and

either of the conditions mentioned in subsection (6ZA) below is met.

(6ZA) The conditions referred to in subsection (6) above are—

(a) the person has not had his fingerprints taken since he was convicted or cautioned;

(b) he has had his fingerprints taken since then but subsection (3A)(a) or (b) above applies.

(6ZB) Fingerprints may only be taken as specified in subsection (6) above with the authorisation of an officer of at least the rank of inspector.

(6ZC) An officer may only give an authorisation under subsection (6ZB) above if the officer is satisfied that taking the fingerprints is necessary to assist in the prevention or detection of crime.

(6A) A constable may take a person's fingerprints without the appropriate consent if—

(a) the constable reasonably suspects that the person is committing or attempting to commit an offence, or has committed or attempted to commit an offence; and

(b) either of the two conditions mentioned in subsection (6B) is met.

(6B) The conditions are that—

(a) the name of the person is unknown to, and cannot be readily ascertained by, the constable;

(b) the constable has reasonable grounds for doubting whether a name furnished by the person as his name is his real name.

(6C) The taking of fingerprints by virtue of subsection (6A) does not count for any of the purposes of this Act as taking them in the course of the investigation of an offence by the police.

(6D) Subject to this section, the fingerprints of a person may be taken without the appropriate consent if—

(a) under the law in force in a country or territory outside England and Wales the person has been convicted of an offence under that law (whether before or after the coming into force of this subsection and whether or not he has been punished for it);

(b) the act constituting the offence would constitute a qualifying offence if done in England and Wales (whether or not it constituted such an offence when the person was convicted); and

(c) either of the conditions mentioned in subsection (6E) below is met.

(6E) The conditions referred to in subsection (6D)(c) above are—

(a) the person has not had his fingerprints taken on a previous occasion under subsection (6D) above;

(b) he has had his fingerprints taken on a previous occasion under that subsection but subsection (3A)(a) or (b) above applies.

(6F) Fingerprints may only be taken as specified in subsection (6D) above with the authorisation of an officer of at least the rank of inspector.

(6G) An officer may only give an authorisation under subsection (6F) above if the officer is satisfied that taking the fingerprints is necessary to assist in the prevention or detection of crime.

(7) Where a person's fingerprints are taken without the appropriate consent by virtue of any power conferred by this section—

(a) before the fingerprints are taken, the person shall be informed of—

(i) the reason for taking the fingerprints;

(ii) the power by virtue of which they are taken; and

(iii) in a case where the authorisation of the court or an officer is required for the exercise of the power, the fact that the authorisation has been given; and

(b) those matters shall be recorded as soon as practicable after the fingerprints are taken.

(7A) If a person's fingerprints are taken at a police station or by virtue of subsection (4A), (6A) at a place other than a police station, whether with or without the appropriate consent—

(a) before the fingerprints are taken, an officer (or, where by virtue of subsection (4A), (6A) or (6BA) the fingerprints are taken at a place other than a police station, the constable taking the fingerprints) shall inform him that they may be the subject of a speculative search; and

(b) the fact that the person has been informed of this possibility shall be recorded as soon as is practicable after the fingerprints have been taken.

(8) If he is detained at a police station when the fingerprints are taken, the matters referred to in subsection (7)(a)(i) to (iii) above and, in the case falling within subsection (7A) above, the fact referred to in paragraph (b) of that subsection shall be recorded on his custody record.

(8B) Any power under this section to take the fingerprints of a person without the appropriate consent, if not otherwise specified to be exercisable by a constable, shall be exercisable by a constable.

(9) Nothing in this section—

(a) affects any power conferred by paragraph 18(2) of Schedule 2 to the Immigration Act 1971; or

(b) applies to a person arrested or detained under the terrorism provisions or under section 27 of the National Security Act 2023, or detained under Part 1 of Schedule 3 to the Counter-Terrorism and Border Security Act 2019.

(10) Nothing in this section applies to a person arrested under an extradition arrest power.

61A Impressions of footwear

(1) Except as provided by this section, no impression of a person's footwear may be taken without the appropriate consent.

(2) Consent to the taking of an impression of a person's footwear must be in writing if it is given at a time when he is at a police station.

(3) Where a person is detained at a police station, an impression of his footwear may be taken without the appropriate consent if—

(a) he is detained in consequence of his arrest for a recordable offence, or has been charged with a recordable offence, or informed that he will be reported for a recordable offence; and

(b) he has not had an impression taken of his footwear in the course of the investigation of the offence by the police.

(4) Where a person mentioned in paragraph (a) of subsection (3) above has already had an impression taken of his footwear in the course of the investigation of the offence by the police, that fact shall be disregarded for the purposes of that subsection if the impression of his footwear taken previously is—

(a) incomplete; or

(b) is not of sufficient quality to allow satisfactory analysis, comparison or matching (whether in the case in question or generally).

(5) If an impression of a person's footwear is taken at a police station, whether with or without the appropriate consent—

(a) before it is taken, an officer shall inform him that it may be the subject of a speculative search; and

(b) the fact that the person has been informed of this possibility shall be recorded as soon as is practicable after the impression has been taken, and if he is detained at a police station, the record shall be made on his custody record.

(6) In a case where, by virtue of subsection (3) above, an impression of a person's footwear is taken without the appropriate consent—

(a) he shall be told the reason before it is taken; and

(b) the reason shall be recorded on his custody record as soon as is practicable after the impression is taken.

(7) The power to take an impression of the footwear of a person detained at a police station without the appropriate consent shall be exercisable by any constable.

(8) Nothing in this section applies to any person—

(a) arrested or detained under the terrorism provisions or detained under Part 1 of Schedule 3 to the Counter-Terrorism and Border Security Act 2019;
(b) arrested under an extradition arrest power.

62 Intimate samples

(1) Subject to section 63B below an intimate sample may be taken from a person in police detention only—
(a) if a police officer of at least the rank of inspector authorises it to be taken; and
(b) if the appropriate consent is given.

(1A) An intimate sample may be taken from a person who is not in police detention but from whom, in the course of the investigation of an offence, two or more non-intimate samples suitable for the same means of analysis have been taken which have proved insufficient—
(a) if a police officer of at least the rank of inspector authorises it to be taken; and
(b) if the appropriate consent is given.

(2) An officer may only give an authorisation under subsection (1) or (1A) above if he has reasonable grounds—
(a) for suspecting the involvement of the person from whom the sample is to be taken in a recordable offence; and
(b) for believing that the sample will tend to confirm or disprove his involvement.

(2A) An intimate sample may be taken from a person where—
(a) two or more non-intimate samples suitable for the same means of analysis have been taken from the person under section 63(3E) below (persons convicted of offences outside England and Wales etc.) but have proved insufficient;
(b) a police officer of at least the rank of inspector authorises it to be taken; and
(c) the appropriate consent is given.

(2B) An officer may only give an authorisation under subsection (2A) above if the officer is satisfied that taking the sample is necessary to assist in the prevention or detection of crime.

(3) An officer may give an authorisation under subsection (1) or (1A) or (2A) above orally or in writing but, if he gives it orally, he shall confirm it in writing as soon as is practicable.

(4) The appropriate consent must be given in writing.

(5) Before an intimate sample is taken from a person, an officer shall inform him of the following—
(a) the reason for taking the sample;
(b) the fact that authorisation has been given and the provision of this section under which it has been given; and
(c) if the sample was taken at a police station, the fact that the sample may be the subject of a speculative search.

(6) The reason referred to in subsection (5)(a) above must include, except in a case where the sample is taken under subsection (2A) above, a statement of the nature of the offence in which it is suspected that the person has been involved.

(7) After an intimate sample has been taken from a person, the following shall be recorded as soon as practicable—
(a) the matters referred to in subsection (5)(a) and (b) above;
(b) if the sample was taken at a police station, the fact that the person has been informed as specified in subsection (5)(c) above; and
(c) the fact that the appropriate consent was given.

(8) If an intimate sample is taken from a person detained at a police station, the matters required to be recorded by subsection (7) above shall be recorded in his custody record.

(9) In the case of an intimate sample which is a dental impression, the sample may be taken from a person only by a registered dentist.

(9A) In the case of any other form of intimate sample, except in the case of a sample of urine, the sample may be taken from a person only by—
(a) a registered medical practitioner; or
(b) a registered health care professional.

(10) Where the appropriate consent to the taking of an intimate sample from a person was refused without good cause, in any proceedings against that person for an offence—

(a) the court, in determining—

(ii) whether there is a case to answer; and

(aa) a judge, in deciding whether to grant an application made by the accused under paragraph 2 of Schedule 3 to the Crime and Disorder Act 1998 (applications for dismissal); and

(b) the court or jury, in determining whether that person is guilty of the offence charged,

may draw such inferences from the refusal as appear proper.

(11) Nothing in this section applies to the taking of a specimen for the purposes of any of the provisions of sections 4 to 11 of the Road Traffic Act 1988 or of sections 26 to 38 of the Transport and Works Act 1992.

(12) Nothing in this section applies to a person arrested or detained under the terrorism provisions; and subsection (1A) shall not apply where the non-intimate samples mentioned in that subsection were taken under paragraph 10 of Schedule 8 to the Terrorism Act 2000.

(13) Nothing in this section applies to a person detained under Part 1 of Schedule 3 to the Counter-Terrorism and Border Security Act 2019; and subsection (1A) does not apply where the non-intimate samples mentioned in that subsection were taken under Part 2 of that Schedule.

(14) Nothing in this section applies to a person arrested or detained under section 27 of the National Security Act 2023; and subsection (1A) does not apply where the non-intimate samples mentioned in that subsection were taken under paragraph 10 of Schedule 6 to that Act.

63 Other samples

(1) Except as provided by this section, a non-intimate sample may not be taken from a person without the appropriate consent.

(2) Consent to the taking of a non-intimate sample must be given in writing.

(2A) A non-intimate sample may be taken from a person without the appropriate consent if two conditions are satisfied.

(2B) The first is that the person is in police detention in consequence of his arrest for a recordable offence.

(2C) The second is that—

(a) he has not had a non-intimate sample of the same type and from the same part of the body taken in the course of the investigation of the offence by the police, or

(b) he has had such a sample taken but it proved insufficient.

(3) A non-intimate sample may be taken from a person without the appropriate consent if—

(a) he is being held in custody by the police on the authority of a court; and

(b) an officer of at least the rank of inspector authorises it to be taken without the appropriate consent.

(3ZA) A non-intimate sample may be taken from a person without the appropriate consent if (before or after the coming into force of this subsection) he has been arrested for a recordable offence and released and—

(a) he has not had a non-intimate sample of the same type and from the same part of the body taken from him in the course of the investigation of the offence by the police; or

(b) he has had a non-intimate sample taken from him in the course of that investigation but—

(i) it was not suitable for the same means of analysis, or

(ii) it proved insufficient, or

(iii) subsection (3AA) below applies.

(3A) A non-intimate sample may be taken from a person (whether or not he is in police detention or held in custody by the police on the authority of a court) without the appropriate consent if he has been charged with a recordable offence or informed that he will be reported for such an offence and—

(a) he has not had a non-intimate sample taken from him in the course of the investigation of the offence by the police; or

(b) he has had a non-intimate sample taken from him in the course of that investigation but—
(i) it was not suitable for the same means of analysis, or
(ii) it proved insufficient, or
(iii) subsection (3AA) below applies; or
(c) he has had a non-intimate sample taken from him in the course of that investigation and—
(i) the sample has been destroyed pursuant to section 63R below or any other enactment, and
(ii) it is disputed, in relation to any proceedings relating to the offence, whether a DNA profile relevant to the proceedings is derived from the sample.

(3AA) This subsection applies where the investigation was discontinued but subsequently resumed, and before the resumption of the investigation—
(a) any DNA profile derived from the sample was destroyed pursuant to section 63D(3) below, and
(b) the sample itself was destroyed pursuant to section 63R(4), (5) or (12) below.

(3B) Subject to this section, a non-intimate sample may be taken from a person without the appropriate consent if (before or after the coming into force of this subsection)—
(a) he has been convicted of a recordable offence, or
(b) he has been given a caution in respect of a recordable offence which, at the time of the caution, he has admitted, and

either of the conditions mentioned in subsection (3BA) below is met.

(3BA) The conditions referred to in subsection (3B) above are—
(a) a non-intimate sample has not been taken from the person since he was convicted or cautioned;
(b) such a sample has been taken from him since then but—
(i) it was not suitable for the same means of analysis, or
(ii) it proved insufficient.

(3BB) A non-intimate sample may only be taken as specified in subsection (3B) above with the authorisation of an officer of at least the rank of inspector.

(3BC) An officer may only give an authorisation under subsection (3BB) above if the officer is satisfied that taking the sample is necessary to assist in the prevention or detection of crime.

(3C) A non-intimate sample may also be taken from a person without the appropriate consent if he is a person to whom section 2 of the Criminal Evidence (Amendment) Act 1997 applies (persons detained following acquittal on grounds of insanity or finding of unfitness to plead).

(3E) Subject to this section, a non-intimate sample may be taken without the appropriate consent from a person if—
(a) under the law in force in a country or territory outside England and Wales the person has been convicted of an offence under that law (whether before or after the coming into force of this subsection and whether or not he has been punished for it);
(b) the act constituting the offence would constitute a qualifying offence if done in England and Wales (whether or not it constituted such an offence when the person was convicted); and
(c) either of the conditions mentioned in subsection (3F) below is met.

(3F) The conditions referred to in subsection (3E)(c) above are—
(a) the person has not had a non-intimate sample taken from him on a previous occasion under subsection (3E) above;
(b) he has had such a sample taken from him on a previous occasion under that subsection but—
(i) the sample was not suitable for the same means of analysis, or
(ii) it proved insufficient.

(3G) A non-intimate sample may only be taken as specified in subsection (3E) above with the authorisation of an officer of at least the rank of inspector.

(3H) An officer may only give an authorisation under subsection (3G) above if the officer is satisfied that taking the sample is necessary to assist in the prevention or detection of crime.

(4) An officer may only give an authorisation under subsection (3) above if he has reasonable grounds—

(a) for suspecting the involvement of the person from whom the sample is to be taken in a recordable offence; and

(b) for believing that the sample will tend to confirm or disprove his involvement.

(5) An officer may give an authorisation under subsection (3) above orally or in writing but, if he gives it orally, he shall confirm it in writing as soon as is practicable.

(5A) An officer shall not give an authorisation under subsection (3) above for the taking from any person of a non-intimate sample consisting of a skin impression if—

(a) a skin impression of the same part of the body has already been taken from that person in the course of the investigation of the offence; and

(b) the impression previously taken is not one that has proved insufficient.

(6) Where a non-intimate sample is taken from a person without the appropriate consent by virtue of any power conferred by this section—

(a) before the sample is taken, an officer shall inform him of—

(i) the reason for taking the sample;

(ii) the power by virtue of which it is taken; and

(iii) in a case where the authorisation of an officer is required for the exercise of the power, the fact that the authorisation has been given; and

(b) those matters shall be recorded as soon as practicable after the sample is taken.

(7) The reason referred to in subsection (6)(a)(i) above must include, except in a case where the non-intimate sample is taken under subsection (3B) or (3E) above, a statement of the nature of the offence in which it is suspected that the person has been involved.

(8B) If a non-intimate sample is taken from a person at a police station, whether with or without the appropriate consent—

(a) before the sample is taken, an officer shall inform him that it may be the subject of a speculative search; and

(b) the fact that the person has been informed of this possibility shall be recorded as soon as practicable after the sample has been taken.

(9) If a non-intimate sample is taken from a person detained at a police station, the matters required to be recorded by subsection (6) or (8B) above shall be recorded in his custody record.

(9ZA) The power to take a non-intimate sample from a person without the appropriate consent shall be exercisable by any constable.

(9A) Subsection (3B) above shall not apply to

(a) any person convicted before 10th April 1995 unless he is a person to whom section 1 of the Criminal Evidence (Amendment) Act 1997 applies (persons imprisoned or detained by virtue of pre-existing conviction for sexual offence etc.); or

(b) a person given a caution before 10th April 1995.

(10) Nothing in this section applies to a person arrested or detained under the terrorism provisions or detained under Part 1 of Schedule 3 to the Counter-Terrorism and Border Security Act 2019.

(10A) Nothing in this section applies to a person arrested or detained under section 27 of the National Security Act 2023.

(11) Nothing in this section applies to a person arrested under an extradition arrest power.

63A Fingerprints and samples: supplementary provisions

(1) Where a person has been arrested on suspicion of being involved in a recordable offence or has been charged with such an offence or has been informed that he will be reported for such an offence, fingerprints, impressions of footwear or samples or the information derived from samples taken under any power conferred by this Part of this Act from the person may be checked against—

(a) other fingerprints impressions of footwear or samples to which the person seeking to check has access and which are held by or on behalf of any one or more relevant law-enforcement authorities or which are held in connection with or as a result of an investigation of an offence;

(b) information derived from other samples if the information is contained in records to which the person seeking to check has access and which are held as mentioned in paragraph (a) above.

(1ZA) Fingerprints taken by virtue of section 61(6A) above may be checked against other fingerprints to which the person seeking to check has access and which are held by or on behalf of any one or more relevant law-enforcement authorities or which are held in connection with or as a result of an investigation of an offence.

(1A) In subsection (1) and (1ZA) above 'relevant law-enforcement authority' means—

(a) a police force;

(b) the National Crime Agency;

(ba) the tri-service serious crime unit;

(d) a public authority (not falling within paragraphs (a) to (ba)) with functions in any part of the British Islands which consist of or include the investigation of crimes or the charging of offenders;

(e) any person with functions in any country or territory outside the United Kingdom which—

(i) correspond to those of a police force; or

(ii) otherwise consist of or include the investigation of conduct contrary to the law of that country or territory, or the apprehension of persons guilty of such conduct;

(f) any person with functions under any international agreement which consist of or include the investigation of conduct which is—

(i) unlawful under the law of one or more places,

(ii) prohibited by such an agreement, or

(iii) contrary to international law,

or the apprehension of persons guilty of such conduct.

(1B) The reference in subsection (1A) above to a police force is a reference to any of the following—

(a) any police force maintained under section 2 of the Police Act 1996 (police forces in England and Wales outside London);

(b) the metropolitan police force;

(c) the City of London police force;

(d)–(o) ...*

(1BA) In subsection (1A) 'tri-service serious crime unit' means the unit described in section 375(1A) of the Armed Forces Act 2006.

(1C) Where—

(a) fingerprints, impressions of footwear or samples have been taken from any person in connection with the investigation of an offence but otherwise than in circumstances to which subsection (1) above applies, and

(b) that person has given his consent in writing to the use in a speculative search of the fingerprints, of the impressions of footwear or of the samples and of information derived from them,

the fingerprints or impressions of footwear or, as the case may be, those samples and that information may be checked against any of the fingerprints, impressions of footwear, samples or information mentioned in paragraph (a) or (b) of that subsection.

(1D) A consent given for the purposes of subsection (1C) above shall not be capable of being withdrawn.

(1E) Where fingerprints or samples have been taken from any person under section 61(6) or 63(3B) above (persons convicted etc.), the fingerprints or samples, or information derived from the samples, may be checked against any of the fingerprints, samples or information mentioned in subsection (1)(a) or (b) above.

* **Editor's Note:** Applies to other forces.

(1F) Where fingerprints or samples have been taken from any person under section 61(6D), 62(2A) or 63(3E) above (offences outside England and Wales etc.), the fingerprints or samples, or information derived from the samples, may be checked against any of the fingerprints, samples or information mentioned in subsection (1)(a) or (b) above.

(2) Where a sample of hair other than pubic hair is to be taken the sample may be taken either by cutting hairs or by plucking hairs with their roots so long as no more are plucked than the person taking the sample reasonably considers to be necessary for a sufficient sample.

(3) Where any power to take a sample is exercisable in relation to a person the sample may be taken in a prison or other institution to which the Prison Act 1952 applies.

(3A) Where—

- (a) the power to take a non-intimate sample under section 63(3B) above is exercisable in relation to any person who is detained under Part III of the Mental Health Act 1983 in pursuance of—
  - (i) a hospital order or interim hospital order made following his conviction for the recordable offence in question, or
  - (ii) a transfer direction given at a time when he was detained in pursuance of any sentence or order imposed following that conviction, or
- (b) the power to take a non-intimate sample under section 63(3C) above is exercisable in relation to any person,

the sample may be taken in the hospital in which he is detained under that Part of that Act.

Expressions used in this subsection and in the Mental Health Act 1983 have the same meaning as in that Act.

(3B) Where the power to take a non-intimate sample under section 63(3B) above is exercisable in relation to a person detained in pursuance of directions of the Secretary of State under section 92 of the Powers of Criminal Courts (Sentencing) Act 2000 or section 260 of the Sentencing Code, the sample may be taken at the place where he is so detained.

(4) Schedule 2A (fingerprinting and samples: power to require attendance at police station) shall have effect.

63AA Inclusion of DNA profiles on National DNA Database

(1) This section applies to a DNA profile which is derived from a DNA sample and which is retained under any power conferred by any of sections 63E to 63L (including those sections as applied by section 63P).

(2) A DNA profile to which this section applies must be recorded on the National DNA Database.

63AB National DNA Database Strategy Board

(1) The Secretary of State must make arrangements for a National DNA Database Strategy Board to oversee the operation of the National DNA Database.

(2) The National DNA Database Strategy Board must issue guidance about the destruction of DNA profiles which are, or may be, retained under this Part of this Act.

(3) A chief officer of a police force in England and Wales must act in accordance with guidance issued under subsection (2).

(4) The National DNA Database Strategy Board may issue guidance about the circumstances in which applications may be made to the Commissioner for the Retention and Use of Biometric Material under section 63G.

(5) Before issuing any such guidance, the National DNA Database Strategy Board must consult the Commissioner for the Retention and Use of Biometric Material.

(6) The Secretary of State must publish the governance rules of the National DNA Database Strategy Board and lay a copy of the rules before Parliament.

(7) The National DNA Database Strategy Board must make an annual report to the Secretary of State about the exercise of its functions.

(8) The Secretary of State must publish the report and lay a copy of the published report before Parliament.

(9) The Secretary of State may exclude from publication any part of the report if, in the opinion of the Secretary of State, the publication of that part would be contrary to the public interest or prejudicial to national security.

63B Testing for presence of Class A drugs

(1) A sample of urine or a non-intimate sample may be taken from a person in police detention for the purpose of ascertaining whether he has any specified Class A drug in his body if—

(a) either the arrest condition or the charge condition is met;

(b) both the age condition and the request condition are met; and

(c) the notification condition is met in relation to the arrest condition, the charge condition or the age condition (as the case may be).

(1A) The arrest condition is that the person concerned has been arrested for an offence but has not been charged with that offence and either—

(a) the offence is a trigger offence; or

(b) a police officer of at least the rank of inspector has reasonable grounds for suspecting that the misuse by that person of a specified Class A drug caused or contributed to the offence and has authorised the sample to be taken.

(2) The charge condition is either—

(a) that the person concerned has been charged with a trigger offence; or

(b) that the person concerned has been charged with an offence and a police officer of at least the rank of inspector, who has reasonable grounds for suspecting that the misuse by that person of any specified Class A drug caused or contributed to the offence, has authorised the sample to be taken.

(3) The age condition is—

(a) if the arrest condition is met, that the person concerned has attained the age of 18;

(b) if the charge condition is met, that he has attained the age of 14.

(4) The request condition is that a police officer has requested the person concerned to give the sample.

(4A) The notification condition is that—

(a) the relevant chief officer has been notified by the Secretary of State that appropriate arrangements have been made for the police area as a whole, or for the particular police station, in which the person is in police detention, and

(b) the notice has not been withdrawn.

(4B) For the purposes of subsection (4A) above, appropriate arrangements are arrangements for the taking of samples under this section from whichever of the following is specified in the notification—

(a) persons in respect of whom the arrest condition is met;

(b) persons in respect of whom the charge condition is met;

(c) persons who have not attained the age of 18.

(5) Before requesting the person concerned to give a sample, an officer must—

(a) warn him that if, when so requested, he fails without good cause to do so he may be liable to prosecution, and

(b) in a case within subsection (1A)(b) or (2)(b) above, inform him of the giving of the authorisation and of the grounds in question.

(5A) In the case of a person who has not attained the age of 18—

(a) the making of the request under subsection (4) above;

(b) the giving of the warning and (where applicable) the information under subsection (5) above; and

(c) the taking of the sample,

may not take place except in the presence of an appropriate adult.

(5B) If a sample is taken under this section from a person in respect of whom the arrest condition is met no other sample may be taken from him under this section during the same continuous period of detention but—

(a) if the charge condition is also met in respect of him at any time during that period, the sample must be treated as a sample taken by virtue of the fact that the charge condition is met;

(b) the fact that the sample is to be so treated must be recorded in the person's custody record.

(5C) Despite subsection (1)(a) above, a sample may be taken from a person under this section if—

(a) he was arrested for an offence (the first offence),

(b) the arrest condition is met but the charge condition is not met,

(c) before a sample is taken by virtue of subsection (1) above he would (but for his arrest as mentioned in paragraph (d) below) be required to be released from police detention,

(d) he continues to be in police detention by virtue of his having been arrested for an offence not falling within subsection (1A) above, and

(e) the sample is taken before the end of the period of 24 hours starting with the time when his detention by virtue of his arrest for the first offence began.

(5D) A sample must not be taken from a person under this section if he is detained in a police station unless he has been brought before the custody officer.

(6) A sample may be taken under this section only by a person prescribed by regulations made by the Secretary of State by statutory instrument.

No regulations shall be made under this subsection unless a draft has been laid before, and approved by resolution of, each House of Parliament.

(6A) The Secretary of State may by order made by statutory instrument amend—

(a) paragraph (a) of subsection (3) above, by substituting for the age for the time being specified a different age specified in the order, or different ages so specified for different police areas so specified;

(b) paragraph (b) of that subsection, by substituting for the age for the time being specified a different age specified in the order.

(6B) A statutory instrument containing an order under subsection (6A) above shall not be made unless a draft of the instrument has been laid before, and approved by a resolution of, each House of Parliament.

(7) Information obtained from a sample taken under this section may be disclosed—

(a) for the purpose of informing any decision about granting bail in criminal proceedings (within the meaning of the Bail Act 1976) to the person concerned;

(aa) for the purpose of informing any decision about the giving of a diversionary caution under Part 6 of the Police, Crime, Sentencing and Courts Act 2022 or a youth conditional caution under Chapter 1 of Part 4 of the Crime and Disorder Act 1998 to the person concerned;

(b) where the person concerned is in police detention or is remanded in or committed to custody by an order of a court or has been granted such bail, for the purpose of informing any decision about his supervision;

(c) where the person concerned is convicted of an offence, for the purpose of informing any decision about the appropriate sentence to be passed by a court and any decision about his supervision or release;

(ca) for the purpose of an assessment which the person concerned is required to attend by virtue of section 9(2) or 10(2) of the Drugs Act 2005;

(cb) for the purpose of proceedings against the person concerned for an offence under section 12(3) or 14(3) of that Act;

(d) for the purpose of ensuring that appropriate advice and treatment is made available to the person concerned.

(8) A person who fails without good cause to give any sample which may be taken from him under this section shall be guilty of an offence.

(10) In this section—

'appropriate adult', in relation to a person who has not attained the age of 18, means—
(a) his parent or guardian or, if he is in the care of a local authority or voluntary organisation, a person representing that authority or organisation; or
(b) a social worker of a local authority; or
(c) if no person falling within paragraph (a) or (b) is available, any responsible person aged 18 or over who is not a police officer or a person employed for, or engaged on, police purposes; and 'police purposes' has the meaning given by section 101(2) of the Police Act 1996;

'relevant chief officer' means—
(a) in relation to a police area, the chief officer of police of the police force for that police area; or
(b) in relation to a police station, the chief officer of police of the police force for the police area in which the police station is situated.

63C Testing for presence of Class A drugs: supplementary

(1) A person guilty of an offence under section 63B above shall be liable on summary conviction to imprisonment for a term not exceeding three months, or to a fine not exceeding level 4 on the standard scale, or to both.

(2) A police officer may give an authorisation under section 63B above orally or in writing but, if he gives it orally, he shall confirm it in writing as soon as is practicable.

(3) If a sample is taken under section 63B above by virtue of an authorisation, the authorisation and the grounds for the suspicion shall be recorded as soon as is practicable after the sample is taken.

(4) If the sample is taken from a person detained at a police station, the matters required to be recorded by subsection (3) above shall be recorded in his custody record.

(5) Subsections (11) and (12) of section 62 above apply for the purposes of section 63B above as they do for the purposes of that section; and section 63B above does not prejudice the generality of sections 62 and 63 above.

(6) In section 63B above—

'Class A drug' and 'misuse' have the same meanings as in the Misuse of Drugs Act 1971;

'specified' (in relation to a Class A drug) and 'trigger offence' have the same meanings as in Part III of the Criminal Justice and Court Services Act 2000.

63D Destruction of fingerprints and DNA profiles

(1) This section applies to—
(a) fingerprints—
(i) taken from a person under any power conferred by this Part of this Act, or
(ii) taken by the police, with the consent of the person from whom they were taken, in connection with the investigation of an offence by the police, and
(b) a DNA profile derived from a DNA sample taken as mentioned in paragraph (a)(i) or (ii).

(2) Fingerprints and DNA profiles to which this section applies ('section 63D material') must be destroyed if it appears to the responsible chief officer of police that—
(a) the taking of the fingerprint or, in the case of a DNA profile, the taking of the sample from which the DNA profile was derived, was unlawful, or
(b) the fingerprint was taken, or, in the case of a DNA profile, was derived from a sample taken, from a person in connection with that person's arrest and the arrest was unlawful or based on mistaken identity.

(3) In any other case, section 63D material must be destroyed unless it is retained under any power conferred by sections 63E to 63O (including those sections as applied by section 63P).

(4) Section 63D material which ceases to be retained under a power mentioned in subsection (3) may continue to be retained under any other such power which applies to it.

(5) Nothing in this section prevents a speculative search, in relation to section 63D material, from being carried out within such time as may reasonably be required for the search if the responsible chief officer of police considers the search to be desirable.

63E Retention of section 63D material pending investigation or proceedings

(1) This section applies to section 63D material taken (or, in the case of a DNA profile, derived from a sample taken) in connection with the investigation of an offence in which it is suspected that the person to whom the material relates has been involved.

(2) The material may be retained until the conclusion of the investigation of the offence or, where the investigation gives rise to proceedings against the person for the offence, until the conclusion of those proceedings.

63F Retention of section 63D material: persons arrested for or charged with a qualifying offence

(1) This section applies to section 63D material which—

- (a) relates to a person who is arrested for, or charged with, a qualifying offence but is not convicted of that offence, and
- (b) was taken (or, in the case of a DNA profile, derived from a sample taken) in connection with the investigation of the offence.

(2) If the person has previously been convicted of a recordable offence which is not an excluded offence, or is so convicted before the material is required to be destroyed by virtue of this section, the material may be retained indefinitely.

(2A) In subsection (2), references to a recordable offence include an offence under the law of a country or territory outside England and Wales where the act constituting the offence would constitute a recordable offence if done in England and Wales (and, in the application of subsection (2) where a person has previously been convicted, this applies whether or not the act constituted such an offence when the person was convicted).

(3) Otherwise, material falling within subsection (4), (5) or (5A) may be retained until the end of the retention period specified in subsection (6).

(4) Material falls within this subsection if it—

- (a) relates to a person who is charged with a qualifying offence but is not convicted of that offence, and
- (b) was taken (or, in the case of a DNA profile, derived from a sample taken) in connection with the investigation of the offence.

(5) Material falls within this subsection if—

- (a) it relates to a person who is arrested for a qualifying offence, other than a terrorism-related qualifying offence or a national security-related qualifying offence, but is not charged with that offence,
- (b) it was taken (or, in the case of a DNA profile, derived from a sample taken) in connection with the investigation of the offence, and
- (c) the Commissioner for the Retention and Use of Biometric Material has consented under section 63G to the retention of the material.

(5A) Material falls within this subsection if—

- (a) it relates to a person who is arrested for a terrorism-related qualifying offence or a national security-related qualifying offence but is not charged with that offence, and
- (b) it was taken (or, in the case of a DNA profile, derived from a sample taken) in connection with the investigation of the offence.

(6) The retention period is—

- (a) in the case of fingerprints, the period of 3 years beginning with the date on which the fingerprints were taken, and
- (b) in the case of a DNA profile, the period of 3 years beginning with the date on which the DNA sample from which the profile was derived was taken (or, if the profile was derived from more than one DNA sample, the date on which the first of those samples was taken).

(7) The responsible chief officer of police or a specified chief officer of police may apply to a District Judge (Magistrates' Courts) for an order extending the retention period.

(8) An application for an order under subsection (7) must be made within the period of 3 months ending on the last day of the retention period.

(9) An order under subsection (7) may extend the retention period by a period which—
(a) begins with the end of the retention period, and
(b) ends with the end of the period of 2 years beginning with the end of the retention period.

(10) The following persons may appeal to the Crown Court against an order under subsection (7), or a refusal to make such an order—
(a) the responsible chief officer of police;
(b) a specified chief officer of police;
(c) the person from whom the material was taken.

(11) In this section—
'excluded offence', in relation to a person, means a recordable offence—
(a) which—
(i) is not a qualifying offence,
(ii) is the only recordable offence of which the person has been convicted, and
(iii) was committed when the person was aged under 18, and
(b) for which the person was not given a relevant custodial sentence of 5 years or more,
'national security-related qualifying offence' means—
(a) an offence under section 18 of the National Security Act 2023 or for the time being listed in section 33(3)(a) of that Act, or
(b) an ancillary offence, as defined in section 65A(5), relating to an offence for the time being listed in section 33(3)(a) of that Act,
'relevant custodial sentence' has the meaning given by section 63K(6),
'a specified chief officer of police' means—
(a) the chief officer of the police force of the area in which the person from whom the material was taken resides, or
(b) a chief officer of police who believes that the person is in, or is intending to come to, the chief officer's police area.
'terrorism-related qualifying offence' means—
(a) an offence for the time being listed in section 41(1) of the Counter-Terrorism Act 2008 (see section 65A(2)(r) below), or
(b) an ancillary offence, as defined by section 65A(5) below, relating to an offence for the time being listed in section 41(1) of that Act.

(12) For the purposes of the definition of 'excluded offence' in subsection (11)—
(a) references to a recordable offence or a qualifying offence include an offence under the law of a country or territory outside England and Wales where the act constituting the offence would constitute a recordable offence or (as the case may be) a qualifying offence if done in England and Wales (whether or not it constituted such an offence when the person was convicted), and
(b) in the application of paragraph (b) of that definition in relation to an offence under the law of a country or territory outside England and Wales, the reference to a relevant custodial sentence of 5 years or more is to be read as a reference to a sentence of imprisonment or other form of detention of 5 years or more.

63G Retention of section 63D material by virtue of section 63F(5): consent of Commissioner

(1) The responsible chief officer of police may apply under subsection (2) or (3) to the Commissioner for the Retention and Use of Biometric Material for consent to the retention of section 63D material which falls within section 63F(5)(a) and (b).

(2) The responsible chief officer of police may make an application under this subsection if the responsible chief officer of police considers that the material was taken (or, in the case of a DNA profile, derived from a sample taken) in connection with the investigation of an offence where any alleged victim of the offence was, at the time of the offence—
(a) under the age of 18,
(b) a vulnerable adult, or

(c) associated with the person to whom the material relates.

(3) The responsible chief officer of police may make an application under this subsection if the responsible chief officer of police considers that—

(a) the material is not material to which subsection (2) relates, but

(b) the retention of the material is necessary to assist in the prevention or detection of crime.

(4) The Commissioner may, on an application under this section, consent to the retention of material to which the application relates if the Commissioner considers that it is appropriate to retain the material.

(5) But where notice is given under subsection (6) in relation to the application, the Commissioner must, before deciding whether or not to give consent, consider any representations by the person to whom the material relates which are made within the period of 28 days beginning with the day on which the notice is given.

(6) The responsible chief officer of police must give to the person to whom the material relates notice of—

(a) an application under this section, and

(b) the right to make representations.

(7) A notice under subsection (6) may, in particular, be given to a person by—

(a) leaving it at the person's usual or last known address (whether residential or otherwise),

(b) sending it to the person by post at that address, or

(c) sending it to the person by email or other electronic means.

(8) The requirement in subsection (6) does not apply if the whereabouts of the person to whom the material relates is not known and cannot, after reasonable inquiry, be ascertained by the responsible chief officer of police.

(9) An application or notice under this section must be in writing.

(10) In this section—

'victim' includes intended victim,

'vulnerable adult' means a person aged 18 or over whose ability to protect himself or herself from violence, abuse or neglect is significantly impaired through physical or mental disability or illness, through old age or otherwise,

and the reference in subsection (2)(c) to a person being associated with another person is to be read in accordance with section 62(3) to (7) of the Family Law Act 1996.

63H Retention of section 63D material: persons arrested for or charged with a minor offence

(1) This section applies to section 63D material which—

(a) relates to a person who—

(i) is arrested for or charged with a recordable offence other than a qualifying offence,

(ii) if arrested for or charged with more than one offence arising out of a single course of action, is not also arrested for or charged with a qualifying offence, and

(iii) is not convicted of the offence or offences in respect of which the person is arrested or charged, and

(b) was taken (or, in the case of a DNA profile, derived from a sample taken) in connection with the investigation of the offence or offences in respect of which the person is arrested or charged.

(2) If the person has previously been convicted of a recordable offence which is not an excluded offence, the material may be retained indefinitely.

(2A) In subsection (2), the reference to a recordable offence includes an offence under the law of a country or territory outside England and Wales where the act constituting the offence would constitute a recordable offence if done in England and Wales (whether or not it constituted such an offence when the person was convicted).

(3) In this section 'excluded offence' has the meaning given by section 63F(11) (read with section 63F(12)).

63I Retention of material: persons convicted of a recordable offence

(1) This section applies, subject to subsection (3), to—

(a) section 63D material which—

(i) relates to a person who is convicted of a recordable offence, and

(ii) was taken (or, in the case of a DNA profile, derived from a sample taken) in connection with the investigation of the offence, or

(b) material taken under section 61(6) or 63(3B) which relates to a person who is convicted of a recordable offence.

(2) The material may be retained indefinitely.

(3) This section does not apply to section 63D material to which section 63K applies.

63IA Retention of material: persons convicted of an offence outside England and Wales after taking of section 63D material

(1) This section applies where—

(a) section 63D material is taken (or, in the case of a DNA profile, derived from a sample taken) in connection with the investigation of an offence,

(b) at any time before the material is required to be destroyed by virtue of this Part of this Act, the person is convicted of an offence under the law of a country or territory outside England and Wales, and

(c) the act constituting the offence mentioned in paragraph (b) would constitute a recordable offence if done in England and Wales.

(2) The material may be retained indefinitely.

(3) This section does not apply where section 63KA applies

63J Retention of material: persons convicted of an offence outside England and Wales: other cases

(1) This section applies to material falling within subsection (2) relating to a person who is convicted of an offence under the law of any country or territory outside England and Wales.

(2) Material falls within this subsection if it is—

(a) fingerprints taken from the person under section 61(6D) (power to take fingerprints without consent in relation to offences outside England and Wales), or

(b) a DNA profile derived from a DNA sample taken from the person under section 62(2A) or 63(3E) (powers to take intimate and non-intimate samples in relation to offences outside England and Wales).

(3) The material may be retained indefinitely.

63K Retention of section 63D material: exception for persons under 18 convicted of first minor offence

(1) This section applies to section 63D material which—

(a) relates to a person who—

(i) is convicted of a recordable offence other than a qualifying offence,

(ii) has not previously been convicted of a recordable offence, and

(iii) is aged under 18 at the time of the offence, and

(b) was taken (or, in the case of a DNA profile, derived from a sample taken) in connection with the investigation of the offence.

(1A) In subsection (1)(a)(ii), the reference to a recordable offence includes an offence under the law of a country or territory outside England and Wales where the act constituting the offence would constitute a recordable offence if done in England and Wales (whether or not it constituted such an offence when the person was convicted).

(2) Where the person is given a relevant custodial sentence of less than 5 years in respect of the offence, the material may be retained until the end of the period consisting of the term of the sentence plus 5 years.

(3) Where the person is given a relevant custodial sentence of 5 years or more in respect of the offence, the material may be retained indefinitely.

(4) Where the person is given a sentence other than a relevant custodial sentence in respect of the offence, the material may be retained until—

(a) in the case of fingerprints, the end of the period of 5 years beginning with the date on which the fingerprints were taken, and

(b) in the case of a DNA profile, the end of the period of 5 years beginning with—

(i) the date on which the DNA sample from which the profile was derived was taken, or

(ii) if the profile was derived from more than one DNA sample, the date on which the first of those samples was taken.

(5) But if, before the end of the period within which material may be retained by virtue of this section, the person is again convicted of a recordable offence, the material may be retained indefinitely.

(5A) In subsection (5), the reference to a recordable offence includes an offence under the law of a country or territory outside England and Wales where the act constituting the offence would constitute a recordable offence if done in England and Wales.

(6) In this section, 'relevant custodial sentence' means any of the following—

(a) a custodial sentence within the meaning of section 76 of the Powers of Criminal Courts (Sentencing) Act 2000 or section 222 of the Sentencing Code;

(b) a sentence of a period of detention and training (excluding any period of supervision) which a person is liable to serve under an order under section 211 of the Armed Forces Act 2006 or a secure training order.

63KA Retention of section 63D material under section 63IA: exception for persons under 18 convicted of first minor offence outside England and Wales

(1) This section applies where—

(a) section 63D material is taken (or, in the case of a DNA profile, derived from a sample taken) in connection with the investigation of an offence,

(b) at any time before the material is required to be destroyed by virtue of this Part of this Act, the person is convicted of an offence under the law of a country or territory outside England and Wales,

(c) the act constituting the offence mentioned in paragraph (b) would constitute a recordable offence if done in England and Wales but would not constitute a qualifying offence,

(d) the person is aged under 18 at the time of the offence mentioned in paragraph (b), and

(e) the person has not previously been convicted of a recordable offence.

(2) In subsection (1)(e), the reference to a recordable offence includes an offence under the law of a country or territory outside England and Wales where the act constituting the offence would constitute a recordable offence if done in England and Wales (whether or not it constituted such an offence when the person was convicted).

(3) Where the person is sentenced to imprisonment or another form of detention for less than 5 years in respect of the offence mentioned in subsection (1)(b), the section 63D material may be retained until the end of the period consisting of the term of the sentence plus 5 years.

(4) Where the person is sentenced to imprisonment or another form of detention for 5 years or more in respect of the offence mentioned in subsection (1)(b), the material may be retained indefinitely.

(5) Where the person is given a sentence other than a sentence of imprisonment or other form of detention in respect of the offence mentioned in subsection (1)(b), the material may be retained until the end of the period of 5 years beginning with the date on which the person was arrested for the offence (or, if the person was not arrested for the offence, the date on which the person was charged with it).

(6) But if, before the end of the period within which material may be retained by virtue of this section, the person is again convicted of a recordable offence, the material may be retained indefinitely.

(7) In subsection (6), the reference to a recordable offence includes an offence under the law of a country or territory outside England and Wales where the act constituting the offence would constitute a recordable offence if done in England and Wales.

63M Retention of section 63D material for purposes of national security

(1) Section 63D material may be retained for as long as a national security determination made by a chief officer of police has effect in relation to it.

(2) A national security determination is made if a chief officer of police determines that it is necessary for any section 63D material to be retained for the purposes of national security.

(3) A national security determination—

(a) must be made in writing,

(b) has effect for a maximum of 5 years beginning with the date on which it is made, and

(c) may be renewed.

63N Retention of section 63D material given voluntarily

(1) This section applies to the following section 63D material—

(a) fingerprints taken with the consent of the person from whom they were taken, and

(b) a DNA profile derived from a DNA sample taken with the consent of the person from whom the sample was taken.

(2) Material to which this section applies may be retained until it has fulfilled the purpose for which it was taken or derived.

(3) Material to which this section applies which relates to—

(a) a person who is convicted of a recordable offence, or

(b) a person who has previously been convicted of a recordable offence (other than a person who has only one exempt conviction),

may be retained indefinitely.

(4) For the purposes of subsection (3)(b), a conviction is exempt if it is in respect of a recordable offence, other than a qualifying offence, committed when the person is aged under 18.

(5) The reference to a recordable offence in subsection (3)(a) includes an offence under the law of a country or territory outside England and Wales where the act constituting the offence would constitute a recordable offence if done in England and Wales.

(6) The reference to a recordable offence in subsections (3)(b) and (4), and the reference to a qualifying offence in subsection (4), includes an offence under the law of a country or territory outside England and Wales where the act constituting the offence would constitute a recordable offence or (as the case may be) a qualifying offence if done in England and Wales (whether or not it constituted such an offence when the person was convicted).

63O Retention of section 63D material with consent

(1) This section applies to the following material—

(a) fingerprints (other than fingerprints taken under section 61(6A)) to which section 63D applies, and

(b) a DNA profile to which section 63D applies.

(2) If the person to whom the material relates consents to material to which this section applies being retained, the material may be retained for as long as that person consents to it being retained.

(3) Consent given under this section—

(a) must be in writing, and

(b) can be withdrawn at any time.

63P Retention of 63D material in connection with different offence

(1) Subsection (2) applies if—

(a) section 63D material is taken (or, in the case of a DNA profile, derived from a sample taken) from a person in connection with the investigation of an offence, and

(b) the person is subsequently arrested for or charged with a different offence, or convicted of or given a penalty notice for a different offence.

(2) Sections 63E to 63O and sections 63Q and 63T have effect in relation to the material as if the material were also taken (or, in the case of a DNA profile, derived from a sample taken)—

(a) in connection with the investigation of the offence mentioned in subsection (1)(b),

(b) on the date on which the person was arrested for that offence (or charged with it or given a penalty notice for it, if the person was not arrested).

63PA Retention of further sets of fingerprints

(1) This section applies where section 63D material is or includes a person's fingerprints ('the original fingerprints').

(2) A constable may make a determination under this section in respect of any further fingerprints taken from the same person ('the further fingerprints') if any of conditions 1 to 3 are met.

(3) Condition 1 is met if—

(a) the further fingerprints are section 63D material, and

(b) the further fingerprints or the original fingerprints were taken in connection with a terrorist investigation.

(4) Condition 2 is met if the further fingerprints were taken from the person in England or Wales under—

(a) paragraph 10 of Schedule 8 to the Terrorism Act 2000,

(b) paragraph 1 of Schedule 6 to the Terrorism Prevention and Investigation Measures Act 2011, or

(c) paragraph 34 of Schedule 3 to the Counter-Terrorism and Border Security Act 2019.

(d) paragraph 10 of Schedule 6 to the National Security Act 2023, or

(e) paragraph 1 of Schedule 12 to that Act.

(5) Condition 3 is met if the further fingerprints—

(a) are material to which section 18 of the Counter-Terrorism Act 2008 applies, and

(b) are held under the law of England and Wales.

(6) Where a determination under this section is made in respect of the further fingerprints—

(a) the further fingerprints may be retained for as long as the original fingerprints are retained under a power conferred by sections 63E to 63O (including those sections as applied by section 63P), and

(b) a requirement under any enactment to destroy the further fingerprints does not apply for as long as their retention is authorised by paragraph (a).

(7) Subsection 6)(a) does not prevent the further fingerprints being retained after the original fingerprints fall to be destroyed if the continued retention of the further fingerprints is authorised under any enactment.

(8) A written record must be made of a determination under this section.

63Q Destruction of copies of section 63D material

(1) If fingerprints are required by section 63D to be destroyed, any copies of the fingerprints held by the police must also be destroyed.

(2) If a DNA profile is required by that section to be destroyed, no copy may be retained by the police except in a form which does not include information which identifies the person to whom the DNA profile relates.

63R Destruction of samples

(1) This section applies to samples—

(a) taken from a person under any power conferred by this Part of this Act, or

(b) taken by the police, with the consent of the person from whom they were taken, in connection with the investigation of an offence by the police.

(2) Samples to which this section applies must be destroyed if it appears to the responsible chief officer of police that—

(a) the taking of the samples was unlawful, or

(b) the samples were taken from a person in connection with that person's arrest and the arrest was unlawful or based on mistaken identity.

(3) Subject to this, the rule in subsection (4) or (as the case may be) (5) applies.

(4) A DNA sample to which this section applies must be destroyed—

(a) as soon as a DNA profile has been derived from the sample, or

(b) if sooner, before the end of the period of 6 months beginning with the date on which the sample was taken.

(5) Any other sample to which this section applies must be destroyed before the end of the period of 6 months beginning with the date on which it was taken.

(6) The responsible chief officer of police may apply to a District Judge (Magistrates' Courts) for an order to retain a sample to which this section applies beyond the date on which the sample would otherwise be required to be destroyed by virtue of subsection (4) or (5) if—

(a) the sample was taken from a person in connection with the investigation of a qualifying offence, and

(b) the responsible chief officer of police considers that the condition in subsection (7) is met.

(7) The condition is that, having regard to the nature and complexity of other material that is evidence in relation to the offence, the sample is likely to be needed in any proceedings for the offence for the purposes of—

(a) disclosure to, or use by, a defendant, or

(b) responding to any challenge by a defendant in respect of the admissibility of material that is evidence on which the prosecution proposes to rely.

(8) An application under subsection (6) must be made before the date on which the sample would otherwise be required to be destroyed by virtue of subsection (4) or (5).

(9) If, on an application made by the responsible chief officer of police under subsection (6), the District Judge (Magistrates' Courts) is satisfied that the condition in subsection (7) is met, the District Judge may make an order under this subsection which—

(a) allows the sample to be retained for a period of 12 months beginning with the date on which the sample would otherwise be required to be destroyed by virtue of subsection (4) or (5), and

(b) may be renewed (on one or more occasions) for a further period of not more than 12 months from the end of the period when the order would otherwise cease to have effect.

(10) An application for an order under subsection (9) (other than an application for renewal)—

(a) may be made without notice of the application having been given to the person from whom the sample was taken, and

(b) may be heard and determined in private in the absence of that person.

(11) A sample retained by virtue of an order under subsection (9) must not be used other than for the purposes of any proceedings for the offence in connection with which the sample was taken.

(12) A sample that ceases to be retained by virtue of an order under subsection (9) must be destroyed.

(13) Nothing in this section prevents a speculative search, in relation to samples to which this section applies, from being carried out within such time as may reasonably be required for the search if the responsible chief officer of police considers the search to be desirable.

63S Destruction of impressions of footwear

(1) This section applies to impressions of footwear—

(a) taken from a person under any power conferred by this Part of this Act, or

(b) taken by the police, with the consent of the person from whom they were taken, in connection with the investigation of an offence by the police.

(2) Impressions of footwear to which this section applies must be destroyed unless they are retained under subsection (3).

(3) Impressions of footwear may be retained for as long as is necessary for purposes related to the prevention or detection of crime, the investigation of an offence or the conduct of a prosecution.

63T Use of retained material

(1) Any material to which section 63D, 63R or 63S applies must not be used other than—

(a) in the interests of national security,

(b) for the purposes of a terrorist investigation,

(c) for purposes related to the prevention or detection of crime, the investigation of an offence or the conduct of a prosecution, or

(d) for purposes related to the identification of a deceased person or of the person to whom the material relates.

(2) Material which is required by section 63D, 63R or 63S to be destroyed must not at any time after it is required to be destroyed be used—

(a) in evidence against the person to whom the material relates, or

(b) for the purposes of the investigation of any offence.

(3) In this section—

(a) the reference to using material includes a reference to allowing any check to be made against it and to disclosing it to any person,

(b) the reference to crime includes a reference to any conduct which—

(i) constitutes one or more criminal offences (whether under the law of England and Wales or of any country or territory outside England and Wales), or

(ii) is, or corresponds to, any conduct which, if it all took place in England and Wales, would constitute one or more criminal offences, and

(c) the references to an investigation and to a prosecution include references, respectively, to any investigation outside England and Wales of any crime or suspected crime and to a prosecution brought in respect of any crime in a country or territory outside England and Wales.

63U Exclusions for certain regimes

(1) Sections 63D to 63T do not apply to material to which paragraphs 20A to 20J of Schedule 8 to the Terrorism Act 2000 (destruction, retention and use of material taken from terrorist suspects) apply.

(2) Any reference in those sections to a person being arrested for, or charged with, an offence does not include a reference to a person—

(a) being arrested under section 41 of the Terrorism Act 2000, or

(b) being charged with an offence following an arrest under that section.

(3) Sections 63D to 63T do not apply to material to which paragraph 8 of Schedule 4 to the International Criminal Court Act 2001 (requirement to destroy material) applies.

(4) Sections 63D to 63T do not apply to material to which paragraph 6 of Schedule 6 to the Terrorism Prevention and Investigation Measures Act 2011 (requirement to destroy material) applies.

(4A) Sections 63D to 63T do not apply to material to which paragraphs 43 to 51 of Schedule 3 to the Counter-Terrorism and Border Security Act 2019 (destruction, retention and use of material) apply.

(4B) Sections 63D to 63T do not apply to material to which—

(a) Par2t 4 of Schedule 6 to the National Security Act 2023 applies, or

(b) paragraph 6 of Schedule 12 to that Act applies.

(5) Sections 63D to 63T do not apply to material which is, or may become, disclosable under—

(a) the Criminal Procedure and Investigations Act 1996, or

(b) a code of practice prepared under section 23 of that Act and in operation by virtue of an order under section 25 of that Act.

(5A) A sample that—

(a) falls within subsection (5), and

(b) but for that subsection would be required to be destroyed under section 63R,

must not be used other than for the purposes of any proceedings for the offence in connection with which the sample was taken.

(5B) A sample that once fell within subsection (5) but no longer does, and so becomes a sample to which section 63R applies, must be destroyed immediately if the time specified for its destruction under that section has already passed.

(6) Sections 63D to 63T do not apply to material which—

(a) is taken from a person, but

(b) relates to another person.

(7) Nothing in sections 63D to 63T affects any power conferred by—

(a) paragraph 18(2) of Schedule 2 to the Immigration Act 1971 (power to take reasonable steps to identify a person detained), or

(b) section 20 of the Immigration and Asylum Act 1999 (disclosure of police information to the Secretary of State for use for immigration purposes).

64A Photographing of suspects etc.

(1) A person who is detained at a police station may be photographed—

(a) with the appropriate consent; or

(b) if the appropriate consent is withheld or it is not practicable to obtain it, without it.

(1A) A person falling within subsection (1B) below may, on the occasion of the relevant event referred to in subsection (1B), be photographed elsewhere than at a police station—

(a) with the appropriate consent; or

(b) if the appropriate consent is withheld or it is not practicable to obtain it, without it.

(1B) A person falls within this subsection if he has been—

(a) arrested by a constable for an offence;

(b) taken into custody by a constable after being arrested for an offence by a person other than a constable;

(c) made subject to a requirement to wait with a community support officer or a community support volunteer under paragraph 7 of Schedule 3B to the Police Reform Act 2002 ('the 2002 Act').

(ca) given a direction by a constable under section 35 of the Anti-social Behaviour, Crime and Policing Act 2014;

(cb) given a diversionary or community caution under Part 6 of the Police, Crime, Sentencing and Courts Act 2022;

(d) given a penalty notice by a constable under section 444A of the Education Act 1996, or a fixed penalty notice by a constable in uniform under section 54 of the Road Traffic Offenders Act 1988;

(e) given a fixed penalty notice by a community support officer or community support volunteer who is authorised to give the notice by virtue of his or her designation under section 38 of the Police Reform Act 2002; or

(f) given a notice in relation to a relevant fixed penalty offence (within the meaning of paragraph 1 of Schedule 5 to the 2002 Act) by an accredited person by virtue of accreditation specifying that that paragraph applies to him; or

(g) given a notice in relation to a relevant fixed penalty offence (within the meaning of Schedule 5A to the 2002 Act) by an accredited inspector by virtue of accreditation specifying that paragraph 1 of Schedule 5A to the 2002 Act applies to him.

(1C) A person to whom subsection (1) or (1A) does not apply may be photographed at a police station without the appropriate consent if that person falls within subsection (1D), (1F) or (1H).

(1D) A person falls within this subsection if (before or after the coming into force of this subsection) that person has been—

(a) arrested for a recordable offence and released,

(b) charged with a recordable offence, or

(c) informed that they will be reported for such an offence,

and either of the conditions in subsection (1E) is met in relation to that person.

(1E) The conditions referred to in subsection (1D) are—

(a) that the person has not been photographed in the course of the investigation of the offence by the police, or
offence by the police, or

(b) that the person has been so photographed but—
  (i) any photograph taken on such a previous occasion is unavailable or inadequate, and
  (ii) a constable considers that taking a further photograph is necessary to assist in the prevention or detection of crime.

(1F) A person falls within this subsection if (before or after the coming into force of this subsection) that person has been—

(a) convicted of a recordable offence, or
(b) given a caution in respect of a recordable offence which, at the time of the caution they have admitted,

and either of the conditions in subsection (1G) is met in relation to that person.

(1G) The conditions referred to in subsection (1F) are—

(a) that the person has not been photographed since being convicted or cautioned, or
(b) that the person has been so photographed but—
  (i) any photograph taken on such a previous occasion is unavailable or inadequate, and
  (ii) a constable considers that taking a further photograph is necessary to assist in the prevention or detection of crime.

(1H) A person falls within this subsection if—

(a) under the law in force in a country or territory outside England and Wales the person has been convicted of an offence under that law (whether before or after the coming into force of this subsection and whether or not they have been punished for it),
(b) the act constituting the offence would constitute a qualifying offence if done in England and Wales (whether or not it constituted such an offence when the person was convicted), and
(c) either of the conditions in subsection (1I) is met in relation to that person.

(1I) The conditions referred to in subsection (1H) are—

(a) that the person has not been photographed on a previous occasion by virtue of being a person falling within subsection (1H), or
(b) that the person has been so photographed but—
  (i) any photograph taken on such a previous occasion is unavailable or inadequate, and
  (ii) a constable considers that taking a further photograph is necessary to assist in the prevention or detection of crime.

(1J) A person who falls within subsection (1F) or (1H) may be photographed under subsection (1C) only with the authorisation of an officer of at least the rank of inspector.

(1K) An officer may only give an authorisation under subsection (1J) if the officer is satisfied that taking the photograph is necessary to assist in the prevention or detection of crime.

(1L) In subsections (1E), (1G) and (1I) —

(a) references to a photograph being unavailable include references to a photograph being lost or destroyed, and
(b) references to a photograph being inadequate include references to a photograph being—
  (i) unclear,
  (ii) an incomplete photograph of the subject, or
  (iii) no longer an accurate representation of the subject's appearance.

(1M) In subsections (1E), (1G), (1I) and (1K) references to crime include references to any conduct which—

(a) constitutes one or more criminal offences (whether under the law of a part of the United Kingdom or of a country or territory outside the United Kingdom), or
(b) is, or corresponds to, any conduct which, if it all took place in any one part of the United Kingdom, would constitute one or more criminal offences.

(2) A person proposing to take a photograph of any person under this section—

(a) may, for the purpose of doing so, require the removal of any item or substance worn on or over the whole or any part of the head or face of the person to be photographed; and

(b) if the requirement is not complied with, may remove the item or substance himself.

(3) Where a photograph may be taken under this section, the only persons entitled to take the photograph are constables.

(4) A photograph taken under this section—

(a) may be used by, or disclosed to, any person for any purpose related to the prevention or detection of crime, the investigation of an offence or the conduct of a prosecution or to the enforcement of a sentence; and

(b) after being so used or disclosed, may be retained but may not be used or disclosed except for a purpose so related.

(5) In subsection (4)—

(a) the reference to crime includes a reference to any conduct which—

(i) constitutes one or more criminal offences (whether under the law of a part of the United Kingdom or of a country or territory outside the United Kingdom); or

(ii) is, or corresponds to, any conduct which, if it all took place in any one part of the United Kingdom, would constitute one or more criminal offences;

and

(b) the references to an investigation and to a prosecution include references, respectively, to any investigation outside the United Kingdom of any crime or suspected crime and to a prosecution brought in respect of any crime in a country or territory outside the United Kingdom; and

(c) 'sentence' includes any order made by a court in England and Wales when dealing with an offender in respect of his offence.

(6) References in this section to taking a photograph include references to using any process by means of which a visual image may be produced; and references to photographing a person shall be construed accordingly.

(6A) In this section, a 'photograph' includes a moving image, and corresponding expressions shall be construed accordingly.

(7) Nothing in this section applies to a person arrested under an extradition arrest power.

65 Part V—supplementary

(1) In this Part of this Act—

'analysis', in relation to a skin impression, includes comparison and matching;

'appropriate consent' means—

(a) in relation to a person who has attained the age of 18 years, the consent of that person;

(b) in relation to a person who has not attained that age but has attained the age of 14 years, the consent of that person and his parent or guardian; and

(c) in relation to a person who has not attained the age of 14 years, the consent of his parent or guardian;

'DNA profile' means any information derived from a DNA sample;

'DNA sample' means any material that has come from a human body and consists of or includes human cells;

'extradition arrest power' means any of the following—

(a) a Part 1 warrant (within the meaning given by the Extradition Act 2003) in respect of which a certificate under section 2 of that Act has been issued;

(b) section 5 of that Act;

(c) a warrant issued under section 71 of that Act;

(d) a provisional warrant (within the meaning given by that Act);

(e) section 74A of that Act;

'fingerprints', in relation to any person, means a record (in any form and produced by any method) of the skin pattern and other physical characteristics or features of—

(a) any of that person's fingers; or

(b) either of his palms;

'intimate sample' means—

(a) a sample of blood, semen or any other tissue fluid, urine or pubic hair;
(b) a dental impression;
(c) a swab taken from any part of a person's genitals (including pubic hair) or from a person's body orifice other than the mouth;

'intimate search' means a search which consists of the physical examination of a person's body orifices other than the mouth;

'non-intimate sample' means—

(a) a sample of hair other than pubic hair;
(b) a sample taken from a nail on from under a nail;
(c) a swab taken from any part of a person's body other than a part from which a swab taken would be an intimate sample;
(d) saliva;
(e) a skin impression;

'offence', in relation to any country or territory outside England and Wales, includes an act punishable under the law of that country or territory, however it is described;

'registered dentist' has the same meaning as in the Dentists Act 1984;

'registered health care professional' means a person (other than a medical practitioner) who is—

(a) a registered nurse; or
(b) a registered member of a health care profession which is designated for the purposes of this paragraph by an order made by the Secretary of State;

'the responsible chief officer of police', in relation to material to which section 63D or 63R applies, means the chief officer of police for the police area—

(a) in which the material concerned was taken, or
(b) in the case of a DNA profile, in which the sample from which the DNA profile was derived was taken;

'section 63D material' means fingerprints or DNA profiles to which section 63D applies;

'skin impression', in relation to any person, means any record (other than a fingerprint) which is a record (in any form and produced by any method) of the skin pattern and other physical characteristics or features of the whole or any part of his foot or of any other part of his body;

'speculative search', in relation to a person's fingerprints or samples, means such a check against other fingerprints or samples or against information derived from other samples as is referred to in section 63A(1) above;

'sufficient' and 'insufficient', in relation to a sample, means (subject to subsection (2) below) sufficient or insufficient (in point of quantity or quality) for the purpose of enabling information to be produced by the means of analysis used or to be used in relation to the sample.

'the terrorism provisions' means section 41 and 43B of the Terrorism Act 2000, and any provision of Schedule 7 to that Act conferring a power of detention; and

'terrorism' has the meaning given in section 1 of that Act;

'terrorist investigation' has the meaning given by section 32 of that Act;

(1A) A health care profession is any profession mentioned in section 60(2) of the Health Act 1999 other than the profession of practising medicine and the profession of nursing.

(1B) An order under subsection (1) shall be made by statutory instrument and shall be subject to annulment in pursuance of a resolution of either House of Parliament.

(2) References in this Part of this Act to a sample's proving insufficient include references to where, as a consequence of—

(a) the loss, destruction or contamination of the whole or any part of the sample,
(b) any damage to the whole or a part of the sample, or
(c) the use of the whole or a part of the sample for an analysis which produced no results or which produced results some or all of which must be regarded, in the circumstances, as unreliable, the sample has become unavailable or insufficient for the purpose of

enabling information, or information of a particular description, to be obtained by means of analysis of the sample.

(2A) In subsection (2), the reference to the destruction of a sample does not include a reference to the destruction of a sample under section 63R (requirement to destroy samples).

(2B) Any reference in sections 63F, 63H, 63P or 63U to a person being charged with an offence includes a reference to a person being informed that the person will be reported for an offence.

(3) For the purposes of this Part, a person has in particular been convicted of an offence under the law of a country or territory outside England and Wales if—

(a) a court exercising jurisdiction under the law of that country or territory has made in respect of such an offence a finding equivalent to a finding that the person is not guilty by reason of insanity; or

(b) such a court has made in respect of such an offence a finding equivalent to a finding that the person is under a disability and did the act charged against him in respect of the offence.

65A Qualifying offence

(1) In this Part, 'qualifying offence' means—

(a) an offence specified in subsection (2) below, or

(b) an ancillary offence relating to such an offence.

(2) The offences referred to in subsection (1)(a) above are—

(a) murder;

(b) manslaughter;

(c) false imprisonment;

(d) kidnapping;

(da) an offence of indecent exposure;

(db) an offence under section 4 of the Vagrancy Act 1824, committed by a person by wilfully, openly, lewdly, and obscenely exposing his person with intent to insult any female;

(dc) an offence under section 28 of the Town Police Clauses Act 1847, committed by a person by wilfully and indecently exposing his person;

(e) an offence under section 4, 16, 18, 20 to 24 or 47 of the Offences Against the Person Act 1861;

(f) an offence under section 2 or 3 of the Explosive Substances Act 1883;

(fa) an offence under section 1 of the Infant Life (Preservation) Act 1929;

(g) an offence under section 1 of the Children and Young Persons Act 1933;

(ga) an offence under section 1 of the Infanticide Act 1938;

(gb) an offence under section 12 or 13 of the Sexual Offences Act 1956, other than an offence committed by a person where the other person involved in the conduct constituting the offence consented to it and was aged 16 or over;

(gc) an offence under any other section of that Act, other than sections 18 and 32;

(gd) an offence under section 128 of the Mental Health Act 1959;

(ge) an offence under section 1 of the Indecency with Children Act 1960;

(h) an offence under section 4(1) of the Criminal Law Act 1967 committed in relation to murder;

(ha) an offence under section 5 of the Sexual Offences Act 1967;

(i) an offence under sections 16 to 18 of the Firearms Act 1968;

(j) an offence under section 8, 9 or 10 of the Theft Act 1968 or an offence under section 12A of that Act involving an accident which caused a person's death;

(ja) an offence under section 1(1) of the Genocide Act 1969;

(k) an offence under section 1 of the Criminal Damage Act 1971 required to be charged as arson;

(ka) an offence under section 54 of the Criminal Law Act 1977;

(l) an offence under section 1 of the Protection of Children Act 1978;

(m) an offence under section 1 of the Aviation Security Act 1982;
(n) an offence under section 2 of the Child Abduction Act 1984;
(na) an offence under section 1 of the Prohibition of Female Circumcision Act 1985;
(nb) an offence under section 1 of the Public Order Act 1986;
(o) an offence under section 9 of the Aviation and Maritime Security Act 1990;
(oa) an offence under section 3 of the Sexual Offences (Amendment) Act 2000;
(ob) an offence under section 51 of the International Criminal Court Act 2001;
(oc) an offence under section 1, 2 or 3 of the Female Genital Mutilation Act 2003;
(p) an offence under any of sections 1 to 19, 25, 26, 30 to 41, 47 to 50, 52, 53, 57 to 59A, 61 to 66A, 66B(2) and (3), 67, 69 and 70 of the Sexual Offences Act 2003;
(q) an offence under section 5 of the Domestic Violence, Crime and Victims Act 2004;
(r) an offence for the time being listed in section 41(1) of the Counter-Terrorism Act 2008;
(ra) an offence under section 75A of the Serious Crime Act 2015 (strangulation or suffocation);
(s) an offence under section 2 of the Modern Slavery Act 2015 (human trafficking);
(t) an offence under paragraph 1 of Schedule 4 to the Space Industry Act 2018;
(u) an offence under any of sections 136 to 138 and 148 to 150 of the Health and Care Act 2022 (offences relating to virginity testing and hymenoplasty);
(v) an offence under section 18 of the National Security Act 2023 or for the time being listed in section 33(3)(a) of that Act.

(3) The Secretary of State may by order made by statutory instrument amend subsection (2) above.

(4) A statutory instrument containing an order under subsection (3) above shall not be made unless a draft of the instrument has been laid before, and approved by resolution of, each House of Parliament.

(5) In subsection (1)(b) above 'ancillary offence', in relation to an offence, means—
(a) aiding, abetting, counselling or procuring the commission of the offence;
(b) an offence under Part 2 of the Serious Crime Act 2007 (encouraging or assisting crime) in relation to the offence (including, in relation to times before the commencement of that Part, an offence of incitement);
(c) attempting or conspiring to commit the offence.

65B Persons convicted of an offence

(1) For the purposes of this Part, any reference to a person who is convicted of an offence includes a reference to—
(a) a person who has been given a caution in respect of the offence which, at the time of the caution, the person has admitted,
(b) a person who has been warned or reprimanded under section 65 of the Crime and Disorder Act 1998 for the offence,
(c) a person who has been found not guilty of the offence by reason of insanity, or
(d) a person who has been found to be under a disability and to have done the act charged in respect of the offence.

(2) This Part, so far as it relates to persons convicted of an offence, has effect despite anything in the Rehabilitation of Offenders Act 1974.

(3) But a person is not to be treated as having been convicted of an offence if that conviction is a disregarded conviction or caution by virtue of section 92 of the Protection of Freedoms Act 2012.

(4) If a person is convicted of more than one offence arising out of a single course of action, those convictions are to be treated as a single conviction for the purposes of calculating under sections 63F, 63H and 63N whether the person has been convicted of only one offence.

(5) ...*

* **Editor's Note:** Applies to countries outside England and Wales.

PART VI CODES OF PRACTICE—GENERAL

66 Codes of practice

The Secretary of State shall issue codes of practice in connection with—

(a) the exercise by police officers of statutory powers—

(i) to search a person without first arresting him;

(ii) to search a vehicle without making an arrest; or

(iii) to arrest a person;

(b) the detention, treatment, questioning and identification of persons by police officers;

(c) searches of premises by police officers; and

(d) the seizure of property found by police officers on persons or premises.

(2) Codes shall (in particular) include provision in connection with the exercise by police officers of powers under section 63B above.

(3) ...*

67 Codes of practice—supplementary

(1) In this section, 'code' means a code of practice under section 60, 60A or 66.

(2) The Secretary of State may at any time revise the whole or any part of a code.

(3) A code may be made, or revised, so as to—

(a) apply only in relation to one or more specified areas,

(b) have effect only for a specified period,

(c) apply only in relation to specified offences or descriptions of offender.

(4) Before issuing a code, or any revision of a code, the Secretary of State must consult—

(a) such persons as appear to the Secretary of State to represent the views of police and crime commissioners,

(aa) the Mayor's Office for Policing and Crime,

(ab) the Common Council of the City of London,

(b) The National Police Chiefs' Council,

(c) the General Council of the Bar,

(d) the Law Society of England and Wales,

(e) the Institute of Legal Executives, and

(f) such other persons as he thinks fit.

(4A) The duty to consult under subsection (4) does not apply to a revision of a code where the Secretary of State considers that—

(a) the revision is necessary in consequence of legislation, and

(b) the Secretary of State has no discretion as to the nature of the revision.

(4B) Where, in consequence of subsection (4A), a revision of a code is issued without prior consultation with the persons mentioned in subsection (4), the Secretary of State must (at the same time as issuing the revision) publish a statement that, in his or her opinion, paragraphs (a) and (b) of subsection (4A) apply to the revision.

(4C) In subsection (4A), 'legislation' means any provision of—

(a) an Act,

(b) subordinate legislation within the meaning of the Interpretation Act 1978.

(5) A code, or a revision of a code, does not come into operation until the Secretary of State by order so provides.

(6) The power conferred by subsection (5) is exercisable by statutory instrument.

(7) An order bringing a code into operation may not be made unless a draft of the order has been laid before Parliament and approved by a resolution of each House.

(7A) An order bringing a revision of a code into operation must be laid before Parliament if the order has been made without a draft having been so laid and approved by a resolution of each House.

* **Editor's Note:** Applies to terrorism.

(7B) When an order or draft of an order is laid, the code or revision of a code to which it relates must also be laid.

(7C) No order or draft of an order may be laid until the consultation required by subsection (4) has taken place.

(7D) An order bringing a code, or a revision of a code, into operation may include transitional or saving provisions.

(9) Persons other than police officers who are charged with the duty of investigating offences or charging offenders shall in the discharge of that duty have regard to any relevant provision of a code.

(9A) Persons on whom powers are conferred by—

(a) any designation under section 38 or 39 of the Police Reform Act 2002 (police powers for civilian staff and volunteers), or

(b) any accreditation under section 41 of that Act (accreditation under community safety accreditation schemes),

shall have regard to any relevant provision of a code in the exercise or performance of the powers and duties conferred or imposed on them by that designation or accreditation.

(10) A failure on the part—

(a) of a police officer to comply with any provision of a code;

(b) of any person other than a police officer who is charged with the duty of investigating offences or charging offenders to have regard to any relevant provision of a code in the discharge of that duty; or

(c) of a person designated under section 38 or 39 or accredited under section 41 of the Police Reform Act 2002 to have regard to any relevant provision of a code in the exercise or performance of the powers and duties conferred or imposed on him by that designation or accreditation,

shall not of itself render him liable to any criminal or civil proceedings.

(11) In all criminal and civil proceedings any code shall be admissible in evidence; and if any provision of a code appears to the court or tribunal conducting the proceedings to be relevant to any question arising in the proceedings it shall be taken into account in determining that question.

(12) In subsection (11) 'criminal proceedings' includes service proceedings.

(13) . . .*

PART VII DOCUMENTARY EVIDENCE IN CRIMINAL PROCEEDINGS

71 Microfilm copies

In any proceedings the contents of a document may (whether or not the document is still in existence) be proved by the production of an enlargement of a microfilm copy of that document or of the material part of it, authenticated in such manner as the court may approve.

72 Part VII—supplementary

(1) In this Part of this Act—

'copy' in relation to a document means anything onto which information recorded in the document has been copied, by whatever means and whether directly or indirectly, and 'statement' means any representation of fact however made; and

'proceedings' means criminal proceedings, including service proceedings

(1A) . . .**

(2) Nothing in this Part of this Act shall prejudice any power of a court to exclude evidence (whether by preventing questions from being put or otherwise) at its discretion.

* **Editor's Note:** Applies to service proceedings.

** **Editor's Note:** Defines 'service proceedings'.

PART VIII EVIDENCE IN CRIMINAL PROCEEDINGS—GENERAL

Convictions and acquittals

73 Proof of convictions and acquittals

(1) Where in any proceedings the fact that a person has in the United Kingdom been convicted or acquitted of an offence otherwise than by a Service court is admissible in evidence, it may be proved by producing a certificate of conviction or, as the case may be, of acquittal relating to that offence, and proving that the person named in the certificate as having been convicted or acquitted of the offence is the person whose conviction or acquittal of the offence is to be proved.

(2) For the purposes of this section a certificate of conviction or of acquittal—

(a) shall, as regards a conviction or acquittal on indictment, consist of a certificate, signed by the proper officer of the court where the conviction or acquittal took place, giving the substance and effect (omitting the formal parts) of the indictment and of the conviction or acquittal; and

(b) shall, as regards a conviction or acquittal on a summary trial, consist of a copy of the conviction or of the dismissal of the information, signed by the proper officer of the court where the conviction or acquittal took place or by the proper officer of the court, if any, to which a memorandum of the conviction or acquittal was sent;

and a document purporting to be a duly signed certificate of conviction or acquittal under this section shall be taken to be such a certificate unless the contrary is proved.

(3) In subsection (2) above 'proper officer' means:

(a) in relation to a magistrates' court in England and Wales, the designated officer for the court and

(b) in relation to any other court, the clerk of the court, his deputy or any other person having the custody of the court record.

(4) The method of proving a conviction or acquittal authorised by this section shall be in addition to and not to the exclusion of any other authorised manner of proving a conviction or acquittal.

74 Conviction as evidence of commission of offence

(1) In any proceedings the fact that a person other than the accused has been convicted of an offence by or before any court in the United Kingdom or by a Service court outside the United Kingdom shall be admissible in evidence for the purpose of proving that that person committed that offence, where evidence of his having done so is admissible, whether or not any other evidence of his having committed that offence is given.

(2) In any proceedings in which by virtue of this section a person other than the accused is proved to have been convicted of an offence by or before any court in the United Kingdom or by a Service court outside the United Kingdom, he shall be taken to have committed that offence unless the contrary is proved.

(3) In any proceedings where evidence is admissible of the fact that the accused has committed an offence, if the accused is proved to have been convicted of the offence—

(a) by or before any court in the United Kingdom; or

(b) by a Service court outside the United Kingdom,

he shall be taken to have committed that offence unless the contrary is proved.

(4) Nothing in this section shall prejudice—

(a) the admissibility in evidence of any conviction which would be admissible apart from this section; or

(b) the operation of any enactment whereby a conviction or a finding of fact in any proceedings is for the purposes of any other proceedings made conclusive evidence of any fact.

75 Provisions supplementary to section 74

(1) Where evidence that a person has been convicted of an offence is admissible by virtue of section 74 above, then without prejudice to the reception of any other admissible evidence for the purpose of identifying the facts on which the conviction was based—

(a) the contents of any document which is admissible as evidence of the conviction; and
(b) the contents of the information, complaint, indictment or charge-sheet on which the person in question was convicted,

shall be admissible in evidence for that purpose.

(2) Where in any proceedings the contents of any document are admissible in evidence by virtue of subsection (1) above, a copy of that document, or of the material part of it, purporting to be certified or otherwise authenticated by or on behalf of the court or authority having custody of that document shall be admissible in evidence and shall be taken to be a true copy of that document or part unless the contrary is shown.

(3) Nothing in any of the following—

(a) section 14 of the Powers of Criminal Courts (Sentencing) Act 2000 or section 82 of the Sentencing Code (under which a conviction leading to discharge is to be disregarded except as mentioned in that section);
(aa) . . .*
(b), (c) . . .**

shall affect the operation of section 74 above; . . .

(4) Nothing in section 74 above shall be construed as rendering admissible in any proceedings evidence of any conviction other than a subsisting one.

Confessions

76 Confessions

(1) In any proceedings a confession made by an accused person may be given in evidence against him in so far as it is relevant to any matter in issue in the proceedings and is not excluded by the court in pursuance of this section.

(2) If, in any proceedings where the prosecution proposes to give in evidence a confession made by an accused person, it is represented to the court that the confession was or may have been obtained—

(a) by oppression of the person who made it; or
(b) in consequence of anything said or done which was likely, in the circumstances existing at the time, to render unreliable any confession which might be made by him in consequence thereof,

the court shall not allow the confession to be given in evidence against him except in so far as the prosecution proves to the court beyond reasonable doubt that the confession (notwithstanding that it may be true) was not obtained as aforesaid.

(3) In any proceedings where the prosecution proposes to give in evidence a confession made by an accused person, the court may of its own motion require the prosecution, as a condition of allowing it to do so, to prove that the confession was not obtained as mentioned in subsection (2) above.

(4) The fact that a confession is wholly or partly excluded in pursuance of this section shall not affect the admissibility in evidence—

(a) of any facts discovered as a result of the confession; or
(b) where the confession is relevant as showing that the accused speaks, writes or expresses himself in a particular way, of so much of the confession as is necessary to show that he does so.

(5) Evidence that a fact to which this subsection applies was discovered as a result of a statement made by an accused person shall not be admissible unless evidence of how it was discovered is given by him or on his behalf.

(6) Subsection (5) above applies—

(a) to any fact discovered as a result of a confession which is wholly excluded in pursuance of this section; and

* **Editor's Note:** Applies to service convictions.

** **Editor's Note:** Apply to Scotland and Northern Ireland only.

(b) to any fact discovered as a result of a confession which is partly so excluded, if the fact is discovered as a result of the excluded part of the confession.

(7) Nothing in Part VII of this Act shall prejudice the admissibility of a confession made by an accused person.

(8) In this section 'oppression' includes torture, inhuman or degrading treatment, and the use or threat of violence (whether or not amounting to torture).

76A Confessions may be given in evidence for co-accused

(1) In any proceedings a confession made by an accused person may be given in evidence for another person charged in the same proceedings (a co-accused) in so far as it is relevant to any matter in issue in the proceedings and is not excluded by the court in pursuance of this section.

(2) If, in any proceedings where a co-accused proposes to give in evidence a confession made by an accused person, it is represented to the court that the confession was or may have been obtained—

(a) by oppression of the person who made it; or

(b) in consequence of anything said or done which was likely, in the circumstances existing at the time, to render unreliable any confession which might be made by him in consequence thereof,

the court shall not allow the confession to be given in evidence for the co-accused except in so far as it is proved to the court on the balance of probabilities that the confession (notwithstanding that it may be true) was not so obtained.

(3) Before allowing a confession made by an accused person to be given in evidence for a co-accused in any proceedings, the court may of its own motion require the fact that the confession was not obtained as mentioned in subsection (2) above to be proved in the proceedings on the balance of probabilities.

(4) The fact that a confession is wholly or partly excluded in pursuance of this section shall not affect the admissibility in evidence—

(a) of any facts discovered as a result of the confession; or

(b) where the confession is relevant as showing that the accused speaks, writes or expresses himself in a particular way, of so much of the confession as is necessary to show that he does so.

(5) Evidence that a fact to which this subsection applies was discovered as a result of a statement made by an accused person shall not be admissible unless evidence of how it was discovered is given by him or on his behalf.

(6) Subsection (5) above applies—

(a) to any fact discovered as a result of a confession which is wholly excluded in pursuance of this section; and

(b) to any fact discovered as a result of a confession which is partly so excluded, if the fact is discovered as a result of the excluded part of the confession.

(7) In this section 'oppression' includes torture, inhuman or degrading treatment, and the use or threat of violence (whether or not amounting to torture).

77 Confessions by mentally handicapped persons

(1) Without prejudice to the general duty of the court at a trial on indictment with a jury to direct the jury on any matter on which it appears to the court appropriate to do so, where at such a trial—

(a) the case against the accused depends wholly or substantially on a confession by him; and

(b) the court is satisfied—

(i) that he is mentally handicapped; and

(ii) that the confession was not made in the presence of an independent person;

the court shall warn the jury that there is special need for caution before convicting the accused in reliance on the confession, and shall explain that the need arises because of the circumstances mentioned in paragraphs (a) and (b) above.

(2) In any case where at the summary trial of a person for an offence it appears to the court that a warning under subsection (1) above would be required if the trial were on indictment with a jury, the court shall treat the case as one in which there is a special need for caution before convicting the accused on his confession.

(2A) In any case where at the trial on indictment without a jury of a person for an offence it appears to the court that a warning under subsection (1) above would be required if the trial were with a jury, the court shall treat the case as one in which there is a special need for caution before convicting the accused on his confession.

(3) In this section—

'independent person' does not include a police officer or a person employed for, or engaged on, police purposes;

'mentally handicapped', in relation to a person, means that he is in a state of arrested or incomplete development of mind which includes significant impairment of intelligence and social functioning; and

'police purposes' has the meaning assigned to it by section 101(2) of the Police Act 1996.

78 Exclusion of unfair evidence

(1) In any proceedings the court may refuse to allow evidence on which the prosecution proposes to rely to be given if it appears to the court that, having regard to all the circumstances, including the circumstances in which the evidence was obtained, the admission of the evidence would have such an adverse effect on the fairness of the proceedings that the court ought not to admit it.

(2) Nothing in this section shall prejudice any rule of law requiring a court to exclude evidence.

79 Time for taking accused's evidence

If at the trial of any person for an offence—

- (a) the defence intends to call two or more witnesses to the facts of the case; and
- (b) those witnesses include the accused,

the accused shall be called before the other witness or witnesses unless the court in its discretion otherwise directs.

80 Competence and compellability of accused's spouse or civil partner

(2) In any proceedings the spouse or civil partner of a person charged in the proceedings shall, subject to subsection (4) below, be compellable to give evidence on behalf of that person.

(2A) In any proceedings the spouse or civil partner of a person charged in the proceedings shall, subject to subsection (4) below, be compellable—

- (a) to give evidence on behalf of any other person charged in the proceedings but only in respect of any specified offence with which that other person is charged; or
- (b) to give evidence for the prosecution but only in respect of any specified offence with which any person is charged in the proceedings.

(3) In relation to the spouse or civil partner of a person charged in any proceedings, an offence is a specified offence for the purposes of subsection (2A) above if—

- (a) it involves an assault on, or injury or a threat of injury to, the spouse or civil partner or a person who was at the material time under the age of 16;
- (b) it is a sexual offence alleged to have been committed in respect of a person who was at the material time under that age; or
- (c) it consists of attempting or conspiring to commit, or of aiding, abetting, counselling, procuring or inciting the commission of, an offence falling within paragraph (a) or (b) above.

(4) No person who is charged in any proceedings shall be compellable by virtue of subsection (2) or (2A) above to give evidence in the proceedings.

(4A) References in this section to a person charged in any proceedings do not include a person who is not, or is no longer, liable to be convicted of any offence in the proceedings (whether as a result of pleading guilty or for any other reason).

(5) In any proceedings a person who has been but is no longer married to the accused shall be compellable to give evidence as if that person and the accused had never been married.

(5A) In any proceedings a person who has been but is no longer the civil partner of the accused shall be compellable to give evidence as if that person and the accused had never been civil partners.

(6) Where in any proceedings the age of any person at any time is material for the purposes of subsection (3) above, his age at the material time shall for the purposes of that provision be deemed to be or to have been that which appears to the court to be or to have been his age at that time.

(7) In subsection (3)(b) above 'sexual offence' means an offence under the Protection of Children Act 1978 or Part I of the Sexual Offences Act 2003 or an offence under section 2 of the Modern Slavery Act 2015 (human trafficking) committed with a view to exploitation that consists of or includes behaviour within section 3(3) of that Act (sexual exploitation).

(9) Section 1(d) of the Criminal Evidence Act 1898 (communications between husband and wife) and section 43(1) of the Matrimonial Causes Act 1965 (evidence as to marital intercourse) shall cease to have effect.

80A Rule where accused's spouse or civil partner not compellable

The failure of the spouse or civil partner of a person charged in any proceedings to give evidence in the proceedings shall not be made the subject of any comment by the prosecution.

81 Advance notice of expert evidence in Crown Court

(1) Criminal Procedure Rules may make provision for—

- (a) requiring any party to proceedings before the court to disclose to the other party or parties any expert evidence which he proposes to adduce in the proceedings; and
- (b) prohibiting a party who fails to comply in respect of any evidence with any requirement imposed by virtue of paragraph (a) above from adducing that evidence without the leave of the court.

(2) Criminal Procedure Rules made by virtue of this section may specify the kinds of expert evidence to which they apply and may exempt facts or matters of any description specified in the rules.

PART VIII SUPPLEMENTARY

82 Part VIII—interpretation

(1) In this Part of this Act—

'confession' includes any statement wholly or partly adverse to the person who made it, whether made to a person in authority or not and whether made in words or otherwise;

'proceedings' means criminal proceedings, including service proceedings.

'Service court' means the Court Martial or the Service Civilian Court.

(1A) . . .*

(3) Nothing in this Part of this Act shall prejudice any power of a court to exclude evidence (whether by preventing questions from being put or otherwise) at its discretion.

PART X POLICE—GENERAL

107 Police officers performing duties of higher rank

(1) For the purpose of any provision of this Act or any other Act under which a power in respect of the investigation of offences or the treatment of persons in police custody is exercisable only by or with the authority of a police officer of at least the rank of superintendent, an officer of the rank of chief inspector shall be treated as holding the rank of superintendent if—

* **Editor's Note:** Defines 'service proceedings'.

(a) he has been authorised by an officer holding a rank above the rank of superintendent to exercise the power or, as the case may be, to give his authority for its exercise, or

(b) he is acting during the absence of an officer holding the rank of superintendent who has authorised him, for the duration of that absence, to exercise the power, or as the case may be, to give his authority for its exercise.

(2) For the purpose of any provision of this Act or any other Act under which such a power is exercisable only by or with the authority of an officer of at least the rank of inspector, an officer of the rank of sergeant shall be treated as holding the rank of inspector if he has been authorised by an officer of at least the rank of superintendent to exercise the power or, as the case may be, to give his authority for its exercise.

111 Regulations for Police Forces and Police Cadets—Scotland

. . .*

PART XI MISCELLANEOUS AND SUPPLEMENTARY

117 Power of constable to use reasonable force

Where any provision of this Act—

(a) confers a power on a constable; and

(b) does not provide that the power may only be exercised with the consent of some person, other than a police officer,

the officer may use reasonable force, if necessary, in the exercise of the power.

118 General interpretation**

(1) In this Act—

'designated police station' has the meaning assigned to it by section 35 above;

'document' means anything in which information of any description is recorded;

'item subject to legal privilege' has the meaning assigned to it by section 10 above;

'parent or guardian' means—

(a) in the case of a child or young person in the care of a local authority, that authority;

'premises' has the meaning assigned to it by section 27 above;

'recordable offence' means any offence to which regulations under section 23 above apply;

'vessel' includes any ship, boat, raft or other apparatus constructed or adapted for floating on water.

(2) Subject to subsection (2A) a person is in police detention for the purposes of this Act if—

(a) he has been taken to a police station after being arrested for an offence or after being arrested under section 41 or 43B of the Terrorism Act 2000 or section 27 of the National Security Act 2023; or

(b) he is arrested at a police station after attending voluntarily at the station or accompanying a constable to it,

and is detained there or is detained elsewhere in the charge of a constable, except that a person who is at a court after being charged is not in police detention for those purposes.

(2A) Where a person is in another's lawful custody by virtue of paragraph 34(1) or 35(3) of Schedule 4 to the Police Reform Act 2002, he shall be treated as in police detention.

122 Short title

This Act may be cited as the Police and Criminal Evidence Act 1984.

* **Editor's Note:** Applies to Scotland.

** **Editor's Note:** This section has effect in relation to powers of entry for the enforcement of social security offences under the Social Security Administration Act 1992, section 109D and the Public Authorities (Fraud, Error and Recovery) Act 2025, section 7.

SCHEDULE 2A

FINGERPRINTING, SAMPLES AND PHOTOGRAPHS: POWER TO REQUIRE ATTENDANCE AT POLICE STATION

PART 1 FINGERPRINTING

Persons arrested and released

1 (1) A constable may require a person to attend a police station for the purpose of taking his fingerprints under section 61(5A).

(2) The power under sub-paragraph (1) above may not be exercised in a case falling within section 61(5A)(b)(i) (fingerprints taken on previous occasion insufficient etc.) after the end of the period of six months beginning with the day on which the appropriate officer was informed that section 61(3A)(a) or (b) applied.

(3) In sub-paragraph (2) above 'appropriate officer' means the officer investigating the offence for which the person was arrested.

(4) The power under sub-paragraph (1) above may not be exercised in a case falling within section 61(5A)(b)(ii) (fingerprints destroyed where investigation interrupted) after the end of the period of six months beginning with the day on which the investigation was resumed.

Persons charged etc.

2 (1) A constable may require a person to attend a police station for the purpose of taking his fingerprints under section 61(5B).

(2) The power under sub-paragraph (1) above may not be exercised after the end of the period of six months beginning with—

(a) in a case falling within section 61(5B)(a) (fingerprints not taken previously), the day on which the person was charged or informed that he would be reported, or

(b) in a case falling within section 61(5B)(b)(i) (fingerprints taken on previous occasion insufficient etc.), the day on which the appropriate officer was informed that section 61(3A)(a) or (b) applied or

(c) in a case falling within section 61(5B)(b)(ii) (fingerprints destroyed where investigation interrupted), the day on which the investigation was resumed.

(3) In sub-paragraph (2)(b) above 'appropriate officer' means the officer investigating the offence for which the person was charged or informed that he would be reported.

Persons convicted etc. of an offence in England and Wales

3 (1) A constable may require a person to attend a police station for the purpose of taking his fingerprints under section 61(6).

(2) Where the condition in section 61(6ZA)(a) is satisfied (fingerprints not taken previously), the power under sub-paragraph (1) above may not be exercised after the end of the period of two years beginning with—

(a) the day on which the person was convicted or cautioned, or

(b) if later, the day on which this Schedule comes into force.

(3) Where the condition in section 61(6ZA)(b) is satisfied (fingerprints taken on previous occasion insufficient etc.), the power under sub-paragraph (1) above may not be exercised after the end of the period of two years beginning with—

(a) the day on which an appropriate officer was informed that section 61(3A)(a) or (b) applied, or

(b) if later, the day on which this Schedule comes into force.

(4) In sub-paragraph (3)(a) above 'appropriate officer' means an officer of the police force which investigated the offence in question.

(5) Sub-paragraphs (2) and (3) above do not apply where the offence is a qualifying offence (whether or not it was such an offence at the time of the conviction or caution).

Persons convicted etc. of an offence outside England and Wales

5 A constable may require a person to attend a police station for the purpose of taking his fingerprints under section 61(6D).

Multiple attendance

6 (1) Where a person's fingerprints have been taken under section 61 on two occasions in relation to any offence, he may not under this Schedule be required to attend a police station to have his fingerprints taken under that section in relation to that offence on a subsequent occasion without the authorisation of an officer of at least the rank of inspector.

(2) Where an authorisation is given under sub-paragraph (1) above—

(a) the fact of the authorisation, and

(b) the reasons for giving it,

shall be recorded as soon as practicable after it has been given.

PART 2 INTIMATE SAMPLES

Persons suspected to be involved in an offence

7 A constable may require a person to attend a police station for the purpose of taking an intimate sample from him under section 62(1A) if, in the course of the investigation of an offence, two or more non-intimate samples suitable for the same means of analysis have been taken from him but have proved insufficient.

Persons convicted etc. of an offence outside England and Wales

8 A constable may require a person to attend a police station for the purpose of taking a sample from him under section 62(2A) if two or more non-intimate samples suitable for the same means of analysis have been taken from him under section 63(3E) but have proved insufficient.

PART 3 NON-INTIMATE SAMPLES

Persons arrested and released

9 (1) A constable may require a person to attend a police station for the purpose of taking a non-intimate sample from him under section 63(3ZA).

(2) The power under sub-paragraph (1) above may not be exercised in a case falling within section 63(3ZA)(b)(i) or (ii) (sample taken on a previous occasion not suitable etc.) after the end of the period of six months beginning with the day on which the appropriate officer was informed of the matters specified in section 63(3ZA)(b)(i) or (ii).

(3) In sub-paragraph (2) above, 'appropriate officer' means the officer investigating the offence for which the person was arrested.

(4) The power under sub-paragraph (1) above may not be exercised in a case falling within section 63(3ZA)(b)(iii) (sample, and any DNA profile, destroyed where investigation interrupted) after the end of the period of six months beginning with the day on which the investigation was resumed.

Persons charged etc.

10 (1) A constable may require a person to attend a police station for the purpose of taking a non-intimate sample from him under section 63(3A).

(2) The power under sub-paragraph (1) above may not be exercised in a case falling within section 63(3A)(a) (sample not taken previously) after the end of the period of six months beginning with the day on which he was charged or informed that he would be reported.

(3) The power under sub-paragraph (1) above may not be exercised in a case falling within section 63(3A)(b)(i) or (ii) (sample taken on a previous occasion not suitable etc.) after the end of the period of six months beginning with the day on which the appropriate officer was informed of the matters specified in section 63(3A)(b)(i) or (ii).

(4) In sub-paragraph (3) above 'appropriate officer' means the officer investigating the offence for which the person was charged or informed that he would be reported.

(5) The power under sub-paragraph (1) above may not be exercised in a case falling within section 63(3A)(b)(iii) (sample, and any DNA profile, destroyed where investigation interrupted) after the end of the period of six months beginning with the day on which the investigation was resumed.

Persons convicted etc. of an offence in England and Wales

11 (1) A constable may require a person to attend a police station for the purpose of taking a non-intimate sample from him under section 63(3B).

(2) Where the condition in section 63(3BA)(a) is satisfied (sample not taken previously), the power under sub-paragraph (1) above may not be exercised after the end of the period of two years beginning with—

- (a) the day on which the person was convicted or cautioned, or
- (b) if later, the day on which this Schedule comes into force.

(3) Where the condition in section 63(3BA)(b) is satisfied (sample taken on a previous occasion not suitable etc.), the power under sub-paragraph (1) above may not be exercised after the end of the period of two years beginning with—

- (a) the day on which an appropriate officer was informed of the matters specified in section 63(3BA)(b)(i) or (ii), or
- (b) if later, the day on which this Schedule comes into force.

(4) In sub-paragraph (3)(a) above 'appropriate officer' means an officer of the police force which investigated the offence in question.

(5) Sub-paragraphs (2) and (3) above do not apply where—

- (a) the offence is a qualifying offence (whether or not it was such an offence at the time of the conviction or caution), or
- (b) he was convicted before 10th April 1995 and is a person to whom section 1 of the Criminal Evidence (Amendment) Act 1997 applies.

Persons convicted etc. of an offence outside England and Wales

13 A constable may require a person to attend a police station for the purpose of taking a non-intimate sample from him under section 63(3E).

Multiple exercise of power

14 (1) Where a non-intimate sample has been taken from a person under section 63 on two occasions in relation to any offence, he may not under this Schedule be required to attend a police station to have another such sample taken from him under that section in relation to that offence on a subsequent occasion without the authorisation of an officer of at least the rank of inspector.

(2) Where an authorisation is given under sub-paragraph (1) above—

- (a) the fact of the authorisation, and
- (b) the reasons for giving it,

shall be recorded as soon as practicable after it has been given.

PART 3A PHOTOGRAPHS

Persons arrested and released

14A (1) A constable may require a person who falls within section 64A(1D)(a) to attend a police station to be photographed under section 64A(1C).

(2) The power under sub-paragraph (1) may not be exercised in a case where section 64A(1E)(b) applies (photograph taken on a previous occasion unavailable or inadequate) after the end of the period of six months beginning with the day on which the appropriate officer was informed that section 64(1E)(b)(i) applied.

(3) In sub-paragraph (2) the 'appropriate officer' means the officer investigating the offence for which the person was arrested.

Persons charged etc.

14B (1) A constable may require a person who falls within section 64A(1D)(b) or (c) to attend a police station to be photographed under section 64A(1C).

(2) The power under sub-paragraph (1) may not be exercised after the end of the period of six months beginning with—

- (a) in a case where section 64A(1E)(a) applies (photograph not previously taken), the day on which the person was charged or informed that they would be reported, or
- (b) in a case where section 64A(1E)(b) applies (photograph taken on a previous occasion unavailable or inadequate), the day on which the appropriate officer was informed that section 64A(1E)(b)(i) applied.

(3) In sub-paragraph (2)(b) the 'appropriate officer' means the officer investigating the offence for which the person was charged or informed that they would be reported.

Persons convicted of an offence etc. in England and Wales

14C (1) A constable may require a person who falls within section 64A(1F) to attend a police station to be photographed under section 64A(1C).

(2) Where section 64A(1G)(a) applies (photographs not previously taken), the power under sub-paragraph (1) may not be exercised after the end of the period of two years beginning with—

- (a) the day on which the person was convicted or cautioned, or
- (b) if later, the day on which this Part comes into force.

(3) Where section 64A(1G)(b) applies (photograph taken on previous occasion unavailable or inadequate), the power under sub-paragraph (1) may not be exercised after the end of the period of two years beginning with—

- (a) the day on which an appropriate officer was informed that section 64A(1G)(b)(i) applied, or
- (b) if later, the day on which this Part comes into force.

(4) In sub-paragraph (3)(a), 'appropriate officer' means an officer of the police force which investigated the offence in question.

(5) Sub-paragraphs (2) and (3) do not apply where the offence is a qualifying offence (whether or not it was such an offence at the time of the conviction or caution).

Persons convicted of an offence etc. outside England and Wales

14D A constable may require a person falling within section 64A(1H) to attend at a police station to be photographed under section 64A(1C).

Multiple exercise of power

14E (1) Where a photograph is taken of a person under section 64A on two occasions in relation to any offence, the person may not under this Schedule be required to attend a police station to be photographed under that section in relation to that offence on a subsequent occasion without the authorisation of an officer of at least the rank of inspector.

(2) Where an authorisation is given under sub-paragraph (1) —

- (a) the fact of the authorisation, and
- (b) the reasons for giving it,

must be recorded as soon as practicable after it has been given.

PART 4 GENERAL AND SUPPLEMENTARY

Requirement to have power to take fingerprints,sample or photograph

15 A power conferred by this Schedule to require a person to attend a police station for the purposes of taking fingerprints, a sample or a photograph under any provision of this Act may be exercised only in a case where the fingerprints, sample or photograph may be taken from the person under that provision (and, in particular, if any necessary authorisation for taking the fingerprints, sample or photograph under that provision has been obtained).

Date and time of attendance

16 (1) A requirement under this Schedule—

(a) must direct the person to attend the police station on a specified date; and

(b) may either direct the person to attend the police station at a specified time on that date or direct the person to attend the police station between specified times on that date.

(2) In specifying a date, time or times for the purposes of sub-paragraph (1) above, the constable shall consider whether the fingerprints, sample or photograph could reasonably be taken at a time when the person is for any other reason required to attend the police station.

(5) If the constable giving a requirement under this Schedule and the person to whom it is given so agree, it may be varied so as to specify any date, time at which or times between which the person must attend; but a variation shall not have effect unless confirmed by the constable in writing.

Enforcement

17 A constable may arrest without warrant a person who has failed to comply with a requirement under this Schedule.

Criminal Justice Act 1988

(1988, c. 33)

PART III OTHER PROVISIONS ABOUT EVIDENCE IN CRIMINAL PROCEEDINGS

30 Expert reports

(1) An expert report shall be admissible as evidence in criminal proceedings, whether or not the person making it attends to give oral evidence in those proceedings.

(2) If it is proposed that the person making the report shall not give oral evidence, the report shall only be admissible with the leave of the court.

(3) For the purpose of determining whether to give leave the court shall have regard—

(a) to the contents of the report;

(b) to the reasons why it is proposed that the person making the report shall not give oral evidence;

(c) to any risk, having regard in particular to whether it is likely to be possible to controvert statements in the report if the person making it does not attend to give oral evidence in the proceedings, that its admission or exclusion will result in unfairness to the accused or, if there is more than one, to any of them; and

(d) to any other circumstances that appear to the court to be relevant.

(4) An expert report, when admitted, shall be evidence of any fact or opinion of which the person making it could have given oral evidence.

(5) In this section 'expert report' means a written report by a person dealing wholly or mainly with matters on which he is (or would if living be) qualified to give expert evidence.

31 Form of evidence and glossaries

For the purpose of helping members of juries to understand complicated issues of fact or technical terms Criminal Procedure Rules may make provision:

(a) as to the furnishing of evidence in any form, notwithstanding the existence of admissible material from which the evidence to be given in that form would be derived; and

(b) as to the furnishing of glossaries for such purposes as may be specified;

in any case where the court gives leave for, or requires, evidence or a glossary to be so furnished.

32 Evidence through television links when witness abroad: service courts

(A1) This section applies only so far as provided by an order under paragraph 8 of Schedule 13.

(1) A person other than the accused may give evidence through a live television link in proceedings to which subsection (1A) below applies if—

(a) the witness is outside the United Kingdom;

but evidence may not be so given without the leave of the court.

(1A) This subsection applies—

(a) to trials on indictment, appeals to the criminal division of the Court of Appeal and hearings of references under section 9 of the Criminal Appeal Act 1995; and

(b) to proceedings in youth courts, appeals to the Crown Court arising out of such proceedings and hearings of references under section 11 of the Criminal Appeal Act 1995 so arising.

(3) A statement made on oath by a witness outside the United Kingdom and given in evidence through a link by virtue of this section shall be treated for the purposes of section 1 of the Perjury Act 1911 as having been made in the proceedings in which it is given in evidence.

(4) Without prejudice to the generality of any enactment conferring power to make Criminal Procedure Rules to which this subsection applies, such rules may make such provision as appears to the authority making them to be necessary or expedient for the purposes of this section.]

34 Abolition of requirement of corroboration for unsworn evidence of children

(2) Any requirement whereby at a trial on indictment it is obligatory for the court to give the jury a warning about convicting the accused on the uncorroborated evidence of a child is abrogated.

(3) Unsworn evidence admitted by virtue of section 56 of the Youth Justice and Criminal Evidence Act 1999 may corroborate evidence (sworn or unsworn) given by any other person.

Sexual Offences (Amendment) Act 1992

(1992, c. 34)

1 Anonymity of victims of certain offences

(1) Where an allegation has been made that an offence to which this Act applies has been committed against a person, no matter relating to that person shall during that person's lifetime be included in any publication if it is likely to lead members of the public to identify that person as the person against whom the offence is alleged to have been committed.

(2) Where a person is accused of an offence to which this Act applies, no matter likely to lead members of the public to identify a person as the person against whom the offence is alleged to have been committed ('the complainant') shall during the complainant's lifetime be included in any publication.

(3) This section—

(a) does not apply in relation to a person by virtue of subsection (1) at any time after a person has been accused of the offence, and

(b) in its application in relation to a person by virtue of subsection (2), has effect subject to any direction given under section 3.

(3A) The matters relating to a person in relation to which the restrictions imposed by subsection (1) or (2) apply (if their inclusion in any publication is likely to have the result mentioned in that subsection) include in particular—

(a) the person's name,
(b) the person's address,
(c) the identity of any school or other educational establishment attended by the person,
(d) the identity of any place of work, and
(e) any still or moving picture of the person.

(4) Nothing in this section prohibits the inclusion in a publication of matter consisting only of a report of criminal proceedings other than proceedings at, or intended to lead to, or on an appeal arising out of, a trial at which the accused is charged with the offence.

2 Offences to which this Act applies

(1) This Act applies to the following offences against the law of England and Wales—

(aa) rape;
(ab) burglary with intent to rape;
(a) any offence under any of the provisions of the Sexual Offences Act 1956 mentioned in subsection (2);
(b) any offence under section 128 of the Mental Health Act 1959 (intercourse with mentally handicapped person by hospital staff etc.);
(c) any offence under section 1 of the Indecency with Children Act 1960 (indecent conduct towards young child);
(d) any offence under section 54 of the Criminal Law Act 1977 (incitement by man of his grand-daughter, daughter or sister under the age of 16 to commit incest with him);
(da) any offence under any of the provisions of Part 1 of the Sexual Offences Act 2003 except section 64, 65, 69 or 71;
(db) any offence under section 2 of the Modern Slavery Act 2015 (human trafficking);
(e) any attempt to commit any of the offences mentioned in paragraphs (aa) to (db);
(f) any conspiracy to commit any of those offences;
(g) any incitement of another to commit any of those offences;
(h) aiding, abetting, counselling or procuring the commission of any of the offences mentioned in paragraphs (aa) to (e) and (g);

(2) The provisions of the Act of 1956 are—

(a) section 2 (procurement of a woman by threats);
(b) section 3 (procurement of a woman by false pretences);
(c) section 4 (administering drugs to obtain intercourse with a woman);
(d) section 5 (intercourse with a girl under the age of 13);
(e) section 6 (intercourse with a girl between the ages of 13 and 16);
(f) section 7 (intercourse with a mentally handicapped person);
(g) section 9 (procurement of a mentally handicapped person);
(h) section 10 (incest by a man);
(i) section 11 (incest by a woman);
(j) section 12 (buggery);
(k) section 14 (indecent assault on a woman);
(l) section 15 (indecent assault on a man);
(m) section 16 (assault with intent to commit buggery);
(n) section 17 (abduction of woman by force).

(3) . . .*

(4) . . .**

* **Editor's Note:** Applies to Northern Ireland.

** **Editor's Note:** Applies to armed forces.

Criminal Justice and Public Order Act 1994

(1994, c. 33)

Corroboration

32 Abolition of corroboration rules

(1) Any requirement whereby at a trial on indictment it is obligatory for the court to give the jury a warning about convicting the accused on the uncorroborated evidence of a person merely because that person is—

(a) an alleged accomplice of the accused, or

(b) where the offence charged is a sexual offence, the person in respect of whom it is alleged to have been committed,

is hereby abrogated.

(2) . . .

(3) Any requirement that—

(a) is applicable at the summary trial of a person for an offence, and

(b) corresponds to the requirement mentioned in subsection (1) above or that mentioned in section 34(2) of the Criminal Justice Act 1988,

is hereby abrogated.

(4) Nothing in this section applies in relation to—

(a) any trial, or

(b) any proceedings before a magistrates' court as examining justices,

which began before the commencement of this section.

33 Abolition of corroboration requirements under Sexual Offences Act 1956

(1) The following provisions of the Sexual Offences Act 1956 (which provide that a person shall not be convicted of the offence concerned on the evidence of one witness only unless the witness is corroborated) are hereby repealed—

(a) section 2(2) (procurement of woman by threats),

(b) section 3(2) (procurement of woman by false pretences),

(c) section 4(2) (administering drugs to obtain or facilitate intercourse),

(d) section 22(2) (causing prostitution of women), and

(e) section 23(2) (procuration of girl under twenty-one).

(2) Nothing in this section applies in relation to—

(a) any trial, or

(b) any proceedings before a magistrates' court as examining justices,

which began before the commencement of this section.

Inferences from accused's silence

34 Effect of accused's failure to mention facts when questioned or charged

(1) Where, in any proceedings against a person for an offence, evidence is given that the accused—

(a) at any time before he was charged with the offence, on being questioned under caution by a constable trying to discover whether or by whom the offence had been committed, failed to mention any fact relied on in his defence in those proceedings; or

(b) on being charged with the offence or officially informed that he might be prosecuted for it, failed to mention any such fact, or

. . .*

being a fact which in the circumstances existing at the time the accused could reasonably have been expected to mention when so questioned, charged or informed, as the case may be, subsection (2) below applies.

* **Editor's Note:** Applies to terrorism.

(2) Where this subsection applies—

(b) a judge, in deciding whether to grant an application made by the accused under paragraph 2 of Schedule 3 to the Crime and Disorder Act 1998;

(c) the court, in determining whether there is a case to answer; and

(d) the court or jury, in determining whether the accused is guilty of the offence charged,

may draw such inferences from the failure as appear proper.

(2A) Where the accused was at an authorised place of detention at the time of failure, subsections (1) and (2) above do not apply if he had not been allowed an opportunity to consult a solicitor prior to being questioned, charged or informed as mentioned in subsection (1) above.

(3) Subject to any directions by the court, evidence tending to establish the failure may be given before or after evidence tending to establish the fact which the accused is alleged to have failed to mention.

(4) This section applies in relation to questioning by persons (other than constables) charged with the duty of investigating offences or charging offenders as it applies in relation to questioning by constables; and in subsection (1) above 'officially informed' means informed by a constable or any such person.

(5) This section does not—

(a) prejudice the admissibility in evidence of the silence or other reaction of the accused in the face of anything said in his presence relating to the conduct in respect of which he is charged, in so far as evidence thereof would be admissible apart from this section; or

(b) preclude the drawing of any inference from any such silence or other reaction of the accused which could properly be drawn apart from this section.

(6) This section does not apply in relation to a failure to mention a fact if the failure occurred before the commencement of this section.

35 Effect of accused's silence at trial

(1) At the trial of any person for an offence, subsections (2) and (3) below apply unless—

(a) the accused's guilt is not in issue; or

(b) it appears to the court that the physical or mental condition of the accused makes it undesirable for him to give evidence;

but subsection (2) below does not apply if, at the conclusion of the evidence for the prosecution, his legal representative informs the court that the accused will give evidence or, where he is unrepresented, the court ascertains from him that he will give evidence.

(2) Where this subsection applies, the court shall, at the conclusion of the evidence for the prosecution, satisfy itself (in the case of proceedings on indictment with a jury, in the presence of the jury) that the accused is aware that the stage has been reached at which evidence can be given for the defence and that he can, if he wishes, give evidence and that, if he chooses not to give evidence, or having been sworn, without good cause refuses to answer any question, it will be permissible for the court or jury to draw such inferences as appear proper from his failure to give evidence or his refusal, without good cause, to answer any question.

(3) Where this subsection applies, the court or jury, in determining whether the accused is guilty of the offence charged, may draw such inferences as appear proper from the failure of the accused to give evidence or his refusal, without good cause, to answer any question.

(4) This section does not render the accused compellable to give evidence on his own behalf, and he shall accordingly not be guilty of contempt of court by reason of a failure to do so.

(5) For the purposes of this section a person who, having been sworn, refuses to answer any question shall be taken to do so without good cause unless—

(a) he is entitled to refuse to answer the question by virtue of any enactment, whenever passed or made, or on the ground of privilege; or

(b) the court in the exercise of its general discretion excuses him from answering it.

(7) This section applies—

(a) in relation to proceedings on indictment for an offence, only if the person charged with the offence is arraigned on or after the commencement of this section;

(b) in relation to proceedings in a magistrates' court, only if the time when the court begins to receive evidence in the proceedings falls after the commencement of this section.

36 Effect of accused's failure or refusal to account for objects, substances or marks

(1) Where—

(a) a person is arrested by a constable, and there is—

(i) on his person; or

(ii) in or on his clothing or footwear; or

(iii) otherwise in his possession; or

(iv) in any place in which he is at the time of his arrest,

any object, substance or mark, or there is any mark on any such object; and

(b) that or another constable investigating the case reasonably believes that the presence of the object, substance or mark may be attributable to the participation of the person arrested in the commission of an offence specified by the constable; and

(c) the constable informs the person arrested that he so believes, and requests him to account for the presence of the object, substance or mark; and

(d) the person fails or refuses to do so,

then if, in any proceedings against the person for the offence so specified, evidence of those matters is given, subsection (2) below applies.

(2) Where this subsection applies—

(b) a judge, in deciding whether to grant an application made by the accused under paragraph 2 of Schedule 3 to the Crime and Disorder Act 1998;

(c) the court, in determining whether there is a case to answer; and

(d) the court or jury, in determining whether the accused is guilty of the offence charged,

may draw such inferences from the failure or refusal as appear proper.

(3) Subsections (1) and (2) above apply to the condition of clothing or footwear as they apply to a substance or mark thereon.

(4) Subsections 1 and 2 above do not apply unless the accused was told in ordinary language by the constable when making the request mentioned in subsection (1)(c) above what the effect of this section would be if he failed or refused to comply with the request.

(4A) Where the accused was at an authorised place of detention at the time of the failure or refusal, subsections (1) and (2) above do not apply if he had not been allowed an opportunity to consult a solicitor prior to the request being made.

(5) This section applies in relation to officers of customs and excise as it applies in relation to constables.

(5A) This section applies in relation to enforcement officers who—

(a) are appointed by the Secretary of State under section 90 of the Employment Rights Act 2025, and

(b) are acting in the exercise of functions conferred on them by virtue of section 114B of the Police and Criminal Evidence Act 1984,

as it applies in relation to constables.

(6) This section does not preclude the drawing of any inference from a failure or refusal of the accused to account for the presence of an object, substance or mark or from the condition of clothing or footwear which could properly be drawn apart from this section.

(7) This section does not apply in relation to a failure or refusal which occurred before the commencement of this section.

37 Effect of accused's failure or refusal to account for presence at a particular place

(1) Where—

(a) a person arrested by a constable was found by him at a place at or about the time the offence for which he was arrested is alleged to have been committed; and

(b) that or another constable investigating the offence reasonably believes that the presence of the person at that place and at that time may be attributable to his participation in the commission of the offence; and

(c) the constable informs the person that he so believes, and requests him to account for that presence; and

(d) the person fails or refuses to do so, then if, in any proceedings against the person for the offence, evidence of those matters is given, subsection (2) below applies.

(2) Where this subsection applies—

(b) a judge, in deciding whether to grant an application made by the accused under paragraph 2 of Schedule 3 to the Crime and Disorder Act 1998;

(c) the court, in determining whether there is a case to answer, and

(d) the court or jury, in determining whether the accused is guilty of the offence charged,

may draw such inferences from the failure or refusal as appear proper.

(3) Subsections (1) and (2) do not apply unless the accused was told in ordinary language by the constable when making the request mentioned in subsection (1)(c) above what the effect of this section would be if he failed or refused to comply with the request.

(3A) Where the accused was at an authorised place of detention at the time of the failure or refusal, subsections (1) and (2) do not apply if he had not been allowed an opportunity to consult a solicitor prior to the request being made.

(4) This section applies in relation to officers of customs and excise as it applies in relation to constables.

(4A) This section applies in relation to enforcement officers who—

(a) are appointed by the Secretary of State under section 90 of the Employment Rights Act 2025, and

(b) are acting in the exercise of functions conferred on them by virtue of section 114B of the Police and Criminal Evidence Act 1984,

as it applies in relation to constables.

(5) This section does not preclude the drawing of any inference from a failure or refusal of the accused to account for his presence at a place which could properly be drawn apart from this section.

(6) This section does not apply in relation to a failure or refusal which occurred before the commencement of this section.

38 Interpretation and savings for sections 34, 35, 36 and 37

(1) In sections 34, 35, 36 and 37 of this Act—

'legal representative' means a person who, for the purposes of the Legal Services Act 2007, is an authorised person in relation to an activity which constitutes the exercise of a right of audience or the conduct of litigation (within the meaning of that Act); and

'place' includes any building or part of a building, any vehicle, vessel, aircraft or hovercraft and any other place whatsoever.

(2) In sections 34(2), 35(3), 36(2) and 37(2), references to an offence charged include references to any other offence of which the accused could lawfully be convicted on that charge.

(2A) In each of sections 34(2A), 36(4A) and 37(3A) 'authorised place of detention' means—

(a) a police station; or

(b) any other place prescribed for the purposes of that provision by order made by the Secretary of State;

and the power to make an order under this subsection shall be exercisable by statutory instrument which shall be subject to annulment on pursuance of a resolution of either House of Parliament.

(3) A person shall not have the proceedings against him transferred to the Crown Court for trial, have a case to answer or be convicted of an offence solely on an inference drawn from such a failure or refusal as is mentioned in section 34(2), 35(3), 36(2) or 37(2).

(4) A judge shall not refuse to grant such an application as is mentioned in section 34(2)(b), 36(2)(b) and 37(2)(b) solely on an inference drawn from such a failure as is mentioned in section 34(2), 36(2) or 37(2).

(5) Nothing in sections 34, 35, 36 or 37 prejudices the operation of a provision of an enactment which provides (in whatever words) that any answer or evidence given by a person in specified circumstances shall not be admissible in evidence against him or some other person in any proceedings or class of proceedings (however described, and whether civil or criminal).

In this subsection, the reference to giving evidence is a reference to giving evidence in any manner, whether by furnishing information, making discovery, producing documents or otherwise.

(6) Nothing in sections 34, 35, 36 or 37 prejudices any power of a court, in any proceedings, to exclude evidence (whether by preventing questions being put or otherwise) at its discretion.

Criminal Evidence (Amendment) Act 1997

(1997, c. 17)

Extension of power to take non-intimate body samples without consent

1 Persons imprisoned or detained by virtue of pre-existing conviction for sexual offence etc.

(1) This section has effect for removing, in relation to persons to whom this section applies, the restriction on the operation of section 63(3B) of the Police and Criminal Evidence Act 1984 (power to take non-intimate samples without the appropriate consent from persons convicted of recordable offences)—

(a) which is imposed by the subsection (10) inserted in section 63 by section 55(6) of the Criminal Justice and Public Order Act 1994, and

(b) by virtue of which section 63(3B) does not apply to persons convicted before 10 April 1995.

(2) . . .*

(3) This section applies to a person who was convicted of a recordable offence before 10 April 1995 if—

(a) that offence was one of the offences listed in Schedule 1 to this Act (which lists certain sexual, violent and other offences), and

(b) he has at any time served or at the relevant time he is serving a sentence of imprisonment in respect of that offence.

(4) This section also applies to a person who was convicted of a recordable offence before 10 April 1995 if—

(a) that offence was one of the offences listed in Schedule 1 to this Act, and

(b) he has at any time been detained or at the relevant time he is detained under Part III of the Mental Health Act 1983 in pursuance of—

(i) a hospital order or interim hospital order made following that conviction.

Expressions used in this subsection and in the Mental Health Act 1983 have the same meaning as in that Act.

(5) Where a person convicted of a recordable offence before 10 April 1995 was, following his conviction for that and any other offence or offences, sentenced to two or more terms of imprisonment (whether taking effect consecutively or concurrently), he shall be treated for the purposes of this section as serving a sentence of imprisonment in respect of that offence at any time when serving any of those terms.

(6) For the purposes of this section, references to a person serving a sentence of imprisonment include references—

(a) to his being detained in any institution to which the Prison Act 1952 applies in pursuance of any other sentence or order for detention imposed by a court in criminal proceedings, or

(b) to his being detained (otherwise than in any such institution) in pursuance of directions of the Secretary of State under section 92 of the Powers of Criminal Courts (Sentencing) Act 2000;

and any reference to a term of imprisonment shall be construed accordingly.

* **Editor's Note:** Amends the Police and Criminal Evidence Act 1984, section 63(3)(B) for limited purposes of subsection (1) above.

2 Persons detained following acquittal on grounds of insanity or finding of unfitness to plead

(1) This section has effect for enabling non-intimate samples to be taken from persons under section 63 of the 1984 Act without the appropriate consent where they are persons to whom this section applies.

(2) . . .*

(3) This section applies to a person if—

(a) he has at any time been detained or at the relevant time he is detained under Part III of the Mental Health Act 1983 in pursuance of an order made under—

(i) section 5(2)(a) of the Criminal Procedure (Insanity) Act 1964 or section 6 or 14 of the Criminal Appeal Act 1968 (finding of insanity or unfitness to plead), or

(ii) section 37(3) of the Mental Health Act 1983 (power of magistrates' court to make hospital order without convicting accused); and

that order was made on or after the date of the passing of this Act in respect of a recordable offence.

(4) This section also applies to a person if—

(a) he has at any time been detained or at the relevant time he is detained under Part III of the Mental Health Act 1983 in pursuance of an order made under—

(i) any of the provisions mentioned in subsection (3)(a), or

(ii) section 5(1) of the Criminal Procedure (Insanity) Act 1964 as originally enacted; and

(b) that order was made before the date of the passing of this Act in respect of any offence listed in Schedule 1 to this Act.

(5) Subsection (4)(a)(i) does not apply to any order made under section 14(2) of the Criminal Appeal Act 1968 as originally enacted.

(6) For the purposes of this section an order falling within subsection (3) or (4) shall be treated as having been made in respect of an offence of a particular description—

(a) if, where the order was made following—

(i) a finding of not guilty by reason of insanity, or

(ii) a finding that the person in question was under a disability and did the act or made the omission charged against him, or

(iii) a finding for the purposes of section 37(3) of the Mental Health Act 1983 that the person in question did the act or made the omission charged against him, or

(iv) (in the case of an order made under section 5(1) of the Criminal Procedure (Insanity) Act 1964 as originally enacted) a finding that he was under a disability,

that finding was recorded in respect of an offence of that description; or

(b) if, where the order was made following the Court of Appeal forming such opinion as is mentioned in section 6(1) or 14(1) of the Criminal Appeal Act 1968, that opinion was formed on an appeal brought in respect of an offence of that description.

(7) In this section any reference to an Act 'as originally enacted' is a reference to that Act as it had effect without any of the amendments made by the Criminal Procedure (Insanity and Unfitness to Plead) Act 1991.

Supplementary

5 Interpretation

In this Act—

'the 1984 Act' means the Police and Criminal Evidence Act 1984;

'appropriate consent' has the meaning given by section 65 of the 1984 Act;

'non-intimate sample' has the meaning given by section 65 of the 1984 Act;

'recordable offence' means any offence to which regulations under section 27 of the 1984 Act (fingerprinting) apply;

* **Editor's Note:** Amends the Police and Criminal Evidence Act 1984, section 63(3)(C) for limited purposes of subsection (1) above.

'the relevant time' means, in relation to the exercise of any power to take a non-intimate sample from a person, the time when it is sought to take the sample.

SCHEDULE 1
LIST OF OFFENCES

Sexual offences and offences of indecency

1. Any offence under the Sexual Offences Act 1956, other than an offence under section 30, 31 or 33 to 36 of that Act.

2. Any offence under section 128 of the Mental Health Act 1959 (intercourse with mentally handicapped person by hospital staff etc.).

3. Any offence under section 1 of the Indecency with Children Act 1960 (indecent conduct towards young child).

4. Any offence under section 54 of the Criminal Law Act 1977 (incitement by man of his grand-daughter, daughter or sister under the age of 16 to commit incest with him).

5. Any offence under section 1 of the Protection of Children Act 1978.

Violent and other offences

6. Any of the following offences—
   (a) murder;
   (b) manslaughter;
   (c) false imprisonment; and
   (d) kidnapping.

7. Any offence under any of the following provisions of the Offences Against the Person Act 1861—
   (a) section 4 (conspiring or soliciting to commit murder);
   (b) section 16 (threats to kill);
   (c) section 18 (wounding with intent to cause grievous bodily harm);
   (d) section 20 (causing grievous bodily harm);
   (e) section 21 (attempting to choke etc. in order to commit or assist in the committing of any indictable offence);
   (f) section 22 (using chloroform etc. to commit or assist in the committing of any indictable offence);
   (g) section 23 (maliciously administering poison etc. so as to endanger life or inflict grievous bodily harm);
   (h) section 24 (maliciously administering poison etc. with intent to injure etc.); and
   (i) section 47 (assault occasioning actual bodily harm).

8. Any offence under either of the following provisions of the Explosive Substances Act 1883—
   (a) section 2 (causing explosion likely to endanger life or property); and
   (b) section 3 (attempt to cause explosion, or making or keeping explosive with intent to endanger life or property).

9. Any offence under section 1 of the Children and Young Persons Act 1933 (cruelty to person under 16).

10. Any offence under section 4(1) of the Criminal Law Act 1967 (assisting offender) committed in relation to the offence of murder.

11. Any offence under any of the following provisions of the Firearms Act 1968—
    (a) section 16 (possession of firearm with intent to injure);
    (b) section 17 (use of firearm to resist arrest); and
    (c) section 18 (carrying firearm with criminal intent).

12. Any offence under either of the following provisions of the Theft Act 1968—
    (a) section 9 (burglary); and

(b) section 10 (aggravated burglary);

and any offence under section 12A of that Act (aggravated vehicle-taking) involving an accident which caused the death of any person.

13. Any offence under section 1 of the Criminal Damage Act 1971 (destroying or damaging property) required to be charged as arson.

14. Any offence under section 2 of the Child Abduction Act 1984 (abduction of child by person other than parent).

Conspiracy, incitement and attempts

15. Any offence under section 1 of the Criminal Law Act 1977 of conspiracy to commit any of the offences mentioned in paragraphs 1 to 14.

16. Any offence under section 1 of the Criminal Attempts Act 1981 of attempting to commit any of those offences.

17. Any offence of inciting another to commit any of those offences.

Youth Justice and Criminal Evidence Act 1999

(1999, c. 23)

PART II GIVING OF EVIDENCE OR INFORMATION FOR PURPOSES OF CRIMINAL PROCEEDINGS

Chapter I Special measures directions in case of vulnerable and intimidated witnesses

Preliminary

16 Witnesses eligible for assistance on grounds of age or incapacity

(1) For the purposes of this Chapter a witness in criminal proceedings (other than the accused) is eligible for assistance by virtue of this section—

(a) if under the age of 18 at the time of the hearing; or

(b) if the court considers that the quality of evidence given by the witness is likely to be diminished by reason of any circumstances falling within subsection (2).

(2) The circumstances falling within this subsection are—

(a) that the witness—

(i) suffers from mental disorder within the meaning of the Mental Health Act 1983, or

(ii) otherwise has a significant impairment of intelligence and social functioning;

(b) that the witness has a physical disability or is suffering from a physical disorder.

(3) In subsection (1)(a) 'the time of the hearing', in relation to a witness, means the time when it falls to the court to make a determination for the purposes of section 19(2) in relation to the witness.

(4) In determining whether a witness falls within subsection (1)(b) the court must consider any views expressed by the witness.

(5) In this Chapter references to the quality of a witness's evidence are to its quality in terms of completeness, coherence and accuracy; and for this purpose 'coherence' refers to a witness's ability in giving evidence to give answers which address the questions put to the witness and can be understood both individually and collectively.

17 Witnesses eligible for assistance on grounds of fear or distress about testifying

(1) For the purposes of this Chapter a witness in criminal proceedings (other than the accused) is eligible for assistance by virtue of this subsection if the court is satisfied that the quality of evidence given by the witness is likely to be diminished by reason of fear or distress on the part of the witness in connection with testifying in the proceedings.

(2) In determining whether a witness falls within subsection (1) the court must take into account, in particular—

- (a) the nature and alleged circumstances of the offence to which the proceedings relate;
- (b) the age of the witness;
- (c) such of the following matters as appear to the court to be relevant, namely—
  - (i) the social and cultural background and ethnic origins of the witness,
  - (ii) the domestic and employment circumstances of the witness, and
  - (iii) any religious beliefs or political opinions of the witness;
- (d) any behaviour towards the witness on the part of—
  - (i) the accused,
  - (ii) members of the family or associates of the accused, or
  - (iii) any other person who is likely to be an accused or a witness in the proceedings.

(3) In determining that question the court must in addition consider any views expressed by the witness.

(4) Where the complainant in respect of a sexual offence or an offence under section 1 or 2 of the Modern Slavery Act 2015 an offence listed in subsection (4A) is a witness in proceedings relating to that offence (or to that offence and any other offences), the witness is eligible for assistance in relation to those proceedings by virtue of this subsection unless the witness has informed the court of the witness's wish not to be so eligible by virtue of this subsection.

(4A) The offences are—

- (a) a sexual offence;
- (b) an offence under section 1 or 2 of the Modern Slavery Act 2015;
- (c) any other offence where it is alleged that the behaviour of the accused amounted to domestic abuse within the meaning of the Domestic Abuse Act 2021 (see section 1 of that Act).

(5) A witness in proceedings relating to a relevant offence (or to a relevant offence and any other offences) is eligible for assistance in relation to those proceedings by virtue of this subsection unless the witness has informed the court of the witness's wish not to be so eligible by virtue of this subsection.

(6) For the purposes of subsection (5) an offence is a relevant offence if it is an offence described in Schedule 1A.

(7) The Secretary of State may by order amend Schedule 1A.

18 Special measures available to eligible witnesses

(1) For the purposes of this Chapter—

- (a) the provision which may be made by a special measures direction by virtue of each of sections 23 to 30 is a special measure available in relation to a witness eligible for assistance by virtue of section 16; and
- (b) the provision which may be made by such a direction by virtue of each of sections 23 to 28 is a special measure available in relation to a witness eligible for assistance by virtue of section 17;

but this subsection has effect subject to subsection (2).

(2) Where (apart from this subsection) a special measure would, in accordance with subsection (1)(a) or (b), be available in relation to a witness in any proceedings, it shall not be taken by a court to be available in relation to the witness unless—

(a) the court has been notified by the Secretary of State that relevant arrangements may be made available in the area in which it appears to the court that the proceedings will take place, and

(b) the notice has not been withdrawn.

(3) In subsection (2) 'relevant arrangements' means arrangements for implementing the measure in question which cover the witness and the proceedings in question.

(4) The withdrawal of a notice under that subsection relating to a special measure shall not affect the availability of that measure in relation to a witness if a special measures direction providing for that measure to apply to the witness's evidence has been made by the court before the notice is withdrawn.

(5) The Secretary of State may by order make such amendments of this Chapter as he considers appropriate for altering the special measures which, in accordance with subsection (1)(a) or (b), are available in relation to a witness eligible for assistance by virtue of section 16 or (as the case may be) section 17, whether—

(a) by modifying the provisions relating to any measure for the time being available in relation to such a witness,

(b) by the addition—

(i) (with or without modifications) of any measure which is for the time being available in relation to a witness eligible for assistance by virtue of the other of those sections, or

(ii) of any new measure, or

(c) by the removal of any measure.

Special measures directions

19 Special measures direction relating to eligible witness

(1) This section applies where in any criminal proceedings—

(a) a party to the proceedings makes an application for the court to give a direction under this section in relation to a witness in the proceedings other than the accused, or

(b) the court of its own motion raises the issue whether such a direction should be given.

(2) Where the court determines that the witness is eligible for assistance by virtue of section 16 or 17, the court must then—

(a) determine whether any of the special measures available in relation to the witness (or any combination of them) would, in its opinion, be likely to improve the quality of evidence given by the witness; and

(b) if so—

(i) determine which of those measures (or combination of them) would, in its opinion, be likely to maximise so far as practicable the quality of such evidence; and

(ii) give a direction under this section providing for the measure or measures so determined to apply to evidence given by the witness.

(3) In determining for the purposes of this Chapter whether any special measure or measures would or would not be likely to improve, or to maximise so far as practicable, the quality of evidence given by the witness, the court must consider all the circumstances of the case, including in particular—

(a) any views expressed by the witness; and

(b) whether the measure or measures might tend to inhibit such evidence being effectively tested by a party to the proceedings.

(4) A special measures direction must specify particulars of the provision made by the direction in respect of each special measure which is to apply to the witness's evidence.

(5) In this Chapter 'special measures direction' means a direction under this section.

(6) Nothing in this Chapter is to be regarded as affecting any power of a court to make an order or give leave of any description (in the exercise of its inherent jurisdiction or otherwise)—

(a) in relation to a witness who is not an eligible witness, or

(b) in relation to an eligible witness where (as, for example, in a case where a foreign language interpreter is to be provided) the order is made or the leave is given otherwise than by reason of the fact that the witness is an eligible witness.

20 Further provisions about directions: general

(1) Subject to subsection (2) and section 21(8), a special measures direction has binding effect from the time it is made until the proceedings for the purposes of which it is made are either—

(a) determined (by acquittal, conviction or otherwise), or

(b) abandoned,

in relation to the accused or (if there is more than one) in relation to each of the accused.

(2) The court may discharge or vary (or further vary) a special measures direction if it appears to the court to be in the interests of justice to do so, and may do so either—

(a) on an application made by a party to the proceedings, if there has been a material change of circumstances since the relevant time, or

(b) of its own motion.

(3) In subsection (2) 'the relevant time' means—

(a) the time when the direction was given, or

(b) if a previous application has been made under that subsection, the time when the application (or last application) was made.

(4) Nothing in section 24(2) and (3), 27(4) to (7) or 28(4) to (6) is to be regarded as affecting the power of the court to vary or discharge a special measures direction under subsection (2).

(5) The court must state in open court its reasons for—

(a) giving or varying,

(b) refusing an application for, or for the variation or discharge of, or

(c) discharging,

a special measures direction and, if it is a magistrates' court, must cause them to be entered in the register of its proceedings.

(6) Criminal Procedure Rules may make provision—

(a) for uncontested applications to be determined by the court without a hearing;

(b) for preventing the renewal of an unsuccessful application for a special measures direction except where there has been a material change of circumstances;

(c) for expert evidence to be given in connection with an application for, or for varying or discharging, such a direction;

(d) for the manner in which confidential or sensitive information is to be treated in connection with such an application and in particular as to its being disclosed to, or withheld from, a party to the proceedings.

21 Special provisions relating to child witnesses

(1) For the purposes of this section—

(a) a witness in criminal proceedings is a 'child witness' if he is an eligible witness by reason of section 16(1)(a) (whether or not he is an eligible witness by reason of any other provision of section 16 or 17); and

(c) a 'relevant recording', in relation to a child witness, is a video recording of an interview of the witness made with a view to its admission as evidence in chief of the witness.

(2) Where the court, in making a determination for the purposes of section 19(2), determines that a witness in criminal proceedings is a child witness, the court must—

(a) first have regard to subsections (3) to (4C) below; and

(b) then have regard to section 19(2);

and for the purposes of section 19(2), as it then applies to the witness, any special measures required to be applied in relation to him by virtue of this section shall be treated as if they were measures determined by the court, pursuant to section 19(2)(a) and (b)(i), to be ones that (whether on their own or with any other special measures) would be likely to maximise, so far as practicable, the quality of his evidence.

(3) The primary rule in the case of a child witness is that the court must give a special measures direction in relation to the witness which complies with the following requirements—

(a) it must provide for any relevant recording to be admitted under section 27 (video recorded evidence in chief); and

(b) it must provide for any evidence given by the witness in the proceedings which is not given by means of a video recording (whether in chief or otherwise) to be given by means of a live link in accordance with section 24.

(4) The primary rule is subject to the following limitations—

(a) the requirement contained in subsection (3)(a) or (b) has effect subject to the availability (within the meaning of section 18(2)) of the special measure in question in relation to the witness;

(b) the requirement contained in subsection (2)(a) also has effect subject to section 27(2);

(ba) if the witness informs the court of the witness's wish that the rule should not apply or should apply only in part, the rule does not apply to the extent that the court is satisfied that not complying with the rule would not diminish the quality of the witness's evidence; and

(c) the rule does not apply to the extent that the court is satisfied that compliance with it would not be likely to maximise the quality of the witness's evidence so far as practicable (whether because the application to that evidence of one or more other special measures available in relation to the witness would have that result or for any other reason).

(4A) Where as a consequence of all or part of the primary rule being disapplied under subsection (4)(ba) a witness's evidence or any part of it would fall to be given as testimony in court, the court must give a special measures direction making such provision as is described in section 23 for the evidence or that part of it.

(4B) The requirement in subsection (4A) is subject to the following limitations—

(a) if the witness informs the court of the witness's wish that the requirement in subsection (4A) should not apply, the requirement does not apply to the extent that the court is satisfied that not complying with it would not diminish the quality of the witness's evidence; and

(b) the requirement does not apply to the extent that the court is satisfied that making such a provision would not be likely to maximise the quality of the witness's evidence so far as practicable (whether because the application to that evidence of one or more other special measures available in relation to the witness would have that result or for any other reason).

(4C) In making a decision under subsection (4)(ba) or (4B)(a), the court must take into account the following factors (and any others it considers relevant)—

(a) the age and maturity of the witness;

(b) the ability of the witness to understand the consequences of giving evidence otherwise than in accordance with the requirements in subsection (3) or (as the case may be) in accordance with the requirement in subsection (4A);

(c) the relationship (if any) between the witness and the accused;

(d) the witness's social and cultural background and ethnic origins;

(e) the nature and alleged circumstances of the offence to which the proceedings relate.

(8) Where a special measures direction is given in relation to a child witness who is an eligible witness by reason only of section 16(1)(a), then—

(a) subject to subsection (9) below, and

(b) except where the witness has already begun to give evidence in the proceedings,

the direction shall cease to have effect at the time when the witness attains the age of 18.

(9) Where a special measures direction is given in relation to a child witness who is an eligible witness by reason only of section 16(1)(a) and—

(a) the direction provides—

(i) for any relevant recording to be admitted under section 27 as evidence in chief of the witness, or

(ii) for the special measure available under section 28 to apply in relation to the witness, and

(b) if it provides for that special measure to so apply, the witness is still under the age of 18 when the video recording is made for the purposes of section 28,

then, so far as it provides as mentioned in paragraph (a)(i) or (ii) above, the direction shall continue to have effect in accordance with section 20(1) even though the witness subsequently attains that age.

22 Extension of provisions of section 21 to certain witness over 18

(1) For the purposes of this section—

(a) a witness in criminal proceedings (other than the accused) is a 'qualifying witness' if he—

(i) is not an eligible witness at the time of the hearing (as defined by section 16(3)), but

(ii) was under the age of 18 when a relevant recording was made;

and

(c) a 'relevant recording', in relation to a witness, is a video recording of an interview of the witness made with a view to its admission as evidence in chief of the witness.

(2) Subsections (2) to (4) and (4C) of section 21, so far as relating to the giving of a direction complying with the requirement contained in section 21(3)(a), apply to a qualifying witness in respect of the relevant recording as they apply to a child witness (within the meaning of that section).

22A Special provisions relating to sexual offences

(1) This section applies where in criminal proceedings relating to a sexual offence (or to a sexual offence and other offences) the complainant in respect of that offence is a witness in the proceedings.

(2) This section does not apply if the place of trial is a magistrates' court.

(3) This section does not apply if the complainant is an eligible witness by reason of section 16(1)(a) (whether or not the complainant is an eligible witness by reason of any other provision of section 16 or 17).

(4) If a party to the proceedings makes an application under section 19(1)(a) for a special measures direction in relation to the complainant, the party may request that the direction provide for any relevant recording to be admitted under section 27 (video recorded evidence in chief).

(5) Subsection (6) applies if—

(a) a party to the proceedings makes a request under subsection (4) with respect to the complainant, and

(b) the court determines for the purposes of section 19(2) that the complainant is eligible for assistance by virtue of section 16(1)(b) or 17.

(6) The court must—

(a) first have regard to subsections (7) to (9); and

(b) then have regard to section 19(2);

and for the purposes of section 19(2), as it then applies to the complainant, any special measure required to be applied in relation to the complainant by virtue of this section is to be treated as if it were a measure determined by the court, pursuant to section 19(2)(a) and (b)(i), to be one that (whether on its own or with any other special measures) would be likely to maximise, so far as practicable, the quality of the complainant's evidence.

(7) The court must give a special measures direction in relation to the complainant that provides for any relevant recording to be admitted under section 27.

(8) The requirement in subsection (7) has effect subject to section 27(2).

(9) The requirement in subsection (7) does not apply to the extent that the court is satisfied that compliance with it would not be likely to maximise the quality of the complainant's evidence

so far as practicable (whether because the application to that evidence of one or more other special measures available in relation to the complainant would have that result or for any other reason).

(10) In this section 'relevant recording', in relation to a complainant, is a video recording of an interview of the complainant made with a view to its admission as the evidence in chief of the complainant.

Special measures

23 Screening witness from accused

(1) A special measures direction may provide for the witness, while giving testimony or being sworn in court, to be prevented by means of a screen or other arrangement from seeing the accused.

(2) But the screen or other arrangement must not prevent the witness from being able to see, and to be seen by—

(a) the judge or justices (or both) and the jury (if there is one);

(b) legal representatives acting in the proceedings; and

(c) any interpreter or other person appointed (in pursuance of the direction or otherwise) to assist the witness.

(3) Where two or more legal representatives are acting for a party to the proceedings, subsection (2)(b) is to be regarded as satisfied in relation to those representatives if the witness is able at all material times to see and be seen by at least one of them.

24 Evidence by live link

(1) A special measures direction may provide for the witness to give evidence by means of a live link.

(1A) Such a direction may also provide for a specified person to accompany the witness while the witness is giving evidence by live link.

(1B) In determining who may accompany the witness, the court must have regard to the wishes of the witness.

(2) Where a direction provides for the witness to give evidence by means of a live link, the witness may not give evidence in any other way without the permission of the court.

(3) The court may give permission for the purposes of subsection (2) if it appears to the court to be in the interests of justice to do so, and may do so either—

(a) on an application by a party to the proceedings, if there has been a material change of circumstances since the relevant time, or

(b) of its own motion.

(4) In subsection (3) 'the relevant time' means—

(a) the time when the direction was given, or

(b) if a previous application has been made under that subsection, the time when the application (or last application) was made.

(8) In this Chapter 'live link' means a live television link or other arrangement whereby a witness, while absent from the courtroom or other place where the proceedings are being held, is able to see and hear a person there and to be such and heard by the persons specified in section 23(2)(a) to (c).

25 Evidence given in private

(1) A special measures direction may provide for the exclusion from the court, during the giving of the witness's evidence, of persons of any description specified in the direction.

(2) The persons who may be so excluded do not include—

(a) the accused,

(b) legal representatives acting in the proceedings, or

(c) any interpreter or other person appointed (in pursuance of the direction or otherwise) to assist the witness.

(3) A special measures direction providing for representatives of news gathering or reporting organisations to be so excluded shall be expressed not to apply to one named person who—

(a) is a representative of such an organisation, and
(b) has been nominated for the purpose by one or more such organisations,

unless it appears to the court that no such nomination has been made.

(4) A special measures direction may only provide for the exclusion of persons under this section where—

(a) the proceedings relate to a sexual offence or an offence under section 1 or 2 of the Modern Slavery Act 2015 an offence listed in section 17(4A); or
(b) it appears to the court that there are reasonable grounds for believing that any person other than the accused has sought, or will seek, to intimidate the witness in connection with testifying in the proceedings.

(5) Any proceedings from which persons are excluded under this section (whether or not those persons include representatives of news gathering or reporting organisations) shall nevertheless be taken to be held in public for the purposes of any privilege or exemption from liability available in respect of fair, accurate and contemporaneous reports of legal proceedings held in public.

26 Removal of wigs and gowns

A special measures direction may provide for the wearing of wigs or gowns to be dispensed with during the giving of the witness's evidence.

27 Video recorded evidence in chief

(1) A special measures direction may provide for a video recording of an interview of the witness to be admitted as evidence in chief of the witness.

(2) A special measures direction may, however, not provide for a video recording, or a part of such a recording, to be admitted under this section if the court is of the opinion, having regard to all the circumstances of the case, that in the interests of justice the recording, or that part of it, should not be so admitted.

(3) In considering for the purposes of subsection (2) whether any part of a recording should not be admitted under this section, the court must consider whether any prejudice to the accused which might result from that part being so admitted is outweighed by the desirability of showing the whole, or substantially the whole, of the recorded interview.

(4) Where a special measures direction provides for a recording to be admitted under this section, the court may nevertheless subsequently direct that it is not to be so admitted if—

(a) it appears to the court that—
  (i) the witness will not be available for cross-examination (whether conducted in the ordinary way or in accordance with any such direction), and
  (ii) the parties to the proceedings have not agreed that there is no need for the witness to be so available; or
(b) any Criminal Procedure Rules requiring disclosure of the circumstances in which the recording was made have not been complied with to the satisfaction of the court.

(5) Where a recording is admitted under this section—

(a) the witness must be called by the party tendering it in evidence, unless—
  (i) a special measures direction provides for the witness's evidence on cross-examination to be given in any recording admissible under section 28, or
  (ii) the parties to the proceedings have agreed as mentioned in subsection (4)(a)(ii); and
(b) the witness may not without the permission of the court give evidence in chief otherwise than by means of the recording as to any matter which, in the opinion of the court, is dealt with in the witness's recorded testimony.

(6) Where in accordance with subsection (2) a special measures direction provides for part only of a recording to be admitted under this section, references in subsection (4) and (5) to the recording or to the witness's recorded testimony are references to the part of the recording or testimony which is to be so admitted.

(7) The court may give permission for the purposes of subsection (5)(b) if it appears to the court to be in the interests of justice to do so, and may do so either—

(a) on an application by a party to the proceedings, or

(b) of its own motion.

(9) The court may, in giving permission for the purposes of subsection (5)(b), direct that the evidence in question is to be given by the witness by means of a live link;

(9A) If the court directs under subsection (9) that evidence is to be given by live link, it may also make such provision in that direction as it could make under section 24(1A) in a special measures direction.

(11) Nothing in this section affects the admissibility of any video recording which would be admissible apart from this section.

28 Video recorded cross-examination or re-examination

(1) Where a special measures direction provides for a video recording to be admitted under section 27 as evidence in chief of the witness, the direction may also provide—

(a) for any cross-examination of the witness, and any re-examination, to be recorded by means of a video recording; and

(b) for such a recording to be admitted, so far as it relates to any such cross-examination or re-examination, as evidence of the witness under cross-examination or on re-examination, as the case may be.

(2) Such a recording must be made in the presence of such persons as Criminal Procedure Rules or the direction may provide and in the absence of the accused, but in circumstances in which—

(a) the judge or justices (or both) and legal representatives acting in the proceedings are able to see and hear the examination of the witness and to communicate with the persons in whose presence the recording is being made, and

(b) the accused is able to see and hear any such examination and to communicate with any legal representative acting for him.

(3) Where two or more legal representatives are acting for a party to the proceedings, subsection (2)(a) and (b) are to be regarded as satisfied in relation to those representatives if at all material times they are satisfied in relation to at least one of them.

(4) Where a special measures direction provides for a recording to be admitted under this section, the court may nevertheless subsequently direct that it is not to be so admitted if any requirement of subsection (2) or Criminal Procedure Rules or the direction has not been complied with to the satisfaction of the court.

(5) Where in pursuance of subsection (1) a recording has been made of any examination of the witness, the witness may not be subsequently cross-examined or re-examined in respect of any evidence given by the witness in the proceedings (whether in any recording admissible under section 27 or this section or otherwise than in such a recording) unless the court gives a further special measures direction making such provision as is mentioned in subsection (1)(a) and (b) in relation to any subsequent cross-examination, and re-examination, of the witness.

(6) The court may only give such a further direction if it appears to the court—

(a) that the proposed cross-examination is sought by a party to the proceedings as a result of that party having become aware, since the time when the original recording was made in pursuance of subsection (1), of a matter which that party could not with reasonable diligence have ascertained by then, or

(b) that for any other reason it is in the interests of justice to give the further direction.

(7) Nothing in this section shall be read as applying in relation to any cross-examination of the witness by the accused in person (in a case where the accused is to be able to conduct any such cross-examination).

29 Examination of witness through intermediary

(1) A special measures direction may provide for any examination of the witness (however and wherever conducted) to be conducted through an interpreter or other person approved by the court for the purposes of this section ('an intermediary').

(2) The function of an intermediary is to communicate—

(a) to the witness, questions put to the witness, and

(b) to any person asking such questions, the answers given by the witness in reply to them,

and to explain such questions or answers so far as necessary to enable them to be understood by the witness or person in question.

(3) Any examination of the witness in pursuance of subsection (1) must take place in the presence of such persons as Criminal Procedure Rules or the direction may provide, but in circumstances in which—

(a) the judge or justices (or both) and legal representatives acting in the proceedings are able to see and hear the examination of the witness and to communicate with the intermediary, and

(b) (except in the case of a video recorded examination) the jury (if there is one) are able to see and hear the examination of the witness.

(4) Where two or more legal representatives are acting for a party to the proceedings, subsection (3)(a) is to be regarded as satisfied in relation to those representatives if at all material times it is satisfied in relation to at least one of them.

(5) A person may not act as an intermediary in a particular case except after making a declaration, in such form as may be prescribed by Criminal Procedure Rules, that he will faithfully perform his function as intermediary.

(6) Subsection (1) does not apply to an interview of the witness which is recorded by means of a video recording with a view to its admission as evidence in chief of the witness; but a special measures direction may provide for such a recording to be admitted under section 27 if the interview was conducted through an intermediary and—

(a) that person complied with subsection (5) before the interview began, and

(b) the court's approval for the purposes of this action is given before the direction is given.

(7) Section 1 of the Perjury Act 1911 (perjury) shall apply in relation to a person acting as an intermediary as it applies in relation to a person lawfully sworn as an interpreter in a judicial proceeding; and for this purpose, where a person acts as an intermediary in any proceeding which is not a judicial proceeding for the purposes of that section, that proceeding shall be taken to be part of the judicial proceeding in which the witness's evidence is given.

30 Aids to communication

A special measures direction may provide for the witness, while giving evidence (whether by testimony in court or otherwise), to be provided with such device as the court considers appropriate with a view to enabling questions or answers to be communicated to or by the witness despite any disability or disorder or other impairment which the witness has or suffers from.

Supplementary

31 Status of evidence given under Chapter 1

(1) Subsections (2) to (4) apply to a statement made by a witness in criminal proceedings which, in accordance with a special measures direction, is not made by the witness in direct oral testimony in court but forms part of the witness's evidence in those proceedings.

(2) The statement shall be treated as if made by the witness in direct oral testimony in court; and accordingly—

(a) it is admissible evidence of any fact of which such testimony from the witness would be admissible;

(b) it is not capable of corroborating any other evidence given by the witness.

(3) Subsection (2) applies to a statement admitted under section 27 or 28 which is not made by the witness on oath even though it would have been required to be made on oath if made by the witness in direct oral testimony in court.

(4) In estimating the weight (if any) to be attached to the statement, the court must have regard to all the circumstances from which an inference can reasonably be drawn (as to the accuracy of the statement or otherwise).

(5) Nothing in this Chapter (apart from subsection (3)) affects the operation of any rule of law relating to evidence in criminal proceedings.

(6) Where any statement made by a person on oath in any proceeding which is not a judicial proceeding for the purposes of section 1 of the Perjury Act 1911 (perjury) is received in evidence in pursuance of a special measures direction, that proceeding shall be taken for the purposes of that section to be part of the judicial proceeding in which the statement is so received in evidence.

(7) Where in any proceeding which is not a judicial proceeding for the purposes of that Act—

(a) a person wilfully makes a false statement otherwise than on oath which is subsequently received in evidence in pursuance of a special measures direction, and

(b) the statement is made in such circumstances that had it been given on oath in any such judicial proceeding that person would have been guilty of perjury, he shall be guilty of an offence and liable to any punishment which might be imposed on conviction of an offence under section 57(2) (giving of false unsworn evidence in criminal proceedings).

(8) In this section 'statement' includes any representation of fact, whether made in words or otherwise.

32 Warning to jury

Where on a trial on indictment with a jury evidence has been given in accordance with a special measures direction, the judge must give the jury such warning (if any) as the judge considers necessary to ensure that the fact that the direction was given in relation to the witness does not prejudice the accused.

33 Interpretation etc. of Chapter 1

(1) In this Chapter—

'eligible witness' means a witness eligible for assistance by virtue of section 16 or 17;

'live link' has the meaning given by section 24(8);

'quality', in relation to the evidence of a witness, shall be construed in accordance with section 16(5);

'special measures direction' means (in accordance with section 19(5)) a direction under section 19.

(2) In this Chapter references to the special measures available in relation to a witness shall be construed in accordance with section 18.

(3) In this Chapter references to a person being able to see or hear, or be seen or heard by, another person are to be read as not applying to the extent that either of them is unable to see or hear by reason of any impairment of eyesight or hearing.

(4) In the case of any proceedings in which there is more than one accused—

(a) any reference to the accused in sections 23 to 28 may be taken by a court, in connection with the giving of a special measures direction, as a reference to all or any of the accused, as the court may determine, and

(b) any such direction may be given on the basis of any such determination.

(5) For the purposes of this Chapter as it applies in relation to a witness who is the complainant in respect of a relevant offence, where the age of the witness is uncertain and there are reasons to believe that the witness is under the age of 18, that witness is presumed to be under the age of 18.

(6) In subsection (5) 'relevant offence' means—

(a) a sexual offence;

(b) an offence under section 1 of the Protection of Children Act 1978;

(c) an offence under section 160 of the Criminal Justice Act 1988;

(d) an offence under section 1 or 2 of the Modern Slavery Act 2015.

Chapter 1A Use of live link and intermediary for evidence of certain accused persons

33A Live link directions

(1) This section applies to proceedings in a service against a person for an offence, if and so far as provided by an order under subsection 61(1).

(2) The court may, on the application of the accused, give a live link direction if it is satisfied—

(a) that the conditions in subsection (4) or, as the case may be, subsection (5) are met in relation to the accused, and

(b) that it is in the interests of justice for the accused to give evidence through a live link.

(3) A live link direction is a direction that any oral evidence to be given before the court by the accused is to be given through a live link.

(4) Where the accused is aged under 18 when the application is made, the conditions are that—

(a) his ability to participate effectively in the proceedings as a witness giving oral evidence in court is compromised by his level of intellectual ability or social functioning, and

(b) use of a live link would enable him to participate more effectively in the proceedings as a witness (whether by improving the quality of his evidence or otherwise).

(5) Where the accused has attained the age of 18 at that time, the conditions are that—

(a) he suffers from a mental disorder (within the meaning of the Mental Health Act 1983) or otherwise has a significant impairment of intelligence and social function,

(b) he is for that reason unable to participate effectively in the proceedings as a witness giving oral evidence in court, and

(c) use of a live link would enable him to participate more effectively in the proceedings as a witness (whether by improving the quality of his evidence or otherwise).

(6) While a live link direction has effect the accused may not give oral evidence before the court in the proceedings otherwise than through a live link.

(7) The court may discharge a live link direction at any time before or during any hearing to which it applies if it appears to the court to be in the interests of justice to do so (but this does not affect the power to give a further live link direction in relation to the accused).

The court may exercise this power of its own motion or on an application by a party.

(8) The court must state in open court its reasons for—

(a) giving or discharging a live link direction, or

(b) refusing an application for or for the discharge of a live link direction,

and, if it is a magistrates' court, it must cause those reasons to be entered in the register of its proceedings.

33B Section 33A: meaning of 'live link'

(1) In section 33A 'live link' means an arrangement by which the accused, while absent from the place where the proceedings are being held, is able—

(a) to see and hear a person there, and

(b) to be seen and heard by the persons mentioned in subsection (2),

and for this purpose any impairment of eyesight or hearing is to be disregarded.

(2) The persons are—

(a) the judge or justices (or both) and the jury (if there is one),

(b) where there are two or more accused in the proceedings, each of the other accused,

(c) legal representatives acting in the proceedings, and

(d) any interpreter or other person appointed by the court to assist the accused.

33C Saving

Nothing in this Chapter affects—

(a) any power of a court to make an order, give directions or give leave of any description in relation to any witness (including an accused), or

(b) the operation of any rule of law relating to evidence in criminal proceedings.

Chapter II Protection of witnesses from cross-examination by accused in person

General prohibitions

34 Complainants in proceedings for sexual offences

No person charged with a sexual offence may in any criminal proceedings cross-examine in person a witness who is the complainant, either—

(a) in connection with that offence, or

(b) in connection with any other offence (or whatever nature) with which that person is charged in the proceedings.

35 Child complainants and other child witnesses

(1) No person charged with an offence to which this section applies may in any criminal proceedings cross-examine in person a protected witness, either—

(a) in connection with that offence, or

(b) in connection with any other offence (of whatever nature) with which that person is charged in the proceedings.

(2) For the purposes of subsection (1) a 'protected witness' is a witness who—

(a) either is the complainant or is alleged to have been a witness to the commission of the offence to which this section applies, and

(b) either is a child or falls to be cross-examined after giving evidence in chief (whether wholly or in part)—

(i) by means of a video recording made (for the purposes of section 27) at a time when the witness was a child, or

(ii) in any other way at any such time.

(3) the offences to which this section applies are—

(a) any offence under—

(iva) any of sections 33 to 36 of the Sexual Offences Act 1956

(v) the Protection of Children Act 1978;

(vi) Part I of the Sexual Offences Act 2003 or any relevant superseded enactment; or

(vii) sections 1 and 2 of the Modern Slavery Act 2015.

(b) kidnapping, false imprisonment or an offence under section 1 or 2 of the Child Abduction Act 1984;

(c) any offence under section 1 of the Children and Young Persons Act 1933;

(d) any offence (not within any of the preceding paragraphs) which involves an assault on, or injury or a threat of injury to, any person.

(3A) In subsection (3)(a)(vi) 'relevant superseded enactment' means—

(a) any of sections 1 to 32 of the Sexual Offences Act 1956;

(b) the Indecency with Children Act 1960;

(c) the Sexual Offences Act 1967;

(d) section 54 of the Criminal Law Act 1977.

(4) In this section 'child' means—

(a) where the offence falls within subsection (3)(a), a person under the age of 18; or

(b) where the offence falls within subsection (3)(b), (c) or (d), a person under the age of 14.

(5) For the purposes of this section 'witness' includes a witness who is charged with an offence in the proceedings.

Prohibition imposed by court

36 Direction prohibiting accused from cross-examining particular witness

(1) This section applies where, in a case where neither of sections 34 and 35 operates to prevent an accused in any criminal proceedings from cross-examining a witness in person—

(a) the prosecutor makes an application for the court to give a direction under this section in relation to the witness, or

(b) the court of its own motion raises the issue whether such a direction should be given.

(2) If it appears to the court—

(a) that the quality of evidence given by the witness on cross-examination—

(i) is likely to be diminished if the cross-examination (or further cross-examination) is conducted by the accused in person, and

(ii) would be likely to be improved if a direction were given under this section,

and

(b) that it would not be contrary to the interests of justice to give such a direction, the court may give a direction prohibiting the accused from cross-examining (or further cross-examining) the witness in person.

(3) In determining whether subsection (2)(a) applies in the case of a witness the court must have regard, in particular, to—

(a) any views expressed by the witness as to whether or not the witness is content to be cross-examined by the accused in person;

(b) the nature of the questions likely to be asked, having regard to the issues in the proceedings and the defence case advanced so far (if any);

(c) any behaviour on the part of the accused at any stage of the proceedings, both generally and in relation to the witness;

(d) any relationship (of whatever nature) between the witness and the accused;

(e) whether any person (other than the accused) is or has at any time been charged in the proceedings with a sexual offence or an offence to which section 35 applies, and (if so) whether section 34 or 35 operates or would have operated to prevent that person from cross-examining the witness in person;

(f) any direction under section 19 which the court has given, or proposes to give, in relation to the witness.

(4) For the purposes of this section—

(a) 'witness', in relation to an accused, does not include any other person who is charged with an offence in the proceedings; and

(b) any reference to the quality of a witness's evidence shall be construed in accordance with section 16(5).

37 Further provisions about directions under section 36

(1) Subject to subsection (2), a direction has binding effect from the time it is made until the witness to whom it applies is discharged.

In this section 'direction' means a direction under section 36.

(2) The court may discharge a direction if it appears to the court to be in the interests of justice to do so, and may do so either—

(a) on an application made by a party to the proceedings, if there has been a material change of circumstances since the relevant time, or

(b) of its own motion.

(3) In subsection (2) 'the relevant time' means—

(a) the time when the direction was given, or

(b) if a previous application has been made under that subsection, the time when the application (or last application) was made.

(4) The court must state in open court its reasons for—

(a) giving, or

(b) refusing an application for, or for the discharge of, or

(c) discharging,

a direction and, if it is a magistrates' court, must cause them to be entered in the register of its proceedings.

(5) Criminal Procedure Rules may make provision—

(a) for uncontested applications to be determined by the court without a hearing;

(b) for preventing the renewal of an unsuccessful application for a direction except where there has been a material change of circumstances;
(c) for expert evidence to be given in connection with an application for, or for discharging, a direction;
(d) for the manner in which confidential or sensitive information is to be treated in connection with such an application and in particular as to its being disclosed to, or withheld from, a party to the proceedings.

Cross-examination on behalf of accused

38 Defence representation for purposes of cross-examination

(1) This section applies where an accused is prevented from cross-examining a witness in person by virtue of section 34, 35 or 36.

(2) Where it appears to the court that this section applies, it must—
(a) invite the accused to arrange for a legal representative to act for him for the purpose of cross-examining the witness; and
(b) require the accused to notify the court, by the end of such period as it may specify, whether a legal representative is to act for him for that purpose.

(3) If by the end of the period mentioned in subsection (2)(b) either—
(a) the accused has notified the court that no legal representative is to act for him for the purpose of cross-examining the witness, or
(b) no notification has been received by the court and it appears to the court that no legal representative is to so act,

the court must consider whether it is necessary in the interests of justice for the witness to be cross-examined by a legal representative appointed to represent the interests of the accused.

(4) If the court decides that it is necessary in the interests of justice for the witness to be so cross-examined, the court must appoint a qualified legal representative (chosen by the court) to cross-examine the witness in the interests of the accused.

(5) A person so appointed shall not be responsible to the accused.

(6) Criminal Procedure Rules may make provision—
(a) as to the time when, and the manner in which, subsection (2) is to be complied with;
(b) in connection with the appointment of a legal representative under subsection (4), and in particular for securing that a person so appointed is provided with evidence or other material relating to the proceedings.

(7) Criminal Procedure Rules made in pursuance of subsection (6)(b) may make provision for the application, with such modifications as are specified in the rules, of any of the provisions of—
(a) Part I of the Criminal Procedure and Investigations Act 1996 (disclosure of material in connection with criminal proceedings), or
(b) the Sexual Offences (Protected Material) Act 1997.

(8) For the purposes of this section—
(a) any reference to cross-examination includes (in a case where a direction is given under section 36 after the accused has begun cross-examining the witness) a reference to further cross-examination; and
(b) 'qualified legal representative' means a legal representative who has a right of audience (within the meaning of the Courts and Legal Services Act 1990) in relation to the proceedings before the court.

39 Warning to jury

(1) Where on a trial on indictment with a jury an accused is prevented from cross-examining a witness in person by virtue of section 34, 35 or 36, the judge must give the jury such warning (if any) as the judge considers necessary to ensure that the accused is not prejudiced—
(a) by any inferences that might be drawn from the fact that the accused has been prevented from cross-examining the witness in person;

(b) where the witness has been cross-examined by a legal representative appointed under section 38(4), by the fact that the cross-examination was carried out by such a legal representative and not by a person acting as the accused's own legal representative.

(2) Subsection (8)(a) of section 38 applies for the purposes of this section as it applies for the purposes of section 38.

Chapter III Protection of complainants in proceedings for sexual offences

41 Restriction on evidence or questions about complainant's sexual history

(1) If at a trial a person is charged with a sexual offence, then, except with the leave of the court—

(a) no evidence may be adduced, and

(b) no question may be asked in cross-examination,

by or on behalf of any accused at the trial, about any sexual behaviour of the complainant.

(2) The court may give leave in relation to any evidence or question only on an application made by or on behalf of an accused, and may not give such leave unless it is satisfied—

(a) that subsection (3) or (5) applies, and

(b) that a refusal of leave might have the result of rendering unsafe a conclusion of the jury or (as the case may be) the court on any relevant issue in the case.

(3) This subsection applies if the evidence or question relates to a relevant issue in the case and either—

(a) that issue is not an issue of consent; or

(b) it is an issue of consent and the sexual behaviour of the complainant to which the evidence or question relates is alleged to have taken place at or about the same time as the event which is the subject matter of the charge against the accused; or

(c) it is an issue of consent and the sexual behaviour of the complainant to which the evidence or question relates is alleged to have been, in any respect, so similar—

(i) to any sexual behaviour of the complainant which (according to evidence adduced or to be adduced by or on behalf of the accused) took place as part of the event which is the subject matter of the charge against the accused, or

(ii) to any other sexual behaviour of the complainant which (according to such evidence) took place at or about the same time as the event,

that the similarity cannot reasonably be explained as a coincidence.

(4) For the purposes of subsection (3) no evidence or question shall be regarded as relating to a relevant issue in the case if it appears to the court to be reasonable to assume that the purpose (or main purpose) for which it would be adduced or asked is to establish or elicit material for impugning the credibility of the complainant as a witness.

(5) This subsection applies if the evidence or question—

(a) relates to any evidence adduced by the prosecution about any sexual behaviour of the complainant; and

(b) in the opinion of the court, would go no further than is necessary to enable the evidence adduced by the prosecution to be rebutted or explained by or on behalf of the accused.

(6) For the purposes of subsections (3) and (5) the evidence or question must relate to a specific instance (or specific instances) of alleged sexual behaviour on the part of the complainant (and accordingly nothing in those subsections is capable of applying in relation to the evidence or question to the extent that it does not so relate).

(7) Where this section applies in relation to a trial by virtue of the fact that one or more of a number of persons charged in the proceedings is or are charged with a sexual offence—

(a) it shall cease to apply in relation to the trial if the prosecutor decides not to proceed with the case against that person or those persons in respect of that charge; but

(b) it shall not cease to do so in the event of that person or those persons pleading guilty to, or being convicted of, that charge.

(8) Nothing in this section authorises any evidence to be adduced or any question to be asked which cannot be adduced or asked apart from this section.

42 Interpretation and application of section 41

(1) In section 41—

(a) 'relevant issue in the case' means any issue falling to be proved by the prosecution or defence in the trial of the accused;

(b) 'issue of consent' means any issue whether the complainant in fact consented to the conduct constituting the offence with which the accused is charged (and accordingly does not include any issue as to the belief of the accused that the complainant so consented);

(c) 'sexual behaviour' means any sexual behaviour or other sexual experience, whether or not involving any accused or other person, but excluding (except in section 41(3)(c)(i) and (5)(a)) anything alleged to have taken place as part of the event which is the subject matter of the charge against the accused; and

(d) subject to any other made under subsection (2), 'sexual offence' shall be construed in accordance with section 62.

(2) The Secretary of State may by order make such provision as he considers appropriate for adding or removing, for the purposes of section 41, any offence to or from the offences which are sexual offences for the purposes of this Act by virtue of section 62.

(3) Section 41 applies in relation to the following proceedings as it applies to a trial, namely—

(c) the hearing of an application under paragraph 2(1) of Schedule 3 to the Crime and Disorder Act 1998 (application to dismiss charge by person sent for trial under section 51 or 51A of that Act),

(d) any hearing held, between conviction and sentencing, for the purpose of determining matters relevant to the court's decision as to how the accused is to be dealt with, and

(e) the hearing of an appeal,

and references (in section 41 or this section) to a person charged with an offence accordingly include a person convicted of an offence.

43 Procedure on applications under section 41

(1) An application for leave shall be heard in private and in the absence of the complainant. In this section 'leave' means leave under section 41.

(2) Where such an application has been determined, the court must state in open court (but in the absence of the jury, if there is one)—

(a) its reasons for giving, or refusing, leave, and

(b) if it gives leave, the extent to which evidence may be adduced or questions asked in pursuance of the leave,

and, if it is a magistrates' court, must cause those matters to be entered in the register of its proceedings.

(3) Criminal Procedure Rules may make provision—

(a) requiring applications for leave to specify, in relation to each item of evidence or question to which they relate, particulars of the grounds on which it is asserted that leave should be given by virtue of subsection (3) or (5) or section 41;

(b) enabling the court to request a party to the proceedings to provide the court with information which it considers would assist it in determining an application for leave;

(c) for the manner in which confidential or sensitive information is to be treated in connection with such an application, and in particular as to its being disclosed to, or withheld from, parties to the proceedings.

Chapter IV Reporting restrictions

Reports relating to persons under 18

44 Restrictions on reporting alleged offences involving persons under 18

(1) This section applies (subject to subsection (3)) where a criminal investigation has begun in respect of—

(a) an alleged offence against the law of—

(i) England and Wales, or

. . .

(b) . . .

(2) No matter relating to any person involved in the offence shall while he is under the age of 18 be included in any publication if it is likely to lead members of the public to identify him as a person involved in the offence.

(3) The restrictions imposed by subsection (2) cease to apply once there are proceedings in a court . . . in respect of the offence.

(4) For the purposes of subsection (2) any reference to a person involved in the offence is to—

(a) a person by whom the offence is alleged to have been committed . . .; or

(b) if this paragraph applies to the publication in question by virtue of subsection (5)—

(i) a person against or in respect of whom the offence is alleged to have been committed, or

(ii) a person who is alleged to have been a witness to the commission of the offence;

except that paragraph (b)(i) does not include a person in relation to whom section 1 of the Sexual Offences (Amendment) Act 1992 (anonymity of victims of certain sexual offences) applies in connection with the offence.

(5) Subsection (4)(b) applies to a publication if—

(a) where it is a relevant programme, it is transmitted, or

(b) in the case of any other publication, it is published,

on or after such date as may be specified in an order made by the Secretary of State.

(5A) . . .

(6) The matters relating to a person in relation to which the restrictions imposed by subsection (2) apply (if their inclusion in any publication is likely to have the result mentioned in that subsection) include in particular—

(a) his name,

(b) his address,

(c) the identity of any school or other educational establishment attended by him,

(d) the identity of any place of work, and

(e) any still or moving picture of him.

(7) Any appropriate criminal court may by order dispense, to any extent specified in the order, with the restrictions imposed by subsection (2) in relation to a person if it is satisfied that it is necessary in the interests of justice to do so.

(8) However, when deciding whether to make such an order dispensing (to any extent) with the restrictions imposed by subsection (2) in relation to a person, the court shall have regard to the welfare of that person.

(9) In subsection (7) 'appropriate criminal court' means—

(a) in a case where this section applies by virtue of subsection (1)(a)(i) or (ii), any court . . . which has any jurisdiction in, or in relation to, any criminal proceedings (but not a service court unless the offence is alleged to have been committed by a person subject to service law);

(b) in a case where this section applies by virtue of subsection (1)(b), any court falling within paragraph (a) or a service court.

(10) The power under subsection (7) of a magistrates' court in England and Wales may be exercised by a single justice.

(11) In the case of a decision of a magistrates' court . . . to make or refuse to make an order under subsection (7), the following persons, namely—

(a) any person who was a party to the proceedings on the application for the order, and
(b) with the leave of the Crown Court, . . . any other person,

may, in accordance with Criminal Procedure Rules . . ., appeal to the Crown Court against that decision or appear or be represented at the hearing of such an appeal.

(12) On such an appeal the Crown Court . . .—

(a) may make such order as is necessary to give effect to its determination of the appeal; and
(b) may also make such incidental or consequential orders as appear to it to be just.

(13) In this section—

(a) 'civil offence' means an act or omission which, if committed in England and Wales, would be an offence against the law of England and Wales;
(b) any reference to a criminal investigation, in relation to an alleged offence, is to an investigation conducted by police officers, or other persons charged with the duty of investigation offences, with a view to it being ascertained whether a person should be charged with the offence;

. . .

45 Power to restrict reporting of criminal proceedings involving persons under 18

(1) This section applies (subject to subsection (2)) in relation to—

(a) any criminal proceedings in any court (other than a service court) . . .; and

. . .

(2) This section does not apply in relation to any proceedings to which section 49 of the Children and Young Persons Act 1933 applies.

(3) The court may direct that no matter relating to any person concerned in the proceedings shall while he is under the age of 18 be included in any publication if it is likely to lead members of the public to identify him as a person concerned in the proceedings.

(4) The court or an appellate court may by direction ('an excepting direction') dispense, to any extent specified in the excepting direction, with the restrictions imposed by a direction under subsection (3) if it is satisfied that it is necessary in the interests of justice to do so.

(5) The court or an appellate court may also by direction ('an excepting direction') dispense, to any extent specified in the excepting direction, with the restrictions imposed by a direction under subsection (3) if it is satisfied—

(a) that their effect is to impose a substantial and unreasonable restriction on the reporting of the proceedings, and
(b) that it is in the public interest to remove or relax that restriction;

but no excepting direction shall be given under this subsection by reason only of the fact that the proceedings have been determined in any way or have been abandoned.

(6) When deciding whether to make—

(a) a direction under subsection (3) in relation to a person, or
(b) an excepting direction under subsection (4) or (5) by virtue of which the restrictions imposed by a direction under subsection (3) would be dispensed with (to any extent) in relation to a person,

the court or (as the case may be) the appellate court shall have regard to the welfare of that person.

(7) For the purposes of subsection (3) any reference to a person concerned in the proceedings is to a person—

(a) against or in respect of whom the proceedings are taken, or
(b) who is a witness in the proceedings.

(8) the matters relating to a person in relation to which the restrictions imposed by a direction under subsection (3) apply (if their inclusion in any publication is likely to have the result mentioned in that subsection) include in particular—

(a) his name,
(b) his address,
(c) the identity of any school or other educational establishment attended by him,
(d) the identity of any place of work, and
(e) any still or moving picture of him.

(9) A direction under subsection (3) may be revoked by the court or an appellate court.

(10) An excepting direction—
(a) may be given at the time the direction under subsection (3) is given or subsequently; and
(b) may be varied or revoked by the court or an appellate court.

(11) In this section 'appellate court', in relation to any proceedings in a court, means a court dealing with an appeal (including an appeal by way of case stated) arising out of the proceedings or with any further appeal.

45A Power to restrict reporting of criminal proceedings for lifetime of witnesses and victims under 18

(1) This section applies in relation to—
(a) any criminal proceedings in any court (other than a service court) . . ., and
(b) . . .

(2) The court may make a direction ('a reporting direction') that no matter relating to a person mentioned in subsection (3) shall during that person's lifetime be included in any publication if it is likely to lead members of the public to identify that person as being concerned in the proceedings.

(3) A reporting direction may be made only in respect of a person who is under the age of 18 when the proceedings commence and who is—
(a) a witness, other than an accused, in the proceedings;
(b) a person against whom the offence, which is the subject of the proceedings, is alleged to have been committed.

(4) For the purposes of subsection (2), matters relating to a person in respect of whom the reporting direction is made include—
(a) the person's name,
(b) the person's address,
(c) the identity of any school or other educational establishment attended by the person,
(d) the identity of any place of work of the person, and
(e) any still or moving picture of the person.

(5) The court may make a reporting direction in respect of a person only if it is satisfied that—
(a) the quality of any evidence given by the person, or
(b) the level of co-operation given by the person to any party to the proceedings in connection with that party's preparation of its case,

is likely to be diminished by reason of fear or distress on the part of the person in connection with being identified by members of the public as a person concerned in the proceedings.

(6) In determining whether subsection (5) is satisfied, the court must in particular take into account—
(a) the nature and alleged circumstances of the offence to which the proceedings relate;
(b) the age of the person;
(c) such of the following as appear to the court to be relevant—
(i) the social and cultural background and ethnic origins of the person,
(ii) the domestic, educational and employment circumstances of the person, and
(iii) any religious beliefs or political opinions of the person;
(d) any behaviour towards the person on the part of—
(i) an accused,
(ii) members of the family or associates of an accused, or
(iii) any other person who is likely to be an accused or a witness in the proceedings.

(7) In determining that question the court must in addition consider any views expressed—

(a) by the person in respect of whom the reporting restriction may be made, and

(b) where that person is under the age of 16, by an appropriate person other than an accused.

(8) In determining whether to make a reporting direction in respect of a person, the court must have regard to—

(a) the welfare of that person,

(b) whether it would be in the interests of justice to make the direction, and

(c) the public interest in avoiding the imposition of a substantial and unreasonable restriction on the reporting of the proceedings.

(9) A reporting direction may be revoked by the court or an appellate court.

(10) The court or an appellate court may by direction ('an excepting direction') dispense, to any extent specified in the excepting direction, with the restrictions imposed by a reporting direction.

(11) The court or an appellate court may only make an excepting direction if—

(a) it is satisfied that it is necessary in the interests of justice to do so, or

(b) it is satisfied that—

(i) the effect of the reporting direction is to impose a substantial and unreasonable restriction on the reporting of the proceedings, and

(ii) it is in the public interest to remove or relax that restriction.

(12) No excepting direction shall be given under subsection (11)(b) by reason only of the fact that the proceedings have been determined in any way or have been abandoned.

(13) In determining whether to make an excepting direction in respect of a person, the court or the appellate court must have regard to the welfare of that person.

(14) An excepting direction—

(a) may be given at the time the reporting direction is given or subsequently, and

(b) may be varied or revoked by the court or an appellate court.

(15) For the purposes of this section—

(a) criminal proceedings in a court . . . commence when proceedings are instituted for the purposes of Part 1 of the Prosecution of Offences Act 1985, in accordance with section 15(2) of that Act;

(b) . . .

(16) In this section—

(a) 'appellate court', in relation to any proceedings in a court, means a court dealing with an appeal (including an appeal by way of case stated) arising out of the proceedings or with any further appeal;

(b) 'appropriate person' has the same meaning as in section 50;

(c) references to the quality of evidence given by a person are to its quality in terms of completeness, coherence and accuracy (and for this purpose 'coherence' refers to a person's ability in giving evidence to give answers which address the questions put to the person and can be understood both individually and collectively);

(d) references to the preparation of the case of a party to any proceedings include, where the party is the prosecution, the carrying out of investigations into any offence at any time charged in the proceedings.

Reports relating to adult witnesses

46 Power to restrict reports about certain adult witnesses in criminal proceedings

(1) This section applies where—

(a) in any criminal proceedings in any court (other than a service court) . . . or

(b) . . .

a party to the proceedings makes an application for the court to give a reporting direction in relation to a witness in the proceedings (other than the accused) who has attained the age of 18.

In this section 'reporting direction' has the meaning given by subsection (6).

(2) If the court determines—

(a) that the witness is eligible for protection, and

(b) that giving a reporting direction in relation to the witness is likely to improve—

(i) the quality of evidence given by the witness, or

(ii) the level of co-operation given by the witness to any party to the proceedings in connection with that party's preparation of its case,

the court may give a reporting direction in relation to the witness.

(3) For the purposes of this section a witness is eligible for protection if the court is satisfied—

(a) that the quality of evidence given by the witness, or

(b) the level of co-operation given by the witness to any party to the proceedings in connection with that party's preparation of its case,

is likely to be diminished by reason of fear or distress on the part of the witness in connection with being identified by members of the public as a witness in the proceedings.

(4) In determining whether a witness is eligible for protection the court must take into account, in particular—

(a) the nature and alleged circumstances of the offence to which the proceedings relate;

(b) the age of the witness;

(c) such of the following matters as appear to the court to be relevant, namely—

(i) the social and cultural background and ethnic origins of the witness,

(ii) the domestic and employment circumstances of the witness, and

(iii) any religious beliefs or political opinions of the witness;

(d) any behaviour towards the witness on the part of—

(i) the accused,

(ii) members of the family or associates of the accused, or

(iii) any other person who is likely to be an accused or a witness in the proceedings.

(5) In determining that question the court must in addition consider any views expressed by the witness.

(6) For the purposes of this section a reporting direction in relation to a witness is a direction that no matter relating to the witness shall during the witness's lifetime be included in any publication if it is likely to lead members of the public to identify him as being a witness in the proceedings.

(7) The matters relating to a witness in relation to which the restrictions imposed by a reporting direction apply (if their inclusion in any publication is likely to have the result mentioned in subsection (6)) include in particular—

(a) the witness's name,

(b) the witness's address,

(c) the identity of any educational establishment attended by the witness,

(d) the identity of any place of work, and

(e) any still or moving picture of the witness.

(8) In determining whether to give a reporting direction the court shall consider—

(a) whether it would be in the interests of justice to do so, and

(b) the public interest in avoiding the imposition of a substantial and unreasonable restriction on the reporting of the proceedings.

(9) The court or an appellate court may by direction ('an excepting direction') dispense, to any extent specified in the excepting direction, with the restrictions imposed by a reporting direction if—

(a) it is satisfied that it is necessary in the interests of justice to do so, or

(b) it is satisfied—

(i) that the effect of those restrictions is to impose a substantial and unreasonable restriction on the reporting of the proceedings, and

(ii) that it is in the public interest to remove or relax that restriction;

but no excepting direction shall be given under paragraph (b) by reason only of the fact that the proceedings have been determined in any way or have been abandoned.

(10) A reporting direction may be revoked by the court or an appellate court.

(11) An excepting direction—

(a) may be given at the time the reporting direction is given or subsequently; and

(b) may be varied or revoked by the court or an appellate court.

(12) In this section—

(a) 'appellate court', in relation to any proceedings in a court, means a court dealing with an appeal (including an appeal by way of case stated) arising out of the proceedings or with any further appeal;

(b) references to the quality of a witness's evidence are to its quality in terms of completeness, coherence and accuracy (and for this purpose 'coherence' refers to a witness's ability in giving evidence to give answers which address the questions put to the witness and can be understood both individually and collectively);

(c) references to the preparation of the case of a party to any proceedings include, where the party is the prosecution, the carrying out of investigations into any offence at any time charged in the proceedings.

Reports relating to directions under Chapter 1, 1A or 2

47 Restrictions on reporting directions under Chapter 1, 1A or 2

(1) Except as provided by this section, no publication shall include a report of a matter falling within subsection (2).

(2) The matters falling within this subsection are—

(a) a direction under section 19, 33A or 36 or an order discharging, or (in the case of a direction under section 19) varying, such a direction;

(aa) . . .

(b) proceedings—

(i) on an application for such a direction or order, or

(ii) where the court acts of its own motion to determine whether to give or make any such direction or order.

(3) The court dealing with a matter falling within subsection (2) may order that subsection (1) is not to apply, or is not to apply to a specified extent, to a report of that matter.

(4) Where—

(a) there is only one accused in the relevant proceedings, and

(b) he objects to the making of an order under subsection (3),

the court shall make the order if (and only if) satisfied after considering (in the case of proceedings in England and Wales) or hearing (in the case of other proceedings) the representations of the accused that it is in the interests of justice to do so; and if the order is made it shall not apply to the extent that a report deals with any such objections or representations.

(5) Where—

(a) there are two or more accused in the relevant proceedings, and

(b) one or more of them object to the making of an order under subsection (3),

the court shall make the order if (and only if) satisfied after considering (in the case of proceedings in England and Wales) or hearing (in the case of other proceedings) the representations of each of the accused that it is in the interests of justice to do so; and if the order is made it shall not apply to the extent that a report deals with any such objections or representations.

(6) Subsection (1) does not apply to the inclusion in a publication of a report of matters after the relevant proceedings are either—

(a) determined (by acquittal, conviction or otherwise), or

(b) abandoned,

in relation to the accused or (if there is more than one) in relation to each of the accused.

(7) In this section 'the relevant proceedings' means the proceedings to which any such direction as is mentioned in subsection (2) relates or would relate.

(8) Nothing in this section affects any prohibition or restriction by virtue of any other enactment on the inclusion of matter in a publication.

Other restrictions

48 Amendments relating to other reporting restrictions

Schedule 2, which contains amendments relating to reporting restrictions under—

(a) the Children and Young Persons Act 1933,
(b) the Sexual Offences (Amendment) Act 1976,
(c) . . .
(d) the Sexual Offences (Amendment) Act 1992, and
(e) . . .

shall have effect.

Offences

49 Offences under Chapter IV

(1) This section applies if a publication—

(a) includes any matter in contravention of section 44(2) or of a direction under section 45(3) or 46(2); or
(b) includes a report in a contravention of section 47.

(1A) This section also applies—

(a) . . .;
(b) in England and Wales, if a publication includes any matter in contravention of a direction under section 45A(2) made by a court other than a service court.

(2) Where the publication is a newspaper or periodical, any proprietor, any editor and any publisher of the newspaper or periodical is guilty of an offence.

(3) Where the publication is a relevant programme—

(a) any body corporate . . . engaged in providing the programme service in which the programme is included, and
(b) any person having functions in relation to the programme corresponding to those of an editor of a newspaper,

is guilty of an offence.

(4) In the case of any other publication, any person publishing it is guilty of an offence.

(5) A person guilty of an offence under this section is liable on summary conviction to a fine not exceeding level 5 on the standard scale.

(6) Proceedings for an offence under this section in respect of a publication falling within subsection (1)(b) may not be instituted—

(a) in England and Wales otherwise than by or with the consent of the Attorney General,
(b) . . .

(7) Schedule 2A makes special provision in connection with the operation of this section, so far as it relates to a publication that includes matter in contravention of a direction under section 45A(2), in relation to persons providing information society services.

50 Defences

(1) Where a person is charged with an offence under section 49 it shall be a defence to prove that at the time of the alleged offence he was not aware, and neither suspected nor had reason to suspect, that the publication included in the matter or report in question.

(2) Where—

(a) a person is charged with an offence under section 49, and
(b) the offence relates to the inclusion of any matter in a publication in contravention of section 44(2),

it shall be a defence to prove that at the time of the alleged offence he was not aware, and neither suspected nor had reason to suspect, that the criminal investigation in question had begun.

(3) Where—

(a) paragraphs (a) and (b) or subsection (2) apply, and

(b) the contravention of section 44(2) does not relate to either—

(i) the person by whom the offence mentioned in that provision is alleged to have been committed, or

(ii) (where that offence is one in relation to which section 1 of the Sexual Offences (Amendment) Act 1992 applies) a person who is alleged to be a witness to the commission of the offence,

it shall be a defence to show to the satisfaction of the court that the inclusion in the publication of the matter in question was in the public interest on the ground that, to the extent that they operated to prevent that matter from being so included, the effect of the restrictions imposed by section 44(2) was to impose a substantial and unreasonable restriction on the reporting of matters connected with that offence.

(4) Subsection (5) applies where—

(a) paragraphs (a) and (b) of subsection (2) apply, and

(b) the contravention of section 44(2) relates to a person ('the protected person') who is neither—

(i) the person mentioned in subsection (3)(b)(i), nor

(ii) a person within subsection (3)(b)(ii) who is under the age of 16.

(5) In such a case it shall be a defence, subject to subsection (6), to prove that written consent to the inclusion of the matter in question in the publication had been given—

(a) by an appropriate person, if at the time when the consent was given the protected person was under the age of 16, or

(b) by the protected person, if that person was aged 16 or 17 at that time,

and (where the consent was given by an appropriate person) that written notice had been previously given to that person drawing to his attention the need to consider the welfare of the protected person when deciding whether to give consent.

(6) The defence provided by subsection (5) is not available if—

(a) (where the consent was given by an appropriate person) it is proved that written or other notice withdrawing the consent—

(i) was given to the appropriate recipient by any other appropriate person or by the protected person, and

(ii) was so given in sufficient time to enable the inclusion in the publication of the matter in question to be prevented; or

(b) subsection (8) applies.

(6A) Where—

(a) a person is charged with an offence under section 49, and

(b) the offence relates to the inclusion of any matter in a publication in contravention of a direction under section 45A(2),

it shall be a defence, unless subsection (6B) or (8) applies, to prove that the person in relation to whom the direction was given had given written consent to the inclusion of that matter in the publication.

(6B) Written consent is not a defence by virtue of subsection (6A) if the person was under the age of 18 at the time the consent was given.

(7) Where—

(a) a person is charged with an offence under section 49, and

(b) the offence relates to the inclusion of any matter in a publication in contravention of a direction under section 46(2), it shall be a defence, unless subsection (8) applies, to prove that the person in relation to whom the direction was given had given written consent to the inclusion of that matter in the publication.

(8) Written consent is not a defence by virtue of subsections (5) to (7) if it is proved that any person interfered—

(a) with the peace or comfort of the person giving the consent, or

(b) (where the consent was given by an appropriate person) with the peace or comfort of either that person or the protected person,

with intent to obtain the consent.

(9) In this section—

'an appropriate person' means (subject to subsections (10) to (12))—

(a) . . . a person who is a parent or guardian of the protected person,

(b) . . .

'guardian', in relation to the protected person, means any person who is not a parent of the protected person but who has parental responsibility for the protected person within the meaning of—

(a) . . . the Children Act 1989, or

(b) . . .

(10) Where the protected person is (within the meaning of the Children Act 1989) . . . a child who is looked after by a local authority, 'an appropriate person' means a person who is—

(a) a representative of that authority, or

(b) a parent or guardian of the protected person with whom the protected person is allowed to live.

. . .

(13) However, no person by whom the offence mentioned in section 44(2) is alleged to have been committed is, by virtue of subsection (9) to (12), an appropriate person for the purposes of this section.

(14) In this section 'the appropriate recipient', in relation to a notice under subsection (6)(a), means—

(a) the person to whom the notice giving consent was given,

(b) (if different) the person by whom the matter in question was published, or

(c) any other person exercising, on behalf of the person mentioned in paragraph (b), any responsibility in relation to the publication of that matter;

and for this purpose 'person' includes a body of persons and a partnership.

51 Offences committed by bodies corporate or Scottish partnerships

(1) If an offence under section 49 committed by a body corporate is proved—

(a) to have been committed with the consent or connivance of, or

(b) to be attributable to any neglect on the part of,

an officer, the officer as well as the body corporate is guilty of the offence and liable to be proceeded against and punished accordingly.

(2) In subsection (1) 'officer' means a director, manager, secretary or other similar officer of the body, or a person purporting to act in any such capacity.

(3) If the affairs of a body corporate are managed by its members, 'director' in subsection (2) means a member of that body.

(4) . . .

Supplementary

52 Decisions as to public interest for purposes of Chapter IV

(1) Where for the purposes of any provision of this Chapter it falls to a court to determine whether anything is (or, as the case may be, was) in the public interest, the court must have regard, in particular, to the matters referred to in subsection (2) (so far as relevant).

(2) Those matters are—

(a) the interest in each of the following—
(i) the open reporting of crime,
(ii) the open reporting of matters relating to human health or safety, and
(iii) the prevention and exposure of miscarriages of justice;
(b) the welfare of any person in relation to whom the relevant restrictions imposed by or under this Chapter apply or would apply (or, as the case may be, applied); and
(c) any views expressed—
(i) by an appropriate person on behalf of a person within paragraph (b) who is under the age of 16 ('the protected person'), or
(ii) by a person within that paragraph who has attained that age.

(3) In subsection (2) 'an appropriate person', in relation to the protected person, has the same meaning as it has for the purposes of section 50.

Chapter V Competence of witnesses and capacity to be sworn

Competence of witnesses

53 Competence of witnesses to give evidence

(1) At every stage in criminal proceedings all persons are (whatever their age) competent to give evidence.

(2) Subsection (1) has effect subject to subsections (3) and (4).

(3) A person is not competent to give evidence in criminal proceedings if it appears to the court that he is not a person who is able to—
(a) understand questions put to him as a witness, and
(b) give answers to them which can be understood.

(4) A person charged in criminal proceedings is not competent to give evidence in the proceedings for the prosecution (whether he is the only person, or is one of two or more persons, charged in the proceedings).

(5) In subsection (4) the reference to a person charged in criminal proceedings does not include a person who is not, or is no longer, liable to be convicted of any offence in the proceedings (whether as a result of pleading guilty or for any other reason).

54 Determining competence of witnesses

(1) Any question whether a witness in criminal proceedings is competent to give evidence in the proceedings, whether raised—
(a) by a party to the proceedings, or
(b) by the court of its own motion,
shall be determined by the court in accordance with this section.

(2) It is for the party calling the witness to satisfy the court that, on a balance of probabilities, the witness is competent to give evidence in the proceedings.

(3) In determining the question mentioned in subsection (1) the court shall treat the witness as having the benefit of any directions under section 19 which the court has given, or proposes to give, in relation to the witness.

(4) Any proceedings held for the determination of the question shall take place in the absence of the jury (if there is one).

(5) Expert evidence may be received on the question.

(6) Any questioning of the witness (where the court considers that necessary) shall be conducted by the court in the presence of the parties.

Giving of sworn or unsworn evidence

55 Determining whether witness to be sworn

(1) Any question whether a witness in criminal proceedings may be sworn for the purpose of giving evidence on oath, whether raised—

(a) by a party to the proceedings, or

(b) by the court of its own motion,

shall be determined by the court in accordance with this section.

(2) The witness may not be sworn for that purpose unless—

(a) he has attained the age of 14, and

(b) he has a sufficient appreciation of the solemnity of the occasion and of the particular responsibility to tell the truth which is involved in taking an oath.

(3) The witness shall, if he is able to give intelligible testimony, be presumed to have a sufficient appreciation of those matters if no evidence tending to show the contrary is adduced (by any party).

(4) If any such evidence is adduced, it is for the party seeking to have the witness sworn to satisfy the court that, on a balance of probabilities, the witness has attained the age of 14 and has a sufficient appreciation of the matters mentioned in subsection (2)(b).

(5) Any proceedings held for the determination of the question mentioned in subsection (1) shall take place in the absence of the jury (if there is one).

(6) Expert evidence may be received on the question.

(7) Any questioning of the witness (where the court considers that necessary) shall be conducted by the court in the presence of the parties.

(8) For the purposes of this section a person is able to give intelligible testimony if he is able to—

(a) understand questions put to him as a witness, and

(b) give answers to them which can be understood.

56 Reception of unsworn evidence

(1) Subsections (2) and (3) apply to a person (of any age) who—

(a) is competent to give evidence in criminal proceedings, but

(b) (by virtue of section 55(2)) is not permitted to be sworn for the purpose of giving evidence on oath in such proceedings.

(2) The evidence in criminal proceedings of a person to whom this subsection applies shall be given unsworn.

(3) A deposition of unsworn evidence given by a person to whom this subsection applies may be taken for the purposes of criminal proceedings as if that evidence had been given on oath.

(4) A court in criminal proceedings shall accordingly receive in evidence any evidence given unsworn in pursuance of subsection (2) or (3).

(5) Where a person ('the witness') who is competent to give evidence in criminal proceedings gives evidence in such proceedings unsworn, no conviction, verdict or finding in those proceedings shall be taken to be unsafe for the purposes of any of sections 2(1), 13(1) and 16(1) of the Criminal Appeal Act 1968 (grounds for allowing appeals) by reason only that it appears to the Court of Appeal that the witness was a person falling within section 55(2) (and should accordingly have given his evidence on oath).

57 Penalty for giving false unsworn evidence

(1) This section applies where a person gives unsworn evidence in criminal proceedings in pursuance of section 56(2) or (3).

(2) If such a person wilfully gives false evidence in such circumstances that, had the evidence been given on oath, he would have been guilty of perjury, he shall be guilty of an offence and liable on summary conviction to—

(a) imprisonment for a term not exceeding 6 months, or

(b) a fine not exceeding £1,000,

or both.

(3) In relation to a person under the age of 14, subsection (2) shall have effect as if for the words following 'on summary conviction' there were substituted 'to a fine not exceeding £250'.

59 Restriction on use of answers etc. obtained under compulsion

Schedule 3, which amends enactments providing for the use of answers and statements given under compulsion so as to restrict in criminal proceedings their use in evidence against the persons giving them, shall have effect.

Chapter VII General

62 Meaning of 'sexual offence' and other references to offences

(1) In this Part 'sexual offence' means any offence under—

(a) Part 1 of the Sexual Offences Act 2003 or any relevant superseded offence; or

(b) section 2 of the Modern Slavery Act 2015 (human trafficking) committed with a view to exploitation that consists of or includes behaviour within section 3(3) of that Act (sexual exploitation).

(1A) In subsection (1) 'relevant superseded offence' means—

(a) rape or burglary with intent to rape;

(b) an offence under any of sections 2 to 12 and 14 to 17 of the Sexual Offences Act 1956 (unlawful intercourse, indecent assault, forcible abduction etc.);

(c) an offence under section 128 of the Mental Health Act 1959 (unlawful intercourse with person receiving treatment for mental disorder by member of hospital staff etc.);

(d) an offence under section 1 of the Indecency with Children Act 1960 (indecent conduct towards child under 14);

(e) an offence under section 54 of the Criminal Law Act 1977 (incitement of child under 16 to commit incest).

(2) In this part any reference (including a reference having effect by virtue of this subsection) to an offence of any description ('the substantive offence') is to be taken to include a reference to an offence which consists of attempting or conspiring to commit, or of aiding, abetting, counselling, procuring or inciting* the commission of, the substantive offence.

63 General interpretation etc. of Part II

(1) In this Part (except where the context otherwise requires)—

'accused', in relation to any criminal proceedings, means any person charged with an offence to which the proceedings relate (whether or not he has been convicted);

'the complainant', in relation to any offence (or alleged offence), means a person against or in relation to whom the offence was (or is alleged to have been) committed;

'court' (except in Chapter IV or V or subsection (2)) means a magistrates' court, the Crown Court or criminal division of the Court of Appeal;

'legal representative' means a person who, for the purposes of the Legal Services Act 2007, is an authorised person in relation to an activity which constitutes the exercise of a right of audience or the conduct of litigation (within the meaning of that Act);

'picture' includes a likeness however produced;

'the prosecutor' means any person acting as prosecutor, whether an individual or body;

'publication' includes any speech, writing, relevant programme or other communication in whatever form, which is addressed to the public at large or any section of the public (and for this purpose every relevant programme shall be taken to be so addressed), but does not include an indictment or other document prepared for use in particular legal proceedings;

* **Editor's Note:** The common law offence of inciting a crime was abolished by the Serious Crime Act 2007. Schedule 6, Part 1, section 37 applies to subsection (2) above.

'relevant programme' means a programme included in a programme service, within the meaning of the Broadcasting Act 1990;

'service court' means—

. . .

'video recording' means any recording, on any medium, from which a moving image may by any means be produced, and includes the accompanying sound-track;

'witness', in relation to any criminal proceedings, means any person called, or proposed to be called, to give evidence in the proceedings.

(2) Nothing in this Part shall affect any power of a court to exclude evidence at its discretion (whether by preventing questions being put or otherwise) which is exercisable apart from this Part.

SCHEDULE 1A

RELEVANT OFFENCES FOR THE PURPOSES OF SECTION 17

Murder and manslaughter

1 Murder in a case where it is alleged that a firearm or knife was used to cause the death in question.

2 Manslaughter in a case where it is alleged that a firearm or knife was used to cause the death in question.

3 Murder or manslaughter in a case (other than a case falling within paragraph 1 or 2) where it is alleged that—

(a) the accused was carrying a firearm or knife at any time during the commission of the offence, and

(b) a person other than the accused knew or believed at any time during the commission of the offence that the accused was carrying a firearm or knife.

Offences against the Person Act 1861

4 An offence under section 18 of the Offences against the Person Act 1861 (wounding with intent to cause grievous bodily harm etc.) in a case where it is alleged that a firearm or knife was used to cause the wound or harm in question.

5 An offence under section 20 of that Act (malicious wounding) in a case where it is alleged that a firearm or knife was used to cause the wound or inflict the harm in question.

6 An offence under section 38 of that Act (assault with intent to resist arrest) in a case where it is alleged that a firearm or knife was used to carry out the assault in question.

7 An offence under section 47 of the Offences against the Person Act 1861 (assault occasioning actual bodily harm) in a case where it is alleged that a firearm or knife was used to inflict the harm in question.

8 An offence under section 18, 20, 38 or 47 of the Offences against the Person Act 1861 in a case (other than a case falling within any of paragraphs 4 to 7) where it is alleged that—

(a) the accused was carrying a firearm or knife at any time during the commission of the offence, and

(b) a person other than the accused knew or believed at any time during the commission of the offence that the accused was carrying a firearm or knife.

Prevention of Crime Act 1953

9 An offence under section 1 of the Prevention of Crime Act 1953 (having an offensive weapon in a public place).

9A An offence under section 1A (threatening with offensive weapon in public).

Firearms Act 1968

10 An offence under section 1 of the Firearms Act 1968 (requirement of firearm certificate).

11 An offence under section 2(1) of that Act (possession etc. of a shot gun without a certificate).

12 An offence under section 3 of that Act (business and other transactions with firearms and ammunition).

13 An offence under section 4 of that Act (conversion of weapons).

14 An offence under section 5(1) of that Act (weapons subject to general prohibition).

15 An offence under section 5(1A) of that Act (ammunition subject to general prohibition).

16 An offence under section 16 of that Act (possession with intent to injure).

17 An offence under section 16A of that Act (possession with intent to cause fear of violence).

18 An offence under section 17 of that Act (use of firearm to resist arrest).

19 An offence under section 18 of that Act (carrying firearm with criminal intent).

20 An offence under section 19 of that Act (carrying firearm in a public place).

21 An offence under section 20 of that Act (trespassing with firearm).

22 An offence under section 21 of that Act (possession of firearms by person previously convicted of crime).

23 An offence under section 21A of that Act (firing an air weapon beyond premises).

24 An offence under section 24A of that Act (supplying imitation firearms to minors).

Criminal Justice Act 1988

25 An offence under section 139 of the Criminal Justice Act 1988 (having article with blade or point in public place).

26 An offence under section 139A of that Act (having article with blade or point (or offensive weapon) on school premises).

26A An offence under section 139AA of that Act (threatening with article with blade or point or offensive weapon).

Violent Crime Reduction Act 2006

27 An offence under section 28 of the Violent Crime Reduction Act 2006 (using someone to mind a weapon).

28 An offence under section 32 of that Act (sales of air weapons by way of trade or business to be face to face).

29 An offence under section 36 of that Act (manufacture, import and sale of realistic imitation firearms).

Serious Crime Act 2015

29A An offence under section 75A of the Serious Crime Act 2015 (strangulation or suffocation) in a case where it is alleged that—

- (a) the accused was carrying a firearm or knife at any time during the commission of the offence, and
- (b) a person other than the accused knew or believed at any time during the commission of the offence that the accused was carrying a firearm or knife.

General

30 A reference in any of paragraphs 1 to 8 and 29A to an offence ('offence A') includes—

- (a) a reference to an attempt to commit offence A in a case where it is alleged that it was attempted to commit offence A in the manner or circumstances described in that paragraph,
- (b) a reference to a conspiracy to commit offence A in a case where it is alleged that the conspiracy was to commit offence A in the manner or circumstances described in that paragraph,
- (c) a reference to an offence under Part 2 of the Serious Crime Act 2007 in relation to which offence A is the offence (or one of the offences) which the person intended or believed would be committed in a case where it is alleged that the person intended or believed offence A would be committed in the manner or circumstances described in that paragraph, and

(d) a reference to aiding, abetting, counselling or procuring the commission of offence A in a case where it is alleged that offence A was committed, or the act or omission charged in respect of offence A was done or made, in the manner or circumstances described in that paragraph.

31 A reference in any of paragraphs 9 to 29 to an offence ('offence A') includes—

(a) a reference to an attempt to commit offence A,

(b) a reference to a conspiracy to commit offence A,

(c) a reference to an offence under Part 2 of the Serious Crime Act 2007 in relation to which offence A is the offence (or one of the offences) which the person intended or believed would be committed, and

(d) a reference to aiding, abetting, counselling or procuring the commission of offence A.

Interpretation

32 In this Schedule—

'firearm' has the meaning given by section 57 of the Firearms Act 1968;

'knife' has the meaning given by section 10 of the Knives Act 1997.

Sexual Offences Act 2003

(2003, c. 42)

75 Evidential presumptions about consent

(1) If in proceedings for an offence to which this section applies it is proved—

(a) that the defendant did the relevant act,

(b) that any of the circumstances specified in subsection (2) existed, and

(c) that the defendant knew that those circumstances existed,

the complainant is to be taken not to have consented to the relevant act unless sufficient evidence is adduced to raise an issue as to whether he consented, and the defendant is to be taken not to have reasonably believed that the complainant consented unless sufficient evidence is adduced to raise an issue as to whether he reasonably believed it.

(2) The circumstances are that—

(a) any person was, at the time of the relevant act or immediately before it began, using violence against the complainant or causing the complainant to fear that immediate violence would be used against him;

(b) any person was, at the time of the relevant act or immediately before it began, causing the complainant to fear that violence was being used, or that immediate violence would be used, against another person;

(c) the complainant was, and the defendant was not, unlawfully detained at the time of the relevant act;

(d) the complainant was asleep or otherwise unconscious at the time of the relevant act;

(e) because of the complainant's physical disability, the complainant would not have been able at the time of the relevant act to communicate to the defendant whether the complainant consented;

(f) any person had administered to or caused to be taken by the complainant, without the complainant's consent, a substance which, having regard to when it was administered or taken, was capable of causing or enabling the complainant to be stupefied or overpowered at the time of the relevant act.

(3) In subsection (2)(a) and (b), the reference to the time immediately before the relevant act began is, in the case of an act which is one of a continuous series of sexual activities, a reference to the time immediately before the first sexual activity began.

76 Conclusive presumptions about consent

(1) If in proceedings for an offence to which this section applies it is proved that the defendant did the relevant act and that any of the circumstances specified in subsection (2) existed, it is to be conclusively presumed—

(a) that the complainant did not consent to the relevant act, and
(b) that the defendant did not believe that the complainant consented to the relevant act.

(2) The circumstances are that—

(a) the defendant intentionally deceived the complainant as to the nature or purpose of the relevant act;
(b) the defendant intentionally induced the complainant to consent to the relevant act by impersonating a person known personally to the complainant.

77 Sections 75 and 76: relevant acts

In relation to an offence to which sections 75 and 76 apply, references in those sections to the relevant act and to the complainant are to be read as follows—

Offence	Relevant Act
An offence under section 1 (rape).	The defendant intentionally penetrating, with his penis, the vagina, anus or mouth of another person ('the complainant').
An offence under section 2 (assault by penetration).	The defendant intentionally penetrating, with a part of his body or anything else, the vagina or anus of another person ('the complainant'), where the penetration is sexual.
An offence under section 3 (sexual assault).	The defendant intentionally touching another person ('the complainant'), where the touching is sexual.
An offence under section 4 (causing a person to engage in sexual activity without consent).	The defendant intentionally causing another person ('the complainant') to engage in an activity, where the activity is sexual.

78 'Sexual'

For the purposes of this Part (except sections 15A, 66B to 66D, and 71), penetration, touching or any other activity is sexual if a reasonable person would consider that—

(a) whatever its circumstances or any person's purpose in relation to it, it is because of its nature sexual, or
(b) because of its nature it may be sexual and because of its circumstances or the purpose of any person in relation to it (or both) it is sexual.

79 Part 1: general interpretation

(1) The following apply for the purposes of this Part.

(2) Penetration is a continuing act from entry to withdrawal.

(3) References to a part of the body include references to a part surgically constructed (in particular, through gender reassignment surgery).

(4) 'Image' means a moving or still image and includes an image produced by any means and, where the context permits, a three-dimensional image.

(5) References to an image of a person (except in sections 66E, 66F, and 66G) include references to an image of an imaginary person.

(6) 'Mental disorder' has the meaning given by section 1 of the Mental Health Act 1983.

(7) References to observation (however expressed) are to observation whether direct or by looking at an image.

(8) Touching includes touching—

(a) with any part of the body,
(b) with anything else,
(c) through anything,

and in particular includes touching amounting to penetration.

(9) 'Vagina' includes vulva.

(10) In relation to an animal, references to the vagina or anus include references to any similar part.

Criminal Justice Act 2003

(2003, c. 44)

PART 8 LIVE LINKS

51 Directions for live links in criminal proceedings

(1) The court may, by a direction, require or permit a person to take part in eligible criminal proceedings through—

(a) a live audio link, or

(b) a live video link.

(2) A direction under this section may be given in relation to a member of a jury only if the direction requires all members of the jury to take part through a live video link while present at the same place.

(3) In this Part 'eligible criminal proceedings' means—

(a) a preliminary hearing (see section 56(1)),

(b) a summary trial,

(c) a criminal appeal to the Crown Court and any proceedings that are preliminary or incidental to such an appeal,

(d) a trial on indictment or any other trial in the Crown Court for an offence,

(e) proceedings under section 4A or 5 of the Criminal Procedure (Insanity) Act 1964,

(f) proceedings under Part 3 of the Mental Health Act 1983,

(g) proceedings under—

(i) section 11 of the Powers of Criminal Courts (Sentencing) Act 2000, or

(ii) section 81(1)(g) of the Senior Courts Act 1981 or section 16 of this Act in respect of a person who has been remanded by a magistrates' court on adjourning a case under that section of the 2000 Act,

(h) an appeal to the criminal division of the Court of Appeal and any proceedings that are preliminary or incidental to such an appeal,

(i) a reference to the Court of Appeal by the Attorney General under Part 4 of the Criminal Justice Act 1988 and any proceedings that are preliminary or incidental to such a reference,

(j) the hearing of a reference under section 9 or 11 of the Criminal Appeal Act 1995 and any proceedings that are preliminary or incidental to such a hearing,

(k) a hearing before a magistrates' court or the Crown Court which is held after the defendant has entered a plea of guilty,

(l) a hearing under section 142(1) or (2) of the Magistrates' Courts Act 1980,

(m) a hearing before the Court of Appeal under section 80 of this Act and any proceedings that are preliminary or incidental to such a hearing,

(n) any hearing following conviction held for the purpose of making a decision about bail in respect of the person convicted,

(o) a sentencing hearing (see section 56(1)), or

(p) an enforcement hearing (see section 56(1)).

(4) The court may not give a direction under this section unless—

(a) the court is satisfied that it is in the interests of justice for the person to whom the direction relates to take part in the proceedings in accordance with the direction through the live audio link or live video link,

(b) the parties to the proceedings have been given the opportunity to make representations, and

(c) if so required by section 52(9), the relevant youth offending team has been given the opportunity to make representations.

(5) In deciding whether to give a direction under this section, the court must consider—

(a) any guidance given by the Lord Chief Justice, and
(b) all the circumstances of the case.

(6) Those circumstances include in particular—
(a) the availability of the person to whom the direction would relate,
(b) any need for that person to attend in person,
(c) the views of that person,
(d) the suitability of the facilities at the place where that person would take part in the proceedings in accordance with the direction,
(e) whether that person would be able to take part in the proceedings effectively if the person took part in accordance with the direction,
(f) in the case of a direction relating to a witness—
(i) the importance of the witness's evidence to the proceedings, and
(ii) whether the direction might tend to inhibit any party to the proceedings from effectively testing the witness's evidence, and
(g) the arrangements that would or could be put in place for members of the public to see or hear the proceedings as conducted in accordance with the direction.

52 Further provision about the effect of live-link directions

(1) The power conferred by section 51 includes power to give—
(a) a direction that is applicable to several, or all, of the persons taking part in particular eligible criminal proceedings;
(b) a direction that is applicable to a particular person in respect of only some aspects of particular eligible criminal proceedings (such as giving evidence or attending the proceedings when not giving evidence);
(c) a direction requiring or permitting a person who is outside England and Wales (whether in the United Kingdom or elsewhere) to take part in eligible criminal proceedings through a live audio link or a live video link.

(2) The court may vary or rescind a direction under section 51 at any time before or during the eligible criminal proceedings to which it relates (but this does not affect the court's power to give a further direction under that section in relation to the proceedings).

(3) A direction under section 51 may not be rescinded unless—
(a) the court is satisfied that it is in the interests of justice for the direction to be rescinded,
(b) the parties to the proceedings have been given the opportunity to make representations, and
(c) if so required by subsection (9), the relevant youth offending team has been given the opportunity to make representations.

(4) In relation to the variation of a direction given under section 51—
(a) so far as the effect of the variation would be to allow a person to take part in eligible criminal proceedings through a live audio link or a live video link, or to alter (without removing) a person's ability to do so, sections 51(4) and 53(1) to (3) apply as they apply to the giving of a direction;
(b) so far as the effect of the variation would be to remove a person's ability to take part in eligible criminal proceedings through a live audio link or a live video link, subsection (3) applies as it applies to the rescission of a direction.

(5) Section 51(5) and (6) applies in relation to the variation or rescission of a direction given under section 51 as it applies to the giving of a direction under that section.

(6) A direction under section 51 may be given, varied or rescinded—
(a) on an application by a party to the proceedings, or
(b) of the court's own motion.

But a party may not apply for a variation or rescission unless there has been a material change of circumstances since the direction was given or last varied.

(7) The court must state in open court its reasons for refusing an application for the giving, variation or rescission of a direction under section 51 and, if it is a magistrates' court, must cause them to be entered in the register of its proceedings.

(8) If a hearing takes place in relation to the giving, variation or rescission of a direction under section 51, the court may require or permit a person to take part in that hearing through—

(a) a live audio link, or

(b) a live video link.

(9) The requirement referred to in section 51(4)(c) and subsection (3)(c) arises in a case where—

(a) the defendant is a party to the proceedings, and

(b) either—

(i) the defendant has not attained the age of 18 years, or

(ii) the defendant has attained the age of 18 years but the court is dealing with the case as if the defendant had not attained that age.

52A Further provision about the effect of live-link directions

(1) A person who takes part in eligible criminal proceedings in accordance with a direction under section 51 is to be treated as complying with any requirement (however imposed or expressed) for that person to attend or appear before court, or to surrender to the custody of the court, for the purposes of that participation in those proceedings.

(2) A person who takes part in eligible criminal proceedings in accordance with a direction under section 51 is to be treated as present in court for the purposes of those proceedings.

(3) If eligible criminal proceedings are conducted with one or more persons taking part in accordance with a direction under section 51, the proceedings are to be regarded as taking place—

(a) if at least one member of the court is taking part in the proceedings while in a courtroom, in that courtroom (or, if more than one courtroom falls within this paragraph, such of them as the court directs),

(b) if no member of the court, but at least one other person, is taking part in the proceedings while in a courtroom, in that courtroom (or, if more than one courtroom falls within this paragraph, such of them as the court directs), or

(c) if no person is taking part in the proceedings while in a courtroom, at such place as the court directs (being a place where the court could lawfully sit for the purposes of those proceedings).

(4) In subsection (3), 'courtroom' includes any place where proceedings of the sort in question might ordinarily be held (if no person were taking part in the proceedings in accordance with a direction under section 51).

(5) A statement made on oath by a witness outside the United Kingdom and given in evidence through a live audio link or a live video link in accordance with a direction under section 51 is to be treated for the purposes of section 1 of the Perjury Act 1911 as having been made in the proceedings in which it is given in evidence.

53 Further provisions about live links in magistrate's courts

(1) Subsections (2) and (3) apply where—

(a) a magistrates' court is minded to give a direction under section 51 requiring or permitting a person to take part in proceedings before the court through a live audio link or a live video link, and

(b) suitable facilities for such participation are not available at any place at which the court can (apart from subsection (2)) lawfully sit.

(2) The court may sit for the purposes of the whole or any part of the proceedings at any place at which such facilities are available and which has been authorised by a direction under section 30 of the Courts Act 2003.

(3) If the place mentioned in subsection (2) is outside the local justice area in which the justices act it shall be deemed to be in that area for the purpose of the jurisdiction of the justices acting in that area.

(4) The following functions of a magistrates' court may be discharged by a single justice—

(a) giving a direction under section 51 or varying such a direction under section 52(2);

(b) rescinding under section 52(2) a direction given under section 51 before the eligible criminal proceedings concerned begin;

(c) requiring or permitting, under section 52(8), a person to take part by live audio link or live video link in a hearing about a matter within paragraph (a) or (b).

54 Warning to jury

(1) This section applies where, as a result of a direction under section 51, evidence has been given through a live audio link or a live video link by a witness (including the defendant) in proceedings before the Crown Court.

(2) The judge may give the jury (if there is one) such direction as he thinks necessary to ensure that the jury gives the same weight to the evidence as if it had been given by the witness in the courtroom or other place where the proceedings are held.

55 Rules of court

(1) Criminal Procedure Rules may make such provision as appears to the Criminal Procedure Rules Authority to be necessary or expedient for the purposes of this Part.

(2) Criminal Procedure Rules may in particular make provision—

(a) as to the procedure to be followed in connection with applications under section 52(6), and

(b) as to the arrangements or safeguards to be put in place in connection with the operation of live audio links and live video links.

(3) The provision which may be made by virtue of subsection (2)(a) includes provision—

(a) for applications to be determined by the court without a hearing,

(b) for preventing the renewal of an unsuccessful application under section 52(6) unless there has been a material change of circumstances,

(c) for the manner in which confidential or sensitive information is to be treated in connection with an application under section 52(6) and in particular as to its being disclosed to, or withheld from, a party to the proceedings.

(4) Nothing in this section is to be taken as affecting the generality of any enactment conferring power to make Criminal Procedure Rules.

56 Interpretation of Part 8

(1) In this Part—

'bail' includes remand to local authority accommodation in accordance with Chapter 3 of Part 3 of the Legal Aid, Sentencing and Punishment of Offenders Act 2012,

'defendant' includes the person accused or convicted of an offence and, in the case of an enforcement hearing, the person liable to pay the sum or financial penalty concerned,

'eligible criminal proceedings' has the meaning given in section 51(3),

'enforcement hearing' means a hearing relating to collection, discharge, satisfaction or enforcement of—

(a) a sum that has been adjudged to be paid on conviction for an offence by a magistrates' court or the Crown Court, or

(b) a financial penalty that is enforceable in accordance with section 85(6) and (7) of the Criminal Justice and Immigration Act 2008 as if it were such a sum (including a hearing to determine whether a financial penalty is so enforceable),

'live audio link', in relation to a person (P) taking part in proceedings, means a live telephone link or other arrangement which—

(a) enables P to hear all other persons taking part in the proceedings who are not in the same location as P, and

(b) enables all other persons taking part in the proceedings who are not in the same location as P to hear P,

'live video link', in relation to a person (P) taking part in proceedings, means a live television link or other arrangement which—

(a) enables P to see and hear all other persons taking part in the proceedings who are not in the same location as P, and

(b) enables all other persons taking part in the proceedings who are not in the same location as P to see and hear P, 'local justice area' has the same meaning as in the Courts Act 2003,

'preliminary hearing' means a hearing in proceedings for an offence held before the start of the trial (within the meaning of subsection (11A) or (11B) of section 22 of the Prosecution of Offences Act 1985), including, in the case of proceedings in the Crown Court, a preparatory hearing held under—

(a) section 7 of the Criminal Justice Act 1987 (cases of serious or complex fraud), or

(b) section 29 of the Criminal Procedure and Investigations Act 1996 (other serious, complex or lengthy cases),

'relevant youth offending team' means the youth offending team (established under section 39 of the Crime and Disorder Act 1998) whose functions are exercisable in relation to the defendant concerned,

'sentencing hearing' means any hearing following conviction for an offence which is held for the purpose of—

(a) proceedings (in a magistrates' court) relating to committal to the Crown Court for sentencing,

(b) sentencing the offender or determining how the court should deal with the offender in respect of the offence (including reviewing, amending or revoking such a sentence or determination), or

(c) determining—

(i) how the offender has complied with a sentence given in respect of the offence, or

(ii) how the offender should be dealt with in respect of compliance with such a sentence,

and here 'sentence' includes any way in which a court has determined that the offender should be dealt with in respect of the offence,

'witness', in relation to any criminal proceedings, means a person called, or proposed to be called, to give evidence in the proceedings.

(1A) In this Part, reference to taking part in proceedings means taking part in whatever capacity, including hearing the proceedings as a member of the court.

(1B) In the application of this Part in relation to a witness, a reference to taking part in proceedings includes attending those proceedings for a purpose preliminary or incidental to the giving of evidence.

(4) The following matters are to be disregarded for the purposes of the definitions of 'live audio link' and 'live video link' in subsection (1)—

(a) the extent (if any) to which a person is unable to see or hear by reason of any impairment of eyesight or hearing;

(b) the effect of any direction or order which provides for one person taking part in proceedings to be prevented by means of a screen or other arrangement from seeing another person taking part in the proceedings.

(5) Nothing in this Part is to be regarded as affecting any power of a court—

(a) to make an order, give directions or give leave of any description in relation to any witness (including the defendant or defendants), or

(b) to exclude evidence at its discretion (whether by preventing questions being put or otherwise).

PART 9 PROSECUTION APPEALS

Introduction

57 Introduction

(1) In relation to a trial on indictment, the prosecution is to have the rights of appeal for which provision is made by this Part.

(2) But the prosecution is to have no right of appeal under this Part in respect of—

(a) a ruling that a jury be discharged, or

(b) a ruling from which an appeal lies to the Court of Appeal by virtue of any other enactment.

(3) An appeal under this Part is to lie to the Court of Appeal.

(4) Such an appeal may be brought only with the leave of the judge or the Court of Appeal.

General right of appeal in respect of rulings

58 General right of appeal in respect of rulings

(1) This section applies where a judge makes a ruling in relation to a trial on indictment at an applicable time and the ruling relates to one or more offences included in the indictment.

(2) The prosecution may appeal in respect of the ruling in accordance with this section.

(3) The ruling is to have no effect whilst the prosecution is able to take any steps under subsection (4).

(4) The prosecution may not appeal in respect of the ruling unless—

(a) following the making of the ruling, it—

(i) informs the court that it intends to appeal, or

(ii) requests an adjournment to consider whether to appeal, and

(b) if such an adjournment is granted, it informs the court following the adjournment that it intends to appeal.

(5) If the prosecution requests an adjournment under subsection (4)(a)(ii), the judge may grant such an adjournment.

(6) Where the ruling relates to two or more offences—

(a) any one or more of those offences may be the subject of the appeal, and

(b) if the prosecution informs the court in accordance with subsection (4) that it intends to appeal, it must at the same time inform the court of the offence or offences which are the subject of the appeal.

(7) Where—

(a) the ruling is a ruling that there is no case to answer, and

(b) the prosecution, at the same time that it informs the court in accordance with subsection (4) that it intends to appeal, nominates one or more other rulings which have been made by a judge in relation to the trial on indictment at an applicable time and which relate to the offence or offences which are the subject of the appeal,

that other ruling, or those other rulings, are also to be treated as the subject of the appeal.

(8) The prosecution may not inform the court in accordance with subsection (4) that it intends to appeal, unless, at or before that time, it informs the court that it agrees that, in respect of the offence or each offence which is the subject of the appeal, the defendant in relation to that offence should be acquitted of that offence if either of the conditions mentioned in subsection (9) is fulfilled.

(9) Those conditions are—

(a) that leave to appeal to the Court of Appeal is not obtained, and

(b) that the appeal is abandoned before it is determined by the Court of Appeal.

(10) If the prosecution informs the court in accordance with subsection (4) that it intends to appeal, the ruling mentioned in subsection (1) is to continue to have no effect in relation to the offence or offences which are the subject of the appeal whilst the appeal is pursued.

(11) If and to the extent that a ruling has no effect in accordance with this section—

(a) any consequences of the ruling are also to have no effect,

(b) the judge may not take any steps in consequence of the ruling, and

(c) if he does so, any such steps are also to have no effect.

(12) Where the prosecution has informed the court of its agreement under subsection (8) and either of the conditions mentioned in subsection (9) is fulfilled, the judge or the Court of Appeal must order that the defendant in relation to the offence or each offence concerned be acquitted of that offence.

(13) In this section 'applicable time', in relation to a trial on indictment, means any time (whether before or after the commencement of the trial) before the time when the judge starts his summing-up to the jury.

(14) The reference in subsection (13) to the time when the judge starts his summing-up to the jury includes the time when the judge would start his summing-up to the jury but for the making of an order under Part 7.

59 Expedited and non-expedited appeals

(1) Where the prosecution informs the court in accordance with section 58(4) that it intends to appeal, the judge must decide whether or not the appeal should be expedited.

(2) If the judge decides that the appeal should be expedited, he may order an adjournment.

(3) If the judge decides that the appeal should not be expedited, he may—

(a) order an adjournment, or

(b) discharge the jury (if one has been sworn).

(4) If he decides that the appeal should be expedited, he or the Court of Appeal may subsequently reverse that decision and, if it is reversed, the judge may act as mentioned in subsection (3)(a) or (b).

60 Continuation of proceedings for offences not affected by ruling

(1) This section applies where the prosecution informs the court in accordance with section 58(4) that it intends to appeal.

(2) Proceedings may be continued in respect of any offence which is not the subject of the appeal.

61 Determination of appeal by Court of Appeal

(1) On an appeal under section 58, the Court of Appeal may confirm, reverse or vary any ruling to which the appeal relates.

(2) Subsections (3) to (5) apply where the appeal relates to a single ruling.

(3) Where the Court of Appeal confirms the ruling, it must, in respect of the offence or each offence which is the subject of the appeal, order that the defendant in relation to that offence be acquitted of that offence.

(4) Where the Court of Appeal reverses or varies the ruling, it must, in respect of the offence or each offence which is the subject of the appeal, do any of the following—

(a) order that proceedings for that offence may be resumed in the Crown Court,

(b) order that a fresh trial may take place in the Crown Court for that offence,

(c) order that the defendant in relation to that offence be acquitted of that offence.

(5) But the Court of Appeal may not make an order under subsection (4)(c) in respect of an offence unless it considers that the defendant could not receive a fair trial if an order were made under subsection (4)(a) or (b).

(6) Subsections (7) and (8) apply where the appeal relates to a ruling that there is no case to answer and one or more other rulings.

(7) Where the Court of Appeal confirms the ruling that there is no case to answer, it must, in respect of the offence or each offence which is the subject of the appeal, order that the defendant in relation to that offence be acquitted of that offence.

(8) Where the Court of Appeal reverses or varies the ruling that there is no case to answer, it must in respect of the offence or each offence which is the subject of the appeal, make any of the orders mentioned in subsection (4)(a) to (c) (but subject to subsection (5)).

Miscellaneous and supplemental

67 Reversal of rulings

The Court of Appeal may not reverse a ruling on an appeal under this Part unless it is satisfied—

(a) that the ruling was wrong in law,

(b) that the ruling involved an error of law or principle, or

(c) that the ruling was a ruling that it was not reasonable for the judge to have made.

PART 10 RETRIAL FOR SERIOUS OFFENCES

Cases that may be retried

75 Cases that may be retried

(1) This Part applies where a person has been acquitted of a qualifying offence in proceedings—
- (a) on indictment in England and Wales,
- (b) on appeal against a conviction, verdict or finding in proceedings on indictment in England and Wales, or
- (c) on appeal from a decision on such an appeal.

(2) A person acquitted of an offence in proceedings mentioned in subsection (1) is treated for the purposes of that subsection as also acquitted of any qualifying offence of which he could have been convicted in the proceedings because of the first-mentioned offence being charged in the indictment, except an offence—
- (a) of which he has been convicted,
- (b) of which he has been found not guilty by reason of insanity, or
- (c) in respect of which, in proceedings where he has been found to be under a disability (as defined by section 4 of the Criminal Procedure (Insanity) Act 1964), a finding has been made that he did the act or made the omission charged against him.

(3) References in subsections (1) and (2) to a qualifying offence do not include references to an offence which, at the time of the acquittal, was the subject of an order under section 77(1) or (3).

(4) This Part also applies where a person has been acquitted, in proceedings elsewhere than in the United Kingdom, of an offence under the law of the place where the proceedings were held, if the commission of the offence as alleged would have amounted to or included the commission (in the United Kingdom or elsewhere) of a qualifying offence.

(5) Conduct punishable under the law in force elsewhere than in the United Kingdom is an offence under that law for the purposes of subsection (4), however it is described in that law.

(6) This Part applies whether the acquittal was before or after the passing of this Act.

(7) References in this Part to acquittal are to acquittal in circumstances within subsection (1) or (4).

(8) In this Part 'qualifying offence' means an offence listed in Part 1 of Schedule 5.

Application for retrial

76 Application to court of appeal

(1) A prosecutor may apply to the Court of Appeal for an order—
- (a) quashing a person's acquittal in proceedings within section 75(1), and
- (b) ordering him to be retried for the qualifying offence.

(2) A prosecutor may apply to the Court of Appeal, in the case of a person acquitted elsewhere than in the United Kingdom, for—
- (a) a determination whether the acquittal is a bar to the person being tried in England and Wales for the qualifying offence, and
- (b) if it is, an order that the acquittal is not to be a bar.

(3) A prosecutor may make an application under subsection (1) or (2) only with the written consent of the Director of Public Prosecutions.

(4) The Director of Public Prosecutions may give his consent only if satisfied that—
- (a) there is evidence as respects which the requirements of section 78 appear to be met,
- (b) it is in the public interest for the application to proceed, and
- (c) any trial pursuant to an order on the application would not be inconsistent with obligations of the United Kingdom under Article 31 or 34 of the Treaty on European Union (as it had effect before 1 December 2009) or Article 82, 83 or 85 of the Treaty on the Functioning of the European Union relating to the principle of *ne bis in idem*.

(5) Not more than one application may be made under subsection (1) or (2) in relation to an acquittal.

77 Determination by Court of Appeal

(1) On an application under section 76(1), the Court of Appeal—

(a) if satisfied that the requirements of sections 78 and 79 are met, must make the order applied for;

(b) otherwise, must dismiss the application.

(2) Subsections (3) and (4) apply to an application under section 76(2).

(3) Where the Court of Appeal determines that the acquittal is a bar to the person being tried for the qualifying offence, the court—

(a) if satisfied that the requirements of sections 78 and 79 are met, must make the order applied for;

(b) otherwise, must make a declaration to the effect that the acquittal is a bar to the person being tried for the offence.

(4) Where the Court of Appeal determines that the acquittal is not a bar to the person being tried for the qualifying offence, it must make a declaration to that effect.

78 New and compelling evidence

(1) The requirements of this section are met if there is new and compelling evidence against the acquitted person in relation to the qualifying offence.

(2) Evidence is new if it was not adduced in the proceedings in which the person was acquitted (nor, if those were appeal proceedings, in earlier proceedings to which the appeal related).

(3) Evidence is compelling if—

(a) it is reliable,

(b) it is substantial, and

(c) in the context of the outstanding issues, it appears highly probative of the case against the acquitted person.

(4) The outstanding issues are the issues in dispute in the proceedings in which the person was acquitted and, if those were appeal proceedings, any other issues remaining in dispute from earlier proceedings to which the appeal related.

(5) For the purposes of this section, it is irrelevant whether any evidence would have been admissible in earlier proceedings against the acquitted person.

79 Interests of justice

(1) The requirements of this section are met if in all the circumstances it is in the interests of justice for the court to make the order under section 77.

(2) That question is to be determined having regard in particular to—

(a) whether existing circumstances make a fair trial unlikely;

(b) for the purposes of that question and otherwise, the length of time since the qualifying offence was allegedly committed;

(c) whether it is likely that the new evidence would have been adduced in the earlier proceedings against the acquitted person but for a failure by an officer or by a prosecutor to act with due diligence or expedition;

(d) whether, since those proceedings or, if later, since the commencement of this Part, any officer or prosecutor has failed to act with due diligence or expedition.

(3) In subsection (2) references to an officer or prosecutor include references to a person charged with corresponding duties under the law in force elsewhere than in England and Wales.

(4) Where the earlier prosecution was conducted by a person other than a prosecutor, subsection (2)(c) applies in relation to that person as well as in relation to a prosecutor.

80 Procedure and evidence

(1) A prosecutor who wishes to make an application under section 76(1) or (2) must give notice of the application to the Court of Appeal.

(2) Within two days beginning with the day on which any such notice is given, notice of the application must be served by the prosecutor on the person to whom the application relates,

charging him with the offence to which it relates or, if he has been charged with it in accordance with section 87(4), stating that he has been so charged.

(3) Subsection (2) applies whether the person to whom the application relates is in the United Kingdom or elsewhere, but the Court of Appeal may, on application by the prosecutor, extend the time for service under that subsection if it considers it necessary to do so because of that person's absence from the United Kingdom.

(4) The Court of Appeal must consider the application at a hearing.

(5) The person to whom the application relates—

(a) is entitled to be present at the hearing, although he may be in custody, unless he is in custody elsewhere than in England and Wales or Northern Ireland, and

(b) is entitled to be represented at the hearing, whether he is present or not.

(6) For the purposes of the application, the Court of Appeal may, if it thinks it necessary or expedient in the interests of justice—

(a) order the production of any document, exhibit or other thing, the production of which appears to the court to be necessary for the determination of the application, and

(b) order any witness who would be a compellable witness in proceedings pursuant to an order or declaration made on the application to attend for examination and be examined before the court.

(7) The Court of Appeal may at one hearing consider more than one application (whether or not relating to the same person), but only if the offences concerned could be tried on the same indictment.

PART 11 EVIDENCE

Chapter 1 Evidence of bad character

Introductory

98 'Bad character'

References in this Chapter to evidence of a person's 'bad character' are to evidence of, or of a disposition towards, misconduct on his part, other than evidence which—

(a) has to do with the alleged facts of the offence with which the defendant is charged, or

(b) is evidence of misconduct in connection with the investigation or prosecution of that offence.

99 Abolition of common law rules

(1) The common law rules governing the admissibility of evidence of bad character in criminal proceedings are abolished.

(2) Subsection (1) is subject to section 118(1) in so far as it preserves the rule under which in criminal proceedings a person's reputation is admissible for the purposes of proving his bad character.

Persons other than defendants

100 Non-defendant's bad character

(1) In criminal proceedings evidence of the bad character of a person other than the defendant is admissible if and only if—

(a) it is important explanatory evidence,

(b) it has substantial probative value in relation to a matter which—

(i) is a matter in issue in the proceedings, and

(ii) is of substantial importance in the context of the case as a whole,

or

(c) all parties to the proceedings agree to the evidence being admissible.

(2) For the purposes of subsection (1)(a) evidence is important explanatory evidence if—

(a) without it, the court or jury would find it impossible or difficult properly to understand other evidence in the case, and

(b) its value for understanding the case as a whole is substantial.

(3) In assessing the probative value of evidence for the purposes of subsection (1)(b) the court must have regard to the following factors (and to any others it considers relevant)—

(a) the nature and number of the events, or other things, to which the evidence relates;

(b) when those events or things are alleged to have happened or existed;

(c) where—

(i) the evidence is evidence of a person's misconduct, and

(ii) it is suggested that the evidence has probative value by reason of similarity between that misconduct and other alleged misconduct,

the nature and extent of the similarities and the dissimilarities between each of the alleged instances of misconduct;

(d) where—

(i) the evidence is evidence of a person's misconduct,

(ii) it is suggested that that person is also responsible for the misconduct charged, and

(iii) the identity of the person responsible for the misconduct charged is disputed, the extent to which the evidence shows or tends to show that the same person was responsible each time.

(4) Except where subsection (1)(c) applies, evidence of the bad character of a person other than the defendant must not be given without leave of the court.

Defendants

101 Defendant's bad character

(1) In criminal proceedings evidence of the defendant's bad character is admissible if, but only if—

(a) all parties to the proceedings agree to the evidence being admissible,

(b) the evidence is adduced by the defendant himself or is given in answer to a question asked by him in cross-examination and intended to elicit it,

(c) it is important explanatory evidence,

(d) it is relevant to an important matter in issue between the defendant and the prosecution,

(e) it has substantial probative value in relation to an important matter in issue between the defendant and a co-defendant,

(f) it is evidence to correct a false impression given by the defendant, or

(g) the defendant has made an attack on another person's character.

(2) Sections 102 to 106 contain provision supplementing subsection (1).

(3) The court must not admit evidence under subsection (1)(d) or (g) if, on an application by the defendant to exclude it, it appears to the court that the admission of the evidence would have such an adverse effect on the fairness of the proceedings that the court ought not to admit it.

(4) On an application to exclude evidence under subsection (3) the court must have regard, in particular, to the length of time between the matters to which that evidence relates and the matters which form the subject of the offence charged.

102 'Important explanatory evidence'

For the purposes of section 101(1)(c) evidence is important explanatory evidence if—

(a) without it, the court or jury would find it impossible or difficult properly to understand other evidence in the case, and

(b) its value for understanding the case as a whole is substantial.

103 'Matter in issue between the defendant and the prosecution'

(1) For the purposes of section 101(1)(d) the matters in issue between the defendant and the prosecution include—

(a) the question whether the defendant has a propensity to commit offences of the kind with which he is charged, except where his having such a propensity makes it no more likely that he is guilty of the offence;

(b) the question whether the defendant has a propensity to be untruthful, except where it is not suggested that the defendant's case is untruthful in any respect.

(2) Where subsection (1)(a) applies, a defendant's propensity to commit offences of the kind with which he is charged may (without prejudice to any other way of doing so) be established by evidence that he has been convicted of—

(a) an offence of the same description as the one with which he is charged, or

(b) an offence of the same category as the one with which he is charged.

(3) Subsection (2) does not apply in the case of a particular defendant if the court is satisfied, by reason of the length of time since the conviction or for any other reason, that it would be unjust for it to apply in his case.

(4) For the purposes of subsection (2)—

(a) two offences are of the same description as each other if the statement of the offence in a written charge or indictment would, in each case, be in the same terms;

(b) two offences are of the same category as each other if they belong to the same category of offences prescribed for the purposes of this section by an order made by the Secretary of State.

(5) A category prescribed by an order under subsection (4)(b) must consist of offences of the same type.

(6) Only prosecution evidence is admissible under section 101(1)(d).

(7)–(11) . . .*

104 'Matter in issue between the defendant and a co-defendant'

(1) Evidence which is relevant to the question whether the defendant has a propensity to be untruthful is admissible on that basis under section 101(1)(e) only if the nature or conduct of his defence is such as to undermine the co-defendant's defence.

(2) Only evidence—

(a) which is to be (or has been) adduced by the co-defendant, or

(b) which a witness is to be invited to give (or has given) in cross-examination by the co-defendant,

is admissible under section 101(1)(e).

105 'Evidence to correct a false impression'

(1) For the purposes of section 101(1)(f)—

(a) the defendant gives a false impression if he is responsible for the making of an express or implied assertion which is apt to give the court or jury a false or misleading impression about the defendant;

(b) evidence to correct such an impression is evidence which has probative value in correcting it.

(2) A defendant is treated as being responsible for the making of an assertion if—

(a) the assertion is made by the defendant in the proceedings (whether or not in evidence given by him),

(b) the assertion was made by the defendant—

(i) on being questioned under caution, before charge, about the offence with which he is charged, or

(ii) on being charged with the offence or officially informed that he might be prosecuted for it,

and evidence of the assertion is given in the proceedings,

(c) the assertion is made by a witness called by the defendant,

(d) the assertion is made by any witness in cross-examination in response to a question asked by the defendant that is intended to elicit it, or is likely to do so, or

* **Editor's Note:** Apply to 'corresponding offences' committed outside England and Wales.

(e) the assertion was made by any person out of court, and the defendant adduces evidence of it in the proceedings.

(3) A defendant who would otherwise be treated as responsible for the making of an assertion shall not be so treated if, or to the extent that, he withdraws it or disassociates himself from it.

(4) Where it appears to the court that a defendant, by means of his conduct (other than the giving of evidence) in the proceedings, is seeking to give the court or jury an impression about himself that is false or misleading, the court may if it appears just to do so treat the defendant as being responsible for the making of an assertion which is apt to give that impression.

(5) In subsection (4) 'conduct' includes appearance or dress.

(6) Evidence is admissible under section 101(1)(f) only if it goes no further than is necessary to correct the false impression.

(7) Only prosecution evidence is admissible under section 101(1)(f).

106 'Attack on another person's character'

(1) For the purposes of section 101(1)(g) a defendant makes an attack on another person's character if—

(a) he adduces evidence attacking the other person's character,

(b) he (or any legal representative appointed under section 38(4) of the Youth Justice and Criminal Evidence Act 1999 to cross-examine a witness in his interests) asks questions in cross-examination that are intended to elicit such evidence, or are likely to do so, or

(c) evidence is given of an imputation about the other person made by the defendant—

(i) on being questioned under caution, before charge, about the offence with which he is charged, or

(ii) on being charged with the offence or officially informed that he might be prosecuted for it.

(2) In subsection (1) 'evidence attacking the other person's character' means evidence to the effect that the other person—

(a) has committed an offence (whether a different offence from the one with which the defendant is charged or the same one), or

(b) has behaved, or is disposed to behave, in a reprehensible way;

and 'imputation about the other person' means an assertion to that effect.

(3) Only prosecution evidence is admissible under section 101(1)(g).

107 Stopping the case where evidence contaminated

(1) If on a defendant's trial before a judge and jury for an offence—

(a) evidence of his bad character has been admitted under any of paragraphs (c) to (g) of section 101(1), and

(b) the court is satisfied at any time after the close of the case for the prosecution that—

(i) the evidence is contaminated, and

(ii) the contamination is such that, considering the importance of the evidence to the case against the defendant, his conviction of the offence would be unsafe,

the court must either direct the jury to acquit the defendant of the offence or, if it considers that there ought to be a retrial, discharge the jury.

(2) Where—

(a) a jury is directed under subsection (1) to acquit a defendant of an offence, and

(b) the circumstances are such that, apart from this subsection, the defendant could if acquitted of that offence be found guilty of another offence,

the defendant may not be found guilty of that other offence if the court is satisfied as mentioned in subsection (1)(b) in respect of it.

(3) If—

(a) a jury is required to determine under section 4A(2) of the Criminal Procedure (Insanity) Act 1964 whether a person charged on an indictment with an offence did the act or made the omission charged,

(b) evidence of the person's bad character has been admitted under any of paragraphs (c) to (g) of section 101(1), and
(c) the court is satisfied at any time after the close of the case for the prosecution that—
(i) the evidence is contaminated, and
(ii) the contamination is such that, considering the importance of the evidence to the case against the person, a finding that he did the act or made the omission would be unsafe,

the court must either direct the jury to acquit the defendant of the offence or, if it considers that there ought to be a rehearing, discharge the jury.

(4) This section does not prejudice any other power a court may have to direct a jury to acquit a person of an offence or to discharge a jury.

(5) For the purposes of this section a person's evidence is contaminated where—
(a) as a result of an agreement or understanding between the person and one or more others, or
(b) as a result of the person being aware of anything alleged by one or more others whose evidence may be, or has been, given in the proceedings,

the evidence is false or misleading in any respect, or is different from what it would otherwise have been.

108 Offences committed by defendant when a child

(1) Section 16(2) and (3) of the Children and Young Persons Act 1963 (offences committed by person under 14 disregarded for purposes of evidence relating to previous convictions) shall cease to have effect.

(2) In proceedings for an offence committed or alleged to have been committed by the defendant when aged 21 or over, evidence of his conviction for an offence when under the age of 14 is not admissible unless—
(a) both of the offences are triable only on indictment, and
(b) the court is satisfied that the interests of justice require the evidence to be admissible.

(2A), (2B) . . .*

(3) Subsection (2) applies in addition to section 101.

General

109 Assumption of truth in assessment of relevance or probative value

(1) Subject to subsection (2), a reference in this Chapter to the relevance or probative value of evidence is a reference to its relevance or probative value on the assumption that it is true.

(2) In assessing the relevance or probative value of an item of evidence for any purpose of this Chapter, a court need not assume that the evidence is true if it appears, on the basis of any material before the court (including any evidence it decides to hear on the matter), that no court or jury could reasonably find it to be true.

110 Court's duty to give reasons for rulings

(1) Where the court makes a relevant ruling—
(a) it must state in open court (but in the absence of the jury, if there is one) its reasons for the ruling;
(b) if it is a magistrates' court, it must cause the ruling and the reasons for it to be entered in the register of the court's proceedings.

(2) In this section 'relevant ruling' means—
(a) a ruling on whether an item of evidence is evidence of a person's bad character;
(b) a ruling on whether an item of such evidence is admissible under section 100 or 101 (including a ruling on an application under section 101(3));
(c) a ruling under section 107.

* **Editor's Note:** Apply to corresponding offences committed outside England and Wales.

111 Rules of court

(1) Rules of court may make such provision as appears to the appropriate authority to be necessary or expedient for the purposes of this Act; and the appropriate authority is the authority entitled to make the rules.

(2) The rules may, and, where the party in question is the prosecution, must, contain provision requiring a party who—

(a) proposes to adduce evidence of a defendant's bad character, or

(b) proposes to cross-examine a witness with a view to eliciting such evidence,

to serve on the defendant such notice, and such particulars of or relating to the evidence, as may be prescribed.

(3) The rules may provide that the court or the defendant may, in such circumstances as may be prescribed, dispense with a requirement imposed by virtue of subsection (2).

(4) In considering the exercise of its powers with respect to costs, the court may take into account any failure by a party to comply with a requirement imposed by virtue of subsection (2) and not dispensed with by virtue of subsection (3).

(5) The rules may—

(a) limit the application of any provision of the rules to prescribed circumstances;

(b) subject any provision of the rules to prescribed exceptions;

(c) make different provision for different cases or circumstances.

(6) Nothing in this section prejudices the generality of any enactment conferring power to make rules of court; and no particular provision of this section prejudices any general provision of it.

(7) In this section 'prescribed' means prescribed by rules of court.

112 Interpretation of Chapter 1

(1) In this Chapter—

'bad character' is to be read in accordance with section 98;

'criminal proceedings' means criminal proceedings in relation to which the strict rules of evidence apply;

'defendant', in relation to criminal proceedings, means a person charged with an offence in those proceedings; and 'co-defendant', in relation to a defendant, means a person charged with an offence in the same proceedings;

'important matter' means a matter of substantial importance in the context of the case as a whole;

'misconduct' means the commission of an offence or other reprehensible behaviour;

'offence' includes a service offence;

'probative value', and 'relevant' (in relation to an item of evidence), are to be read in accordance with section 109;

'prosecution evidence' means evidence which is to be (or has been) adduced by the prosecution, or which a witness is to be invited to give (or has given) in cross-examination by the prosecution;

. . .

'written charge' has the same meaning as in section 29 and also includes an information.

(2) Where a defendant is charged with two or more offences in the same criminal proceedings, this Chapter (except section 101(3)) has effect as if each offence were charged in separate proceedings; and references to the offence with which the defendant is charged are to be read accordingly.

(3) Nothing in this Chapter affects the exclusion of evidence—

(a) under the rule in section 3 of the Criminal Procedure Act 1865 against a party impeaching the credit of his own witness by general evidence of bad character,

(b) under section 41 of the Youth Justice and Criminal Evidence Act 1999 (restriction on evidence or questions about complainant's sexual history), or

(c) On grounds other than the fact that it is evidence of a person's bad character.

113 Armed Forces

. . .

Chapter 2

114 Admissibility of hearsay evidence

(1) In criminal proceedings a statement not made in oral evidence in the proceedings is admissible as evidence of any matter stated if, but only if—

(a) any provision of this Chapter or any other statutory provision makes it admissible,
(b) any rule of law preserved by section 118 makes it admissible,
(c) all parties to the proceedings agree to it being admissible, or
(d) the court is satisfied that it is in the interests of justice for it to be admissible.

(2) In deciding whether a statement not made in oral evidence should be admitted under subsection (1)(d), the court must have regard to the following factors (and to any others it considers relevant)—

(a) how much probative value the statement has (assuming it to be true) in relation to a matter in issue in the proceedings, or how valuable it is for the understanding of other evidence in the case;
(b) what other evidence has been, or can be, given on the matter or evidence mentioned in paragraph (a);
(c) how important the matter or evidence mentioned in paragraph (a) is in the context of the case as a whole;
(d) the circumstances in which the statement was made;
(e) how reliable the maker of the statement appears to be;
(f) how reliable the evidence of the making of the statement appears to be;
(g) whether oral evidence of the matter stated can be given and, if not, why it cannot;
(h) the amount of difficulty involved in challenging the statement;
(i) the extent to which that difficulty would be likely to prejudice the party facing it.

(3) Nothing in this Chapter affects the exclusion of evidence of a statement on grounds other than the fact that it is a statement not made in oral evidence in the proceedings.

115 Statements and matters stated

(1) In this Chapter references to a statement or to a matter stated are to be read as follows.

(2) A statement is any representation of fact or opinion made by a person by whatever means; and it includes a representation made in a sketch, photofit or other pictorial form.

(3) A matter stated is one to which this Chapter applies if (and only if) the purpose, or one of the purposes, of the person making the statement appears to the court to have been—

(a) to cause another person to believe the matter, or
(b) to cause another person to act or a machine to operate on the basis that the matter is as stated.

Principal categories of admissibility

116 Cases where a witness is unavailable

(1) In criminal proceedings a statement not made in oral evidence in the proceedings is admissible as evidence of any matter stated if—

(a) oral evidence given in the proceedings by the person who made the statement would be admissible as evidence of that matter,
(b) the person who made the statement (the relevant person) is identified to the court's satisfaction, and
(c) any of the five conditions mentioned in subsection (2) is satisfied.

(2) The conditions are—

(a) that the relevant person is dead;
(b) that the relevant person is unfit to be a witness because of his bodily or mental condition;
(c) that the relevant person is outside the United Kingdom and it is not reasonably practicable to secure his attendance;
(d) that the relevant person cannot be found although such steps as it is reasonably practicable to take to find him have been taken;

(e) that through fear the relevant person does not give (or does not continue to give) oral evidence in the proceedings, either at all or in connection with the subject matter of the statement, and the court gives leave for the statement to be given in evidence.

(3) For the purposes of subsection (2)(e) 'fear' is to be widely construed and (for example) includes fear of the death or injury of another person or of financial loss.

(4) Leave may be given under subsection (2)(e) only if the court considers that the statement ought to be admitted in the interests of justice, having regard—

(a) to the statement's contents,
(b) to any risk that its admission or exclusion will result in unfairness to any party to the proceedings (and in particular to how difficult it will be to challenge the statement if the relevant person does not give oral evidence),
(c) in appropriate cases, to the fact that a direction under section 19 of the Youth Justice and Criminal Evidence Act 1999 (special measures for the giving of evidence by fearful witnesses etc.) could be made in relation to the relevant person, and
(d) to any other relevant circumstances.

(5) A condition set out in any paragraph of subsection (2) which is in fact satisfied is to be treated as not satisfied if it is shown that the circumstances described in that paragraph are caused—

(a) by the person in support of whose case it is sought to give the statement in evidence, or
(b) by a person acting on his behalf,

in order to prevent the relevant person giving oral evidence in the proceedings (whether at all or in connection with the subject matter of the statement).

117 Business and other documents

(1) In criminal proceedings a statement contained in a document is admissible as evidence of any matter stated if—

(a) oral evidence given in the proceedings would be admissible as evidence of that matter,
(b) the requirements of subsection (2) are satisfied, and
(c) the requirements of subsection (5) are satisfied, in a case where subsection (4) requires them to be.

(2) The requirements of this subsection are satisfied if—

(a) the document or the part containing the statement was created or received by a person in the course of a trade, business, profession or other occupation, or as the holder of a paid or unpaid office,
(b) the person who supplied the information contained in the statement (the relevant person) had or may reasonably be supposed to have had personal knowledge of the matters dealt with, and
(c) each person (if any) through whom the information was supplied from the relevant person to the person mentioned in paragraph (a) received the information in the course of a trade, business, profession or other occupation, or as the holder of a paid or unpaid office.

(3) The persons mentioned in paragraphs (a) and (b) of subsection (2) may be the same person.

(4) The additional requirements of subsection (5) must be satisfied if the statement—

(a) was prepared for the purposes of pending or contemplated criminal proceedings, or for a criminal investigation, but
(b) was not obtained pursuant to
  (i) a request under section 7 of the Crime (International Co-operation) Act 2003,
  (ii) an order under paragraph 6 of Schedule 13 to the Criminal Justice Act 1988, or
  (iii) an overseas production order under the Crime (Overseas Production Orders) Act 2019

(all of which relate to overseas evidence).

(5) The requirements of this subsection are satisfied if—

(a) any of the five conditions mentioned in section 116(2) is satisfied (absence of relevant person etc.), or

(b) the relevant person cannot reasonably be expected to have any recollection of the matters dealt with in the statement (having regard to the length of time since he supplied the information and all other circumstances).

(6) A statement is not admissible under this section if the court makes a direction to that effect under subsection (7).

(7) The court may make a direction under this subsection if satisfied that the statement's reliability as evidence for the purpose for which it is tendered is doubtful in view of—

(a) its contents,
(b) the source of the information contained in it,
(c) the way in which or the circumstances in which the information was supplied or received, or
(d) the way in which or the circumstances in which the document concerned was created or received.

118 Preservation of certain common law categories of admissibility

(1) The following rules of law are preserved.

Public information etc.

1. Any rule of law under which in criminal proceedings—

(a) published works dealing with matters of a public nature (such as histories, scientific works, dictionaries and maps) are admissible as evidence of facts of a public nature stated in them,
(b) public documents (such as public registers, and returns made under public authority with respect to matters of public interest) are admissible as evidence of facts stated in them,
(c) records (such as the records of certain courts, treaties, Crown grants, pardons and commissions) are admissible as evidence of facts stated in them, or
(d) evidence relating to a person's age or date or place of birth may be given by a person without personal knowledge of the matter.

Reputation as to character

2. Any rule of law under which in criminal proceedings evidence of a person's reputation is admissible for the purpose of proving his good or bad character.

Note

The rule is preserved only so far as it allows the court to treat such evidence as proving the matter concerned.

Reputation or family tradition

3. Any rule of law under which in criminal proceedings evidence of reputation or family tradition is admissible for the purpose of proving or disproving—

(a) pedigree or the existence of a marriage,
(b) the existence of any public or general right, or
(c) the identity of any person or thing.

Note

The rule is preserved only so far as it allows the court to treat such evidence as proving or disproving the matter concerned.

Res gestae

4. Any rule of law under which in criminal proceedings a statement is admissible as evidence of any matter stated if—

(a) the statement was made by a person so emotionally overpowered by an event that the possibility of concoction or distortion can be disregarded,
(b) the statement accompanied an act which can be properly evaluated as evidence only if considered in conjunction with the statement, or
(c) the statement relates to a physical sensation or a mental state (such as intention or emotion).

Confessions etc.

5. Any rule of law relating to the admissibility of confessions or mixed statements in criminal proceedings.

Admissions by agents etc.

6. Any rule of law under which in criminal proceedings—

(a) an admission made by an agent of a defendant is admissible against the defendant as evidence of any matter stated, or

(b) a statement made by a person to whom a defendant refers a person for information is admissible against the defendant as evidence of any matter stated.

Common enterprise

7. Any rule of law under which in criminal proceedings a statement made by a party to a common enterprise is admissible against another party to the enterprise as evidence of any matter stated.

Expert evidence

8. Any rule of law under which in criminal proceedings an expert witness may draw on the body of expertise relevant to his field.

(2) With the exception of the rules preserved by this section, the common law rules governing the admissibility of hearsay evidence in criminal proceedings are abolished.

119 Inconsistent statements

(1) If in criminal proceedings a person gives oral evidence and—

(a) he admits making a previous inconsistent statement, or

(b) a previous inconsistent statement made by him is proved by virtue of section 3, 4 or 5 of the Criminal Procedure Act 1865,

the statement is admissible as evidence of any matter stated of which oral evidence by him would be admissible.

(2) If in criminal proceedings evidence of an inconsistent statement by any person is given under section 124(2)(c), the statement is admissible as evidence of any matter stated in it of which oral evidence by that person would be admissible.

120 Other previous statements of witnesses

(1) This section applies where a person (the witness) is called to give evidence in criminal proceedings.

(2) If a previous statement by the witness is admitted as evidence to rebut a suggestion that his oral evidence has been fabricated, that statement is admissible as evidence of any matter stated of which oral evidence by the witness would be admissible.

(3) A statement made by the witness in a document—

(a) which is used by him to refresh his memory while giving evidence,

(b) on which he is cross-examined, and

(c) which as a consequence is received in evidence in the proceedings,

is admissible as evidence of any matter stated of which oral evidence by him would be admissible.

(4) A previous statement by the witness is admissible as evidence of any matter stated of which oral evidence by him would be admissible, if—

(a) any of the following three conditions is satisfied, and

(b) while giving evidence the witness indicates that to the best of his belief he made the statement, and that to the best of his belief it states the truth.

(5) The first condition is that the statement identifies or describes a person, object or place.

(6) The second condition is that the statement was made by the witness when the matters stated were fresh in his memory but he does not remember them, and cannot reasonably be expected to remember them, well enough to give oral evidence of them in the proceedings.

(7) The third condition is that—

(a) the witness claims to be a person against whom an offence has been committed,

(b) the offence is one to which the proceedings relate,

(c) the statement consists of a complaint made by the witness (whether to a person in authority or not) about conduct which would, if proved, constitute the offence or part of the offence,

(e) before the statement is adduced the witness gives oral evidence in connection with its subject matter.

(8) For the purposes of subsection (7) the fact that the complaint was elicited (for example, by a leading question) is irrelevant unless a threat or a promise was involved.

Supplementary

121 Additional requirement for admissibility of multiple hearsay

(1) A hearsay statement is not admissible to prove the fact that an earlier hearsay statement was made unless—

(a) either of the statements is admissible under section 117, 119 or 120,

(b) all parties to the proceedings so agree, or

(c) the court is satisfied that the value of the evidence in question, taking into account how reliable the statements appear to be, is so high that the interests of justice require the later statement to be admissible for that purpose.

(2) In this section 'hearsay statement' means a statement, not made in oral evidence, that is relied on as evidence of a matter stated in it.

122 Documents produced as exhibits

(1) This section applies if on a trial before a judge and jury for an offence—

(a) a statement made in a document is admitted in evidence under section 119 or 120, and

(b) the document or a copy of it is produced as an exhibit.

(2) The exhibit must not accompany the jury when they retire to consider their verdict unless—

(a) the court considers it appropriate, or

(b) all the parties to the proceedings agree that it should accompany the jury.

123 Capability to make statement

(1) Nothing in section 116, 119 or 120 makes a statement admissible as evidence if it was made by a person who did not have the required capability at the time when he made the statement.

(2) Nothing in section 117 makes a statement admissible as evidence if any person who, in order for the requirements of section 117(2) to be satisfied, must at any time have supplied or received the information concerned or created or received the document or part concerned—

(a) did not have the required capability at that time, or

(b) cannot be identified but cannot reasonably be assumed to have had the required capability at that time.

(3) For the purposes of this section a person has the required capability if he is capable of—

(a) understanding questions put to him about the matters stated, and

(b) giving answers to such questions which can be understood.

(4) Where by reason of this section there is an issue as to whether a person had the required capability when he made a statement—

(a) proceedings held for the determination of the issue must take place in the absence of the jury (if there is one);

(b) in determining the issue the court may receive expert evidence and evidence from any person to whom the statement in question was made;

(c) the burden of proof on the issue lies on the party seeking to adduce the statement, and the standard of proof is the balance of probabilities.

124 Credibility

(1) This section applies if in criminal proceedings—

(a) a statement not made in oral evidence in the proceedings is admitted as evidence of a matter stated, and

(b) the maker of the statement does not give oral evidence in connection with the subject matter of the statement.

(2) In such a case—

(a) any evidence which (if he had given such evidence) would have been admissible as relevant to his credibility as a witness is so admissible in the proceedings;

(b) evidence may with the court's leave be given of any matter which (if he had given such evidence) could have been put to him in cross-examination as relevant to his credibility as a witness but of which evidence could not have been adduced by the cross-examining party;

(c) evidence tending to prove that he made (at whatever time) any other statement inconsistent with the statement admitted as evidence is admissible for the purpose of showing that he contradicted himself.

(3) If as a result of evidence admitted under this section an allegation is made against the maker of a statement, the court may permit a party to lead additional evidence of such description as the court may specify for the purposes of denying or answering the allegation.

(4) In the case of a statement in a document which is admitted as evidence under section 117 each person who, in order for the statement to be admissible, must have supplied or received the information concerned or created or received the document or part concerned is to be treated as the maker of the statement for the purposes of subsections (1) to (3) above.

125 Stopping the case where evidence is unconvincing

(1) If on a defendant's trial before a judge and jury for an offence the court is satisfied at any time after the close of the case for the prosecution that—

(a) the case against the defendant is based wholly or partly on a statement not made in oral evidence in the proceedings, and

(b) the evidence provided by the statement is so unconvincing that, considering its importance to the case against the defendant, his conviction of the offence would be unsafe,

the court must either direct the jury to acquit the defendant of the offence or, if it considers that there ought to be a retrial, discharge the jury.

(2) Where—

(a) a jury is directed under subsection (1) to acquit a defendant of an offence, and

(b) the circumstances are such that, apart from this subsection, the defendant could if acquitted of that offence be found guilty of another offence,

the defendant may not be found guilty of that other offence if the court is satisfied as mentioned in subsection (1) in respect of it.

(3) If—

(a) a jury is required to determine under section 4A(2) of the Criminal Procedure (Insanity) Act 1964 whether a person charged on an indictment with an offence did the act or made the omission charged, and

(b) the court is satisfied as mentioned in subsection (1) above at any time after the close of the case for the prosecution that—

(i) the case against the defendant is based wholly or partly on a statement not made in oral evidence in the proceedings, and

(ii) the evidence provided by the statement is so unconvincing that, considering its importance to the case against the person, a finding that he did the act or made the omission would be unsafe, the court must either direct the jury to acquit the defendant of the offence or, if it considers that there ought to be a rehearing, discharge the jury.

(4) This section does not prejudice any other power a court may have to direct a jury to acquit a person of an offence or to discharge a jury.

126 Court's general discretion to exclude evidence

(1) In criminal proceedings the court may refuse to admit a statement as evidence of a matter stated if—

(a) the statement was made otherwise than in oral evidence in the proceedings, and

(b) the court is satisfied that the case for excluding the statement, taking account of the danger that to admit it would result in undue waste of time, substantially outweighs the case for admitting it, taking account of the value of the evidence.

(2) Nothing in this Chapter prejudices—

(a) any power of a court to exclude evidence under section 78 of the Police and Criminal Evidence Act 1984 (exclusion of unfair evidence), or

(b) any other power of a court to exclude evidence at its discretion (whether by preventing questions from being put or otherwise).

Miscellaneous

127 Expert evidence: preparatory work

(1) This section applies if—

(a) a statement has been prepared for the purposes of criminal proceedings,

(b) the person who prepared the statement had or may reasonably be supposed to have had personal knowledge of the matters stated,

(c) notice is given under the appropriate rules that another person (the expert) will in evidence given in the proceedings orally or under section 9 of the Criminal Justice Act 1967 base an opinion or inference on the statement, and

(d) the notice gives the name of the person who prepared the statement and the nature of the matters stated.

(2) In evidence given in the proceedings the expert may base an opinion or inference on the statement.

(3) If evidence based on the statement is given under subsection (2) the statement is to be treated as evidence of what it states.

(4) This section does not apply if the court, on an application by a party to the proceedings, orders that it is not in the interests of justice that it should apply.

(5) The matters to be considered by the court in deciding whether to make an order under subsection (4) include—

(a) the expense of calling as a witness the person who prepared the statement;

(b) whether relevant evidence could be given by that person which could not be given by the expert;

(c) whether that person can reasonably be expected to remember the matters stated well enough to give oral evidence of them.

(6) Subsections (1) to (5) apply to a statement prepared for the purposes of a criminal investigation as they apply to a statement prepared for the purposes of criminal proceedings, and in such a case references to the proceedings are to criminal proceedings arising from the investigation.

(7) The appropriate rules are Criminal Procedure Rules made by virtue of—

(a) section 81 of the Police and Criminal Evidence Act 1984 (advance notice of expert evidence in Crown Court), or

(b) section 20(3) of the Criminal Procedure and Investigations Act 1996 (advance notice of expert evidence in magistrates' courts).

128 Confessions

(1) . . .*

(2) Subject to subsection (1), nothing in this Chapter makes a confession by a defendant admissible if it would not be admissible under section 76 of the Police and Criminal Evidence Act 1984.

(3) In subsection (2) 'confession' has the meaning given by section 82 of that Act.

129 Representations other than by a person

(1) Where a representation of any fact—

(a) is made otherwise than by a person, but

(b) depends for its accuracy on information supplied (directly or indirectly) by a person,

the representation is not admissible in criminal proceedings as evidence of the fact unless it is proved that the information was accurate.

(2) Subsection (1) does not affect the operation of the presumption that a mechanical device has been properly set or calibrated.

General

132 Rules of court

(1) Rules of court may make such provision as appears to the appropriate authority to be necessary or expedient for the purposes of this Chapter; and the appropriate authority is the authority entitled to make the rules.

(2) The rules may make provision about the procedure to be followed and other conditions to be fulfilled by a party proposing to tender a statement in evidence under any provision of this Chapter.

(3) The rules may require a party proposing to tender the evidence to serve on each party to the proceedings such notice, and such particulars of or relating to the evidence, as may be prescribed.

(4) The rules may provide that the evidence is to be treated as admissible by agreement of the parties if—

(a) a notice has been served in accordance with provision made under subsection (3), and

(b) no counter-notice in the prescribed form objecting to the admission of the evidence has been served by a party.

(5) If a party proposing to tender evidence fails to comply with a prescribed requirement applicable to it—

(a) the evidence is not admissible except with the court's leave;

(b) where leave is given the court or jury may draw such inferences from the failure as appear proper;

(c) the failure may be taken into account by the court in considering the exercise of its powers with respect to costs.

(6) In considering whether or how to exercise any of its powers under subsection (5) the court shall have regard to whether there is any justification for the failure to comply with the requirement.

(7) A person shall not be convicted of an offence solely on an inference drawn under subsection (5)(b).

(8) Rules under this section may—

(a) limit the application of any provision of the rules to prescribed circumstances;

(b) subject any provision of the rules to prescribed exceptions;

(c) make different provision for different cases or circumstances.

(9) Nothing in this section prejudices the generality of any enactment conferring power to make rules of court; and no particular provision of this section prejudices any general provision of it.

(10) In this section 'prescribed' means prescribed by rules of court.

133 Proof of statements in documents

Where a statement in a document is admissible as evidence in criminal proceedings, the statement may be proved by producing either—

* **Editor's Note:** Refers to the Police and Criminal Evidence Act 1984, section 76A.

(a) the document, or
(b) (whether or not the document exists) a copy of the document or of the material part of it,

authenticated in whatever way the court may approve.

134 Interpretation of Chapter 2

(1) In this Chapter—

'copy', in relation to a document, means anything on to which information recorded in the document has been copied, by whatever means and whether directly or indirectly;

'criminal proceedings' means criminal proceedings in relation to which the strict rules of evidence apply;

'defendant', in relation to criminal proceedings, means a person charged with an offence in those proceedings;

'document' means anything in which information of any description is recorded;

'oral evidence' includes evidence which, by reason of any disability, disorder or other impairment, a person called as a witness gives in writing or by signs or by way of any device;

'statutory provision' means any provision contained in, or in an instrument made under, this or any other Act, including any Act passed after this Act.

(2) Section 115 (statements and matters stated) contains other general interpretative provisions.

(3) Where a defendant is charged with two or more offences in the same criminal proceedings, this Chapter has effect as if each offence were charged in separate proceedings.

Chapter 3 Miscellaneous and supplemental

139 Use of documents to refresh memory

(1) A person giving oral evidence in criminal proceedings about any matter may, at any stage in the course of doing so, refresh his memory of it from a document made or verified by him at an earlier time if—

(a) he states in his oral evidence that the document records his recollection of the matter at that earlier time, and
(b) his recollection of the matter is likely to have been significantly better at that time than it is at the time of his oral evidence.

(2) Where—

(a) a person giving oral evidence in criminal proceedings about any matter has previously given an oral account, of which a sound recording was made, and he states in that evidence that the account represented his recollection of the matter at that time,
(b) his recollection of the matter is likely to have been significantly better at the time of the previous account than it is at the time of his oral evidence, and
(c) a transcript has been made of the sound recording,

he may, at any stage in the course of giving his evidence, refresh his memory of the matter from that transcript.

140 Interpretation of Chapter 3

In this Chapter—

'criminal proceedings' means criminal proceedings in relation to which the strict rules of evidence apply;

'defendant', in relation to criminal proceedings, means a person charged with an offence in those proceedings;

'document' means anything in which information of any description is recorded, but not including any recording of sounds or moving images;

'oral evidence' includes evidence which, by reason of any disability, disorder or other impairment, a person called as a witness gives in writing or by signs or by way of any device;

'video recording' means any recording, on any medium, from which a moving image may by any means be produced, and includes the accompanying sound-track.

SCHEDULE 5

QUALIFYING OFFENCES FOR PURPOSES OF PART 10

PART 1 LIST OF OFFENCES FOR ENGLAND AND WALES

Offences against the person

Murder

1. Murder.

Attempted murder

2. An offence under section 1 of the Criminal Attempts Act 1981 of attempting to commit murder.

Soliciting murder

3. An offence under section 4 of the Offences against the Person Act 1861.

Manslaughter

4. Manslaughter.

Corporate manslaughter

4A. An offence under section 1 of the Corporate Manslaughter and Corporate Homicide Act 2007.

Kidnapping

5. Kidnapping.

Sexual offences

Rape

6. An offence under section 1 of the Sexual Offences Act 1956 or section 1 of the Sexual Offences Act 2003.

Attempted rape

7. An offence under section 1 of the Criminal Attempts Act 1981 of attempting to commit an offence under section 1 of the Sexual Offences Act 1956 or section 1 of the Sexual Offences Act 2003.

Intercourse with a girl under thirteen

8. An offence under section 5 of the Sexual Offences Act 1956.

Incest by a man with a girl under thirteen

9. An offence under section 10 of the Sexual Offences Act 1956 alleged to have been committed with a girl under thirteen.

Assault by penetration

10. An offence under section 2 of the Sexual Offences Act 2003.

Causing a person to engage in sexual activity without consent

11. An offence under section 4 of the Sexual Offences Act 2003 where it is alleged that the activity caused involved penetration within subsection (4)(a) to (d) of that section.

Rape of a child under thirteen

12. An offence under section 5 of the Sexual Offences Act 2003.

Attempted rape of a child under thirteen

13. An offence under section 1 of the Criminal Attempts Act 1981 of attempting to commit an offence under section 5 of the Sexual Offences Act 2003.

Assault of a child under thirteen by penetration

14. An offence under section 6 of the Sexual Offences Act 2003.

Causing a child under thirteen to engage in sexual activity

15. An offence under section 8 of the Sexual Offences Act 2003 where it is alleged that an activity involving penetration within subsection (2)(a) to (d) of that section was caused.

Sexual activity with a person with a mental disorder impeding choice

16. An offence under section 30 of the Sexual Offences Act 2003 where it is alleged that the touching involved penetration within subsection (3)(a) to (d) of that section.

Causing a person with a mental disorder impeding choice to engage in sexual activity

17. An offence under section 31 of the Sexual Offences Act 2003 where it is alleged that an activity involving penetration within subsection (3)(a) to (d) of that section was caused.

Drugs offences

Unlawful importation of Class A drug

18. An offence under section 50(2) of the Customs and Excise Management Act 1979 alleged to have been committed in respect of a Class A drug (as defined by section 2 of the Misuse of Drugs Act 1971).

Unlawful exportation of Class A drug

19. An offence under section 68(2) of the Customs and Excise Management Act 1979 alleged to have been committed in respect of a Class A drug (as defined by section 2 of the Misuse of Drugs Act 1971).

Fraudulent evasion in respect of Class A drug

20. An offence under section 170(1) or (2) of the Customs and Excise Management Act 1979 alleged to have been committed in respect of a Class A drug (as defined by section 2 of the Misuse of Drugs Act 1971).

Producing or being concerned in production of Class A drug

21. An offence under section 4(2) of the Misuse of Drugs Act 1971 alleged to have been committed in relation to a Class A drug (as defined by section 2 of that Act).

Criminal damage offences

Arson endangering life

22. An offence under section 1(2) of the Criminal Damage Act 1971 alleged to have been committed by destroying or damaging property by fire.

Causing explosion likely to endanger life or property

23. An offence under section 2 of the Explosive Substances Act 1883.

Intent or conspiracy to cause explosion likely to endanger life or property

24. An offence under section 3(1)(a) of the Explosive Substances Act 1883.

War crimes and terrorism

Genocide, crimes against humanity and war crimes

25. An offence under section 51 or 52 of the International Criminal Court Act 2001.

Grave breaches of the Geneva conventions

26. An offence under section 1 of the Geneva Conventions Act 1957.

Directing terrorist organisation

27. An offence under section 56 of the Terrorism Act 2000.

Hostage-taking

28. An offence under section 1 of the Taking of Hostages Act 1982.

Conspiracy

Conspiracy

29. An offence under section 1 of the Criminal Law Act 1977 of conspiracy to commit an offence listed in this Part of this Schedule.

Domestic Violence, Crime and Victims Act 2004

(2004, c. 28)

PART 1 DOMESTIC VIOLENCE ETC.

Causing or allowing the death of a child or vulnerable adult

5 The offence

(1) A person ('D') is guilty of an offence if—

(a) a child or vulnerable adult ('V') dies or suffers serious physical harm as a result of the unlawful act of a person who—

(i) was a member of the same household as V, and

(ii) had frequent contact with him,

(b) D was such a person at the time of that act,

(c) at that time there was a significant risk of serious physical harm being caused to V by the unlawful act of such a person, and

(d) either D was the person whose act caused the death or serious physical harm or—

(i) D was, or ought to have been, aware of the risk mentioned in paragraph (c),

(ii) D failed to take such steps as he could reasonably have been expected to take to protect V from the risk, and

(iii) the act occurred in circumstances of the kind that D foresaw or ought to have foreseen.

(2) The prosecution does not have to prove whether it is the first alternative in subsection (1)(d) or the second (sub-paragraphs (i) to (iii)) that applies.

(3) If D was not the mother or father of V—

(a) D may not be charged with an offence under this section if he was under the age of 16 at the time of the act that caused the death or serious physical harm;

(b) for the purposes of subsection (1)(d)(ii) D could not have been expected to take any such step as is referred to there before attaining that age.

(4) For the purposes of this section—

(a) a person is to be regarded as a 'member' of a particular household, even if he does not live in that household, if he visits it so often and for such periods of time that it is reasonable to regard him as a member of it;

(b) where V lived in different households at different times, 'the same household as V' refers to the household in which V was living at the time of the act that caused the death or serious physical harm.

(5) For the purposes of this section an 'unlawful' act is one that—

(a) constitutes an offence, or

(a) would constitute an offence but for being the act of—

(i) a person under the age of ten, or

(ii) a person entitled to rely on a defence of insanity.

Paragraph (b) does not apply to an act of D.

(6) In this section—

'act' includes a course of conduct and also includes omission;

'child' means a person under the age of 16;

'serious' harm means harm that amounts to grievous bodily harm for the purposes of the Offences against the Person Act 1861;

'vulnerable adult' means a person aged 16 or over whose ability to protect himself from violence, abuse or neglect is significantly impaired through physical or mental disability or illness, through old age or otherwise.

(7) A person guilty of an offence under this section of causing or allowing a person's death is liable—

(a) on conviction on indictment in England and Wales, to imprisonment for life or to a fine, or to both;

(b) on conviction on indictment in Northern Ireland, to imprisonment for a term not exceeding 14 years or to a fine, or to both.

(8) A person guilty of an offence under this section of causing or allowing a person to suffer serious physical harm is liable—

(a) on conviction on indictment in England and Wales, to imprisonment for a term not exceeding 14 years or to a fine, or to both;

(b) on conviction on indictment in Northern Ireland, to imprisonment for a term not exceeding 10 years or to a fine, or to both.

6 Evidence and procedure in cases of death: England and Wales

(1) Subsections (2) to (4) apply where a person ('the defendant') is charged in the same proceedings with an offence of murder or manslaughter and with an offence under section 5 in respect of the same death ('the section 5 offence').

(2) Where by virtue of section 35(3) of the Criminal Justice and Public Order Act 1994 a court or jury is permitted, in relation to the section 5 offence, to draw such inferences as appear proper from the defendant's failure to give evidence or refusal to answer a question, the court or jury may also draw such inferences in determining whether he is guilty—

(a) of murder or manslaughter, or

(b) of any other offence of which he could lawfully be convicted on the charge of murder or manslaughter,

even if there would otherwise be no case for him to answer in relation to that offence.

(3) The charge of murder or manslaughter is not to be dismissed under paragraph 2 of Schedule 3 to the Crime and Disorder Act 1998 (unless the section 5 offence is dismissed).

(4) At the defendant's trial the question whether there is a case for the defendant to answer on the charge of murder or manslaughter is not to be considered before the close of all the evidence (or, if at some earlier time he ceases to be charged with the section 5 offence, before that earlier time).

(5) An offence under section 5 of causing or allowing a person's death is an offence of homicide for the purposes of the following enactments—

sections 24 and 25 of the Magistrates' Courts Act 1980 (c. 43) (mode of trial of child or young person for indictable offence);

section 51A of the Crime and Disorder Act 1998 (sending cases to the Crown Court: children and young persons);

section 25 of the Sentencing Code (power and duty to remit young offenders to youth courts for sentence).

6A Evidence and procedure in cases of serious physical harm: England and Wales

(1) Subsections (3) to (5) apply where a person ('the defendant') is charged in the same proceedings with a relevant offence and with an offence under section 5 in respect of the same harm ('the section 5 offence').

(2) In this section 'relevant offence' means—

(a) an offence under section 18 or 20 of the Offences against the Person Act 1861 (grievous bodily harm etc.);

(b) an offence under section 1 of the Criminal Attempts Act 1981 of attempting to commit murder;

(c) an offence under section 75A of the Serious Crime Act 2015 (strangulation or suffocation).

(3) Where by virtue of section 35(3) of the Criminal Justice and Public Order Act 1994 a court or jury is permitted, in relation to the section 5 offence, to draw such inferences as appear proper from the defendant's failure to give evidence or refusal to answer a question, the court or jury may also draw such inferences in determining whether the defendant is guilty of a relevant offence, even if there would otherwise be no case for the defendant to answer in relation to that offence.

(4) The charge of the relevant offence is not to be dismissed under paragraph 2 of Schedule 3 to the Crime and Disorder Act 1998 (unless the section 5 offence is dismissed).

(5) At the defendant's trial the question whether there is a case for the defendant to answer on the charge of the relevant offence is not to be considered before the close of all the evidence (or, if at some earlier time the defendant ceases to be charged with the section 5 offence, before that earlier time).

Coroners and Justice Act 2009

(2009, c. 25)

PART 2 CRIMINAL OFFENCES

Chapter 1 Murder, Infanticide and Suicide

Partial defence to murder: loss of control

54 Partial defence to murder: loss of control

(1) Where a person ('D') kills or is a party to the killing of another ('V'), D is not to be convicted of murder if—

(a) D's acts and omissions in doing or being a party to the killing resulted from D's loss of self-control,

(b) the loss of self-control had a qualifying trigger, and

(c) a person of D's sex and age, with a normal degree of tolerance and self-restraint and in the circumstances of D, might have reacted in the same or in a similar way to D.

(2) For the purposes of subsection (1)(a), it does not matter whether or not the loss of control was sudden.

(3) In subsection (1)(c) the reference to 'the circumstances of D' is a reference to all of D's circumstances other than those whose only relevance to D's conduct is that they bear on D's general capacity for tolerance or self-restraint.

(4) Subsection (1) does not apply if, in doing or being a party to the killing, D acted in a considered desire for revenge.

(5) On a charge of murder, if sufficient evidence is adduced to raise an issue with respect to the defence under subsection (1), the jury must assume that the defence is satisfied unless the prosecution proves beyond reasonable doubt that it is not.

(6) For the purposes of subsection (5), sufficient evidence is adduced to raise an issue with respect to the defence if evidence is adduced on which, in the opinion of the trial judge, a jury, properly directed, could reasonably conclude that the defence might apply.

(7) A person who, but for this section, would be liable to be convicted of murder is liable instead to be convicted of manslaughter.

(8) The fact that one party to a killing is by virtue of this section not liable to be convicted of murder does not affect the question whether the killing amounted to murder in the case of any other party to it.

55 Meaning of 'qualifying trigger'

(1) This section applies for the purposes of section 54.

(2) A loss of self-control had a qualifying trigger if subsection (3), (4) or (5) applies.

(3) This subsection applies if D's loss of self-control was attributable to D's fear of serious violence from V against D or another identified person.

(4) This subsection applies if D's loss of self-control was attributable to a thing or things done or said (or both) which—

(a) constituted circumstances of an extremely grave character, and

(b) caused D to have a justifiable sense of being seriously wronged.

(5) This subsection applies if D's loss of self-control was attributable to a combination of the matters mentioned in subsections (3) and (4).

(6) In determining whether a loss of self-control had a qualifying trigger—

(a) D's fear of serious violence is to be disregarded to the extent that it was caused by a thing which D incited to be done or said for the purpose of providing an excuse to use violence;

(b) a sense of being seriously wronged by a thing done or said is not justifiable if D incited the thing to be done or said for the purpose of providing an excuse to use violence;

(c) the fact that a thing done or said constituted sexual infidelity is to be disregarded.

(7) In this section references to 'D' and 'V' are to be construed in accordance with section 54.

Chapter 2 Anonymity of Witnesses

Witness anonymity orders

86 Witness anonymity orders

(1) In this Chapter a 'witness anonymity order' is an order made by a court that requires such specified measures to be taken in relation to a witness in criminal proceedings as the court considers appropriate to ensure that the identity of the witness is not disclosed in or in connection with the proceedings.

(2) The kinds of measures that may be required to be taken in relation to a witness include measures for securing one or more of the following—

(a) that the witness's name and other identifying details may be—

(i) withheld;

(ii) removed from materials disclosed to any party to the proceedings;

(b) that the witness may use a pseudonym;

(c) that the witness is not asked questions of any specified description that might lead to the identification of the witness;

(d) that the witness is screened to any specified extent;

(e) that the witness's voice is subjected to modulation to any specified extent.

(3) Subsection (2) does not affect the generality of subsection (1).

(4) Nothing in this section authorises the court to require—

(a) the witness to be screened to such an extent that the witness cannot be seen by—

(i) the judge or other members of the court (if any), or

(ii) the jury (if there is one);

(b) the witness's voice to be modulated to such an extent that the witness's natural voice cannot be heard by any persons within paragraph (a)(i) or (ii).

(5) In this section 'specified' means specified in the witness anonymity order concerned.

87 Applications

(1) An application for a witness anonymity order to be made in relation to a witness in criminal proceedings may be made to the court by the prosecutor or the defendant.

(2) Where an application is made by the prosecutor, the prosecutor—

(a) must (unless the court directs otherwise) inform the court of the identity of the witness, but

(b) is not required to disclose in connection with the application—

(i) the identity of the witness, or

(ii) any information that might enable the witness to be identified,

to any other party to the proceedings or his or her legal representatives.

(3) Where an application is made by the defendant, the defendant—

(a) must inform the court and the prosecutor of the identity of the witness, but

(b) (if there is more than one defendant) is not required to disclose in connection with the application—
(i) the identity of the witness, or
(ii) any information that might enable the witness to be identified,
to any other defendant or his or her legal representatives.

(4) Accordingly, where the prosecutor or the defendant proposes to make an application under this section in respect of a witness, any relevant material which is disclosed by or on behalf of that party before the determination of the application may be disclosed in such a way as to prevent—
(a) the identity of the witness, or
(b) any information that might enable the witness to be identified,
from being disclosed except as required by subsection (2)(a) or (3)(a).

(5) 'Relevant material' means any document or other material which falls to be disclosed, or is sought to be relied on, by or on behalf of the party concerned in connection with the proceedings or proceedings preliminary to them.

(6) The court must give every party to the proceedings the opportunity to be heard on an application under this section.

(7) But subsection (6) does not prevent the court from hearing one or more parties in the absence of a defendant and his or her legal representatives, if it appears to the court to be appropriate to do so in the circumstances of the case.

(8) Nothing in this section is to be taken as restricting any power to make rules of court.

88 Conditions for making order

(1) This section applies where an application is made for a witness anonymity order to be made in relation to a witness in criminal proceedings.

(2) The court may make such an order only if it is satisfied that Conditions A to C below are met.

(3) Condition A is that the proposed order is necessary—
(a) in order to protect the safety of the witness or another person or to prevent any serious damage to property, or
(b) in order to prevent real harm to the public interest (whether affecting the carrying on of any activities in the public interest or the safety of a person involved in carrying on such activities, or otherwise).

(4) Condition B is that, having regard to all the circumstances, the effect of the proposed order would be consistent with the defendant receiving a fair trial.

(5) Condition C is that the importance of the witness's testimony is such that in the interests of justice the witness ought to testify and—
(a) the witness would not testify if the proposed order were not made, or
(b) there would be real harm to the public interest if the witness were to testify without the proposed order being made.

(6) In determining whether the proposed order is necessary for the purpose mentioned in subsection (3)(a), the court must have regard (in particular) to any reasonable fear on the part of the witness—
(a) that the witness or another person would suffer death or injury, or
(b) that there would be serious damage to property,
if the witness were to be identified.

89 Relevant considerations

(1) When deciding whether Conditions A to C in section 88 are met in the case of an application for a witness anonymity order, the court must have regard to—
(a) the considerations mentioned in subsection (2) below, and
(b) such other matters as the court considers relevant.

(2) The considerations are—
(a) the general right of a defendant in criminal proceedings to know the identity of a witness in the proceedings;
(b) the extent to which the credibility of the witness concerned would be a relevant factor when the weight of his or her evidence comes to be assessed;

(c) whether evidence given by the witness might be the sole or decisive evidence implicating the defendant;
(d) whether the witness's evidence could be properly tested (whether on grounds of credibility or otherwise) without his or her identity being disclosed;
(e) whether there is any reason to believe that the witness—
(i) has a tendency to be dishonest, or
(ii) has any motive to be dishonest in the circumstances of the case,
having regard (in particular) to any previous convictions of the witness and to any relationship between the witness and the defendant or any associates of the defendant;
(f) whether it would be reasonably practicable to protect the witness by any means other than by making a witness anonymity order specifying the measures that are under consideration by the court.

90 Warning to jury

(1) Subsection (2) applies where, on a trial on indictment with a jury, any evidence has been given by a witness at a time when a witness anonymity order applied to the witness.

(2) The judge must give the jury such warning as the judge considers appropriate to ensure that the fact that the order was made in relation to the witness does not prejudice the defendant.

Discharge and variation

91 Discharge or variation of order

(1) A court that has made a witness anonymity order in relation to any criminal proceedings may in those proceedings subsequently discharge or vary (or further vary) the order if it appears to the court to be appropriate to do so in view of the provisions of sections 88 and 89 that apply to the making of an order.

(2) The court may do so—
(a) on an application made by a party to the proceedings if there has been a material change of circumstances since the relevant time, or
(b) on its own initiative.

(3) The court must give every party to the proceedings the opportunity to be heard—
(a) before determining an application made to it under subsection (2);
(b) before discharging or varying the order on its own initiative.

(4) But subsection (3) does not prevent the court hearing one or more of the parties to the proceedings in the absence of a defendant in the proceedings and his or her legal representatives, if it appears to the court to be appropriate to do so in the circumstances of the case.

(5) 'The relevant time' means—
(a) the time when the order was made, or
(b) if a previous application has been made under subsection (2), the time when the application (or the last application) was made.

92 Discharge or variation after proceedings

(1) This section applies if—
(a) a court has made a witness anonymity order in relation to a witness in criminal proceedings ('the old proceedings'), and
(b) the old proceedings have come to an end.

(2) The court that made the order may discharge or vary (or further vary) the order if it appears to the court to be appropriate to do so in view of—
(a) the provisions of sections 88 and 89 that apply to the making of a witness anonymity order, and
(b) such other matters as the court considers relevant.

(3) The court may do so—
(a) on an application made by a party to the old proceedings if there has been a material change of circumstances since the relevant time, or
(b) on an application made by the witness if there has been a material change of circumstances since the relevant time.

(4) The court may not determine an application made to it under subsection (3) unless in the case of each of the parties to the old proceedings and the witness—

(a) it has given the person the opportunity to be heard, or

(b) it is satisfied that it is not reasonably practicable to communicate with the person.

(5) Subsection (4) does not prevent the court hearing one or more of the persons mentioned in that subsection in the absence of a person who was a defendant in the old proceedings and that person's legal representatives, if it appears to the court to be appropriate to do so in the circumstances of the case.

(6) 'The relevant time' means—

(a) the time when the old proceedings came to an end, or

(b) if a previous application has been made under subsection (3), the time when the application (or the last application) was made.

93 Discharge or variation by appeal court

(1) This section applies if—

(a) a court has made a witness anonymity order in relation to a witness in criminal proceedings ('the trial proceedings'), and

(b) a defendant in the trial proceedings has in those proceedings—

(i) been convicted,

(ii) been found not guilty by reason of insanity, or

(iii) been found to be under a disability and to have done the act charged in respect of an offence.

(2) The appeal court may in proceedings on or in connection with an appeal by the defendant from the trial proceedings discharge or vary (or further vary) the order if it appears to the court to be appropriate to do so in view of—

(a) the provisions of sections 88 and 89 that apply to the making of a witness anonymity order, and

(b) such other matters as the court considers relevant.

(3) The appeal court may not discharge or vary the order unless in the case of each party to the trial proceedings—

(a) it has given the person the opportunity to be heard, or

(b) it is satisfied that it is not reasonably practicable to communicate with the person.

(4) But subsection (3) does not prevent the appeal court hearing one or more of the parties to the trial proceedings in the absence of a person who was a defendant in the trial proceedings and that person's legal representatives, if it appears to the court to be appropriate to do so in the circumstances of the case.

(5) In this section a reference to the doing of an act includes a reference to a failure to act.

(6) 'Appeal court' means—

(a) the Court of Appeal,

(b) the Court of Appeal in Northern Ireland, or

(c) the Court Martial Appeal Court.

Police, Crime, Sentencing and Courts Act 2022

(2022, c. 32)

Chapter 3 Extraction of Information from Electronic Devices

37 Extraction of information from electronic devices; investigations of crime etc

(1) An authorised person may extract information stored on an electronic device from that device if—

(a) a user of the device has voluntarily provided the device to an authorised person, and

(b) that user has agreed to the extraction of information from the device by an authorised person.

(2) The power in subsection (1) may be exercised only for the purposes of—

(a) preventing, detecting, investigating or prosecuting crime,

(b) helping to locate a missing person, or

(c) protecting a child or an at-risk adult from neglect or physical, mental or emotional harm.

(3) The reference in subsection (2) to crime is a reference to—

(a) conduct which constitutes one or more criminal offences in any part of the United Kingdom, or

(b) conduct which, if it took place in any part of the United Kingdom, would constitute one or more criminal offences.

(4) For the purposes of subsection (2) an adult is an at-risk adult if the authorised person reasonably believes that the adult—

(a) is experiencing, or at risk of, neglect or physical, mental or emotional harm, and

(b) is unable to protect themselves against the neglect or harm or the risk of it.

(5) An authorised person may exercise the power in subsection (1) only if—

(a) in a case where the authorised person proposes to exercise the power for a purpose within subsection (2)(a), the authorised person reasonably believes that information stored on the electronic device is relevant to a reasonable line of enquiry which is being, or is to be, pursued by an authorised person,

(b) in a case where the authorised person proposes to exercise the power for a purpose within subsection (2)(b) or (c), the authorised person reasonably believes that information stored on the electronic device is relevant to that purpose, and

(c) in any case, the authorised person is satisfied that exercise of the power is necessary and proportionate to achieve the purpose within subsection (2) for which the person proposes to exercise the power.

(6) Subsection (7) applies if the authorised person thinks that, in exercising the power, there is a risk of obtaining information other than—

(a) information necessary for a purpose within subsection (2) for which the authorised person may exercise the power, or

(b) information necessary for a purpose within subsection (2) of section 41 (investigations of death) for which the authorised person may exercise the power in subsection (1) of that section.

(7) The authorised person must, to be satisfied that the exercise of the power in subsection (1) is proportionate, be satisfied that—

(a) there are no other means of obtaining the information sought by the authorised person which avoid that risk, or

(b) there are such other means, but it is not reasonably practicable to use them.

(8) Subsection (9) applies if the authorised person thinks that, in exercising the power in subsection (1), there is a risk of obtaining confidential information.

(9) The authorised person must, to be satisfied that the exercise of the power is proportionate—

(a) have regard to the matters in subsection (10), and

(b) be satisfied that—

(i) there are no other means of obtaining the information sought by the authorised person which avoid that risk, or

(ii) there are such other means, but it is not reasonably practicable to use them.

(10) The matters referred to in subsection (9)(a) are—

(a) the amount of confidential information likely to be stored on the device, and

(b) the potential relevance of the confidential information to—

(i) a purpose within subsection (2) for which the authorised person may exercise the power, or

(ii) a purpose within subsection (2) of section 41 for which the authorised person may exercise the power in subsection (1) of that section.

(11) An authorised person must have regard to the code of practice for the time being in force under section 42 in exercising, or deciding whether to exercise, the power in subsection (1).

(12) This section does not affect any power relating to the extraction or production of information, or any power to seize any item or obtain any information, conferred by an enactment or rule of law.

(13) In this Chapter—

'adult' means a person aged 18 or over;

'authorised person' has the meaning given by subsection (1) of section 44 (subject to subsections (2) and (3) of that section);

'child means a person aged under 18;

'confidential information' has the meaning given by section 43;

'criminal offence' includes—

(a) a service offence within the meaning of the Armed Forces Act 2006, and
(b) an SDA offence within the meaning of the Armed Forces Act 2006 (Transitional Provisions etc) Order 2009 (S.I. 2009/1059);

'electronic device' means any device on which information is capable of being stored electronically and includes any component of such a device;

'enactment' includes—

(a) an enactment contained in subordinate legislation within the meaning of the Interpretation Act 1978,
(b) an enactment contained in, or in an instrument made under, an Act of the Scottish Parliament,
(c) an enactment contained in, or in an instrument made under, an Act or Measure of Senedd Cymru, and
(d) an enactment contained in, or in an instrument made under, Northern Ireland legislation;

'information' includes moving or still images and sounds;

'user', in relation to an electronic device, means a person who ordinarily uses the device.

(14) References in this Chapter to the extraction of information include its reproduction in any form.

(15) This section is subject to sections 38 (children, and adults without capacity), 39 (requirements for voluntary provision and agreement) and 40 (persons who have died etc).

38 Application of section 37 to children and adults without capacity

(1) A child is not to be treated for the purposes of section 37(1) as being capable of—

(a) voluntarily providing an electronic device to an authorised person for those purposes, or
(b) agreeing for those purposes to the extraction of information from the device by an authorised person.

(2) If a child is a user of an electronic device, a person who is not a user of the device but is listed in subsection (3) may—

(a) voluntarily provide the device to an authorised person for the purposes of section 37(1), and
(b) agree for those purposes to the extraction of information from the device by an authorised person.

(3) The persons mentioned in subsection (2) are—

(a) a parent or guardian of the child or, if the child is in the care of a relevant authority or voluntary organisation, a person representing that authority or organisation, or
(b) if no person within paragraph (a) is available, any responsible person who is aged 18 or over other than a relevant authorised person.

(4) Before exercising the power under section 37(1) by virtue of subsection (2), an authorised person must, so far as it is reasonably practicable to do so—

(a) ascertain the views of the child, and
(b) have regard to any views so ascertained, taking account of the child's age and maturity.

(5) If an authorised person ('A') exercises the power under section 37(1) as a result of action taken under subsection (2) by a person within subsection (3)(b), A must, unless A considers that it is not appropriate to do so, inform a person within subsection (3)(a) that A has exercised the power.

(6) An adult without capacity is not to be treated for the purposes of section 37(1) as being capable of—

(a) voluntarily providing an electronic device to an authorised person for those purposes, or

(b) agreeing for those purposes to the extraction of information from the device by an authorised person.

(7) If a user of an electronic device is an adult without capacity, a person who is not a user of the device but is listed in subsection (8) may—

(a) voluntarily provide the device to an authorised person for the purposes of section 37(1), and

(b) agree for those purposes to the extraction of information from the device by an authorised person.

(8) The persons mentioned in subsection (7) are—

(a) a parent or guardian of the adult without capacity or, if the adult without capacity is in the care of a relevant authority or voluntary organisation, a person representing that authority or organisation,

(b) a registered social worker,

(c) a person who, under a power of attorney, may make decisions for the purposes of subsection (7)(a) and (b) on behalf of the adult without capacity,

(d) . . .*

(e) . . .** or

(f) if no person within any of paragraphs (a) to (e) is available, any responsible person who is aged 18 or over other than a relevant authorised person.

(9) Nothing in this section prevents any other user of an electronic device who is not a child or an adult without capacity from—

(a) voluntarily providing the device to an authorised person for the purposes of section 37(1), or

(b) agreeing for those purposes to the extraction of information from the device by an authorised person.

(10) For the purposes of this Chapter a person is an adult without capacity if—

(a) in relation to England and Wales, the person is an adult who, within the meaning of the Mental Capacity Act 2005, lacks capacity to do the things mentioned in section 37(1)(a) and (b);

(b) . . .***

(c) . . .****

(11) In this Chapter—

'local authority'—

(a) in relation to England, means a county council, a district council for an area for which there is no county council, a London borough council or the Common Council of the City of London in its capacity as a local authority;

(b) in relation to Wales, means a county council or a county borough council;

(c) . . .*****

'registered social worker' means a person registered as a social worker in a register maintained by—

(a) Social Work England,

(b) the Care Council for Wales,

* **Editor's Note:** Applies to Northern Ireland.

** **Editor's Note:** Applies to Scotland.

*** **Editor's Note:** Applies to Scotland.

**** **Editor's Note:** Applies to Northern Ireland.

***** **Editor's Note:** Applies to Scotland.

(c) . . .*
(d) . . .**

'relevant authorised person', in relation to the extraction of information from an electronic device for a particular purpose, means an authorised person who may extract the information from the device for that purpose;

'relevant authority'—
(a) in relation to England and Wales and Scotland, means a local authority;
(b) . . .***

'voluntary organisation'—
(a) in relation to England and Wales, has the same meaning as in the Children Act 1989;
(b) . . .****
(c) . . .*****

(12) This section is subject to section 39 (requirements for voluntary provision and agreement).

39 Requirements for voluntary provision and agreement

(1) A person ('P') is to be treated for the purposes of section 37 or 38 as having—
(a) voluntarily provided an electronic device to an authorised person, and
(b) agreed to the extraction of information from the device by an authorised person,
only if the requirements of this section have been met.

(2) An authorised person must not have placed undue pressure on P to provide the device or agree to the extraction of information from it.

(3) An authorised person must have given P notice in writing—
(a) specifying or describing the information that is sought,
(b) specifying the reason why the information is sought,
(c) specifying how the information will be dealt with once it has been extracted,
(d) stating that P may refuse to provide the device or agree to the extraction of information from it, and
(e) stating that the investigation or enquiry for the purposes of which the information is sought will not be brought to an end merely because P refuses to provide the device or agree to the extraction of information from it.

(4) Subject to subsection (5), P must have confirmed in writing that P has—
(a) voluntarily provided the device to an authorised person, and
(b) agreed to the extraction of information from the device by an authorised person.

(5) If P was unable to provide that confirmation in writing as a result of P's physical impairment or lack of literacy skills—
(a) P must have given that confirmation orally, and
(b) an authorised person must have recorded P's confirmation in writing.

(6) If P's confirmation was given in writing and in hard copy form, the authorised person must have given P a copy of that confirmation (in hard copy or electronic form).

(7) If P's confirmation was given orally, the authorised person must have given P a copy of the record of that confirmation (in hard copy or electronic form).

40 Application of section 37 where user has died etc

(1) If any of conditions A to C is met, an authorised person may exercise the power in section 37(1) to extract information stored on an electronic device from that device even though—
(a) the device has not been voluntarily provided to an authorised person by a user of the device, or

* **Editor's Note:** Applies to Scotland.
** **Editor's Note:** Applies to Northern Ireland.
*** **Editor's Note:** Applies to Northern Ireland.
**** **Editor's Note:** Applies to Scotland.
***** **Editor's Note:** Applies to Northern Ireland.

(b) no user of the device has agreed to the extraction of information from the device by an authorised person.

(2) Condition A is that—

(a) a person who was a user of the electronic device has died, and

(b) the person was a user of the device immediately before their death.

(3) Condition B is that—

(a) a user of the electronic device is a child or an adult without capacity, and

(b) an authorised person reasonably believes that the user's life is at risk or there is a risk of serious harm to the user.

(4) Condition C is that—

(a) a person who was a user of the electronic device is missing,

(b) the person was a user of the device immediately before they went missing, and

(c) an authorised person reasonably believes that the person's life is at risk or there is a risk of serious harm to the person.

(5) The exercise of the power in subsection (1) of section 37 by virtue of this section is subject to that section.

41 Extraction of information from electronic devices: investigations of death

(1) An authorised person may extract information stored on an electronic device from that device if—

(a) a person who was a user of the electronic device has died, and

(b) the person was a user of the device immediately before their death.

(2) The power in subsection (1) may be exercised only for the purposes of—

(a) an investigation into the person's death under Chapter 1 of Part 1 of the Coroners and Justice Act 2009,

(b) . . .*

(c) . . .**

(3) References in subsection (2) to the exercise of the power in subsection (1) for the purposes of an investigation or inquest include references to the exercise of that power for the purposes of determining whether an investigation should be conducted or an inquest should be held.

(4) An authorised person may exercise the power in subsection (1) only if—

(a) the authorised person reasonably believes that information stored on the electronic device is relevant to a purpose within subsection (2), and

(b) the authorised person is satisfied that exercise of the power is necessary and proportionate to achieve that purpose.

(5) Subsection (6) applies if the authorised person thinks that, in exercising the power, there is a risk of obtaining information other than—

(a) information necessary for a purpose within subsection (2), or

(b) information necessary for a purpose within section 37(2).

(6) The authorised person must, to be satisfied that the exercise of the power is proportionate, be satisfied that—

(a) there are no other means of obtaining the information sought by the authorised person which avoid that risk, or

(b) there are such other means, but it is not reasonably practicable to use them.

(7) Subsection (8) applies if the authorised person thinks that, in exercising the power in subsection (1), there is a risk of obtaining confidential information.

(8) The authorised person must, to be satisfied that the exercise of the power is proportionate—

(a) have regard to the matters in subsection (9), and

(b) be satisfied that—

* **Editor's Note:** Applies to Northern Ireland.

** **Editor's Note:** Applies to Scotland.

(i) there are no other means of obtaining the information sought by the authorised person which avoid that risk, or
(ii) there are such other means, but it is not reasonably practicable to use them.

(9) The matters referred to in subsection (8)(a) are—
(a) the amount of confidential information likely to be stored on the device, and
(b) the potential relevance of the confidential information to a purpose within subsection (2) or section 37(2).

(10) An authorised person must have regard to the code of practice for the time being in force under section 42 in exercising, or deciding whether to exercise, the power in subsection (1).

(11) This section does not affect any power relating to the extraction or production of information, or any power to seize any item or obtain any information, conferred by an enactment or rule of law.

42 Code of practice about the extraction of information

(1) The Secretary of State must prepare a code of practice containing guidance about the exercise of the powers in sections 37(1) and 41(1).

(2) The code may make different provision for different purposes or areas.

(3) In preparing the code, the Secretary of State must consult—
(a) the Information Commissioner,
(b) the Scottish Ministers,
(c) the Department of Justice in Northern Ireland,
(d) the Commissioner for Victims and Witnesses,
(e) the Domestic Abuse Commissioner,
(f) the Commission for Victims and Survivors for Northern Ireland, and
(g) such other persons as the Secretary of State considers appropriate.

(4) . . .*

(5) After preparing the code, the Secretary of State must lay it before Parliament and publish it.

(6) The code is to be brought into force by regulations made by statutory instrument.

(7) A statutory instrument containing regulations under subsection (6) is subject to annulment in pursuance of a resolution of either House of Parliament.

(8) After the code has come into force the Secretary of State may from time to time revise it.

(9) A failure on the part of an authorised person to act in accordance with the code does not of itself render the person liable to any criminal or civil proceedings.

(10) But the code is admissible in evidence in criminal or civil proceedings and a court may take into account a failure to act in accordance with it in determining a question in the proceedings.

(11) References in subsections (2) to (10) to the code include a revised code, subject to subsection (12).

(12) The duty to consult in subsection (3) does not apply in relation to the preparation of a revised code if the Secretary of State considers that the proposed revisions are insubstantial.

43 Confidential information

(1) In this Chapter 'confidential information' means information which constitutes or may constitute—
(a) confidential journalistic material within the meaning of the Investigatory Powers Act 2016 (see section 264(6) and (7) of that Act), or
(b) protected material.

(2) In subsection (1)(b) 'protected material'—
(a) in relation to England and Wales means—
(i) items subject to legal privilege, within the meaning of the Police and Criminal Evidence Act 1984 (see section 10 of that Act),
(ii) material falling within section 11(1)(a) of that Act (certain personal records held in confidence), or

* **Editor's Note:** Applies to Northern Ireland.

(iii) material to which section 14(2) of that Act applies (other material acquired in the course of a trade etc that is held in confidence);

(b) . . .*

(c) . . .**

44 Authorised persons

(1) Subject to subsections (2) and (3), in this Chapter 'authorised person' means a person listed in Schedule 3.

(2) The power in subsection (1) of section 37 may be exercised for a purpose mentioned in subsection (2)(b) or (c) of that section only by a person listed in Part 1 or 2 of Schedule 3.

(3) The power in section 41(1) may be exercised only by a person listed in Part 1 of Schedule 3.

(4) The Secretary of State may by regulations made by statutory instrument amend Schedule 3—

(a) so as to add a reference to a person;

(b) so as to remove a reference to a person;

(c) so as to modify a description of a person mentioned in that Schedule.

(5) Regulations under subsection (4) may contain transitional, transitory or saving provision.

(6) . . .***

(7) . . .****

(8) Subject to subsection (9), a statutory instrument containing regulations under subsection (4)(a) (whether alone or with other provision) may not be made unless a draft of the instrument has been laid before and approved by a resolution of each House of Parliament.

(9) Subsection (8) does not apply to a statutory instrument containing regulations which—

(a) remove a reference to a person from Part 1 of Schedule 3 and add a reference to that person to Part 2 or 3 of that Schedule, or

(b) remove a reference to a person from Part 2 of that Schedule and add a reference to that person to Part 3 of that Schedule.

(10) A statutory instrument containing—

(a) regulations under subsection (4)(a) to which subsection (9) applies, or

(b) regulations under subsection (4)(b) or (c),

and which is not a statutory instrument to which subsection (8) applies is subject to annulment in pursuance of a resolution of either House of Parliament.

* **Editor's Note:** Applies to Scotland.

** **Editor's Note:** Applies to Northern Ireland.

*** **Editor's Note:** Applies to Scotland.

**** **Editor's Note:** Applies to Northern Ireland.

Part II

Criminal Proceedings—Codes, Rules, and Guidelines

Code of Practice for the Detention, Treatment and Questioning of Persons by Police Officers (Code C)

(2023)

1 General

1.0 The powers and procedures in this Code must be used fairly, responsibly, with respect for the people to whom they apply and without unlawful discrimination. Under the Equality Act 2010, section 149 (Public sector Equality Duty), police forces must, in carrying out their functions, have due regard to the need to eliminate unlawful discrimination, harassment, victimisation and any other conduct which is prohibited by that Act, to advance equality of opportunity between people who share a relevant protected characteristic and people who do not share it, and to foster good relations between those persons. The Equality Act *also* makes it unlawful for police officers to discriminate against, harass or victimise any person on the grounds of the 'protected characteristics' of age, disability, gender reassignment, race, religion or belief, sex and sexual orientation, marriage and civil partnership, pregnancy and maternity, when using their powers. See *Notes 1A* and *1AA*.

1.1 All persons in custody must be dealt with expeditiously, and released as soon as the need for detention no longer applies.

1.1A A custody officer must perform the functions in this Code as soon as practicable. A custody officer will not be in breach of this Code if delay is justifiable and reasonable steps are taken to prevent unnecessary delay. The custody record shall show when a delay has occurred and the reason. See *Note 1H*.

1.2 This Code of Practice must be readily available at all police stations for consultation by:

- police officers;
- police staff;
- detained persons;
- members of the public.

1.3 The provisions of this Code:

- include the *Annexes*
- do not include the *Notes for Guidance* which form guidance to police officers and others about its application and interpretation.

1.4 If at any time an officer has any reason to suspect that a person of any age may be vulnerable (see *paragraph 1.13(d)*), in the absence of clear evidence to dispel that suspicion, that person shall be treated as such for the purposes of this Code and to establish whether any such reason may exist in relation to a person suspected of committing an offence (see *paragraph 10.1 and Note 10A*), the custody officer in the case of a detained person, or the officer investigating the offence in the case of a person who has not been arrested or detained, shall take, or cause to be taken, (see *paragraph 3.5* and *Note 3F*) the following action:

(a) reasonable enquiries shall be made to ascertain what information is available that is relevant to any of the factors described in *paragraph 1.13(d)* as indicating that the person may be vulnerable might apply;

(b) a record shall be made describing whether any of those factors appear to apply and provide any reason to suspect that the person may be vulnerable or (as the case may be) may not be vulnerable; and
(c) the record mentioned in sub-paragraph (b) shall be made available to be taken into account by police officers, police staff and any others who, in accordance with the provisions of this or any other Code, are required or entitled to communicate with the person in question. This would include any solicitor, appropriate adult and health care professional and is particularly relevant to communication by telephone or by means of a live link (see *paragraphs 12.9A* (interviews), *13.12* (interpretation), and *15.3C, 15.11A, 15.11B, 15.11C* and *15.11D* (reviews and extension of detention)).

See *Notes 1G, 1GA, 1GB* and *1GC*.

1.5 Anyone who appears to be under 18, shall, in the absence of clear evidence that they are older be treated as a juvenile for the purposes of this Code and any other Code. *See Note 1L*

1.5A *Not used.*

1.6 If a person appears to be blind, seriously visually impaired, deaf, unable to read or speak or has difficulty orally because of a speech impediment, they shall be treated as such for the purposes of this Code in the absence of clear evidence to the contrary.

1.7 'The appropriate adult' means, in the case of a:

(a) juvenile:
  (i) the parent, guardian or, if the juvenile is in the care of a local authority or voluntary organisation, a person representing that authority or organisation (see *Note 1B*);
  (ii) a social worker of a local authority (see *Note 1C*);
  (iii) failing these, some other responsible adult aged 18 or over who is *not*:
    ~ a police officer;
    ~ employed by the police;
    ~ under the direction or control of the chief officer of a police force;
    ~ a person who provides services under contractual arrangements (but without being employed by the chief officer of a police force), to assist that force in relation to the discharge of its chief officer's functions,

  whether or not they are on duty at the time.

  See *Note 1F.*

(b) person who is vulnerable (See *paragraph 1.4* and *Note 1D*):
  (i) a relative, guardian or other person responsible for their care or custody;
  (ii) someone experienced in dealing with vulnerable persons but who is not:
    ~ a police officer;
    ~ employed by the police;
    ~ under the direction or control of the chief officer of a police force; or
    ~ a person who provides services under contractual arrangements (but without being employed by the chief officer of a police force), to assist that force in relation to the discharge of its chief officer's functions,

  whether or not they are on duty at the time;
  (iii) failing these, some other responsible adult aged 18 or over other than a person described in the bullet points in *sub-paragraph (b)(ii)* above.

  See *Note 1F.*

1.7A The role of the appropriate adult is to safeguard the rights, entitlements and welfare of juveniles and vulnerable persons (see *paragraphs 1.4* and *1.5*) to whom the provisions of this and any other Code of Practice apply. For this reason, the appropriate adult is expected, amongst other things, to:

- support, advise and assist them when, in accordance with this Code or any other Code of Practice, they are given or asked to provide information or participate in any procedure;
- observe whether the police are acting properly and fairly to respect their rights and entitlements, and inform an officer of the rank of inspector or above if they consider that they are not;

- assist them to communicate with the police whilst respecting their right to say nothing unless they want to as set out in the terms of the caution (*see paragraphs 10.5* and *10.6*);
- *help them to understand their rights and ensure that those rights are protected and respected* (*see paragraphs 3.15, 3.17, 6.5A* and *11.17*).

1.8 If this Code requires a person be given certain information, they do not have to be given it if at the time they are incapable of understanding what is said, are violent or may become violent or in urgent need of medical attention, but they must be given it as soon as practicable.

1.9 References to a custody officer include any police officer who, for the time being, is performing the functions of a custody officer.

1.9A When this Code requires the prior authority or agreement of an officer of at least inspector or superintendent rank, that authority may be given by a sergeant or chief inspector authorised to perform the functions of the higher rank under the Police and Criminal Evidence Act 1984 (PACE), section 107.

1.10 Subject to *paragraph 1.12*, this Code applies to people in custody at police stations in England and Wales, whether or not they have been arrested, and to those removed to a police station as a place of safety under the Mental Health Act 1983, sections 135 and 136, as amended by the Policing and Crime Act 2017 (see paragraph 3.16). *Section 15* applies solely to people in police detention, e.g. those brought to a police station under arrest or arrested at a police station for an offence after going there voluntarily.

1.11 No part of this Code applies to a detained person:

(a) to whom PACE Code H applies because:
- they are detained following arrest under section 41 of the Terrorism Act 2000 (TACT) and not charged; or
- an authorisation has been given under section 22 of the Counter-Terrorism Act 2008 (CTACT) (post-charge questioning of terrorist suspects) to interview them.

(ab) to whom PACE Code I applies because they are detained following arrest under section 27 of the National Security Act 2023.

(ac) to whom the Code of Practice issued under paragraph 56 of Schedule 3 to the Counter-Terrorism and Border Security Act 2019 applies because they are detained for examination under that Schedule.

(b) to whom the Code of Practice issued under paragraph 6 of Schedule 14 to TACT applies because they are detained for examination under Schedule 7 to TACT.

1.12 This Code does not apply to people in custody:

(i) arrested by officers under the Criminal Justice and Public Order Act 1994, section 136(2) on warrants issued in Scotland, or arrested or detained without warrant under section 137(2) by officers from a police force in Scotland. In these cases, police powers and duties and the person's rights and entitlements whilst at a police station in England or Wales are the same as those in Scotland;

(ii) arrested under the Immigration and Asylum Act 1999, section 142(3) in order to have their fingerprints taken;

(iii) whose detention has been authorised under Schedules 2 or 3 to the Immigration Act 1971 or section 62 of the Nationality, Immigration and Asylum Act 2002;

(iv) who are convicted or remanded prisoners held in police cells on behalf of the Prison Service under the Imprisonment (Temporary Provisions) Act 1980;

(v) *Not used.*

(vi) detained for searches under stop and search powers except as required by Code A.

The provisions on conditions of detention and treatment in *sections 8* and *9* must be considered as the minimum standards of treatment for such detainees.

1.13 In this Code:

(a) 'designated person' means a person other than a police officer, who has specified powers and duties conferred or imposed on them by designation under section 38 or 39 of the Police Reform Act 2002;

(b) reference to a police officer includes a designated person acting in the exercise or performance of the powers and duties conferred or imposed on them by their designation;

(c) if there is doubt as to whether the person should be treated, or continue to be treated, as being male or female in the case of:

(i) a search carried out or observed by a person of the same sex as the detainee; or

(ii) any other procedure which requires action to be taken or information to be given that depends on whether the person is to be treated as being male or female;

then the gender of the detainee and other parties concerned should be established and recorded in line with Annex L of this Code.

(d) 'vulnerable' applies to any person who, because of a mental health condition or mental disorder (see *Notes 1G and 1GB*):

(i) may have difficulty understanding or communicating effectively about the full implications for them of any procedures and processes connected with:

- their arrest and detention; or (as the case may be)
- their voluntary attendance at a police station or their presence elsewhere (see *paragraph 3.21*), for the purpose of a voluntary interview; and
- the exercise of their rights and entitlements.

(ii) does not appear to understand the significance of what they are told, of questions they are asked or of their replies:

(iii) appears to be particularly prone to:

- becoming confused and unclear about their position;
- providing unreliable, misleading or incriminating information without knowing or wishing to do so;
- accepting or acting on suggestions from others without consciously knowing or wishing to do so; or
- readily agreeing to suggestions or proposals without any protest or question.

(e) 'Live link' means:

(i) for the purpose of *paragraph 12.9A*; an arrangement by means of which the *interviewing officer* who is not present at the police station where the detainee is held, is able to see and hear, and to be seen and heard by, the detainee concerned, the detainee's solicitor, appropriate adult and interpreter (as applicable) and the officer who has custody of that detainee (see *Note 1N*).

(ii) for the purpose of *paragraph 15.9A*; an arrangement by means of which the *review officer* who is not present at the police station where the detainee is held, is able to see and hear, and to be seen and heard by, the detainee concerned and the detainee's solicitor, appropriate adult and interpreter (as applicable) (see *Note 1N*). The use of live link for decisions about detention under *section 45A of PACE* is subject to regulations made by the Secretary of State being in force.

(iii) for the purpose of *paragraph 15.11A*;an arrangement by means of which the *authorising officer* who is not present at the police station where the detainee is held, is able to see and hear, and to be seen and heard by, the detainee concerned and the detainee's solicitor, appropriate adult and interpreter (as applicable) (see *Note 1N*).

(iv) for the purpose of *paragraph 15.11C*; an arrangement by means of which the *detainee* when not present in the court where the hearing is being held, is able to see and hear, and to be seen and heard by, the court during the hearing (see *Note 1N*).

Note: Chief officers must be satisfied that live link used in their force area for the above purposes provides for accurate and secure communication between the detainee, the detainee's solicitor, appropriate adult and interpreter (as applicable). This includes ensuring that at any time during which the live link is being used: a person cannot see, hear or otherwise obtain access to any such communications unless so authorised or allowed by the custody officer or, in the case of an interview, the interviewer and that as applicable, the confidentiality of any private consultation between a suspect and their solicitor and appropriate adult is maintained.

1.14 Designated persons are entitled to use reasonable force as follows:

(a) when exercising a power conferred on them which allows a police officer exercising that power to use reasonable force, a designated person has the same entitlement to use force; and

(b) at other times when carrying out duties conferred or imposed on them that also entitle them to use reasonable force, for example:

- when at a police station carrying out the duty to keep detainees for whom they are responsible under control and to assist any police officer or designated person to keep any detainee under control and to prevent their escape;
- when securing, or assisting any police officer or designated person in securing, the detention of a person at a police station;
- when escorting, or assisting any police officer or designated person in escorting, a detainee within a police station;
- for the purpose of saving life or limb;
- or preventing serious damage to property.

1.15 Nothing in this Code prevents the custody officer, or other police officer or designated person (see *paragraph 1.13(a)*) given custody of the detainee by the custody officer, from allowing another person (see *(a)* and *(b)* below) to carry out individual procedures or tasks at the police station if the law allows. However, the officer or designated person given custody remains responsible for making sure the procedures and tasks are carried out correctly in accordance with the Codes of Practice (see *paragraph 3.5* and *Note 3F*). The other person who is allowed to carry out the procedures or tasks must be someone who *at that time*, is:

(a) under the direction and control of the chief officer of the force responsible for the police station in question; or

(b) providing services under contractual arrangements (but without being employed by the chief officer the police force), to assist a police force in relation to the discharge of its chief officer's functions.

1.16 Designated persons and others mentioned in *sub-paragraphs (a)* and *(b)* of *paragraph 1.15*, must have regard to any relevant provisions of the Codes of Practice.

1.17 In any provision of this or any other Code which allows or requires police officers or police staff to make a record in their report book, the reference to report book shall include any official report book or electronic recording device issued to them that enables the record in question to be made and dealt with in accordance with that provision. References in this and any other Code to written records, forms and signatures include electronic records and forms and electronic confirmation that identifies the person making the record or completing the form.

Chief officers must be satisfied as to the integrity and security of the devices, records and forms to which this *paragraph* applies and that use of those devices, records and forms satisfies relevant data protection legislation.

Notes for Guidance

1A Although certain sections of this Code apply specifically to people in custody at police stations, a person who attends a police station or other location voluntarily to assist with an investigation should be treated with no less consideration, e.g. offered or allowed refreshments at appropriate times, and enjoy an absolute right to obtain legal advice or communicate with anyone outside the police station or other location (see paragraphs 3.21 and 3.22).

*1AA In paragraph 1.0, under the Equality Act 2010, section 149, the 'relevant protected characteristics' are age, disability, gender reassignment, pregnancy and maternity, race, religion/belief and sex and sexual orientation. For further detailed guidance and advice on the Equality Act, see: https://*www.gov.uk/guidance/equality-act-2010-guidance.

1B A person, including a parent or guardian, should not be an appropriate adult if they:

- are:
  - ~ *suspected of involvement in the offence;*
  - ~ *the victim;*
  - ~ *a witness;*
  - ~ *involved in the investigation.*

- received admissions prior to attending to act as the appropriate adult.

Note: If a juvenile's parent is estranged from the juvenile, they should not be asked to act as the appropriate adult if the juvenile expressly and specifically objects to their presence.

1C If a juvenile admits an offence to, or in the presence of, a social worker or member of a youth offending team other than during the time that person is acting as the juvenile's appropriate adult, another appropriate adult should be appointed in the interest of fairness.

1D In the case of someone who is vulnerable, it may be more satisfactory if the appropriate adult is someone experienced or trained in their care rather than a relative lacking such qualifications. But if the person prefers a relative to a better qualified stranger or objects to a particular person their wishes should, if practicable, be respected.

1E A detainee should always be given an opportunity, when an appropriate adult is called to the police station, to consult privately with a solicitor in the appropriate adult's absence if they want. An appropriate adult is not subject to legal privilege.

1F An appropriate adult who is not a parent or guardian in the case of a juvenile, or a relative, guardian or carer in the case of a vulnerable person, must be independent of the police as their role is to safeguard the person's rights and entitlements. Additionally, a solicitor or independent custody visitor who is present at the police station and acting in that capacity, may not be the appropriate adult.

1G A person may be vulnerable as a result of a having a mental health condition or mental disorder. Similarly, simply because an individual does not have, or is not known to have, any such condition or disorder, does not mean that they are not vulnerable for the purposes of this Code. It is therefore important that the custody officer in the case of a detained person or the officer investigating the offence in the case of a person who has not been arrested or detained, as appropriate, considers on a case by case basis, whether any of the factors described in paragraph 1.13(d) might apply to the person in question. In doing so, the officer must take into account the particular circumstances of the individual and how the nature of the investigation might affect them and bear in mind that juveniles, by virtue of their age will always require an appropriate adult.

1GA For the purposes of paragraph 1.4(a), examples of relevant information that may be available include:

- *the behaviour of the adult or juvenile;*
- *the mental health and capacity of the adult or juvenile;*
- *what the adult or juvenile says about themselves;*
- *information from relatives and friends of the adult or juvenile;*
- *information from police officers and staff and from police records;*
- *information from health and social care (including liaison and diversion services) and other professionals who know, or have had previous contact with, the individual and may be able to contribute to assessing their need for help and support from an appropriate adult. This includes contacts and assessments arranged by the police or at the request of the individual or (as applicable) their appropriate adult or solicitor.*

1GB The Mental Health Act 1983 Code of Practice at page 26 describes the range of clinically recognised conditions which can fall with the meaning of mental disorder for the purpose of paragraph 1.13(d). The Code is published here:

https://www.gov.uk/government/publications/code-of-practice-mental-health-act-1983.

1GC When a person is under the influence of drink and/or drugs, it is not intended that they are to be treated as vulnerable and requiring an appropriate adult for the purpose of paragraph 1.4 unless other information indicates that any of the factors described in paragraph 1.13(d) may apply to that person. When the person has recovered from the effects of drink and/or drugs, they should be re-assessed in accordance with paragraph 1.4. See paragraph 15.4A for application to live link.

1H Paragraph 1.1A is intended to cover delays which may occur in processing detainees e.g. if:

- *a large number of suspects are brought into the station simultaneously to be placed in custody;*
- *interview rooms are all being used;*
- *there are difficulties contacting an appropriate adult, solicitor or interpreter.*

1I The custody officer must remind the appropriate adult and detainee about the right to legal advice and record any reasons for waiving it in accordance with section 6.

1J Not used.

1K This Code does not affect the principle that all citizens have a duty to help police officers to prevent crime and discover offenders. This is a civic rather than a legal duty; but when police officers are trying to discover whether, or by whom, offences have been committed they are entitled to question any person from whom they think useful information can be obtained, subject to the restrictions imposed by this Code. A person's declaration that they are unwilling to reply does not alter this entitlement.

1L Paragraph 1.5 reflects the statutory definition of 'arrested juvenile' in section 37(15) of PACE. This section was amended by section 42 of the Criminal Justice and Courts Act 2015 with effect from 26 October 2015, and includes anyone who appears to be under the age of 18. This definition applies for the purposes of the detention and bail provisions in sections 34 to 51 of PACE. With effect from 3 April 2017, amendments made by the Policing and Crime Act 2017 require persons under the age of 18 to be treated as juveniles for the purposes of all other provisions of PACE and the Codes.

1M Not used.

1N For the purpose of the provisions of PACE that allow a live link to be used, any impairment of the detainee's eyesight or hearing is to be disregarded. This means that if a detainee's eyesight or hearing is impaired, the arrangements which would be needed to ensure effective communication if all parties were physically present in the same location, for example, using sign language, would apply to the live link arrangements.

2 Custody records

2.1A When a person:

- is brought to a police station under arrest
- is arrested at the police station having attended there voluntarily or attends a police station to answer bail

they must be brought before the custody officer as soon as practicable after their arrival at the station or if applicable, following their arrest after attending the police station voluntarily. This applies to both designated and non-designated police stations. A person is deemed to be 'at a police station' for these purposes if they are within the boundary of any building or enclosed yard which forms part of that police station.

2.1 A separate custody record must be opened as soon as practicable for each person brought to a police station under arrest or arrested at the station having gone there voluntarily or attending a police station in answer to street bail. All information recorded under this Code must be recorded as soon as practicable in the custody record unless otherwise specified. Any audio or video recording made in the custody area is not part of the custody record.

2.2 If any action requires the authority of an officer of a specified rank, subject to *paragraph 2.6A*, their name and rank must be noted in the custody record.

2.3 The custody officer is responsible for the custody record's accuracy and completeness and for making sure the record or copy of the record accompanies a detainee if they are transferred to another police station. The record shall show the:

- time and reason for transfer;
- time a person is released from detention.

2.3A If a person is arrested and taken to a police station as a result of a search in the exercise of any stop and search power to which PACE Code A (Stop and search) or the 'search powers code' issued under TACT applies, the officer carrying out the search is responsible for ensuring that the record of that stop and search is made as part of the person's custody record. The custody officer must then ensure that the person is asked if they want a copy of the search record and if they do, that they are given a copy as soon as practicable. The person's entitlement to a copy of the search record which is made as part of their custody record is in addition to, and does not affect, their entitlement to a copy of their custody record or any other provisions of section 2 (Custody records) of this Code. (See Code A *paragraph 4.2B* and the TACT search powers code *paragraph 5.3.5*).

2.4 The detainee's solicitor and appropriate adult must be permitted to inspect the whole of the detainee's custody record as soon as practicable after their arrival at the station and at any other time on request, whilst the person is detained. This includes the following *specific* records relating to the reasons for the detainee's arrest and detention and the offence concerned to which *paragraph 3.1(b)* refers:

(a) The information about the circumstances and reasons for the detainee's arrest as recorded in the custody record in accordance with *paragraph 4.3 of Code G*. This applies to any further offences for which the detainee is arrested whilst in custody;

(b) The record of the grounds for each authorisation to keep the person in custody. The authorisations to which this applies are the same as those described at items *(i)(a)* to *(d)* in the table in *paragraph 2* of *Annex M* of this Code.

Access to the records in *sub-paragraphs (a)* and *(b)* is *in addition* to the requirements in *paragraphs 3.4(b), 11.1A, 15.0, 15,7A(c) and 16.7A* to make certain documents and materials available and to provide information about the offence and the reasons for arrest and detention.

Access to the custody record for the purposes of this paragraph must be arranged and agreed with the custody officer and may not unreasonably interfere with the custody officer's duties. A record shall be made when access is allowed and whether it includes the records described in *sub-paragraphs (a)* and *(b)* above.

2.4A When a detainee leaves police detention or is taken before a court they, their legal representative or appropriate adult shall be given, on request, a copy of the custody record as soon as practicable. This entitlement lasts for 12 months after release.

2.5 The detainee, appropriate adult or legal representative shall be permitted to inspect the original custody record after the detainee has left police detention provided they give reasonable notice of their request. Any such inspection shall be noted in the custody record.

2.6 Subject to *paragraph 2.6A*, all entries in custody records must be timed and signed by the maker. Records entered on computer shall be timed and contain the operator's identification.

2.6A Nothing in this Code requires the identity of officers or other police staff to be recorded or disclosed:

(a) *Not used.*

(b) if the officer or police staff reasonably believe recording or disclosing their name might put them in danger.

In these cases, they shall use their warrant or other identification numbers and the name of their police station. See *Note 2A*.

2.7 The fact and time of any detainee's refusal to sign a custody record, when asked in accordance with this Code, must be recorded.

Note for Guidance

2A The purpose of paragraph 2.6A(b) is to protect those involved in serious organised crime investigations or arrests of particularly violent suspects when there is reliable information that those arrested or their associates may threaten or cause harm to those involved. In cases of doubt, an officer of inspector rank or above should be consulted.

3 Initial action

(A) Detained persons—normal procedure

3.1 When a person is brought to a police station under arrest or arrested at the station having gone there voluntarily, the custody officer must make sure the person is told clearly about:

(a) the following continuing rights, which may be exercised at any stage during the period in custody:

(i) their right to consult privately with a solicitor and that free independent legal advice is available as in *section 6*;

(ii) their right to have someone informed of their arrest as in *section 5*;

(iii) their right to consult the Codes of Practice (see *Note 3D*); and

(iv) if applicable, their right to interpretation and translation (see *paragraph 3.12*) and their right to communicate with their High Commission, Embassy or Consulate (see *paragraph 3.12A*).

(b) their right to be informed about the offence and (as the case may be) any further offences for which they are arrested whilst in custody and why they have been arrested and detained in accordance with *paragraphs 2.4, 3.4(a)* and *11.1A* of this Code and *paragraph 3.3* of *Code G*.

3.2 The detainee must also be given a written notice, which contains information:

(a) to allow them to exercise their rights by setting out:

(i) their rights under *paragraph 3.1, paragraph 3.12* and *3.12A*;

(ii) the arrangements for obtaining legal advice, see section 6;

(iii) their right to a copy of the custody record as in *paragraph 2.4A*;

(iv) their right to remain silent as set out in the caution in the terms prescribed in section 10;

(v) their right to have access to materials and documents which are essential to effectively challenging the lawfulness of their arrest and detention for any offence and (as the case may be) any further offences for which they are arrested whilst in custody, in accordance with *paragraphs 3.4(b), 15.0, 15.7A(c)* and *16.7A* of this Code;

(vi) the maximum period for which they may be kept in police detention without being charged, when detention must be reviewed and when release is required;

(vii) their right to medical assistance in accordance with *section 9* of this Code;

(viii) their right, if they are prosecuted, to have access to the evidence in the case before their trial in accordance with the Criminal Procedure and Investigations Act 1996, the Attorney General's Guidelines on Disclosure, the common law and the Criminal Procedure Rules; and

(b) briefly setting out their other entitlements while in custody, by:

(i) mentioning:

~ the provisions relating to the conduct of interviews;

~ the circumstances in which an appropriate adult should be available to assist the detainee and their statutory rights to make representations whenever the need for their detention is reviewed;

(ii) listing the entitlements in this Code, concerning;

~ reasonable standards of physical comfort;

~ adequate food and drink;

~ access to toilets and washing facilities, clothing, medical attention, and exercise when practicable;

~ personal needs relating to health, hygiene and welfare concerning the provision of menstrual and any other health, hygiene and welfare products needed by the detainee in question and speaking about these in private to a member of the custody staff (see *paragraphs 9.3A* and *9.3B*).

See *Note 3A*.

3.2A The detainee must be given an opportunity to read the notice and shall be asked to sign the custody record to acknowledge receipt of the notice. Any refusal to sign must be recorded on the custody record.

3.3 *Not used*.

3.3A An 'easy read' illustrated version should also be provided if available (see *Note 3A*).

3.4 (a) The custody officer shall:

- record the offence(s) that the detainee has been arrested for and the reason(s) for the arrest on the custody record. See *paragraph 10.3 and Code G paragraphs 2.2 and 4.3*;
- note on the custody record any comment the detainee makes in relation to the arresting officer's account but shall not invite comment. If the arresting officer is not physically present when the detainee is brought to a police station, the arresting officer's account must be made available to the custody officer remotely or by a third party on the arresting officer's behalf. If the custody officer authorises a person's detention, subject to *paragraph 1.8*, that officer must record the grounds for detention in the detainee's presence and at the same time, inform them of the grounds. The detainee must be informed of the grounds for their detention before they are questioned about any offence;

- note any comment the detainee makes in respect of the decision to detain them but shall not invite comment;
- not put specific questions to the detainee regarding their involvement in any offence, nor in respect of any comments they may make in response to the arresting officer's account or the decision to place them in detention. Such an exchange is likely to constitute an interview as in *paragraph 11.1A* and require the associated safeguards in *section 11*.

Note: This *sub-paragraph* also applies to any further offences and grounds for detention which come to light whilst the person is detained.
See *paragraph 11.13* in respect of unsolicited comments.

(b) Documents and materials which are essential to effectively challenging the lawfulness of the detainee's arrest and detention must be made available to the detainee or their solicitor. Documents and materials will be 'essential' for this purpose if they are capable of undermining the reasons and grounds which make the detainee's arrest and detention necessary. The decision about whether particular documents or materials must be made available for the purpose of this requirement therefore rests with the custody officer who determines whether detention is necessary, in consultation with the investigating officer who has the knowledge of the documents and materials in a particular case necessary to inform that decision. A note should be made in the detainee's custody record of the *fact* that documents or materials have been made available under this sub-paragraph and when. The investigating officer should make a separate note of what is made available and how it is made available in a particular case. This sub-paragraph also applies (with modifications) for the purposes of *sections 15 (Reviews and extensions of detention)* and *16 (Charging detained persons)*. See *Note 3ZA* and *paragraphs 15.0* and *16.7A*.

3.5 The custody officer or other custody staff as directed by the custody officer shall:

(a) ask the detainee whether at this time, they:
  (i) would like legal advice, see *paragraph 6.5*;
  (ii) want someone informed of their detention, see *section 5*;
(b) ask the detainee to sign the custody record to confirm their decisions in respect of *(a)*;
(c) determine whether the detainee:
  (i) is, or might be, in need of medical treatment or attention, see *section 9*;
  (ii) is a juvenile and/or vulnerable and therefore requires an appropriate adult (see *paragraphs 1.4, 1.5*, and *3.15*);
  (iia) wishes to speak in private with a member of the custody staff who may be of the same sex about any matter concerning their personal needs relating to health, hygiene and welfare (see *paragraph 9.3A*);
  (iii) requires:
  - help to check documentation (see *paragraph 3.20*);
  - an interpreter (see paragraph 3.12 and Note 13B).
(ca) if the detainee is a female aged 18 or over, ask if they require or are likely to require any menstrual products whilst they are in custody (see *paragraph 9.3B*). For girls under 18, see *paragraph 3.20A*;
(d) record the decision and actions taken as applicable in respect of (c) and *(ca)*.

Where any duties under this paragraph have been carried out by custody staff at the direction of the custody officer, the outcomes shall, as soon as practicable, be reported to the custody officer who retains overall responsibility for the detainee's care and treatment and ensuring that it complies with this Code. See *Note 3F*.

3.6 When the needs mentioned in *paragraph 3.5(c)* are being determined, the custody officer is responsible for initiating an assessment to consider whether the detainee is likely to present specific risks to custody staff, any individual who may have contact with detainee (e.g. legal advisers, medical staff) or themselves. This risk assessment must include the taking of reasonable steps to establish the detainee's identity and to obtain information about the detainee that is relevant to their safe custody, security and welfare and risks to others. Such assessments should therefore always include a check on the Police National Computer (PNC), to be carried out as soon as practicable, to identify any risks that have been highlighted in relation to the detainee. Although such assessments are primarily the custody officer's responsibility, it may be necessary for them to consult and involve others, e.g. the arresting officer or an appropriate healthcare professional, see *paragraph 9.13*. Other records held by or on behalf of the police and other UK law enforcement authorities that might provide information relevant to the detainee's safe custody, security and welfare and risk to others and to confirming their identity should also be checked. Reasons for delaying the initiation or completion of the assessment must be recorded.

3.7 Chief officers should ensure that arrangements for proper and effective risk assessments required by *paragraph 3.6* are implemented in respect of all detainees at police stations in their area.

3.8 Risk assessments must follow a structured process which clearly defines the categories of risk to be considered and the results must be incorporated in the detainee's custody record. The custody officer is responsible for making sure those responsible for the detainee's custody are appropriately briefed about the risks. If no specific risks are identified by the assessment, that should be noted in the custody record. See *Note 3E* and *paragraph 9.14*.

3.8A The content of any risk assessment and any analysis of the level of risk relating to the person's detention is not required to be shown or provided to the detainee or any person acting on behalf of the detainee. But information should not be withheld from any person acting on the detainee's behalf, for example, an appropriate adult, solicitor or interpreter, if to do so might put that person at risk.

3.9 The custody officer is responsible for implementing the response to any specific risk assessment, e.g.:

- reducing opportunities for self harm;
- calling an appropriate healthcare professional;
- increasing levels of monitoring or observation;
- reducing the risk to those who come into contact with the detainee. See *Note 3E*.

3.10 Risk assessment is an ongoing process and assessments must always be subject to review if circumstances change.

3.11 If video cameras are installed in the custody area, notices shall be prominently displayed showing cameras are in use. Any request to have video cameras switched off shall be refused.

(B) Detained persons—special groups

3.12 If the detainee appears to be someone who does not speak or understand English or who has a hearing or speech impediment, the custody officer must ensure:

(a) that without delay, arrangements (see *paragraph 13.1ZA*) are made for the detainee to have the assistance of an interpreter in the action under *paragraphs 3.1* to *3.5*. If the person appears to have a hearing or speech impediment, the reference to 'interpreter' includes appropriate assistance necessary to comply with *paragraphs 3.1* to *3.5*. See *paragraph 13.1C* if the detainee is in Wales. See *section 13* and *Note 13B*;

(b) that in addition to the continuing rights set out in *paragraph 3.1(a)(i)* to *(iv)*, the detainee is told clearly about their right to interpretation and translation;

(c) that the written notice given to the detainee in accordance with *paragraph 3.2* is in a language the detainee understands and includes the right to interpretation and translation together with information about the provisions in *section 13* and *Annex M*, which explain how the right applies (see *Note 3A*); and

(d) that if the translation of the notice is not available, the information in the notice is given through an interpreter and a written translation provided without undue delay.

3.12A If the detainee is a citizen of an independent Commonwealth country or a national of a foreign country, including the Republic of Ireland, the custody officer must ensure that in addition to the continuing rights set out in *paragraph 3.1(a)(i)* to *(iv)*, they are informed as soon as practicable about their rights of communication with their High Commission, Embassy or Consulate set out in *section 7*. This right must be included in the written notice given to the detainee in accordance with *paragraph 3.2*.

3.13 If the detainee is a juvenile, the custody officer must, if it is practicable, ascertain the identity of a person responsible for their welfare. That person:

- may be:
  - ~ the parent or guardian;
  - ~ if the juvenile is in local authority or voluntary organisation care, or is otherwise being looked after under the Children Act 1989, a person appointed by that authority or organisation to have responsibility for the juvenile's welfare;
  - ~ any other person who has, for the time being, assumed responsibility for the juvenile's welfare.
- must be informed as soon as practicable that the juvenile has been arrested, why they have been arrested and where they are detained. This right is in addition to the juvenile's right in *section 5* not to be held incommunicado. See *Note 3C*.

3.14 If a juvenile is known to be subject to a court order under which a person or organisation is given any degree of statutory responsibility to supervise or otherwise monitor them, reasonable steps must also be taken to notify that person or organisation (the 'responsible officer'). The responsible officer will normally be a member of a Youth Offending Team, except for a curfew order which involves electronic monitoring when the contractor providing the monitoring will normally be the responsible officer.

3.15 If the detainee is a juvenile or a vulnerable person, the custody officer must, as soon as practicable ensure that:

- the detainee is informed of the decision that an appropriate adult is required and the reason for that decision (see *paragraph 3.5(c)(ii)*) and;
- the detainee is advised:
  - ~ of the duties of the appropriate adult as described in *paragraph 1.7A*; and
  - ~ that they can consult privately with the appropriate adult at any time.
- the appropriate adult, who in the case of a juvenile may or may not be a person responsible for their welfare, as in *paragraph 3.13*, is informed of:
  - ~ the grounds for their detention;
  - ~ their whereabouts; and
- the attendance of the appropriate adult at the police station to see the detainee is secured.

3.16 It is imperative that a person detained under the Mental Health Act 1983, section 135 or 136, be assessed as soon as possible within the permitted period of detention specified in that Act. A police station may only be used as a place of safety in accordance with The Mental Health Act 1983 (Places of Safety) Regulations 2017. If that assessment is to take place at the police station, an approved mental health professional and a registered medical practitioner shall be called to the station as soon as possible to carry it out. See *Note 9D*. The appropriate adult has no role in the assessment process and their presence is not required. Once the detainee has been assessed and suitable arrangements made for their treatment or care, they can no longer be detained under section 135 or 136. A detainee must be immediately discharged from detention if a registered medical practitioner, having examined them, concludes they are not mentally disordered within the meaning of the Act.

3.17 If the appropriate adult is:

- already at the police station, the provisions of *paragraphs 3.1* to *3.5* must be complied with in the appropriate adult's presence;
- not at the station when these provisions are complied with, they must be complied with again in the presence of the appropriate adult when they arrive,

and a copy of the notice given to the detainee in accordance with *paragraph 3.2*, shall also be given to the appropriate adult.

3.17A The custody officer must ensure that at the time the copy of the notice is given to the appropriate adult, or as soon as practicable thereafter, the appropriate adult is advised of the duties of the appropriate adult as described in *paragraph 1.7A*.

3.18 *Not used.*

3.19 If the detainee, or appropriate adult on the detainee's behalf, asks for a solicitor to be called to give legal advice, the provisions of *section 6* apply (see *paragraph 6.5A* and *Note 3H*).

3.20 If the detainee is blind, seriously visually impaired or unable to read, the custody officer shall make sure their solicitor, relative, appropriate adult or some other person likely to take an interest in them and not involved in the investigation is available to help check any documentation. When this Code requires written consent or signing the person assisting may be asked to sign instead, if the detainee prefers. This paragraph does not require an appropriate adult to be called solely to assist in checking and signing documentation for a person who is not a juvenile, or is not vulnerable (see *paragraph 3.15* and *Note 13C*).

3.20A The Children and Young Persons Act 1933, section 31, requires that arrangements must be made for ensuring that a girl under the age of 18, while detained in a police station, is under the care of a woman. The custody officer must ensure that the woman under whose care the girl is, makes the enquiries and provides the information concerning personal needs relating to their health, hygiene and welfare described in *paragraph 9.3A* and menstrual products described in *paragraph 9.3B*. See *Note 3G*. The section also requires arrangements must be made for preventing any person under 18, while being detained in a police station, from associating with an adult charged with any offence, unless that adult is a relative or the adult is jointly charged with the same offence as the person under 18.

(C) Detained persons—Documentation

3.20B The grounds for a person's detention shall be recorded, in the persons' presence if practicable. See *paragraph 1.8*.

3.20C Action taken under *paragraphs 3.12* to *3.20A* shall be recorded.

(D) Persons attending a police station or elsewhere voluntarily

3.21 Anybody attending a police station or other location (see *paragraph 3.22* and *Note 3I*) voluntarily to assist police with the investigation of an offence may leave at will unless arrested. See *Notes 1A* and *1K*. The person may only be prevented from leaving at will if their arrest on suspicion of committing the offence is necessary in accordance with Code G. See *Code G Note 2G*.

Action if arrest becomes necessary

(a) If during a person's voluntary attendance at a police station or other location it is decided for any reason that their arrest is necessary, they must:

- be informed at once that they are under arrest and of the grounds and reasons as required by *Code G*, and
- be brought before the custody officer at the police station where they are arrested or, as the case may be, at the police station to which they are taken after being arrested elsewhere. The custody officer is then responsible for making sure that a custody record is opened and that they are notified of their rights in the same way as other detainees as required by this Code.

Information to be given when arranging a voluntary interview:

(b) If the suspect's arrest is not necessary but they are cautioned as required in *section 10*, the person who, after describing the nature and circumstances of the suspected offence, gives the caution must at the same time, inform them that they are not under arrest and that they are not obliged to remain at the station or other location (see *paragraph 3.22* and *Note 3I*). The rights, entitlements and safeguards that apply to the conduct and recording of interviews with suspects are not diminished simply because the interview is arranged on a voluntary basis. For the purpose of arranging a voluntary interview (see *Code G Note 2F*), the duty of the interviewer reflects that of the custody officer with regard to detained suspects. As a result:

(i) the requirement in *paragraph 3.5(c)(ii)* to determine whether a detained suspect requires an appropriate adult, help to check documentation or an interpreter shall apply equally to a suspect who has not been arrested; and

(ii) the suspect must not be asked to give their informed consent to be interviewed until *after* they have been informed of the rights, entitlements and safeguards that apply to voluntary interviews. These are set out in *paragraph 3.21A* and the interviewer is responsible for ensuring that the suspect is so informed and for explaining these rights, entitlements and safeguards.

3.21A The interviewer must inform the suspect that the purpose of the voluntary interview is to question them to obtain evidence about their involvement or suspected involvement in the offence(s) described when they were cautioned and told that they were not under arrest. The interviewer shall then inform the suspect that the following matters will apply if they agree to the voluntary interview proceeding:

(a) Their right to information about the offence(s) in question by providing sufficient information to enable them to understand the nature of any such offence(s) and why they are suspected of committing it. This is in order to allow for the effective exercise of the rights of the defence as required by *paragraph 11.1A*. It applies whether or not they ask for legal advice and includes any further offences that come to light and are pointed out during the voluntary interview and for which they are cautioned.

(b) Their right to free *(see Note 3J)* legal advice by:

(i) explaining that they may obtain free and independent legal advice if they want it, and that this includes the right to speak with a solicitor on the telephone and to have the solicitor present during the interview;

(ii) asking if they want legal advice and recording their reply; and

(iii) if the person requests advice, securing its provision before the interview by contacting the Defence Solicitor Call Centre and explaining that the time and place of the interview will be arranged to enable them to obtain advice and that the interview will be delayed until they have received the advice unless, in accordance with *paragraph 6.6(c)* (Nominated solicitor not available and duty solicitor declined) or *paragraph 6.6(d)* (Change of mind), an officer of the rank of inspector or above agrees to the interview proceeding; or

(iv) if the person declines to exercise the right, asking them why and recording any reasons given (see *Note 6K*).

Note: When explaining the right to legal advice and the arrangements, the interviewer must take care not to indicate, except to answer a direct question, that the time taken to arrange and complete the voluntary interview might be reduced if:

- the suspect does not ask for legal advice or does not want a solicitor present when they are interviewed; or
- the suspect asks for legal advice or (as the case may be) asks for a solicitor to be present when they are interviewed, but changes their mind and agrees to be interviewed without waiting for a solicitor.

(c) Their right, if in accordance with *paragraph 3.5(c)(ii)* the interviewer determines:

(i) that they are a juvenile or are vulnerable; or

(ii) that they need help to check documentation (see *paragraph 3.20*), to have the appropriate adult present or (as the case may be) to have the necessary help to check documentation; and that the interview will be delayed until the presence of the appropriate adult or the necessary help, is secured.

(d) If they are a juvenile or vulnerable and do not want legal advice, their appropriate adult has the right to ask for a solicitor to attend if this would be in their best interests and the appropriate adult must be so informed. In this case, action to secure the provision of advice if so requested by their appropriate adult will be taken without delay in the same way as if requested by the person (see *sub-paragraph (b)(iii))*. However, they cannot be forced to see the solicitor if they are adamant that they do not wish to do so (see *paragraphs 3.19* and *6.5A*).

(e) Their right to an interpreter, if in accordance with, *paragraphs 3.5(c)(ii)* and *3.12*, the interviewer determines that they require an interpreter and that if they require an interpreter, making the necessary arrangements in accordance with *paragraph 13.1ZA* and that the interview will be delayed to make the arrangements.

(f) That interview will be arranged for a time and location (see *paragraph 3.22* and *Note 3I*) that enables:

(i) the suspect's rights described above to be fully respected; and

(ii) the whole of the interview to be recorded using an authorised recording device in accordance with Code E (Code of Practice on Audio recording of interviews with suspects) or (as the case may be) Code F (Code of Practice on visual recording with sound of interviews with suspects); and

(g) That their agreement to take part in the interview also signifies their agreement for that interview to be audio-recorded or (as the case may be) visually recorded with sound.

3.21B The provision by the interviewer of factual information described in *paragraph 3.21A* and, if asked by the suspect, further such information, does not constitute an interview for the purpose of this Code and *when that information is provided*:

(a) the interviewer must remind the suspect about the caution as required in *section 10* but must not *invite* comment about the offence or put specific questions to the suspect regarding their involvement in any offence, nor in respect of any comments they may make when given the information. Such an exchange is itself likely to constitute an interview as in *paragraph 11.1A* and require the associated interview safeguards in *section 11.*

(b) Any comment the suspect makes when the information is given which might be relevant to the offence, must be recorded and dealt with in accordance with *paragraph 11.13.*

(c) The suspect must be given a notice summarising the matters described in *paragraph 3.21A* and which includes the arrangements for obtaining legal advice. If a specific notice is not available, the notice given to detained suspects with references to detention-specific requirements and information redacted, may be used.

(d) For juvenile and vulnerable suspects (see *paragraphs 1.4* and *1.5*):

(i) the information must be provided or (as the case may be) provided again, together with the notice, in the presence of the appropriate adult;

(ii) if cautioned in the absence of the appropriate adult, the caution must be repeated in the appropriate adult's presence (see *paragraph 10.12*);

(iii) the suspect must be informed of the decision that an appropriate is required and the reason (see *paragraph 3.5(c)(ii)*;

(iv) the suspect *and* the appropriate adult shall be advised:

- that the duties of the appropriate adult include giving advice and assistance in accordance with *paragraphs 1.7A* and *11.17*; and
- that they can consult privately at any time.

(v) their informed agreement to be interviewed voluntarily must be sought and given in the *presence* of the appropriate adult and for a juvenile, the agreement of a parent or guardian of the juvenile is also required.

3.22 If the other location mentioned in *paragraph 3.21* is any place or premises for which the interviewer requires the informed consent of the suspect and/or occupier (if different) to remain, for example, the suspect's home (see *Note 3I*), then the references that the person is 'not obliged to remain' and that they 'may leave at will' mean that the suspect and/or occupier (if different) may also withdraw their consent and require the interviewer to leave.

Commencement of voluntary interview—general

3.22A Before asking the suspect any questions about their involvement in the offence they are suspected of committing, the interviewing officer must ask them to confirm that they agree to the interview proceeding. This confirmation shall be recorded in the interview record made in accordance with section 11 of this Code (written record) or Code E or Code F.

Documentation

3.22B Action taken under *paragraphs 3.21A* to *3.21B* shall be recorded. The record shall include the date time and place the action was taken, who was present and anything said to or by the suspect and to or by those present.

3.23 *Not used.*

3.24 *Not used.*

(E) Persons answering street bail

3.25 When a person is answering street bail, the custody officer should link any documentation held in relation to arrest with the custody record. Any further action shall be recorded on the custody record in accordance with *paragraphs 3.20B* and *3.20C* above.

(F) Requirements for suspects to be informed of certain rights

3.26 The provisions of this section identify the information which must be given to suspects who have been cautioned in accordance with *section 10 of this Code* according to whether or not they have been arrested and detained. It includes information required by *EU Directive 2012/13* on the right to information in criminal proceedings. If a complaint is made by or on behalf of such a suspect that the information and (as the case may be) access to records and documents has not been provided as required, the matter shall be reported to an inspector to deal with as a complaint for the purposes of *paragraph 9.2,* or *paragraph 12.9* if the challenge is made during an interview. This would include, for example:

(a) in the case of a detained suspect:
- not informing them of their rights (see *paragraph 3.1*);
- not giving them a copy of the Notice (see *paragraph 3.2(a)*);
- not providing an opportunity to read the notice (see *paragraph 3.2A*);
- not providing the required information (see *paragraphs 3.2(a)*, *3.12(b)* and, *3.12A*;
- not allowing access to the custody record (see *paragraph 2.4*);
- not providing a translation of the Notice (see *paragraph 3.12(c)* and *(d)*); and

(b) in the case of a suspect who is not detained:
- not informing them of their rights or providing the required information (see *paragraphs 3.21(b)* to *3.21B*).

Notes for Guidance

3ZA For the purposes of paragraphs 3.4(b) and 15.0:

(a) Investigating officers are responsible for bringing to the attention of the officer who is responsible for authorising the suspect's detention or (as the case may be) continued detention (before or after charge), any documents and materials in their possession or control which appear to undermine the need to keep the suspect in custody. In accordance with Part IV of PACE, this officer will be either the custody officer, the officer reviewing the need for detention before or after charge (PACE, section 40), or the officer considering the need to extend detention without charge from 24 to 36 hours (PACE, section 42) who is then responsible for determining, which, if any, of those documents and materials are capable of undermining the need to detain the suspect and must therefore be made available to the suspect or their solicitor.

(b) the way in which documents and materials are 'made available', is a matter for the investigating officer to determine on a case by case basis and having regard to the nature and volume of the documents and materials involved. For example, they may be made available by supplying a copy or allowing supervised access to view. However, for view only access, it will be necessary to demonstrate that sufficient time is allowed for the suspect and solicitor to view and consider the documents and materials in question.

3A For access to currently available notices, including 'easy-read' versions, see https://www.gov.uk/guidance/notice-of-rights-and-entitlements-a-persons-rights-in-police-detention.

3B Not used.

3C If the juvenile is in local authority or voluntary organisation care but living with their parents or other adults responsible for their welfare, although there is no legal obligation to inform them, they should normally be contacted, as well as the authority or organisation unless they are suspected of involvement in the offence concerned. Even if the juvenile is not living with their parents, consideration should be given to informing them.

3D The right to consult the Codes of Practice does not entitle the person concerned to delay unreasonably any necessary investigative or administrative action whilst they do so. Examples of action which need not be delayed unreasonably include:

- *procedures requiring the provision of breath, blood or urine specimens under the Road Traffic Act 1988 or the Transport and Works Act 1992;*
- *searching detainees at the police station;*
- *taking fingerprints, footwear impressions or non-intimate samples without consent for evidential purposes.*

3E The Detention and Custody Authorised Professional Practice (APP) produced by the College of Policing (see http://www.app.college.police.uk) provides more detailed guidance on risk assessments and identifies key risk areas which should always be considered. See Home Office Circular 34/2007 (Safety of solicitors and probationary representatives at police stations).

3F A custody officer or other officer who, in accordance with this Code, allows or directs the carrying out of any task or action relating to a detainee's care, treatment, rights and entitlements to another officer or any other person, must be satisfied that the officer or person concerned is suitable, trained and competent to carry out the task or action in question.

3G Guidance for police officers and police staff on the operational application of section 31 of the Children and Young Persons Act 1933 has been published by the College of Policing and is available at: https://www.app.college.police.uk/app-content/detention-and-custody-2/detainee-care/children-and-young-persons/#girls.

3H The purpose of the provisions at paragraphs 3.19 and 6.5A is to protect the rights of juvenile and vulnerable persons who may not understand the significance of what is said to them. They should always be given an opportunity, when an appropriate adult is called to the police station, to consult privately with a solicitor in the absence of the appropriate adult if they want.

3I An interviewer who is not sure, or has any doubt, about whether a place or location elsewhere than a police station is suitable for carrying out a voluntary interview, particularly in the case of a juvenile or vulnerable person, should consult an officer of the rank of sergeant or above for advice. Detailed guidance for police officers and staff concerning the conduct and recording of voluntary interviews is being developed by the College of Policing. It follows a review of operational issues arising when voluntary interviews need to be arranged. The aim is to ensure the effective implementation of the safeguards in paragraphs 3.21 to 3.22B particularly concerning the rights of suspects, the location for the interview and supervision.

3J For voluntary interviews conducted by non-police investigators, the provision of legal advice is set out by the Legal Aid Agency at paragraph 9.54 of the 2017 Standard Crime Contract Specification. This is published at https://www.gov.uk/government/publications/standard-crime-contract-2017 and the rules mean that a non-police interviewer who does not have their own statutory power of arrest would have to inform the suspect that they have a right to seek legal advice if they wish, but payment would be a matter for them to arrange with the solicitor.

4 Detainee's property

(A) Action

4.1 The custody officer is responsible for:

(a) ascertaining what property a detainee:

(i) has with them when they come to the police station, whether on:

- arrest or re-detention on answering to bail;
- commitment to prison custody on the order or sentence of a court;
- lodgement at the police station with a view to their production in court from prison custody;

- transfer from detention at another station or hospital;
- detention under the Mental Health Act 1983, section 135 or 136;
- remand into police custody on the authority of a court.

(ii) might have acquired for an unlawful or harmful purpose while in custody;

(b) the safekeeping of any property taken from a detainee which remains at the police station.

The custody officer may search the detainee or authorise their being searched to the extent they consider necessary, provided a search of intimate parts of the body or involving the removal of more than outer clothing is only made as in *Annex A*. A search may only be carried out by an officer of the same sex as the detainee. See *Note 4A* and *Annex L*.

4.2 Subject to *paragraph 4.3A*, detainees may retain clothing and personal effects at their own risk unless the custody officer considers they may use them to cause harm to themselves or others, interfere with evidence, damage property, effect an escape or they are needed as evidence. In this event the custody officer may withhold such articles as they consider necessary and must tell the detainee why.

4.3 Personal effects are those items a detainee may lawfully need, use or refer to while in detention but do not include cash and other items of value.

4.3A For the purposes of *paragraph 4.2*, the reference to clothing and personal effects shall be treated as including menstrual and any other health, hygiene and welfare products needed by the detainee in question (see *paragraphs 9.3A* and *9.3B*) and a decision to withhold any such products must be subject to a further specific risk assessment.

(B) Documentation

4.4 It is a matter for the custody officer to determine whether a record should be made of the property a detained person has with him or had taken from him on arrest. Any record made is not required to be kept as part of the custody record but the custody record should be noted as to where such a record exists and that record shall be treated as being part of the custody record for the purpose of this and any other Code of Practice (see *paragraphs 2.4, 2.4A* and *2.5*). Whenever a record is made the detainee shall be allowed to check and sign the record of property as correct. Any refusal to sign shall be recorded.

4.5 If a detainee is not allowed to keep any article of clothing or personal effects, the reason must be recorded.

Notes for Guidance

4A PACE, Section 54(1) and paragraph 4.1 require a detainee to be searched when it is clear the custody officer will have continuing duties in relation to that detainee or when that detainee's behaviour or offence makes an inventory appropriate. They do not require every detainee to be searched, e.g. if it is clear a person will only be detained for a short period and is not to be placed in a cell, the custody officer may decide not to search them. In such a case the custody record will be endorsed 'not searched', paragraph 4.4 will not apply, and the detainee will be invited to sign the entry. If the detainee refuses, the custody officer will be obliged to ascertain what property they have in accordance with paragraph 4.1.

4B Paragraph 4.4 does not require the custody officer to record on the custody record property in the detainee's possession on arrest if, by virtue of its nature, quantity or size, it is not practicable to remove it to the police station.

4C Paragraph 4.4 does not require items of clothing worn by the person to be recorded unless withheld by the custody officer as in paragraph 4.2.

5 Right not to be held incommunicado

(A) Action

5.1 Subject to *paragraph 5.7B*, any person arrested and held in custody at a police station or other premises may, on request, have one person known to them or likely to take an interest in their welfare informed at public expense of their whereabouts as soon as practicable. If the person cannot be contacted the detainee may choose up to two alternatives. If they cannot be contacted, the person in charge of detention or the investigation has discretion to allow further attempts until the information has been conveyed. See *Notes 5C* and *5D*.

5.2 The exercise of the above right in respect of each person nominated may be delayed only in accordance with *Annex B*.

5.3 The above right may be exercised each time a detainee is taken to another police station.

5.4 If the detainee agrees, they may at the custody officer's discretion, receive visits from friends, family or others likely to take an interest in their welfare, or in whose welfare the detainee has an interest. See *Note 5B*.

5.5 If a friend, relative or person with an interest in the detainee's welfare enquires about their whereabouts, this information shall be given if the suspect agrees and *Annex B* does not apply. See *Note 5D*.

5.6 The detainee shall be given writing materials, on request, and allowed to telephone one person for a reasonable time, see *Notes 5A* and *5E*. Either or both of these privileges may be denied or delayed if an officer of inspector rank or above considers sending a letter or making a telephone call may result in any of the consequences in:

(a) *Annex B paragraphs 1* and *2* and the person is detained in connection with an indictable offence;

(b) *Not used*.

Nothing in this paragraph permits the restriction or denial of the rights in *paragraphs 5.1* and *6.1*.

5.7 Before any letter or message is sent, or telephone call made, the detainee shall be informed that what they say in any letter, call or message (other than in a communication to a solicitor) may be read or listened to and may be given in evidence. A telephone call may be terminated if it is being abused. The costs can be at public expense at the custody officer's discretion.

5.7A Any delay or denial of the rights in this section should be proportionate and should last no longer than necessary.

5.7B In the case of a person in police custody for specific purposes and periods in accordance with a direction under the Crime (Sentences) Act 1997, Schedule 1 (productions from prison etc.), the exercise of the rights in this section shall be subject to any additional conditions specified in the direction for the purpose of regulating the detainee's contact and communication with others whilst in police custody. See *Note 5F*.

(B) Documentation

5.8 A record must be kept of any:

(a) request made under this section and the action taken;

(b) letters, messages or telephone calls made or received or visit received;

(c) refusal by the detainee to have information about them given to an outside enquirer. The detainee must be asked to countersign the record accordingly and any refusal recorded.

Notes for Guidance

5A A person may request an interpreter to interpret a telephone call or translate a letter.

5B At the custody officer's discretion and subject to the detainee's consent, visits should be allowed when possible, subject to having sufficient personnel to supervise a visit and any possible hindrance to the investigation.

5C If the detainee does not know anyone to contact for advice or support or cannot contact a friend or relative, the custody officer should bear in mind any local voluntary bodies or other organisations who might be able to help. Paragraph 6.1 applies if legal advice is required.

5D In some circumstances it may not be appropriate to use the telephone to disclose information under paragraphs 5.1 and 5.5.

5E The telephone call at paragraph 5.6 is in addition to any communication under paragraphs 5.1 and 6.1.

5F Prison Service Instruction 26/2012 (Production of Prisoners at the Request of Warranted Law Enforcement Agencies) provides detailed guidance and instructions for police officers and Governors and Directors of Prisons regarding applications for prisoners to be transferred to police custody and their safe custody and treatment while in police custody.

6 Right to legal advice

(A) Action

6.1 Unless *Annex B* applies, all detainees must be informed that they may at any time consult and communicate privately with a solicitor, whether in person, in writing or by telephone, and that free independent legal advice is available. See *paragraph 3.1, Notes 1I, 6B and 6J.*

6.2 *Not used.*

6.3 A poster advertising the right to legal advice must be prominently displayed in the charging area of every police station. See *Note 6H.*

6.4 No police officer should, at any time, do or say anything with the intention of dissuading any person who is entitled to legal advice in accordance with this Code, whether or not they have been arrested and are detained, from obtaining legal advice. See *Note 6ZA.*

6.5 The exercise of the right of access to legal advice may be delayed only as in *Annex B.* Whenever legal advice is requested, and unless *Annex B* applies, the custody officer must act without delay to secure the provision of such advice. If the detainee has the right to speak to a solicitor in person but declines to exercise the right the officer should point out that the right includes the right to speak with a solicitor on the telephone. If the detainee continues to waive this right, or a detainee whose right to free legal advice is limited to telephone advice from the Criminal Defence Service (CDS) Direct (*see Note 6B*) declines to exercise that right, the officer should ask them why and any reasons should be recorded on the custody record or the interview record as appropriate. Reminders of the right to legal advice must be given as in *paragraphs 3.5, 11.2, 15.4, 16.4, 16.5, 2B of Annex A, 3 of Annex K* and *5 of Annex M* of this Code and Code D, *paragraphs 3.17(ii)* and *6.3.* Once it is clear a detainee does not want to speak to a solicitor in person or by telephone they should cease to be asked their reasons. See *Note 6K.*

6.5A In the case of a person who is a juvenile or is vulnerable, an appropriate adult should consider whether legal advice from a solicitor is required. If such a detained person wants to exercise the right to legal advice, the appropriate action should be taken and should not be delayed until the appropriate adult arrives. If the person indicates that they do not want legal advice, the appropriate adult has the right to ask for a solicitor to attend if this would be in the best interests of the person and must be so informed. In this case, action to secure the provision of advice if so requested by the appropriate adult shall be taken without delay in the same way as when requested by the person. However, the person cannot be forced to see the solicitor if they are adamant that they do not wish to do so.

6.6 A detainee who wants legal advice may not be interviewed or continue to be interviewed until they have received such advice unless:

(a) delay in access to legal advice has been authorised, as set out in Annex B, by an officer of superintendent rank or above who has reasonable grounds for believing the exercise of the right to consult a solicitor will have one of the following consequences:
   (i) interference with or harm to evidence of an indictable offence;
   (ii) interference with or physical injury to any person;
   (iii) the alerting of persons who are suspected of having committed an indictable offence but who have not been arrested for it;
   (iv) the hindering of the recovery of property obtained as a result of an indictable offence;
   (v) the detained person has benefited from their criminal conduct (in accordance with Part 2 or 4 of the Proceeds of Crime Act 2002) and the recovery of the value of the property constituting the benefit will be hindered.

   See Note 6A

(b) It is authorised by an officer of superintendent rank or above who has reasonable grounds for believing that delaying the interview to await legal advice will have any of the relevant consequences set out in (a) above.

   Note: In these cases the restriction on drawing adverse inferences from silence in *Annex C* will apply because the detainee is not allowed an opportunity to consult a solicitor.

(c) the solicitor the detainee has nominated or selected from a list:
   (i) cannot be contacted;
   (ii) has previously indicated they do not wish to be contacted; or
   (iii) having been contacted, has declined to attend; and
      - the detainee has been advised of the Duty Solicitor Scheme but has declined to ask for the duty solicitor;
      - in these circumstances the interview may be started or continued without further delay provided an officer of inspector rank or above has agreed to the interview proceeding.

   Note: The restriction on drawing adverse inferences from silence in *Annex C* will not apply because the detainee is allowed an opportunity to consult the duty solicitor;

(d) the detainee changes their mind about wanting legal advice or (as the case may be) about wanting a solicitor present at the interview and states that they no longer wish to speak to a solicitor. In these circumstances, the interview may be started or continued without delay provided that:
   (i) an officer of inspector rank or above:
      - speaks to the detainee to enquire about the reasons for their change of mind (see *Note 6K*), and
      - makes, or directs the making of, reasonable efforts to ascertain the solicitor's expected time of arrival and to inform the solicitor that the suspect has stated that they wish to change their mind and the reason (if given);
   (ii) the detainee's reason for their change of mind (if given) and the outcome of the action in (i) are recorded in the custody record;
   (iii) the detainee, after being informed of the outcome of the action in (i) above, confirms in writing that they want the interview to proceed without speaking or further speaking to a solicitor or (as the case may be) without a solicitor being present and do not wish to wait for a solicitor by signing an entry to this effect in the custody record;
   (iv) an officer of inspector rank or above is satisfied that it is proper for the interview to proceed in these circumstances and:
      - gives authority in writing for the interview to proceed and, if the authority is not recorded in the custody record, the officer must ensure that the custody record shows the date and time of the authority and where it is recorded, and
      - takes, or directs the taking of, reasonable steps to inform the solicitor that the authority has been given and the time when the interview is expected to commence and records or causes to be recorded, the outcome of this action in the custody record.
   (v) When the interview starts and the interviewer reminds the suspect of their right to legal advice (see *paragraph 11.2*, Code E *paragraph 4.5* and Code F *paragraph 4.5*), the interviewer shall then ensure that the following is recorded in the written interview record or the interview record made in accordance with Code E or F:
      - confirmation that the detainee has changed their mind about wanting legal advice or (as the case may be) about wanting a solicitor present and the reasons for it if given;
      - the fact that authority for the interview to proceed has been given and, subject to *paragraph 2.6A,* the name of the authorising officer;
      - that if the solicitor arrives at the station before the interview is completed, the detainee will be so informed without delay and *a break will be taken* to allow them to speak to the solicitor if they wish, unless *paragraph 6.6(a)* applies, and
      - that at any time during the interview, the detainee may again ask for legal advice and that if they do, a break will be taken to allow them to speak to the solicitor, unless *paragraph 6.6(a), (b), or (c)* applies.

Note: In these circumstances, the restriction on drawing adverse inferences from silence in *Annex C* will not apply because the detainee is allowed an opportunity to consult a solicitor if they wish.

6.7 If *paragraph 6.6(a)* applies, where the reason for authorising the delay ceases to apply, there may be no further delay in permitting the exercise of the right in the absence of a further authorisation unless *paragraph 6.6(b), (c)* or *(d)* applies. If *paragraph 6.6(b)* applies, once sufficient information has been obtained to avert the risk, questioning must cease until the detainee has received legal advice unless *paragraph 6.6(a), (b), (c)* or *(d)* applies.

6.8 A detainee who has been permitted to consult a solicitor shall be entitled on request to have the solicitor present when they are interviewed unless one of the exceptions in *paragraph 6.6* applies.

6.9 The solicitor may only be required to leave the interview if their conduct is such that the interviewer is unable properly to put questions to the suspect. See *Notes 6D* and *6E*.

6.10 If the interviewer considers a solicitor is acting in such a way, they will stop the interview and consult an officer not below superintendent rank, if one is readily available, and otherwise an officer not below inspector rank not connected with the investigation. After speaking to the solicitor, the officer consulted will decide if the interview should continue in the presence of that solicitor. If they decide it should not, the suspect will be given the opportunity to consult another solicitor before the interview continues and that solicitor given an opportunity to be present at the interview. *See Note 6E*.

6.11 The removal of a solicitor from an interview is a serious step and, if it occurs, the officer of superintendent rank or above who took the decision will consider if the incident should be reported to the Solicitors Regulatory Authority. If the decision to remove the solicitor has been taken by an officer below superintendent rank, the facts must be reported to an officer of superintendent rank or above, who will similarly consider whether a report to the Solicitors Regulatory Authority would be appropriate. When the solicitor concerned is a duty solicitor, the report should be both to the Solicitors Regulatory Authority and to the Legal Aid Agency.

6.12 'Solicitor' in this Code means:

- a solicitor who holds a current practising certificate;
- an accredited or probationary representative included on the register of representatives maintained by the Legal Aid Agency.

6.12A An accredited or probationary representative sent to provide advice by, and on behalf of, a solicitor shall be admitted to the police station for this purpose unless an officer of inspector rank or above considers such a visit will hinder the investigation and directs otherwise. Hindering the investigation does not include giving proper legal advice to a detainee as in *Note 6D*. Once admitted to the police station, *paragraphs 6.6* to *6.10* apply.

6.13 In exercising their discretion under *paragraph 6.12A*, the officer should take into account in particular:

- whether:
  - ~ the identity and status of an accredited or probationary representative have been satisfactorily established;
  - ~ they are of suitable character to provide legal advice, e.g. a person with a criminal record is unlikely to be suitable unless the conviction was for a minor offence and not recent.
- any other matters in any written letter of authorisation provided by the solicitor on whose behalf the person is attending the police station. See *Note 6F*.

6.14 If the inspector refuses access to an accredited or probationary representative or a decision is taken that such a person should not be permitted to remain at an interview, the inspector must notify the solicitor on whose behalf the representative was acting and give them an opportunity to make alternative arrangements. The detainee must be informed and the custody record noted.

6.15 If a solicitor arrives at the station to see a particular person, that person must, unless *Annex B* applies, be so informed whether or not they are being interviewed and asked if they would like to see the solicitor. This applies even if the detainee has declined legal advice or, having requested it, subsequently agreed to be interviewed without receiving advice. The solicitor's attendance and the detainee's decision must be noted in the custody record.

(B) Documentation

6.16 Any request for legal advice and the action taken shall be recorded.

6.17 A record shall be made in the interview record if a detainee asks for legal advice and an interview is begun either in the absence of a solicitor or their representative, or they have been required to leave an interview.

Notes for Guidance

6ZA No police officer or police staff shall indicate to any suspect, except to answer a direct question, that the period for which they are liable to be detained, or if not detained, the time taken to complete the interview, might be reduced:

- *if they do not ask for legal advice or do not want a solicitor present when they are interviewed; or*
- *if they have asked for legal advice or (as the case may be) asked for a solicitor to be present when they are interviewed but change their mind and agree to be interviewed without waiting for a solicitor.*

6A In considering if paragraph 6.6(b) applies, the officer should, if practicable, ask the solicitor for an estimate of how long it will take to come to the station and relate this to the time detention is permitted, the time of day (i.e. whether the rest period under paragraph 12.2 is imminent) and the requirements of other investigations. If the solicitor is on their way or is to set off immediately, it will not normally be appropriate to begin an interview before they arrive. If it appears necessary to begin an interview before the solicitor's arrival, they should be given an indication of how long the police would be able to wait before 6.6(b) applies so there is an opportunity to make arrangements for someone else to provide legal advice.

6B A detainee has a right to free legal advice and to be represented by a solicitor. This Note for Guidance explains the arrangements which enable detainees to obtain legal advice. An outline of these arrangements is also included in the Notice of Rights and Entitlements given to detainees in accordance with paragraph 3.2. The arrangements also apply, with appropriate modifications, to persons attending a police station or other location (see paragraph 3.22 and Notes 3I and 3J) voluntarily who are cautioned prior to being interviewed. See paragraph 3.21.

When a detainee asks for free legal advice, the Defence Solicitor Call Centre (DSCC) must be informed of the request.

Free legal advice will be limited to telephone advice provided by CDS Direct if a detainee is:

- *detained for a non-imprisonable offence;*
- *arrested on a bench warrant for failing to appear and being held for production at court (except where the solicitor has clear documentary evidence available that would result in the client being released from custody);*
- *arrested for drink driving (driving/in charge with excess alcohol, failing to provide a specimen, driving/in charge whilst unfit through drink), or*
- *detained in relation to breach of police or court bail conditions*

unless one or more exceptions apply, in which case the DSCC should arrange for advice to be given by a solicitor at the police station, for example:

- *the police want to interview the detainee or carry out an eye-witness identification procedure;*
- *the detainee needs an appropriate adult;*
- *the detainee is unable to communicate over the telephone;*
- *the detainee alleges serious misconduct by the police;*
- *the investigation includes another offence not included in the list,*
- *the solicitor to be assigned is already at the police station.*

When free advice is not limited to telephone advice, a detainee can ask for free advice from a solicitor they know or if they do not know a solicitor or the solicitor they know cannot be contacted, from the duty solicitor.

To arrange free legal advice, the police should telephone the DSCC. The call centre will decide whether legal advice should be limited to telephone advice from CDS Direct, or whether a solicitor known to the detainee or the duty solicitor should speak to the detainee.

When a detainee wants to pay for legal advice themselves:

- *the DSCC will contact a solicitor of their choice on their behalf;*
- *they may, when free advice is only available by telephone from CDS Direct, still speak to a solicitor of their choice on the telephone for advice, but the solicitor would not be paid by legal aid and may ask the person to pay for the advice;*
- *they should be given an opportunity to consult a specific solicitor or another solicitor from that solicitor's firm. If this solicitor is not available, they may choose up to two alternatives. If these alternatives are not available, the custody officer has discretion to allow further attempts until a solicitor has been contacted and agreed to provide advice;*
- *they are entitled to a private consultation with their chosen solicitor on the telephone or the solicitor may decide to come to the police station;*
- *If their chosen solicitor cannot be contacted, the DSCC may still be called to arrange free legal advice.*

Apart from carrying out duties necessary to implement these arrangements, an officer must not advise the suspect about any particular firm of solicitors.

6B1 Not used.

6B2 Not used.

6C Not used.

6D The solicitor's only role in the police station is to protect and advance the legal rights of their client. On occasions this may require the solicitor to give advice which has the effect of the client avoiding giving evidence which strengthens a prosecution case. The solicitor may intervene in order to seek clarification, challenge an improper question to their client or the manner in which it is put, advise their client not to reply to particular questions, or if they wish to give their client further legal advice. Paragraph 6.9 only applies if the solicitor's approach or conduct prevents or unreasonably obstructs proper questions being put to the suspect or the suspect's response being recorded. Examples of unacceptable conduct include answering questions on a suspect's behalf or providing written replies for the suspect to quote.

6E An officer who takes the decision to exclude a solicitor must be in a position to satisfy the court the decision was properly made. In order to do this they may need to witness what is happening.

6F If an officer of at least inspector rank considers a particular solicitor or firm of solicitors is persistently sending probationary representatives who are unsuited to provide legal advice, they should inform an officer of at least superintendent rank, who may wish to take the matter up with the Solicitors Regulation Authority.

6G Subject to the constraints of Annex B, a solicitor may advise more than one client in an investigation if they wish. Any question of a conflict of interest is for the solicitor under their professional code of conduct. If, however, waiting for a solicitor to give advice to one client may lead to unreasonable delay to the interview with another, the provisions of paragraph 6.6(b) may apply.

6H In addition to a poster in English, a poster or posters containing translations into Welsh, the main minority ethnic languages and the principal European languages should be displayed wherever they are likely to be helpful and it is practicable to do so.

6I Not used.

6J Whenever a detainee exercises their right to legal advice by consulting or communicating with a solicitor, they must be allowed to do so in private. This right to consult or communicate in private is fundamental. If the requirement for privacy is compromised because what is said or written by the detainee or solicitor for the purpose of giving and receiving legal advice is overheard, listened to, or read by others without the informed consent of the detainee, the right will effectively have been denied. When a detainee speaks to a solicitor on the telephone, they should be allowed to do so in private unless this is impractical because of the design and layout of the custody area or the location of telephones. However, the normal expectation should be that facilities will be available, unless they are being used, at all police stations to enable detainees to speak in private to a solicitor either face to face or over the telephone.

6K A detainee is not obliged to give reasons for declining legal advice and should not be pressed to do so.

7 Citizens of independent Commonwealth countries or foreign nationals

(A) Action

7.1 A detainee who is a citizen of an independent Commonwealth country or a national of a foreign country, including the Republic of Ireland, has the right, upon request, to communicate at any time with the appropriate High Commission, Embassy or Consulate. That detainee must be informed as soon as practicable of this right and asked if they want to have their High Commission, Embassy or Consulate told of their whereabouts and the grounds for their detention. Such a request should be acted upon as soon as practicable. See *Note 7A*.

7.2 A detainee who is a citizen of a country with which a bilateral consular convention or agreement is in force requiring notification of arrest must also be informed that subject to *paragraph 7.4,* notification of their arrest will be sent to the appropriate High Commission, Embassy or Consulate as soon as practicable, whether or not they request it. A list of the countries to which this requirement currently applies and contact details for the relevant High Commissions, Embassies and Consulates can be obtained from the Consular Directorate of the Foreign and Commonwealth Office (FCO) as follows:

- from the FCO web pages:
  - *https://gov.uk/government/publications/table-of-consular-conventions-and-mandatory-notification-obligations, and*
  - https://www.gov.uk/government/publications/foreign-embassies-in-the-uk
- by telephone to 020 7008 3100,
- by email to fcocorrespondence@fco.gov.uk.
- by letter to the Foreign and Commonwealth Office, King Charles Street, London, SW1A 2AH.

7.3 Consular officers may, if the detainee agrees, visit one of their nationals in police detention to talk to them and, if required, to arrange for legal advice. Such visits shall take place out of the hearing of a police officer.

7.4 Notwithstanding the provisions of consular conventions, if the detainee claims that they are a refugee or have applied or intend to apply for asylum, the custody officer must ensure that UK Visas and Immigration (UKVI) (formerly the UK Border Agency) is informed as soon as practicable of the claim. UKVI will then determine whether compliance with relevant international obligations requires notification of the arrest to be sent and will inform the custody officer as to what action police need to take.

(B) Documentation

7.5 A record shall be made:

- when a detainee is informed of their rights under this section and of any requirement in paragraph 7.2;
- of any communications with a High Commission, Embassy or Consulate, and
- of any communications with UKVI about a detainee's claim to be a refugee or to be seeking asylum and the resulting action taken by police.

Note for Guidance

7A The exercise of the rights in this section may not be interfered with even though Annex B applies.

8 Conditions of detention

(A) Action

8.1 So far as it is practicable, not more than one detainee should be detained in each cell. See *Note 8C*.

8.2 Cells in use must be adequately heated, cleaned and ventilated. They must be adequately lit, subject to such dimming as is compatible with safety and security to allow people detained overnight to sleep. No additional restraints shall be used within a locked cell unless absolutely necessary and then only restraint equipment, approved for use in that force by the chief officer, which is reasonable and necessary in the circumstances having regard to the detainee's demeanour and with a view to ensuring their safety and the safety of others. If a detainee is deaf or a vulnerable person, particular care must be taken when deciding whether to use any form of approved restraints.

8.3 Blankets, mattresses, pillows and other bedding supplied shall be of a reasonable standard and in a clean and sanitary condition. See *Note 8A*.

8.4 Access to toilet and washing facilities must be provided. This must take account of the dignity of the detainee. See *Note 8D*.

8.5 If it is necessary to remove a detainee's clothes for the purposes of investigation, for hygiene, health reasons or cleaning, removal shall be conducted with proper regard to the dignity, sensitivity and vulnerability of the detainee and replacement clothing of a reasonable standard of comfort and cleanliness shall be provided. A detainee may not be interviewed unless adequate clothing has been offered.

8.6 At least two light meals and one main meal should be offered in any 24-hour period. See *Note 8B*. Drinks should be provided at meal times and upon reasonable request between meals. Whenever necessary, advice shall be sought from the appropriate healthcare professional, see *Note 9A*, on medical and dietary matters. As far as practicable, meals provided shall offer a varied diet and meet any specific dietary needs or religious beliefs the detainee may have. The detainee may, at the custody officer's discretion, have meals supplied by their family or friends at their expense. See *Note 8A*.

8.7 Brief outdoor exercise shall be offered daily if practicable.

8.8 A juvenile shall not be placed in a police cell unless no other secure accommodation is available and the custody officer considers it is not practicable to supervise them if they are not placed in a cell or that a cell provides more comfortable accommodation than other secure accommodation in the station. A juvenile may not be placed in a cell with a detained adult.

(B) Documentation

8.9 A record must be kept of replacement clothing and meals offered.

8.10 If a juvenile is placed in a cell, the reason must be recorded.

8.11 The use of any restraints on a detainee whilst in a cell, the reasons for it and, if appropriate, the arrangements for enhanced supervision of the detainee whilst so restrained, shall be recorded. See paragraph 3.9.

Notes for Guidance

8A The provisions in paragraph 8.3 and 8.6 respectively are of particular importance in the case of a person likely to be detained for an extended period. In deciding whether to allow meals to be supplied by family or friends, the custody officer is entitled to take account of the risk of items being concealed in any food or package and the officer's duties and responsibilities under food handling legislation.

8B Meals should, so far as practicable, be offered at recognised meal times, or at other times that take account of when the detainee last had a meal.

8C The Detention and Custody Authorised Professional Practice (APP) produced by the College of Policing (see http://www.app.college.police.uk) provides more detailed guidance on matters concerning detainee healthcare and treatment and associated forensic issues which should be read in conjunction with sections 8 and 9 of this Code.

8D In cells subject to CCTV monitoring, privacy in the toilet area should be ensured by any appropriate means and detainees should be made aware of this when they are placed in the cell. If a detainee or appropriate adult on their behalf, expresses doubts about the effectiveness of the means used, reasonable steps should be taken to allay those doubts, for example, by explaining or demonstrating the means used.

9 Care and treatment of detained persons

(A) General

9.1 Nothing in this section prevents the police from calling an appropriate healthcare professional to examine a detainee for the purposes of obtaining evidence relating to any offence in which the detainee is suspected of being involved. See *Notes 9A and 8C.*

9.2 If a complaint is made by, or on behalf of, a detainee about their treatment since their arrest, or it comes to notice that a detainee may have been treated improperly, a report must be made as soon as practicable to an officer of inspector rank or above not connected with the investigation. If the matter concerns a possible assault or the possibility of the unnecessary or unreasonable use of force, an appropriate healthcare professional must also be called as soon as practicable.

9.3 Subject to *paragraph 9.6* in the case of a person to whom The Mental Health Act 1983 (Places of Safety) Regulations 2017 apply, detainees should be visited at least every hour. If no reasonably foreseeable risk was identified in a risk assessment, see *paragraphs 3.6 to 3.10,* there is no need to wake a sleeping detainee. Those suspected of being under the influence of drink or drugs or both or of having swallowed drugs, see *Note 9CA,* or whose level of consciousness causes concern must, subject to any clinical directions given by the appropriate healthcare professional, see *paragraph 9.13*:

- be visited and roused at least every half hour;
- have their condition assessed as in *Annex H;*
- and clinical treatment arranged if appropriate.

See *Notes 9B, 9C* and *9H*

9.3A As soon as practicable after arrival at the police station, each detainee must be given an opportunity to speak in private with a member of the custody staff who if they wish may be of the same sex as the detainee (see *paragraph 1.13(c)*), about any matter concerning the detainee's personal needs relating to their health, hygiene and welfare that might affect or concern them whilst in custody. If the detainee wishes to take this opportunity, the necessary arrangements shall be made as soon as practicable. In the case of a juvenile or vulnerable person, the appropriate adult must be involved in accordance with *paragraph 3.17* and in the case of a girl under 18, see *paragraph 3.20A* (see *Note 9CB*).

9.3B Each female detainee aged 18 or over shall be asked in private if possible and at the earliest opportunity, if they require or are likely to require any menstrual products whilst they are in custody. They must be told that they will be provided free of charge and that replacement products are available. At the custody officer's discretion, detainees may have menstrual products supplied by their family or friends at their expense (see *Note 9CC*). For girls under 18, see *paragraph 3.20A.*

9.4 When arrangements are made to secure clinical attention for a detainee, the custody officer must make sure all relevant information which might assist in the treatment of the detainee's condition is made available to the responsible healthcare professional. This applies whether or not the healthcare professional asks for such information. Any officer or police staff with relevant information must inform the custody officer as soon as practicable.

(B) Clinical treatment and attention

9.5 The custody officer must make sure a detainee receives appropriate clinical attention as soon as reasonably practicable if the person:

(a) appears to be suffering from physical illness; or
(b) is injured; or
(c) appears to be suffering from a mental disorder; or
(d) appears to need clinical attention.

9.5A This applies even if the detainee makes no request for clinical attention and whether or not they have already received clinical attention elsewhere. If the need for attention appears urgent, e.g. when indicated as in *Annex H,* the nearest available healthcare professional or an ambulance must be called immediately.

9.5B The custody officer must also consider the need for clinical attention as set out in *Note 9C* in relation to those suffering the effects of alcohol or drugs.

9.6 Paragraph 9.5 is not meant to prevent or delay the transfer to a hospital if necessary of a person detained under the Mental Health Act 1983, sections 135 and 136, as amended by the Policing and Crime Act 2017. See *Note 9D*. When an assessment under that Act is to take place at a police station (see *paragraph 3.16*) the custody officer must also ensure that in accordance with The Mental Health Act 1983 (Places of Safety) Regulations 2017, a health professional is present and available to the person throughout the period they are detained at the police station and that at the welfare of the detainee is checked by the health professional at least once every thirty minutes and any appropriate action for the care and treatment of the detainee taken.

9.7 If it appears to the custody officer, or they are told, that a person brought to a station under arrest may be suffering from an infectious disease or condition, the custody officer must take reasonable steps to safeguard the health of the detainee and others at the station. In deciding what action to take, advice must be sought from an appropriate healthcare professional. See *Note 9E*. The custody officer has discretion to isolate the person and their property until clinical directions have been obtained.

9.8 If a detainee requests a clinical examination, an appropriate healthcare professional must be called as soon as practicable to assess the detainee's clinical needs. If a safe and appropriate care plan cannot be provided, the appropriate healthcare professional's advice must be sought. The detainee may also be examined by a medical practitioner of their choice at their expense.

9.9 If a detainee is required to take or apply any medication in compliance with clinical directions prescribed before their detention, the custody officer must consult the appropriate healthcare professional before the use of the medication. Subject to the restrictions in *paragraph 9.10*, the custody officer is responsible for the safekeeping of any medication and for making sure the detainee is given the opportunity to take or apply prescribed or approved medication. Any such consultation and its outcome shall be noted in the custody record.

9.10 No police officer may administer or supervise the self-administration of medically prescribed controlled drugs of the types and forms listed in the Misuse of Drugs Regulations 2001, Schedule 2 or 3. A detainee may only self-administer such drugs under the personal supervision of the registered medical practitioner authorising their use or other appropriate healthcare professional. The custody officer may supervise the self-administration of, or authorise other custody staff to supervise the self-administration of, drugs listed in Schedule 4 or 5 if the officer has consulted the appropriate healthcare professional authorising their use and both are satisfied self-administration will not expose the detainee, police officers or anyone else to the risk of harm or injury.

9.11 When appropriate healthcare professionals administer drugs or authorise the use of other medications, supervise their self-administration or consult with the custody officer about allowing self-administration of drugs listed in Schedule 4 or 5, it must be within current medicines legislation and the scope of practice as determined by their relevant statutory regulatory body.

9.12 If a detainee has in their possession, or claims to need, medication relating to a heart condition, diabetes, epilepsy or a condition of comparable potential seriousness then, even though *paragraph 9.5* may not apply, the advice of the appropriate healthcare professional must be obtained.

9.13 Whenever the appropriate healthcare professional is called in accordance with this section to examine or treat a detainee, the custody officer shall ask for their opinion about:

- any risks or problems which police need to take into account when making decisions about the detainee's continued detention;
- when to carry out an interview if applicable; and
- the need for safeguards.

9.14 When clinical directions are given by the appropriate healthcare professional, whether orally or in writing, and the custody officer has any doubts or is in any way uncertain about any aspect of the directions, the custody officer shall ask for clarification. It is particularly important that directions concerning the frequency of visits are clear, precise and capable of being implemented. See *Note 9F*.

(C) Documentation

9.15 A record must be made in the custody record of:

(a) the arrangements made for an examination by an appropriate healthcare professional under *paragraph 9.2* and of any complaint reported under that paragraph together with any relevant remarks by the custody officer;

(b) any arrangements made in accordance with *paragraph 9.5*;

(c) any request for a clinical examination under *paragraph 9.8* and any arrangements made in response;

(d) the injury, ailment, condition or other reason which made it necessary to make the arrangements in *(a)* to *(c)*; See *Note 9G.*

(e) any clinical directions and advice, including any further clarifications, given to police by a healthcare professional concerning the care and treatment of the detainee in connection with any of the arrangements made in *(a)* to *(c)*; See *Notes 9E* and *9F.*

(f) if applicable, the responses received when attempting to rouse a person using the procedure in *Annex H.* See *Note 9H.*

9.16 If a healthcare professional does not record their clinical findings in the custody record, the record must show where they are recorded. See *Note 9G.* However, information which is necessary to custody staff to ensure the effective ongoing care and well being of the detainee must be recorded openly in the custody record, see *paragraph 3.8* and *Annex G, paragraph 7.*

9.17 Subject to the requirements of *Section 4*, the custody record shall include:

- a record of all medication a detainee has in their possession on arrival at the police station;
- a note of any such medication they claim to need but do not have with them.

Notes for Guidance

9A A 'healthcare professional' means a clinically qualified person working within the scope of practice as determined by their relevant statutory regulatory body. Whether a healthcare professional is 'appropriate' depends on the circumstances of the duties they carry out at the time.

9B Whenever possible detained juveniles and vulnerable persons should be visited more frequently.

9C A detainee who appears drunk or behaves abnormally may be suffering from illness, the effects of drugs or may have sustained injury, particularly a head injury which is not apparent. A detainee needing or dependent on certain drugs, including alcohol, may experience harmful effects within a short time of being deprived of their supply. In these circumstances, when there is any doubt, police should always act urgently to call an appropriate healthcare professional or an ambulance. Paragraph 9.5 does not apply to minor ailments or injuries which do not need attention. However, all such ailments or injuries must be recorded in the custody record and any doubt must be resolved in favour of calling the appropriate healthcare professional.

9CA Paragraph 9.3 would apply to a person in police custody by order of a magistrates' court under the Criminal Justice Act 1988, section 152 (as amended by the Drugs Act 2005, section 8) to facilitate the recovery of evidence after being charged with drug possession or drug trafficking and suspected of having swallowed drugs. In the case of the healthcare needs of a person who has swallowed drugs, the custody officer, subject to any clinical directions, should consider the necessity for rousing every half hour. This does not negate the need for regular visiting of the suspect in the cell.

9CB Matters concerning personal needs to which paragraph 9.3A applies include any requirement for menstrual products incontinence products and colostomy appliances, where these needs have not previously been identified (see paragraph 3.5(c)). It also enables adult women to speak in private to a female officer about their requirements for menstrual products if they decline to respond to the more direct enquiry envisaged under paragraph 9.3B. This contact should be facilitated at any time, where possible.

9CC Detailed guidance for police officers and staff concerning menstruating female detainees in police custody is included in the College of Policing Authorised Professional Practice (APP).

9D Except as allowed for under The Mental Health Act 1983 (Places of Safety) Regulations 2017, a police station must not be used as a place of safety for persons detained under section 135 or 136 of that Act. Chapter 16 of the Mental Health Act 1983 Code of Practice (as revised), provides more detailed guidance about arranging assessments under the Mental Health Act and transferring detainees from police stations to other places of safety. Additional guidance in relation to amendments made to the Mental Health Act in 2017 are published at https://www.gov.uk/government/publications/mental-health-act-1983-implementing-changes-to-police-powers.

9E It is important to respect a person's right to privacy and information about their health must be kept confidential and only disclosed with their consent or in accordance with clinical advice when it is necessary to protect the detainee's health or that of others who come into contact with them.

9F The custody officer should always seek to clarify directions that the detainee requires constant observation or supervision and should ask the appropriate healthcare professional to explain precisely what action needs to be taken to implement such directions.

9G Paragraphs 9.15 and 9.16 do not require any information about the cause of any injury, ailment or condition to be recorded on the custody record if it appears capable of providing evidence of an offence.

9H The purpose of recording a person's responses when attempting to rouse them using the procedure in Annex H is to enable any change in the individual's consciousness level to be noted and clinical treatment arranged if appropriate.

10 Cautions

(A) When a caution must be given

10.1 A person whom there are grounds to suspect of an offence, see *Note 10A,* must be cautioned before any questions about an offence, or further questions if the answers provide the grounds for suspicion, are put to them if either the suspect's answers or silence, (i.e. failure or refusal to answer or answer satisfactorily) may be given in evidence to a court in a prosecution. A person need not be cautioned if questions are for other necessary purposes, e.g.:

- (a) solely to establish their identity or ownership of any vehicle;
- (b) to obtain information in accordance with any relevant statutory requirement, see *paragraph 10.9*;
- (c) in furtherance of the proper and effective conduct of a search, e.g. to determine the need to search in the exercise of powers of stop and search or to seek co-operation while carrying out a search; or
- (d) to seek verification of a written record as in *paragraph 11.13.*
- (e) *Not used.*

10.2 Whenever a person not under arrest is initially cautioned, or reminded that they are under caution, that person must at the same time be told they are not under arrest and must be informed of the provisions of *paragraphs 3.21* to *3.21B* which explain that they need to agree to be interviewed, how they may obtain legal advice according to whether they are at a police station or elsewhere and the other rights and entitlements that apply to a voluntary interview. See *Note 10C.*

10.3 A person who is arrested, or further arrested, must be informed at the time if practicable or, if not, as soon as it becomes practicable thereafter, that they are under arrest and of the grounds and reasons for their arrest, see paragraph 3.4, *Note 10B* and *Code G, paragraphs 2.2 and 4.3.*

10.4 As required by *Code G, section 3,* a person who is arrested, or further arrested, must also be cautioned unless:

- (a) it is impracticable to do so by reason of their condition or behaviour at the time;
- (b) they have already been cautioned immediately prior to arrest as in *paragraph 10.1.*

(B) Terms of the cautions

10.5 The caution which must be given on:

- (a) arrest; or
- (b) all other occasions before a person is charged or informed they may be prosecuted; see *section 16,*

should, unless the restriction on drawing adverse inferences from silence applies, see *Annex C*, be in the following terms:

'You do not have to say anything. But it may harm your defence if you do not mention when questioned something which you later rely on in Court. Anything you do say may be given in evidence.'

Where the use of the Welsh Language is appropriate, a constable may provide the caution directly in Welsh in the following terms:

'Does dim rhaid i chi ddweud dim byd. Ond gall niweidio eich amddiffyniad os na fyddwch chi'n sôn, wrth gael eich holi, am rywbeth y byddwch chi'n dibynnu arno nes ymlaen yn y Llys. Gall unrhyw beth yr ydych yn ei ddweud gael ei roi fel tystiolaeth.'

See *Note 10G*

10.6 *Annex C, paragraph 2* sets out the alternative terms of the caution to be used when the restriction on drawing adverse inferences from silence applies.

10.7 Minor deviations from the words of any caution given in accordance with this Code do not constitute a breach of this Code, provided the sense of the relevant caution is preserved. See *Note 10D*.

10.8 After any break in questioning under caution, the person being questioned must be made aware they remain under caution. If there is any doubt the relevant caution should be given again in full when the interview resumes. See *Note 10E*.

10.9 When, despite being cautioned, a person fails to co-operate or to answer particular questions which may affect their immediate treatment, the person should be informed of any relevant consequences and that those consequences are not affected by the caution. Examples are when a person's refusal to provide:

- their name and address when charged may make them liable to detention;
- particulars and information in accordance with a statutory requirement, e.g. under the Road Traffic Act 1988, may amount to an offence or may make the person liable to a further arrest.

(C) Special warnings under the Criminal Justice and Public Order Act 1994, sections 36 and 37

10.10 When a suspect interviewed at a police station or authorised place of detention after arrest fails or refuses to answer certain questions, or to answer satisfactorily, after due warning, see *Note 10F*, a court or jury may draw such inferences as appear proper under the Criminal Justice and Public Order Act 1994, sections 36 and 37. Such inferences may only be drawn when:

(a) the restriction on drawing adverse inferences from silence, see *Annex C*, does not apply; and

(b) the suspect is arrested by a constable and fails or refuses to account for any objects, marks or substances, or marks on such objects found:

- on their person;
- in or on their clothing or footwear;
- otherwise in their possession;
- or in the place they were arrested;

(c) the arrested suspect was found by a constable at a place at or about the time the offence for which that officer has arrested them is alleged to have been committed, and the suspect fails or refuses to account for their presence there.

When the restriction on drawing adverse inferences from silence applies, the suspect may still be asked to account for any of the matters in *(b)* or *(c)* but the special warning described in *paragraph 10.11* will not apply and must not be given.

10.11 For an inference to be drawn when a suspect fails or refuses to answer a question about one of these matters or to answer it satisfactorily, the suspect must first be told in ordinary language:

(a) what offence is being investigated;

(b) what fact they are being asked to account for;

(c) this fact may be due to them taking part in the commission of the offence;
(d) a court may draw a proper inference if they fail or refuse to account for this fact; and
(e) a record is being made of the interview and it may be given in evidence if they are brought to trial.

(D) Juveniles and vulnerable persons

10.11A The information required in paragraph 10.11 must not be given to a suspect who is a juvenile or a vulnerable person unless the appropriate adult is present.

10.12 If a juvenile or a vulnerable person is cautioned in the absence of the appropriate adult, the caution must be repeated in the appropriate adult's presence.

10.12A *Not used.*

(E) Documentation

10.13 A record shall be made when a caution is given under this section, either in the interviewer's report book or in the interview record.

Notes for Guidance

10A There must be some reasonable, objective grounds for the suspicion, based on known facts or information which are relevant to the likelihood the offence has been committed and the person to be questioned committed it.

10B An arrested person must be given sufficient information to enable them to understand that they have been deprived of their liberty and the reason they have been arrested, e.g. when a person is arrested on suspicion of committing an offence they must be informed of the suspected offence's nature, when and where it was committed. The suspect must also be informed of the reason or reasons why the arrest is considered necessary. Vague or technical language should be avoided.

10C The restriction on drawing inferences from silence, see Annex C, paragraph 1, does not apply to a person who has not been detained and who therefore cannot be prevented from seeking legal advice if they want, see paragraph 3.21.

10D If it appears a person does not understand the caution, the person giving it should explain it in their own words.

10E It may be necessary to show to the court that nothing occurred during an interview break or between interviews which influenced the suspect's recorded evidence. After a break in an interview or at the beginning of a subsequent interview, the interviewer should summarise the reason for the break and confirm this with the suspect.

10F The Criminal Justice and Public Order Act 1994, sections 36 and 37 apply only to suspects who have been arrested by a constable or an officer of Revenue and Customs and are given the relevant warning by the police or Revenue and Customs officer who made the arrest or who is investigating the offence. They do not apply to any interviews with suspects who have not been arrested.

10G Nothing in this Code requires a caution to be given or repeated when informing a person not under arrest they may be prosecuted for an offence. However, a court will not be able to draw any inferences under the Criminal Justice and Public Order Act 1994, section 34, if the person was not cautioned.

11 Interviews—general

(A) Action

11.1A An interview is the questioning of a person regarding their involvement or suspected involvement in a criminal offence or offences which, under paragraph 10.1, must be carried out under caution. Before a person is interviewed, they and, if they are represented, their solicitor must be given sufficient information to enable them to understand the nature of any such offence, and why they are suspected of committing it (see *paragraphs 3.4(a)* and *10.3*), in order to allow for the effective exercise of the rights of the defence. However, whilst the information must always be sufficient for the person to understand the nature of any offence (see *Note 11ZA*), this does not require the disclosure of details at a time which might prejudice the criminal investigation. The decision about what needs to be disclosed for the purpose of this requirement therefore rests with the investigating officer who has sufficient knowledge of the case to make that decision. The officer who discloses the information shall make a record of the information disclosed and when it was disclosed. This record may be made in the interview record, in the officer's report book or other form provided for this purpose. Procedures under the Road Traffic Act 1988, section 7 or the Transport and Works Act 1992, section 31 do not constitute interviewing for the purpose of this Code.

11.1 Following a decision to arrest a suspect, they must not be interviewed about the relevant offence except at a police station or other authorised place of detention, unless the consequent delay would be likely to:

(a) lead to:
- interference with, or harm to, evidence connected with an offence;
- interference with, or physical harm to, other people; or
- serious loss of, or damage to, property;

(b) lead to alerting other people suspected of committing an offence but not yet arrested for it; or

(c) hinder the recovery of property obtained in consequence of the commission of an offence.

Interviewing in any of these circumstances shall cease once the relevant risk has been averted or the necessary questions have been put in order to attempt to avert that risk.

11.2 Immediately prior to the commencement or re-commencement of any interview at a police station or other authorised place of detention, the interviewer should remind the suspect of their entitlement to free legal advice and that the interview can be delayed for legal advice to be obtained, unless one of the exceptions in *paragraph 6.6* applies. It is the interviewer's responsibility to make sure all reminders are recorded in the interview record.

11.3 *Not used.*

11.4 At the beginning of an interview the interviewer, after cautioning the suspect, see *section 10*, shall put to them any significant statement or silence which occurred in the presence and hearing of a police officer or other police staff before the start of the interview and which have not been put to the suspect in the course of a previous interview. See *Note 11A*. The interviewer shall ask the suspect whether they confirm or deny that earlier statement or silence and if they want to add anything.

11.4A A significant statement is one which appears capable of being used in evidence against the suspect, in particular a direct admission of guilt. A significant silence is a failure or refusal to answer a question or answer satisfactorily when under caution, which might, allowing for the restriction on drawing adverse inferences from silence, see *Annex C,* give rise to an inference under the Criminal Justice and Public Order Act 1994, Part III.

11.5 No interviewer may try to obtain answers or elicit a statement by the use of oppression. Except as in *paragraph 10.9*, no interviewer shall indicate, except to answer a direct question, what action will be taken by the police if the person being questioned answers questions, makes a statement or refuses to do either. If the person asks directly what action will be taken if they answer questions, make a statement or refuse to do either, the interviewer may inform them what action the police propose to take provided that action is itself proper and warranted.

11.6 The interview or further interview of a person about an offence with which that person has not been charged or for which they have not been informed they may be prosecuted, must cease when:

(a) the officer in charge of the investigation is satisfied all the questions they consider relevant to obtaining accurate and reliable information about the offence have been put to the suspect, this includes allowing the suspect an opportunity to give an innocent explanation and asking questions to test if the explanation is accurate and reliable, e.g. to clear up ambiguities or clarify what the suspect said;

(b) the officer in charge of the investigation has taken account of any other available evidence; and

(c) the officer in charge of the investigation, or in the case of a detained suspect, the custody officer, see *paragraph 16.1,* reasonably believes there is sufficient evidence to provide a realistic prospect of conviction for that offence. See *Note 11B.*

This paragraph does not prevent officers in revenue cases or acting under the confiscation provisions of the Criminal Justice Act 1988 or the Drug Trafficking Act 1994 from inviting suspects to complete a formal question and answer record after the interview is concluded.

(B) Interview records

11.7 (a) An accurate record must be made of each interview, whether or not the interview takes place at a police station.

(b) The record must state the place of interview, the time it begins and ends, any interview breaks and, subject to *paragraph 2.6A*, the names of all those present; and must be made on the forms provided for this purpose or in the interviewer's report book or in accordance with Codes of Practice E or F.

(c) Any written record must be made and completed during the interview, unless this would not be practicable or would interfere with the conduct of the interview, and must constitute either a verbatim record of what has been said or, failing this, an account of the interview which adequately and accurately summarises it.

11.8 If a written record is not made during the interview it must be made as soon as practicable after its completion.

11.9 Written interview records must be timed and signed by the maker.

11.10 If a written record is not completed during the interview the reason must be recorded in the interview record.

11.11 Unless it is impracticable, the person interviewed shall be given the opportunity to read the interview record and to sign it as correct or to indicate how they consider it inaccurate. If the person interviewed cannot read or refuses to read the record or sign it, the senior interviewer present shall read it to them and ask whether they would like to sign it as correct or make their mark or to indicate how they consider it inaccurate. The interviewer shall certify on the interview record itself what has occurred. See *Note 11E*.

11.12 If the appropriate adult or the person's solicitor is present during the interview, they should also be given an opportunity to read and sign the interview record or any written statement taken down during the interview.

11.13 A record shall be made of any comments made by a suspect, including unsolicited comments, which are outside the context of an interview but which might be relevant to the offence. Any such record must be timed and signed by the maker. When practicable the suspect shall be given the opportunity to read that record and to sign it as correct or to indicate how they consider it inaccurate. See *Note 11E*.

11.14 Any refusal by a person to sign an interview record when asked in accordance with this Code must itself be recorded.

(C) Juveniles and vulnerable persons

11.15 A juvenile or vulnerable person must not be interviewed regarding their involvement or suspected involvement in a criminal offence or offences, or asked to provide or sign a written statement under caution or record of interview, in the absence of the appropriate adult unless *paragraphs 11.1* or *11.18* to *11.20* apply. See *Note 11C*.

11.16 Juveniles may only be interviewed at their place of education in exceptional circumstances and only when the principal or their nominee agrees. Every effort should be made to notify the parent(s) or other person responsible for the juvenile's welfare and the appropriate adult, if this is a different person, that the police want to interview the juvenile and reasonable time should be allowed to enable the appropriate adult to be present at the interview. If awaiting the appropriate adult would cause unreasonable delay, and unless the juvenile is suspected of an offence against the educational establishment, the principal or their nominee can act as the appropriate adult for the purposes of the interview.

11.17 If an appropriate adult is present at an interview, they shall be informed:

- that they are not expected to act simply as an observer; and
- that the purpose of their presence is to:

~ advise the person being interviewed;
~ observe whether the interview is being conducted properly and fairly; and
~ facilitate communication with the person being interviewed.

See *paragraph 1.7A*.

11.17A The appropriate adult may be required to leave the interview if their conduct is such that the interviewer is unable properly to put questions to the suspect. This will include situations where the appropriate adult's approach or conduct prevents or unreasonably obstructs proper questions being put to the suspect or the suspect's responses being recorded (see *Note 11F*). If the interviewer considers an appropriate adult is acting in such a way, they will stop the interview and consult an officer not below superintendent rank, if one is readily available, and otherwise an officer not below inspector rank not connected with the investigation. After speaking to the appropriate adult, the officer consulted must remind the adult that their role under *paragraph 11.17* does not allow them to obstruct proper questioning and give the adult an opportunity to respond. The officer consulted will then decide if the interview should continue without the attendance of that appropriate adult. If they decide it should, another appropriate adult must be obtained before the interview continues, unless the provisions of *paragraph 11.18* below apply.

(D) Vulnerable suspects—urgent interviews at police stations

11.18 The following interviews may take place only if an officer of superintendent rank or above considers delaying the interview will lead to the consequences in *paragraph 11.1(a)* to *(c)*, and is satisfied the interview would not significantly harm the person's physical or mental state (see *Annex G*):

(a) an interview of a detained juvenile or vulnerable person without the appropriate adult being present (see *Note 11C*);
(b) an interview of anyone detained other than in *(a)* who appears unable to:
  - appreciate the significance of questions and their answers; or
  - understand what is happening because of the effects of drink, drugs or any illness, ailment or condition;
(c) an interview, without an interpreter having been arranged, of a detained person whom the custody officer has determined requires an interpreter (see *paragraphs 3.5(c)(ii)* and *3.12*) which is carried out by an interviewer speaking the suspect's own language or (as the case may be) otherwise establishing effective communication which is sufficient to enable the necessary questions to be asked and answered in order to avert the consequences. See *paragraphs 13.2* and *13.5*.

11.19 These interviews may not continue once sufficient information has been obtained to avert the consequences in *paragraph 11.1(a)* to *(c)*.

11.20 A record shall be made of the grounds for any decision to interview a person under *paragraph 11.18*.

(E) Conduct and recording of Interviews at police stations—use of live link

11.21 When a suspect in police detention is interviewed using a live link by a police officer who is not at the police station where the detainee is held, the provisions of this section that govern the conduct and making a written record of that interview, shall be subject to *paragraph 12.9B* of this Code.

(F) Witnesses

11.22 The provisions of this Code and Codes E and F which govern the conduct and recording of interviews do not apply to interviews with, or taking statements from, witnesses.

Notes for Guidance

11ZA The requirement in paragraph 11.1A for a suspect to be given sufficient information about the offence applies prior to the interview and whether or not they are legally represented. What is sufficient will depend on the circumstances of the case, but it should normally include, as a minimum, a description of the facts relating to the suspected offence that are known to the officer, including the time and place in question. This aims to avoid suspects being confused or unclear about what they are supposed to have done and to help an innocent suspect to clear the matter up more quickly.

11A Paragraph 11.4 does not prevent the interviewer from putting significant statements and silences to a suspect again at a later stage or a further interview.

11B The Criminal Procedure and Investigations Act 1996 Code of Practice, paragraph 3.5 states 'In conducting an investigation, the investigator should pursue all reasonable lines of enquiry, whether these point towards or away from the suspect. What is reasonable will depend on the particular circumstances.' Interviewers should keep this in mind when deciding what questions to ask in an interview.

11C Although juveniles or vulnerable persons are often capable of providing reliable evidence, they may, without knowing or wishing to do so, be particularly prone in certain circumstances to providing information that may be unreliable, misleading or self-incriminating. Special care should always be taken when questioning such a person, and the appropriate adult should be involved if there is any doubt about a person's age, mental state or capacity. Because of the risk of unreliable evidence it is also important to obtain corroboration of any facts admitted whenever possible. Because of the risks, which the presence of the appropriate adult is intended to minimise, officers of superintendent rank or above should exercise their discretion under paragraph 11.18(a) to authorise the commencement of an interview in the appropriate adult's absence only in exceptional cases, if it is necessary to avert one or more of the specified risks in paragraph 11.1.

11D Juveniles should not be arrested at their place of education unless this is unavoidable. When a juvenile is arrested at their place of education, the principal or their nominee must be informed.

11E Significant statements described in paragraph 11.4 will always be relevant to the offence and must be recorded. When a suspect agrees to read records of interviews and other comments and sign them as correct, they should be asked to endorse the record with, e.g. 'I agree that this is a correct record of what was said' and add their signature. If the suspect does not agree with the record, the interviewer should record the details of any disagreement and ask the suspect to read these details and sign them to the effect that they accurately reflect their disagreement. Any refusal to sign should be recorded.

11F The appropriate adult may intervene if they consider it is necessary to help the suspect understand any question asked and to help the suspect to answer any question. Paragraph 11.17A only applies if the appropriate adult's approach or conduct prevents or unreasonably obstructs proper questions being put to the suspect or the suspect's response being recorded. Examples of unacceptable conduct include answering questions on a suspect's behalf or providing written replies for the suspect to quote. An officer who takes the decision to exclude an appropriate adult must be in a position to satisfy the court the decision was properly made. In order to do this they may need to witness what is happening and give the suspect's solicitor (if they have one) who witnessed what happened, an opportunity to comment.

12 Interviews in police stations

(A) Action

When interviewer and suspect are present at the same police station

12.1 If a police officer wants to interview or conduct enquiries which require the presence of a detainee, the custody officer is responsible for deciding whether to deliver the detainee into the officer's custody. An investigating officer who is given custody of a detainee takes over responsibility for the detainee's care and safe custody for the purposes of this Code until they return the detainee to the custody officer when they must report the manner in which they complied with the Code whilst having custody of the detainee.

12.2 Except as below, in any period of 24 hours a detainee must be allowed a continuous period of at least 8 hours for rest, free from questioning, travel or any interruption in connection with the investigation concerned. This period should normally be at night or other appropriate time which takes account of when the detainee last slept or rested. If a detainee is arrested at a police station after going there voluntarily, the period of 24 hours runs from the time of their arrest and not the time of arrival at the police station. The period may not be interrupted or delayed, except:

(a) when there are reasonable grounds for believing not delaying or interrupting the period would:
   (i) involve a risk of harm to people or serious loss of, or damage to, property;
   (ii) delay unnecessarily the person's release from custody; or
   (iii) otherwise prejudice the outcome of the investigation;
(b) at the request of the detainee, their appropriate adult or legal representative;
(c) when a delay or interruption is necessary in order to:
   (i) comply with the legal obligations and duties arising under section 15; or
   (ii) to take action required under *section 9* or in accordance with medical advice.

If the period is interrupted in accordance with *(a)*, a fresh period must be allowed. Interruptions under *(b)* and *(c)* do not require a fresh period to be allowed.

12.3 Before a detainee is interviewed, the custody officer, in consultation with the officer in charge of the investigation and appropriate healthcare professionals as necessary, shall assess whether the detainee is fit enough to be interviewed. This means determining and considering the risks to the detainee's physical and mental state if the interview took place and determining what safeguards are needed to allow the interview to take place. See *Annex G.* The custody officer shall not allow a detainee to be interviewed if the custody officer considers it would cause significant harm to the detainee's physical or mental state. Vulnerable suspects listed at *paragraph 11.18* shall be treated as always being at some risk during an interview and these persons may not be interviewed except in accordance with *paragraphs 11.18* to *11.20.*

12.4 As far as practicable interviews shall take place in interview rooms which are adequately heated, lit and ventilated.

12.5 A suspect whose detention without charge has been authorised under PACE because the detention is necessary for an interview to obtain evidence of the offence for which they have been arrested may choose not to answer questions but police do not require the suspect's consent or agreement to interview them for this purpose. If a suspect takes steps to prevent themselves being questioned or further questioned, e.g. by refusing to leave their cell to go to a suitable interview room or by trying to leave the interview room, they shall be advised that their consent or agreement to be interviewed is not required. The suspect shall be cautioned as in *section 10,* and informed if they fail or refuse to co-operate, the interview may take place in the cell and that their failure or refusal to co-operate may be given in evidence. The suspect shall then be invited to co-operate and go into the interview room. If they refuse and the custody officer considers, on reasonable grounds, that the interview should not be delayed, the custody officer has discretion to direct that the interview be conducted in a cell.

12.6 People being questioned or making statements shall not be required to stand.

12.7 Before the interview commences each interviewer shall, subject to *paragraph 2.6A,* identify themselves and any other persons present to the interviewee.

12.8 Breaks from interviewing should be made at recognised meal times or at other times that take account of when an interviewee last had a meal. Short refreshment breaks shall be provided at approximately two hour intervals, subject to the interviewer's discretion to delay a break if there are reasonable grounds for believing it would:
   (i) involve a:
      - risk of harm to people;
      - serious loss of, or damage to, property;
   (ii) unnecessarily delay the detainee's release; or
   (iii) otherwise prejudice the outcome of the investigation.

See *Note 12B*

12.9 If during the interview a complaint is made by or on behalf of the interviewee concerning the provisions of any of the Codes, or it comes to the interviewer's notice that the interviewee may have been treated improperly, the interviewer should:
   (i) record the matter in the interview record; and
   (ii) inform the custody officer, who is then responsible for dealing with it as in *section 9.*

Interviewer not present at the same station as the detainee—use of live link

12.9A Amendments to PACE, section 39, allow a person in police detention to be interviewed using a live link (see *paragraph 1.13(e)(i)*) by a police officer who is not at the police station where the detainee is held. Subject to *sub-paragraphs (a)* to *(f)* below, the custody officer is responsible for deciding on a case by case basis whether a detainee is fit to be interviewed (see *paragraph 12.3)* and should be delivered into the physical custody of an officer who is not involved in the investigation, for the purpose of enabling another officer who is investigating the offence for which the person is detained and who is not at the police station where the person is detained, to interview the detainee by means of a live link (see *Note 12ZA*).

(a) The custody officer must be satisfied that the live link to be used provides for accurate and secure communication with the suspect. The provisions of *paragraph 13.13* shall apply to communications between the interviewing officer, the suspect and anyone else whose presence at the interview or, (as the case may be) whose access to any communications between the suspect and the interviewer, has been authorised by the custody officer or the interviewing officer.

(b) Each decision must take account of the age, gender and vulnerability of the suspect, the nature and circumstances of the offence and the investigation and the impact on the suspect of carrying out the interview by means of a live link. For this reason, the custody officer must consider whether the ability of the particular suspect, to communicate confidently and effectively for the purpose of the interview is likely to be adversely affected or otherwise undermined or limited if the interviewing officer is not physically present and a live-link is used (see *Note 12ZB*). Although a suspect for whom an appropriate adult is required may be more likely to be adversely affected as described, it is important to note that a person who does not require an appropriate adult may also be adversely impacted if interviewed by means of a live link.

(c) If the custody officer is satisfied that interviewing the detainee by means of a live link *would not* adversely affect or otherwise undermine or limit the suspect's ability to communicate confidently and effectively for the purpose of the *interview*, the officer must so inform the suspect, their solicitor and (if applicable) the appropriate adult. At the same time, the operation of the live-link must be explained and demonstrated to them (see *Note 12ZC*), they must be advised of the chief officer's obligations concerning the security of live-link communications under *paragraph 13.13* and they must be asked if they wish to make representations that the live-link should not be used or if they require more information about the operation of the arrangements. They must also be told that at any time live-link is in use, they may make representations to the custody officer or the interviewer that its operation should cease and that the physical presence of the interviewer should be arranged.

When the authority of an inspector is required

(d) If:

(i) representations are made that a live-link should not be used to carry out the interview, or that at any time it is in use, its operation should cease and the physical presence of the interviewer arranged; and

(ii) the custody officer in consultation with the interviewer is unable to allay the concerns raised;

then live-link may not be used, or (as the case may be) continue to be used, unless authorised in writing by an officer of the rank of inspector or above in accordance with *sub-paragraph (e)*.

(e) Authority may be given if the officer is satisfied that interviewing the detainee by means of a live link is necessary and justified. In making this decision, the officer must have regard to:

(i) the circumstances of the suspect;

(ii) the nature and seriousness of the offence;

(iii) the requirements of the investigation, including its likely impact on both the suspect and any victim(s);
(iv) the representations made by the suspect, their solicitor and (if applicable) the appropriate adult that a live-link should not be used (see *sub-paragraph (b);*
(v) the impact on the investigation of making arrangements for the physical presence of the interviewer (see *Note 12ZD*); and
(vi) the risk if the interviewer is not *physically* present, evidence obtained using link interpretation might be excluded in subsequent criminal proceedings; and
(vii) the likely impact on the suspect and the investigation of any consequential delay to arrange for the interviewer to be *physically* present with the suspect.

(f) The officer given custody of the detainee *and* the interviewer take over responsibility for the detainee's care, treatment and safe custody for the purposes of this Code until the detainee is returned to the custody officer. On that return, both must report the manner in which they complied with the Code during period in question.

12.9B When a suspect detained at a police station is interviewed using a live link in accordance with *paragraph 12.9A*, the officer given custody of the detainee at the police station *and* the interviewer who is not present at the police station, take over responsibility for ensuring compliance with the provisions of *sections 11* and *12* of this Code, or *Code E* (Audio recording) or *Code F* (Audio visual recording) that govern the conduct and recording of that interview. In these circumstances:

(a) *the interviewer who is not at the police station where the detainee is held* must direct the officer having physical custody of the suspect at the police station, to take the action required by those provisions and which the interviewer would be required to take if they were present at the police station.
(b) *the officer having physical custody of the suspect at the police station* must take the action required by those provisions and which would otherwise be required to be taken by the interviewer if they were present at the police station. This applies whether or not the officer has been so directed by the interviewer but in such a case, the officer must inform the interviewer of the action taken.
(c) *during the course of the interview,* the officers in (a) and (b) may consult each other as necessary to clarify any action to be taken and to avoid any misunderstanding. Such consultations must, if in the hearing of the suspect and any other person present with the suspect (for example, a solicitor, appropriate adult or interpreter) be recorded in the interview record.

(B) Documentation

12.10 A record must be made of the:

- time a detainee is not in the custody of the custody officer, and why
- reason for any refusal to deliver the detainee out of that custody.

12.11 A record shall be made of the following:

(a) the reasons it was not practicable to use an interview room;
(b) any action taken as in *paragraph 12.5*, and
(c) the actions, decisions, authorisations, representations and outcomes arising from the requirements of *paragraphs 12.9A* and *12.9B*.

The record shall be made on the custody record or in the interview record for action taken whilst an interview record is being kept, with a brief reference to this effect in the custody record.

12.12 Any decision to delay a break in an interview must be recorded, with reasons, in the interview record.

12.13 All written statements made at police stations under caution shall be written on forms provided for the purpose.

12.14 All written statements made under caution shall be taken in accordance with *Annex D*. Before a person makes a written statement under caution at a police station, they shall be reminded about the right to legal advice. See *Note 12A*.

Notes for Guidance

12ZA 'Live link' means an arrangement by means of which the interviewing officer who is not at the police station is able to see and hear, and to be seen and heard by, the detainee concerned, the detainee's solicitor, any appropriate adult present and the officer who has custody of that detainee. See paragraphs 13.12 to 13.14 and Annex N for application to live-link interpretation.

12ZB In considering whether the use of the live link is appropriate in a particular case, the custody officer, in consultation with the interviewer, should make an assessment of the detainee's ability to understand and take part in the interviewing process and make a record of the outcome. If the suspect has asked for legal advice, their solicitor should be involved in the assessment and in the case of a juvenile or vulnerable person, the appropriate adult should be involved.

12ZC The explanation and demonstration of live-link interpretation is intended to help the suspect, solicitor and appropriate adult make an informed decision and to allay any concerns they may have.

12ZD Factors affecting the arrangements for the interviewer to be physically present will include the location of the police station where the interview would take place and the availability of an interviewer with sufficient knowledge of the investigation who can attend that station and carry out the interview.

12A It is not normally necessary to ask for a written statement if the interview was recorded in writing and the record signed in accordance with paragraph 11.11 or audibly or visually recorded in accordance with Code E or F. Statements under caution should normally be taken in these circumstances only at the person's express wish. A person may however be asked if they want to make such a statement.

12B Meal breaks should normally last at least 45 minutes and shorter breaks after two hours should last at least 15 minutes. If the interviewer delays a break in accordance with paragraph 12.8 and prolongs the interview, a longer break should be provided. If there is a short interview and another short interview is contemplated, the length of the break may be reduced if there are reasonable grounds to believe this is necessary to avoid any of the consequences in paragraph 12.8(i) to (iii).

13 Interpreters

(A) General

13.1 Chief officers are responsible for making arrangements (see *paragraph 13.1ZA*) to provide appropriately qualified independent persons to act as interpreters and to provide translations of essential documents for:

- (a) detained suspects who, in accordance with *paragraph 3.5(c)(ii)*, the custody officer has determined require an interpreter, and
- (b) suspects who are not under arrest but are cautioned as in *section 10* who, in accordance with *paragraph 3.21(b)*, the interviewer has determined require an interpreter. In these cases, the responsibilities of the custody officer are, if appropriate, assigned to the interviewer. An interviewer who has any doubts about whether and what arrangements for an interpreter must be made or about how the provisions of this section should be applied to a suspect who is not under arrest should seek advice from an officer of the rank of sergeant or above.

If the suspect has a hearing or speech impediment, references to 'interpreter' and 'interpretation' in this Code include arrangements for appropriate assistance necessary to establish effective communication with that person. See *paragraph 13.1C* below if the person is in Wales.

13.1ZA References in *paragraph 13.1* above and elsewhere in this Code (see *paragraphs 3.12(a), 13.2, 13.2A, 13.5, 13.6, 13.9, 13.10, 13.10A, 13.10D and 13.11* below and in any other Code, to making arrangements for an interpreter to assist a suspect, mean making arrangements for the interpreter to be *physically* present in the same location as the suspect *unless* the provisions in *paragraph 13.12* below, and Part 1 of *Annex N*, allow live-link interpretation to be used.

13.1A The arrangements must comply with the minimum requirements set out in *Directive 2010/64/EU* of the European Parliament and of the Council of 20 October 2010 on the right to interpretation and translation in criminal proceedings (see *Note 13A*). The provisions *of this* Code implement the requirements for those to whom this Code applies. These requirements include the following:

- That the arrangements made and the quality of interpretation and translation provided shall be sufficient to 'safeguard the fairness of the proceedings, in particular by ensuring that suspected or accused persons have knowledge of the cases against them and are able to exercise their right of defence'. This term which is used by the Directive means that the suspect must be able to understand their position and be able to communicate effectively with police officers, interviewers, solicitors and appropriate adults as provided for by this and any other Code in the same way as a suspect who can speak and understand English and who does not have a hearing or speech impediment and who would therefore not require an interpreter. See *paragraphs 13.12 to 13.14* and *Annex N* for application to live-link interpretation.
- The provision of a written translation of all documents considered essential for the person to exercise their right of defence and to *'safeguard the fairness of the proceedings'* as described above. For the purposes of this Code, this includes any decision to authorise a person to be detained and details of any offence(s) with which the person has been charged or for which they have been told they may be prosecuted, see *Annex M*.
- Procedures to help determine:
  - ~ whether a suspect can speak and understand English and needs the assistance of an interpreter, see *paragraph 13.1* and *Notes 13B* and *13C*; and
  - ~ whether another interpreter should be arranged or another translation should be provided when a suspect complains about the quality of either or both, see *paragraphs 13.10A* and *13.10C*.

13.1B All reasonable attempts should be made to make the suspect understand that interpretation and translation will be provided at public expense.

13.1C With regard to persons in Wales, nothing in this or any other Code affects the application of the Welsh Language Schemes produced by police and crime commissioners in Wales in accordance with the Welsh Language Act 1993. See *paragraphs 3.12 and 13.1.*

(B) Interviewing suspects—foreign languages

13.2 Unless *paragraphs 11.1 or 11.18(c)* apply, a suspect who for the purposes of this Code requires an interpreter because they do not appear to speak or understand English (see *paragraphs 3.5(c)(ii)* and *3.12*) must not be interviewed unless arrangements are made for a person capable of interpreting to assist the suspect to understand and communicate.

13.2A If a person who is a juvenile or a vulnerable person is interviewed and the person acting as the appropriate adult does not appear to speak or understand English, arrangements must be made for an interpreter to assist communication between the person, the appropriate adult and the interviewer, unless the interview is urgent and *paragraphs 11.1 or 11.18(c)* apply.

13.3 When a written record of the interview is made (see *paragraph 11.7*), the interviewer shall make sure the interpreter makes a note of the interview at the time in the person's language for use in the event of the interpreter being called to give evidence, and certifies its accuracy. The interviewer should allow sufficient time for the interpreter to note each question and answer after each is put, given and interpreted. The person should be allowed to read the record or have it read to them and sign it as correct or indicate the respects in which they consider it inaccurate. If an audio or visual record of the interview is made, the arrangements in Code E or F shall apply. See *paragraphs 13.12* to *13.14* and Annex N for application to live-link interpretation.

13.4 In the case of a person making a statement under caution (see *Annex D)* to a police officer or other police staff in a language other than English:

(a) the interpreter shall record the statement in the language it is made;
(b) the person shall be invited to sign it;
(c) an official English translation shall be made in due course. See *paragraphs* 13.12 to *13.14* and Annex N for application to live-link interpretation.

(C) Interviewing suspects who have a hearing or speech impediment

13.5 Unless *paragraphs 11.1 or 11.18(c)* (urgent interviews) apply, a suspect who for the purposes of this Code requires an interpreter or other appropriate assistance to enable effective communication with them because they appear to have a hearing or speech impediment (see *paragraphs 3.5(c)(ii)* and *3.12*) must not be interviewed without arrangements having been made to provide an independent person capable of interpreting or of providing other appropriate assistance.

13.6 An interpreter should also be arranged if a person who is a juvenile or a vulnerable person is interviewed and the person who is present as the appropriate adult, appears to have a hearing or speech impediment, unless the interview is urgent and *paragraphs 11.1 or 11.18(c)* apply.

13.7 If a written record of the interview is made, the interviewer shall make sure the interpreter is allowed to read the record and certify its accuracy in the event of the interpreter being called to give evidence. If an audio or visual recording is made, the arrangements in Code E or F apply.

See *paragraphs 13.12* to *13.14* and Annex N for application to live-link interpretation.

(D) Additional rules for detained persons

13.8 *Not used.*

13.9 If *paragraph 6.1* applies and the detainee cannot communicate with the solicitor because of language, hearing or speech difficulties, arrangements must be made for an interpreter to enable communication. A police officer or any other police staff may not be used for this purpose.

13.10 After the custody officer has determined that a detainee requires an interpreter (see *paragraph 3.5(c)(ii)*) and following the initial action in *paragraphs 3.1 to 3.5*, arrangements must also be made for an interpreter to:

- explain the grounds and reasons for any authorisation for their *continued* detention, before or after charge and any information about the authorisation given to them by the authorising officer and which is recorded in the custody record. See *paragraphs 15.3, 15.4* and *15.16(a)* and *(b)*;
- to provide interpretation at the magistrates' court for the hearing of an application for a warrant of further detention or any extension or further extension of such warrant to explain any grounds and reasons for the application and any information about the authorisation of their further detention given to them by the court (see PACE, sections 43 and 44 and *paragraphs 15.2* and *15.16(c)*); and
- explain any offence with which the detainee is charged or for which they are informed they may be prosecuted and any other information about the offence given to them by or on behalf of the custody officer, see *paragraphs 16.1* and *16.3*.

13.10A If a detainee complains that they are not satisfied with the quality of interpretation, the custody officer or (as the case may be) the interviewer, is responsible for deciding whether to make arrangements for a different interpreter in accordance with the procedures set out in the arrangements made by the chief officer, *see paragraph 13.1A*.

(E) Translations of essential documents

13.10B Written translations, oral translations and oral summaries of essential documents in a language the detainee understands shall be provided in accordance with Annex M (Translations of documents and records).

13.10C If a detainee complains that they are not satisfied with the quality of the translation, the custody officer or (as the case may be) the interviewer, is responsible for deciding whether a further translation should be provided in accordance with the procedures set out in the arrangements made by the chief officer, see *paragraph 13.1A*.

(F) Decisions not to provide interpretation and translation.

13.10D If a suspect challenges a decision:

- made by the custody officer or (as the case may be) by the interviewer, in accordance with this Code (see *paragraphs 3.5(c)(ii)* and *3.21(b)*) that they do not require an interpreter, or

- made in accordance with *paragraphs 13.10A, 13.10B* or *13.10C* not to make arrangements to provide a different interpreter or another translation or not to translate a requested document,

the matter shall be reported to an inspector to deal with as a complaint for the purposes of *paragraph 9.2* or *paragraph 12.9* if the challenge is made during an interview.

(G) Documentation

13.11 The following must be recorded in the custody record or, as applicable, the interview record:

(a) Action taken to arrange for an interpreter, including the live-link requirements in *Annex N* as applicable;

(b) Action taken when a detainee is not satisfied about the standard of interpretation or translation provided, see *paragraphs 13.10A* and *13.10C*;

(c) When an urgent interview is carried out in accordance with *paragraph 13.2* or *13.5* in the absence of an interpreter;

(d) When a detainee has been assisted by an interpreter for the purpose of providing or being given information or being interviewed;

(e) Action taken in accordance with *Annex M* when:

- a written translation of an essential document is provided;
- an oral translation or oral summary of an essential document is provided instead of a written translation and the authorising officer's reason(s) why this would not prejudice the fairness of the proceedings (see *Annex M, paragraph 3*);
- a suspect waives their right to a translation of an essential document (see *Annex M, paragraph 4*);
- when representations that a document which is not included in the table is essential and that a translation should be provided are refused and the reason for the refusal (see *Annex M, paragraph 8*).

(H) Live-link interpretation

13.12 In this section and in *Annex N*, 'live-link interpretation' means an arrangement to enable communication between the suspect and an interpreter who is not *physically* present with the suspect. The arrangement must ensure that anything said by any person in the suspect's presence and hearing can be interpreted in the same way as if the interpreter was physically present at that time. The communication must be by audio *and* visual means for the purpose of an interview, and for all other purposes it may be *either*; by audio and visual means, or by audio means *only*, as follows:

(a) **Audio and visual communication**

This applies for the purposes of an interview conducted and recorded in accordance with Code E (Audio recording) or Code F (Visual recording) and during that interview, live link interpretation must *enable*:

(i) the suspect, the interviewer, solicitor, appropriate adult and any other person *physically* present with the suspect at any time during the interview and an interpreter who is not *physically* present, to *see* and *hear* each other; and

(ii) the interview to be conducted and recorded in accordance with the provisions of Codes C, E and F, subject to the modifications in Part 2 of Annex N.

(b) **Audio and visual or audio without visual communication.**

This applies to communication for the purposes of any provision of this or any other Code except as described in (a), which requires or permits information to be given to, sought from, or provided by a suspect, whether orally or in writing, which would include communication between the suspect and their solicitor and/or appropriate adult, and for these cases, live link interpretation must:

(i) *enable* the suspect, the person giving or seeking that information, any other person *physically* present with the suspect at that time and an interpreter who is not so present, to either *see* and *hear* each other, or to *hear without seeing* each other (for example by using a telephone); and

(ii) enable that information to be given to, sought from, or provided by, the suspect in accordance with the provisions of this or any other Code that apply to that information, as modified for the purposes of the live-link, by *Part 2 of Annex N.*

13.12A The requirement in *sub-paragraphs 13.12(a)(ii)* and *(b)(ii),* that live-link interpretation must enable compliance with the relevant provisions of the Codes C, E and F, means that the arrangements must provide for any written or electronic record of what the suspect says in their own language which is made by the interpreter, to be securely transmitted without delay so that the suspect can be invited to read, check and if appropriate, sign or otherwise confirm that the record is correct or make corrections to the record.

13.13 Chief officers must be satisfied that live-link interpretation used in their force area for the purposes of *paragraphs 13.12(a)* and *(b),* provides for accurate and secure communication with the suspect. This includes ensuring that at any time during which live link interpretation is being used: a person cannot see, hear or otherwise obtain access to any communications between the suspect and interpreter or communicate with the suspect or interpreter unless so authorised or allowed by the custody officer or, in the case of an interview, the interviewer and that as applicable, the confidentiality of any private consultation between a suspect and their solicitor and appropriate adult (see *paragraphs 13.2A, 13.6* and *13.9)* is maintained. See *Annex N paragraph 4.*

Notes for Guidance

13A Chief officers have discretion when determining the individuals or organisations they use to provide interpretation and translation services for their forces provided that these are compatible with the requirements of the Directive. One example which chief officers may wish to consider is the Ministry of Justice commercial agreements for interpretation and translation services.

13B A procedure for determining whether a person needs an interpreter might involve a telephone interpreter service or using cue cards or similar visual aids which enable the detainee to indicate their ability to speak and understand English and their preferred language. This could be confirmed through an interpreter who could also assess the extent to which the person can speak and understand English.

13C There should also be a procedure for determining whether a suspect who requires an interpreter requires assistance in accordance with paragraph 3.20 to help them check and if applicable, sign any documentation.

14 Questioning—special restrictions

14.1 If a person is arrested by one police force on behalf of another and the lawful period of detention in respect of that offence has not yet commenced in accordance with PACE, section 41, no questions may be put to them about the offence while they are in transit between the forces except to clarify any voluntary statement they make.

14.2 If a person is in police detention at a hospital, they may not be questioned without the agreement of a responsible doctor. See *Note 14A.*

Note for Guidance

14A If questioning takes place at a hospital under paragraph 14.2, or on the way to or from a hospital, the period of questioning concerned counts towards the total period of detention permitted.

15 Reviews and extensions of detention

(A) Persons detained under PACE

15.0 The requirement in *paragraph 3.4(b)* that documents and materials essential to challenging the lawfulness of the detainee's arrest and detention must be made available to the detainee or their solicitor, applies for the purposes of this section as follows:

(a) The officer reviewing the need for detention without charge (*PACE, section 40*), or (as the case may be) the officer considering the need to extend detention without charge from 24 to 36 hours (*PACE, section 42*), is responsible, in consultation with the investigating officer, for deciding which documents and materials are essential and must be made available.

(b) When *paragraph 15.7A* applies (application for a warrant of further detention or extension of such a warrant), the officer making the application is responsible for deciding which documents and materials are essential and must be made available *before* the hearing. See *Note 3ZA*.

15.1 The review officer is responsible under PACE, section 40 for periodically determining if a person's detention, before or after charge, continues to be necessary. This requirement continues throughout the detention period and, except when a telephone or a live link is used in accordance with paragraphs 15.9 to 15.11C, the review officer must be present at the police station holding the detainee. See *Notes 15A* and *15B*.

15.2 Under PACE, section 42, an officer of superintendent rank or above who is responsible for the station holding the detainee may give authority any time after the second review to extend the maximum period the person may be detained without charge by up to 12 hours. Except when a live link is used as in *paragraph 15.11A*, the superintendent must be present at the station holding the detainee. Further detention without charge may be authorised only by a magistrates' court in accordance with PACE, sections 43 and 44 and unless the court has given a live link direction as in *paragraph 15.11B*, the detainee must be brought before the court for the hearing. See *Notes 15C, 15D* and *15E.*

15.2A An authorisation under section 42(1) of PACE extends the maximum period of detention permitted before charge for indictable offences from 24 hours to 36 hours. Detaining a juvenile or a vulnerable person for longer than 24 hours will be dependent on the circumstances of the case and with regard to the person's:

(a) special vulnerability;
(b) the legal obligation to provide an opportunity for representations to be made prior to a decision about extending detention;
(c) the need to consult and consider the views of any appropriate adult; and
(d) any alternatives to police custody.

15.3 Before deciding whether to authorise continued detention the officer responsible under *paragraph 15.1* or *15.2* shall give an opportunity to make representations about the detention to:

(a) the detainee, unless in the case of a review as in *paragraph 15.1*, the detainee is asleep;
(b) the detainee's solicitor if available at the time; and
(c) the appropriate adult if available at the time. See *Note 15CA*

15.3A Other people having an interest in the detainee's welfare may also make representations at the authorising officer's discretion.

15.3B Subject to *paragraph 15.10*, the representations may be made orally in person or by telephone or in writing. The authorising officer may, however, refuse to hear oral representations from the detainee if the officer considers them unfit to make representations because of their condition or behaviour. See *Note 15C.*

15.3C The decision on whether the review takes place in person or by telephone or by live link (see *paragraph 1.13(e)(ii)*) is a matter for the review officer. In determining the form the review may take, the review officer must always take full account of the needs of the person in custody. The benefits of carrying out a review in person should always be considered, based on the individual circumstances of each case with specific additional consideration if the person is:

(a) a juvenile (and the age of the juvenile); or
(b) a vulnerable person; or
(c) in need of medical attention for other than routine minor ailments; or
(d) subject to presentational or community issues around their detention.

See paragraph 1.4(c)

15.4 Before conducting a review or determining whether to extend the maximum period of detention without charge, the officer responsible must make sure the detainee is reminded of their entitlement to free legal advice, see *paragraph 6.5,* unless in the case of a review the person is asleep. When determining whether to extend the maximum period of detention without charge, it should also be pointed out that for the purposes of *paragraph 15.2*, the superintendent or (as the case may be) the court, responsible for authorising any such extension, will not be able to use a live link unless the detainee has *received* legal advice on the use of the live link (see *paragraphs 15.11A(ii)* and *15.11C(ii)*) and given consent to its use (see *paragraphs 15.11A(iii)* and *15.11C(iii)*. The detainee must also be given information about how the live link is used.

15.4A Following sections 45ZA and 45ZB of PACE, when the reminder and information concerning legal advice and about the use of the live link is given and the detainee's consent is sought, the presence of an appropriate adult is required if the detainee in question is a juvenile (see *paragraph 1.5*) or is a *vulnerable adult* by virtue of being a person aged 18 or over who, because of a mental disorder established in accordance *paragraphs 1.4* and *1.13(d)* or for *any other reason* (see *paragraph 15.4B*), may have difficulty understanding the purpose of:

(a) an authorisation under section 42 of PACE or anything that occurs in connection with a decision whether to give it (see *paragraphs 15.2* and *15.2A*); or
(b) a court hearing under section 43 or 44 of PACE or what occurs at the hearing it (see *paragraphs 15.2* and *15.7A*).

15.4B For the purpose of using a live link in accordance with sections 45ZA and 45ZB of PACE to authorise detention without charge (see *paragraphs 15.11A* and *15.11C*), the reference to '*any other reason*' would extend to difficulties in understanding the purposes mentioned in paragraph 15.4A that might arise if the person happened to be under the influence of drink or drugs at the time the live link is to be used. This does not however apply for the purposes of *paragraphs 1.4* and *1.13(d)* (see *Note 1GC*).

15.5 If, after considering any representations, the review officer under *paragraph 15.1* decides to keep the detainee in detention or the superintendent under *paragraph 15.2* extends the maximum period for which they may be detained without charge, then any comment made by the detainee shall be recorded. If applicable, the officer shall be informed of the comment as soon as practicable. See also *paragraphs 11.4* and *11.13*.

15.6 No officer shall put specific questions to the detainee:

- regarding their involvement in any offence; or
- in respect of any comments they may make:
  - ~ when given the opportunity to make representations; or
  - ~ in response to a decision to keep them in detention or extend the maximum period of detention.

Such an exchange could constitute an interview as in *paragraph 11.1A* and would be subject to the associated safeguards in *section 11* and, in respect of a person who has been charged, *paragraph 16.5*. See also *paragraph 11.13*.

15.7 A detainee who is asleep at a review, see *paragraph 15.1*, and whose continued detention is authorised must be informed about the decision and reason as soon as practicable after waking.

15.7A When an application is made to a magistrates' court under PACE, section 43 for a warrant of further detention to extend detention without charge of a person arrested for an *indictable offence*, or under section 44, to extend or further extend that warrant, the detainee:

(a) must, unless the court has given a live link direction as in *paragraph 15.11C*, be brought to court for the hearing of the application (see *Note 15D*);
(b) is entitled to be legally represented if they wish, in which case, *Annex B* cannot apply; and
(c) must be given a copy of the information which supports the application and states:
  (i) the nature of the offence for which the person to whom the application relates has been arrested;
  (ii) the general nature of the evidence on which the person was arrested;
  (iii) what inquiries about the offence have been made and what further inquiries are proposed;
  (iv) the reasons for believing continued detention is necessary for the purposes of the further inquiries;

Note: A warrant of further detention can only be issued or extended if the court has reasonable grounds for believing that the person's further detention is necessary for the purpose of obtaining evidence of an indictable offence for which the person has been arrested and that the investigation is being conducted diligently and expeditiously.

See *paragraph 15.0(b)*.

15.8 *Not used.*

(B) Review of detention by telephone or by using a live link (section 40A and 45A)

15.9 PACE, section 40A provides that the officer responsible under section 40 for reviewing the detention of a person who has not been charged, need not attend the police station holding the detainee and may carry out the review by telephone.

15.9A PACE, section 45A(2) provides that the officer responsible under section 40 for reviewing the detention of a person who has not been charged, need not attend the police station holding the detainee and may carry out the review using a live link. See *paragraph 1.13(e)(ii)*.

15.9B A telephone review is not permitted where facilities for review using a live link exist and it is practicable to use them.

15.9C The review officer can decide at any stage that a telephone review or review by live link should be terminated and that the review will be conducted in person. The reasons for doing so should be noted in the custody record. See *Note 15F*.

15.10 When a review is carried out by telephone or by using a live link, an officer at the station holding the detainee shall be required by the review officer to fulfil that officer's obligations under PACE section 40 and this Code by:

(a) making any record connected with the review in the detainee's custody record;
(b) if applicable, making the record in (*a*) in the presence of the detainee; and
(c) for a review by telephone, giving the detainee information about the review.

15.11 When a review is carried out by telephone or by using a live link, or the requirement in *paragraph 15.3* will be satisfied:

(a) if facilities exist for the immediate transmission of written representations to the review officer, e.g. fax or email message, by allowing those who are given the opportunity to make representations, to make their representations:
    (i) orally by telephone or (as the case may be) by means of the live link; or
    (ii) in writing using the facilities for the immediate transmission of written representations; and
(b) in all other cases, by allowing those who are given the opportunity to make representations, to make their representations orally by telephone or by means of the live link.

(C) Authorisation to extend detention using live link (sections 45ZA and 45ZB)

15.11A For the purpose of *paragraphs 15.2* and *15.2A*, a superintendent who is not present at the police station where the detainee is being held but who has access to the use of a live link (see *paragraph 1.13(e)(iii)*) may, using that live link, give authority to extend the maximum period of detention permitted before charge, if, and only if, the following conditions are satisfied:

(i) the custody officer considers that the use of the live link is appropriate (see *Note 15H*);
(ii) the detainee in question has requested and received legal advice on the use of the live link (see *paragraph 15.4*).
(iii) the detainee has given their consent to the live link being used (see *paragraph 15.11D*)

15.11B When a live link is used:

(a) the authorising superintendent shall, with regard to any record connected with the authorisation which PACE, section 42 and this Code require to be made by the authorising officer, require an officer at the station holding the detainee to make that record in the detainee's custody record;
(b) the requirement in *paragraph 15.3* (allowing opportunity to make representations) will be satisfied:
    (i) if facilities exist for the immediate transmission of written representations to the authorising officer, e.g. fax or email message, by allowing those who are given the opportunity to make representations, to make their representations:

- in writing by means of those facilities or
- orally by means of the live link; or

(ii) in all other cases, by allowing those who are given the opportunity to make representations, to make their representations orally by means of the live link.

(c) The authorising officer can decide at any stage to terminate the live link and attend the police station where the detainee is held to carry out the procedure in person. The reasons for doing so should be noted in the custody record.

15.11C For the purpose of *paragraph 15.7A* and the hearing of an application to a magistrates' court under PACE, section 43 for a warrant of further detention to extend detention without charge of a person arrested for an *indictable offence*, or under PACE, section 44, to extend or further extend that warrant, the magistrates' court may give a direction that a live link (see *paragraph 1.13(e)(iv)*) be used for the purposes of the hearing if, and only if, the following conditions are satisfied:

(i) the custody officer considers that the use of the live link for the purpose of the hearing is appropriate (see *Note 15H*);

(ii) the detainee in question has requested and received legal advice on the use of the live link (see *paragraph 15.4*);

(iii) the detainee has given their consent to the live link being used (see *paragraph 15.11D*); and

(iv) it is not contrary to the interests of justice to give the direction.

15.11D References in *paragraphs 15.11A(iii)* and *15.11C(iii)* to the consent of the detainee mean:

(a) if detainee is aged 18 or over, the consent of that detainee;

(b) if the detainee is aged 14 and under 18, the consent of the detainee and their parent or guardian; and

(c) if the detainee is aged under 14, the consent of their parent or guardian.

15.11E The consent described in *paragraph 15.11D* will only be valid if:

(i) in the case of a detainee aged 18 or over *who is a vulnerable adult* as described in *paragraph 15.4A*), information about how the live link is used and the reminder about their right to legal advice mentioned in *paragraph 15.4* and their consent, are given in the *presence of the appropriate adult*; and

(ii) in the case of a *juvenile:*

- if information about how the live link is used and the reminder about their right to legal advice mentioned in *paragraph 15.4* are given in the *presence of the appropriate adult* (who may or may not be their parent or guardian); and
- if the juvenile is aged 14 or over, their consent is given in the *presence of the appropriate adult* (who may or may not be their parent or guardian).

Note: If the juvenile is aged under 14, the consent of their parent or guardian is sufficient in its own right (see *Note 15I*).

(D) Documentation

15.12 It is the officer's responsibility to make sure all reminders given under *paragraph 15.4* are noted in the custody record.

15.13 The grounds for, and extent of, any delay in conducting a review shall be recorded.

15.14 When a review is carried out by telephone or video conferencing facilities, a record shall be made of:

(a) the reason the review officer did not attend the station holding the detainee;

(b) the place the review officer was;

(c) the method representations, oral or written, were made to the review officer, see *paragraph 15.11*.

15.15 Any written representations shall be retained.

15.16 A record shall be made as soon as practicable of:

(a) the outcome of each review of detention before or after charge, and if *paragraph 15.7* applies, of when the person was informed and by whom;
(b) the outcome of any determination under PACE, section 42 by a superintendent whether to extend the maximum period of detention without charge beyond 24 hours from the relevant time. If an authorisation is given, the record shall state the number of hours and minutes by which the detention period is extended or further extended.
(c) the outcome of each application under PACE, section 43, for a warrant of further detention or under section 44, for an extension or further extension of that warrant. If a warrant for further detention is granted under section 43 or extended or further extended under 44, the record shall state the detention period authorised by the warrant and the date and time it was granted or (as the case may be) the period by which the warrant is extended or further extended.

Note: Any period during which a person is released on bail does not count towards the maximum period of detention without charge allowed under PACE, sections 41 to 44.

Notes for Guidance

15A Review officer for the purposes of:

- *PACE, sections 40, 40A and 45A means, in the case of a person arrested but not charged, an officer of at least inspector rank not directly involved in the investigation and, if a person has been arrested and charged, the custody officer.*

15B The detention of persons in police custody not subject to the statutory review requirement in paragraph 15.1 should still be reviewed periodically as a matter of good practice. Such reviews can be carried out by an officer of the rank of sergeant or above. The purpose of such reviews is to check the particular power under which a detainee is held continues to apply, any associated conditions are complied with and to make sure appropriate action is taken to deal with any changes. This includes the detainee's prompt release when the power no longer applies, or their transfer if the power requires the detainee be taken elsewhere as soon as the necessary arrangements are made. Examples include persons:

(a) arrested on warrant because they failed to answer bail to appear at court;
(b) arrested under the Bail Act 1976, section 7(3) for breaching a condition of bail granted after charge;
(c) in police custody for specific purposes and periods under the Crime (Sentences) Act 1997, Schedule 1;
(d) convicted, or remand prisoners, held in police stations on behalf of the Prison Service under the Imprisonment (Temporary Provisions) Act 1980, section 6;
(e) being detained to prevent them causing a breach of the peace;
(f) detained at police stations on behalf of Immigration Enforcement (formerly the UK Immigration Service);
(g) detained by order of a magistrates' court under the Criminal Justice Act 1988, section 152 (as amended by the Drugs Act 2005, section 8) to facilitate the recovery of evidence after being charged with drug possession or drug trafficking and suspected of having swallowed drugs.

The detention of persons remanded into police detention by order of a court under the Magistrates' Courts Act 1980, section 128 is subject to a statutory requirement to review that detention. This is to make sure the detainee is taken back to court no later than the end of the period authorised by the court or when the need for their detention by police ceases, whichever is the sooner.

15C In the case of a review of detention, but not an extension, the detainee need not be woken for the review. However, if the detainee is likely to be asleep, e.g. during a period of rest allowed as in paragraph 12.2, at the latest time a review or authorisation to extend detention may take place, the officer should, if the legal obligations and time constraints permit, bring forward the procedure to allow the detainee to make representations. A detainee not asleep during the review must be present when the grounds for their continued detention are recorded and must at the same time be informed of those grounds unless the review officer considers the person is incapable of understanding what is said, violent or likely to become violent or in urgent need of medical attention.

15CA In paragraph 15.3(b) and (c), 'available' includes being contactable in time to enable them to make representations remotely by telephone or other electronic means or in person by attending the station. Reasonable efforts should therefore be made to give the solicitor and appropriate adult sufficient notice of the time the decision is expected to be made so that they can make themselves available.

15D An application to a Magistrates' Court under PACE, sections 43 or 44 for a warrant of further detention or its extension should be made between 10am and 9pm, and if possible during normal court hours. It will not usually be practicable to arrange for a court to sit specially outside the hours of 10am to 9pm. If it appears a special sitting may be needed outside normal court hours but between 10am and 9pm, the clerk to the justices should be given notice and informed of this possibility, while the court is sitting if possible.

15E In paragraph 15.2, the officer responsible for the station holding the detainee includes a superintendent or above who, in accordance with their force operational policy or police regulations, is given that responsibility on a temporary basis whilst the appointed long-term holder is off duty or otherwise unavailable.

15F The provisions of PACE, section 40A allowing telephone reviews do not apply to reviews of detention after charge by the custody officer. When use of a live link is not required, they allow the use of a telephone to carry out a review of detention before charge.

15G Not used.

15H In considering whether the use of the live link is appropriate in the case of a juvenile or vulnerable person, the custody officer and the superintendent should have regard to the detainee's ability to understand the purpose of the authorisation or (as the case may be) the court hearing, and be satisfied that the suspect is able to take part effectively in the process (see paragraphs 1.4(c)). The appropriate adult should always be involved.

15I For the purpose of paragraphs 15.11D and 15.11E, the consent required from a parent or guardian may, for a juvenile in the care of a local authority or voluntary organisation, be given by that authority or organisation. In the case of a juvenile, nothing in paragraphs 15.11D and 15.11E require the parent, guardian or representative of a local authority or voluntary organisation to be present with the juvenile to give their consent, unless they are acting as the appropriate adult. However, it is important that the parent, guardian or representative of a local authority or voluntary organisation who is not present is fully informed before being asked to consent. They must be given the same information as that given to the juvenile and the appropriate adult in accordance with paragraph 15.11E. They must also be allowed to speak to the juvenile and the appropriate adult if they wish. Provided the consent is fully informed and is not withdrawn, it may be obtained at any time before the live link is used.

16 Charging detained persons

(A) Action

16.1 When the officer in charge of the investigation reasonably believes there is sufficient evidence to provide a realistic prospect of conviction for the offence (see *paragraph 11.6)*, they shall without delay, and subject to the following qualification, inform the custody officer who will be responsible for considering whether the detainee should be charged. See *Notes 11B* and *16A*. When a person is detained in respect of more than one offence it is permissible to delay informing the custody officer until the above conditions are satisfied in respect of all the offences, but see *paragraph 11.6*. If the detainee is a juvenile, or a vulnerable person, any resulting action shall be taken in the presence of the appropriate adult if they are present at the time.

See *Notes 16B* and *16C*.

16.1A Where guidance issued by the Director of Public Prosecutions under PACE, section 37A is in force the custody officer must comply with that Guidance in deciding how to act in dealing with the detainee. See *Notes 16AA* and *16AB*.

16.1B Where in compliance with the DPP's Guidance the custody officer decides that the case should be immediately referred to the CPS to make the charging decision, consultation should take place with a Crown Prosecutor as soon as is reasonably practicable. Where the Crown Prosecutor is unable to make the charging decision on the information available at that time, the detainee may be released without charge and on bail (with conditions if necessary) under section 37(7)(a). In such circumstances, the detainee should be informed that they are being released to enable the Director of Public Prosecutions to make a decision under section 37B.

16.2 When a detainee is charged with or informed they may be prosecuted for an offence, see *Note 16B,* they shall, unless the restriction on drawing adverse inferences from silence applies, see *Annex C,* be cautioned as follows:

> *'You do not have to say anything. But it may harm your defence if you do not mention now something which you later rely on in court. Anything you do say may be given in evidence.'*

Where the use of the Welsh Language is appropriate, a constable may provide the caution directly in Welsh in the following terms:

> *'Does dim rhaid i chi ddweud dim byd. Ond gall niweidio eich amddiffyniad os na fyddwch chi'n sôn, yn awr, am rywbeth y byddwch chi'n dibynnu arno nes ymlaen yn y llys. Gall unrhyw beth yr ydych yn ei ddweud gael ei roi fel tystiolaeth.'*

Annex C, paragraph 2 sets out the alternative terms of the caution to be used when the restriction on drawing adverse inferences from silence applies.

16.3 When a detainee is charged they shall be given a written notice showing particulars of the offence and, subject to *paragraph 2.6A,* the officer's name and the case reference number. As far as possible the particulars of the charge shall be stated in simple terms, but they shall also show the precise offence in law with which the detainee is charged. The notice shall begin:

> *'You are charged with the offence(s) shown below.'* Followed by the caution.

If the detainee is a juvenile, mentally disordered or otherwise mentally vulnerable, a copy of the notice should also be given to the appropriate adult.

16.4 If, after a detainee has been charged with or informed they may be prosecuted for an offence, an officer wants to tell them about any written statement or interview with another person relating to such an offence, the detainee shall either be handed a true copy of the written statement or the content of the interview record brought to their attention. Nothing shall be done to invite any reply or comment except to:

(a) caution the detainee, *'You do not have to say anything, but anything you do say may be given in evidence.'*;

Where the use of the Welsh Language is appropriate, caution the detainee in the following terms:

'Does dim rhaid i chi ddweud dim byd, ond gall unrhyw beth yr ydych yn ei ddweud gael ei roi fel tystiolaeth.'

and

(b) remind the detainee about their right to legal advice.

16.4A If the detainee:

- cannot read, the document may be read to them;
- is a juvenile, mentally disordered or otherwise mentally vulnerable, the appropriate adult shall also be given a copy, or the interview record shall be brought to their attention.

16.5 A detainee may not be interviewed about an offence after they have been charged with, or informed they may be prosecuted for it, unless the interview is necessary:

- to prevent or minimise harm or loss to some other person, or the public
- to clear up an ambiguity in a previous answer or statement
- in the interests of justice for the detainee to have put to them, and have an opportunity to comment on, information concerning the offence which has come to light since they were charged or informed they might be prosecuted

Before any such interview, the interviewer shall:

(a) caution the detainee, *'You do not have to say anything, but anything you do say may be given in evidence.'*

Where the use of the Welsh Language is appropriate, the interviewer shall caution the detainee: *'Does dim rhaid i chi ddweud dim byd, ond gall unrhyw beth yr ydych yn ei ddweud gael ei roi fel tystiolaeth.'*

(b) remind the detainee about their right to legal advice.

See *Note 16B*

16.6 The provisions of *paragraphs 16.2* to *16.5* must be complied with in the appropriate adult's presence if they are already at the police station. If they are not at the police station then these provisions must be complied with again in their presence when they arrive unless the detainee has been released. See *Note 16C.*

16.7 When a juvenile is charged with an offence and the custody officer authorises their continued detention after charge, the custody officer must make arrangements for the juvenile to be taken into the care of a local authority to be detained pending appearance in court *unless* the custody officer certifies in accordance with PACE, section 38(6), that:

(a) for any juvenile; it is impracticable to do so and the reasons why it is impracticable must be set out in the certificate that must be produced to the court; or,

(b) in the case of a juvenile of at least 12 years old, no secure accommodation is available and other accommodation would not be adequate to protect the public from serious harm from that juvenile. See *Note 16D.*

Note: Chief officers should ensure that the operation of these provisions at police stations in their areas is subject to supervision and monitoring by an officer of the rank of inspector or above. See *Note 16E.*

16.7A The requirement in *paragraph 3.4(b)* that documents and materials essential to effectively challenging the lawfulness of the detainee's arrest and detention must be made available to the detainee and, if they are represented, their solicitor, applies for the purposes of this section and a person's detention after charge. This means that the custody officer making the bail decision (PACE, section 38) or reviewing the need for detention after charge (*PACE, section 40*), is responsible for determining what, if any, documents or materials are essential and must be made available to the detainee or their solicitor. See *Note 3ZA.*

(B) Documentation

16.8 A record shall be made of anything a detainee says when charged.

16.9 Any questions put in an interview after charge and answers given relating to the offence shall be recorded in full during the interview on forms for that purpose and the record signed by the detainee or, if they refuse, by the interviewer and any third parties present. If the questions are audibly recorded or visually recorded the arrangements in Code E or F apply.

16.10 If arrangements for a juvenile's transfer into local authority care as in *paragraph 16.7* are not made, the custody officer must record the reasons in a certificate which must be produced before the court with the juvenile. See *Note 16D.*

Notes for Guidance

16A The custody officer must take into account alternatives to prosecution under the Crime and Disorder Act 1998 applicable to persons under 18, and in national guidance on the cautioning of offenders applicable to persons aged 18 and over.

16AA When a person is arrested under the provisions of the Criminal Justice Act 2003 which allow a person to be re-tried after being acquitted of a serious offence which is a qualifying offence specified in Schedule 5 to that Act and not precluded from further prosecution by virtue of section 75(3) of that Act the detention provisions of PACE are modified and make an officer of the rank of superintendent or above who has not been directly involved in the investigation responsible for determining whether the evidence is sufficient to charge.

16AB Where Guidance issued by the Director of Public Prosecutions under section 37B is in force, a custody officer who determines in accordance with that Guidance that there is sufficient evidence to charge the detainee, may detain that person for no longer than is reasonably necessary to decide how that person is to be dealt with under PACE, section 37(7)(a) to (d), including, where appropriate, consultation with the Duty Prosecutor. The period is subject to the maximum period of detention before charge determined by PACE, sections 41 to 44. Where in accordance with the Guidance the case is referred to the CPS for decision, the custody officer should ensure that an officer involved in the investigation sends to the CPS such information as is specified in the Guidance.

16B The giving of a warning or the service of the Notice of Intended Prosecution required by the Road Traffic Offenders Act 1988, section 1 does not amount to informing a detainee they may be prosecuted for an offence and so does not preclude further questioning in relation to that offence.

16C There is no power under PACE to detain a person and delay action under paragraphs 16.2 to 16.5 solely to await the arrival of the appropriate adult. Reasonable efforts should therefore be made to give the appropriate adult sufficient notice of the time the decision (charge etc.) is to be implemented so that they can be present. If the appropriate adult is not, or cannot be, present at that time, the detainee should be released on bail to return for the decision to be implemented when the adult is present, unless the custody officer determines that the absence of the appropriate adult makes the detainee unsuitable for bail for this purpose. After charge, bail cannot be refused, or release on bail delayed, simply because an appropriate adult is not available, unless the absence of that adult provides the custody officer with the necessary grounds to authorise detention after charge under PACE, section 38.

16D Except as in paragraph 16.7, neither a juvenile's behaviour nor the nature of the offence provides grounds for the custody officer to decide it is impracticable to arrange the juvenile's transfer to local authority care. Impracticability concerns the transport and travel requirements and the lack of secure accommodation which is provided for the purposes of restricting liberty does not make it impracticable to transfer the juvenile. Rather, 'impracticable' should be taken to mean that exceptional circumstances render movement of the child impossible or that the juvenile is due at court in such a short space of time that transfer would deprive them of rest or cause them to miss a court appearance. When the reason for not transferring the juvenile is an imminent court appearance, details of the travelling and court appearance times which justify the decision should be included in the certificate. The availability of secure accommodation is only a factor in relation to a juvenile aged 12 or over when other local authority accommodation would not be adequate to protect the public from serious harm from them. The obligation to transfer a juvenile to local authority accommodation applies as much to a juvenile charged during the daytime as to a juvenile to be held overnight, subject to a requirement to bring the juvenile before a court under PACE, section 46.

16E The Concordat on Children in Custody published by the Home Office in 2017 provides detailed guidance with the aim of preventing the detention of children in police stations following charge. It is available here: https://www.gov.uk/government/publications/concordat-on-children-in-custody.

17 Testing persons for the presence of specified Class A drugs

(A) Action

17.1 This section of Code C applies only in selected police stations in police areas where the provisions for drug testing under section 63B of PACE (as amended by section 5 of the Criminal Justice Act 2003 and section 7 of the Drugs Act 2005) are in force and in respect of which the Secretary of State has given a notification to the relevant chief officer of police that arrangements for the taking of samples have been made. Such a notification will cover either a police area as a whole or particular stations within a police area. The notification indicates whether the testing applies to those arrested or charged or under the age of 18 as the case may be and testing can only take place in respect of the persons so indicated in the notification. Testing cannot be carried out unless the relevant notification has been given and has not been withdrawn. See *Note 17F.*

17.2 A sample of urine or a non-intimate sample may be taken from a person in police detention for the purpose of ascertaining whether they have any specified Class A drug in their body only where they have been brought before the custody officer and:

(a) either the arrest condition, see *paragraph 17.3*, or the charge condition, see *paragraph 17.4* is met;
(b) the age condition see *paragraph 17.5*, is met;
(c) the notification condition is met in relation to the arrest condition, the charge condition, or the age condition, as the case may be. (Testing on charge and/or arrest must be specifically provided for in the notification for the power to apply. In addition, the fact that testing of under 18s is authorised must be expressly provided for in the notification before the power to test such persons applies.). See *paragraph 17.1*; and
(d) a police officer has requested the person concerned to give the sample (the request condition).

17.3 The arrest condition is met where the detainee:
(a) has been arrested for a trigger offence, see *Note 17E*, but not charged with that offence; or
(b) has been arrested for any other offence but not charged with that offence and a police officer of inspector rank or above, who has reasonable grounds for suspecting that their misuse of any specified Class A drug caused or contributed to the offence, has authorised the sample to be taken.

17.4 The charge condition is met where the detainee:
(a) has been charged with a trigger offence, or
(b) has been charged with any other offence and a police officer of inspector rank or above, who has reasonable grounds for suspecting that the detainee's misuse of any specified Class A drug caused or contributed to the offence, has authorised the sample to be taken.

17.5 The age condition is met where:
(a) in the case of a detainee who has been arrested but not charged as in *paragraph 17.3*, they are aged 18 or over;
(b) in the case of a detainee who has been charged as in *paragraph 17.4*, they are aged 14 or over.

17.6 Before requesting a sample from the person concerned, an officer must:
(a) inform them that the purpose of taking the sample is for drug testing under PACE. This is to ascertain whether they have a specified Class A drug present in their body;
(b) warn them that if, when so requested, they fail without good cause to provide a sample they may be liable to prosecution;
(c) where the taking of the sample has been authorised by an inspector or above in accordance with *paragraph 17.3(b)* or *17.4(b)* above, inform them that the authorisation has been given and the grounds for giving it;
(d) remind them of the following rights, which may be exercised at any stage during the period in custody:
  (i) the right to have someone informed of their arrest [see section 5];
  (ii) the right to consult privately with a solicitor and that free independent legal advice is available [see section 6]; and
  (iii) the right to consult these Codes of Practice [see section 3].

17.7 In the case of a person who has not attained the age specified in section 63B(5A) of PACE—
(a) the making of the request for a sample under *paragraph 17.2(d)* above;
(b) the giving of the warning and the information under *paragraph 17.6* above; and
(c) the taking of the sample,

may not take place except in the presence of an appropriate adult. See *Note 17G*.

17.8 Authorisation by an officer of the rank of inspector or above within *paragraph 17.3(b)* or *17.4(b)* may be given orally or in writing but, if it is given orally, it must be confirmed in writing as soon as practicable.

17.9 If a sample is taken from a detainee who has been arrested for an offence but not charged with that offence as in *paragraph 17.3*, no further sample may be taken during the same continuous period of detention. If during that same period the charge condition is also met in respect of that detainee, the sample which has been taken shall be treated as being taken by virtue of the charge condition, see *paragraph 17.4*, being met.

17.10 A detainee from whom a sample may be taken may be detained for up to six hours from the time of charge if the custody officer reasonably believes the detention is necessary to enable a sample to be taken. Where the arrest condition is met, a detainee whom the custody officer has decided to release on bail without charge may continue to be detained, but not beyond 24 hours from the relevant time (as defined in section 41(2) of PACE), to enable a sample to be taken.

17.11 A detainee in respect of whom the arrest condition is met, but not the charge condition, see *paragraphs 17.3* and *17.4*, and whose release would be required before a sample can be taken had they not continued to be detained as a result of being arrested for a further offence which does not satisfy the arrest condition, may have a sample taken at any time within 24 hours after the arrest for the offence that satisfies the arrest condition.

(B) Documentation

17.12 The following must be recorded in the custody record:

(a) if a sample is taken following authorisation by an officer of the rank of inspector or above, the authorisation and the grounds for suspicion;
(b) the giving of a warning of the consequences of failure to provide a sample;
(c) the time at which the sample was given; and
(d) the time of charge or, where the arrest condition is being relied upon, the time of arrest and, where applicable, the fact that a sample taken after arrest but before charge is to be treated as being taken by virtue of the charge condition, where that is met in the same period of continuous detention. See *paragraph 17.9*.

(C) General

17.13 A sample may only be taken by a prescribed person. See *Note 17C*.

17.14 Force may not be used to take any sample for the purpose of drug testing.

17.15 The terms 'Class A drug' and 'misuse' have the same meanings as in the Misuse of Drugs Act 1971. 'Specified' (in relation to a Class A drug) and 'trigger offence' have the same meanings as in Part III of the Criminal Justice and Court Services Act 2000.

17.16 Any sample taken:

(a) may not be used for any purpose other than to ascertain whether the person concerned has a specified Class A drug present in his body; and
(b) can be disposed of as clinical waste unless it is to be sent for further analysis in cases where the test result is disputed at the point when the result is known, including on the basis that medication has been taken, or for quality assurance purposes.

(D) Assessment of misuse of drugs

17.17 Under the provisions of Part 3 of the Drugs Act 2005, where a detainee has tested positive for a specified Class A drug under section 63B of PACE a police officer may, at any time before the person's release from the police station, impose a requirement on the detainee to attend an initial assessment of their drug misuse by a suitably qualified person and to remain for its duration. Where such a requirement is imposed, the officer must, at the same time, impose a second requirement on the detainee to attend and remain for a follow-up assessment. The officer must inform the detainee that the second requirement will cease to have effect if, at the initial assessment they are informed that a follow-up assessment is not necessary These requirements may only be imposed on a person if:

(a) they have reached the age of 18

(b) notification has been given by the Secretary of State to the relevant chief officer of police that arrangements for conducting initial and follow-up assessments have been made for those from whom samples for testing have been taken at the police station where the detainee is in custody.

17.18 When imposing a requirement to attend an initial assessment and a follow-up assessment the police officer must:

(a) inform the person of the time and place at which the initial assessment is to take place;
(b) explain that this information will be confirmed in writing; and
(c) warn the person that they may be liable to prosecution if they fail without good cause to attend the initial assessment and remain for its duration and if they fail to attend the follow-up assessment and remain for its duration (if so required).

17.19 Where a police officer has imposed a requirement to attend an initial assessment and a follow-up assessment in accordance with *paragraph 17.17*, he must, before the person is released from detention, give the person notice in writing which:

(a) confirms their requirement to attend and remain for the duration of the assessments; and
(b) confirms the information and repeats the warning referred to in *paragraph 17.18*.

17.20 The following must be recorded in the custody record:

(a) that the requirement to attend an initial assessment and a follow-up assessment has been imposed; and
(b) the information, explanation, warning and notice given in accordance with *paragraphs 17.17* and *17.19*.

17.21 Where a notice is given in accordance with paragraph 17.19, a police officer can give the person a further notice in writing which informs the person of any change to the time or place at which the initial assessment is to take place and which repeats the warning referred to in *paragraph 17.18(c)*.

17.22 Part 3 of the Drugs Act 2005 also requires police officers to have regard to any guidance issued by the Secretary of State in respect of the assessment provisions.

Notes for Guidance

17A When warning a person who is asked to provide a urine or non-intimate sample in accordance with paragraph 17.6(b), the following form of words may be used:

'You do not have to provide a sample, but I must warn you that if you fail or refuse without good cause to do so, you will commit an offence for which you may be imprisoned, or fined, or both'.

Where the Welsh language is appropriate, the following form of words may be used:

'Does dim rhaid i chi roi sampl, ond mae'n rhaid i mi eich rhybuddio y byddwch chi'n cyflawni trosedd os byddwch chi'n methu neu yn gwrthod gwneud hynny heb reswm da, ac y gellir, oherwydd hynny, eich carcharu, eich dirwyo, neu'r ddau.'

17B A sample has to be sufficient and suitable. A sufficient sample is sufficient in quantity and quality to enable drug-testing analysis to take place. A suitable sample is one which by its nature, is suitable for a particular form of drug analysis.

17C A prescribed person in paragraph 17.13 is one who is prescribed in regulations made by the Secretary of State under section 63B(6) of the Police and Criminal Evidence Act 1984. [The regulations are currently contained in regulation SI 2001 No. 2645, the Police and Criminal Evidence Act 1984 (Drug Testing Persons in Police Detention) (Prescribed Persons) Regulations 2001.]

17D Samples, and the information derived from them, may not be subsequently used in the investigation of any offence or in evidence against the persons from whom they were taken.

17E Trigger offences are:

1. *Offences under the following provisions of the Theft Act 1968:*

section 1	*(theft)*
section 8	*(robbery)*
section 9	*(burglary)*

section 10 (aggravated burglary)
section 12 (taking a motor vehicle or other conveyance without authority)
section 12A (aggravated vehicle-taking)
section 22 (handling stolen goods)
section 25 (going equipped for stealing etc.)

2. *Offences under the following provisions of the Misuse of Drugs Act 1971, if committed in respect of a specified Class A drug:—*
section 4 (restriction on production and supply of controlled drugs)
section 5(2) (possession of a controlled drug)
section 5(3) (possession of a controlled drug with intent to supply)

3. *Offences under the following provisions of the Fraud Act 2006:*
section 1 (fraud)
section 6 (possession etc. of articles for use in frauds)
section 7 (making or supplying articles for use in frauds)

3A. *An offence under section 1(1) of the Criminal Attempts Act 1981 if committed in respect of an offence under*
(a) any of the following provisions of the Theft Act 1968:
section 1 (theft)
section 8 (robbery)
section 9 (burglary)
section 22 (handling stolen goods)
(b) section 1 of the Fraud Act 2006 (fraud)

4. *Offences under the following provisions of the Vagrancy Act 1824:*
section 3 (begging)
section 4 (persistent begging)

17F The power to take samples is subject to notification by the Secretary of State that appropriate arrangements for the taking of samples have been made for the police area as a whole or for the particular police station concerned for whichever of the following is specified in the notification:
(a) persons in respect of whom the arrest condition is met;
(b) persons in respect of whom the charge condition is met;
(c) persons who have not attained the age of 18.

Note: Notification is treated as having been given for the purposes of the charge condition in relation to a police area, if testing (on charge) under section 63B(2) of PACE was in force immediately before section 7 of the Drugs Act 2005 was brought into force; and for the purposes of the age condition, in relation to a police area or police station, if immediately before that day, notification that arrangements had been made for the taking of samples from persons under the age of 18 (those aged 14-17) had been given and had not been withdrawn.

17G Appropriate adult in paragraph 17.7 means the person's–
(a) parent or guardian or, if they are in the care of a local authority or voluntary organisation, a person representing that authority or organisation; or
(b) a social worker of a local authority; or
(c) if no person falling within (a) or (b) above is available, any responsible person aged 18 or over who is not:
~ a police officer;
~ employed by the police;
~ under the direction or control of the chief officer of police force; or
~ a person who provides services under contractual arrangements (but without being employed by the chief officer of a police force), to assist that force in relation to the discharge of its chief officer's functions;

whether or not they are on duty at the time.

Annex A Intimate and Strip Searches

A Intimate search

1. An intimate search consists of the physical examination of a person's body orifices other than the mouth. The intrusive nature of such searches means the actual and potential risks associated with intimate searches must never be underestimated.

(a) Action

2. Body orifices other than the mouth may be searched only:

(a) if authorised by an officer of inspector rank or above who has reasonable grounds for believing that the person may have concealed on themselves:

(i) anything which they could and might use to cause physical injury to themselves or others at the station; or

(ii) a Class A drug which they intended to supply to another or to export;

and the officer has reasonable grounds for believing that an intimate search is the only means of removing those items; and

(b) if the search is under *paragraph 2(a)(ii)* (a drug offence search), the detainee's appropriate consent has been given in writing.

2A. Before the search begins, a police officer or designated detention officer, must tell the detainee:—

(a) that the authority to carry out the search has been given;

(b) the grounds for giving the authorisation and for believing that the article cannot be removed without an intimate search.

2B. Before a detainee is asked to give appropriate consent to a search under *paragraph 2(a)(ii)* (a drug offence search) they must be warned that if they refuse without good cause their refusal may harm their case if it comes to trial, see *Note A6*. This warning may be given by a police officer or member of police staff. In the case of a juvenile or a vulnerable person, the seeking and giving of consent must take place in the presence of the appropriate adult. A juvenile's consent is only valid if their parent's or guardian's consent is also obtained unless the juvenile is under 14, when their parent's or guardian's consent is sufficient in its own right. A detainee who is not legally represented must be reminded of their entitlement to have free legal advice, see Code C, *paragraph 6.5*, and the reminder noted in the custody record.

3. An intimate search may only be carried out by a registered medical practitioner or registered nurse, unless an officer of at least inspector rank considers this is not practicable and the search is to take place under *paragraph 2(a)(i)*, in which case a police officer may carry out the search. See *Notes A1* to *A5*.

3A. Any proposal for a search under *paragraph 2(a)(i)* to be carried out by someone other than a registered medical practitioner or registered nurse must only be considered as a last resort and when the authorising officer is satisfied the risks associated with allowing the item to remain with the detainee outweigh the risks associated with removing it. See *Notes A1* to *A5*.

4. An intimate search under:

- *paragraph 2(a)(i)* may take place only at a hospital, surgery, other medical premises or police station;
- *paragraph 2(a)(ii)* may take place only at a hospital, surgery or other medical premises and must be carried out by a registered medical practitioner or a registered nurse.

5. An intimate search at a police station of a juvenile or vulnerable person may take place only in the presence of an appropriate adult of the same sex (see *Annex L*), unless the detainee specifically requests a particular appropriate adult of the opposite sex who is readily available. In the case of a juvenile, the search may take place in the absence of the appropriate adult only if the juvenile signifies in the presence of the appropriate adult they do not want the appropriate adult present during the search and the appropriate adult agrees. A record shall be made of the juvenile's decision and signed by the appropriate adult.

6. When an intimate search under *paragraph 2(a)(i)* is carried out by a police officer, the officer must be of the same sex as the detainee (see *Annex L*). A minimum of two people, other than the detainee, must be present during the search. Subject to *paragraph 5*, no person of the opposite sex who is not a medical practitioner or nurse shall be present, nor shall anyone whose presence is unnecessary. The search shall be conducted with proper regard to the dignity, sensitivity and vulnerability of the detainee including in particular, their health, hygiene and welfare needs to which *paragraphs 9.3A* and *9.3B* apply.

(b) Documentation

7. In the case of an intimate search, the following shall be recorded as soon as practicable in the detainee's custody record:

(a) for searches under paragraphs 2(a)(i) and (ii);
- the authorisation to carry out the search;
- the grounds for giving the authorisation;
- the grounds for believing the article could not be removed without an intimate search;
- which parts of the detainee's body were searched;
- who carried out the search;
- who was present;
- the result.

(b) for searches under paragraph 2(a)(ii):
- the giving of the warning required by *paragraph 2B*;
- the fact that the appropriate consent was given or (as the case may be) refused, and if refused, the reason given for the refusal (if any).

8. If an intimate search is carried out by a police officer, the reason why it was impracticable for a registered medical practitioner or registered nurse to conduct it must be recorded.

B Strip search

9. A strip search is a search involving the removal of more than outer clothing. In this Code, outer clothing includes shoes and socks.

(a) Action

10. A strip search may take place only if it is considered necessary to remove an article which a detainee would not be allowed to keep and the officer reasonably considers the detainee might have concealed such an article. Strip searches shall not be routinely carried out if there is no reason to consider that articles are concealed.

The conduct of strip searches

11. When strip searches are conducted:

(a) a police officer carrying out a strip search must be the same sex as the detainee (see *Annex L*);

(b) the search shall take place in an area where the detainee cannot be seen by anyone who does not need to be present, nor by a member of the opposite sex (see *Annex L*) except an appropriate adult who has been specifically requested by the detainee;

(c) except in cases of urgency, where there is risk of serious harm to the detainee or to others, whenever a strip search involves exposure of intimate body parts, there must be at least two people present other than the detainee, and if the search is of a juvenile or vulnerable person, one of the people must be the appropriate adult. Except in urgent cases as above, a search of a juvenile may take place in the absence of the appropriate adult only if the juvenile signifies in the presence of the appropriate adult that they do not want the appropriate adult to be present during the search and the appropriate adult agrees. A record shall be made of the juvenile's decision and signed by the appropriate adult. The presence of more than two people, other than an appropriate adult, shall be permitted only in the most exceptional circumstances;

(d) the search shall be conducted with proper regard to the dignity, sensitivity and vulnerability of the detainee in these circumstances, including in particular, their health, hygiene and welfare needs to which *paragraphs 9.3A* and *9.3B* apply. Every reasonable effort shall be made to secure the detainee's co-operation, maintain their dignity and minimise embarrassment. Detainees who are searched shall not normally be required to remove all their clothes at the same time, e.g. a person should be allowed to remove clothing above the waist and redress before removing further clothing;

(e) if necessary to assist the search, the detainee may be required to hold their arms in the air or to stand with their legs apart and bend forward so a visual examination may be made of the genital and anal areas provided no physical contact is made with any body orifice;

(f) if articles are found, the detainee shall be asked to hand them over. If articles are found within any body orifice other than the mouth, and the detainee refuses to hand them over, their removal would constitute an intimate search, which must be carried out as in *Part A*;

(g) a strip search shall be conducted as quickly as possible, and the detainee allowed to dress as soon as the procedure is complete.

(b) Documentation

12. A record shall be made on the custody record of a strip search including the reason it was considered necessary, those present and any result.

Notes for Guidance

A1 Before authorising any intimate search, the authorising officer must make every reasonable effort to persuade the detainee to hand the article over without a search. If the detainee agrees, a registered medical practitioner or registered nurse should whenever possible be asked to assess the risks involved and, if necessary, attend to assist the detainee.

A2 If the detainee does not agree to hand the article over without a search, the authorising officer must carefully review all the relevant factors before authorising an intimate search. In particular, the officer must consider whether the grounds for believing an article may be concealed are reasonable.

A3 If authority is given for a search under paragraph 2(a)(i), a registered medical practitioner or registered nurse shall be consulted whenever possible. The presumption should be that the search will be conducted by the registered medical practitioner or registered nurse and the authorising officer must make every reasonable effort to persuade the detainee to allow the medical practitioner or nurse to conduct the search.

A4 A constable should only be authorised to carry out a search as a last resort and when all other approaches have failed. In these circumstances, the authorising officer must be satisfied the detainee might use the article for one or more of the purposes in paragraph 2(a)(i) and the physical injury likely to be caused is sufficiently severe to justify authorising a constable to carry out the search.

A5 If an officer has any doubts whether to authorise an intimate search by a constable, the officer should seek advice from an officer of superintendent rank or above.

A6 In warning a detainee who is asked to consent to an intimate drug offence search, as in paragraph 2B, the following form of words may be used:

'You do not have to allow yourself to be searched, but I must warn you that if you refuse without good cause, your refusal may harm your case if it comes to trial.'

Where the use of the Welsh Language is appropriate, the following form of words may be used:

'Nid oes rhaid i chi roi caniatâd i gael eich archwilio, ond mae'n rhaid i mi eich rhybuddio os gwrthodwch heb reswm da, y gallai eich penderfyniad i wrthod wneud niwed i'ch achos pe bai'n dod gerbron llys.'

Annex B Delay in Notification of Arrest and Whereabouts or Allowing Access to Legal Advice

A Persons detained under PACE

1. The exercise of the rights in *Section 5* or *Section 6,* or both, may be delayed if the person is in police detention, as in PACE, section 118(2), in connection with an indictable offence, has not yet been charged with an offence and an officer of superintendent rank or above, or inspector rank or above only for the rights in *Section 5,* has reasonable grounds for believing their exercise will:

(i) lead to:
- interference with, or harm to, evidence connected with an indictable offence; or
- interference with, or physical harm to, other people; or

(ii) lead to alerting other people suspected of having committed an indictable offence but not yet arrested for it; or

(iii) hinder the recovery of property obtained in consequence of the commission of such an offence.

2. These rights may also be delayed if the officer has reasonable grounds to believe that:

(i) the person detained for an indictable offence has benefited from their criminal conduct (decided in accordance with Part 2 of the Proceeds of Crime Act 2002); and

(ii) the recovery of the value of the property constituting that benefit will be hindered by the exercise of either right.

3. Authority to delay a detainee's right to consult privately with a solicitor may be given only if the authorising officer has reasonable grounds to believe the solicitor the detainee wants to consult will, inadvertently or otherwise, pass on a message from the detainee or act in some other way which will have any of the consequences specified under *paragraphs 1 or 2.* In these circumstances, the detainee must be allowed to choose another solicitor. See *Note B3.*

4. If the detainee wishes to see a solicitor, access to that solicitor may not be delayed on the grounds they might advise the detainee not to answer questions or the solicitor was initially asked to attend the police station by someone else. In the latter case, the detainee must be told the solicitor has come to the police station at another person's request, and must be asked to sign the custody record to signify whether they want to see the solicitor.

5. The fact the grounds for delaying notification of arrest may be satisfied does not automatically mean the grounds for delaying access to legal advice will also be satisfied.

6. These rights may be delayed only for as long as grounds exist and in no case beyond 36 hours after the relevant time as in PACE, section 41. If the grounds cease to apply within this time, the detainee must, as soon as practicable, be asked if they want to exercise either right, the custody record must be noted accordingly, and action taken in accordance with the relevant section of the Code.

7. A detained person must be permitted to consult a solicitor for a reasonable time before any court hearing.

B Not used

C Documentation

13. The grounds for action under this Annex shall be recorded and the detainee informed of them as soon as practicable.

14. Any reply given by a detainee under *paragraphs 6* or *11* must be recorded and the detainee asked to endorse the record in relation to whether they want to receive legal advice at this point.

D Cautions and special warnings

15. When a suspect detained at a police station is interviewed during any period for which access to legal advice has been delayed under this Annex, the court or jury may not draw adverse inferences from their silence.

Notes for Guidance

B1 Even if Annex B applies in the case of a juvenile, or a vulnerable person, action to inform the appropriate adult and the person responsible for a juvenile's welfare, if that is a different person, must nevertheless be taken as in paragraph 3.13 and 3.15.

B2 In the case of Commonwealth citizens and foreign nationals, see Note 7A.

B3 A decision to delay access to a specific solicitor is likely to be a rare occurrence and only when it can be shown the suspect is capable of misleading that particular solicitor and there is more than a substantial risk that the suspect will succeed in causing information to be conveyed which will lead to one or more of the specified consequences.

Annex C Restriction on Drawing Adverse Inferences from Silence and Terms of the Caution when the Restriction Applies

(a) The restriction on drawing adverse inferences from silence

1. The Criminal Justice and Public Order Act 1994, sections 34, 36 and 37 as amended by the Youth Justice and Criminal Evidence Act 1999, section 58 describe the conditions under which adverse inferences may be drawn from a person's failure or refusal to say anything about their involvement in the offence when interviewed, after being charged or informed they may be prosecuted. These provisions are subject to an overriding restriction on the ability of a court or jury to draw adverse inferences from a person's silence. This restriction applies:

(a) to any detainee at a police station, see *Note 10C* who, before being interviewed, see *section 11* or being charged or informed they may be prosecuted, see *section 16,* has:
- (i) asked for legal advice, see *section 6, paragraph 6*.1;
- (ii) not been allowed an opportunity to consult a solicitor, including the duty solicitor, as in this Code; and
- (iii) not changed their mind about wanting legal advice, see *section 6, paragraph 6.6(d).*

Note the condition in (ii) will:
- ~ apply when a detainee who has asked for legal advice is interviewed before speaking to a solicitor as in *section 6, paragraph 6.6(a)* or *(b)*;
- ~ not apply if the detained person declines to ask for the duty solicitor, see *section 6, paragraphs 6.6(c)* and *(d).*

(b) to any person charged with, or informed they may be prosecuted for, an offence who:
- (i) has had brought to their notice a written statement made by another person or the content of an interview with another person which relates to that offence, see *section 16, paragraph 16.4*;
- (ii) is interviewed about that offence, see *section 16, paragraph 16.5*; or
- (iii) makes a written statement about that offence, see *Annex D paragraphs 4* and *9.*

(b) Terms of the caution when the restriction applies

2. When a requirement to caution arises at a time when the restriction on drawing adverse inferences from silence applies, the caution shall be:

'You do not have to say anything, but anything you do say may be given in evidence.'

Where the use of the Welsh Language is appropriate, the caution may be used directly in Welsh in the following terms:

'Does dim rhaid i chi ddweud dim byd, ond gall unrhyw beth yr ydych chi'n ei ddweud gael ei roi fel tystiolaeth.'

3. Whenever the restriction either begins to apply or ceases to apply after a caution has already been given, the person shall be re-cautioned in the appropriate terms. The changed position on drawing inferences and that the previous caution no longer applies shall also be explained to the detainee in ordinary language. See *Note C2.*

Notes for Guidance

C1 The restriction on drawing inferences from silence does not apply to a person who has not been detained and who therefore cannot be prevented from seeking legal advice if they want to, see paragraphs 10.2 and 3.21.

C2 The following is suggested as a framework to help explain changes in the position on drawing adverse inferences if the restriction on drawing adverse inferences from silence:

(a) begins to apply:

'The caution you were previously given no longer applies. This is because after that caution:

(i) you asked to speak to a solicitor but have not yet been allowed an opportunity to speak to a solicitor. See paragraph 1(a); or

(ii) you have been charged with/informed you may be prosecuted. See paragraph 1(b).

'This means that from now on, adverse inferences cannot be drawn at court and your defence will not be harmed just because you choose to say nothing. Please listen carefully to the caution I am about to give you because it will apply from now on. You will see that it does not say anything about your defence being harmed.'

(b) ceases to apply before or at the time the person is charged or informed they may be prosecuted, see paragraph 1(a);

'The caution you were previously given no longer applies. This is because after that caution you have been allowed an opportunity to speak to a solicitor. Please listen carefully to the caution I am about to give you because it will apply from now on. It explains how your defence at court may be affected if you choose to say nothing.'

Annex D Written Statements Under Caution

(a) Written by a person under caution

1. A person shall always be invited to write down what they want to say.

2. A person who has not been charged with, or informed they may be prosecuted for, any offence to which the statement they want to write relates, shall:

(a) unless the statement is made at a time when the restriction on drawing adverse inferences from silence applies, see Annex C, be asked to write out and sign the following before writing what they want to say:

'I make this statement of my own free will. I understand that I do not have to say anything but that it may harm my defence if I do not mention when questioned something which I later rely on in court. This statement may be given in evidence.';

(b) if the statement is made at a time when the restriction on drawing adverse inferences from silence applies, be asked to write out and sign the following before writing what they want to say;

'I make this statement of my own free will. I understand that I do not have to say anything. This statement may be given in evidence.'

3. When a person, on the occasion of being charged with or informed they may be prosecuted for any offence, asks to make a statement which relates to any such offence and wants to write it they shall:

(a) unless the restriction on drawing adverse inferences from silence, see *Annex C,* applied when they were so charged or informed they may be prosecuted, be asked to write out and sign the following before writing what they want to say:

'I make this statement of my own free will. I understand that I do not have to say anything but that it may harm my defence if I do not mention when questioned something which I later rely on in court. This statement may be given in evidence.';

(b) if the restriction on drawing adverse inferences from silence applied when they were so charged or informed they may be prosecuted, be asked to write out and sign the following before writing what they want to say:

'I make this statement of my own free will. I understand that I do not have to say anything. This statement may be given in evidence.'

4. When a person who has already been charged with or informed they may be prosecuted for any offence asks to make a statement which relates to any such offence and wants to write it, they shall be asked to write out and sign the following before writing what they want to say:

'I make this statement of my own free will. I understand that I do not have to say anything. This statement may be given in evidence.';

5. Any person writing their own statement shall be allowed to do so without any prompting except a police officer or other police staff may indicate to them which matters are material or question any ambiguity in the statement.

(b) Written by a police officer or other police staff

6. If a person says they would like someone to write the statement for them, a police officer, or other police staff shall write the statement.

7. If the person has not been charged with, or informed they may be prosecuted for, any offence to which the statement they want to make relates they shall, before starting, be asked to sign, or make their mark, to the following:

(a) unless the statement is made at a time when the restriction on drawing adverse inferences from silence applies, see *Annex C*:

'I, ..., wish to make a statement. I want someone to write down what I say. I understand that I do not have to say anything but that it may harm my defence if I do not mention when questioned something which I later rely on in court. This statement may be given in evidence.';

(b) if the statement is made at a time when the restriction on drawing adverse inferences from silence applies:

'I, ..., wish to make a statement. I want someone to write down what I say. I understand that I do not have to say anything. This statement may be given in evidence.'

8. If, on the occasion of being charged with or informed they may be prosecuted for any offence, the person asks to make a statement which relates to any such offence they shall before starting be asked to sign, or make their mark to, the following:

(a) unless the restriction on drawing adverse inferences from silence applied, see *Annex C*, when they were so charged or informed they may be prosecuted:

'I, ..., wish to make a statement. I want someone to write down what I say. I understand that I do not have to say anything but that it may harm my defence if I do not mention when questioned something which I later rely on in court. This statement may be given in evidence.';

(b) if the restriction on drawing adverse inferences from silence applied when they were so charged or informed they may be prosecuted:

'I, ..., wish to make a statement. I want someone to write down what I say. I understand that I do not have to say anything. This statement may be given in evidence.'

9. If, having already been charged with or informed they may be prosecuted for any offence, a person asks to make a statement which relates to any such offence they shall before starting, be asked to sign, or make their mark to:

'I, ..., wish to make a statement. I want someone to write down what I say. I understand that I do not have to say anything. This statement may be given in evidence.'

10. The person writing the statement must take down the exact words spoken by the person making it and must not edit or paraphrase it. Any questions that are necessary, e.g. to make it more intelligible, and the answers given must be recorded at the same time on the statement form.

11. When the writing of a statement is finished the person making it shall be asked to read it and to make any corrections, alterations or additions they want. When they have finished reading

they shall be asked to write and sign or make their mark on the following certificate at the end of the statement:

'I have read the above statement, and I have been able to correct, alter or add anything I wish. This statement is true. I have made it of my own free will.'

12. If the person making the statement cannot read, or refuses to read it, or to write the above mentioned certificate at the end of it or to sign it, the person taking the statement shall read it to them and ask them if they would like to correct, alter or add anything and to put their signature or make their mark at the end. The person taking the statement shall certify on the statement itself what has occurred.

Annex E Summary of Provisions Relating to Vulnerable Persons

1. If at any time an officer has reason to suspect that a person of any age may be vulnerable (see *paragraph 1.13(d)*), in the absence of clear evidence to dispel that suspicion that person shall be treated as such for the purposes of this Code and to establish whether any such reason may exist in relation to a person suspected of committing an offence (see *paragraph 10.1* and *Note 10A*), the custody officer in the case of a detained person, or the officer investigating the offence in the case of a person who has not been arrested or detained, shall take, or cause to be taken, (see *paragraph 3.5* and *Note 3F*) the following action:

(a) reasonable enquiries shall be made to ascertain what information is available that is relevant to any of the factors described in *paragraph 1.13(d)* as indicating that the person may be vulnerable might apply;

(b) a record shall be made describing whether any of those factors appear to apply and provide any reason to suspect that the person may be vulnerable or (as the case may be) may not be vulnerable; and

(c) the record mentioned in sub-paragraph (b) shall be made available to be taken into account by police officers, police staff and any others who, in accordance with the provisions of this or any other Code, are entitled to communicate with the person in question. This would include any solicitor, appropriate adult and health care professional and is particularly relevant to communication by telephone or by means of a live link (see *paragraphs 12.9A* (interviews), *13.12* (interpretation), and *15.3C, 15.11A, 15.11B, 15.11C* and *15.11D* (reviews and extension of detention)).

See *Notes 1G, E5, E6* and *E7.*

2. In the case of a person who is vulnerable, 'the appropriate adult' means:

(i) a relative, guardian or other person responsible for their care or custody;

(ii) someone experienced in dealing with vulnerable persons but who is not:

~ a police officer;

~ employed by the police;

~ under the direction or control of the chief officer of a police force;

~ a person who provides services under contractual arrangements (but without being employed by the chief officer of a police force), to assist that force in relation to the discharge of its chief officer's functions,

whether or not they are on duty at the time.

(iii) failing these, some other responsible adult aged 18 or over who is other than a person described in the bullet points in *sub-paragraph (ii)* above.

See *paragraph 1.7(b)* and *Notes 1D* and *1F.*

2A The role of the appropriate adult is to safeguard the rights, entitlements and welfare of 'vulnerable persons' (see *paragraph 1)* to whom the provisions of this and any other Code of Practice apply. For this reason, the appropriate adult is expected, amongst other things, to:

- support, advise and assist them when, in accordance with this Code or any other Code of Practice, they are given or asked to provide information or participate in any procedure;

- observe whether the police are acting properly and fairly to respect their rights and entitlements, and inform an officer of the rank of inspector or above if they consider that they are not;
- assist them to communicate with the police whilst respecting their right to say nothing unless they want to as set out in the terms of the caution (see *paragraphs 10.5* and *10.6*); and
- help them understand their rights and ensure that those rights are protected and respected (see *paragraphs 3.15, 3.17, 6.5A* and *11.17*).

See *paragraph 1.7A*.

3. If the custody officer authorises the detention of a vulnerable person, the custody officer must as soon as practicable inform the appropriate adult of the grounds for detention and the person's whereabouts, and secure the attendance of the appropriate adult at the police station to see the detainee. If the appropriate adult:
   - is already at the station when information is given as in *paragraphs 3.1* to *3.5* the information must be given in their presence;
   - is not at the station when the provisions of *paragraph 3.1* to *3.5* are complied with these provisions must be complied with again in their presence once they arrive.

See *paragraphs 3.15* to *3.17*

4. If the appropriate adult, having been informed of the right to legal advice, considers legal advice should be taken, the provisions of *section 6* apply as if the vulnerable person had requested access to legal advice. See *paragraphs 3.19, 6.5A* and *Note E1*.

5. The custody officer must make sure a person receives appropriate clinical attention as soon as reasonably practicable if the person appears to be suffering from a mental disorder or in urgent cases immediately call the nearest appropriate healthcare professional or an ambulance. See Code C *paragraphs 3.16, 9.5* and *9.6* which apply when a person is detained under the Mental Health Act 1983, sections 135 and 136, as amended by the Policing and Crime Act 2017.

6. *Not used.*

7. If a vulnerable person is cautioned in the absence of the appropriate adult, the caution must be repeated in the appropriate adult's presence. See *paragraph 10.12*.

8. A vulnerable person must not be interviewed or asked to provide or sign a written statement in the absence of the appropriate adult unless the provisions of *paragraphs 11.1* or *11.18* to *11.20* apply. Questioning in these circumstances may not continue in the absence of the appropriate adult once sufficient information to avert the risk has been obtained. A record shall be made of the grounds for any decision to begin an interview in these circumstances. See *paragraphs 11.1, 11.15* and *11.18* to *11.20*.

9. If the appropriate adult is present at an interview, they shall be informed they are not expected to act simply as an observer and the purposes of their presence are to:
   - advise the interviewee;
   - observe whether or not the interview is being conducted properly and fairly;
   - facilitate communication with the interviewee.

See *paragraph 11.17*

10. If the detention of a vulnerable person is reviewed by a review officer or a superintendent, the appropriate adult must, if available at the time, be given an opportunity to make representations to the officer about the need for continuing detention. See *paragraph 15.3*.

11. If the custody officer charges a vulnerable person with an offence or takes such other action as is appropriate when there is sufficient evidence for a prosecution this must be carried out in the presence of the appropriate adult if they are at the police station. A copy of the written notice embodying any charge must also be given to the appropriate adult. See *paragraphs 16.1* to *16.4A*

12. An intimate or strip search of a vulnerable person may take place only in the presence of the appropriate adult of the same sex, unless the detainee specifically requests the presence of a particular adult of the opposite sex. A strip search may take place in the absence of an appropriate

adult only in cases of urgency when there is a risk of serious harm to the detainee or others. See *Annex A, paragraphs 5* and *11(c)*.

13. Particular care must be taken when deciding whether to use any form of approved restraints on a vulnerable person in a locked cell. See *paragraph 8.2*.

Notes for Guidance

E1 The purpose of the provisions at paragraphs 3.19 and 6.5A is to protect the rights of a vulnerable person who does not understand the significance of what is said to them. A vulnerable person should always be given an opportunity, when an appropriate adult is called to the police station, to consult privately with a solicitor in the absence of the appropriate adult if they want.

E2 Although vulnerable persons are often capable of providing reliable evidence, they may, without knowing or wanting to do so, be particularly prone in certain circumstances to provide information that may be unreliable, misleading or self-incriminating. Special care should always be taken when questioning such a person, and the appropriate adult should be involved if there is any doubt about a person's mental state or capacity. Because of the risk of unreliable evidence, it is important to obtain corroboration of any facts admitted whenever possible.

E3 Because of the risks referred to in Note E2, which the presence of the appropriate adult is intended to minimise, officers of superintendent rank or above should exercise their discretion to authorise the commencement of an interview in the appropriate adult's absence only in exceptional cases, if it is necessary to avert one or more of the specified risks in paragraph 11.1. See paragraphs 11.1 and 11.18 to 11.20.

E4 When a person is detained under section 136 of the Mental Health Act 1983 for assessment, the appropriate adult has no role in the assessment process and their presence is not required.

E5 For the purposes of Annex E paragraph 1, examples of relevant information that may be available include:

- *the behaviour of the adult or juvenile;*
- *the mental health and capacity of the adult or juvenile;*
- *what the adult or juvenile says about themselves;*
- *information from relatives and friends of the adult or juvenile;*
- *information from police officers and staff and from police records;*
- *information from health and social care (including liaison and diversion services) and other professionals who know, or have had previous contact with, the individual and may be able to contribute to assessing their need for help and support from an appropriate adult. This includes contacts and assessments arranged by the police or at the request of the individual or (as applicable) their appropriate adult or solicitor.*

E6 The Mental Health Act 1983 Code of Practice at page 26 describes the range of clinically recognised conditions which can fall with the meaning of mental disorder for the purpose of paragraph 1.13(d). The Code is published here: https://www.gov.uk/government/publications/code-of-practice-mental-health-act-1983.

E7 When a person is under the influence of drink and/or drugs, it is not intended that they are to be treated as vulnerable and requiring an appropriate adult for the purpose of Annex E paragraph 1 unless other information indicates that any of the factors described in paragraph 1.13(d) may apply to that person. When the person has recovered from the effects of drink and/or drugs, they should be re-assessed in accordance with Annex E paragraph 1. See paragraph 15.4A for application to live link.

Annex F *Not used*

Annex G Fitness to be Interviewed

1. This Annex contains general guidance to help police officers and healthcare professionals assess whether a detainee might be at risk in an interview.

2. A detainee may be at risk in an interview if it is considered that:
   (a) conducting the interview could significantly harm the detainee's physical or mental state;
   (b) anything the detainee says in the interview about their involvement or suspected involvement in the offence about which they are being interviewed **might** be considered unreliable in subsequent court proceedings because of their physical or mental state.

3. In assessing whether the detainee should be interviewed, the following must be considered:
   (a) how the detainee's physical or mental state might affect their ability to understand the nature and purpose of the interview, to comprehend what is being asked and to appreciate the significance of any answers given and make rational decisions about whether they want to say anything;
   (b) the extent to which the detainee's replies may be affected by their physical or mental condition rather than representing a rational and accurate explanation of their involvement in the offence;
   (c) how the nature of the interview, which could include particularly probing questions, might affect the detainee.

4. It is essential healthcare professionals who are consulted consider the functional ability of the detainee rather than simply relying on a medical diagnosis, e.g. it is possible for a person with severe mental illness to be fit for interview.

5. Healthcare professionals should advise on the need for an appropriate adult to be present, whether reassessment of the person's fitness for interview may be necessary if the interview lasts beyond a specified time, and whether a further specialist opinion may be required.

6. When healthcare professionals identify risks they should be asked to quantify the risks. They should inform the custody officer:

- whether the person's condition:
  - ~ is likely to improve;
  - ~ will require or be amenable to treatment; and
- indicate how long it may take for such improvement to take effect.

7. The role of the healthcare professional is to consider the risks and advise the custody officer of the outcome of that consideration. The healthcare professional's determination and any advice or recommendations should be made in writing and form part of the custody record.

8. Once the healthcare professional has provided that information, it is a matter for the custody officer to decide whether or not to allow the interview to go ahead and if the interview is to proceed, to determine what safeguards are needed. Nothing prevents safeguards being provided in addition to those required under the Code. An example might be to have an appropriate healthcare professional present during the interview, in addition to an appropriate adult, in order constantly to monitor the person's condition and how it is being affected by the interview.

Annex H Detained Person: Observation List

1. If any detainee fails to meet any of the following criteria, an appropriate healthcare professional or an ambulance must be called.

2. When assessing the level of rousability, consider:

Rousability—can they be woken?

- go into the cell
- call their name
- shake gently

Response to questions—can they give appropriate answers to questions such as:

- What's your name?
- Where do you live?
- Where do you think you are?

Response to commands—can they respond appropriately to commands such as:

- Open your eyes!
- Lift one arm, now the other arm!

3. Remember to take into account the possibility or presence of other illnesses, injury, or mental condition; a person who is drowsy and smells of alcohol may also have the following:

- Diabetes
- Epilepsy
- Head injury
- Drug intoxication or overdose
- Stroke

Annex I *Not used*

Annex J *Not used*

Annex K X-Rays and Ultrasound Scans

(a) Action

1. PACE, section 55A allows a person who has been arrested and is in police detention to have an X-ray taken of them or an ultrasound scan to be carried out on them (or both) if:

(a) authorised by an officer of inspector rank or above who has reasonable grounds for believing that the detainee:

(i) may have swallowed a Class A drug; and

(ii) was in possession of that Class A drug with the intention of supplying it to another or to export; and

(b) the detainee's appropriate consent has been given in writing.

2. Before an x-ray is taken or an ultrasound scan carried out, a police officer or designated detention officer must tell the detainee:-

(a) that the authority has been given; and

(b) the grounds for giving the authorisation.

3. Before a detainee is asked to give appropriate consent to an x-ray or an ultrasound scan, they must be warned that if they refuse without good cause their refusal may harm their case if it comes to trial, see *Notes K1* and *K2*. This warning may be given by a police officer or member of police staff. In the case of juveniles and vulnerable persons, the seeking and giving of consent must take place in the presence of the appropriate adult. A juvenile's consent is only valid if their parent's or guardian's consent is also obtained unless the juvenile is under 14, when their parent's or guardian's consent is sufficient in its own right. A detainee who is not legally represented must be reminded of their entitlement to have free legal advice, see Code C, *paragraph 6.5*, and the reminder noted in the custody record.

4. An x-ray may be taken, or an ultrasound scan may be carried out, only by a registered medical practitioner or registered nurse, and only at a hospital, surgery or other medical premises.

(b) Documentation

5. The following shall be recorded as soon as practicable in the detainee's custody record:

(a) the authorisation to take the x-ray or carry out the ultrasound scan (or both);

(b) the grounds for giving the authorisation;

(c) the giving of the warning required by *paragraph 3*; and

(d) the fact that the appropriate consent was given or (as the case may be) refused, and if refused, the reason given for the refusal (if any); and

(e) if an x-ray is taken or an ultrasound scan carried out:
where it was taken or carried out;
- who took it or carried it out;
- who was present;
- the result.

6. *Not used.*

Notes for Guidance

K1 If authority is given for an x-ray to be taken or an ultrasound scan to be carried out (or both), consideration should be given to asking a registered medical practitioner or registered nurse to explain to the detainee what is involved and to allay any concerns the detainee might have about the effect which taking an x-ray or carrying out an ultrasound scan might have on them. If appropriate consent is not given, evidence of the explanation may, if the case comes to trial, be relevant to determining whether the detainee had a good cause for refusing.

K2 In warning a detainee who is asked to consent to an X-ray being taken or an ultrasound scan being carried out (or both), as in paragraph 3, the following form of words may be used:

'You do not have to allow an x-ray of you to be taken or an ultrasound scan to be carried out on you, but I must warn you that if you refuse without good cause, your refusal may harm your case if it comes to trial.'

Where the use of the Welsh Language is appropriate, the following form of words may be provided in Welsh:

'Does dim rhaid i chi ganiatáu cymryd sgan uwchsain neu belydr-x (neu'r ddau) arnoch, ond mae'n rhaid i mi eich rhybuddio os byddwch chi'n gwrthod gwneud hynny heb reswm da, fe allai hynny niweidio eich achos pe bai'n dod gerbron llys.'

Annex L Establishing Gender of Persons for the Purpose of Searching and Certain other Procedures

1. Certain provisions of this and other PACE Codes explicitly state that searches and other procedures may only be carried out by, or in the presence of, persons of the same sex as the person subject to the search or other procedure or require action to be taken or information to be given which depends on whether the detainee is treated as being male or female. See *Note L1*.

2. All such searches, procedures and requirements must be carried out with courtesy, consideration and respect for the person concerned. Police officers should show particular sensitivity when dealing with transgender individuals (including transsexual persons) and transvestite persons (see *Notes L2, L3 and L4*).

(a) Consideration

3. In law, the gender (and accordingly the sex) of an individual is their gender as registered at birth unless they have been issued with a Gender Recognition Certificate (GRC) under the Gender Recognition Act 2004 (GRA), in which case the person's gender is their acquired gender. This means that if the acquired gender is the male gender, the person's sex becomes that of a man and, if it is the female gender, the person's sex becomes that of a woman and they must be treated as their acquired gender.

4. When establishing whether the person concerned should be treated as being male or female for the purposes of these searches, procedures and requirements, the following approach which is designed to maintain their dignity, minimise embarrassment and secure their co-operation should be followed:

(a) The person must not be asked whether they have a GRC (see paragraph 8);

(b) If there is no doubt as to as to whether the person concerned should be treated as being male or female, they should be dealt with as being of that sex.

(c) If at any time (including during the search or carrying out the procedure or requirement) there is doubt as to whether the person should be treated, or continue to be treated, as being male or female:

(i) the person should be asked what gender they consider themselves to be. If they express a preference to be dealt with as a particular gender, they should be asked to indicate and confirm their preference by signing the custody record or, if a custody record has not been opened, the search record or the officer's notebook. Subject to (ii) below, the person should be treated according to their preference except with regard to the requirements to provide that person with information concerning menstrual products and their personal needs relating to health, hygiene and welfare described in *paragraph 3.20A* (if aged under 18) and *paragraphs 9.3A* and *9.3B* (if aged 18 or over). In these cases, a person whose confirmed preference is to be dealt with as being male should be asked in private whether they wish to speak in private with a member of the custody staff of a gender of their choosing about the provision of menstrual products and their personal needs, notwithstanding their confirmed preference (see *Note L3A*);

(ii) if there are grounds to doubt that the preference in (i) accurately reflects the person's predominant lifestyle, for example, if they ask to be treated as a woman but documents and other information make it clear that they live predominantly as a man, or vice versa, they should be treated according to what appears to be their predominant lifestyle and not their stated preference;

(iii) If the person is unwilling to express a preference as in (i) above, efforts should be made to determine their predominant lifestyle and they should be treated as such. For example, if they appear to live predominantly as a woman, they should be treated as being female except with regard to the requirements to provide that person with information concerning menstrual products and their personal needs relating to health, hygiene and welfare described in *paragraph 3.20A* (if aged under 18) and *paragraphs 9.3A* and *9.3B* (if aged 18 or over). In these cases, a person whose predominant lifestyle has been determined to be male should be asked in private whether they wish to speak in private with a member of the custody staff of a gender of their choosing about the provision of menstrual products and their personal needs, notwithstanding their determined predominant lifestyle (see *Note L3A*); or

(iv) if none of the above apply, the person should be dealt with according to what reasonably appears to have been their sex as registered at birth.

5. Once a decision has been made about which gender an individual is to be treated as, each officer responsible for the search, procedure or requirement should where possible be advised before the search or procedure starts of any doubts as to the person's gender and the person informed that the doubts have been disclosed. This is important so as to maintain the dignity of the person and any officers concerned.

(b) Documentation

6. The person's gender as established under *paragraph 4(c)(i)* to *(iv)* above must be recorded in the person's custody record or, if a custody record has not been opened, on the search record or in the officer's notebook.

7. Where the person elects which gender they consider themselves to be under *paragraph 4(b)(i)* but, following *4(b)(ii)* is not treated in accordance with their preference, the reason must be recorded in the search record, in the officer's notebook or, if applicable, in the person's custody record.

(c) Disclosure of information

8. Section 22 of the GRA defines any information relating to a person's application for a GRC or to a successful applicant's gender before it became their acquired gender as 'protected information'. Nothing in this Annex is to be read as authorising or permitting any police officer or any police staff who has acquired such information when acting in their official capacity to disclose that information to any other person in contravention of the GRA. Disclosure includes making a record of 'protected information' which is read by others.

Notes for Guidance

L1 Provisions to which paragraph 1 applies include:

- *In Code C; paragraphs 3.20A, 4.1 and Annex A paragraphs 5, 6, and 11 (searches, strip and intimate searches of detainees under sections 54 and 55 of PACE) and 9.3B;*
- *In Code A; paragraphs 2.8 and 3.6 and Note 4;*
- *In Code D; paragraph 5.5 and Note 5F (searches, examinations and photographing of detainees under section 54A of PACE) and paragraph 6.9 (taking samples);*
- *In Code H; paragraphs 3.21, 4.1 and Annex A paragraphs 6, 7 and 12 (searches, strip and intimate searches under sections 54 and 55 of PACE of persons arrested under section 41 of the Terrorism Act 2000) and 9.4B.*

L2 While there is no agreed definition of transgender (or trans), it is generally used as an umbrella term to describe people whose gender identity (self-identification as being a woman, man, neither or both) differs from the sex they were registered as at birth. The term includes, but is not limited to, transsexual people.

L3 Transsexual means a person who is proposing to undergo, is undergoing or has undergone a process (or part of a process) for the purpose of gender reassignment, which is a protected characteristic under the Equality Act 2010 (see paragraph 1.0), by changing physiological or other attributes of their sex. This includes aspects of gender such as dress and title. It would apply to a woman making the transition to being a man and a man making the transition to being a woman, as well as to a person who has only just started out on the process of gender reassignment and to a person who has completed the process. Both would share the characteristic of gender reassignment with each having the characteristics of one sex, but with certain characteristics of the other sex.

L3A The reason for the exception is to modify the same sex/gender approach for searching to acknowledge the possible needs of transgender individuals in respect of menstrual products and other personal needs relating to health, hygiene and welfare and ensure that they are not overlooked.

L4 Transvestite means a person of one gender who dresses in the clothes of a person of the opposite gender. However, a transvestite does not live permanently in the gender opposite to their birth sex.

L5 Chief officers are responsible for providing corresponding operational guidance and instructions for the deployment of transgender officers and staff under their direction and control to duties which involve carrying out, or being present at, any of the searches and procedures described in paragraph 1. The guidance and instructions must comply with the Equality Act 2010 and should therefore complement the approach in this Annex.

Annex M Documents and Records to be Translated

1. For the purposes of Directive 2010/64/EU of the European Parliament and of the Council of 20 October 2010 and this Code, essential documents comprise records required to be made in accordance with this Code which are relevant to decisions to deprive a person of their liberty, to any charge and to any record considered necessary to enable a detainee to defend themselves in criminal proceedings and to safeguard the fairness of the proceedings. Passages of essential documents which are not relevant need not be translated. See *Note M1*

2. The table below lists the documents considered essential for the purposes of this Code and when (subject to paragraphs 3 to 7) written translations must be created and provided. See *paragraphs 13.12* to *13.14* and *Annex N* for application to live-link interpretation.

Table of essential documents:

	ESSENTIAL DOCUMENTS FOR THE PURPOSES OF THIS CODE	WHEN TRANSLATION TO BE CREATED	WHEN TRANSLATION TO BE PROVIDED.
(i)	The grounds for each of the following authorisations to keep the person in custody as they are described and referred to in the custody record: (a) Authorisation for detention before and after charge given by the custody officer and by the review officer, see Code C paragraphs 3.4 and 15.16(a). (b) Authorisation to extend detention without charge beyond 24 hours given by a superintendent, see Code C paragraph 15.16(b). (c) A warrant of further detention issued by a magistrates' court and any extension(s) of the warrant, see Code C paragraph 15.16(c). (d) An authority to detain in accordance with the directions in a warrant of arrest issued in connection with criminal proceedings including the court issuing the warrant.	As soon as practicable after each authorisation has been recorded in the custody record.	As soon as practicable after the translation has been created, whilst the person is detained or after they have been released (see Note M3).
(ii)	Written notice showing particulars of the offence charged required by Code C paragraph 16.3 or the offence for which the suspect has been told they may be prosecuted.	As soon as practicable after the person has been charged or reported.	
(iii)	Written interview records: Code C11.11, 13.3, 13.4 & Code E4.7 Written statement under caution: Code C Annex D.	To be created contemporaneously by the interpreter for the person to check and sign.	As soon as practicable after the person has been charged or told they may be prosecuted.

3. The custody officer may authorise an oral translation or oral summary of documents (i) to (ii) in the table (but not (iii)) to be provided (through an interpreter) instead of a written translation. Such an oral translation or summary may only be provided if it would not prejudice the fairness of the proceedings by in any way adversely affecting or otherwise undermining or limiting the ability of the suspect in question to understand their position and to communicate effectively with police officers, interviewers, solicitors and appropriate adults with regard to

their detention and the investigation of the offence in question and to defend themselves in the event of criminal proceedings. The quantity and complexity of the information in the document should always be considered and specific additional consideration given if the suspect is vulnerable or is a juvenile (see *Code C paragraph 1.5*). The reason for the decision must be recorded (see *paragraph 13.11(e)*)

4. Subject to paragraphs 5 to 7 below, a suspect may waive their right to a written translation of the essential documents described in the table but only if they do so voluntarily after receiving legal advice or having full knowledge of the consequences and give their unconditional and fully informed consent in writing (see *paragraph 9*).

5. The suspect may be asked if they wish to waive their right to a written translation and before giving their consent, they must be reminded of their right to legal advice and asked whether they wish to speak to a solicitor.

6. No police officer or police staff should do or say anything with the intention of persuading a suspect who is entitled to a written translation of an essential document to waive that right. See *Notes M2 and M3*.

7. For the purpose of the waiver:

(a) the consent of a vulnerable person is only valid if the information about the circumstances under which they can waive the right and the reminder about their right to legal advice mentioned in *paragraphs 3* to *5* and their consent is given in the presence of the appropriate adult.

(b) the consent of a juvenile is only valid if their parent's or guardian's consent is also obtained unless the juvenile is under 14, when their parent's or guardian's consent is sufficient in its own right and the information and reminder mentioned in *sub-paragraph (a)* above and their consent is also given in the presence of the appropriate adult (who may or may not be a parent or guardian).

8. The detainee, their solicitor or appropriate adult may make representations to the custody officer that a document which is not included in the table is essential and that a translation should be provided. The request may be refused if the officer is satisfied that the translation requested is not essential for the purposes described in *paragraph 1* above.

9. If the custody officer has any doubts about

- providing an oral translation or summary of an essential document instead of a written translation (see paragraph 3);
- whether the suspect fully understands the consequences of waiving their right to a written translation of an essential document (see paragraph 4), or
- about refusing to provide a translation of a requested document (see *paragraph 7*), the officer should seek advice from an inspector or above.

Documentation

10. Action taken in accordance with this Annex shall be recorded in the detainee's custody record or interview record as appropriate (see *Code C paragraph 13.11(e)*).

Notes for Guidance

M1 It is not necessary to disclose information in any translation which is capable of undermining or otherwise adversely affecting any investigative processes, for example, by enabling the suspect to fabricate an innocent explanation or to conceal lies from the interviewer.

M2 No police officer or police staff shall indicate to any suspect, except to answer a direct question, whether the period for which they are liable to be detained or if not detained, the time taken to complete the interview, might be reduced:

- *if they do not ask for legal advice before deciding whether they wish to waive their right to a written translation of an essential document; or*
- *if they decide to waive their right to a written translation of an essential document.*

M3 There is no power under PACE to detain a person or to delay their release solely to create and provide a written translation of any essential document.

Annex N Live-Link Interpretation (para. 13.12)

Part 1: When the physical presence of the interpreter is not required.

1. EU Directive 2010/64 (see *paragraph 13.1*), Article 2(6) provides 'Where appropriate, communication technology such as videoconferencing, telephone or the Internet may be used, unless the physical presence of the interpreter is required in order to safeguard the fairness of the proceedings.' This Article permits, but does not require the use of a live-link, and the following provisions of this Annex determine whether the use of a live-link is appropriate in any particular case.

2. Decisions in accordance with this Annex that the physical presence of the interpreter is not required and to permit live-link interpretation, must be made on a case by case basis. Each decision must take account of the age, gender and vulnerability of the suspect, the nature and circumstances of the offence and the investigation and the impact on the suspect according to the particular purpose(s) for which the suspect requires the assistance of an interpreter and the time(s) when that assistance is required (see *Note N1*). For this reason, the custody officer in the case of a detained suspect, or in the case of a suspect who has not been arrested, the interviewer (subject to *paragraph 13.1(b)*), must consider whether the ability of the particular suspect, to communicate confidently and effectively for the purpose in question (see *paragraph 3*) is likely to be adversely affected or otherwise undermined or limited if the interpreter is not physically present and live-link interpretation is used. Although a suspect for whom an appropriate adult is required may be more likely to be adversely affected as described, it is important to note that a person who does not require an appropriate adult may also be adversely impacted by the use of live-link interpretation.

3. Examples of purposes referred to in *paragraph 2* include:

(a) understanding and appreciating their position having regard to any information given to them, or sought from them, in accordance with this or any other Code of Practice which, in particular, include:

- the caution (see *paragraphs C10.1* and *10.12*).
- the special warning (see *paragraphs 10.10* to *10.12*).
- information about the offence (see *paragraphs 10.3, 11.1A* and *Note 11ZA*).
- the grounds and reasons for detention (see *paragraphs 13.10* and *13.10A*).
- the translation of essential documents (see *paragraph 13.10B* and *Annex M*).
- their rights and entitlements (see *paragraph 3.12 and C3.21(b)*).
- intimate and non-intimate searches of detained persons at police stations.
- provisions and procedures to which Code D (Identification) applies concerning, for example, eye-witness identification, taking fingerprints, samples and photographs.

(b) understanding and seeking clarification from the interviewer of questions asked during an interview conducted and recorded in accordance with Code E or Code F and of anything else that is said by the interviewer and answering the questions.

(c) consulting privately with their solicitor and (if applicable) the appropriate adult (see *paragraphs 3.18, 13.2A, 13.6 and 13.9*):

(i) to help decide whether to answer questions put to them during interview; and

(ii) about any other matter concerning their detention and treatment whilst in custody.

(d) communicating with practitioners and others who have some formal responsibility for, or an interest in, the health and welfare of the suspect. Particular examples include appropriate healthcare professionals (see *section 9* of this Code), Independent Custody Visitors and drug arrest referral workers.

4. If the custody officer or the interviewer (subject to *paragraph 13.1(b)*) is satisfied that for a particular purpose as described in *paragraphs 2 and 3 above*, the live-link interpretation *would not* adversely affect or otherwise undermine or limit the suspect's ability to communicate confidently and effectively for *that* purpose, they must so inform the suspect, their solicitor and (if applicable) the appropriate adult. At the same time, the operation of live-link interpretation must be explained

and demonstrated to them, they must be advised of the chief officer's obligations concerning the security of live-link communications under *paragraph 13.13* (see *Note N2*) and they must be asked if they wish to make representations that live-link interpretation should not be used or if they require more information about the operation of the arrangements. They must also be told that at any time live-link interpretation is in use, they may make representations to the custody officer or the interviewer that its operation should cease and that the physical presence of an interpreter should be arranged.

When the authority of an inspector is required

If:

(i) representations are made that live-link interpretation should not be used, or that at any time live-link interpretation is in use, its operation should cease and the physical presence of an interpreter arranged; and

(ii) the custody officer or interviewer (subject to paragraph 13.1(b)) is unable to allay the concerns raised;

then live-link interpretation may not be used, or (as the case may be) continue to be used, unless authorised in writing by an officer of the rank of inspector or above, in accordance with *paragraph* 6.

6. Authority may be given if the officer is satisfied that for the purpose(s) in question at the time an interpreter is required, live-link interpretation is necessary and justified. In making this decision, the officer must have regard to:

(a) the circumstances of the suspect;

(b) the nature and seriousness of the offence;

(c) the requirements of the investigation, including its likely impact on both the suspect and any victim(s);

(d) the representations made by the suspect, their solicitor and (if applicable) the appropriate adult that live-link interpretation should not be used (see *paragraph 5*);

(e) the availability of a suitable interpreter to be *physically* present compared with the availability of a suitable interpreter for live-link interpretation (see *Note N3*); and

(f) the risk if the interpreter is not *physically* present, evidence obtained using link interpretation might be excluded in subsequent criminal proceedings; and

(g) the likely impact on the suspect and the investigation of any consequential delay to arrange for the interpreter to be *physically* present with the suspect.

7. For the purposes of Code E and live-link interpretation, there is no requirement to make a visual recording which shows the interpreter as viewed by the suspect and others present at the interview. The audio recording required by that Code is sufficient. However, the authorising officer, in consultation with the officer in charge of the investigation, may direct that the interview is conducted and recorded in accordance with Code F. This will require the visual record to show the live-link interpretation arrangements and the interpreter as seen and experienced by the suspect during the interview. This should be considered if it appears that the admissibility of interview evidence might be challenged because the interpreter was not *physically* present or if the suspect, solicitor or appropriate adult make representations that Code F should be applied.

Documentation

8. A record must be made of the actions, decisions, authorisations and outcomes arising from the requirements of this Annex. This includes representations made in accordance with *paragraphs 4* and *7*.

Part 2: Modifications for live-link interpretation

9. The following modification shall apply for the purposes of live-link interpretation:

(a) Code C paragraph 13.3:

For the third sentence, *substitute:* 'A clear legible copy of the complete record shall be sent without delay via the live-link to the interviewer. The interviewer, after confirming with the suspect that the copy is legible and complete, shall allow the suspect to read the record, or have the record read to them by the interpreter and to sign the copy as correct or indicate the respects in which they consider it inaccurate. The interviewer is responsible for ensuring that that the signed copy and the original record made by the interpreter are retained with the case papers for use in evidence if required and must advise the interpreter of their obligation to keep the original record securely for that purpose.';

(b) Code C paragraph 13.4:

For sub-paragraph (b), *substitute*: 'A clear legible copy of the complete statement shall be sent without delay via the live-link to the interviewer. The interviewer, after confirming with the suspect that the copy is legible and complete, shall invite the suspect to sign it. The interviewer is responsible for ensuring that that the signed copy and the original record made by the interpreter are retained with the case papers for use in evidence if required and must advise the interpreter of their obligation to keep the original record securely for that purpose.';

(c) Code C paragraph 13.7:

After the first sentence, *insert:* 'A clear legible copy of the certified record must be sent without delay via the live-link to the interviewer. The interviewer is responsible for ensuring that the original certified record and the copy are retained with the case papers for use as evidence if required and must advise the interpreter of their obligation to keep the original record securely for that purpose.'

(d) Code C paragraph 11.2, Code E paragraphs 3.4 and 4.3 and Code F paragraph 2.5.—interviews

At the beginning of each paragraph, *insert*: 'Before the interview commences, the operation of live-link interpretation shall be explained and demonstrated to the suspect, their solicitor and appropriate adult, unless it has been previously explained and demonstrated (see Code C Annex N *paragraph 4*).'

(e) Code E, paragraph 3.20 (signing master recording label)

After the *third sentence,* insert, 'If live-link interpretation has been used, the interviewer should ask the interpreter to observe the removal and sealing of the master recording and to confirm in writing that they have seen it sealed and signed by the interviewer. A clear legible copy of the confirmation signed by the interpreter must be sent via the live-link to the interviewer. The interviewer is responsible for ensuring that the original confirmation and the copy are retained with the case papers for use in evidence if required and must advise the interpreter of their obligation to keep the original confirmation securely for that purpose.'

Note: By virtue of *paragraphs 2.1* and *2.3 of Code F,* this applies when a visually recording to which Code F applies is made.

Notes for Guidance

N1 For purposes other than an interview, audio-only live-link interpretation, for example by telephone (see Code C paragraph 13.12(b)) may provide an appropriate option until an interpreter is physically present or audio-visual live-link interpretation becomes available. A particular example would be the initial action required when a detained suspect arrives at a police station to inform them of, and to explain, the reasons for their arrest and detention and their various rights and entitlements. Another example would be to inform the suspect by telephone, that an interpreter they will be able to see and hear is being arranged. In these circumstances, telephone live-link interpretation may help to allay the suspect's concerns and contribute to the completion of the risk assessment (see Code C paragraph 3.6).

N2 The explanation and demonstration of live-link interpretation is intended to help the suspect, solicitor and appropriate adult make an informed decision and to allay any concerns they may have.

N3 Factors affecting availability of a suitable interpreter will include the location of the police station and the language and type of interpretation (oral or sign language) required.

Code of Practice for the Identification of Persons by Police Officers (Code D)

(2023)

1 Introduction

1.1 This Code of Practice concerns the principal methods used by police to identify people in connection with the investigation of offences and the keeping of accurate and reliable criminal records. The powers and procedures in this code must be used fairly, responsibly, with respect for the people to whom they apply and without unlawful discrimination. Under the Equality Act 2010, section 149 (Public sector Equality Duty), police forces must, in carrying out their functions, have due regard to the need to eliminate unlawful discrimination, harassment, victimisation and any other conduct which is prohibited by that Act, to advance equality of opportunity between people who share a relevant protected characteristic and people who do not share it, and to foster good relations between those persons. The Equality Act also makes it unlawful for police officers to discriminate against, harass or victimise any person on the grounds of the 'protected characteristics' of age, disability, gender reassignment, race, religion or belief, sex and sexual orientation, marriage and civil partnership, pregnancy and maternity when using their powers. See *Note 1A*.

1.2 In this Code, identification by an eye-witness arises when a witness who has seen the offender committing the crime and is given an opportunity to identify a person suspected of involvement in the offence in a video identification, identification parade or similar procedure. These eye-witness identification procedures which are in Part A of section 3 below, are designed to:

- test the eye-witness' ability to identify the suspect as the person they saw on a previous occasion
- provide safeguards against mistaken identification.

While this Code concentrates on visual identification procedures, it does not prevent the police making use of aural identification procedures such as a 'voice identification parade', where they judge that appropriate. See *Note 1B*.

1.2A In this Code, separate provisions in Part B of section 3 below, apply when any person, including a police officer, is asked if they recognise anyone they see in an image as being someone who is known to them and to test their claim that they recognise that person. These separate provisions are not subject to the eye-witnesses identification procedures described in *paragraph 1.2*.

1.2B Part C applies when a film, photograph or image relating to the offence or any description of the suspect is broadcast or published in any national or local media or on any social networking site or on any local or national police communication systems.

1.3 Identification by fingerprints applies when a person's fingerprints are taken to: compare with fingerprints found at the scene of a crime

- check and prove convictions
- help to ascertain a person's identity.

1.3A Identification using footwear impressions applies when a person's footwear impressions are taken to compare with impressions found at the scene of a crime.

1.4 Identification by body samples and impressions includes taking samples such as a cheek swab, hair or blood to generate a DNA profile for comparison with material obtained from the scene of a crime, or a victim.

1.5 Taking photographs of arrested people applies to recording and checking identity and locating and tracing persons who:

- are wanted for offences
- fail to answer their bail.

1.6 Another method of identification involves searching and examining detained suspects to find, e.g., marks such as tattoos or scars which may help establish their identity or whether they have been involved in committing an offence.

1.7 The provisions of the Police and Criminal Evidence Act 1984 (PACE) and this Code are designed to make sure fingerprints, samples, impressions and photographs are taken, used and retained, and identification procedures carried out, only when justified and necessary for preventing, detecting or investigating crime. If these provisions are not observed, the application of the relevant procedures in particular cases may be open to question.

1.8 The provisions of this Code do not authorise, or otherwise permit, fingerprints or samples to be taken from a person detained solely for the purposes of assessment under section 136 of the Mental Health Act 1983.

Note for Guidance

*1A In paragraph 1.1, under the Equality Act 1949, section 149, the 'relevant protected characteristics' are: age, disability, gender reassignment, pregnancy and maternity, race, religion/belief, sex and sexual orientation. For further detailed guidance and advice on the Equality Act, see: https://www.gov.uk/guidance/equality-act-2010-guidance.**

1B See Home Office Circular 57/2003 *'Advice on the use of voice identification parades'.*

2 General

2.1 This Code must be readily available at all police stations for consultation by:

- police officers and police staff
- detained persons
- members of the public

2.2 The provisions of this Code:

- include the Annexes
- do not include the Notes for guidance.

2.3 Code C, paragraph 1.4 and the *Notes for guidance* applicable to those provisions apply to this Code with regard to a suspected person who may be mentally disordered or otherwise mentally vulnerable.

2.4 Code C, paragraphs 1.5 and 1.5A and the *Notes for guidance* applicable to those provisions apply to this Code with regard to a suspected person who appears to be under the age of 18.

2.5 Code C, paragraph 1.6 applies to this Code with regard to a suspected person who appears to be blind, seriously visually impaired, deaf, unable to read or speak or has difficulty communicating orally because of a speech impediment.

2.6 In this Code:

- 'appropriate adult' means the same as in Code C, *paragraph 1.7*
- 'solicitor' means the same as in Code C, *paragraph 6.12*

and the *Notes for guidance* applicable to those provisions apply to this Code.

- where a search or other procedure under this Code may only be carried out or observed by a person of the same sex as the person to whom the search or procedure applies, the gender of the detainee and other persons present should be established and recorded in line with Annex L of Code C.

2.7 References to a custody officer include any police officer who, for the time being, is performing the functions of a custody officer, see *paragraph 1.9* of Code C.

2.8 When a record of any action requiring the authority of an officer of a specified rank is made under this Code, subject to *paragraph 2.18,* the officer's name and rank must be recorded.

2.9 When this Code requires the prior authority or agreement of an officer of at least inspector or superintendent rank, that authority may be given by a sergeant or chief inspector who has been authorised to perform the functions of the higher rank under PACE, section 107.

2.10 Subject to *paragraph 2.18,* all records must be timed and signed by the maker.

2.11 Records must be made in the custody record, unless otherwise specified. In any provision of this Code which allows or requires police officers or police staff to make a record in their report book, the reference to 'report book' shall include any official report book or electronic recording device issued to them that enables the record in question to be made and dealt with in accordance with that provision. References in this Code to written records, forms and signatures include

* **Editor's Note:** The relevant legislation is erroneously recorded in the Code. The relevant legislation is the Equality Act 2010, section 149. The text above is taken directly from the Code.

electronic records and forms and electronic confirmation that identifies the person completing the record or form.

Chief officers must be satisfied as to the integrity and security of the devices, records and forms to which this *paragraph* applies and that use of those devices, records and forms satisfies relevant data protection legislation.

(taken from *Code C paragraph 1.17).*

2.12 If any procedure in this Code requires a person's consent, the consent of a:

- mentally disordered or otherwise mentally vulnerable person is only valid if given in the presence of the appropriate adult
- juvenile is only valid if their parent's or guardian's consent is also obtained unless the juvenile is under 14, when their parent's or guardian's consent is sufficient in its own right. If the only obstacle to an identification procedure in *section 3* is that a juvenile's parent or guardian refuses consent or reasonable efforts to obtain it have failed, the identification officer may apply the provisions of paragraph 3.21 (suspect known but not available). See *Note 2A*.

2.13 If a person is blind, seriously visually impaired or unable to read, the custody officer or identification officer shall make sure their solicitor, relative, appropriate adult or some other person likely to take an interest in them and not involved in the investigation is available to help check any documentation. When this Code requires written consent or signing, the person assisting may be asked to sign instead, if the detainee prefers. This paragraph does not require an appropriate adult to be called solely to assist in checking and signing documentation for a person who is not a juvenile, or mentally disordered or otherwise mentally vulnerable (see *Note 2B* and Code C *paragraph 3.15*).

2.14 If any procedure in this Code requires information to be given to or sought from a suspect, it must be given or sought in the appropriate adult's presence if the suspect is mentally disordered, otherwise mentally vulnerable or a juvenile. If the appropriate adult is not present when the information is first given or sought, the procedure must be repeated in the presence of the appropriate adult when they arrive. If the suspect appears deaf or there is doubt about their hearing or speaking ability or ability to understand English, the custody officer or identification officer must ensure that the necessary arrangements in accordance with Code C are made for an interpreter to assist the suspect.

2.15 Any procedure in this Code involving the participation of a suspect who is mentally disordered, otherwise mentally vulnerable or a juvenile must take place in the presence of the appropriate adult. See Code C *paragraph 1.4*.

2.15A Any procedure in this Code involving the participation of a witness who is or appears to be mentally disordered, otherwise mentally vulnerable or a juvenile should take place in the presence of a pre-trial support person unless the witness states that they do not want a support person to be present. A support person must not be allowed to prompt any identification of a suspect by a witness. See *Note 2AB*.

2.16 References to:

- 'taking a photograph', include the use of any process to produce a single, still or moving, visual image
- 'photographing a person', should be construed accordingly
- 'photographs', 'films', 'negatives' and 'copies' include relevant visual images recorded, stored, or reproduced through any medium
- 'destruction' includes the deletion of computer data relating to such images or making access to that data impossible

2.17 This Code does not affect or apply to, the powers and procedures:

(i) for requiring and taking samples of breath, blood and urine in relation to driving offences, etc., when under the influence of drink, drugs or excess alcohol under the:
   - Road Traffic Act 1988, sections 4 to 11
   - Road Traffic Offenders Act 1988, sections 15 and 16
   - Transport and Works Act 1992, sections 26 to 38;

(ii) under the Immigration Act 1971, Schedule 2, paragraph 18, for taking photographs, measuring and identifying and taking biometric information (not including DNA) from persons detained or liable to be detained under that Act, Schedule 2, paragraph 16 (Administrative Provisions as to Control on Entry etc.); or for taking fingerprints in accordance with the Immigration and Asylum Act 1999, sections 141 and 142(4), or other methods for collecting information about a person's external physical characteristics provided for by regulations made under that Act, section 144;

(iii) under the Terrorism Act 2000, Schedule 8, for taking photographs, fingerprints, skin impressions, body samples or impressions from people:
- arrested under that Act, section 41,
- detained for the purposes of examination under that Act, Schedule 7, and to whom the Code of Practice issued under that Act, Schedule 14, paragraph 6, applies ('the terrorism provisions')

(iv) for taking photographs, fingerprints, skin impressions, body samples or impressions from people who have been:
- arrested on warrants issued in Scotland, by officers exercising powers mentioned in Part X of the Criminal Justice and Public Order Act 1994;
- arrested or detained without warrant by officers from a police force in Scotland exercising their powers of arrest or detention mentioned in Part X of the Criminal Justice and Public Order Act 1994.

Note: In these cases, police powers and duties and the person's rights and entitlements whilst at a police station in England and Wales are the same as if the person had been arrested in Scotland by a Scottish police officer.

2.18 Nothing in this Code requires the identity of officers or police staff to be recorded or disclosed:

(a) in the case of enquiries linked to national security including terrorism;

(b) if the officers or police staff reasonably believe recording or disclosing their names might put them in danger.

In these cases, they shall use their warrant or other identification numbers and the name of their police station. *See Note 2D.*

2.19 In this Code:

(a) 'designated person' means a person other than a police officer, who has specified powers and duties conferred or imposed on them by designation under section 38 or 39 of the Police Reform Act 2002;

(b) any reference to a police officer includes a designated person acting in the exercise or performance of the powers and duties conferred or imposed on them by their designation.

2.20 If a power conferred on a designated person:

(a) allows reasonable force to be used when exercised by a police officer, a designated person exercising that power has the same entitlement to use force;

(b) includes power to use force to enter any premises, that power is not exercisable by that designated person except:

(i) in the company, and under the supervision, of a police officer; or

(ii) for the purpose of:
- saving life or limb; or
- preventing serious damage to property.

2.21 In the case of a detained person, nothing in this Code prevents the custody officer, or other police officer or designated person given custody of the detainee by the custody officer for the purposes of the investigation of an offence for which the person is detained, from allowing another person (see *(a)* and *(b)* below) to carry out individual procedures or tasks at the police station if the law allows. However, the officer or designated person given custody remains responsible for making sure the procedures and tasks are carried out correctly in accordance with the Codes of Practice. The other person who is allowed to carry out the procedures or tasks must be *someone who at that time* is:

- (a) under the direction and control of the chief officer of the force responsible for the police station in question; or;
- (b) providing services under contractual arrangements (but without being employed by the chief officer the police force), to assist a police force in relation to the discharge of its chief officer's functions.

2.22 Designated persons and others mentioned in *sub-paragraphs (a)* and *(b)* of *paragraph 2.21* must have regard to any relevant provisions of the Codes of Practice.

Notes for guidance

2A For the purposes of paragraph 2.12, the consent required from a parent or guardian may, for a juvenile in the care of a local authority or voluntary organisation, be given by that authority or organisation. In the case of a juvenile, nothing in paragraph 2.12 requires the parent, guardian or representative of a local authority or voluntary organisation to be present to give their consent, unless they are acting as the appropriate adult under paragraphs 2.14 or 2.15. However, it is important that a parent or guardian not present is fully informed before being asked to consent. They must be given the same information about the procedure and the juvenile's suspected involvement in the offence as the juvenile and appropriate adult. The parent or guardian must also be allowed to speak to the juvenile and the appropriate adult if they wish. Provided the consent is fully informed and is not withdrawn, it may be obtained at any time before the procedure takes place.

2AB The Youth Justice and Criminal Evidence Act 1999 guidance 'Achieving Best Evidence in Criminal Proceedings' indicates that a pre-trial support person should accompany a vulnerable witness during any identification procedure unless the witness states that they do not want a support person to be present. It states that this support person should not be (or not be likely to be) a witness in the investigation.

2B People who are seriously visually impaired or unable to read may be unwilling to sign police documents. The alternative, i.e. their representative signing on their behalf, seeks to protect the interests of both police and suspects.

2C Not used

2D The purpose of paragraph 2.18(b) is to protect those involved in serious organised crime investigations or arrests of particularly violent suspects when there is reliable information that those arrested or their associates may threaten or cause harm to the officers. In cases of doubt, an officer of inspector rank or above should be consulted.

3 Identification and recognition of suspects

Part (A) Identification of a suspect by an eye-witness

3.0 This part applies when an eye-witness has seen a person committing a crime or in any other circumstances which tend to prove or disprove the involvement of the person they saw in a crime, for example, close to the scene of the crime, immediately before or immediately after it was committed. It sets out the procedures to be used to test the ability of that eye-witness to identify a person suspected of involvement in the offence ('the suspect') as the person they saw on the previous occasion. This part does not apply to the procedure described in Part B (see Note 3AA) which is used to test the ability of someone who is not an eye-witness, to recognise anyone whose image they see.

3.1 A record shall be made of the description of the suspect as first given by the eye-witness. This record must:

- (a) be made and kept in a form which enables details of that description to be accurately produced from it, in a visible and legible form, which can be given to the suspect or the suspect's solicitor in accordance with this Code; and
- (b) unless otherwise specified, be made before the eye-witness takes part in any identification procedures under *paragraphs 3.5 to 3.10, 3.21, 3.23* or Annex E (Showing Photographs to Eye-Witnesses).

A copy of the record shall where practicable, be given to the suspect or their solicitor before any procedures under *paragraphs 3.5* to *3.10, 3.21 or 3.23* are carried out. See *Note 3E.*

3.1A References in this Part:

(a) to the identity of the suspect being 'known' mean that there is sufficient information known to the police to establish, in accordance with Code G (Arrest), that there are reasonable grounds to suspect a particular person of involvement in the offence;

(b) to the suspect being 'available' mean that the suspect is immediately available, or will be available within a reasonably short time, in order that they can be invited to take part in at least one of the eye-witness identification procedures under *paragraphs 3.5* to *3.10* and it is practicable to arrange an effective procedure under *paragraphs 3.5 to 3.10*; and

(c) to the eye-witness identification procedures under *paragraphs 3.5* to *3.10* mean:

- Video identification (*paragraphs 3.5* and *3.6*);
- Identification parade (*paragraphs 3.7* and *3.8*); and
- Group identification (*paragraphs 3.9* and *3.10*).

(a) Cases when the suspect's identity is not known

3.2 In cases when the suspect's identity is not known, an eye-witness may be taken to a particular neighbourhood or place to see whether they can identify the person they saw on a previous occasion. Although the number, age, sex, race, general description and style of clothing of other people present at the location and the way in which any identification is made cannot be controlled, the principles applicable to the formal procedures under *paragraphs 3.5* to *3.10* shall be followed as far as practicable. For example:

(a) where it is practicable to do so, a record should be made of the eye-witness' description of the person they saw on the previous occasion, as in *paragraph 3.1(a),* before asking the eye-witness to make an identification;

(b) Care must be taken not provide the eye-witness with any information concerning the description of the suspect (if such information is available) and not to direct the eye-witness' attention to any individual unless, taking into account all the circumstances, this cannot be avoided. However, this does not prevent an eye-witness being asked to look carefully at the people around at the time or to look towards a group or in a particular direction, if this appears necessary to make sure that the witness does not overlook a possible suspect simply because the eye-witness is looking in the opposite direction and also to enable the eye-witness to make comparisons between any suspect and others who are in the area;

(c) where there is more than one eye-witness, every effort should be made to keep them separate and eye-witnesses should be taken to see whether they can identify a person independently;

(d) once there is sufficient information to establish, in accordance with *paragraph 3.1A(a),* that the suspect is 'known', e.g. after the eye-witness makes an identification, the provisions set out from *paragraph 3.4* onwards shall apply for that and any other eye-witnesses in relation to that individual;

(e) the officer or police staff accompanying the eye-witness must record, in their report book, the action taken as soon as practicable and in as much detail, as possible. The record should include:

(i) the date, time and place of the relevant occasion when the eye-witness claims to have previously seen the person committing the offence in question or in any other circumstances which tend to prove or disprove the involvement of the person they saw in a crime (see *paragraph 3.0*); and

(ii) where any identification was made:

- how it was made and the conditions at the time (e.g., the distance the eye-witness was from the suspect, the weather and light);

- if the eye-witness's attention was drawn to the suspect; the reason for this; and
- anything said by the eye-witness or the suspect about the identification or the conduct of the procedure.

See Note 3F

3.3 An eye-witness must not be shown photographs, computerised or artist's composite likenesses or similar likenesses or pictures (including 'E-fit' images) if in accordance with *paragraph 3.1A*, the identity of the suspect is known and they are available to take part in one of the procedures under *paragraphs 3.5* to *3.10*. If the suspect's identity is not known, the showing of any such images to an eye-witness to see if they can identify a person whose image they are shown as the person they saw on a previous occasion must be done in accordance with *Annex E*.

(b) Cases when the suspect is known and available

3.4 If the suspect's identity is known to the police (see *paragraph 3.1A(a)*) and they are available (see *paragraph 3.1A(b)*), the identification procedures that may be used are set out in *paragraphs 3.5* to *3.10* below as follows:

(i) video identification;
(ii) identification parade; or
(iii) group identification.

(i) Video identification

3.5 A 'video identification' is when the eye-witness is shown images of a known suspect, together with similar images of others who resemble the suspect. *Moving* images must be used unless the conditions in sub-paragraph (a) or (b) below apply:

(a) this sub-paragraph applies if:
   (i) the identification officer, in consultation with the officer in charge of the investigation, is satisfied that because of aging, or other physical changes or differences, the appearance of the suspect has significantly changed since the previous occasion when the eye-witness claims to have seen the suspect (see *paragraph 3.0* and *Note 3ZA*);
   (ii) an image (moving or still) is available which the identification officer and the officer in charge of the investigation reasonably believe shows the appearance of the suspect as it was at the time the suspect was seen by the eye-witness; and
   (iii) having regard to the extent of change and the purpose of eye-witness identification procedures (see *paragraph 3.0*), the identification officer believes that that such an image should be shown to the eye-witness.

   In such a case, the identification officer may arrange a video identification procedure using the image described in (ii). In accordance with the 'Notice to suspect' (see *paragraph 3.17(vi)*), the suspect must first be given an opportunity to provide their own image(s) for use in the procedure but it is for the identification officer and officer in charge of the investigation to decide whether, following (ii) and (iii), any image(s) provided by the suspect should be used.

   A video identification using an image described above may, at the discretion of the identification officer be arranged in addition to, or as an alternative to, a video identification using *moving* images taken after the suspect has been given the information and notice described in *paragraphs 3.17* and *3.18*.

   See paragraph 3.21 and Note 3D in any case where the suspect deliberately takes steps to frustrate the eye-witness identification arrangements and procedures.

(b) this sub-paragraph applies if, in accordance with *paragraph 2A* of *Annex A* of this Code, the identification officer does not consider that replication of a physical feature or concealment of the location of the feature can be achieved using a moving image. In these cases, still images may be used.

3.6 Video identifications must be carried out in accordance with *Annex A*.

(ii) Identification parade

3.7 An 'identification parade' is when the eye-witness sees the suspect in a line of others who resemble the suspect.

3.8 Identification parades must be carried out in accordance with *Annex B*.

(iii) Group identification

3.9 A 'group identification' is when the eye-witness sees the suspect in an informal group of people.

3.10 Group identifications must be carried out in accordance with *Annex C*.

Arranging eye-witness identification procedures—duties of identification officer

3.11 Except as provided for in *paragraph 3.19*, the arrangements for, and conduct of, the eye-witness identification procedures in *paragraphs 3.5 to 3.10* and circumstances in which any such identification procedure must be held shall be the responsibility of an officer not below inspector rank who is not involved with the investigation ('the identification officer'). The identification officer may direct another officer or police staff, see *paragraph 2.21*, to make arrangements for, and to conduct, any of these identification procedures and except as provided for in *paragraph 7* of *Annex A*, any reference in this section to the identification officer includes the officer or police staff to whom the arrangements for, and/or conduct of, any of these procedure has been delegated. In delegating these arrangements and procedures, the identification officer must be able to supervise effectively and either intervene or be contacted for advice. Where any action referred to in this paragraph is taken by another officer or police staff at the direction of the identification officer, the outcome shall, as soon as practicable, be reported to the identification officer. For the purpose of these procedures, the identification officer retains overall responsibility for ensuring that the procedure complies with this Code and in addition, in the case of detained suspect, their care and treatment until returned to the custody officer. Except as permitted by this Code, no officer or any other person involved with the investigation of the case against the suspect may take any part in these procedures or act as the identification officer.

This paragraph does not prevent the identification officer from consulting the officer in charge of the investigation to determine which procedure to use. When an identification procedure is required, in the interest of fairness to suspects and eye-witnesses, it must be held as soon as practicable.

Circumstances in which an eye-witness identification procedure must be held

3.12 If, before any identification procedure set out in *paragraphs 3.5* to *3.10* has been held

(a) an eye-witness has identified a suspect or purported to have identified them; or

(b) there is an eye-witness available who expresses an ability to identify the suspect; or

(c) there is a reasonable chance of an eye-witness being able to identify the suspect,

and the eye-witness in (a) to (c) has not been given an opportunity to identify the suspect in any of the procedures set out in *paragraphs 3.5* to *3.10*, then an identification procedure shall be held if the suspect disputes being the person the eye-witness claims to have seen on a previous occasion (see *paragraph 3.0*), unless:

(i) it is not practicable to hold any such procedure; or

(ii) any such procedure would serve no useful purpose in proving or disproving whether the suspect was involved in committing the offence, for example

- where the suspect admits being at the scene of the crime and gives an account of what took place and the eye-witness does not see anything which contradicts that; or
- when it is not disputed that the suspect is already known to the eye-witness who claims to have recognised them when seeing them commit the crime.

3.13 An eye-witness identification procedure may also be held if the officer in charge of the investigation, after consultation with the identification officer, considers it would be useful.

Selecting an eye-witness identification procedure

3.14 If, because of paragraph 3.12, an identification procedure is to be held, the suspect shall initially be invited to take part in a video identification unless:

(a) a video identification is not practicable; or
(b) an identification parade is both practicable and more suitable than a video identification; or
(c) *paragraph 3.16* applies.

The identification officer and the officer in charge of the investigation shall consult each other to determine which option is to be offered. An identification parade may not be practicable because of factors relating to the witnesses, such as their number, state of health, availability and travelling requirements. A video identification would normally be more suitable if it could be arranged and completed sooner than an identification parade. Before an option is offered the suspect must also be reminded of their entitlement to have free legal advice, see Code C, *paragraph 6.5.*

3.15 A suspect who refuses the identification procedure in which the suspect is first invited to take part shall be asked to state their reason for refusing and may get advice from their solicitor and/or if present, their appropriate adult. The suspect, solicitor and/or appropriate adult shall be allowed to make representations about why another procedure should be used. A record should be made of the reasons for refusal and any representations made. After considering any reasons given, and representations made, the identification officer shall, if appropriate, arrange for the suspect to be invited to take part in an alternative which the officer considers suitable and practicable. If the officer decides it is not suitable and practicable to invite the suspect to take part in an alternative identification procedure, the reasons for that decision shall be recorded.

3.16 A suspect may initially be invited to take part in a group identification if the officer in charge of the investigation considers it is more suitable than a video identification or an identification parade and the identification officer considers it practicable to arrange.

Notice to suspect

3.17 Unless *paragraph 3.20* applies, before any eye-witness identification procedure set out in *paragraphs 3.5* to *3.10* is arranged, the following shall be explained to the suspect:

(i) the purpose of the procedure (see *paragraph 3.0*);
(ii) their entitlement to free legal advice; see Code C, *paragraph 6.5*;
(iii) the procedures for holding it, including their right, subject to *Annex A, paragraph 9*, to have a solicitor or friend present;
(iv) that they do not have to consent to or co-operate in the procedure;
(v) that if they do not consent to, and co-operate in, a procedure, their refusal may be given in evidence in any subsequent trial and police may proceed covertly without their consent or make other arrangements to test whether an eye-witness can identify them, see *paragraph 3.21*;
(vi) whether, for the purposes of a video identification procedure, images of them have previously been obtained either:
- in accordance with *paragraph 3.20*, and if so, that they may co-operate in providing further, suitable images to be used instead; or
- in accordance with *paragraph 3.5(a)*, and if so, that they may provide their own images for the identification officer to consider using.

(vii) if appropriate, the special arrangements for juveniles;
(viii) if appropriate, the special arrangements for mentally disordered or otherwise mentally vulnerable people;
(ix) that if they significantly alter their appearance between being offered an identification procedure and any attempt to hold an identification procedure, this may be given in evidence if the case comes to trial, and the identification officer may then consider other forms of identification, see *paragraph 3.21* and *Note 3C*;

(x) that a moving image or photograph may be taken of them when they attend for any identification procedure;

(xi) whether, before their identity became known, the eye-witness was shown photographs, a computerised or artist's composite likeness or similar likeness or image by the police, see *Note 3B;*

(xii) that if they change their appearance before an identification parade, it may not be practicable to arrange one on the day or subsequently and, because of the appearance change, the identification officer may consider alternative methods of identification, see *Note 3C*;

(xiii) that they or their solicitor will be provided with details of the description of the suspect as first given by any eye-witnesses who are to attend the procedure or confrontation, see *paragraph 3.1.*

3.18 This information must also be recorded in a written notice handed to the suspect. The suspect must be given a reasonable opportunity to read the notice, after which, they should be asked to sign a copy of the notice to indicate if they are willing to co-operate with the making of a video or take part in the identification parade or group identification. The signed copy shall be retained by the identification officer.

3.19 In the case of a detained suspect, the duties under *paragraphs 3.17* and *3.18* may be performed by the custody officer or by another officer or police staff not involved in the investigation as directed by the custody officer, if:

(a) it is proposed to release the suspect in order that an identification procedure can be arranged and carried out and an inspector is not available to act as the identification officer, see *paragraph 3.11*, before the suspect leaves the station; or

(b) it is proposed to keep the suspect in police detention whilst the procedure is arranged and carried out and waiting for an inspector to act as the identification officer, see *paragraph 3.11,* would cause unreasonable delay to the investigation.

The officer concerned shall inform the identification officer of the action taken and give them the signed copy of the notice. See *Note 3C.*

3.20 If the identification officer and officer in charge of the investigation suspect, on reasonable grounds that if the suspect was given the information and notice as in *paragraphs 3.17* and *3.18*, they would then take steps to avoid being seen by a witness in any identification procedure, the identification officer may arrange for images of the suspect suitable for use in a video identification procedure to be obtained before giving the information and notice. If suspect's images are obtained in these circumstances, the suspect may, for the purposes of a video identification procedure, co-operate in providing new images which if suitable, would be used instead, see *paragraph 3.17(vi).*

(c) Cases when the suspect is known but not available

3.21 When a known suspect is not available or has ceased to be available, see *paragraph 3.1A*, the identification officer may make arrangements for a video identification (see paragraph 3.5 and Annex A). If necessary, the identification officer may follow the video identification procedures using any suitable moving or still images and these may be obtained covertly if necessary. Alternatively, the identification officer may make arrangements for a group identification without the suspect's consent (see Annex C *paragraph 34*). See *Note 3D*. These provisions may also be applied to juveniles where the consent of their parent or guardian is either refused or reasonable efforts to obtain that consent have failed (see *paragraph 2.12*).

3.22 Any covert activity should be strictly limited to that necessary to test the ability of the eye-witness to identify the suspect as the person they saw on the relevant previous occasion.

3.23 The identification officer may arrange for the suspect to be confronted by the eye-witness if none of the options referred to in *paragraphs 3.5* to *3.10* or *3.21* are practicable. A 'confrontation' is when the suspect is directly confronted by the eye-witness. A confrontation does not require the suspect's consent. Confrontations must be carried out in accordance with Annex D.

3.24 Requirements for information to be given to, or sought from, a suspect or for the suspect to be given an opportunity to view images before they are shown to an eye-witness, do not apply if the suspect's lack of co-operation prevents the necessary action.

(d) Documentation

3.25 A record shall be made of the video identification, identification parade, group identification or confrontation on forms provided for the purpose.

3.26 If the identification officer considers it is not practicable to hold a video identification or identification parade requested by the suspect, the reasons shall be recorded and explained to the suspect.

3.27 A record shall be made of a person's failure or refusal to co-operate in a video identification, identification parade or group identification and, if applicable, of the grounds for obtaining images in accordance with *paragraph 3.20.*

(e) Not used

3.28 *Not used.*

3.29 *Not used.*

(f) Destruction and retention of photographs taken or used in eye-witness identification procedures

3.30 PACE, section 64A, see *paragraph 5.12,* provides powers to take photographs of suspects and allows these photographs to be used or disclosed only for purposes related to the prevention or detection of crime, the investigation of offences or the conduct of prosecutions by, or on behalf of, police or other law enforcement and prosecuting authorities inside and outside the United Kingdom or the enforcement of a sentence. After being so used or disclosed, they may be retained but can only be used or disclosed for the same purposes.

3.31 Subject to *paragraph 3.33,* the photographs (and all negatives and copies), of suspects *not* taken in accordance with the provisions in *paragraph 5.12* which are taken for the purposes of, or in connection with, the identification procedures in *paragraphs 3.5* to *3.10, 3.21 or 3.23* must be destroyed unless the suspect:

(a) is charged with, or informed they may be prosecuted for, a recordable offence;
(b) is prosecuted for a recordable offence;
(c) is cautioned for a recordable offence or given a warning or reprimand in accordance with the Crime and Disorder Act 1998 for a recordable offence; or
(d) gives informed consent, in writing, for the photograph or images to be retained for purposes described in *paragraph 3.30.*

3.32 When *paragraph 3.31* requires the destruction of any photograph, the person must be given an opportunity to witness the destruction or to have a certificate confirming the destruction if they request one within five days of being informed that the destruction is required.

3.33 Nothing in *paragraph 3.31* affects any separate requirement under the Criminal Procedure and Investigations Act 1996 to retain material in connection with criminal investigations.

Part (B) Recognition by controlled showing of films, photographs and images

3.34 This Part of this section applies when, for the purposes of obtaining evidence of recognition, arrangements are made for a person, including a police officer, who is not an eye-witness (see *Note 3AA)*:

(a) to view a film, photograph or any other visual medium; and
(b) on the occasion of the viewing, to be asked whether they recognise anyone whose image is shown in the material as someone who is known to them.

The arrangements for such viewings may be made by the officer in charge of the relevant investigation. Although there is no requirement for the identification officer to make the arrangements or to be consulted about the arrangements, nothing prevents this. See *Notes 3AA* and *3G.*

3.35 To provide safeguards against mistaken recognition and to avoid any possibility of collusion, on the occasion of the viewing, the arrangements should ensure:

(a) that the films, photographs and other images are shown on an individual basis;
(b) that any person who views the material;
  (i) is unable to communicate with any other individual to whom the material has been, or is to be, shown;
  (ii) is not reminded of any photograph or description of any individual whose image is shown or given any other indication as to the identity of any such individual;
  (iii) is not be told whether a previous witness has recognised any one;
(c) that immediately before a person views the material, they are told that:
  (i) an individual who is known to them may, or may not, appear in the material they are shown and that if they do not recognise anyone, they should say so;
  (ii) at any point, they may ask to see a particular part of the material frozen for them to study and there is no limit on how many times they can view the whole or any part or parts of the material; and
(d) that the person who views the material is not asked to make any decision as to whether they recognise anyone whose image they have seen as someone known to them until they have seen the whole of the material at least twice, unless the officer in charge of the viewing decides that because of the number of images the person has been invited to view, it would not be reasonable to ask them to view the whole of the material for a second time. A record of this decision must be included in the record that is made in accordance with *paragraph 3.36*.

(see *Note 3G*).

3.36 A record of the circumstances and conditions under which the person is given an opportunity to recognise an individual must be made and the record must include:

(a) whether the person knew or was given information concerning the name or identity of any suspect;
(b) what the person has been told *before* the viewing about the offence, the person(s) depicted in the images or the offender and by whom;
(c) how and by whom the witness was asked to view the image or look at the individual;
(d) whether the viewing was alone or with others and if with others, the reason for it;
(e) the arrangements under which the person viewed the film or saw the individual and by whom those arrangements were made;
(f) subject to *paragraph 2.18*, the name and rank of the officer responsible for deciding that the viewing arrangements should be made in accordance with this Part;
(g) the date time and place images were viewed or further viewed or the individual was seen;
(h) the times between which the images were viewed or the individual was seen;
(i) how the viewing of images or sighting of the individual was controlled and by whom;
(j) whether the person was familiar with the location shown in any images or the place where they saw the individual and if so, why;
(k) whether or not, on this occasion, the person claims to recognise any image shown, or any individual seen, as being someone known to them, and if they do:
  (i) the reason;
  (ii) the words of recognition;
  (iii) any expressions of doubt; and
  (iv) what features of the image or the individual triggered the recognition.

3.37 The record required under *paragraph 3.36* may be made by the person who views the image or sees the individual and makes the recognition; and if applicable, by the officer or police staff in charge of showing the images to that person or in charge of the conditions under which that person sees the individual. The person must be asked to read and check the completed record and as applicable, confirm that it is correctly and accurately reflects the part they played in the viewing (see *Note 3H*).

Part (C) Recognition by uncontrolled viewing of films, photographs and images

3.38 This Part applies when, for the purpose of identifying and tracing suspects, films and photographs of incidents or other images are:

(a) shown to the public (which may include police officers and police staff as well as members of the public) through the national or local media or any social media networking site; or

(b) circulated through local or national police communication systems for viewing by police officers and police staff; and

the viewing is not formally controlled and supervised as set out in Part B.

3.39 A copy of the relevant material released to the national or local media for showing as described in sub-paragraph 3.38(a), shall be kept. The suspect or their solicitor shall be allowed to view such material before any eye-witness identification procedure under *paragraphs 3.5* to *3.10*, *3.21* or *3.23* of Part A are carried out, provided it is practicable and would not unreasonably delay the investigation. This paragraph does not affect any separate requirement under the Criminal Procedure and Investigations Act 1996 to retain material in connection with criminal investigations that might apply to *sub-paragraphs 3.38(a)* and *(b)*.

3.40 Each eye-witness involved in any eye-witness identification procedure under *paragraphs 3.5* to *3.10*, *3.21* or *3.23* shall be asked, *after they have taken part*, whether they have seen any film, photograph or image relating to the offence or any description of the suspect which has been broadcast or published as described in *paragraph 3.38(a)* and their reply recorded. If they have, they should be asked to give details of the circumstances and subject to the eye-witness's recollection, the record described in *paragraph 3.41* should be completed.

3.41 As soon as practicable after an individual (member of the public, police officer or police staff) indicates in response to a viewing that they may have information relating to the identity and whereabouts of anyone they have seen in that viewing, arrangements should be made to ensure that they are asked to give details of the circumstances and, subject to the individual's recollection, a record of the circumstances and conditions under which the viewing took place is made. This record shall be made in accordance with the provisions of *paragraph 3.36* insofar as they can be applied to the viewing in question (see *Note 3H*).

Notes for guidance

3AA The eye-witness identification procedures in Part A should not be used to test whether a witness can recognise a person as someone they know and would be able to give evidence of recognition along the lines that 'On (describe date, time, location and circumstances) I saw an image of an individual who I recognised as AB.' In these cases, the procedures in Part B shall apply if the viewing is controlled and the procedure in Part C shall apply if the viewing is not controlled.

3ZA In paragraph 3.5(a)(i), examples of physical changes or differences that the identification officer may wish to consider include hair style and colour, weight, facial hair, wearing or removal of spectacles and tinted contact lenses, facial injuries, tattoos and makeup.

3A Except for the provisions of Annex E, paragraph 1, a police officer who is a witness for the purposes of this part of the Code is subject to the same principles and procedures as a civilian witness.

3B When an eye-witness attending an identification procedure has previously been shown photographs, or been shown or provided with computerised or artist's composite likenesses, or similar likenesses or pictures, it is the officer in charge of the investigation's responsibility to make the identification officer aware of this.

3C The purpose of paragraph 3.19 is to avoid or reduce delay in arranging identification procedures by enabling the required information and warnings, see sub-paragraphs 3.17(ix) and 3.17(xii), to be given at the earliest opportunity.

3D Paragraph 3.21 would apply when a known suspect becomes 'unavailable' and thereby delays or frustrates arrangements for obtaining identification evidence. It also applies when a suspect refuses or fails to take part in a video identification, an identification parade or a group identification, or refuses or fails to take part in the only practicable options from that list. It enables any suitable images of the suspect, moving or still, which are available or can be obtained, to be used in an identification procedure. Examples include images from custody and other CCTV systems and from visually recorded interview records, see Code F Note for Guidance 2D.

3E When it is proposed to show photographs to a witness in accordance with Annex E, it is the responsibility of the officer in charge of the investigation to confirm to the officer responsible for supervising and directing the showing, that the first description of the suspect given by that eye-witness has been recorded. If this description has not been recorded, the procedure under Annex E must be postponed, see Annex E paragraph 2.

3F The admissibility and value of identification evidence obtained when carrying out the procedure under paragraph 3.2 may be compromised if:

- *(a) before a person is identified, the eye-witness' attention is specifically drawn to that person; or*
- *(b) the suspect's identity becomes known before the procedure.*

3G The admissibility and value of evidence of recognition obtained when carrying out the procedures in Part B may be compromised if, before the person is recognised, the witness who has claimed to know them is given or is made, or becomes aware of, information about the person which was not previously known to them personally but which they have purported to rely on to support their claim that the person is in fact known to them.

3H It is important that the record referred to in paragraphs 3.36 and 3.41 is made as soon as practicable after the viewing and whilst it is fresh in the mind of the individual who makes the recognition.

4 Identification by fingerprints and footwear impressions

(A) Taking fingerprints in connection with a criminal investigation

(a) General

4.1 References to 'fingerprints' means any record, produced by any method, of the skin pattern and other physical characteristics or features of a person's:

- (i) fingers; or
- (ii) palms.

(b) Action

4.2 A person's fingerprints may be taken in connection with the investigation of an offence only with their consent or if *paragraph 4.3* applies. If the person is at a police station, consent must be in writing.

4.3 PACE, section 61, provides powers to take fingerprints without consent from any person aged ten or over as follows:

- (a) under *section 61(3)*, from a person detained at a police station in consequence of being arrested for a recordable offence, see *Note 4A*, if they have not had their fingerprints taken in the course of the investigation of the offence unless those previously taken fingerprints are not a complete set or some or all of those fingerprints are not of sufficient quality to allow satisfactory analysis, comparison or matching.
- (b) under *section 61(4)*, from a person detained at a police station who has been charged with a recordable offence, see *Note 4A*, or informed they will be reported for such an offence if they have not had their fingerprints taken in the course of the investigation of the offence unless those previously taken fingerprints are not a complete set or some or all of those fingerprints are not of sufficient quality to allow satisfactory analysis, comparison or matching.
- (c) under *section 61(4A)*, from a person who has been bailed to appear at a court or police station if the person:
  - (i) has answered to bail for a person whose fingerprints were taken previously and there are reasonable grounds for believing they are not the same person; or
  - (ii) who has answered to bail claims to be a different person from a person whose fingerprints were previously taken;

and in either case, the court or an officer of inspector rank or above, authorises the fingerprints to be taken at the court or police station (an inspector's authority may be given in writing or orally and confirmed in writing, as soon as practicable);

(ca) under *section 61(5A)* from a person who has been arrested for a recordable offence and released if the person:

(i) is on bail and has not had their fingerprints taken in the course of the investigation of the offence, or;

(ii) has had their fingerprints taken in the course of the investigation of the offence, but they do not constitute a complete set or some, or all, of the fingerprints are not of sufficient quality to allow satisfactory analysis, comparison or matching.

(cb) under *section 61(5B)* from a person not detained at a police station who has been charged with a recordable offence or informed they will be reported for such an offence if:

(i) they have not had their fingerprints taken in the course of the investigation; or

(ii) their fingerprints have been taken in the course of the investigation of the offence but either:

- they do not constitute a complete set or some, or all, of the fingerprints are not of sufficient quality to allow satisfactory analysis, comparison or matching; or
- the investigation was discontinued but subsequently resumed and, before the resumption, their fingerprints were destroyed pursuant to section 63D(3).

(d) under *section 61(6)*, from a person who has been:

(i) convicted of a recordable offence; or

(ii) given a caution in respect of a recordable offence (see Note 4A) which, at the time of the caution, the person admitted;

if, since being convicted or cautioned:

- their fingerprints have not been taken; or
- their fingerprints which have been taken do not constitute a complete set or some, or all, of the fingerprints are not of sufficient quality to allow satisfactory analysis, comparison or matching;

and in either case, an officer of inspector rank or above is satisfied that taking the fingerprints is necessary to assist in the prevention or detection of crime and authorises the taking;

(e) under *section 61(6A)* from a person a constable reasonably suspects is committing or attempting to commit, or has committed or attempted to commit, any offence if either:

(i) the person's name is unknown to, and cannot be readily ascertained by, the constable; or

(ii) the constable has reasonable grounds for doubting whether a name given by the person as their name is their real name.

Note: fingerprints taken under this power are not regarded as having been taken in the course of the investigation of an offence.

[See *Note 4C*]

(f) under *section 61(6D)* from a person who has been convicted outside England and Wales of an offence which if committed in England and Wales would be a qualifying offence as defined by PACE, section 65A (see Note 4AB) if:

(i) the person's fingerprints have not been taken previously under this power or their fingerprints have been so taken on a previous occasion but they do not constitute a complete set or some, or all, of the fingerprints are not of sufficient quality to allow satisfactory analysis, comparison or matching; and

(ii) a police officer of inspector rank or above is satisfied that taking fingerprints is necessary to assist in the prevention or detection of crime and authorises them to be taken.

4.4 PACE, section 63A(4) and Schedule 2A provide powers to:

(a) make a requirement (in accordance with Annex G) for a person to attend a police station to have their fingerprints taken in the exercise of one of the following powers (described in *paragraph 4.3* above) within certain periods as follows:

(i) *section 61(5A)*—Persons arrested for a recordable offence and released, see *paragraph 4.3(ca)*: In the case of a person whose fingerprints were taken in the course of the investigation but those fingerprints do not constitute a complete set or some, or all, of the fingerprints are not of sufficient quality, the requirement may not be made more than six months from the day the investigating officer was informed that the fingerprints previously taken were incomplete or below standard. In the case of a person whose fingerprints were destroyed prior to the resumption of the investigation, the requirement may not be made more than six months from the day on which the investigation resumed.

(ii) *section 61(5B)*—Persons not detained at a police station charged etc. with a recordable offence, see *paragraph 4.3(cb)*: The requirement may not be made more than six months from:

- the day the person was charged or informed that they would be reported, if fingerprints have not been taken in the course of the investigation of the offence; or
- the day the investigating officer was informed that the fingerprints previously taken were incomplete or below standard, if fingerprints have been taken in the course of the investigation but those fingerprints do not constitute a complete set or some, or all, of the fingerprints are not of sufficient quality; or
- the day on which the investigation was resumed, in the case of a person whose fingerprints were destroyed prior to the resumption of the investigation.

(iii) *section 61(6)*—Persons convicted or cautioned for a recordable offence in England and Wales, see *paragraph 4.3(d)*: Where the offence for which the person was convicted or cautioned is a qualifying offence (see Note 4AB), there is no time limit for the exercise of this power. Where the conviction or caution is for a recordable offence which is not a qualifying offence, the requirement may not be made more than two years from:

- in the case of a person who has not had their fingerprints taken since the conviction or caution, the day on which the person was convicted or cautioned, or, if later, the day on which Schedule 2A came into force (March 7, 2011); or
- in the case of a person whose fingerprints have been taken in the course of the investigation but those fingerprints do not constitute a complete set or some, or all, of the fingerprints are not of sufficient quality, the day on which an officer from the force investigating the offence was informed that the fingerprints previously taken were incomplete or below standard, or, if later, the day on which Schedule 2A came into force (March 7, 2011).

(iv) *section 61(6D)*—A person who has been convicted of a qualifying offence (see *Note 4AB*) outside England and Wales, see *paragraph 4.3(g)*: There is no time limit for making the requirement.

Note: A person who has had their fingerprints taken under any of the powers in section 61 mentioned in *paragraph 4.3* on two occasions in relation to any offence may not be required under Schedule 2A to attend a police station for their fingerprints to be taken again under section 61 in relation to that offence, unless authorised by an officer of inspector rank or above. The fact of the authorisation and the reasons for giving it must be recorded as soon as practicable.

(b) arrest, without warrant, a person who fails to comply with the requirement.

4.5 A person's fingerprints may be taken, as above, electronically.

4.6 Reasonable force may be used, if necessary, to take a person's fingerprints without their consent under the powers as in *paragraphs 4.3* and *4.4*.

4.7 Before any fingerprints are taken:

(a) without consent under any power mentioned in *paragraphs 4.3* and *4.4* above, the person must be informed of:

(i) the reason their fingerprints are to be taken;

(ii) the power under which they are to be taken; and

(iii) the fact that the relevant authority has been given if any power mentioned in *paragraph 4.3(c), (d)* or *(f)* applies

(b) with or without consent at a police station or elsewhere, the person must be informed:

(i) that their fingerprints may be subject of a speculative search against other fingerprints, see *Note 4B*; and

(ii) that their fingerprints may be retained in accordance with *Annex F, Part (a)* unless they were taken under the power mentioned in paragraph 4.3(e) when they must be destroyed after they have being checked (See *Note 4C*).

(c) Documentation

4.8A A record must be made as soon as practicable after the fingerprints are taken, of:

- the matters in paragraph 4.7(a)(i) to (iii) and the fact that the person has been informed of those matters; and
- the fact that the person has been informed of the matters in paragraph 4.7(b)(i) and (ii).

The record must be made in the person's custody record if they are detained at a police station when the fingerprints are taken.

4.8 If force is used, a record shall be made of the circumstances and those present.

4.9 *Not used*

(B) *Not used*

4.10 *Not used*

4.11 *Not used*

4.12 *Not used*

4.13 *Not used*

4.14 *Not used*

4.15 *Not used*

(C) *Taking footwear impressions in connection with a criminal investigation*

(a) Action

4.16 Impressions of a person's footwear may be taken in connection with the investigation of an offence only with their consent or if *paragraph 4.17* applies. If the person is at a police station consent must be in writing.

4.17 PACE, section 61A, provides power for a police officer to take footwear impressions without consent from any person over the age of ten years who is detained at a police station:

(a) in consequence of being arrested for a recordable offence, see *Note 4A*; or if the detainee has been charged with a recordable offence, or informed they will be reported for such an offence; and

(b) the detainee has not had an impression of their footwear taken in the course of the investigation of the offence unless the previously taken impression is not complete or is not of sufficient quality to allow satisfactory analysis, comparison or matching (whether in the case in question or generally).

4.18 Reasonable force may be used, if necessary, to take a footwear impression from a detainee without consent under the power in *paragraph 4.17.*

4.19 Before any footwear impression is taken with, or without, consent as above, the person must be informed:

(a) of the reason the impression is to be taken;

(b) that the impression may be retained and may be subject of a speculative search against other impressions, see *Note 4B*, unless destruction of the impression is required in accordance with *Annex F, Part B*.

(b) Documentation

4.20 A record must be made, as soon as possible, of the reason for taking a person's footwear impressions without consent. If force is used, a record shall be made of the circumstances and those present.

4.21 A record shall be made when a person has been informed under the terms of *paragraph 4.19(b)*, of the possibility that their footwear impressions may be subject of a speculative search.

Notes for guidance

4A References to 'recordable offences' in this Code relate to those offences for which convictions or cautions may be recorded in national police records. See PACE, section 27(4). The recordable offences current at the time when this Code was prepared, are any offences which carry a sentence of imprisonment on conviction (irrespective of the period, or the age of the offender or actual sentence passed) as well as the non-imprisonable offences under the Vagrancy Act 1824 sections 3 and 4 (begging and persistent begging), the Street Offences Act 1959, section 1 (loitering or soliciting for purposes of prostitution), the Road Traffic Act 1988, section 25 (tampering with motor vehicles), the Criminal Justice and Public Order Act 1994, section 167 (touting for hire car services) and others listed in the National Police Records (Recordable Offences) Regulations 2000 as amended.

4AB A qualifying offence is one of the offences specified in PACE, section 65A. These include offences which involve the use or threat of violence or unlawful force against persons, sexual offences, offences against children and other offences, for example:

- *murder, false imprisonment, kidnapping contrary to Common law*
- *manslaughter, conspiracy to murder, threats to kill, wounding with intent to cause grievous bodily harm (GBH), causing GBH and assault occasioning actual bodily harm contrary to the Offences Against the Person Act 1861;*
- *criminal possession or use of firearms contrary to sections 16 to 18 of the Firearms Act 1968;*
- *robbery, burglary and aggravated burglary contrary to sections 8, 9 or 10 of the Theft Act 1968 or an offence under section 12A of that Act involving an accident which caused a person's death;*
- *criminal damage required to be charged as arson contrary to section 1 of the Criminal Damage Act 1971;*
- *taking, possessing and showing indecent photographs of children contrary to section 1 of the Protection of Children Act 1978;*
- *rape, sexual assault, child sex offences, exposure and other offences contrary to the Sexual Offences Act 2003.*

4B Fingerprints, footwear impressions or a DNA sample (and the information derived from it) taken from a person arrested on suspicion of being involved in a recordable offence, or charged with such an offence, or informed they will be reported for such an offence, may be subject of a speculative search. This means the fingerprints, footwear impressions or DNA sample may be checked against other fingerprints, footwear impressions and DNA records held by, or on behalf of, the police and other law enforcement authorities in, or outside, the UK, or held in connection with, or as a result of, an investigation of an offence inside or outside the UK.

4C The power under section 61(6A) of PACE described in paragraph 4.3(e) allows fingerprints of a suspect who has not been arrested, and whose name is not known or cannot be ascertained, or who gave a doubtful name, to be taken in connection with any offence (whether recordable or not) using a mobile device and then checked on the street against the database containing the national fingerprint collection. Fingerprints taken under this power cannot be retained after they have been checked. The results may make an arrest for the suspected offence based on the name condition unnecessary (See Code G paragraph 2.9(a)) and enable the offence to be disposed of without arrest, for example, by summons/charging by post, penalty notice or words of advice. If arrest for a non-recordable offence is necessary for any other reasons, this power may also be exercised at the station. Before the power is exercised, the officer should:

- *inform the person of the nature of the suspected offence and why they are suspected of committing it.*
- *give them a reasonable opportunity to establish their real name before deciding that their name is unknown and cannot be readily ascertained or that there are reasonable grounds to doubt that a name they have given is their real name.*
- *as applicable, inform the person of the reason why their name is not known and cannot be readily ascertained or of the grounds for doubting that a name they have given is their real name, including, for example, the reason why a particular document the person has produced to verify their real name, is not sufficient.*

4D Not used.

5 Examinations to establish identity and the taking of photographs

(A) Detainees at police stations

(a) Searching or examination of detainees at police stations

5.1 PACE, section 54A(1), allows a detainee at a police station to be searched or examined or both, to establish:

(a) whether they have any marks, features or injuries that would tend to identify them as a person involved in the commission of an offence and to photograph any identifying marks, see *paragraph 5.5*; or

(b) their identity, see *Note 5A.*

A person detained at a police station to be searched under a stop and search power, see Code A, is not a detainee for the purposes of these powers.

5.2 A search and/or examination to find marks under section 54A (1) (a) may be carried out without the detainee's consent, see *paragraph 2.12,* only if authorised by an officer of at least inspector rank when consent has been withheld or it is not practicable to obtain consent, see *Note 5D.*

5.3 A search or examination to establish a suspect's identity under section 54A (1) (b) may be carried out without the detainee's consent, see *paragraph 2.12,* only if authorised by an officer of at least inspector rank when the detainee has refused to identify themselves or the authorising officer has reasonable grounds for suspecting the person is not who they claim to be.

5.4 Any marks that assist in establishing the detainee's identity, or their identification as a person involved in the commission of an offence, are identifying marks. Such marks may be photographed with the detainee's consent, see *paragraph 2.12*; or without their consent if it is withheld or it is not practicable to obtain it, see *Note 5D.*

5.5 A detainee may only be searched, examined and photographed under section 54A, by a police officer of the same sex.

5.6 Any photographs of identifying marks, taken under section 54A, may be used or disclosed only for purposes related to the prevention or detection of crime, the investigation of offences or the conduct of prosecutions by, or on behalf of, police or other law enforcement and prosecuting authorities inside, and outside, the UK. After being so used or disclosed, the photograph may be retained but must not be used or disclosed except for these purposes, see *Note 5B.*

5.7 The powers, as in *paragraph 5.1,* do not affect any separate requirement under the Criminal Procedure and Investigations Act 1996 to retain material in connection with criminal investigations.

5.8 Authority for the search and/or examination for the purposes of *paragraphs 5.2* and *5.3* may be given orally or in writing. If given orally, the authorising officer must confirm it in writing as soon as practicable. A separate authority is required for each purpose which applies.

5.9 If it is established a person is unwilling to co-operate sufficiently to enable a search and/or examination to take place or a suitable photograph to be taken, an officer may use reasonable force to:

(a) search and/or examine a detainee without their consent; and
(b) photograph any identifying marks without their consent.

5.10 The thoroughness and extent of any search or examination carried out in accordance with the powers in section 54A must be no more than the officer considers necessary to achieve the required purpose. Any search or examination which involves the removal of more than the person's outer clothing shall be conducted in accordance with Code C, Annex A, paragraph 11.

5.11 An intimate search may not be carried out under the powers in section 54A.

(b) Photographing detainees at police stations and other persons elsewhere than at a police station

5.12 Under PACE, section 64A, an officer may photograph:

(a) any person whilst they are detained at a police station; and
(b) any person who is elsewhere than at a police station and who has been:
    (i) arrested by a constable for an offence;
    (ii) taken into custody by a constable after being arrested for an offence by a person other than a constable;
    (iii) made subject to a requirement to wait with a community support officer under paragraph 2(3) or (3B) of Schedule 4 to the Police Reform Act 2002;
    (iiia) given a direction by a constable under section 27 of the Violent Crime Reduction Act 2006.
    (iv) given a penalty notice by a constable in uniform under Chapter 1 of Part 1 of the Criminal Justice and Police Act 2001, a penalty notice by a constable under section 444A of the Education Act 1996, or a fixed penalty notice by a constable in uniform under section 54 of the Road Traffic Offenders Act 1988;
    (v) given a notice in relation to a relevant fixed penalty offence (within the meaning of paragraph 1 of Schedule 4 to the Police Reform Act 2002) by a community support officer by virtue of a designation applying that paragraph to him;
    (vi) given a notice in relation to a relevant fixed penalty offence (within the meaning of paragraph 1 of Schedule 5 to the Police Reform Act 2002) by an accredited person by virtue of accreditation specifying that that paragraph applies to him; or
    (vii) given a direction to leave and not return to a specified location for up to 48 hours by a police constable (under section 27 of the Violent Crime Reduction Act 2006).

5.12A Photographs taken under PACE, section 64A:

(a) may be taken with the person's consent, or without their consent if consent is withheld or it is not practicable to obtain their consent, see *Note 5E*; and
(b) may be used or disclosed only for purposes related to the prevention or detection of crime, the investigation of offences or the conduct of prosecutions by, or on behalf of, police or other law enforcement and prosecuting authorities inside and outside the United Kingdom or the enforcement of any sentence or order made by a court when dealing with an offence. After being so used or disclosed, they may be retained but can only be used or disclosed for the same purposes. See *Note 5B*.

5.13 The officer proposing to take a detainee's photograph may, for this purpose, require the person to remove any item or substance worn on, or over, all, or any part of, their head or face. If they do not comply with such a requirement, the officer may remove the item or substance.

5.14 If it is established the detainee is unwilling to co-operate sufficiently to enable a suitable photograph to be taken and it is not reasonably practicable to take the photograph covertly, an officer may use reasonable force, see *Note 5F*.

(a) to take their photograph without their consent; and
(b) for the purpose of taking the photograph, remove any item or substance worn on, or over, all, or any part of, the person's head or face which they have failed to remove when asked.

5.15 For the purposes of this Code, a photograph may be obtained without the person's consent by making a copy of an image of them taken at any time on a camera system installed anywhere in the police station.

(c) Information to be given

5.18 When a person is searched, examined or photographed under the provisions as in *paragraph 5.1* and *5.12*, or their photograph obtained as in *paragraph 5.15*, they must be informed of the:

- (a) purpose of the search, examination or photograph;
- (b) grounds on which the relevant authority, if applicable, has been given; and
- (c) purposes for which the photograph may be used, disclosed or retained.

This information must be given before the search or examination commences or the photograph is taken, except if the photograph is:

- (i) to be taken covertly;
- (ii) obtained as in *paragraph 5.15*, in which case the person must be informed as soon as practicable after the photograph is taken or obtained.

(d) Documentation

5.17 A record must be made when a detainee is searched, examined, or a photograph of the person, or any identifying marks found on them, are taken. The record must include the:

- (a) identity, subject to paragraph 2.18, of the officer carrying out the search, examination or taking the photograph;
- (b) purpose of the search, examination or photograph and the outcome;
- (c) detainee's consent to the search, examination or photograph, or the reason the person was searched, examined or photographed without consent;
- (d) giving of any authority as in *paragraphs 5.2* and *5.3*, the grounds for giving it and the authorising officer.

5.18 If force is used when searching, examining or taking a photograph in accordance with this section, a record shall be made of the circumstances and those present.

(B) Persons at police stations not detained

5.19 When there are reasonable grounds for suspecting the involvement of a person in a criminal offence, but that person is at a police station **voluntarily** and not detained, the provisions of *paragraphs 5.1* to *5.18* should apply, subject to the modifications in the following paragraphs.

5.20 References to the 'person being detained' and to the powers mentioned in *paragraph 5.1* which apply only to detainees at police stations shall be omitted.

5.21 Force may not be used to:

- (a) search and/or examine the person to:
  - (i) discover whether they have any marks that would tend to identify them as a person involved in the commission of an offence; or
  - (ii) establish their identity, see *Note 5A*;
- (b) take photographs of any identifying marks, see *paragraph 5.4*; or
- (c) take a photograph of the person.

5.22 Subject to *paragraph 5.24*, the photographs of persons or of their identifying marks which are not taken in accordance with the provisions mentioned in *paragraphs 5.1* or *5.12*, must be destroyed (together with any negatives and copies) unless the person:

- (a) is charged with, or informed they may be prosecuted for, a recordable offence;
- (b) is prosecuted for a recordable offence;
- (c) is cautioned for a recordable offence or given a warning or reprimand in accordance with the Crime and Disorder Act 1998 for a recordable offence; or
- (d) gives informed consent, in writing, for the photograph or image to be retained as in *paragraph 5.6*.

5.23 When *paragraph 5.22* requires the destruction of any photograph, the person must be given an opportunity to witness the destruction or to have a certificate confirming the destruction provided they so request the certificate within five days of being informed the destruction is required.

5.24 Nothing in *paragraph 5.22* affects any separate requirement under the Criminal Procedure and Investigations Act 1996 to retain material in connection with criminal investigations.

Notes for guidance

5A The conditions under which fingerprints may be taken to assist in establishing a person's identity, are described in Section 4.

5B Examples of purposes related to the prevention or detection of crime, the investigation of offences or the conduct of prosecutions include:

- *(a) checking the photograph against other photographs held in records or in connection with, or as a result of, an investigation of an offence to establish whether the person is liable to arrest for other offences;*
- *(b) when the person is arrested at the same time as other people, or at a time when it is likely that other people will be arrested, using the photograph to help establish who was arrested, at what time and where;*
- *(c) when the real identity of the person is not known and cannot be readily ascertained or there are reasonable grounds for doubting a name and other personal details given by the person, are their real name and personal details. In these circumstances, using or disclosing the photograph to help to establish or verify their real identity or determine whether they are liable to arrest for some other offence, e.g. by checking it against other photographs held in records or in connection with, or as a result of, an investigation of an offence;*
- *(d) when it appears any identification procedure in section 3 may need to be arranged for which the person's photograph would assist;*
- *(e) when the person's release without charge may be required, and if the release is:*
  - *(i) on bail to appear at a police station, using the photograph to help verify the person's identity when they answer their bail and if the person does not answer their bail, to assist in arresting them; or*
  - *(ii) without bail, using the photograph to help verify their identity or assist in locating them for the purposes of serving them with a summons to appear at court in criminal proceedings;*
- *(f) when the person has answered to bail at a police station and there are reasonable grounds for doubting they are the person who was previously granted bail, using the photograph to help establish or verify their identity;*
- *(g) when the person arrested on a warrant claims to be a different person from the person named on the warrant and a photograph would help to confirm or disprove their claim;*
- *(h) when the person has been charged with, reported for, or convicted of, a recordable offence and their photograph is not already on record as a result of (a) to (f) or their photograph is on record but their appearance has changed since it was taken and the person has not yet been released or brought before a court.*

5C There is no power to arrest a person convicted of a recordable offence solely to take their photograph. The power to take photographs in this section applies only where the person is in custody as a result of the exercise of another power, e.g. arrest for fingerprinting under PACE, Schedule 2A, paragraph 17.

5D Examples of when it would not be practicable to obtain a detainee's consent, see paragraph 2.12, to a search, examination or the taking of a photograph of an identifying mark include:

- *(a) when the person is drunk or otherwise unfit to give consent;*
- *(b) when there are reasonable grounds to suspect that if the person became aware a search or examination was to take place or an identifying mark was to be photographed, they would take steps to prevent this happening, e.g. by violently resisting, covering or*

concealing the mark etc. and it would not otherwise be possible to carry out the search or examination or to photograph any identifying mark;

(c) in the case of a juvenile, if the parent or guardian cannot be contacted in sufficient time to allow the search or examination to be carried out or the photograph to be taken.

5E Examples of when it would not be practicable to obtain the person's consent, see paragraph 2.12, to a photograph being taken include:

(a) when the person is drunk or otherwise unfit to give consent;

(b) when there are reasonable grounds to suspect that if the person became aware a photograph, suitable to be used or disclosed for the use and disclosure described in paragraph 5.6, was to be taken, they would take steps to prevent it being taken, e.g. by violently resisting, covering or distorting their face etc., and it would not otherwise be possible to take a suitable photograph;

(c) when, in order to obtain a suitable photograph, it is necessary to take it covertly; and

(d) in the case of a juvenile, if the parent or guardian cannot be contacted in sufficient time to allow the photograph to be taken.

5F The use of reasonable force to take the photograph of a suspect elsewhere than at a police station must be carefully considered. In order to obtain a suspect's consent and co-operation to remove an item of religious headwear to take their photograph, a constable should consider whether in the circumstances of the situation the removal of the headwear and the taking of the photograph should be by an officer of the same sex as the person. It would be appropriate for these actions to be conducted out of public view (see paragraph 1.1 and Note 1A).

6 Identification by body samples and impressions

(A) General

6.1 References to:

(a) an 'intimate sample' mean a dental impression or sample of blood, semen or any other tissue fluid, urine, or pubic hair, or a swab taken from any part of a person's genitals or from a person's body orifice other than the mouth;

(b) a 'non-intimate sample' means:

(i) a sample of hair, other than pubic hair, which includes hair plucked with the root, see *Note 6A*;

(ii) a sample taken from a nail or from under a nail;

(iii) a swab taken from any part of a person's body other than a part from which a swab taken would be an intimate sample;

(iv) saliva;

(v) a skin impression which means any record, other than a fingerprint, which is a record, in any form and produced by any method, of the skin pattern and other physical characteristics or features of the whole, or any part of, a person's foot or of any other part of their body.

(B) Action

(a) Intimate samples

6.2 PACE, section 62, provides that intimate samples may be taken under:

(a) section 62(1), from a person in police detention only:

(i) if a police officer of inspector rank or above has reasonable grounds to believe such an impression or sample will tend to confirm or disprove the suspect's involvement in a recordable offence, see *Note 4A*, and gives authorisation for a sample to be taken; and

(ii) with the suspect's written consent;

(b) section 62(1A), from a person not in police detention but from whom two or more non-intimate samples have been taken in the course of an investigation of an offence and the samples, though suitable, have proved insufficient if:

(i) a police officer of inspector rank or above authorises it to be taken; and
(ii) the person concerned gives their written consent. See *Notes 6B* and *6C*

(c) section 62(2A), from a person convicted outside England and Wales of an offence which if committed in England and Wales would be qualifying offence as defined by PACE, section 65A (see *Note 4AB*) from whom two or more non-intimate samples taken under section 63(3E) (see *paragraph 6.6(h)* have proved insufficient if:
(i) a police officer of inspector rank or above is satisfied that taking the sample is necessary to assist in the prevention or detection of crime and authorises it to be taken; and
(ii) the person concerned gives their written consent.

6.2A PACE, section 63A(4) and Schedule 2A provide powers to:

(a) make a requirement (in accordance with Annex G) for a person to attend a police station to have an intimate sample taken in the exercise of one of the following powers (see *paragraph 6.2*):
(i) *section 62(1A)*—Persons from whom two or more non-intimate samples have been taken and proved to be insufficient, see paragraph 6.2(b): There is no time limit for making the requirement.
(ii) *section 62(2A)*—Persons convicted outside England and Wales from whom two or more non-intimate samples taken under section 63(3E) (see paragraph 6.6(g) have proved insufficient, see *paragraph 6.2(c)*: There is no time limit for making the requirement.

(b) arrest without warrant a person who fails to comply with the requirement

6.3 Before a suspect is asked to provide an intimate sample, they must be:

(a) informed:
(i) of the reason, including the nature of the suspected offence (except if taken under paragraph 6.2(c) from a person convicted outside England and Wales.
(ii) that authorisation has been given and the provisions under which given;
(iii) that a sample taken at a police station may be subject of a speculative search;

(b) warned that if they refuse without good cause their refusal may harm their case if it comes to trial, see *Note 6D*. If the suspect is in police detention and not legally represented, they must also be reminded of their entitlement to have free legal advice, see Code C, *paragraph 6.5*, and the reminder noted in the custody record. If *paragraph 6.2(b)* applies and the person is attending a station voluntarily, their entitlement to free legal advice as in Code C, *paragraph 3.21* shall be explained to them.

6.4 Dental impressions may only be taken by a registered dentist. Other intimate samples, except for samples of urine, may only be taken by a registered medical practitioner or registered nurse or registered paramedic.

(b) Non-intimate samples

6.5 A non-intimate sample may be taken from a detainee only with their written consent or if *paragraph 6.6* applies.

6.6 A non-intimate sample may be taken from a person without the appropriate consent in the following circumstances:

(a) under *section 63(2A)* from a person who is in police detention as a consequence of being arrested for a recordable offence and who has not had a non-intimate sample of the same type and from the same part of the body taken in the course of the investigation of the offence by the police or they have had such a sample taken but it proved insufficient.

(b) Under *section 63(3)* from a person who is being held in custody by the police on the authority of a court if an officer of at least the rank of inspector authorises it to be taken. An authorisation may be given:

(i) if the authorising officer has reasonable grounds for suspecting the person of involvement in a recordable offence and for believing that the sample will tend to confirm or disprove that involvement, and

(ii) in writing or orally and confirmed in writing, as soon as practicable;

but an authorisation may not be given to take from the same part of the body a further non-intimate sample consisting of a skin impression unless the previously taken impression proved insufficient

(c) under *section 63(3ZA)* from a person who has been arrested for a recordable offence and released if:

(i) in the case of a person who is on bail, they have not had a sample of the same type and from the same part of the body taken in the course of the investigation of the offence, or;

(ii) in any case, the person has had such a sample taken in the course of the investigation of the offence, but either:

- it was not suitable or proved insufficient; or
- the investigation was discontinued but subsequently resumed and before the resumption, any DNA profile derived from the sample was destroyed and the sample itself was destroyed pursuant to section 63R(4), (5) or (12).

(d) under *section 63(3A)*, from a person (whether or not in police detention or held in custody by the police on the authority of a court) who has been charged with a recordable offence or informed they will be reported for such an offence if the person:

(i) has not had a non-intimate sample taken from them in the course of the investigation of the offence; or

(ii) has had a sample so taken, but it was not suitable or proved insufficient, see *Note 6B*; or

(iii) has had a sample taken in the course of the investigation of the offence and the sample has been destroyed and in proceedings relating to that offence there is a dispute as to whether a DNA profile relevant to the proceedings was derived from the destroyed sample.

(e) under *section 63(3B)*, from a person who has been:

(i) convicted of a recordable offence; or

(ii) given a caution in respect of a recordable offence which, at the time of the caution, the person admitted;

if, since their conviction or caution a non-intimate sample has not been taken from them or a sample which has been taken since then was not suitable or proved insufficient and in either case, an officer of inspector rank or above, is satisfied that taking the fingerprints is necessary to assist in the prevention or detection of crime and authorises the taking;

(f) under *section 63(3C)* from a person to whom section 2 of the Criminal Evidence (Amendment) Act 1997 applies (persons detained following acquittal on grounds of insanity or finding of unfitness to plead).

(g) under *section 63(3E)* from a person who has been convicted outside England and Wales of an offence which if committed in England and Wales would be a qualifying offence as defined by PACE, section 65A (see *Note 4AB*) if:

(i) a non-intimate sample has not been taken previously under this power or unless a sample was so taken but was not suitable or proved insufficient; and

(ii) a police officer of inspector rank or above is satisfied that taking a sample is necessary to assist in the prevention or detection of crime and authorises it to be taken.

6.6A PACE, *section 63A(4)* and *Schedule 2A* provide powers to:

(a) make a requirement (in accordance with Annex G) for a person to attend a police station to have a non-intimate sample taken in the exercise of one of the following powers (see *paragraph 6.6* above) within certain time limits as follows:

(i) *section 63(3ZA)*—Persons arrested for a recordable offence and released, see paragraph 6.6(c): In the case of a person from whom a non-intimate sample was taken in the course of the investigation but that sample was not suitable or proved insufficient, the requirement may not be made more than six months from the day the investigating officer was informed that the sample previously taken was not suitable or proved insufficient. In the case of a person whose DNA profile and sample was destroyed prior to the resumption of the investigation, the requirement may not be made more than six months from the day on which the investigation resumed.

(ii) *section 63(3A)*—Persons charged etc. with a recordable offence, see paragraph 6.6(d): The requirement may not be made more than six months from:

- the day the person was charged or informed that they would be reported, if a sample has not been taken in the course of the investigation;
- the day the investigating officer was informed that the sample previously taken was not suitable or proved insufficient, if a sample has been taken in the course of the investigation but the sample was not suitable or proved insufficient; or
- the day on which the investigation was resumed, in the case of a person whose DNA profile and sample were destroyed prior to the resumption of the investigation.

(iii) *section 63(3B)*—Person convicted or cautioned for a recordable offence in England and Wales, see paragraph 6.6(e): Where the offence for which the person was convicted etc. is also a qualifying offence (see *Note 4AB*), there is no time limit for the exercise of this power. Where the conviction etc. was for a recordable offence that is not a qualifying offence, the requirement may not be made more than two years from:

- in the case of a person whose sample has not been taken since they were convicted or cautioned, the day the person was convicted or cautioned, , or, if later. the day Schedule 2A came into force (March 7 2011); or
- in the case of a person whose sample has been taken but was not suitable or proved insufficient, the day an officer from the force investigating the offence was informed that the sample previously taken was not suitable or proved insufficient or, if later, the day Schedule 2A came into force (March 7 2011).

(iv) *section 63(3E)*—A person who has been convicted of qualifying offence (see *Note 4AB*) outside England and Wales, see *paragraph 6.6(h)*: There is no time limit for making the requirement.

Note: A person who has had a non-intimate sample taken under any of the powers in section 63 mentioned in paragraph 6.6 on two occasions in relation to any offence may not be required under Schedule 2A to attend a police station for a sample to be taken again under section 63 in relation to that offence, unless authorised by an officer of inspector rank or above. The fact of the authorisation and the reasons for giving it must be recorded as soon as practicable.

(b) arrest, without warrant, a person who fails to comply with the requirement.

6.7 Reasonable force may be used, if necessary, to take a non-intimate sample from a person without their consent under the powers mentioned in *paragraph 6.6*.

6.8 Before any non-intimate sample is taken:

(a) without consent under any power mentioned in paragraphs 6.6 and 6.6A, the person must be informed of:

(i) the reason for taking the sample;

(ii) the power under which the sample is to be taken;

(iii) the fact that the relevant authority has been given if any power mentioned in *paragraph 6.6(b), (e)* or *(g)* applies, including the nature of the suspected offence (except if taken under *paragraph 6.6(e)* from a person convicted or cautioned, or under *paragraph 6.6(g)* if taken from a person convicted outside England and Wales;

(b) with or without consent at a police station or elsewhere, the person must be informed:

(i) that their sample or information derived from it may be subject of a speculative search against other samples and information derived from them, see *Note 6E* and

(ii) that their sample and the information derived from it may be retained in accordance with Annex F, Part (a).

(c) Removal of clothing

6.9 When clothing needs to be removed in circumstances likely to cause embarrassment to the person, no person of the opposite sex who is not a registered medical practitioner or registered health care professional shall be present, (unless in the case of a juvenile, mentally disordered or mentally vulnerable person, that person specifically requests the presence of an appropriate adult of the opposite sex who is readily available) nor shall anyone whose presence is unnecessary. However, in the case of a juvenile, this is subject to the overriding proviso that such a removal of clothing may take place in the absence of the appropriate adult only if the juvenile signifies in their presence, that they prefer the adult's absence and they agree.

(d) Documentation

6.10 A record must be made as soon as practicable after the sample is taken of:

- The matters in *paragraph 6.8(a)(i)* to *(iii)* and the fact that the person has been informed of those matters; and
- The fact that the person has been informed of the matters in paragraph 6.8(b)(i) and (ii).

6.10A If force is used, a record shall be made of the circumstances and those present.

6.11 A record must be made of a warning given as required by *paragraph 6.3.*

6.12 *Not used*

Notes for guidance

6A When hair samples are taken for the purpose of DNA analysis (rather than for other purposes such as making a visual match), the suspect should be permitted a reasonable choice as to what part of the body the hairs are taken from. When hairs are plucked, they should be plucked individually, unless the suspect prefers otherwise and no more should be plucked than the person taking them reasonably considers necessary for a sufficient sample.

6B (a) An insufficient sample is one which is not sufficient either in quantity or quality to provide information for a particular form of analysis, such as DNA analysis. A sample may also be insufficient if enough information cannot be obtained from it by analysis because of loss, destruction, damage or contamination of the sample or as a result of an earlier, unsuccessful attempt at analysis.

(b) An unsuitable sample is one which, by its nature, is not suitable for a particular form of analysis.

6C Nothing in paragraph 6.2 prevents intimate samples being taken for elimination purposes with the consent of the person concerned but the provisions of paragraph 2.12 relating to the role of the appropriate adult, should be applied. Paragraph 6.2(b) does not, however, apply where the non-intimate samples were previously taken under the Terrorism Act 2000, Schedule 8, paragraph 10, or under the National Security Act 2023, Schedule 6, paragraph 10.

6D In warning a person who is asked to provide an intimate sample as in paragraph 6.3, the following form of words may be used:

'You do not have to provide this sample/allow this swab or impression to be taken, but I must warn you that if you refuse without good cause, your refusal may harm your case if it comes to trial.'

6E Fingerprints or a DNA sample and the information derived from it taken from a person arrested on suspicion of being involved in a recordable offence, or charged with such an offence, or informed they will be reported for such an offence, may be subject of a speculative search. This means they may be checked against other fingerprints and DNA records held by, or on behalf of, the police and other law enforcement authorities in or outside the UK or held in connection with, or as a result of, an investigation of an offence inside or outside the UK.

See Annex F regarding the retention and use of fingerprints and samples taken with consent for elimination purposes.

6F Samples of urine and non-intimate samples taken in accordance with sections 63B and 63C of PACE may not be used for identification purposes in accordance with this Code. See Code C Note for guidance 17D.

Annex A Video Identification

(a) General

1. The arrangements for obtaining and ensuring the availability of a suitable set of images to be used in a video identification must be the responsibility of an identification officer (see *paragraph 3.11* of this Code) who has no direct involvement with the case.

2. The set of images must include the suspect and at least eight other people who, so far as possible, and subject to *paragraph 7*, resemble the suspect in age, general appearance and position in life. Only one suspect shall appear in any set unless there are two suspects of roughly similar appearance, in which case they may be shown together with at least twelve other people.

2A If the suspect has an unusual physical feature, e.g., a facial scar, tattoo or distinctive hairstyle or hair colour which does not appear on the images of the other people that are available to be used, steps may be taken to:

(a) conceal the location of the feature on the images of the suspect and the other people; or

(b) replicate that feature on the images of the other people.

For these purposes, the feature may be concealed or replicated electronically or by any other method which it is practicable to use to ensure that the images of the suspect and other people resemble each other. The identification officer has discretion to choose whether to conceal or replicate the feature and the method to be used.

2B If the identification officer decides that a feature should be concealed or replicated, the reason for the decision and whether the feature was concealed or replicated in the images shown to any eye-witness shall be recorded.

2C If the eye-witness requests to view any image where an unusual physical feature has been concealed or replicated without the feature being concealed or replicated, the identification officer has discretion to allow the eye-witness to view such image(s) if they are available.

3. The images used to conduct a video identification shall, as far as possible, show the suspect and other people in the same positions or carrying out the same sequence of movements. They shall also show the suspect and other people under identical conditions unless the identification officer reasonably believes:

(a) because of the suspect's failure or refusal to co-operate or other reasons, it is not practicable for the conditions to be identical; and

(b) any difference in the conditions would not direct an eye-witness' attention to any individual image.

4. The reasons identical conditions are not practicable shall be recorded on forms provided for the purpose.

5. Provision must be made for each person shown to be identified by number.

6. If police officers are shown, any numerals or other identifying badges must be concealed. If a prison inmate is shown, either as a suspect or not, then either all, or none of, the people shown should be in prison clothing.

7. The suspect or their solicitor, friend, or appropriate adult must be given a reasonable opportunity to see the complete set of images before it is shown to any eye-witness. If the suspect has a

reasonable objection to the set of images or any of the participants, the suspect shall be asked to state the reasons for the objection. Steps shall, if practicable, be taken to remove the grounds for objection. If this is not practicable, the suspect and/or their representative shall be told why their objections cannot be met and the objection, the reason given for it and why it cannot be met shall be recorded on forms provided for the purpose. The requirement in *paragraph 2* that the images of the other people 'resemble' the suspect does not require the images to be identical or extremely similar (see *Note A1*).

8. Before the images are shown in accordance with *paragraph 7,* the suspect or their solicitor shall be provided with details of the first description of the suspect by any eye-witnesses who are to attend the video identification. When a broadcast or publication is made, as in *paragraph 3.38(a)*, the suspect or their solicitor must also be allowed to view any material released to the media by the police for the purpose of recognising or tracing the suspect, provided it is practicable and would not unreasonably delay the investigation.

9. No unauthorised people may be present when the video identification is conducted. The suspect's solicitor, if practicable, shall be given reasonable notification of the time and place the video identification is to be conducted. The suspect's solicitor may only be present at the video identification on request and with the prior agreement of the identification officer, if the officer is satisfied that the solicitor's presence will not deter or distract any eye-witness from viewing the images and making an identification. If the identification officer is not satisfied and does not agree to the request, the reason must be recorded. The solicitor must be informed of the decision and the reason for it. and that they may then make representations about why they should be allowed to be present. The representations may be made orally or in writing, in person or remotely by electronic communication and must be recorded. These representations must be considered by an officer of at least the rank of inspector who is not involved with the investigation and responsibility for this may not be delegated under *paragraph 3.11*. If, after considering the representations, the officer is satisfied that the solicitor's presence will deter or distract the eye-witness, the officer shall inform the solicitor of the decision and reason for it and ensure that any response by the solicitor is also recorded. If allowed to be present, the solicitor is not entitled to communicate in any way with an eye-witness during the procedure but this does not prevent the solicitor from communicating with the identification officer. The suspect may not be present when the images are shown to any eye-witness and is not entitled to be informed of the time and place the video identification procedure is to be conducted. The video identification procedure itself shall be recorded on video with sound. The recording must show all persons present within the sight or hearing of the eye-witness whilst the images are being viewed and must include what the eye-witness says and what is said to them by the identification officer and by any other person present at the video identification procedure. A supervised viewing of the recording of the video identification procedure by the suspect and/or their solicitor may be arranged on request, at the discretion of the investigating officer. Where the recording of the video identification procedure is to be shown to the suspect and/or their solicitor, the investigating officer may arrange for anything in the recording that might allow the eye-witness to be identified to be concealed if the investigating officer considers that this is justified (see *Note A2*). In accordance with *paragraph 2.18*, the investigating officer may also arrange for anything in that recording that might allow any police officers or police staff to be identified to be concealed.

(b) Conducting the video identification

10. The identification officer is responsible for making the appropriate arrangements to make sure, before they see the set of images, eye-witnesses are not able to communicate with each other about the case, see any of the images which are to be shown, see, or be reminded of, any photograph or description of the suspect or be given any other indication as to the suspect's identity, or overhear an eye-witness who has already seen the material. There must be no discussion with the eye-witness about the composition of the set of images and they must not be told whether a previous eye-witness has made any identification.

11. Only one eye-witness may see the set of images at a time. Immediately before the images are shown, the eye-witness shall be told that the person they saw on a specified earlier occasion

may, or may not, appear in the images they are shown and that if they cannot make an identification, they should say so. The eye-witness shall be advised that at any point, they may ask to see a particular part of the set of images or to have a particular image frozen for them to study. Furthermore, it should be pointed out to the eye-witness that there is no limit on how many times they can view the whole set of images or any part of them. However, they should be asked not to make any decision as to whether the person they saw is on the set of images until they have seen the whole set at least twice.

12. Once the eye-witness has seen the whole set of images at least twice and has indicated that they do not want to view the images, or any part of them, again, the eye-witness shall be asked to say whether the individual they saw in person on a specified earlier occasion has been shown and, if so, to identify them by number of the image. The eye-witness will then be shown that image to confirm the identification, see *paragraph 17.*

13. Care must be taken not to direct the eye-witness' attention to any one individual image or give any indication of the suspect's identity. Where an eye-witness has previously made an identification by photographs, or a computerised or artist's composite or similar likeness, they must not be reminded of such a photograph or composite likeness once a suspect is available for identification by other means in accordance with this Code. Nor must the eye-witness be reminded of any description of the suspect.

13A. If after the video identification procedure has ended, the eye-witness informs any police officer or police staff involved in the post-viewing arrangements that they wish to change their decision about their identification, or they have not made an identification when in fact they could have made one, an accurate record of the words used by the eye-witness and of the circumstances immediately after the procedure ended, shall be made. If the eye-witness has not had an opportunity to communicate with other people about the procedure, the identification officer has the discretion to allow the eye-witness a second opportunity to make an identification by repeating the video identification procedure using the same images but in different positions.

14. After the procedure, action required in accordance with *paragraph 3.40* applies.

(c) Image security and destruction

15. Arrangements shall be made for all relevant material containing sets of images used for specific identification procedures to be kept securely and their movements accounted for. In particular, no-one involved in the investigation shall be permitted to view the material prior to it being shown to any witness.

16. As appropriate, *paragraph 3.30* or *3.31* applies to the destruction or retention of relevant sets of images.

(d) Documentation

17. A record must be made of all those participating in, or seeing, the set of images whose names are known to the police.

18. A record of the conduct of the video identification must be made on forms provided for the purpose. This shall include anything said by the witness about any identifications or the conduct of the procedure and any reasons it was not practicable to comply with any of the provisions of this Code governing the conduct of video identifications. This record is in addition to any statement that is taken from any eye-witness after the procedure.

Note for guidance

A1 The purpose of the video identification is to test the eye-witness' ability to distinguish the suspect from others and it would not be a fair test if all the images shown were identical or extremely similar to each other. The identification officer is responsible for ensuring that the images shown are suitable for the purpose of this test.

A2 The purpose of allowing the identity of the eye-witness to be concealed is to protect them in cases when there is information that suspects or their associates, may threaten the witness or cause them harm or when the investigating officer considers that special measures may be required to protect their identity during the criminal process.

Annex B Identification Parades

(a) General

1. A suspect must be given a reasonable opportunity to have a solicitor or friend present, and the suspect shall be asked to indicate on a second copy of the notice whether or not they wish to do so.

2. An identification parade may take place either in a normal room or one equipped with a screen permitting witnesses to see members of the identification parade without being seen. The procedures for the composition and conduct of the identification parade are the same in both cases, subject to *paragraph 8* (except that an identification parade involving a screen may take place only when the suspect's solicitor, friend or appropriate adult is present or the identification parade is recorded on video).

3. Before the identification parade takes place, the suspect or their solicitor shall be provided with details of the first description of the suspect by any witnesses who are attending the identification parade. When a broadcast or publication is made as in *paragraph 3.38(a)*, the suspect or their solicitor should also be allowed to view any material released to the media by the police for the purpose of identifying and tracing the suspect, provided it is practicable to do so and would not unreasonably delay the investigation.

(b) Identification parades involving prison inmates

4. If a prison inmate is required for identification, and there are no security problems about the person leaving the establishment, they may be asked to participate in an identification parade or video identification.

5. An identification parade may be held in a Prison Department establishment but shall be conducted, as far as practicable under normal identification parade rules. Members of the public shall make up the identification parade unless there are serious security, or control, objections to their admission to the establishment. In such cases, or if a group or video identification is arranged within the establishment, other inmates may participate. If an inmate is the suspect, they are not required to wear prison clothing for the identification parade unless the other people taking part are other inmates in similar clothing, or are members of the public who are prepared to wear prison clothing for the occasion.

(c) Conduct of the identification parade

6. Immediately before the identification parade, the suspect must be reminded of the procedures governing its conduct and cautioned in the terms of Code C, paragraphs 10.5 or 10.6, as appropriate.

7. All unauthorised people must be excluded from the place where the identification parade is held.

8. Once the identification parade has been formed, everything afterwards, in respect of it, shall take place in the presence and hearing of the suspect and any interpreter, solicitor, friend or appropriate adult who is present (unless the identification parade involves a screen, in which case everything said to, or by, any witness at the place where the identification parade is held, must be said in the hearing and presence of the suspect's solicitor, friend or appropriate adult or be recorded on video).

9. The identification parade shall consist of at least eight people (in addition to the suspect) who, so far as possible, resemble the suspect in age, height, general appearance and position in life. Only one suspect shall be included in an identification parade unless there are two suspects of roughly similar appearance, in which case they may be paraded together with at least twelve other people. In no circumstances shall more than two suspects be included in one identification parade and where there are separate identification parades, they shall be made up of different people.

10. If the suspect has an unusual physical feature, e.g., a facial scar, tattoo or distinctive hairstyle or hair colour which cannot be replicated on other members of the identification parade, steps may be taken to conceal the location of that feature on the suspect and the other members of

the identification parade if the suspect and their solicitor, or appropriate adult, agree. For example, by use of a plaster or a hat, so that all members of the identification parade resemble each other in general appearance.

11. When all members of a similar group are possible suspects, separate identification parades shall be held for each unless there are two suspects of similar appearance when they may appear on the same identification parade with at least twelve other members of the group who are not suspects. When police officers in uniform form an identification parade any numerals or other identifying badges shall be concealed.

12. When the suspect is brought to the place where the identification parade is to be held, they shall be asked if they have any objection to the arrangements for the identification parade or to any of the other participants in it and to state the reasons for the objection. The suspect may obtain advice from their solicitor or friend, if present, before the identification parade proceeds. If the suspect has a reasonable objection to the arrangements or any of the participants, steps shall, if practicable, be taken to remove the grounds for objection. When it is not practicable to do so, the suspect shall be told why their objections cannot be met and the objection, the reason given for it and why it cannot be met, shall be recorded on forms provided for the purpose.

13. The suspect may select their own position in the line, but may not otherwise interfere with the order of the people forming the line. When there is more than one witness, the suspect must be told, after each witness has left the room, that they can, if they wish, change position in the line. Each position in the line must be clearly numbered, whether by means of a number laid on the floor in front of each identification parade member or by other means.

14. Appropriate arrangements must be made to make sure, before witnesses attend the identification parade, they are not able to:

- (i) communicate with each other about the case or overhear a witness who has already seen the identification parade;
- (ii) see any member of the identification parade;
- (iii) see, or be reminded of, any photograph or description of the suspect or be given any other indication as to the suspect's identity; or
- (iv) see the suspect before or after the identification parade.

15. The person conducting a witness to an identification parade must not discuss with them the composition of the identification parade and, in particular, must not disclose whether a previous witness has made any identification.

16. Witnesses shall be brought in one at a time. Immediately before the witness inspects the identification parade, they shall be told the person they saw on a specified earlier occasion may, or may not, be present and if they cannot make an identification, they should say so. The witness must also be told they should not make any decision about whether the person they saw is on the identification parade until they have looked at each member at least twice.

17. When the officer or police staff (see *paragraph 3.11*) conducting the identification procedure is satisfied the witness has properly looked at each member of the identification parade, they shall ask the witness whether the person they saw on a specified earlier occasion is on the identification parade and, if so, to indicate the number of the person concerned, see *paragraph 28*.

18. If the witness wishes to hear any identification parade member speak, adopt any specified posture or move, they shall first be asked whether they can identify any person(s) on the identification parade on the basis of appearance only. When the request is to hear members of the identification parade speak, the witness shall be reminded that the participants in the identification parade have been chosen on the basis of physical appearance only. Members of the identification parade may then be asked to comply with the witness' request to hear them speak, see them move or adopt any specified posture.

19. If the witness requests that the person they have indicated remove anything used for the purposes of *paragraph 10* to conceal the location of an unusual physical feature, that person may be asked to remove it.

20. If the witness makes an identification after the identification parade has ended, the suspect and, if present, their solicitor, interpreter or friend shall be informed. When this occurs, consideration should be given to allowing the witness a second opportunity to identify the suspect.

21. After the procedure, action required in accordance with *paragraph 3.40* applies.

22. When the last witness has left, the suspect shall be asked whether they wish to make any comments on the conduct of the identification parade.

(d) Documentation

23. A video recording must normally be taken of the identification parade. If that is impracticable, a colour photograph must be taken. A copy of the video recording or photograph shall be supplied, on request, to the suspect or their solicitor within a reasonable time.

24. As appropriate, *paragraph 3.30* or *3.31*, should apply to any photograph or video taken as in *paragraph 23*.

25. If any person is asked to leave an identification parade because they are interfering with its conduct, the circumstances shall be recorded.

26. A record must be made of all those present at an identification parade whose names are known to the police.

27. If prison inmates make up an identification parade, the circumstances must be recorded.

28. A record of the conduct of any identification parade must be made on forms provided for the purpose. This shall include anything said by the witness or the suspect about any identifications or the conduct of the procedure, and any reasons it was not practicable to comply with any of this Code's provisions.

Annex C Group Identification

(a) General

1. The purpose of this Annex is to make sure, as far as possible, group identifications follow the principles and procedures for identification parades so the conditions are fair to the suspect in the way they test the witness' ability to make an identification.

2. Group identifications may take place either with the suspect's consent and co-operation or covertly without their consent.

3. The location of the group identification is a matter for the identification officer, although the officer may take into account any representations made by the suspect, appropriate adult, their solicitor or friend.

4. The place where the group identification is held should be one where other people are either passing by or waiting around informally, in groups such that the suspect is able to join them and be capable of being seen by the witness at the same time as others in the group. For example people leaving an escalator, pedestrians walking through a shopping centre, passengers on railway and bus stations, waiting in queues or groups or where people are standing or sitting in groups in other public places.

5. If the group identification is to be held covertly, the choice of locations will be limited by the places where the suspect can be found and the number of other people present at that time. In these cases, suitable locations might be along regular routes travelled by the suspect, including buses or trains or public places frequented by the suspect.

6. Although the number, age, sex, race and general description and style of clothing of other people present at the location cannot be controlled by the identification officer, in selecting the location the officer must consider the general appearance and numbers of people likely to be present. In particular, the officer must reasonably expect that over the period the witness observes the group, they will be able to see, from time to time, a number of others whose appearance is broadly similar to that of the suspect.

7. A group identification need not be held if the identification officer believes, because of the unusual appearance of the suspect, none of the locations it would be practicable to use, satisfy the requirements of *paragraph 6* necessary to make the identification fair.

8. Immediately after a group identification procedure has taken place (with or without the suspect's consent), a colour photograph or video should be taken of the general scene, if practicable, to give a general impression of the scene and the number of people present. Alternatively, if it is practicable, the group identification may be video recorded.

9. If it is not practicable to take the photograph or video in accordance with *paragraph 8,* a photograph or film of the scene should be taken later at a time determined by the identification officer if the officer considers it practicable to do so.

10. An identification carried out in accordance with this Code remains a group identification even though, at the time of being seen by the witness, the suspect was on their own rather than in a group.

11. Before the group identification takes place, the suspect or their solicitor shall be provided with details of the first description of the suspect by any witnesses who are to attend the identification. When a broadcast or publication is made, as in *paragraph 3.38(a),* the suspect or their solicitor should also be allowed to view any material released by the police to the media for the purposes of identifying and tracing the suspect, provided that it is practicable and would not unreasonably delay the investigation.

12. After the procedure, action required in accordance with *paragraph 3.40* applies.

(b) Identification with the consent of the suspect

13. A suspect must be given a reasonable opportunity to have a solicitor or friend present. They shall be asked to indicate on a second copy of the notice whether or not they wish to do so.

14. The witness, the person carrying out the procedure and the suspect's solicitor, appropriate adult, friend or any interpreter for the witness, may be concealed from the sight of the individuals in the group they are observing, if the person carrying out the procedure considers this assists the conduct of the identification.

15. The person conducting a witness to a group identification must not discuss with them the forthcoming group identification and, in particular, must not disclose whether a previous witness has made any identification.

16. Anything said to, or by, the witness during the procedure about the identification should be said in the presence and hearing of those present at the procedure.

17. Appropriate arrangements must be made to make sure, before witnesses attend the group identification, they are not able to:

(i) communicate with each other about the case or overhear a witness who has already been given an opportunity to see the suspect in the group;

(ii) see the suspect; or

(iii) see, or be reminded of, any photographs or description of the suspect or be given any other indication of the suspect's identity.

18. Witnesses shall be brought one at a time to the place where they are to observe the group. Immediately before the witness is asked to look at the group, the person conducting the procedure shall tell them that the person they saw on a specified earlier occasion may, or may not, be in the group and that if they cannot make an identification, they should say so. The witness shall be asked to observe the group in which the suspect is to appear. The way in which the witness should do this will depend on whether the group is moving or stationary.

Moving group

19. When the group in which the suspect is to appear is moving, e.g. leaving an escalator, the provisions of *paragraphs 20* to *24* should be followed.

20. If two or more suspects consent to a group identification, each should be the subject of separate identification procedures. These may be conducted consecutively on the same occasion.

21. The person conducting the procedure shall tell the witness to observe the group and ask them to point out any person they think they saw on the specified earlier occasion.

22. Once the witness has been informed as in *paragraph 21* the suspect should be allowed to take whatever position in the group they wish.

23. When the witness points out a person as in *paragraph 21* they shall, if practicable, be asked to take a closer look at the person to confirm the identification. If this is not practicable, or they cannot confirm the identification, they shall be asked how sure they are that the person they have indicated is the relevant person.

24. The witness should continue to observe the group for the period which the person conducting the procedure reasonably believes is necessary in the circumstances for them to be able to make comparisons between the suspect and other individuals of broadly similar appearance to the suspect as in *paragraph 6*.

Stationary groups

25. When the group in which the suspect is to appear is stationary, e.g. people waiting in a queue, the provisions of *paragraphs 26* to *29* should be followed.

26. If two or more suspects consent to a group identification, each should be subject to separate identification procedures unless they are of broadly similar appearance when they may appear in the same group. When separate group identifications are held, the groups must be made up of different people.

27. The suspect may take whatever position in the group they wish. If there is more than one witness, the suspect must be told, out of the sight and hearing of any witness, that they can, if they wish, change their position in the group.

28. The witness shall be asked to pass along, or amongst, the group and to look at each person in the group at least twice, taking as much care and time as possible according to the circumstances, before making an identification. Once the witness has done this, they shall be asked whether the person they saw on the specified earlier occasion is in the group and to indicate any such person by whatever means the person conducting the procedure considers appropriate in the circumstances. If this is not practicable, the witness shall be asked to point out any person they think they saw on the earlier occasion.

29. When the witness makes an indication as in *paragraph 28*, arrangements shall be made, if practicable, for the witness to take a closer look at the person to confirm the identification. If this is not practicable, or the witness is unable to confirm the identification, they shall be asked how sure they are that the person they have indicated is the relevant person.

All cases

30. If the suspect unreasonably delays joining the group, or having joined the group, deliberately conceals themselves from the sight of the witness, this may be treated as a refusal to co-operate in a group identification.

31. If the witness identifies a person other than the suspect, that person should be informed what has happened and asked if they are prepared to give their name and address. There is no obligation upon any member of the public to give these details. There shall be no duty to record any details of any other member of the public present in the group or at the place where the procedure is conducted.

32. When the group identification has been completed, the suspect shall be asked whether they wish to make any comments on the conduct of the procedure.

33. If the suspect has not been previously informed, they shall be told of any identifications made by the witnesses.

(c) Group Identification without the suspect's consent

34. Group identifications held covertly without the suspect's consent should, as far as practicable, follow the rules for conduct of group identification by consent.

35. A suspect has no right to have a solicitor, appropriate adult or friend present as the identification will take place without the knowledge of the suspect.

36. Any number of suspects may be identified at the same time.

(d) Identifications in police stations

37. Group identifications should only take place in police stations for reasons of safety, security or because it is not practicable to hold them elsewhere.

38. The group identification may take place either in a room equipped with a screen permitting witnesses to see members of the group without being seen, or anywhere else in the police station that the identification officer considers appropriate.

39. Any of the additional safeguards applicable to identification parades should be followed if the identification officer considers it is practicable to do so in the circumstances.

(e) Identifications involving prison inmates

40. A group identification involving a prison inmate may only be arranged in the prison or at a police station.

41. When a group identification takes place involving a prison inmate, whether in a prison or in a police station, the arrangements should follow those in *paragraphs 37* to *39*. If a group identification takes place within a prison, other inmates may participate. If an inmate is the suspect, they do not have to wear prison clothing for the group identification unless the other participants are wearing the same clothing.

(f) Documentation

42. When a photograph or video is taken as in *paragraph 8* or *9*, a copy of the photograph or video shall be supplied on request to the suspect or their solicitor within a reasonable time.

43. *Paragraph 3.30* or *3.31*, as appropriate, shall apply when the photograph or film taken in accordance with *paragraph 8* or *9* includes the suspect.

44. A record of the conduct of any group identification must be made on forms provided for the purpose. This shall include anything said by the witness or suspect about any identifications or the conduct of the procedure and any reasons why it was not practicable to comply with any of the provisions of this Code governing the conduct of group identifications.

Annex D Confrontation by an Eye-Witness

1. Before the confrontation takes place, the eye-witness must be told that the person they saw on a specified earlier occasion may, or may not, be the person they are to confront and that if they are not that person, then the witness should say so.

2. Before the confrontation takes place the suspect or their solicitor shall be provided with details of the first description of the suspect given by any eye-witness who is to attend. When a broadcast or publication is made, as in *paragraph 3.38(a)*, the suspect or their solicitor should also be allowed to view any material released to the media for the purposes of recognising or tracing the suspect, provided it is practicable to do so and would not unreasonably delay the investigation.

3. Force may not be used to make the suspect's face visible to the eye-witness.

4. Confrontation must take place in the presence of the suspect's solicitor, interpreter or friend unless this would cause unreasonable delay.

5. The suspect shall be confronted independently by each eye-witness, who shall be asked 'Is this the person?'. If the eye-witness identifies the person but is unable to confirm the identification, they shall be asked how sure they are that the person is the one they saw on the earlier occasion.

6. The confrontation should normally take place in the police station, either in a normal room or one equipped with a screen permitting the eye-witness to see the suspect without being seen. In both cases, the procedures are the same except that a room equipped with a screen may be used only when the suspect's solicitor, friend or appropriate adult is present or the confrontation is recorded on video.

7. After the procedure, action required in accordance with *paragraph 3.40* applies.

Annex E Showing Photographs to Eye-Witnesses

(a) Action

1. An officer of sergeant rank or above shall be responsible for supervising and directing the showing of photographs. The actual showing may be done by another officer or police staff, see *paragraph 3.11.*

2. The supervising officer must confirm the first description of the suspect given by the eye-witness has been recorded before they are shown the photographs. If the supervising officer is unable to confirm the description has been recorded they shall postpone showing the photographs.

3. Only one eye-witness shall be shown photographs at any one time. Each witness shall be given as much privacy as practicable and shall not be allowed to communicate with any other eye-witness in the case.

4. The eye-witness shall be shown not less than twelve photographs at a time, which shall, as far as possible, all be of a similar type.

5. When the eye-witness is shown the photographs, they shall be told the photograph of the person they saw on a specified earlier occasion may, or may not, be amongst them and if they cannot make an identification, they should say so. The eye-witness shall also be told they should not make a decision until they have viewed at least twelve photographs. The eye-witness shall not be prompted or guided in any way but shall be left to make any selection without help.

6. If an eye-witness makes an identification from photographs, unless the person identified is otherwise eliminated from enquiries or is not available, other eye-witnesses shall not be shown photographs. But both they, and the eye-witness who has made the identification, shall be asked to attend a video identification, an identification parade or group identification unless there is no dispute about the suspect's identification.

7. If the eye-witness makes a selection but is unable to confirm the identification, the person showing the photographs shall ask them how sure they are that the photograph they have indicated is the person they saw on the specified earlier occasion.

8. When the use of a computerised or artist's composite or similar likeness has led to there being a known suspect who can be asked to participate in a video identification, appear on an identification parade or participate in a group identification, that likeness shall not be shown to other potential eye-witnesses.

9. When an eye-witness attending a video identification, an identification parade or group identification has previously been shown photographs or computerised or artist's composite or similar likeness (and it is the responsibility of the officer in charge of the investigation to make the identification officer aware that this is the case), the suspect and their solicitor must be informed of this fact before the identification procedure takes place.

10. None of the photographs shown shall be destroyed, whether or not an identification is made, since they may be required for production in court. The photographs shall be numbered and a separate photograph taken of the frame or part of the album from which the eye-witness made an identification as an aid to reconstituting it.

(b) Documentation

11. Whether or not an identification is made, a record shall be kept of the showing of photographs on forms provided for the purpose. This shall include anything said by the eye-witness about any identification or the conduct of the procedure, any reasons it was not practicable to comply with any of the provisions of this Code governing the showing of photographs and the name and rank of the supervising officer.

12. The supervising officer shall inspect and sign the record as soon as practicable.

Annex F Fingerprints, Samples and Footwear Impressions—Destruction And Speculative Searches

Part A: Fingerprints and samples

Paragraphs 1 to 12 summarise and update information which is available at: https://www.gov.uk/government/publications/protection-of-freedoms-act-2012-dna-and-fingerprint-provisions/protection-of-freedoms-act-2012-how-dna-and-fingerprint-evidence-is-protected-in-law

DNA samples

1. A DNA sample is an individual's biological material, containing all of their genetic information. The Act requires all DNA samples to be destroyed within 6 months of being taken. This allows sufficient time for the sample to be analysed and a DNA profile to be produced for use on the database.

2. The only exception to this is if the sample is or may be required for disclosure as evidence, in which case it may be retained for as long as this need exists under the Criminal Procedure and Investigations Act 1996.

DNA profiles and fingerprints

3. A DNA profile consists of a string of 16 pairs of numbers and 2 letters (XX for women, XY for men) to indicate gender. This number string is stored on the National DNA Database (NDNAD). It allows the person to be identified if they leave their DNA at a crime scene.

4. Fingerprints are usually scanned electronically from the individual in custody and the images stored on IDENT1, the national fingerprint database.

Retention Periods: Fingerprints and DNA profiles

5. The retention period depends on the outcome of the investigation of the recordable offence in connection with which the fingerprints and DNA samples was taken, the age of the person at the time the offence was committed and whether the *recordable* offence is a qualifying offence and whether it is an excluded offence (See Table *Notes (a)* to *(c)*), as follows:

Table—Retention periods

(a) Convictions

Age when offence committed	Outcome	Retention Period
Any age	Convicted or given a caution or youth caution for a recordable offence which is also a qualifying offence	INDEFINITE
18 or over	Convicted or given a caution for a recordable offence which is NOT a qualifying offence	INDEFINITE
Under 18	Convicted or given a youth caution for a recordable offence which is NOT a qualifying offence.	1st conviction or youth caution—5 years plus length of any prison sentence. Indefinite if prison sentence 5 years or more 2nd conviction or youth caution: Indefinite

(b) Non-Convictions

Age when offence committed	Outcome	Retention Period
Any age	Charged but not convicted of a recordable qualifying offence.	3 years plus a 2 year extension if granted by a District Judge (or indefinite if the individual has a previous conviction for a recordable offence which is not excluded)
Any age	Arrested for, but not charged with, a recordable qualifying offence	3 years if granted by the Biometrics Commissioner plus a 2 year extension if granted by a District Judge (or indefinite if the individual has a previous conviction for a recordable offence which is not excluded)
Any age	Arrested for or charged with a recordable offence which is not a qualifying offence.	Indefinite if the person has a previous conviction for a recordable offence which is not excluded (otherwise NO RETENTION)
18 or over	Given Penalty Notice for Disorder for recordable offence	2 years

Table Notes:

(a) *A 'recordable' offence is one for which the police are required to keep a record. Generally speaking, these are imprisonable offences; however, it also includes a number of non-imprisonable offences such as begging and taxi touting. The police are not able to take or retain the DNA or fingerprints of an individual who is arrested for an offence which is not recordable.*

(b) *A 'qualifying' offence is one listed under section 65A of the Police and Criminal Evidence Act 1984 (the list comprises sexual, violent, terrorism and burglary offences).*

(c) *An 'excluded' offence is a recordable offence which is not a qualifying offence, was committed when the individual was under 18, for which they received a sentence of fewer than 5 years imprisonment and is the only recordable offence for which the person has been convicted*

Speculative searches

6. Where the retention framework above requires the deletion of a person's DNA profile and fingerprints, the Act first allows a *speculative search* of their DNA and fingerprints against DNA and fingerprints obtained from crime scenes which are stored on NDNAD and IDENT1. Once the speculative search has been completed, the profile and fingerprints are deleted unless there is a match, in which case they will be retained for the duration of any investigation and thereafter in accordance with the retention framework (e.g. if that investigation led to a conviction for a qualifying offence, they would be retained indefinitely).

Extensions of retention period

7. For qualifying offences, PACE allows chief constables to apply for extensions to the given retention periods for DNA profiles and fingerprints if considered necessary for prevention or detection of crime.

8. Section 20 of the Protection of Freedoms Act 2012 established the independent office of Commissioner for the Retention and Use of Biometric Material ('the 'Biometrics Commissioner'). For details, see https://www.gov.uk/government/organisations/biometrics-commissioner.

9. Where an individual is arrested for, but not charged with, a qualifying offence, their DNA profile and fingerprint record will normally be deleted. However, the police can apply to the Biometrics Commissioner for permission to retain their DNA profile and fingerprint record for a

period of 3 years. The application must be made within 28 days of the decision not to proceed with a prosecution.

10. If the police make such an application, the Biometrics Commissioner would first give both them and the arrested individual an opportunity to make written representations and then, taking into account factors including the age and vulnerability of the victim(s) of the alleged offences, and their relationship to the suspect, make a decision on whether or not retention is appropriate.

11. If after considering the application, the Biometrics Commissioner decides that retention is not appropriate, the DNA profile and fingerprint record in question must be destroyed.

12. If the Biometrics Commissioner agrees to allow retention, the police will be able to retain that individual's DNA profile and fingerprint record for a period of 3 years from the date the samples were taken. At the end of that period, the police will be able to apply to a District Judge (Magistrates' Courts) for a single 2 year extension to the retention period. If the application is rejected, the force must then destroy the DNA profile and fingerprint record.

Part B: Footwear impressions

13. Footwear impressions taken in accordance with section 61A of PACE (see *paragraphs 4.16* to *4.21*) may be retained for as long as is necessary for purposes related to the prevention or detection of crime, the investigation of an offence or the conduct of a prosecution.

Part C: Fingerprints, samples and footwear impressions taken in connection with a criminal investigation from a person *not suspected of committing* the offence under investigation for elimination purposes.

14. When fingerprints, footwear impressions or DNA samples are taken from a person in connection with an investigation and the person is *not suspected of having committed the offence*, see *Note F1*, they must be destroyed as soon as they have fulfilled the purpose for which they were taken unless:

(a) they were taken for the purposes of an investigation of an offence for which a person has been convicted; and

(b) fingerprints, footwear impressions or samples were also taken from the convicted person for the purposes of that investigation.

However, subject to *paragraph 14,* the fingerprints, footwear impressions and samples, and the information derived from samples, may not be used in the investigation of any offence or in evidence against the person who is, or would be, entitled to the destruction of the fingerprints, footwear impressions and samples, see *Note F2.*

15. The requirement to destroy fingerprints, footwear impressions and DNA samples, and information derived from samples and restrictions on their retention and use in *paragraph 14* do not apply if the person gives their written consent for their fingerprints, footwear impressions or sample to be retained and used after they have fulfilled the purpose for which they were taken, see *Note F1.* This consent can be withdrawn at any time.

16. When a person's fingerprints, footwear impressions or sample are to be destroyed:

(a) any copies of the fingerprints and footwear impressions must also be destroyed; and

(b) neither the fingerprints, footwear impressions, the sample, or any information derived from the sample, may be used in the investigation of any offence or in evidence against the person who is, or would be, entitled to its destruction.

Notes for guidance

F1 Fingerprints, footwear impressions and samples given voluntarily for the purposes of elimination play an important part in many police investigations. It is, therefore, important to make sure innocent volunteers are not deterred from participating and their consent to their fingerprints, footwear impressions and DNA being used for the purposes of a specific investigation is fully informed and voluntary. If the police or volunteer seek to have the fingerprints, footwear impressions or samples retained for use after the specific investigation ends, it is important the volunteer's consent to this is also fully informed and voluntary. The volunteer must be told that they may withdraw their consent at any time.

The consent must be obtained in writing using current nationally agreed forms provided for police use according to the purpose for which the consent is given. This purpose may be either:

- *DNA/fingerprints/footwear impressions—to be used only for the purposes of a specific investigation; or*
- *DNA/fingerprints/footwear impressions—to be used in the specific investigation and retained by the police for future use.*

To minimise the risk of confusion:

- *if a police officer or member of police staff has any doubt about:*
  - ~ *how the consent forms should be completed and signed, or*
  - ~ *whether a consent form they propose to use and refer to is fully compliant with the current nationally agreed form,*

  the relevant national police helpdesk (for DNA or fingerprints) should be contacted.
- *in each case, the meaning of consent should be explained orally and care taken to ensure the oral explanation accurately reflects the contents of the written form the person is to be asked to sign.*

F2 The provisions for the retention of fingerprints, footwear impressions and samples in paragraph 15 allow for all fingerprints, footwear impressions and samples in a case to be available for any subsequent miscarriage of justice investigation.

Annex G Requirement for a Person to Attend a Police Station for Fingerprints and Samples (*paragraphs 4.4, 6.2A and 6.6A*).

1. A requirement under Schedule 2A for a person to attend a police station to have fingerprints or samples taken:
   (a) must give the person a period of at least seven days within which to attend the police station; and
   (b) may direct them to attend at a specified time of day or between specified times of day.

2. When specifying the period and times of attendance, the officer making the requirements must consider whether the fingerprints or samples could reasonably be taken at a time when the person is required to attend the police station for any other reason. See *Note G1.*

3. An officer of the rank of inspector or above may authorise a period shorter than 7 days if there is an urgent need for person's fingerprints or sample for the purposes of the investigation of an offence. The fact of the authorisation and the reasons for giving it must be recorded as soon as practicable.

4. The constable making a requirement and the person to whom it applies may agree to vary it so as to specify any period within which, or date or time at which, the person is to attend. However, variation shall not have effect for the purposes of enforcement, unless it is confirmed by the constable in writing.

Notes for guidance

G1 The specified period within which the person is to attend need not fall within the period allowed (if applicable) for making the requirement.

G2 To justify the arrest without warrant of a person who fails to comply with a requirement, (see paragraphs 4.4(b) and 6.7(b) above), the officer making the requirement, or confirming a variation, should be prepared to explain how, when and where the requirement was made or the variation was confirmed and what steps were taken to ensure the person understood what to do and the consequences of not complying with the requirement.

Code of Practice on Audio Recording Interviews with Suspects (Code E)

(2018)

1 General

1.0 The procedures in this Code must be used fairly, responsibly, with respect for the people to whom they apply and without unlawful discrimination. Under the Equality Act 2010, section 149 (Public Sector Equality Duty) police forces must, in carrying out their functions, have due regard to the need to eliminate unlawful discrimination, harassment, victimisation and any other conduct which is prohibited by that Act, to advance equality of opportunity between people who share a relevant protected characteristic and people who do not share it, and to foster good relations between those persons. The Equality Act *also* makes it unlawful for police officers to discriminate against, harass or victimise any person on the grounds of the 'protected characteristics' of age, disability, gender reassignment, race, religion or belief, sex and sexual orientation, marriage and civil partnership, pregnancy and maternity, when using their powers. See *Note 1B*.

1.1 This Code of Practice must be readily available for consultation by:

- police officers
- police staff
- detained persons
- members of the public.

1.2 The *Notes for Guidance* included are not provisions of this Code. They form guidance to police officers and others about its application and interpretation.

1.3 Nothing in this Code shall detract from the requirements of Code C, the Code of Practice for the detention, treatment and questioning of persons by police officers.

1.4 The interviews and other matters to which this Code applies are described in *section 2*. This Code does not apply to the conduct and recording in England and Wales, of:

- interviews of persons detained under section 41 of, or Schedule 7 to, the Terrorism Act 2000, and
- post-charge questioning of persons authorised under section 22 of the Counter-Terrorism Act 2008.

These must be video recorded with sound in accordance with the provisions of the separate Code of Practice issued under *paragraph 3 of Schedule 8 to the Terrorism Act 2000* and under *section 25 of the Counter-Terrorism Act 2008*. If, during the course of an interview or questioning under this Code, it becomes apparent that the interview or questioning should be conducted under that separate Code, the interview should only continue in accordance with that Code.

Note: The provisions of this Code and Code F which govern the conduct and recording of interviews *do not apply* to interviews with, or taking statements from, witnesses.

1.5 In this Code:

- 'appropriate adult' has the same meaning as in Code C, *paragraph 1.7.*
- 'vulnerable person' has the same meaning as described in Code C *paragraph 1.13(d).*
- 'solicitor' has the same meaning as in Code C, *paragraph 6.12.*
- 'interview' has the same meaning as in Code C, *paragraph 11.1A.*

1.5A The provisions of this Code which require interviews with suspects to be audio recorded and the provisions of Code F which permit simultaneous visual recording provide safeguards:

- for suspects against inaccurate recording of the words used in questioning them and of their demeanour during the interview; and;
- for police interviewers against unfounded allegations made by, or on behalf of, suspects about the conduct of the interview and what took place during the interview which might otherwise appear credible.

Recording of interviews must therefore be carried out openly to instil confidence in its reliability as an impartial and accurate record of the interview.

1.5B The provisions of Code C:

- *sections 10 and 11,* and the applicable *Notes for Guidance* apply to the conduct of interviews to which this Code applies.
- *paragraphs 11.7 to 11.14* apply only when a written record is needed.

1.5C Code C, *paragraphs 10.10, 10.11* and *Annex C* describe the restriction on drawing adverse inferences from an arrested suspect's failure or refusal to say anything about their involvement in the offence when interviewed or after being charged or informed they may be prosecuted, and how it affects the terms of the caution and determines if and by whom a special warning under sections 36 and 37 of the Criminal Justice and Public Order Act 1994 can be given.

1.6 In this Code:

(a) in relation to the place where an interview of a suspect to which this Code or (as the case may be) Code F, applies, is conducted and recorded (see *Note 1A*):

(i) '*authorised*' in relation to the recording devices described in (ii) and (iii), means any such device that the chief officer has authorised interviewers under their direction and control to use to record the interview in question at the place in question, provided that the interviewer in question has been trained to set up and operate the device, in compliance with the manufacturer's instructions and subject to the operating procedures required by the chief officer;

(ii) '*removable recording media device*' means a recording device which, when set up and operated in accordance with the manufacturer's instructions and the operating procedures required by the chief officers, uses removable, physical recording media (such as magnetic tape, optical disc or solid state memory card) for the purpose of making a clear and accurate, audio recording or (as the case may be) audio-visual recording, of the interview in question which can then be played back and copied using that device or any other device. A sign or indicator on the device which is visible to the suspect must show when the device is recording;

(iii) '*secure digital recording network device*' means a recording device which, when set up and operated in accordance with the manufacturer's instructions and the operating procedures required by the chief officers, enables a clear and accurate original audio recording or (as the case may be) audio-visual recording, of the interview in question, to be made and stored using non-removable storage, as a digital file or a series of such files that can be securely transferred by a wired or wireless connection to a remote secure network file server system (which may have cloud based storage) which ensures that access to interview recordings for all purposes is strictly controlled and is restricted to those whose access, either generally or in specific cases, is necessary. Examples of access include playing back the whole or part of any original recording and making one or more copies of, the whole or part of that original recording. A sign or indicator on the device which is visible to the suspect must show when the device is recording.

(b) 'designated person' means a person other than a police officer, who has specified powers and duties conferred or imposed on them by designation under section 38 or 39 of the Police Reform Act 2002.

(c) any reference to a police officer includes a designated person acting in the exercise or performance of the powers and duties conferred or imposed on them by their designation.

1.7 Section 2 of this Code sets out the requirement that an authorised recording device, if available, must be used to record a suspect interview and when such a device cannot be used, it allows a 'relevant officer' (see *paragraph 2.3(c)*) to decide that the interview is to be recorded in writing in accordance with Code C. For detained suspects, the 'relevant officer' is the custody officer and for voluntary interviews, the officer is determined according to the type of offence (indictable or summary only) and where the interview takes place (police station or elsewhere).

Provisions in sections 3 and 4 deal with the conduct and recording of interviews according to the type of authorised recording device used. Section 3 applies to *removable recording media devices* (see *paragraph 1.6(a)(i)*) and section 4 applies to *secure digital recording network devices* (see *paragraph 1.6(a)(ii)*). The Annex applies when a voluntary interview is conducted elsewhere than at a police station about one of the four offence types specified in the Annex. For such interviews, the relevant officer is the interviewer.

1.8 Nothing in this Code prevents the custody officer, or other officer given custody of the detainee, from allowing police staff who are not designated persons to carry out individual procedures or tasks at the police station if the law allows. However, the officer remains responsible for making sure the procedures and tasks are carried out correctly in accordance with this Code. Any such police staff must be:

(a) a person employed by a police force and under the control and direction of the Chief Officer of that force; or

(b) employed by a person with whom a police force has a contract for the provision of services relating to persons arrested or otherwise in custody.

1.9 Designated persons and other police staff must have regard to any relevant provisions of the Codes of Practice.

1.10 References to pocket book shall include any official report book or electronic recording device issued to police officers or police staff that enables a record required to be made by any provision of this Code (but which is not an audio record to which *paragraph 2.1* applies) to be made and dealt with in accordance with that provision. References in this Code to written records, forms and signatures include electronic records and forms and electronic confirmation that identifies the person making the record or completing the form.

Chief officers must be satisfied as to the integrity and security of the devices, records and forms to which this paragraph applies and that use of those devices, records and forms satisfies relevant data protection legislation.

1.11 References to a custody officer include those performing the functions of a custody officer as in *paragraph 1.9* of Code C.

1.12 *Not used.*

1.13 Nothing in this Code requires the identity of officers or police staff conducting interviews to be recorded or disclosed if the interviewer reasonably believes recording or disclosing their name might put them in danger. In these cases, the officers and staff should use warrant or other identification numbers and the name of their police station. Such instances and the reasons for them shall be recorded in the custody record or the interviewer's pocket book. (See *Note 1C*.)

Notes for Guidance

1A An interviewer who is not sure, or has any doubt, about whether a place or location elsewhere than a police station is suitable for carrying out an interview of a juvenile or vulnerable person, using a particular recording device, should consult an officer of the rank of sergeant or above for advice. See Code C paragraphs 3.21, 3.22 and Note 3I

1B In paragraph 1.0, under the Equality Act 2010, section 149, the 'relevant protected characteristics' are: age, disability, gender reassignment, pregnancy and maternity, race, religion/belief, and sex and sexual orientation. For further detailed guidance and advice on the Equality Act, see: https://www.gov.uk/guidance/equality-act-2010-guidance.

1C The purpose of paragraph 1.13 is to protect those involved in serious organised crime investigations or arrests of particularly violent suspects when there is reliable information that those arrested or their associates may threaten or cause harm to those involved. In cases of doubt, an officer of the rank of inspector or above should be consulted.

1D Attention is drawn to the provisions set out in Code C about the matters to be considered when deciding whether a detained person is fit to be interviewed.

2 Interviews and other matters to be audio recorded under this Code

(A) Requirement to use authorised audio-recording device when available.

2.1 Subject to *paragraph 2.3*, if an authorised recording device (see *paragraph 1.6(a)*) in working order *and* an interview room or other location (see *Note 1A*) suitable for that device to be used, are available, then that device shall be used to record the following matters:

(a) any interview with a person cautioned in accordance with Code C, *section 10* in respect of any *summary* offence or any *indictable* offence, which includes any offence triable either way, when:

(i) that person (the suspect) is questioned about their involvement or suspected involvement in that offence and they have not been charged or informed they may be prosecuted for that offence; and

(ii) exceptionally, further questions are put to a person about any offence *after* they have been charged with, or told they may be prosecuted for, that offence (see Code C, *paragraph 16.5 and Note 2C*).

(b) when a person who has been charged with, or informed they may be prosecuted for, any offence, is told about any written statement or interview with another person and they are handed a true copy of the written statement or the content of the interview record is brought to their attention in accordance with Code C, *paragraph 16.4 and Note 2D.*

See *Note 2A*

2.2 The whole of each of the matters described in *paragraph 2.1* shall be audio-recorded, including the taking and reading back of any statement as applicable.

2.3 A written record of the matters described in *paragraph 2.1(a)* and *(b)* shall be made in accordance with Code C, *section 11*, only if,

(a) an authorised recording device (see *paragraph 1.6(a)*) in working order is *not available;* or

(b) such a device is available but a location suitable for using that device to make the audio recording of the matter in question is not available; and

(c) the 'relevant officer' described in *paragraph 2.4* considers on reasonable grounds, that the proposed interview or (as the case may be) continuation of the interview or other action, should not be delayed until an authorised recording device in working order *and* a suitable interview room or other location become available (see *Note 2E*) and decides that a written record shall be made;

(d) if in accordance with *paragraph 3.9,* the suspect or the appropriate adult on their behalf, objects to the interview being audibly recorded and the 'relevant officer' described in *paragraph 2.4,* after having regard to the nature and circumstances of the objections (see *Note 2F*), decides that a written record shall be made;

(e) in the case of a detainee who refuses to go into or remain in a suitable interview room and in accordance with Code C *paragraphs 12.5* and *12.11,* the custody officer directs that interview be conducted in a cell and considers that an authorised recording device cannot be safely used in the cell.

Note: When the suspect appears to have a hearing impediment, this paragraph does not affect the separate requirement in *paragraphs 3.7* and *4.4* for the interviewer to make a written note of the interview at the same time as the audio recording.

(B) Meaning of 'relevant officer'

2.4 In *paragraph 2.3(c)*:

(a) if the person to be interviewed is arrested elsewhere than at a police station for an offence and before they arrive at a police station, an urgent interview in accordance with *Code C paragraph 11.1* is necessary to avert one or more of the risks mentioned in *sub-paragraphs (a)* to *(c)* of that paragraph, the 'relevant officer' means the *interviewer,* who may or may not be the arresting officer, who must have regard to the time, place and urgency of the proposed interview.

(b) if the person in question has been taken to a police station after being arrested elsewhere for an offence or is arrested for an offence whilst at a police station after attending voluntarily and is detained at that police station or elsewhere in the charge of a constable, the 'relevant officer' means the *custody officer at the station where the person's detention* was last authorised. The custody officer must have regard to the nature of the investigation and in accordance with *Code C paragraph 1.1*, ensure that the detainee is dealt with expeditiously, and released as soon as the need for their detention no longer applies.

(c) In the case of a voluntary interview (see *Code C paragraph 3.21* to *3.22*) which takes place:

(i) at a police station and the offence in question is an indictable offence, the 'relevant officer' means *an officer of the rank of sergeant or above*, in consultation with the investigating officer;

(ii) at a police station and the offence in question is a summary offence, the 'relevant officer' means *the interviewer* in consultation with the investigating officer if different,

(iii) elsewhere than at a police station and the offence is one of the four indictable offence types which satisfy the conditions in Part 1 of the Annex to this Code, the 'relevant officer' means *the interviewer* in consultation with the investigating officer, if different.

(iv) elsewhere than at a police station and the offence in question is an indictable offence which is not one of the four indictable offence types which satisfy the conditions in Part 1 of the Annex to this Code, the 'relevant officer' means an *officer of the rank of sergeant or above*, in consultation with the investigating officer.

(v) elsewhere than at a police station and the offence in question is a summary only offence, the 'relevant officer' means *the interviewer* in consultation with the investigating officer, if different.

See *Note 2B—Summary table—relevant officer for voluntary interviews*

(C) Duties of the 'relevant officer' and the interviewer

2.5 When, in accordance with *paragraph 2.3*, a written record is made:

(a) the relevant officer must:

(i) record the reasons for not making an audio recording and the date and time the decision in *paragraph 2.3(c)* or (as applicable) *paragraph 2.3(d)* was made; and

(ii) ensure that the suspect is informed that a written record will be made;

(b) the interviewer must ensure that the written record includes:

(i) the date and time the decision in *paragraph 2.3(c)* or (as applicable) *paragraph 2.3(d)* was made, who made it and where the decision is recorded, and

(ii) the fact that the suspect was informed.

(c) the written record shall be made in accordance with Code C, *section 11*;

See *Note 2B*

(D) Remote monitoring of interviews

2.6 If the interview room or other location where the interview takes place is equipped with facilities that enable audio recorded interviews to be remotely monitored as they take place, the interviewer must ensure that suspects, their legal representatives and any appropriate adults are fully aware of what this means and that there is no possibility of privileged conversations being listened to. With this in mind, the following safeguards should be applied:

(a) The remote monitoring system should only be able to operate when the audio recording device has been turned on.

(b) The equipment should incorporate a light, clearly visible to all in the interview room, which is automatically illuminated as soon as remote monitoring is activated.

(c) Interview rooms and other locations fitted with remote monitoring equipment must contain a notice, prominently displayed, referring to the capacity for remote monitoring and to the fact that the warning light will illuminate whenever monitoring is taking place.
(d) At the beginning of the interview, the interviewer must explain the contents of the notice to the suspect and if present, to the solicitor and appropriate adult and that explanation should itself be audio recorded.
(e) The fact that an interview, or part of an interview, was remotely monitored should be recorded in the suspect's custody record or, if the suspect is not in detention, the interviewer's pocket book. That record should include the names of the officers doing the monitoring and the purpose of the monitoring (e.g. for training, to assist with the investigation, etc.)

(E) Use of live link—Interviewer not present at the same station as the detainee

2.7 Code C *paragraphs 12.9A* and *12.9B* set out the conditions which, if satisfied allow a suspect in police detention to be interviewed using a live link by a police officer who is not present at the police station where the detainee is held. These provisions also set out the duties and responsibilities of the custody officer, the officer having physical custody of the suspect and the interviewer and the modifications that apply to ensure that any such interview is conducted and audio recorded in accordance with this Code or (as the case may be) visually recorded in accordance with Code F.

Notes for Guidance

2A Nothing in this Code is intended to preclude audio-recording at police discretion at police stations or elsewhere when persons are charged with, or told they may be prosecuted for, an offence or they respond after being so charged or informed.

2B A decision made in accordance with paragraph 2.3 not to audio-record an interview for any reason may be the subject of comment in court. The 'relevant officer' responsible should be prepared to justify that decision.

Table: Summary of paragraph 2.4(c)—relevant officer for voluntary interviews:

	Location of voluntary Interview	***Offence type***	***Relevant Officer***
(i)	*Police station*	*Any indictable offence*	*Sergeant or above+*
(ii)	*Police station*	*Any summary only offence*	*Interviewer+*
(iii)	*Elsewhere than at a police station*	*Indictable offence type defined by the Annex*	*Interviewer+*
(iv)	*Elsewhere than at a police station*	*Indictable offence type not defined by the Annex*	*Sergeant or above+*
(v)	*Elsewhere than at a police station*	*Summary only*	*Interviewer+*

+ = in consultation with the investigating officer.

2C Code C sets out the circumstances in which a suspect may be questioned about an offence after being charged with it.

2D Code C sets out the procedures to be followed when a person's attention is drawn after charge, to a statement made by another person. One method of bringing the content of an interview with another person to the notice of a suspect may be to play them a recording of that interview. The person may not be questioned about the statement or interview record unless this is allowed in accordance with paragraph 16.5 of Code C.

2E A voluntary interview should be arranged for a time and place when it can be audio recorded and enable the safeguards and requirements set out in Code C paragraphs 3.21 to 3.22B to be implemented. It would normally be reasonable to delay the interview to enable audio recording unless the delay to do so would be likely to compromise the outcome of the interview or investigation, for example if there are grounds to suspect that the suspect would use the delay to fabricate an innocent explanation, influence witnesses or tamper with other material evidence.

2F Objections for the purpose of paragraphs 2.3(d) and 3.9 are meant to apply to objections based on the suspect's genuine and honestly held beliefs and to allow officers to exercise their discretion to decide that a written interview record is to be made according to the circumstances surrounding the suspect and the investigation. Objections that appear to be frivolous with the intentions of frustrating or delaying the investigation would not be relevant.

3 Interview recording using *removable recording media* device

(A) Recording and sealing master recordings—general

3.1 When using an authorised *removable recording media* device (see *paragraph 1.6(a)(i)*), one recording, the master recording, will be sealed in the suspect's presence. A second recording will be used as a working copy. The master recording is any of the recordings made by a multi-deck/drive machine or the only recording made by a single deck/drive machine. The working copy is one of the other recordings made by a multi-deck/drive machine or a copy of the master recording made by a single deck/drive machine.

3.2 The purpose of sealing the master recording before it leaves the suspect's presence is to establish their confidence that the integrity of the recording is preserved. If a single deck/drive machine is used the working copy of the master recording must be made in the suspect's presence and without the master recording leaving their sight. The working copy shall be used for making further copies if needed.

(B) Commencement of Interviews

3.3 When the suspect is brought into the interview room or arrives at the location where the interview is to take place, the interviewer shall, without delay but in the suspect's sight, unwrap or open the new recording media, load the recording device with new recording media and set it to record.

3.4 The interviewer must point out the sign or indicator which shows that the recording equipment is activated and is recording (see *paragraph 1.6(a)(i)*) and shall then:

(a) tell the suspect that the interview is being audibly recorded using an authorised *removable recording media* device and outline the recording process (see *Note 3A*);

(b) subject to *paragraph 1.13*, give their name and rank and that of any other interviewer present;

(c) ask the suspect and any other party present, e.g. the appropriate adult, a solicitor or interpreter, to identify themselves (see *Note 3A*);

(d) state the date, time of commencement and place of the interview;

(e) tell the suspect that:

- they will be given a copy of the recording of the interview in the event that they are charged or informed that they will be prosecuted but if they are not charged or informed that they will be prosecuted they will only be given a copy as agreed with the police or on the order of a court; and
- they will be given a written notice at the end of the interview setting out their right to a copy of the recording and what will happen to the recording and;

(f) if equipment for remote monitoring of interviews as described in *paragraph 2.6* is installed, explain the contents of the notice to the suspect, solicitor and appropriate adult as required by *paragraph 2.6(d)* and point out the light that illuminates automatically as soon as remote monitoring is activated.

3.5 Any person entering the interview room after the interview has commenced shall be invited by the interviewer to identify themselves for the purpose of the audio recording and state the reason why they have entered the interview room.

3.6 The interviewer shall:

- caution the suspect, see Code C *section 10*; and

- if they are detained, remind them of their entitlement to free legal advice, see Code C, *paragraph 11.2*; or
- if they are not detained under arrest, explain this and their entitlement to free legal advice (see Code C, *paragraph 3.21*) and ask the suspect to confirm that they agree to the voluntary interview proceeding (see *Code C paragraph 3.22A*).

3.7 The interviewer shall put to the suspect any significant statement or silence, see Code C, *paragraph 11.4*.

(C) Interviews with suspects who appear to have a hearing impediment

3.8 If the suspect appears to have a hearing impediment, the interviewer shall make a written note of the interview in accordance with Code C, at the same time as audio recording it in accordance with this Code. (See *Notes 3B* and *3C*.)

(D) Objections and complaints by the suspect

3.9 If the suspect or an appropriate adult on their behalf, objects to the interview being audibly recorded either at the outset, during the interview or during a break, the interviewer shall explain that the interview is being audibly recorded and that this Code requires the objections to be recorded on the audio recording. When any objections have been audibly recorded or the suspect or appropriate adult have refused to have their objections recorded, the relevant officer shall decide in accordance with *paragraph 2.3(d)* (which requires the officer to have regard to the nature and circumstances of the objections) whether a written record of the interview or its continuation, is to be made and that audio recording should be turned off. Following a decision that a written record is to be made, the interviewer shall say they are turning off the recorder and shall then make a written record of the interview as in Code C, *section 11*. If, however, following a decision that a written record is not to be made, the interviewer may proceed to question the suspect with the audio recording still on. This procedure also applies in cases where the suspect has previously objected to the interview being visually recorded, see Code F *paragraph 2.7*, and the investigating officer has decided to audibly record the interview. (See *Notes 2F* and *3D*.)

3.10 If in the course of an interview a complaint is made by or on behalf of the person being questioned concerning the provisions of this or any other Codes, or it comes to the interviewer's notice that the person may have been treated improperly, the interviewer shall act as in Code C, *paragraph 12.9*. (See *Notes 3E* and *3F*.)

3.11 If the suspect indicates they want to tell the interviewer about matters not directly connected with the offence of which they are suspected and they are unwilling for these matters to be audio recorded, the suspect should be given the opportunity to tell the interviewer about these matters after the conclusion of the formal interview.

(E) Changing recording media

3.12 When the recorder shows the recording media only has a short time left to run, the interviewer shall so inform the person being interviewed and round off that part of the interview. If the interviewer leaves the room for a second set of recording media, the suspect shall not be left unattended. The interviewer will remove the recording media from the recorder and insert the new recording media which shall be unwrapped or opened in the suspect's presence. The recorder should be set to record on the new media. To avoid confusion between the recording media, the interviewer shall mark the media with an identification number immediately after it is removed from the recorder.

(F) Taking a break during interview

3.13 When a break is taken, the fact that a break is to be taken, the reason for it and the time shall be recorded on the audio recording.

3.14 When the break is taken and the interview room vacated by the suspect, the recording media shall be removed from the recorder and the procedures for the conclusion of an interview followed, see *paragraph 3.19*.

3.15 When a break is a short one and both the suspect and an interviewer remain in the interview room, the recording may be stopped. There is no need to remove the recording media and when the interview recommences the recording should continue on the same recording media. The time the interview recommences shall be recorded on the audio recording.

3.16 After any break in the interview the interviewer must, before resuming the interview, remind the person being questioned of their right to legal advice if they have not exercised it and that they remain under caution or, if there is any doubt, give the caution in full again. (See *Note 3G.*)

(G) Failure of recording equipment

3.17 If there is an equipment failure which can be rectified quickly, e.g. by inserting new recording media, the interviewer shall follow the appropriate procedures as in *paragraph 3.12.* When the recording is resumed the interviewer shall explain what happened and record the time the interview recommences. However, if it is not possible to continue recording using the same recording device or by using a replacement device, the interview should be audio-recorded using a secure digital recording network device as in *paragraph 4.1,* if the necessary equipment is available. If it is not available, the interview may continue and be recorded in writing in accordance with *paragraph 2.3* as directed by the 'relevant officer'. (See *Note 3H.*)

(H) Removing recording media from the recorder

3.18 Recording media which is removed from the recorder during the interview shall be retained and the procedures in *paragraph 3.12* followed.

(I) Conclusion of interview

3.19 At the conclusion of the interview, the suspect shall be offered the opportunity to clarify anything they have said and asked if there is anything they want to add.

3.20 At the conclusion of the interview, including the taking and reading back of any written statement, the time shall be recorded and the recording shall be stopped. The interviewer shall seal the master recording with a master recording label and treat it as an exhibit in accordance with force standing orders. The interviewer shall sign the label and ask the suspect and any third party present during the interview to sign it. If the suspect or third party refuse to sign the label an officer of at least the rank of inspector, or if not available the custody officer, or if the suspect has not been arrested, a sergeant, shall be called into the interview room and asked, subject to *paragraph 1.13,* to sign it.

3.21 The suspect shall be handed a notice which explains:

- how the audio recording will be used;
- the arrangements for access to it;
- that if they are charged or informed they will be prosecuted, a copy of the audio recording will be supplied as soon as practicable or as otherwise agreed between the suspect and the police or on the order of a court.

(J) After the interview

3.22 The interviewer shall make a note in their pocket book that the interview has taken place and that it was audibly recorded, the time it commenced, its duration and date and identification number of the master recording (see *Note 3I*).

3.23 If no proceedings follow in respect of the person whose interview was recorded, the recording media must be kept securely as in *paragraph 3.22* and *Note 3J.*

(K) Master Recording security

(i) General

3.24 The officer in charge of each police station at which interviews with suspects are recorded or as the case may be, where recordings of interviews carried out elsewhere than at a police station are held, shall make arrangements for master recordings to be kept securely and their movements accounted for on the same basis as material which may be used for evidential purposes, in accordance with force standing orders. (See *Note 3J*.)

(ii) Breaking master recording seal for criminal proceedings

3.25 A police officer has no authority to break the seal on a master recording which is required for criminal trial or appeal proceedings. If it is necessary to gain access to the master recording, the police officer shall arrange for its seal to be broken in the presence of a representative of the Crown Prosecution Service. The defendant or their legal adviser should be informed and given a reasonable opportunity to be present. If the defendant or their legal representative is present they shall be invited to re-seal and sign the master recording. If either refuses or neither is present this should be done by the representative of the Crown Prosecution Service. (See *Notes 3K and 3L*.)

(iii) Breaking master recording seal: other cases

3.26 The chief officer of police is responsible for establishing arrangements for breaking the seal of the master copy where no criminal proceedings result, or the criminal proceedings to which the interview relates, have been concluded and it becomes necessary to break the seal. These arrangements should be those which the chief officer considers are reasonably necessary to demonstrate to the person interviewed and any other party who may wish to use or refer to the interview record that the master copy has not been tampered with and that the interview record remains accurate. (See *Note 3M*.)

3.27 Subject to *paragraph 3.29*, a representative of each party must be given a reasonable opportunity to be present when the seal is broken and the master recording copied and resealed.

3.28 If one or more of the parties is not present when the master copy seal is broken because they cannot be contacted or refuse to attend or *paragraph 3.29* applies, arrangements should be made for an independent person such as a custody visitor, to be present. Alternatively, or as an additional safeguard, arrangements should be made to visually record the procedure.

3.29 *Paragraph 3.28* does not require a person to be given an opportunity to be present when;

(a) it is necessary to break the master copy seal for the proper and effective further investigation of the original offence or the investigation of some other offence; and
(b) the officer in charge of the investigation has reasonable grounds to suspect that allowing an opportunity might prejudice such an investigation or criminal proceedings which may be brought as a result or endanger any person. (See *Note 3N*.)

(iv) Documentation

3.30 When the master recording seal is broken, a record must be made of the procedure followed, including the date, time, place and persons present.

Notes for guidance

Commencement of interviews (paragraph 3.3)

3A When outlining the recording process, the interviewer should refer to paragraph 1.6(a)(ii) and (iii) and briefly describe how the recording device being used is operated and how recordings are made. For the purpose of voice identification the interviewer should ask the suspect and any other people present to identify themselves.

Interviews with suspects who appear to have a hearing impediment (paragraph 3.8)

3B This provision is to give a person who is deaf or has impaired hearing equivalent rights of access to the full interview record as far as this is possible using audio recording.

3C The provisions of Code C on interpreters for suspects who do not appear to speak or understand English or who appear to have a hearing or speech impediment, continue to apply.

Objections and complaints by the suspect (paragraph 3.9)

3D The relevant officer should be aware that a decision to continue recording against the wishes of the suspect may be the subject of comment in court.

3E If the custody officer, or in the case of a person who has not been arrested, a sergeant, is called to deal with the complaint, the recorder should, if possible, be left on until the officer has entered the room and spoken to the person being interviewed. Continuation or termination of the interview should be at the interviewer's discretion pending action by an inspector under Code C, paragraph 9.2.

3F If the complaint is about a matter not connected with this Code or Code C, the decision to continue is at the interviewer's discretion. When the interviewer decides to continue the interview, they shall tell the suspect that at the conclusion of the interview, the complaint will be brought to the attention of the custody officer, or in the case of a person who has not been arrested, a sergeant. When the interview is concluded the interviewer must, as soon as practicable, inform the custody officer or, as the case may be, the sergeant, about the existence and nature of the complaint made.

3G In considering whether to caution again after a break, the interviewer should bear in mind that they may have to satisfy a court that the person understood that they were still under caution when the interview resumed. The interviewer should also remember that it may be necessary to show to the court that nothing occurred during a break or between interviews which influenced the suspect's recorded evidence. After a break or at the beginning of a subsequent interview, the interviewer should consider summarising on the record the reason for the break and confirming this with the suspect.

Failure of recording equipment (paragraph 3.17)

3H Where the interview is being recorded and the media or the recording equipment fails the interviewer should stop the interview immediately. Where part of the interview is unaffected by the error and is still accessible on the media, that part shall be copied and sealed in the suspect's presence as a master copy and the interview recommenced using new equipment/media as required. Where the content of the interview has been lost in its entirety, the media should be sealed in the suspect's presence and the interview begun again. If the recording equipment cannot be fixed and no replacement is immediately available, subject to paragraph 2.3, the interview should be recorded in accordance with Code C, section 11.

3I Any written record of an audio recorded interview should be made in accordance with current national guidelines for police officers, police staff and CPS prosecutors concerned with the preparation, processing and submission of prosecution files.

Master Recording Security (paragraphs 3.24 to 3.30)

3J This section is concerned with the security of the master recording sealed at the conclusion of the interview. Care must be taken of working copy recordings because their loss or destruction may lead unnecessarily to the need to access master recordings.

Breaking master recording seal for criminal proceedings (paragraph 3.25)

3K If the master recording has been delivered to the crown court for their keeping after committal for trial the crown prosecutor will apply to the chief clerk of the crown court centre for the release of the recording for unsealing by the crown prosecutor.

3L Reference to the Crown Prosecution Service or to the crown prosecutor in this part of the Code should be taken to include any other body or person with a statutory responsibility for the proceedings for which the police recorded interview is required.

Breaking master recording seal: other cases (paragraphs 3.26 to 3.29)

3M The most common reasons for needing access to master copies that are not required for criminal proceedings arise from civil actions and complaints against police and civil actions between individuals arising out of allegations of crime investigated by police.

3N Paragraph 3.29(b) could apply, for example, when one or more of the outcomes or likely outcomes of the investigation might be; (i) the prosecution of one or more of the original suspects; (ii) the prosecution of someone previously not suspected, including someone who was originally a witness, and (iii) any original suspect being treated as a prosecution witness and when premature disclosure of any police action, particularly through contact with any parties involved, could lead to a real risk of compromising the investigation and endangering witnesses.

4 Interview recording using secure digital recording network device.

(A) General

4.1 An authorised secure digital recording network device (see *paragraph 1.6(a)(iii)* does not use removable media and this section specifies the provisions which will apply when such a device is used. For ease of reference, it repeats in full some of the provisions of section 3 that apply to both types of recording device.

(B) Commencement of interviews

4.2 When the suspect is brought into the interview room or arrives at the location where the interview is to take place, the interviewer shall without delay and in the sight of the suspect, switch on the recording equipment and in accordance with the manufacturer's instructions start recording.

4.3 The interviewer must point out the sign or indicator which shows that the recording equipment is activated and is recording (see *paragraph 1.6(a)(iii)*) and shall then:

(a) tell the suspect that the interview is being audibly recorded using an authorised *secure digital recording network device* and outline the recording process (see *Note 3A*);

(b) subject to *paragraph 1.13*, give their name and rank and that of any other interviewer present;

(c) ask the suspect and any other party present, e.g. the appropriate adult, a solicitor or interpreter, to identify themselves (see *Note 3A*);

(d) state the date, time of commencement and place of the interview; and

(e) inform the person that:

- they will be given access to the recording of the interview in the event that they are charged or informed that they will be prosecuted but if they are not charged or informed that they will be prosecuted they will only be given access as agreed with the police or on the order of a court; and
- they will be given a written notice at the end of the interview setting out their rights to access the recording and what will happen to the recording.

(f) If equipment for remote monitoring of interviews as described in *paragraph 2.6* is installed, explain the contents of the notice to the suspect, solicitor and appropriate adult as required by *paragraph 2.6(d)* and point out the light that illuminates automatically as soon as remote monitoring is activated.

4.4 *Paragraphs 3.5* to 3.7 apply.

(C) Interviews with suspects who appear to have a hearing impediment

4.5 *Paragraph 3.8* applies.

(D) Objections and complaints by the suspect

4.6 *Paragraphs 3.9, 3.10* and *3.11* apply.

(E) Taking a break during interview

4.7 When a break is taken, the fact that a break is to be taken, the reason for it and the time shall be recorded on the audio recording. The recording shall be stopped and the procedures in *paragraphs 4.11* and *4.12* for the conclusion of interview followed.

4.8 When the interview recommences the procedures in *paragraphs 4.2* to *4.3* for commencing an interview shall be followed to create a new file to record the continuation of the interview. The time the interview recommences shall be recorded on the audio recording.

4.9 After any break in the interview the interviewer must, before resuming the interview, remind the person being questioned of their right to legal advice if they have not exercised it and that they remain under caution or, if there is any doubt, give the caution in full again (see *Note 3G*).

(F) Failure of recording equipment

4.10 If there is an equipment failure which can be rectified quickly, e.g. by commencing a new secure digital network recording using the same device or a replacement device, the interviewer shall follow the appropriate procedures as in *paragraphs 4.7 to 4.9 (Taking a break during interview)*. When the recording is resumed, the interviewer shall explain what happened and record the time the interview recommences. However, if it is not possible to continue recording on the same device or by using a replacement device, the interview should be audio-recorded on removable media as in *paragraph 3.3*, if the necessary equipment is available. If it is not available, the interview may continue and be recorded in writing in accordance with *paragraph 2.3* as directed by the 'relevant officer'. (See *Note 3H.*)

(G) Conclusion of interview

4.11 At the conclusion of the interview, the suspect shall be offered the opportunity to clarify anything he or she has said and asked if there is anything they want to add.

4.12 At the conclusion of the interview, including the taking and reading back of any written statement:

(a) the time shall be orally recorded.

(b) the suspect shall be handed a notice (see *Note 4A)* which explains:

- how the audio recording will be used
- the arrangements for access to it
- that if they are charged or informed that they will be prosecuted, they will be given access to the recording of the interview either electronically or by being given a copy on removable recording media, but if they are not charged or informed that they will prosecuted, they will only be given access as agreed with the police or on the order of a court.

(c) the suspect must be asked to confirm that he or she has received a copy of the notice at *sub-paragraph (b)* above. If the suspect fails to accept or to acknowledge receipt of the notice, the interviewer will state for the recording that a copy of the notice has been provided to the suspect and that he or she has refused to take a copy of the notice or has refused to acknowledge receipt.

(d) the time shall be recorded and the interviewer shall ensure that the interview record is saved to the device in the presence of the suspect and any third party present during the interview and notify them accordingly. The interviewer must then explain that the record will be transferred securely to the remote secure network file server (see *paragraph 4.15*). If the equipment is available to enable the record to be transferred there and then in the suspect's presence, then it should be so transferred. If it is transferred at a later time, the time and place of the transfer must be recorded. The suspect should then be informed that the interview is terminated.

(H) After the interview

4.13 The interviewer shall make a note in their pocket book that the interview has taken place and that it was audibly recorded, time it commenced, its duration and date and the identification number, filename or other reference for the recording (see *Note 3I*).

4.14 If no proceedings follow in respect of the person whose interview was recorded, the recordings must be kept securely as in *paragraphs 4.15* and *4.16*.

(I) Security of secure digital network interview records

4.15 The recordings are first saved locally on the device before being transferred to the remote network file server system (see *paragraph 1.6(a)(iii)*). The recording remains on the local device until the transfer is complete. If for any reason the network connection fails, the recording will be transferred when the network connection is restored (see *paragraph 4.12(d)*). The interview record files are stored in read only form on non-removable storage devices, for example, hard disk drives, to ensure their integrity.

4.16 Access to interview recordings, including copying to removable media, must be strictly controlled and monitored to ensure that access is restricted to those who have been given specific permission to access for specified purposes when this is necessary. For example, police officers and CPS lawyers involved in the preparation of any prosecution case, persons interviewed if they have been charged or informed they may be prosecuted and their legal representatives.

Note for Guidance

4A The notice at paragraph 4.12(b) above should provide a brief explanation of the secure digital network and how access to the recording is strictly limited. The notice should also explain the access rights of the suspect, their legal representative, the police and the prosecutor to the recording of the interview. Space should be provided on the form to insert the date, the identification number, filename or other reference for the interview recording.

ANNEX: PARAGRAPH 2.4(C)(III)—FOUR INDICTABLE OFFENCE TYPES FOR WHICH THE INTERVIEWER MAY DECIDE TO MAKE A WRITTEN RECORD OF A VOLUNTARY INTERVIEW ELSEWHERE THAN AT A POLICE STATION WHEN AN AUTHORISED AUDIO RECORDING DEVICE CANNOT BE USED.

[See *Notes 2* and *3*]

Part 1: Four specified indictable offence types—two conditions

1. The **first** condition is that the *indictable* offence in respect of which the person has been cautioned is *one* of the following:

   (a) Possession of a controlled drug contrary to section 5(2) of the Misuse of Drugs Act 1971 if the drug is cannabis as defined by that Act and in a form commonly known as herbal cannabis or cannabis resin (see *Note 5*);

   (b) Possession of a controlled drug contrary to section 5(2) of the Misuse of Drugs Act 1971 if the drug is khat as defined by that Act (see *Note 5*);

   (c) Retail theft (shoplifting) contrary to section 1 of the Theft Act 1968 (see *Note 6)*; and

   (d) Criminal damage to property contrary to section 1(1) of the Criminal Damage Act 1971 (see *Note 6),*

and in this paragraph, the reference to each of the above offences applies to an attempt to commit that offence as defined by section 1 of the Criminal Attempts Act 1981.

2. The **second** condition is that:

   (a) where the person has been cautioned in respect of an offence described in *paragraph 1(a)* (Possession of herbal cannabis or cannabis resin) or *paragraph 1(b)* (Possession of khat), the requirements of *paragraphs 3* and *4* are satisfied; or

   (b) where the person has been cautioned in respect of an offence described in *paragraph 1(c)* (Retail theft), the requirements of *paragraphs 3* and *5* are satisfied; or

   (c) where the person has been cautioned in respect of an offence described in *paragraph 1(d)* (criminal damage), the requirements of *paragraphs 3* and *6* are satisfied.

3. The requirements of this paragraph that apply to all four offences described in *paragraph 1* are that:

   (i) with regard to the person suspected of committing the offence:
   - they appear to be aged 18 or over;
   - there is no reason to suspect that they are a vulnerable person for whom an appropriate adult is required (see *paragraph 1.5* of this Code);
   - they do *not* appear to be unable to understand what is happening because of the effects of drink, drugs or illness, ailment or condition;
   - they do *not* require an interpreter in accordance with *Code C section 13*; and in accordance with Code G (Arrest), their arrest is *not* necessary in order to investigate the offence;

   (ii) it appears that the commission of the offence:
   - has *not* resulted in any injury to any person;
   - has *not* involved any realistic threat or risk of injury to any person; and

- has *not* caused any *substantial* financial or material loss to the private property of any individual; and

(iv) the person is not being interviewed about any other offence.

See *Notes 3 and 8.*

4. The requirements of this paragraph that apply to the offences described in *paragraph 1(a)* (possession of herbal cannabis or cannabis resin) and *paragraph 1(b)* (possession of khat) are that a police officer who is experienced in the recognition of the physical appearance, texture and smell of herbal cannabis, cannabis resin or (as the case may be) khat, is able to say that the substance which has been found in the suspect's possession by that officer or, as the case may be, by any other officer not so experienced and trained:

(i) is a controlled drug being either herbal cannabis, cannabis resin or khat; and

(ii) the quantity of the substance found is consistent with personal use by the suspect and does not provide any grounds to suspect an intention to supply others.

See *Note 5.*

5. The requirements of this paragraph that apply to the offence described in *paragraph 1(c)* (retail theft), are that it appears to the officer:

(i) that the value of the property stolen does not exceed £100 inclusive of VAT;

(ii) that the stolen property has been recovered and remains fit for sale unless the items stolen comprised drink or food and have been consumed; and

(iii) that the person suspected of stealing the property is not employed (whether paid or not) by the person, company or organisation to which the property belongs.

See *Note 3.*

6. The requirements of this paragraph that apply to the offence described in *paragraph 1(d)* (Criminal damage), are that it appears to the officer:

(i) that the value of the criminal damage does *not* exceed £300; and

(ii) that the person suspected of damaging the property is not employed (whether paid or not) by the person, company or organisation to which the property belongs.

See *Note 3.*

Part 2: Other provisions applicable to all interviews to which this Annex applies

7. *Paragraphs 3.21* to *3.22B* of Code C set out the responsibilities of the interviewing officer for ensuring compliance with the provisions of Code C that apply to the conduct and recording of voluntary interviews to which this Annex applies. See *Note 7.*

8. If it appears to the interviewing officer that before the conclusion of an interview, any of the requirements in *paragraphs 3 to 6* of *Part 1* that apply to the offence in question described in *paragraph 1* of Part 1 have ceased to apply; this Annex shall cease to apply. The person being interviewed must be so informed and a break in the interview must be taken. The reason must be recorded in the written interview record and the continuation of the interview shall be audio recorded in accordance with section 2 of this Code. For the purpose of the continuation, the provisions of *paragraphs 3.3* and *4.2* (Commencement of interviews) shall apply. See *Note 8.*

Notes for Guidance

1 Not used.

2 The purpose of allowing the interviewer to decide that a written record is to be made is to support the policy which gives police in England and Wales options for dealing with low-level offences quickly and non-bureaucratically in a proportionate manner. Guidance for police about these options is available at: https://www.app.college.police.uk/app-content/prosecution-and-case-management/justice-outcomes/.

3 A decision in relation to a particular indictable offence that the conditions and requirements in this Annex are satisfied is an operational matter for the interviewing officer according to all the particular circumstances of the case. These circumstances include the outcome of the officer's investigation at that time and any other matters that are relevant to the officer's consideration as to how to deal with the matter.

4 Not used.

5 Under the Misuse of Drugs Act 1971 as at the date this Code comes into force:

(a) cannabis includes any part of the cannabis plant but not mature stalks and seeds separated from the plant, cannabis resin and cannabis oil, but paragraph 1(a) applies only to the possession of herbal cannabis and cannabis resin; and

(b) khat includes the leaves, stems and shoots of the plant.

6 The power to issue a Penalty Notice for Disorder (PND) for an offence contrary to section 1 of the Theft Act 1968 applies when the value of the goods stolen does not exceed £100 inclusive of VAT. The power to issue a PND for an offence contrary to section 1(1) of the Criminal Damage Act 1971 applies when the value of the damage does not exceed £300.

7 The provisions of Code C that apply to the conduct and recording of voluntary interviews to which this Annex applies are described in paragraphs 3.21 to 3.22B of Code C. They include the suspect's right to free legal advice, the provision of information about the offence before the interview (see Code C paragraph 11.1A) and the right to interpretation and translation (see Code C section 13). These and other rights and entitlements are summarised in the notice that must be given to the suspect.

8 The requirements in paragraph 3 of Part 1 will cease to apply if, for example during the course of an interview, as a result of what the suspect says or other information which comes to the interviewing officer's notice:

- *it appears that the suspect:*
  - ~ *is aged under 18;*
  - ~ *does require an appropriate adult;*
  - ~ *is unable to appreciate the significance of questions and their answers;*
  - ~ *is unable to understand what is happening because of the effects of drink, drugs or illness, ailment or condition; or*
  - ~ *requires an interpreter; or*
- *the police officer decides that the suspect's arrest is now necessary (see Code G).*

Code of Practice on Visual Recording with Sound of Interviews with Suspects (Code F)

(2018)

1 General

1.0 The procedures in this Code must be used fairly, responsibly, with respect for the people to whom they apply and without unlawful discrimination. Under the Equality Act 2010, section 149 (Public Sector Equality Duty), police forces must, in carrying out their functions, have due regard to the need to eliminate unlawful discrimination, harassment, victimisation and any other conduct which is prohibited by that Act, to advance equality of opportunity between people who share a relevant protected characteristic and people who do not share it, and to foster good relations between those persons. The Equality Act *also* makes it unlawful for police officers to discriminate against, harass or victimise any person on the grounds of the 'protected characteristics' of age, disability, gender reassignment, race, religion or belief, sex and sexual orientation, marriage and civil partnership, pregnancy and maternity, when using their powers. See *Note 1C*.

1.1 This Code of Practice must be readily available for consultation by police officers and other police staff, detained persons and members of the public.

1.2 The *Notes for Guidance* included are not provisions of this code. They form guidance to police officers and others about its application and interpretation.

1.3 Nothing in this Code shall detract from the requirements of Code C, the Code of Practice for the detention, treatment and questioning of persons by police officers.

1.4 The interviews and matters to which this Code applies and provisions that govern the conduct and recording of those interviews and other matters are described in section 2.

Note: The provisions of this Code and Code E which govern the conduct and recording of interviews *do not apply* to interviews with, or taking statements from, witnesses.

1.5 *Not used.*

1.5A The provisions of Code E which require interviews with suspects to be audio recorded and the provisions of this Code which permit simultaneous visual recording provide safeguards:

- for suspects against inaccurate recording of the words used in questioning them and of their demeanour during the interview; and
- for police interviewers against unfounded allegations made by, or on behalf of, suspects about the conduct of the interview and what took place during the interview which might otherwise appear credible.

The visual recording of interviews must therefore be carried out openly to instil confidence in its reliability as an impartial and accurate record of the interview.

1.6 *Not used.*

1.6A *Not used.*

1.7 *Not used.*

1.8 *Not used.*

Notes for Guidance

1A Not used.

1B Not used.

1C In paragraph 1.0, under the Equality Act 2010, section 149, the 'relevant protected characteristics' are: age, disability, gender reassignment, pregnancy and maternity, race, religion/belief, and sex and sexual orientation. For further detailed guidance and advice on the Equality Act, see: https://www.gov.uk/guidance/equality-act-2010-guidance.

2. When interviews and matters to which Code F applies may be visually recorded with sound and provisions for their conduct and recording.

(A) General

2.1 For the purpose of this Code, a visual recording with sound means an audio recording of an interview or other matter made in accordance with the requirement in *paragraph 2.1* of the Code of Practice on audio recording interviews with suspects (Code E) (see *Note 2A*) during which a *simultaneous* visual recording is made which shows the suspect, the interviewer and those in whose presence and hearing the audio recording was made.

2.2 There is no statutory requirement to make a visual recording, however, the provisions of this Code shall be followed on any occasion that the 'relevant officer' described in *Code E paragraph 2.4* considers that a visual recording of any matters mentioned in *paragraph 2.1* should be made. Having regard to the safeguards described in *paragraph 1.5A*, examples of occasions when the relevant officer is likely to consider that a visual recording should be made include when:

(a) the suspect (whether or not detained) requires an appropriate adult;

(b) the suspect or their solicitor or appropriate adult requests that the interview be recorded visually;

(c) the suspect or other person whose presence is necessary is deaf or deaf/blind or speech impaired and uses sign language to communicate;

(d) the interviewer anticipates that when asking the suspect about their involvement in the offence concerned, they will invite the suspect to demonstrate their actions or behaviour at the time or to examine a particular item or object which is handed to them;

(e) the officer in charge of the investigation believes that a visual recording with sound will assist in the conduct of the investigation, for example, when briefing other officers about the suspect or matters coming to light during the course of the interview; and

(f) the authorised recording device that would be used in accordance with *paragraph 2.1 of Code E* incorporates a camera and creates a combined audio and visual recording and does not allow the visual recording function to operate independently of the audio recording function.

2.3 For the purpose of making such a visual recording, the provisions of Code E and the relevant *Notes for Guidance* shall apply equally to visual recordings with sound as they do to audio-only recordings, subject to the additional provisions in *paragraphs 2.5* to *2.12* below which apply exclusively to visual recordings. (See *Note 2E.*)

2.4 This Code does not apply to the conduct and recording in England and Wales, of:

- interviews of persons detained under section 41 of, or Schedule 7 to, the Terrorism Act 2000, and
- post-charge questioning of persons authorised under section 22 of the Counter-Terrorism Act 2008.

These must be video recorded with sound in accordance with the provisions of the separate Code of Practice issued under paragraph 3 of Schedule 8 to the Terrorism Act 2000 and under section 25 of the Counter-Terrorism Act 2008. If, during the course of an interview or questioning being visually recorded under this Code, it becomes apparent that the interview or questioning should be conducted under that separate Code, the interview should only continue in accordance with that Code (see *Code E paragraph 1.4*).

(B) Application of Code E—additional provisions that apply to visual recording with sound.

(i) General

2.5 Before visual recording commences, the interviewer must inform the suspect that in accordance with *paragraph 2.2,* a visual recording is being made and explain the visual and audio recording arrangements. If the suspect is a juvenile or a vulnerable person (see Code C, *paragraphs 1.4, 1.5* and *1.13(d)*), the information and explanation must be provided or (as the case may be) provided again, in the presence of the appropriate adult.

2.6 The device used to make the visual recording at the same time as the audio recording (see *paragraph 2.1*) must ensure coverage of as much of the room or location where the interview takes place as it is practically possible to achieve whilst the interview takes place (see *Note 2B*).

2.7 In cases to which *paragraph 1.13* of Code E (disclosure of identity of officers or police staff conducting interviews) applies:

(a) the officers and staff may have their backs to the visual recording device; and

(b) when in accordance with Code E *paragraph 3.21* or *4.12* as they apply to this Code, arrangements are made for the suspect to have access to the visual recording, the investigating officer may arrange for anything in the recording that might allow the officers or police staff to be identified to be concealed.

2.8 Following a decision made by the relevant officer in accordance with *paragraph 2.2* that an interview or other matter mentioned in *paragraph 2.1* above should be *visually recorded*, the relevant officer may decide that the interview is not to be visually recorded if it no longer appears that a visual recording should be made or because of a fault in the recording device. However, a decision not to make a *visual recording* does not detract in any way from the requirement for the interview to be *audio recorded* in accordance with *paragraph 2.1 of Code E.* (See *Note 2C.*)

2.9 The provisions in *Code E paragraph 2.6* for remote monitoring of interviews shall apply to visually recorded interviews.

(ii) Objections and complaints by the suspect about visual recording

2.10 If the suspect or an appropriate adult on their behalf objects to the interview being *visually* recorded either at the outset or during the interview or during a break in the interview, the interviewer shall explain that the visual recording is being made in accordance with *paragraph 2.2* and that this Code requires the objections to be recorded on the *visual* recording. When any objections have been recorded or the suspect or the appropriate adult have refused to have their objections recorded visually, the relevant officer shall decide in accordance with *paragraph 2.8* and having regard to the nature and circumstances of the objections, whether visual recording should be turned off (see *Note 2D*). Following a decision that visual recording should be turned off, the interviewer shall say that they are turning off the *visual* recording. The audio recording required to be maintained in accordance with Code E shall continue and the interviewer shall ask the person to record their objections to the interview being *visually* recorded on the audio recording. If the relevant officer considers that visual recording should not be turned off, the interviewer may proceed to question the suspect with the visual recording still on. If the suspect also objects to the interview being audio recorded, *paragraph 3.9* of Code E will apply if a removable recording media device (see Code E *paragraph 1.6(a)(ii)*) is being used) and *paragraph 4.6* of Code E will apply if a secure digital recording device (see Code E *paragraph 1.6(a)(iii)*) is being used.

2.11 If the suspect indicates that they wish to tell the interviewer about matters not directly connected with the offence of which they are suspected and that they are unwilling for these matters to be visually recorded, the suspect should be given the opportunity to tell the interviewer about these matters after the conclusion of the formal interview.

(ii) Failure of visual recording device

2.12 If there is a failure of equipment and it is not possible to continue visual recording using the same type of recording device (i.e. a removable recording media device as in Code E *paragraph 1.6(a)(ii)* or a secure digital recording network device as in Code E *paragraph 1.6(a)(iii)*) or by using a replacement device of either type, the relevant officer may decide that the interview is to continue without being visually recorded. In these circumstances, the continuation of the interview must be conducted and recorded in accordance with the provisions of *Code E* (See *Note 2F.*)

Notes for Guidance

2A Paragraph 2.1 of Code E describes the requirement that authorised audio-recording devices are to be used for recording interviews and other matters.

2B Interviewers will wish to arrange that, as far as possible, visual recording arrangements are unobtrusive. It must be clear to the suspect, however, that there is no opportunity to interfere with the recording equipment or the recording media.

2C A decision made in accordance with paragraph 2.8 not to record an interview visually for any reason may be the subject of comment in court. The 'relevant officer' responsible should therefore be prepared to justify that decision.

2D Objections for the purpose of paragraph 2.10 are meant to apply to objections based on the suspect's genuine and honestly held beliefs and to allow officers to exercise their discretion to decide whether a visual recording is to be made according to the circumstances surrounding the suspect and the investigation. Objections that appear to be frivolous with the intentions of frustrating or delaying the investigation would not be relevant.

2E The visual recording made in accordance with this Code may be used for eye-witness identification procedures to which paragraph 3.21 and Annex E of Code D apply.

2F Where the interview is being visually recorded and the media or the recording device fails, the interviewer should stop the interview immediately. Where part of the interview is unaffected by the error and is still accessible on the media or on the network device, that part shall be copied and sealed in the suspect's presence as a master copy or saved as a new secure digital network recording as appropriate. The interview should then be recommenced using a functioning recording device and new recording media as appropriate. Where the media content of the interview has been lost in its entirety, the media should be sealed in the suspect's presence and the interview begun again. If the visual recording equipment cannot be fixed and a replacement device is not immediately available, the interview should be audio recorded in accordance with Code E.

2G The relevant officer should be aware that a decision to continue visual recording against the wishes of the suspect may be the subject of comment in court.

Code of Practice for the Statutory Power of Arrest by Police Officers (Code G)

(2012)

This Code applies to any arrest made by a police officer after midnight on 12 November 2012

1 Introduction

1.1 This Code of Practice deals with the statutory power of police to arrest a person who is involved, or suspected of being involved, in a criminal offence. The power of arrest must be used fairly, responsibly, with respect for people suspected of committing offences and without unlawful discrimination. The Equality Act 2010 makes it unlawful for police officers to discriminate against, harass or victimise any person on the grounds of the 'protected characteristics' of age, disability, gender reassignment, race, religion or belief, sex and sexual orientation, marriage and civil partnership, pregnancy and maternity when using their powers. When police forces are carrying out their functions they also have a duty to have regard to the need to eliminate unlawful discrimination, harassment and victimisation and to take steps to foster good relations.

1.2 The exercise of the power of arrest represents an obvious and significant interference with the Right to liberty and security under Article 5 of the European Convention on Human Rights set out in Part I of Schedule 1 to the Human Rights Act 1998.

1.3 The use of the power must be fully justified and officers exercising the power should consider if the necessary objectives can be met by other, less intrusive means. Absence of justification for exercising the power of arrest may lead to challenges should the case proceed to court. It could also lead to civil claims against police for unlawful arrest and false imprisonment. When the power of arrest is exercised it is essential that it is exercised in a non-discriminatory and proportionate manner which is compatible with the Right to liberty under Article 5. See *Note 1B*.

1.4 Section 24 of the Police and Criminal Evidence Act 1984 (as substituted by section 110 of the Serious Organised Crime and Police Act 2005) provides the statutory power for a constable to arrest without warrant for all offences. If the provisions of the Act and this Code are not observed, both the arrest and the conduct of any subsequent investigation may be open to question.

1.5 This Code of Practice must be readily available at all police stations for consultation by police officers and police staff, detained persons and members of the public.

1.6 The *Notes for Guidance* are not provisions of this code.

2 Elements of Arrest under section 24 PACE

2.1 A lawful arrest requires two elements:

A person's involvement or suspected involvement or attempted involvement in the commission of a criminal offence;

AND

Reasonable grounds for *believing* that the person's arrest is necessary.

- both elements must be satisfied, and
- it can never be necessary to arrest a person unless there are reasonable grounds to suspect them of committing an offence.

2.2 The arrested person must be informed that they have been arrested, even if this fact is obvious, and of the relevant circumstances of the arrest in relation to both the above elements. The custody officer must be informed of these matters on arrival at the police station. See *paragraphs 2.9, 3.3* and *Note 3* and *Code C paragraph 3.4*.

(a) 'Involvement in the commission of an offence'

2.3 A constable may arrest without warrant in relation to any offence (see *Notes 1* and *1A*) anyone:

- who is about to commit an offence or is in the act of committing an offence;
- whom the officer has reasonable grounds for suspecting is about to commit an offence or to be committing an offence;

- whom the officer has reasonable grounds to suspect of being guilty of an offence which he or she has reasonable grounds for suspecting has been committed;
- anyone who is guilty of an offence which has been committed or anyone whom the officer has reasonable grounds for suspecting to be guilty of that offence.

2.3A There must be some reasonable, objective grounds for the suspicion, based on known facts and information which are relevant to the likelihood the offence has been committed and the person liable to arrest committed it. See *Notes 2* and *2A*.

(b) Necessity criteria

2.4 The power of arrest is **only** exercisable if the constable has reasonable grounds for *believing* that it is necessary to arrest the person. The statutory criteria for what may constitute necessity are set out in paragraph 2.9 and it remains an operational decision at the discretion of the constable to decide:

- which one or more of the necessity criteria (if any) applies to the individual; and
- if any of the criteria do apply, whether to arrest, grant street bail after arrest, report for summons or for charging by post, issue a penalty notice or take any other action that is open to the officer.

2.5 In applying the criteria, the arresting officer has to be satisfied that at least one of the reasons supporting the need for arrest is satisfied.

2.6 Extending the power of arrest to all offences provides a constable with the ability to use that power to deal with any situation. However applying the necessity criteria requires the constable to examine and justify the reason or reasons why a person needs to be arrested or (as the case may be) further arrested, for an offence for the custody officer to decide whether to authorise their detention for that offence. See *Note 2C*

2.7 The criteria in paragraph 2.9 below which are set out in section 24 of PACE as substituted by section 110 of the Serious Organised Crime and Police Act 2005 <u>are</u> exhaustive. However, the circumstances that may satisfy those criteria remain a matter for the operational discretion of individual officers. Some examples are given to illustrate what those circumstances might be and what officers might consider when deciding whether arrest is necessary.

2.8 In considering the individual circumstances, the constable must take into account the situation of the victim, the nature of the offence, the circumstances of the suspect and the needs of the investigative process.

2.9 When it is practicable to tell a person why their arrest is necessary (as required by paragraphs 2.2, 3.3 and *Note 3*), the constable should outline the facts, information and other circumstances which provide the grounds for believing that their arrest is necessary and which the officer considers satisfy one or more of the statutory criteria in sub-paragraphs (a) to (f), namely:

(a) to enable the name of the person in question to be ascertained (in the case where the constable does not know, and cannot readily ascertain, the person's name, or has reasonable grounds for doubting whether a name given by the person as his name is his real name):

An officer might decide that a person's name cannot be readily ascertained if they fail or refuse to give it when asked, particularly after being warned that failure or refusal is likely to make their arrest necessary (see *Note 2D)*. Grounds to doubt a name given may arise if the person appears reluctant or hesitant when asked to give their name or to verify the name they have given.

Where mobile fingerprinting is available and the suspect's name cannot be ascertained or is doubted, the officer should consider using the power under section 61(6A) of PACE (see *Code D paragraph 4.3(e)*) to take and check the fingerprints of a suspect as this may avoid the need to arrest solely to enable their name to be ascertained.

(b) correspondingly as regards the person's address:

An officer might decide that a person's address cannot be readily ascertained if they fail or refuse to give it when asked, particularly after being warned that such a failure or refusal is likely to make their arrest necessary. See *Note 2D*. Grounds to doubt an address given may arise if the person appears reluctant or hesitant when asked to give their address or is unable to provide verifiable details of the locality they claim to live in.

When considering reporting to consider summons or charging by post as alternatives to arrest, an address would be satisfactory if the person will be at it for a sufficiently long period for it to be possible to serve them with the summons or requisition and charge; or, that some other person at that address specified by the person will accept service on their behalf. When considering issuing a penalty notice, the address should be one where the person will be in the event of enforcement action if the person does not pay the penalty or is convicted and fined after a court hearing.

(c) to prevent the person in question:

(i) causing physical injury to himself or any other person;

This might apply where the suspect has already used or threatened violence against others and it is thought likely that they may assault others if they are not arrested. See *Note 2D*

(ii) suffering physical injury;

This might apply where the suspect's behaviour and actions are believed likely to provoke, or have provoked, others to want to assault the suspect unless the suspect is arrested for their own protection. See *Note 2D*

(iii) causing loss or damage to property;

This might apply where the suspect is a known persistent offender with a history of serial offending against property (theft and criminal damage) and it is thought likely that they may continue offending if they are not arrested.

(iv) committing an offence against public decency (only applies where members of the public going about their normal business cannot reasonably be expected to avoid the person in question);

This might apply when an offence against public decency is being committed in a place to which the public have access and is likely to be repeated in that or some other public place at a time when the public are likely to encounter the suspect. See *Note 2D*

(v) causing an unlawful obstruction of the highway;

This might apply to any offence where its commission causes an unlawful obstruction which it is believed may continue or be repeated if the person is not arrested, particularly if the person has been warned that they are causing an obstruction. See *Note 2D*

(d) to protect a child or other vulnerable person from the person in question.

This might apply when the health (physical or mental) or welfare of a child or vulnerable person is likely to be harmed or is at risk of being harmed, if the person is not arrested in cases where it is not practicable and appropriate to make alternative arrangements to prevent the suspect from having any harmful or potentially harmful contact with the child or vulnerable person.

(e) to allow the prompt and effective investigation of the offence or of the conduct of the person in question. See *Note 2E*

This may arise when it is thought likely that unless the person is arrested and then either taken in custody to the police station or granted 'street bail' to attend the station later, see *Note 2J*, further action considered necessary to properly investigate their involvement in the offence would be frustrated, unreasonably delayed or otherwise hindered and therefore be impracticable. Examples of such actions include:

(i) *interviewing the suspect* on occasions when the person's voluntary attendance is not considered to be a practicable alternative to arrest, because for example:

- it is thought unlikely that the person would attend the police station voluntarily to be interviewed.
- it is necessary to interview the suspect about the outcome of other investigative action for which their arrest is necessary, see (ii) to (v) below.

- arrest would enable the special warning to be given in accordance with Code C paragraphs 10.10 and 10.11 when the suspect is found:
  - in possession of incriminating objects, or at a place where such objects are found;
  - at or near the scene of the crime at or about the time it was committed.
- the person has made false statements and/or presented false evidence;
- it is thought likely that the person:
  - may steal or destroy evidence;
  - may collude or make contact with, co-suspects or conspirators;
  - may intimidate or threaten or make contact with, witnesses. See *Notes 2F and 2G*

(ii) when considering arrest in connection with the investigation of an *indictable offence* (see *Note 6*), there is a need:

- to enter and search without a search warrant any premises occupied or controlled by the arrested person or where the person was when arrested or immediately before arrest;
- to prevent the arrested person from having contact with others;
- to detain the arrested person for more than 24 hours before charge.

(iii) when considering arrest in connection with any *recordable offence* and it is necessary to secure or preserve evidence of that offence by taking fingerprints, footwear impressions or samples from the suspect for evidential comparison or matching with other material relating to that offence, for example, from the crime scene. See *Note 2H*

(iv) when considering arrest in connection with any offence and it is necessary to search, examine or photograph the person to obtain evidence. See *Note 2H*

(v) when considering arrest in connection with an offence to which the statutory Class A drug testing requirements in Code C section 17 apply, to enable testing when it is thought that drug misuse might have caused or contributed to the offence. See *Note 2I.*

(f) to prevent any prosecution for the offence from being hindered by the disappearance of the person in question.

This may arise when it is thought that:

- if the person is not arrested they are unlikely to attend court if they are prosecuted;
- the address given is not a satisfactory address for service of a summons or a written charge and requisition to appear at court because the person will not be at it for a sufficiently long period for the summons or charge and requisition to be served and no other person at that specified address will accept service on their behalf.

3 Information to be given on Arrest

(a) Cautions—when a caution must be given

3.1 Code C paragraphs 10.1 and 10.2 set out the requirement for a person whom there are grounds to suspect of an offence (see *Note 2*) to be cautioned before being questioned or further questioned about an offence.

3.2 *Not used.*

3.3 A person who is arrested, or further arrested, must be informed at the time if practicable, or if not, as soon as it becomes practicable thereafter, that they are under arrest and of the grounds and reasons for their arrest, see paragraphs 2.2 and *Note 3.*

3.4 A person who is arrested, or further arrested, must be cautioned unless:

(a) it is impracticable to do so by reason of their condition or behaviour at the time;

(b) they have already been cautioned immediately prior to arrest as in *paragraph 3.1.*

(b) Terms of the caution (Taken from Code C section 10)

3.5 The caution, which must be given on arrest, should be in the following terms:

'You do not have to say anything. But it may harm your defence if you do not mention when questioned something which you later rely on in Court. Anything you do say may be given in evidence.'

Where the use of the Welsh Language is appropriate, a constable may provide the caution directly in Welsh in the following terms:

'Does dim rhaid i chi ddweud dim byd. Ond gall niweidio eich amddiffyniad os na fyddwch chi'n sôn, wrth gael eich holi, am rywbeth y byddwch chi'n dibynnu arno nes ymlaen yn y Llys. Gall unrhyw beth yr ydych yn ei ddweud gael ei roi fel tystiolaeth.'

See *Note 4*

3.6 Minor deviations from the words of any caution given in accordance with this Code do not constitute a breach of this Code, provided the sense of the relevant caution is preserved. See *Note 5*

3.7 *Not used.*

4 Records of Arrest

(a) General

4.1 The arresting officer is required to record in his pocket book or by other methods used for recording information:

- the nature and circumstances of the offence leading to the arrest;
- the reason or reasons why arrest was necessary;
- the giving of the caution; and
- anything said by the person at the time of arrest.

4.2 Such a record should be made at the time of the arrest unless impracticable to do. If not made at that time, the record should then be completed as soon as possible thereafter.

4.3 On arrival at the police station or after being first arrested at the police station, the arrested person must be brought before the custody officer as soon as practicable and a custody record must be opened in accordance with section 2 of Code C. The information given by the arresting officer on the circumstances and reason or reasons for arrest shall be recorded as part of the custody record. Alternatively, a copy of the record made by the officer in accordance with paragraph 4.1 above shall be attached as part of the custody record. See *paragraph 2.2* and *Code C paragraphs 3.4* and *10.3.*

4.4 The custody record will serve as a record of the arrest. Copies of the custody record will be provided in accordance with paragraphs 2.4 and 2.4A of Code C and access for inspection of the original record in accordance with paragraph 2.5 of Code C.

(b) Interviews and arrests

4.5 Records of interview, significant statements or silences will be treated in the same way as set out in sections 10 and 11 of Code C and in Codes E and F (audio and visual recording of interviews).

Notes for guidance

1 For the purposes of this Code, 'offence' means any statutory or common law offence for which a person may be tried by a magistrates' court or the Crown court and punished if convicted. Statutory offences include assault, rape, criminal damage, theft, robbery, burglary, fraud, possession of controlled drugs and offences under road traffic, liquor licensing, gambling and immigration legislation and local government byelaws. Common law offences include murder, manslaughter, kidnapping, false imprisonment, perverting the course of justice and escape from lawful custody.

1A This code does not apply to powers of arrest conferred on constables under any arrest warrant, for example, a warrant issued under the Magistrates' Courts Act 1980, sections 1 or 13, or the Bail Act 1976, section 7(1), or to the powers of constables to arrest without warrant other than under section 24 of PACE for an offence. These other powers to arrest without warrant do not depend on the arrested person committing any specific offence and include:

- *PACE, section 46A, arrest of person who fails to answer police bail to attend police station or is suspected of breaching any condition of that bail for the custody officer to decide whether they should be kept in police detention which applies whether or not the person commits an offence under section 6 of the Bail Act 1976 (e.g. failing without reasonable cause to surrender to custody);*
- *Bail Act 1976, section 7(3), arrest of person bailed to attend court who is suspected of breaching, or is believed likely to breach, any condition of bail to take them to court for bail to be re-considered;*

- *Children & Young Persons Act 1969, section 32(1A) (absconding)—arrest to return the person to the place where they are required to reside;*
- *Immigration Act 1971, Schedule 2 to arrest a person liable to examination to determine their right to remain in the UK;*
- *Mental Health Act 1983, section 136 to remove person suffering from mental disorder to place of safety for assessment;*
- *Prison Act 1952, section 49, arrest to return person unlawfully at large to the prison etc. where they are liable to be detained;*
- *Road Traffic Act 1988, section 6D arrest of driver following the outcome of a preliminary roadside test requirement to enable the driver to be required to provide an evidential sample;*
- *Common law power to stop or prevent a Breach of the Peace—after arrest a person aged 18 or over may be brought before a justice of the peace court to show cause why they should not be bound over to keep the peace—not criminal proceedings.*

1B Juveniles should not be arrested at their place of education unless this is unavoidable. When a juvenile is arrested at their place of education, the principal or their nominee must be informed. (From Code C Note 11D)

2 Facts and information relevant to a person's suspected involvement in an offence should not be confined to those which tend to indicate the person has committed or attempted to commit the offence. Before making a decision to arrest, a constable should take account of any facts and information that are available, including claims of innocence made by the person, that might dispel the suspicion.

2A Particular examples of facts and information which might point to a person's innocence and may tend to dispel suspicion include those which relate to the statutory defence provided by the Criminal Law Act 1967, section 3(1) which allows the use of reasonable force in the prevention of crime or making an arrest and the common law of self-defence. This may be relevant when a person appears, or claims, to have been acting reasonably in defence of themselves or others or to prevent their property or the property of others from being stolen, destroyed or damaged, particularly if the offence alleged is based on the use of unlawful force, e.g. a criminal assault. When investigating allegations involving the use of force by school staff, the power given to all school staff under the Education and Inspections Act 2006, section 93, to use reasonable force to prevent their pupils from committing any offence, injuring persons, damaging property or prejudicing the maintenance of good order and discipline may be similarly relevant. The Association of Chief Police Officers and the Crown Prosecution Service have published joint guidance to help the public understand the meaning of reasonable force and what to expect from the police and CPS in cases which involve claims of self defence. Separate advice for school staff on their powers to use reasonable force is available from the Department for Education

2B If a constable who is dealing with an allegation of crime and considering the need to arrest becomes an investigator for the purposes of the Code of Practice under the Criminal Procedure and Investigations Act 1996, the officer should, in accordance with paragraph 3.5 of that Code, 'pursue all reasonable lines of inquiry, whether these point towards or away from the suspect. What is reasonable in each case will depend on the particular circumstances.'

2C For a constable to have reasonable grounds for believing it necessary to arrest, he or she is not required to be satisfied that there is no viable alternative to arrest. However, it does mean that in all cases, the officer should consider that arrest is the practical, sensible and proportionate option in all the circumstances at the time the decision is made. This applies equally to a person in police detention after being arrested for an offence who is suspected of involvement in a further offence and the necessity to arrest them for that further offence is being considered.

2D Although a warning is not expressly required, officers should if practicable, consider whether a warning which points out their offending behaviour, and explains why, if they do not stop, the resulting consequences may make their arrest necessary. Such a warning might:

- *if heeded, avoid the need to arrest, or*
- *if it is ignored, support the need to arrest and also help prove the mental element of certain offences, for example, the person's intent or awareness, or help to rebut a defence that they were acting reasonably.*

A person who is warned that they may be liable to arrest if their real name and address cannot be ascertained, should be given a reasonable opportunity to establish their real name and address before deciding that either or both are unknown and cannot be readily ascertained or that there are reasonable grounds to doubt that a name and address they have given is their real name and address. They should be told why their name is not known and cannot be readily ascertained and (as the case may be) of the grounds for doubting that a name and address they have given is their real name and address, including, for example, the reason why a particular document the person has produced to verify their real name and/or address, is not sufficient.

2E The meaning of 'prompt' should be considered on a case by case basis taking account of all the circumstances. It indicates that the progress of the investigation should not be delayed to the extent that it would adversely affect the effectiveness of the investigation. The arresting officer also has discretion to release the arrested person on 'street bail' as an alternative to taking the person directly to the station. See Note 2J.

2F An officer who believes that it is necessary to interview the person suspected of committing the offence must then consider whether their arrest is necessary in order to carry out the interview. The officer is not required to interrogate the suspect to determine whether they will attend a police station voluntarily to be interviewed but they must consider whether the suspect's voluntary attendance is a practicable alternative for carrying out the interview. If it is, then arrest would not be necessary. Conversely, an officer who considers this option but is not satisfied that it is a practicable alternative, may have reasonable grounds for deciding that the arrest is necessary at the outset 'on the street'. Without such considerations, the officer would not be able to establish that arrest was necessary in order to interview.

Circumstances which suggest that a person's arrest 'on the street' would not be necessary to interview them might be where the officer:

- *is satisfied as to their identity and address and that they will attend the police station voluntarily to be interviewed, either immediately or by arrangement at a future date and time; and*
- *is not aware of any other circumstances which indicate that voluntary attendance would not be a practicable alternative. See paragraph 2.9(e)(i) to (v).*

When making arrangements for the person's voluntary attendance, the officer should tell the person:

- *that to properly investigate their suspected involvement in the offence they must be interviewed under caution at the police station, but in the circumstances their arrest for this purpose will not be necessary if they attend the police station voluntarily to be interviewed;*
- *that if they attend voluntarily, they will be entitled to free legal advice before, and to have a solicitor present at, the interview;*
- *that the date and time of the interview will take account of their circumstances and the needs of the investigation; and*
- *that if they do not agree to attend voluntarily at a time which meets the needs of the investigation, or having so agreed, fail to attend, or having attended, fail to remain for the interview to be completed, their arrest will be necessary to enable them to be interviewed.*

2G When the person attends the police station voluntarily for interview by arrangement as in Note 2F above, their arrest on arrival at the station prior to interview would only be justified if:

- *new information coming to light after the arrangements were made indicates that from that time, voluntary attendance ceased to be a practicable alternative and the person's arrest became necessary; and*
- *it was not reasonably practicable for the person to be arrested before they attended the station.*

If a person who attends the police station voluntarily to be interviewed decides to leave before the interview is complete, the police would at that point be entitled to consider whether their arrest was necessary to carry out the interview. The possibility that the person might decide to leave during the interview is therefore not a valid reason for arresting them before the interview has commenced. See Code C paragraph 3.21.

2H The necessity criteria do not permit arrest solely to enable the routine taking, checking (speculative searching) and retention of fingerprints, samples, footwear impressions and photographs when there are no prior grounds to believe that checking and comparing the fingerprints etc. or taking a photograph would provide relevant evidence of the person's involvement in the offence concerned or would help to ascertain or verify their real identity.

2I The necessity criteria do not permit arrest for an offence solely because it happens to be one of the statutory drug testing 'trigger offences' (see Code C Note 17E) when there is no suspicion that Class A drug misuse might have caused or contributed to the offence.

2J Having determined that the necessity criteria have been met and having made the arrest, the officer can then consider the use of street bail on the basis of the effective and efficient progress of the investigation of the offence in question. It gives the officer discretion to compel the person to attend a police station at a date/time that best suits the overall needs of the particular investigation. Its use is not confined to dealing with child care issues or allowing officers to attend to more urgent operational duties and granting street bail does not retrospectively negate the need to arrest.

3 An arrested person must be given sufficient information to enable them to understand they have been deprived of their liberty and the reason they have been arrested, as soon as practicable after the arrest, e.g. when a person is arrested on suspicion of committing an offence they must be informed of the nature of the suspected offence and when and where it was committed. The suspect must also be informed of the reason or reasons why arrest is considered necessary. Vague or technical language should be avoided. When explaining why one or more of the arrest criteria apply, it is not necessary to disclose any specific details that might undermine or otherwise adversely affect any investigative processes. An example might be the conduct of a formal interview when prior disclosure of such details might give the suspect an opportunity to fabricate an innocent explanation or to otherwise conceal lies from the interviewer.

4 Nothing in this Code requires a caution to be given or repeated when informing a person not under arrest they may be prosecuted for an offence. However, a court will not be able to draw any inferences under the Criminal Justice and Public Order Act 1994, section 34, if the person was not cautioned.

5 If it appears a person does not understand the caution, the person giving it should explain it in their own words.

6 Certain powers available as the result of an arrest—for example, entry and search of premises, detention without charge beyond 24 hours, holding a person incommunicado and delaying access to legal advice—only apply in respect of indictable offences and are subject to the specific requirements on authorisation as set out in PACE and the relevant Code of Practice.

Criminal Procedure and Investigations Act 1996: Code of Practice under Part II

Preamble

This code of practice is issued under Part II of the Criminal Procedure and Investigations Act 1996 ('the Act'). It sets out the manner in which police officers are to record, retain and reveal to the prosecutor material obtained in a criminal investigation and which may be relevant to the investigation, and related matters.

1. Introduction

1.1 This code of practice applies in respect of criminal investigations conducted by police officers which begin on or after the day on which this code comes into effect. Persons other than police officers who are charged with the duty of conducting an investigation as defined in the Act are to have regard to the relevant provisions of the code, and should take these into account in applying their own operating procedures.

1.2 This code does not apply to persons who are not charged with the duty of conducting an investigation as defined in the Act.

1.3 Nothing in this code applies to material intercepted in obedience to a warrant issued under section 2 of the Interception of Communications Act 1985 or section 5 of the Regulation of Investigatory Powers Act 2000, or to any copy of that material as defined in section 10 of the 1985 Act or section 15 of the 2000 Act and by sections of the Investigatory Powers Act 2016.

1.4 This code extends only to England and Wales.

2. Definitions

2.1 In this code:

1. *a criminal investigation* is an investigation conducted by police officers with a view to it being ascertained whether a person should be charged with an offence, or whether a person charged with an offence is guilty of it. This will include:
   - investigations into crimes that have been committed;
   - investigations whose purpose is to ascertain whether a crime has been committed, with a view to the possible institution of criminal proceedings; and
   - investigations which begin in the belief that a crime may be committed, for example when the police keep premises or individuals under observation for a period of time, with a view to the possible institution of criminal proceedings;
2. charging a person with an offence includes prosecution by way of summons or postal requisition;
3. *an investigator* is any police officer involved in the conduct of a criminal investigation. All investigators have a responsibility for carrying out the duties imposed on them under this code, including in particular recording information, and retaining records of information and other material;
4. the *officer in charge of an investigation* is the police officer responsible for directing a criminal investigation. They are also responsible for ensuring that proper procedures are in place for recording information, and retaining records of information and other material, in the investigation;
5. the *disclosure officer* is the person responsible for examining material retained by the police during the investigation; revealing material to the prosecutor during the investigation and any criminal proceedings resulting from it, and certifying that he has done this; and disclosing material to the accused at the request of the prosecutor;
6. the *prosecutor* is the authority responsible for the conduct, on behalf of the Crown, of criminal proceedings resulting from a specific criminal investigation;
7. *material* is material of any kind, including information and objects, which is obtained or inspected in the course of a criminal investigation and which may be relevant to the investigation. This includes not only material coming into the possession of the investigator (such as documents seized in the course of searching premises) but also material generated by them (such as interview records);
8. material may be *relevant to an investigation* if it appears to an investigator, or to the officer in charge of an investigation, or to the disclosure officer, that it has some bearing on any offence under investigation or any person being investigated, or on the surrounding circumstances of the case, unless it is incapable of having any impact on the case;
9. *sensitive material* is material, the disclosure of which, the disclosure officer believes, would give rise to a real risk of serious prejudice to an important public interest;
10. references to *prosecution disclosure* are to the duty of the prosecutor under sections 3 and 7A of the Act to disclose material which is in their possession or which they have inspected in pursuance of this code, and which might reasonably be considered capable of undermining the case against the accused, or of assisting the case for the accused;
11. references to the disclosure of material to a person accused of an offence include references to the disclosure of material to his legal representative;
12. references to police officers and to the chief officer of police include those employed in a police force as defined in section 3(3) of the Prosecution of Offences Act 1985.

3. General responsibilities

3.1 The functions of the investigator, the officer in charge of an investigation and the disclosure officer are separate. Whether they are undertaken by one, two or more persons will depend on the complexity of the case and the administrative arrangements within each police force. Where they are undertaken by more than one person, close consultation between them is essential to the effective performance of the duties imposed by this code.

3.2 In any criminal investigation, one or more deputy disclosure officers may be appointed to assist the disclosure officer, and a deputy disclosure officer may perform any function of a disclosure officer as defined in paragraph 2.1.

3.3 The chief officer of police for each police force is responsible for putting in place arrangements to ensure that in every investigation the identity of the officer in charge of an investigation and the disclosure officer is recorded. The chief officer of police for each police force shall ensure that disclosure officers and deputy disclosure officers have sufficient skills and authority, commensurate with the complexity of the investigation, to discharge their functions effectively. An individual must not be appointed as disclosure officer, or continue in that role, if that is likely to result in a conflict of interest, for instance, if the disclosure officer is the victim of the alleged crime which is the subject of the investigation. The advice of a more senior officer must always be sought if there is doubt as to whether a conflict of interest precludes an individual acting as disclosure officer. If thereafter the doubt remains, the advice of a prosecutor should be sought.

3.4 The officer in charge of an investigation may delegate tasks to another investigator, to civilians employed by the police force, or to other persons participating in the investigation under arrangements for joint investigations, but they remain responsible for ensuring that these have been carried out and for accounting for any general policies followed in the investigation. In particular, it is an essential part of his duties to ensure that all material which may be relevant to an investigation is retained, and either made available to the disclosure officer or (in exceptional circumstances) revealed directly to the prosecutor.

3.5 In conducting an investigation, the investigator should pursue all reasonable lines of inquiry, whether these point towards or away from the suspect. What is reasonable in each case will depend on the particular circumstances. It is a matter for the investigator, with the assistance of the prosecutor if required, to decide what constitutes a reasonable line of inquiry in each case.

3.6 If the officer in charge of an investigation believes that other persons may be in possession of material that may be relevant to the investigation, and if this has not been obtained under paragraph 3.5 above, they should ask the disclosure officer to inform them of the existence of the investigation and to invite them to retain the material in case they receive a request for its disclosure. The disclosure officer should inform the prosecutor that they may have such material. However, the officer in charge of an investigation is not required to make speculative enquiries of other persons; there must be some reason to believe that they may have relevant material. That reason may come from information provided to the police by the accused or from other inquiries made or from some other source.

3.7 If, during a criminal investigation, the officer in charge of an investigation or disclosure officer for any reason no longer has responsibility for the functions falling to them, either their supervisor or the police officer in charge of criminal investigations for the police force concerned must assign someone else to assume that responsibility. That person's identity must be recorded, as with those initially responsible for these functions in each investigation.

4. Recording of information

4.1 If material which may be relevant to the investigation consists of information which is not recorded in any form, the officer in charge of an investigation must ensure that it is recorded in a durable or retrievable form (whether in writing, on video or audio tape, or on computer disk).

4.2 Where it is not practicable to retain the initial record of information because it forms part of a larger record which is to be destroyed, its contents should be transferred as a true record to a durable and more easily-stored form before that happens.

4.3 Negative information is often relevant to an investigation. If it may be relevant it must be recorded. An example might be a number of people present in a particular place at a particular time who state that they saw nothing unusual.

4.4 Where information which may be relevant is obtained, it must be recorded at the time it is obtained or as soon as practicable after that time. This includes, for example, information obtained in house-to-house enquiries, although the requirement to record information promptly does not require an investigator to take a statement from a potential witness where it would not otherwise be taken.

5. Retention of material

(a) Duty to retain material

5.1 The investigator must retain material obtained in a criminal investigation which may be relevant to the investigation. Material may be photographed, video-recorded, captured digitally or otherwise retained in the form of a copy rather than the original at any time, if the original is perishable; the original was supplied to the investigator rather than generated by them and is to be returned to its owner; or the retention of a copy rather than the original is reasonable in all the circumstances.

5.2 Where material has been seized in the exercise of the powers of seizure conferred by the Police and Criminal Evidence Act 1984, the duty to retain it under this code is subject to the provisions on the retention of seized material in section 22 of that Act.

5.3 If the officer in charge of an investigation becomes aware as a result of developments in the case that material previously examined but not retained (because it was not thought to be relevant) may now be relevant to the investigation, they should, wherever practicable, take steps to obtain it or ensure that it is retained for further inspection or for production in court if required.

5.4 The duty to retain material includes in particular the duty to retain material falling into the following categories:

- Records which are derived from tapes or recordings of telephone messages (for example, 999 calls) containing descriptions of an alleged offence or offender;
- Any incident logs relating to the allegation;
- Contemporaneous records of the incident, such as:
  - crime reports and crime report forms;
  - an investigation log;
  - any record or note made by an investigator (including police notebook entries and other handwritten notes) on which they later make a statement or which relates to contact with suspects, victims or witnesses;
  - an account of an incident or information relevant to an incident noted by an investigator in manuscript or electronically;
  - records of actions carried out by officers (such as house-to-house interviews, CCTV or forensic enquiries) noted by a police officer in manuscript or electronically;
  - CCTV footage, or other imagery, of the incident in action;
- The defendant's custody record or voluntary attendance record;
- Any previous accounts made by a complainant or any other witnesses;
- Interview records (written records, or audio or video tapes, of interviews with actual or potential witnesses or suspects);
- Any material casting doubt on the reliability of a witness e.g. relevant previous convictions and relevant cautions of any prosecution witnesses and any co accused;
- Final versions of witness statements (and draft versions where their content differs from the final version), including any exhibits mentioned (unless these have been returned to their owner on the understanding that they will be produced in court if required);
- Material relating to other suspects in the investigation;
- Communications between the police and experts such as forensic scientists, reports of work carried out by experts, and schedules of scientific material prepared by the expert for the investigator, for the purposes of criminal proceedings;
- Records of the first description of a suspect by each potential witness who purports to identify or describe the suspect, whether or not the description differs from that of subsequent descriptions by that or other witnesses.

5.5 The duty to retain material, where it may be relevant to the investigation, also includes in particular the duty to retain any material which may satisfy the test for prosecution disclosure in the Act, such as:

- information provided by an accused person which indicates an explanation for the offence with which they have been charged;
- any material casting doubt on the reliability of a confession;
- any material casting doubt on the reliability of a prosecution witness.

5.6 The duty to retain material falling into these categories does not extend to items which are purely ancillary to such material and possess no independent significance (for example, duplicate copies of records or reports).

(b) Length of time for which material is to be retained

5.7 All material which may be relevant to the investigation must be retained until a decision is taken whether to institute proceedings against a person for an offence.

5.8 If a criminal investigation results in proceedings being instituted, all material which may be relevant must be retained at least until the accused is acquitted or convicted or the prosecutor decides not to proceed with the case.

5.9 Where the accused is convicted, all material which may be relevant must be retained at least until:

- the convicted person is released from custody, or discharged from hospital, in cases where the court imposes a custodial sentence or a hospital order;
- six months from the date of conviction, in all other cases.

If the court imposes a custodial sentence or hospital order and the convicted person is released from custody or discharged from hospital earlier than six months from the date of conviction, all material which may be relevant must be retained at least until six months from the date of conviction.

5.10 If an appeal against conviction is in progress when the release or discharge occurs, or at the end of the period of six months specified in paragraph 5.9, all material which may be relevant must be retained until the appeal is determined. Similarly, if the Criminal Cases Review Commission is considering an application at that point in time, all material which may be relevant must be retained at least until the Commission decides not to refer the case to the Court.

6. Preparation of material for prosecutor

(a) Schedules of unused material

6.1 The officer in charge of the investigation, the disclosure officer or an investigator may seek advice from the prosecutor about whether any particular item of material may be relevant to the investigation.

6.2 Material which may be relevant to an investigation, which has been retained in accordance with this code, and which the disclosure officer believes will not form part of the prosecution case, must be listed on the appropriate schedule of unused material.

6.3 The disclosure officer must ensure that the appropriate schedule of unused material is prepared in the following circumstances:

- the accused is charged with an offence which is triable only on indictment;
- the accused is charged with an offence which is triable either way, and it is considered that the case is likely to be tried on indictment;
- the accused is charged with an either-way offence that is likely to remain in the magistrates' court, and it is considered that they are likely to plead not guilty;
- the accused is charged with a summary offence and it is considered that they are likely to plead not guilty.

6.4 Where, however, the accused is charged with a summary offence or an either-way offence, and it is considered that they are likely to plead guilty (e.g. because they have admitted the offence), a schedule is not required unless a not guilty plea is subsequently entered or indicated.

6.5 Irrespective of the anticipated plea, the Common Law test for disclosure requires material to be disclosed if there is material known to the disclosure officer that might assist the defence with the early preparation of their case or at a bail hearing (for example, a key prosecution witness has relevant previous convictions or a witness has withdrawn their statement). A note must be made on the case summary for the prosecutor of any such material, which must be revealed to the prosecutor who will review it and consider whether it is disclosable. Where there is no such material, a certificate to that effect must be completed.

6.6 Material in the following list (which where it exists will have been retained or recorded in accordance with paragraph 5.4) is likely to include information which meets the test for prosecution disclosure. This material must therefore, subject to the exception at 6.4 above, be scheduled and provided to the prosecutor. In reviewing this material, disclosure officers and prosecutors are to start with a presumption that it is likely to meet the disclosure test, although the material will need to be carefully considered and the disclosure test applied before a decision is made:

a) records which are derived from tapes or recordings of telephone messages (for example 999 calls) containing descriptions of an alleged offence or offender;
b) any incident logs relating to the allegation;
c) contemporaneous records of the incident, such as:
   - crime reports and crime report forms;
   - an investigation log;
   - any record or note made by an investigator (including police notebook entries and other handwritten notes) on which they later make a statement or which relates to contact with suspects, victims or witnesses;
   - an account of an incident or information relevant to an incident noted by an investigator in manuscript or electronically;
   - records of actions carried out by officers (such as house-to-house interviews, CCTV or forensic enquiries) noted by a police officer in manuscript or electronically;
   - CCTV footage, or other imagery, of the incident in action;
d) the defendant's custody record or voluntary attendance record;
e) any previous accounts made by a complainant or by any other witnesses;
f) interview records (written records, or audio or video tapes, of interviews with actual or potential witnesses or suspects);
g) any material casting doubt on the reliability of a witness e. g. relevant previous convictions and relevant cautions of any prosecution witnesses and any co-accused.

This material must be listed on the schedule by the disclosure officer in addition to all other material which may be relevant to an investigation; it is likely that some of this material will need to be redacted (see 6.12).

(b) Way in which material is to be listed on schedule

6.7 Material which the disclosure officer does not believe is sensitive must be listed on a schedule of non-sensitive material, which must include a statement that the disclosure officer does not believe the material is sensitive. Where there is sensitive unused material, see para 6.13 below.

6.8 The disclosure officer should ensure, subject to paras 6.10-6.11 below, that each item of material is listed separately on the schedule, and is numbered consecutively (which may include numbering by volume and sub-volume).

6.9 The description of each item should make clear the nature of the item and should contain sufficient detail to enable the prosecutor to decide whether they need to inspect the material before deciding whether or not it should be disclosed.

6.10 In some investigations it may be disproportionate to list each item of material separately. These may be listed in a block or blocks and described by quantity and generic title.

6.11 Even if some material is listed in a block, the disclosure officer must ensure that any items among that material which might satisfy the test for prosecution disclosure are listed and described individually.

(c) Redaction of sensitive material

6.12 The disclosure officer should redact any sensitive information contained in material that is likely to satisfy the test for prosecution disclosure. The disclosure officer should also redact any personal, confidential information in material that is to be disclosed. Such could include a person's date of birth, address, email address and phone number.

6.13 Any material which is believed to be sensitive must be listed on a schedule of sensitive material. If there is no sensitive material, the disclosure officer must record this fact on a schedule of sensitive material, or otherwise so indicate.

6.14 Subject to paragraph 6.15 below, the disclosure officer must list on a sensitive schedule any material the disclosure of which they believe would give rise to a real risk of serious prejudice to an important public interest, and the reason for that belief. The schedule must include a statement that the disclosure officer believes the material is sensitive. Depending on the circumstances, examples of such material may include the following, among others:

- material relating to national security;
- material received from the intelligence and security agencies;
- material relating to intelligence from foreign sources which reveals sensitive intelligence gathering methods;
- material given in confidence;
- material relating to the identity or activities of informants, or undercover police officers, or witnesses, or other persons supplying information to the police who may be in danger if their identities are revealed;
- material revealing the location of any premises or other place used for police surveillance, or the identity of any person allowing a police officer to use them for surveillance;
- material revealing, either directly or indirectly, techniques and methods relied upon by a police officer in the course of a criminal investigation, for example covert surveillance techniques, or other methods of detecting crime;
- material whose disclosure might facilitate the commission of other offences or hinder the prevention and detection of crime;
- material upon the strength of which search warrants were obtained;
- material containing details of persons taking part in identification parades;
- material supplied to an investigator during a criminal investigation which has been generated by an official of a body concerned with the regulation or supervision of bodies corporate or of persons engaged in financial activities, or which has been generated by a person retained by such a body;
- material supplied to an investigator during a criminal investigation which relates to a child or young person and which has been generated by a local authority social services department, an Area Child Protection Committee or other party contacted by an investigator during the investigation;
- material relating to the private life of a witness.

6.15 In exceptional circumstances, where an investigator considers that material is so sensitive that its revelation to the prosecutor by means of an entry on the sensitive schedule is inappropriate, the existence of the material must be revealed to the prosecutor separately. This will apply only where compromising the material would be likely to lead directly to the loss of life, or directly threaten national security.

6.16 In such circumstances, the responsibility for informing the prosecutor lies with the investigator who knows the detail of the sensitive material. The investigator should act as soon as is reasonably practicable after the file containing the prosecution case is sent to the prosecutor. The investigator must also ensure that the prosecutor is able to inspect the material so that they can assess whether it is disclosable and, if so, whether it needs to be brought before a court for a ruling on disclosure.

7. Revelation of material to prosecutor

7.1 Where cases have been charged on the Full Code Test and it is anticipated that the defendant will plead not guilty, the disclosure officer should provide the schedules concerning unused material to the prosecutor at the same time as submitting the case file.

7.2 In all other cases the disclosure officer must provide the schedules as soon as possible after a not guilty plea has been either indicated or entered.

7.3 The disclosure officer should draw the attention of the prosecutor to any material an investigator has retained (including material to which paragraph 6.15 applies) which it is considered may satisfy the test for prosecution disclosure in the Act, explaining the reasons for coming to that view.

7.4 The disclosure officer must give the prosecutor a copy of any such material (unless it has already been supplied as part of the file containing the material for the prosecution case), together with any material which falls into the following categories:

- information provided by an accused person which indicates an explanation for the offence with which they has been charged;
- any material casting doubt on the reliability of a confession;
- any material casting doubt on the reliability of a prosecution witness.

7.5 The disclosure officer must give the prosecutor a copy of any material which has been scheduled in accordance with paragraph 6.6, indicating whether it is, or is not, considered to satisfy the test for prosecution disclosure, and in either case explaining the reasons for coming to that view.

7.6 The disclosure officer must comply with a request from the prosecutor to be allowed to inspect material which has not already been copied to them. If the prosecutor asks to be provided with a copy of such material it should be provided, except where (having consulted the officer in charge of the investigation) the disclosure officer believes that the material is too sensitive to be copied and can only be inspected.

7.7 If material consists of information which is recorded other than in writing, whether it should be given to the prosecutor in its original form as a whole, or by way of relevant extracts recorded in the same form, or in the form of a transcript, is a matter for agreement between the disclosure officer and the prosecutor.

8. Subsequent action by disclosure officer

8.1 At the time when a schedule of non-sensitive material is prepared, the disclosure officer may not know exactly what material will form the case against the accused. In addition, the prosecutor may not have given advice about the likely relevance of particular items of material. Once these matters have been determined, the disclosure officer must give the prosecutor, where necessary, an amended schedule listing any additional material:

- which may be relevant to the investigation,
- which does not form part of the case against the accused,
- which is not already listed on the schedule, and
- which they believe is not sensitive, unless they are informed in writing by the prosecutor that the prosecutor intends to disclose the material to the defence.

8.2 Section 7A of the Act imposes a continuing duty on the prosecutor, for the duration of criminal proceedings against the accused, to disclose material which satisfies the test for disclosure (subject to public interest considerations). To enable this to be done, any new material coming to light should be treated in the same way as the earlier material.

8.3 In particular, after a defence statement has been given, or details of the issues in dispute have been recorded on the Preparation for Effective Trial form or the Plea and Trial Preparation Hearing form, the disclosure officer must look again at the material which has been retained and must draw the attention of the prosecutor to any material which might reasonably be considered capable of undermining the case for the prosecution against the accused or of assisting the case for the accused; and must reveal it to them in accordance with paragraphs 7.4 and 7.5 above.

9. Certification by disclosure officer

9.1 The disclosure officer must certify to the prosecutor that, to the best of their knowledge and belief, all relevant material which has been retained and made available to them has been revealed to the prosecutor in accordance with this code. They must sign and date the disclosure officer certificate. It will be necessary to certify not only at the time when the schedule and accompanying material is submitted to the prosecutor, and when relevant material which has been retained is reconsidered after the accused has given a defence statement, but also whenever a schedule is otherwise given or material is otherwise revealed to the prosecutor.

10. Disclosure of material to accused

10.1 A prosecutor must review the schedules of unused material provided by the disclosure officer and endorse the schedule to indicate whether each item of material does or does not meet the test for disclosure. If any of the material does meet the test for disclosure, the prosecutor should record the reason for this decision.

10.2 A prosecutor must additionally review any material provided by the disclosure officer under paragraph 6.6 (material likely to meet the test for disclosure). The prosecutor must endorse the schedule to indicate whether the material does or does not meet the test for disclosure, and must record the reason for the decision.

10.3 When a prosecutor provides material to the defence in accordance with the obligation under section 3 or section 7A of the Criminal Procedure and Investigations Act 1996, the prosecutor must at the same time provide the schedule of non-sensitive material to the defence.

10.4 Other than early disclosure under Common Law, in the magistrates' court the schedule (and any relevant unused material to be disclosed under it) must be disclosed to the accused either:

- at the hearing where a not guilty plea is entered, or
- as soon as possible following a formal indication from the accused or representative that a not guilty plea will be entered at the hearing.

In the Crown Court, initial disclosure should if possible be served prior to the Plea and Trial Preparation Hearing (PTPH). Where this has not been done, it should be served as soon as possible after that hearing and in accordance with any direction made by the Court.

10.5 If material has been copied to the prosecutor, and it is to be disclosed, whether it is disclosed by the prosecutor or the disclosure officer is a matter of agreement between the two of them.

10.6 If material has not already been copied to the prosecutor, and they request its disclosure to the accused on the ground that:

- it satisfies the test for prosecution disclosure, or
- the court has ordered its disclosure after considering an application from the accused,

the disclosure officer must disclose it to the accused.

10.7 The disclosure officer must disclose material to the accused either by giving them a copy or by allowing them to inspect it. If the accused person asks for a copy of any material which they have been allowed to inspect, the disclosure officer must supply it, unless in the opinion of the disclosure officer that is either not practicable (for example because the material consists of an object which cannot be copied, or because the volume of material is so great), or not desirable (for example because the material is a statement by a child witness in relation to a sexual offence).

10.8 If material which the accused has been allowed to inspect consists of information which is recorded other than in writing, whether it should be given to the accused in its original form or in the form of a transcript is a matter for the discretion of the disclosure officer. If the material is transcribed, the disclosure officer must ensure that the transcript is certified to the accused as a true record of the material which has been transcribed.

10.9 If a court concludes that an item of sensitive material satisfies the prosecution disclosure test and that the interests of the defence outweigh the public interest in withholding disclosure, it will be necessary to disclose the material if the case is to proceed. This does not mean that sensitive documents must always be disclosed in their original form: for example, the court may agree that sensitive details still requiring protection should be blocked out, or that documents may be summarised, or that the prosecutor may make an admission about the substance of the material under section 10 of the Criminal Justice Act 1967.

Criminal Procedure Rules 2025

(SI 2025, No. 909)

PART 16 WRITTEN WITNESS STATEMENTS

16.1. When this Part applies

This Part applies where a party wants to introduce a written witness statement in evidence under section 9 of the Criminal Justice Act 1967.

[Note. Under section 9 of the Criminal Justice Act 1967, if the conditions specified in that section are met the written statement of a witness is admissible in evidence to the same extent as if that witness gave evidence in person.]

16.2. Content of written witness statement

The statement must contain—

(a) at the beginning—
  (i) the witness' name, and
  (ii) the witness' age, if under 18;
(b) a declaration by the witness that—
  (i) it is true to the best of the witness' knowledge and belief, and
  (ii) the witness knows that if it is introduced in evidence, then it would be an offence wilfully to have stated in it anything that the witness knew to be false or did not believe to be true;
(c) if the witness cannot read the statement, a signed declaration by someone else that that person read it to the witness; and
(d) the witness' signature.

16.3. Reference to exhibit

Where the statement refers to a document or object as an exhibit, it must identify that document or object clearly.

[Note. See section 9(7) of the Criminal Justice Act 1967.]

16.4. Written witness statement in evidence

(1) A party who wants to introduce in evidence a written witness statement must—
(a) before the hearing at which that party wants to introduce it, serve a copy of the statement on—
  (i) the court officer, and
  (ii) each other party; and
(b) at or before that hearing, serve on the court officer the statement or an authenticated copy.

(2) If that party relies on only part of the statement, that party must mark the copy in such a way as to make that clear.

(3) A prosecutor must serve on a defendant, with the copy of the statement, a notice—
(a) of the right to object to the introduction of the statement in evidence instead of the witness giving evidence in person;
(b) of the time limit for objecting under this rule; and
(c) that if the defendant does not object in time, the court—
  (i) can nonetheless require the witness to give evidence in person, but
  (ii) may decide not to do so.

(4) A party served with a written witness statement who objects to its introduction in evidence must—

(a) serve notice of the objection on—
(i) the party who served it, and
(ii) the court officer; and
(b) serve the notice of objection not more than 7 business days after service of the statement unless—
(i) the court extends that time limit, before or after the statement was served,
(ii) rule 24.8 (Written guilty plea: special rules) applies, in which case the time limit is the later of 7 business days after service of the statement or 5 business days before the hearing date, or
(iii) rule 24.9 (Single justice procedure: special rules) applies, in which case the time limit is 15 business days after service of the statement.

(5) The court may exercise its power to require the witness to give evidence in person—
(a) on application by any party; or
(b) on its own initiative.

(6) A party entitled to receive a copy of a statement may waive that entitlement by so informing—
(a) the party who would have served it; and
(b) the court.

[Note. Under section 9(2A) of the Criminal Justice Act 1967, Criminal Procedure Rules may prescribe the period within which a party served with a written witness statement must object to its introduction in evidence, subject to a minimum period of 7 days from its service.

Under section 133 of the Criminal Justice Act 2003, where a statement in a document is admissible as evidence in criminal proceedings, the statement may be proved by producing either (a) the document, or (b) (whether or not the document exists) a copy of the document or of the material part of it, authenticated in whatever way the court may approve. By section 134 of the 2003 Act, 'document' means anything in which information of any description is recorded.]

PART 17 WITNESS SUMMONSES, WARRANTS AND ORDERS

17.1. When this Part applies

This Part applies in magistrates' courts and in the Crown Court where—
(a) a party wants the court to issue a witness summons, warrant or order under—
(i) section 97 of the Magistrates' Courts Act 1980,
(ii) paragraph 4 of Schedule 3 to the Crime and Disorder Act 1998,
(iii) section 2 or section 4 of the Criminal Procedure (Attendance of Witnesses) Act 1965, or
(iv) section 7 of the Bankers' Books Evidence Act 1879;
(b) the court considers the issue of such a summons, warrant or order on its own initiative as if a party had applied; or
(c) one of those listed in rule 17.7 wants the court to withdraw such a summons, warrant or order.

[Note. A magistrates' court may require the attendance of a witness to give evidence or to produce in evidence a document or thing by a summons, or in some circumstances a warrant for the witness' arrest, under section 97 of the Magistrates' Courts Act 1980 or under paragraph 4 of Schedule 3 to the Crime and Disorder Act 1998. The Crown Court may do so under section 2, 2D or 4 of the Criminal Procedure (Attendance of Witnesses) Act 1965.

Under section 97(4) of the 1980 Act, if any person attending or brought before a magistrates' court refuses without just excuse to be sworn or give evidence, or to produce any document or thing required, the court may (i) commit that person to custody for a maximum of one month, or until that person gives evidence or produces the document or thing, if earlier, or (ii) impose a fine not exceeding £2,500, or (iii) both.

Under section 3 of the 1965 Act, any person who without just excuse disobeys a witness summons requiring that person to attend before any court, or disobeys a requirement made by any court under section 2A of that Act (power to require advance production of document or thing), shall be guilty of contempt of that court and may be punished summarily as if that contempt had been committed in the face of the court. No person shall be liable to committal to custody for a period exceeding three months for such disobedience.

Under paragraph 4(7) of Schedule 3 to the 1998 Act, if any person attending or brought before a magistrates' court refuses without just excuse to have evidence taken as a deposition, or to produce a document or other exhibit required, the potential penalties are the same as under section 97(4) of the 1980 Act.

Under section 227(2) of the Sentencing Act 2020, the committal to custody of a person aged under 21 is generally prohibited but section 108 of the Powers of Criminal Courts (Sentencing) Act 2000 allows the court to commit to detention a person aged at least 18 but under 21 if it is of the opinion that no other method of dealing with that person is appropriate.

A magistrates' court or the Crown Court may order the production in evidence of a copy of an entry in a banker's book without the attendance of an officer of the bank, under sections 6 and 7 of the Bankers' Books Evidence Act 1879. Under section 9(2) of the 1879 Act, expressions in the Act relating to 'bankers' books' include ledgers, day books, cash books, account books and other records used in the ordinary business of the bank, whether those records are in written form or are kept on microfilm, magnetic tape or any other form of mechanical or electronic data retrieval mechanism.

See Part 3 for the court's general powers to consider an application and to give directions.]

17.2. Issue etc. of summons, warrant or order

(1) The court may issue or withdraw a witness summons, warrant or order—

(a) at a hearing, which must be in private unless the court otherwise directs; or

(b) without a hearing.

(2) A summons or warrant issued under section 97 of the Magistrates' Courts Act 1980 or under section 2 or 4 of the Criminal Procedure (Attendance of Witnesses) Act 1965 must specify—

(a) the time and place at which the witness must attend the court to give evidence; and

(b) any document or thing that the witness then must produce.

(3) A warrant issued under section 97 of the 1980 Act may specify a period, not exceeding one month, for which the witness may be committed to custody for refusal without just excuse—

(a) to give evidence; or

(b) to produce any document or thing required.

(4) A summons or warrant issued under paragraph 4 of Schedule 3 to the Crime and Disorder Act 1998—

(a) must specify—

(i) the time and place at which the witness must attend the court to have evidence taken as a deposition, and

(ii) any document or other exhibit that the witness then must produce; and

(b) may specify a period, not exceeding one month, for which the witness may be committed to custody for refusal without just excuse—

(i) to have evidence taken as a deposition, or

(ii) to produce any such document or other exhibit.

[Note. If rule 17.5 applies, a person served with an application for a witness summons will have an opportunity to make representations about whether there should be a hearing of that application before the witness summons is issued.

Under section 97(4) of the Magistrates' Courts Act 1980, a warrant issued under section 97(2) or (3) may specify a maximum period of potential committal to custody, up to one month, for refusal without just excuse to be sworn or give evidence, or to produce any document or thing required.

Under paragraph 4(6) of Schedule 3 to the Crime and Disorder Act 1998, the time specified for attendance in a summons or warrant issued under that paragraph must be such as to allow a deposition to be taken before time expires for the service of prosecution evidence in the Crown Court. Under paragraph 4(7), the summons or warrant may specify a maximum period of potential committal to custody, up to one month, for refusal without just excuse to have evidence taken as a deposition, or to produce a document or other exhibit required.]

17.3. Application for summons, warrant or order: general rules

(1) A party who wants the court to issue a witness summons, warrant or order must apply as soon as practicable after becoming aware of the grounds for doing so.

(2) A party applying for a witness summons or order must—

(a) identify the proposed witness;

(b) explain—

(i) what evidence the proposed witness can give or produce,

(ii) why it is likely to be material evidence, and

(iii) why it would be in the interests of justice to issue a summons or warrant as appropriate; and

(c) in an application by the prosecutor for a summons or warrant to be issued under paragraph 4 of Schedule 3 to the Crime and Disorder Act 1998—

(i) specify the date by which the prosecutor must serve the prosecution evidence in the Crown Court, and

(ii) if applicable, describe such steps as have been taken to apply for an extension or further extension of that period.

(3) A party applying for an order to be allowed to inspect and copy an entry in bank records must—

(a) identify the entry;

(b) explain the purpose for which the entry is required; and

(c) propose—

(i) the terms of the order, and

(ii) the period within which the order should take effect, if 3 days from the date of service of the order would not be appropriate.

(4) The application may be made orally unless—

(a) paragraph (3) of this rule applies (bank records);

(b) rule 17.5 applies (Application for summons to produce a document, etc.: special rules); or

(c) the court otherwise directs.

(5) The applicant must—

(a) serve any order made on the witness to whom, or the bank to which, it is directed; and

(b) notify the witness of the right to take legal advice.

[Note. The court may issue a warrant for a witness' arrest if that witness fails to obey a witness summons: see section 97(3) of the Magistrates' Courts Act 1980, paragraph 4(5) of Schedule 3 to the Crime and Disorder Act 1998 and section 4 of the Criminal Procedure (Attendance of Witnesses) Act 1965. Before a magistrates' court may issue a warrant under section 97(3) of the 1980 Act, the witness must first be paid or offered a reasonable amount for costs and expenses.]

17.4. Written application: form and service

(1) An application in writing under rule 17.3 must be in the form issued under the Practice Direction, containing the same declaration of truth as a witness statement.

(2) The party applying must serve the application—

(a) in every case, on the court officer and as directed by the court; and

(b) as required by rule 17.5, if that rule applies.

[Note. Declarations of truth in witness statements are required by section 9 of the Criminal Justice Act 1967. Section 89 of the 1967 Act makes it an offence to make a written statement under section 9 of that Act which the person making it knows to be false or does not believe to be true.]

17.5. Application for summons to produce a document, etc.: special rules

(1) This rule applies to an application under rule 17.3 for a witness summons requiring the proposed witness—

- (a) to produce in evidence a document or thing; or
- (b) to give evidence about information apparently held in confidence,

that relates to another person.

(2) The application must be in writing in the form required by rule 17.4.

(3) The party applying must serve the application—

- (a) on the proposed witness, unless the court otherwise directs; and
- (b) on one or more of the following, if the court so directs—
  - (i) a person to whom the proposed evidence relates, and
  - (ii) another party.

(4) The court must not issue a witness summons where this rule applies unless—

- (a) everyone served with the application has had at least 10 business days in which to make representations, including representations about whether there should be a hearing of the application before the summons is issued; and
- (b) the court is satisfied that it has been able to take adequate account of the duties and rights, including rights of confidentiality, of the proposed witness and of any person to whom the proposed evidence relates.

[Note. Under section 2A of the Criminal Procedure (Attendance of Witnesses) Act 1965, a witness summons to produce a document or thing issued by the Crown Court may require the witness to produce it for inspection by the applicant before producing it in evidence.]

17.6. Application for summons to produce a document, etc.: court's assessment of relevance and confidentiality

(1) This rule applies where a person served with an application for a witness summons requiring the proposed witness to produce in evidence a document or thing objects to its production on the ground that—

- (a) it is not likely to be material evidence; or
- (b) even if it is likely to be material evidence, the duties or rights, including rights of confidentiality, of the proposed witness or of any person to whom the document or thing relates, outweigh the reasons for issuing a summons.

(2) The court may require the proposed witness to make the document or thing available for the objection to be assessed.

(3) The court may invite—

- (a) the proposed witness or any representative of the proposed witness; or
- (b) a person to whom the document or thing relates or any representative of such a person,

to help the court assess the objection.

17.7. Application to withdraw a summons, warrant or order

(1) The court may withdraw a witness summons, warrant or order if one of the following applies for it to be withdrawn—

- (a) the party who applied for it, on the ground that it no longer is needed;
- (b) the witness, on the grounds that the court received no representations by the witness before the summons, warrant or order was issued and, in the Crown Court, the witness had had no notice of any application for a summons, and—
  - (i) the witness cannot give or produce evidence likely to be material evidence, or
  - (ii) even if the witness could do so, the witness' duties or rights, including rights of confidentiality, or those of any person to whom the evidence relates, outweigh the reasons for the issue of the summons, warrant or order;

(c) any person to whom the proposed evidence relates, on the grounds that the court received no representations by that person before the summons, warrant or order was issued and—
  (i) that evidence is not likely to be material evidence, or
  (ii) even if it is, that person's duties or rights, including rights of confidentiality, or those of the witness, outweigh the reasons for the issue of the summons, warrant or order, or
(d) the bank to which the order is directed, on the ground that a requirement of the Bankers' Books Evidence Act 1879 is not met.

(2) A person applying under the rule must—
(a) apply in writing as soon as practicable after becoming aware of the grounds for doing so, explaining why the court should withdraw the summons, warrant or order; and
(b) serve the application on the court officer and as appropriate on—
  (i) the witness or bank,
  (ii) the party (if any) who applied for the summons, warrant or order, and
  (iii) any other person who was served with the application (if any) for the summons, warrant or order.

(3) Rule 17.6 applies to an application under this rule that concerns a document or thing to be produced by a witness in evidence.

[Note. See sections 2B, 2C and 2E of the Criminal Procedure (Attendance of Witnesses) Act 1965 for the Crown Court's powers to withdraw a witness summons, including the power to order costs.]

17.8. Taking a deposition in a magistrates' court

(1) This rule applies where a witness attends or is brought before a magistrates' court on a summons or warrant issued under paragraph 4 of Schedule 3 to the Crime and Disorder Act 1998—
(a) to have evidence taken as a deposition; or
(b) to produce a document or other exhibit.

(2) The general rule is that the hearing must be in public but the court may exercise any power it has to—
(a) impose a restriction on reporting what takes place, or public access;
(b) withhold information from the public during the hearing; or
(c) order a hearing in private.

(3) The court must, in this sequence—
(a) explain, in terms the witness can understand (with help, if necessary), that—
  (i) the court is required by law to take evidence for use by the prosecutor in the Crown Court,
  (ii) any document or other exhibit that the witness was required to produce by the summons or warrant to attend must be produced to the court unless there is a just excuse for not doing so,
  (iii) the prosecutor will ask questions that the witness must answer unless there is a just excuse for not doing so,
  (iv) the witness' evidence will be recorded in writing in a document called a 'deposition' which will be read to the witness and which the witness will be asked to sign, and
  (v) if the witness refuses to produce a required document or other exhibit, or refuses to answer a question, without just excuse, then the court may commit the witness to custody and may impose a fine;
(b) take possession of any document or other exhibit that the witness was required to produce by the summons or warrant to attend;
(c) require the prosecutor to question the witness;
(d) allow any legal representative of the witness who is present to question the witness;

(e) as a general rule, allow a legal representative of the defendant, if present, to question the witness but only to the extent reasonably required to clarify the witness' answer to a question asked by the prosecutor;
(f) cause the witness' evidence to be recorded in writing in a deposition;
(g) in the event of refusal by the witness to produce a required document or other exhibit, or to answer a question—
  (i) ask the witness to explain why,
  (ii) consider the explanation,
  (iii) if satisfied that there is a just excuse for refusal, cause a record of that conclusion to be included in the deposition,
  (iv) if not so satisfied and the refusal is maintained, deal with the refusal at the end of the hearing; and
(h) certify the accuracy of the deposition by—
  (i) inviting the witness to authenticate it, by any written or electronic means, and
  (ii) whether the witness agrees to do so or not, authenticating the deposition by any such means itself.

(4) A justices' legal adviser must assist the court by preparing the deposition, unless the court—
(a) includes a District Judge (Magistrates' Courts); and
(b) otherwise directs.

(5) The magistrates' court officer must, as soon as practicable, make available to the Crown Court and serve on the prosecutor—
(a) a copy of the deposition;
(b) a copy of any document produced by the witness; and
(c) a description of any object produced by the witness.

[Note. For the functions of a justices' legal adviser, see sections 28 and 29 of the Courts Act 2003. See also rule 2.12 (Duties of justices' legal adviser).]

17.9. Court's power to vary requirements under this Part

(1) The court may—
(a) shorten or extend (even after it has expired) a time limit under this Part; and
(b) where a rule or direction requires an application under this Part to be in writing, allow that application to be made orally instead.

(2) Someone who wants the court to allow an application to be made orally under paragraph (1)(b) of this rule must—
(a) give as much notice as the urgency of his application permits to those on whom the application otherwise should be served; and
(b) in doing so explain the reasons for the application and for wanting the court to consider it orally.

PART 18 MEASURES TO HELP A WITNESS OR DEFENDANT TO GIVE EVIDENCE OR OTHERWISE PARTICIPATE

GENERAL RULES

18.1. When this Part applies

This Part applies—
(a) where the court can give a direction (a 'special measures direction'), under section 19 of the Youth Justice and Criminal Evidence Act 1999, on an application or on its own initiative, for any of the following measures—

- (i) preventing a witness from seeing the defendant (section 23 of the 1999 Act),
- (ii) allowing a witness to give evidence by live link (section 24 of the 1999 Act),
- (iii) hearing a witness' evidence in private (section 25 of the 1999 Act),
- (iv) dispensing with the wearing of wigs and gowns (section 26 of the 1999 Act),
- (v) admitting video recorded evidence (sections 27 and 28 of the 1999 Act),
- (vi) questioning a witness through an intermediary (section 29 of the 1999 Act),
- (vii) using a device to help a witness communicate (section 30 of the 1999 Act);

(b) where the court can vary or discharge such a direction, under section 20 of the 1999 Act;

(c) where the court can—
- (i) make a witness anonymity order, under section 86 of the Coroners and Justice Act 2009, or
- (ii) vary or discharge such an order, under section 91, 92 or 93 of the 2009 Act;

(d) where the court can—
- (i) appoint an intermediary to facilitate a defendant's effective participation in that defendant's trial, when the defendant gives evidence or at any other time, or
- (ii) vary or discharge such an appointment; and

(e) where the court can exercise any other power it has to give, make, vary, rescind, discharge or revoke a direction for a measure to help a witness to give evidence or to help a defendant to participate in that defendant's trial.

[Note. At the end of this Part is a summary of the circumstances in which a witness or defendant may be eligible for the assistance of one of the measures to which this Part applies.]

18.2. Meaning of 'witness' and 'live link'

In this Part, —

(a) 'witness' means anyone (other than a defendant) for whose benefit an application, direction or order is made; and

(b) 'live link', in relation to a witness, means a live television link or other arrangement by which a witness who is absent from the courtroom or other place where the proceedings are being held is able to see and hear a person there and to be seen and heard by—
- (i) the judge or justices (or both) and the jury (if there is one),
- (ii) legal representatives acting in the proceedings, and
- (iii) any interpreter or other person appointed (in pursuance of the direction or otherwise) to assist the witness.

[Note. See section 24(8) of the Youth Justice and Criminal Evidence Act 1999.]

18.3. Meaning of 'intermediary' and 'intermediary's report'

In this Part, —

(a) 'intermediary' means a person who is—
- (i) approved by the court for the purposes of section 29 of the Youth Justice and Criminal Evidence Act 1999 (Examination of witness through intermediary),
- (ii) asked to assess a defendant's communication needs, or
- (iii) appointed by the court to facilitate a defendant's effective participation in the trial, when the defendant gives evidence or at any other time, where otherwise that defendant's communication needs would impede such participation; and

(b) a reference to 'an intermediary's report' means a report by such a person which complies with rule 18.24.

18.4. Making an application for a direction or order

A party who wants the court to exercise its power to give or make a direction or order must—

(a) apply in writing as soon as reasonably practicable, and in any event not more than—
- (i) 20 business days after the defendant pleads not guilty, in a magistrates' court, or
- (ii) 10 business days after the defendant pleads not guilty, in the Crown Court; and

(b) serve the application on—
- (i) the court officer, and
- (ii) each other party.

[Note. See also rule 18.10 (Content of application for a special measures direction), rule 18.15 (Content and conduct of application for a witness anonymity order) and rule 18.19 (Appointment of intermediary to facilitate a defendant's participation).]

18.5. Decisions and reasons

(1) A party who wants to introduce the evidence of a witness who is the subject of an application, direction or order must—

(a) inform the witness of the court's decision as soon as reasonably practicable; and

(b) explain to the witness the arrangements that as a result will be made for him or her to give evidence.

(2) The court must—

(a) promptly determine an application; and

(b) allow a party sufficient time to comply with the requirements of—

(i) paragraph (1), and

(ii) the code of practice issued under section 32 of the Domestic Violence, Crime and Victims Act 2004 or under section 2 of the Victims and Prisoners Act 2024.

(3) The court must announce, at a hearing in public before the witness gives evidence or the defendant's trial begins (as the case may be), the reasons for a decision—

(a) to give, make, vary or discharge a direction or order; or

(b) to refuse to do so.

[Note. See section 20(5) of the Youth Justice and Criminal Evidence Act 1999 and sections 51(8) and 52(7) of the Criminal Justice Act 2003.

Under section 32 of the Domestic Violence, Crime and Victims Act 2004, the Secretary of State for Justice must issue a code of practice as to the services to be provided by specified persons to a victim of criminal conduct. Section 2 of the Victims and Prisoners Act 2024 imposes a corresponding obligation. Under section 2(13) of the 2024 Act, until the first code of practice issued under section 2 is in operation, references in sections 5 to 12 and 32 of that Act to the 'victims' code' are references to the code of practice issued under section 32 of the 2004 Act for the time being in operation.]

18.6. Court's power to vary requirements under this Part

(1) The court may—

(a) shorten or extend (even after it has expired) a time limit under this Part; and

(b) allow an application or representations to be made in a different form to one issued under the Practice Direction, or to be made orally.

(2) A person who wants an extension of time must—

(a) apply when serving the application or representations for which it is needed; and

(b) explain the delay.

18.7. Custody of documents

Unless the court otherwise directs, the court officer may—

(a) keep a written application or representations; or

(b) arrange for the whole or any part to be kept by some other appropriate person, subject to any conditions that the court may impose.

SPECIAL MEASURES DIRECTIONS

18.8. Exercise of court's powers

(1) The court may decide whether to give, vary or discharge a special measures direction—

(a) at a hearing, in public or in private, or without a hearing; and

(b) in a party's absence, if that party—

(i) applied for the direction, variation or discharge, or

(ii) has had at least 10 business days in which to make representations.

(2) Where a direction provides for evidence to be admitted under section 28 of the Youth Justice and Criminal Evidence Act 1999 (Video recorded cross-examination or re-examination) the court must set a timetable that provides for—

(a) the date of any ground rules hearing under rule 3.9;
(b) the date on which the cross-examination and any re-examination will be recorded;
(c) the date by which any application under section 28(5) of the 1999 Act must be made for a direction for further cross-examination or re-examination;
(d) the date by which any application must be made to exclude as evidence any part of the recording; and
(e) the date by which any editing of the recording must be completed.

18.9. Special measures direction without application

(1) This rule applies where —

(a) a party notifies the court that a witness is eligible for assistance under section 16 or section 17 of the Youth Justice and Criminal Evidence Act 1999;
(b) the notice is given at—
    (i) a preparation for trial hearing in a magistrates' court, or
    (ii) a plea and trial preparation hearing in the Crown Court; and
(c) no other party opposes the giving of a special measures direction for the benefit of that witness.

(2) The court may exercise its power to give a special measures direction without requiring an application under rule 18.10.

(3) The party who gives the notice must—

(a) `provide any information that the court may need to assess—
    (i) the measure or measures likely to maximise so far as practicable the quality of the witness' evidence, and
    (ii) the witness' own views; and
(b) where a direction provides for video recorded evidence to be admitted under section 27 of the Youth Justice and Criminal Evidence Act 1999, as soon as reasonably practicable serve such evidence on—
    (i) the court officer, and
    (ii) each other party.

[Note. Under sections 21 and 22 of the Youth Justice and Criminal Evidence Act 1999, a 'child witness' is one who is under 18, and a 'qualifying witness' is one who was a child witness when interviewed.

Under those sections, the 'primary rule' requires the court to give a direction—

(a) for the evidence of a child witness or of a qualifying witness to be admitted—
    (i) by means of a video recording of an interview with the witness, in the place of examination-in-chief, and
    (ii) after that, by live link; or
(b) if one or both of those measures is not taken, for the witness while giving evidence to be screened from seeing the defendant.

The primary rule always applies unless—

(a) the witness does not want it to apply, and the court is satisfied that to omit a measure usually required by that rule would not diminish the quality of the witness' evidence; or
(b) the court is satisfied that to direct one of the measures usually required by that rule would not be likely to maximise, so far as practicable, the quality of the witness' evidence.]

18.10. Content of application for a special measures direction

An applicant for a special measures direction must—

(a) explain how the witness is eligible for assistance;
(b) explain why special measures would be likely to improve the quality of the witness' evidence;

(c) propose the measure or measures that in the applicant's opinion would be likely to maximise, so far as practicable, the quality of that evidence;
(d) report any views that the witness has expressed about—
(i) his or her eligibility for assistance,
(ii) the likelihood that special measures would improve the quality of his or her evidence, and
(iii) the measure or measures proposed by the applicant;
(e) in a case in which a child witness or a qualifying witness does not want the primary rule to apply, provide any information that the court may need to assess the witness' views;
(f) in a case in which the applicant proposes that the witness should give evidence by live link—
(i) identify someone to accompany the witness while the witness gives evidence,
(ii) name that person, if possible, and
(iii) explain why that person would be an appropriate companion for the witness, including the witness' own views;
(g) in a case in which the applicant proposes the admission of video recorded evidence, identify—
(i) the date and duration of the recording, and
(ii) which part the applicant wants the court to admit as evidence, if the applicant does not want the court to admit all of it;
(h) attach any other material on which the applicant relies; and
(i) if the applicant wants a hearing, ask for one, and explain why it is needed.

18.11. Application to vary or discharge a special measures direction

(1) A party who wants the court to vary or discharge a special measures direction must—
(a) apply in writing, as soon as reasonably practicable after becoming aware of the grounds for doing so; and
(b) serve the application on—
(i) the court officer, and
(ii) each other party.
(2) The applicant must—
(a) explain what material circumstances have changed since the direction was given (or last varied, if applicable);
(b) explain why the direction should be varied or discharged; and
(c) ask for a hearing, if the applicant wants one, and explain why it is needed.

[Note. Under section 20 of the Youth Justice and Criminal Evidence Act 1999, the court can vary or discharge a special measures direction—
(a) on application, if there has been a material change of circumstances; or
(b) on the court's own initiative.]

18.12. Application containing information withheld from another party

(1) This rule applies where—
(a) an applicant serves an application for a special measures direction, or for its variation or discharge; and
(b) the application includes information that the applicant thinks ought not be revealed to another party.
(2) The applicant must—
(a) omit that information from the part of the application that is served on that other party;
(b) mark the other part to show that, unless the court otherwise directs, it is only for the court; and

(c) in that other part, explain why the applicant has withheld that information from that other party.

(3) Any hearing of an application to which this rule applies—

(a) must be in private, unless the court otherwise directs; and

(b) if the court so directs, may be, wholly or in part, in the absence of a party from whom information has been withheld.

(4) At any hearing of an application to which this rule applies—

(a) the general rule is that the court must consider, in the following sequence—

(i) representations first by the applicant and then by each other party, in all the parties' presence, and then

(ii) further representations by the applicant, in the absence of a party from whom information has been withheld; but

(b) the court may direct other arrangements for the hearing.

[Note. See section 20 of the Youth Justice and Criminal Evidence Act 1999.]

18.13. Representations in response

(1) This rule applies where a party wants to make representations about—

(a) an application for a special measures direction;

(b) an application for the variation or discharge of such a direction; or

(c) a direction, variation or discharge that the court proposes on its own initiative.

(2) Such a party must—

(a) serve the representations on—

(i) the court officer, and

(ii) each other party;

(b) do so not more than 10 business days after, as applicable—

(i) service of the application, or

(ii) notice of the direction, variation or discharge that the court proposes; and

(c) ask for a hearing, if that party wants one, and explain why it is needed.

(3) Where representations include information that the person making them thinks ought not be revealed to another party, that person must—

(a) omit that information from the representations served on that other party;

(b) mark the information to show that, unless the court otherwise directs, it is only for the court; and

(c) with that information include an explanation of why it has been withheld from that other party.

(4) Representations against a special measures direction must explain, as appropriate—

(a) why the witness is not eligible for assistance;

(b) if the witness is eligible for assistance, why—

(i) no special measure would be likely to improve the quality of the witness' evidence,

(ii) the proposed measure or measures would not be likely to maximise, so far as practicable, the quality of the witness' evidence, or

(iii) the proposed measure or measures might tend to inhibit the effective testing of that evidence; and

(c) in a case in which the admission of video recorded evidence is proposed, why it would not be in the interests of justice for the recording, or part of it, to be admitted as evidence.

(5) Representations against the variation or discharge of a special measures direction must explain why it should not be varied or discharged.

[Note. Under sections 21 and 22 of the Youth Justice and Criminal Evidence Act 1999, where the witness is a child witness or a qualifying witness the special measures that the court usually must direct must be treated as likely to maximise, so far as practicable, the quality of the witness' evidence, irrespective of representations to the contrary.]

WITNESS ANONYMITY ORDERS

18.14. Exercise of court's powers

(1) The court may decide whether to make, vary or discharge a witness anonymity order—

(a) at a hearing (which must be in private, unless the court otherwise directs), or without a hearing (unless any party asks for one); and

(b) in the absence of a defendant.

(2) The court must not exercise its power to make, vary or discharge a witness anonymity order, or to refuse to do so—

(a) before or during the trial, unless each party has had an opportunity to make representations;

(b) on an appeal by the defendant to which applies Part 34 (Appeal to the Crown Court) or Part 39 (Appeal to the Court of Appeal about conviction or sentence), unless in each party's case—

(i) that party has had an opportunity to make representations, or

(ii) the appeal court is satisfied that it is not reasonably practicable to communicate with that party; or

(c) after the trial and any such appeal are over, unless in the case of each party and the witness—

(i) each has had an opportunity to make representations, or

(ii) the court is satisfied that it is not reasonably practicable to communicate with that party or witness.

18.15. Content and conduct of application for a witness anonymity order

(1) An applicant for a witness anonymity order must—

(a) include in the application nothing that might reveal the witness' identity;

(b) describe the measures proposed by the applicant;

(c) explain how the proposed order meets the conditions prescribed by section 88 of the Coroners and Justice Act 2009;

(d) explain why no measures other than those proposed will suffice, such as—

(i) an admission of the facts that would be proved by the witness,

(ii) an order restricting public access to the trial,

(iii) reporting restrictions, in particular under sections 45, 45A or 46 of the Youth Justice and Criminal Evidence Act 1999,

(iv) a direction for a special measure under section 19 of the Youth Justice and Criminal Evidence Act 1999,

(v) introduction of the witness' written statement as hearsay evidence, under section 116 of the Criminal Justice Act 2003, or

(vi) arrangements for the protection of the witness;

(e) attach to the application—

(i) a witness statement setting out the proposed evidence, edited in such a way as not to reveal the witness' identity,

(ii) where the prosecutor is the applicant, any further prosecution evidence to be served, and any further prosecution material to be disclosed under the Criminal Procedure and Investigations Act 1996, similarly edited, and

(iii) any defence statement that has been served, or as much information as may be available to the applicant that gives particulars of the defence; and

(f) ask for a hearing, if the applicant wants one.

(2) At any hearing of the application, the applicant must—

(a) identify the witness to the court, unless at the prosecutor's request the court otherwise directs; and

(b) present to the court, unless it otherwise directs—
  (i) the unedited witness statement from which the edited version has been prepared,
  (ii) where the prosecutor is the applicant, the unedited version of any further prosecution evidence or material from which an edited version has been prepared, and
  (iii) such further material as the applicant relies on to establish that the proposed order meets the conditions prescribed by section 88 of the 2009 Act.

(3) At any such hearing—
  (a) the general rule is that the court must consider, in the following sequence—
    (i) representations first by the applicant and then by each other party, in all the parties' presence, and then
    (ii) information withheld from a defendant, and further representations by the applicant, in the absence of any (or any other) defendant; but
  (b) the court may direct other arrangements for the hearing.

(4) Before the witness gives evidence, the applicant must identify the witness to the court—
  (a) if not already done;
  (b) without revealing the witness' identity to any other party or person; and
  (c) unless at the prosecutor's request the court otherwise directs.

18.16. Duty of court officer to notify the Director of Public Prosecutions

The court officer must notify the Director of Public Prosecutions of an application, unless the prosecutor is, or acts on behalf of, a public authority.

18.17. Application to vary or discharge a witness anonymity order

(1) A party who wants the court to vary or discharge a witness anonymity order, or a witness who wants the court to do so when the case is over, must—
  (a) apply in writing, as soon as reasonably practicable after becoming aware of the grounds for doing so; and
  (b) serve the application on—
    (i) the court officer, and
    (ii) each other party.

(2) The applicant must—
  (a) explain what material circumstances have changed since the order was made (or last varied, if applicable);
  (b) explain why the order should be varied or discharged, taking account of the conditions for making an order; and
  (c) ask for a hearing, if the applicant wants one.

(3) Where an application includes information that the applicant thinks might reveal the witness' identity, the applicant must—
  (a) omit that information from the application that is served on a defendant;
  (b) mark the information to show that it is only for the court and the prosecutor (if the prosecutor is not the applicant); and
  (c) with that information include an explanation of why it has been withheld.

(4) Where a party applies to vary or discharge a witness anonymity order after the trial and any appeal are over, the party who introduced the witness' evidence must serve the application on the witness.

[Note. Under sections 91, 92 and 93 of the Coroners and Justice Act 2009, the court can vary or discharge a witness anonymity order—
  (a) on an application, if there has been a material change of circumstances since it was made or previously varied; or
  (b) on the court's own initiative, unless the trial and any appeal are over.]

18.18. Representations in response

(1) This rule applies where a party or, where the case is over, a witness, wants to make representations about—

(a) an application for a witness anonymity order;
(b) an application for the variation or discharge of such an order; or
(c) a variation or discharge that the court proposes on its own initiative.

(2) Such a party or witness must—

(a) serve the representations on—
   (i) the court officer, and
   (ii) each other party;
(b) do so not more than 10 business days after, as applicable—
   (i) service of the application, or
   (ii) notice of the variation or discharge that the court proposes; and
(c) ask for a hearing, if that party or witness wants one.

(3) Where representations include information that the person making them thinks might reveal the witness' identity, that person must—

(a) omit that information from the representations served on a defendant;
(b) mark the information to show that it is only for the court (and for the prosecutor, if relevant); and
(c) with that information include an explanation of why it has been withheld.

(4) Representations against a witness anonymity order must explain why the conditions for making the order are not met.

(5) Representations against the variation or discharge of such an order must explain why it would not be appropriate to vary or discharge it, taking account of the conditions for making an order.

(6) A prosecutor's representations in response to an application by a defendant must include all information available to the prosecutor that is relevant to the conditions and considerations specified by sections 88 and 89 of the Coroners and Justice Act 2009.

INTERMEDIARY FOR A DEFENDANT

18.19. Appointment of intermediary to facilitate a defendant's participation

(1) The court must exercise its power to appoint an intermediary to facilitate a defendant's effective participation in the trial where—

(a) the defendant's ability to participate is likely to be diminished by reason of—
   (i) age, if the defendant is under 18, or
   (ii) mental disorder (as defined in section 1(2) of the Mental Health Act 1983), a significant impairment of intelligence and social functioning, or a physical disability or disorder; and
(b) the appointment is necessary for that purpose.

(2) In determining whether such an appointment is necessary, who to appoint and the duration or purpose of the appointment, the court must have regard to—

(a) the defendant's communication needs as reported to the court;
(b) the recommendations in any intermediary's report received by the court;
(c) any views that the defendant has expressed about—
   (i) receiving the assistance of an intermediary,
   (ii) other measures or arrangements to facilitate the defendant's effective participation in the trial;

(d) the likely impact of the defendant's age, if under 18, level of intellectual ability or social functioning on the ability to—
  (i) give evidence, and
  (ii) understand what is said and done by the court and other participants;
(e) the likely impact on such participation and on such understanding of any mental disorder or other significant impairment of intelligence or social functioning;
(f) the adequacy of arrangements for questioning the defendant in the absence of an intermediary;
(g) any assistance that the defendant has received in the past—
  (i) while giving evidence in legal proceedings,
  (ii) while being questioned during the investigation of an alleged offence, or
  (iii) as a defendant in a criminal case;
(h) any assessment of the defendant's health by a mental health practitioner acting independently of the parties to assist the court;
(i) any expert medical opinion that the court may have received; and
(j) any other matter that the court thinks relevant.

(3) The court may exercise its power to appoint an intermediary—
(a) for the duration of every hearing that the defendant is due to attend;
(b) for the duration of any specified such hearing or hearings, or for the duration of a specified part of such a hearing; or
(c) for a specified purpose during a hearing.

(4) Unless the court otherwise directs, the appointment of an intermediary extends to facilitating the defendant's communication with that defendant's legal representatives for the duration and for the purpose of the appointment.

(5) The court may decide whether to appoint an intermediary to facilitate a defendant's effective participation in the trial and whether to vary or discharge any such appointment—
(a) on application or on the court's own initiative;
(b) at a hearing, in public or in private, or without a hearing; and
(c) in a party's absence, if that party—
  (i) applied for the appointment, variation or discharge, or
  (ii) has had at least 10 business days in which to make representations.

(6) The court must not exercise its power to vary or discharge a direction for the appointment of an intermediary unless satisfied that—
(a) since the direction was made—
  (i) the defendant's communication needs have changed materially, or
  (ii) any other material circumstance has changed materially; and
(b) the defendant will be able to participate effectively in the trial despite the variation or discharge of the direction.

18.20. Application to vary or discharge the appointment of an intermediary for a defendant

(1) A party who wants the court to vary or discharge the appointment of an intermediary to facilitate a defendant's effective participation in the trial must—
(a) apply in writing, as soon as reasonably practicable after becoming aware of the grounds for doing so; and
(b) serve the application on—
  (i) the court officer, and
  (ii) each other party.

(2) The applicant must—
(a) explain how the criteria listed in rule 18.19(6) are met (variation or discharge of appointment); and
(b) ask for a hearing, if the applicant wants one, and explain why it is needed.

18.21. Representations in response to application or proposal

(1) This rule applies where a party wants to make representations about—
(a) an application or proposal for the appointment of an intermediary to facilitate a defendant's effective participation in the trial; or
(b) an application or proposal for the variation or discharge of such an appointment.

(2) Such a party must—
(a) serve the representations on—
(i) the court officer, and
(ii) each other party;
(b) do so not more than 10 business days after, as applicable—
(i) service of the application, or
(ii) notice of the appointment, variation or discharge that the court proposes; and
(c) ask for a hearing, if that party wants one, and explain why it is needed.

(3) Representations against such an appointment, variation or discharge must explain why the criteria that apply are not met.

DUTIES OF INTERMEDIARIES

18.22. Intermediary's duty to the court

(1) This rule applies to an intermediary who accepts—
(a) approval by the court for the purposes of section 29 of the Youth Justice and Criminal Evidence Act 1999 (Examination of witness through intermediary);
(b) approval by the court for the purposes of section 33BA of the 1999 Act (Examination of accused through intermediary); or
(c) appointment by the court to facilitate a defendant's effective participation in the trial, when the defendant gives evidence or at any other time.

(2) The intermediary must help the court to achieve the overriding objective—
(a) to the best of the intermediary's skill and understanding by—
(i) communicating to the witness or defendant (as the case may be) questions put to them,
(ii) communicating to the questioner and the court the replies, and
(iii) explaining such questions and answers so that they can be understood;
(b) by assessing continually the witness' or the defendant's (as the case may be) ability to participate effectively and intervening if necessary;
(c) where the intermediary is appointed to facilitate a defendant's effective participation, by explaining to the defendant, in terms the defendant can understand, what is said and done by the court and other participants; and
(d) by actively assisting the court in fulfilling its duties under rule 3.2 (Case management; The duty of the court) and rule 3.9 (Case management; Ground rules hearing), in particular by—
(i) complying with directions made by the court, and
(ii) at once informing the court of any significant failure (by the intermediary or another) to take any step required by such a direction.

(3) This duty overrides any obligation to the witness or to the defendant (as the case may be), or to the person by whom the intermediary is paid.

18.23. Declaration by intermediary

(1) This rule applies where—
(a) a video recorded interview with a witness is conducted through an intermediary; or
(b) the court directs the examination of a witness or defendant through an intermediary.

(2) The intermediary must make a declaration—
(a) before such an interview begins; and
(b) before the examination begins (even if such an interview with the witness was conducted through the same intermediary).

(3) The declaration must be in these terms, or in any corresponding terms that the intermediary declares to be binding—

'I swear by Almighty God [*or* I solemnly, sincerely and truly declare and affirm] that I shall faithfully communicate questions and answers and make true explanation of all matters and things required of me according to the best of my skill and understanding.'

18.24. Content of intermediary's report

(1) An intermediary's report must, in every case—
(a) give details of the intermediary's qualifications, relevant experience and any accreditation;
(b) identify the commissioner of the report;
(c) identify those from whom the intermediary has obtained information material to the report;
(d) list the documents received or inspected by the intermediary which contained such information and give an indication of their content;
(e) give the date or dates on which the intermediary met the witness or defendant, as the case may be, for the purpose of preparing the report;
(f) describe the nature and duration of the intermediary's assessment, or assessments, of the witness or defendant;
(g) by reference to examples drawn from the intermediary's assessment of the witness or defendant explain why in this particular case intermediary assistance is necessary;
(h) include an evaluation of—
(i) the impact of any condition or conditions which, whether in isolation or together, may adversely affect the witness' or the defendant's ability to communicate, and
(ii) the extent, if any, to which that impact may be exacerbated by the trial;
(i) if the intermediary is not able to reach an evaluation without qualifying it, state the qualification;
(j) report the views of the witness or defendant, as the case may be, on receiving the assistance of an intermediary;
(k) include in a summary of the intermediary's conclusions any recommendation, with reasons, for—
(i) the approval or appointment of an intermediary,
(ii) the manner and duration of any questioning of the witness or defendant, as the case may be, and
(iii) arrangements for the way in which the intermediary, if approved or appointed, should participate; and
(l) contain a statement that the intermediary—
(i) understands an intermediary's duty to the court, and
(ii) will comply with that duty if approved or appointed.

(2) Where the intermediary is asked to evaluate a defendant's communication needs the report must also—
(a) include an evaluation of the extent to which any measures or arrangements beside the appointment of an intermediary will facilitate the defendant's effective participation in the trial; and
(b) in the summary of the intermediary's conclusions include any recommendation, with reasons, for—

(i) the duration and purpose of any appointment of an intermediary, and
(ii) other measures or arrangements to help the defendant to participate effectively in the trial.

Summary of eligibility for measures to which this Part applies

Special measures direction

Under section 16 of the Youth Justice and Criminal Evidence Act 1999, a witness is eligible for the assistance of a special measures direction given under section 19 of that Act if—

(a) the witness is under 18; or
(b) the witness has—
(i) a mental disorder, or a significant impairment of intelligence and social functioning, or
(ii) a physical disability or disorder
and the court considers that the completeness, coherence and accuracy (the 'quality') of evidence given by the witness is likely to be diminished by reason of those circumstances.

Under section 17 of the 1999 Act, a witness is eligible for such assistance if—

(a) the court is satisfied that the quality of evidence given by the witness is likely to be diminished because of his or her fear or distress in connection with giving evidence, taking account particularly of—
(i) the circumstances of the offence,
(ii) the witness' age, social and cultural background, ethnic origins, domestic and employment circumstances, religious beliefs or political opinions,
(iii) any behaviour towards the witness on the part of the defendant, the defendant's family or associates, or any other potential defendant or witness, and
(iv) the witness' own views;
(b) the witness is the complainant in respect of a sexual offence or other offence specified by the Act, and has not declined such assistance; or
(c) the offence is one of a list of offences involving weapons, and the witness has not declined such assistance.

Section 28 of the 1999 Act (video recorded cross-examination or re-examination) is not yet fully in force. With that exception, all the special measures listed in rule 18.1 potentially are available where the witness is eligible for assistance under section 16 of the Act. Those numbered (i) to (v) are available where the witness is eligible for assistance under section 17.

As a general rule, but with exceptions, the court must give a special measures direction—

(a) under section 21 or 22 of the 1999 Act, where the witness—
(i) is under 18, or
(ii) was under that age when interviewed
whether or not an application for a direction is made;
(b) under section 22A of the 1999 Act(23), where an application is made in the Crown Court for the evidence of a witness who is the complainant of a sexual offence to be admitted by means of a video recording of an interview with the witness in the place of examination-in-chief.

Witness anonymity order

Under section 86 of the Coroners and Justice Act 2009, a witness anonymity order is an order that specifies measures to be taken to ensure that the identity of a witness is not disclosed, such as withholding the witness' name from materials disclosed to a party to the proceedings, the use of a pseudonym, the screening of the witness from view, the modulation of the witness' voice, and the prohibition of questions that might reveal his or her identity. Before making such an order, the court must—

(a) be satisfied that three conditions prescribed by the Act are met (section 88 of the 2009 Act); and
(b) have regard to considerations specified by the Act (section 89 of the 2009 Act).

Intermediary for a defendant

In order to ensure the defendant's effective participation in his or her trial the court has an inherent power to appoint an intermediary to facilitate that participation, including during the giving of evidence by the defendant.

PART 19 EXPERT EVIDENCE

19.1. When this Part applies

(1) This Part applies where a party wants to introduce expert opinion evidence.

(2) A reference to an 'expert' in this Part is a reference to a person who is required to give or prepare expert evidence for the purpose of criminal proceedings, including evidence required to determine fitness to plead or for the purpose of sentencing.

(3) Where evidence that is introduced as evidence of fact within a witness' direct knowledge includes expert opinion the court may direct that the requirements of rules 19.2 (Expert's duty to the court) and 19.3 (Introduction of expert evidence) apply, to the extent and with such adaptations as the court directs.

[Note. Expert medical evidence may be required to determine fitness to plead under section 4 of the Criminal Procedure (Insanity) Act 1964. It may be required also under section 11 of the Powers of Criminal Courts (Sentencing) Act 2000, under Part III of the Mental Health Act 1983 or under Part 12 of the Criminal Justice Act 2003. Those Acts contain requirements about the qualification of medical experts.]

19.2. Expert's duty to the court

(1) An expert must help the court to achieve the overriding objective—

- (a) by giving opinion which is—
  - (i) objective and unbiased, and
  - (ii) within the expert's area or areas of expertise; and
- (b) by actively assisting the court in fulfilling its duty of case management under rule 3.2, in particular by—
  - (i) complying with directions made by the court, and
  - (ii) at once informing the court of any significant failure (by the expert or another) to take any step required by such a direction.

(2) This duty overrides any obligation to the person from whom the expert receives instructions or by whom the expert is paid.

(3) This duty includes obligations—

- (a) to define the expert's area or areas of expertise—
  - (i) in the expert's report, and
  - (ii) when giving evidence in person;
- (b) when giving evidence in person, to draw the court's attention to any question to which the answer would be outside the expert's area or areas of expertise;
- (c) to inform all parties and the court if the expert's opinion changes from that contained in a report served as evidence or given in a statement; and
- (d) to disclose to the party for whom the expert's evidence is commissioned anything—
  - (i) of which the expert is aware, and
  - (ii) of which that party, if aware of it, would be required to give notice under rule 19.3(3)(c).

[Note. The Practice Direction lists examples of matters that should be disclosed under this rule and rule 19.3(3)(c).]

19.3. Introduction of expert evidence

(1) A party who wants another party to admit as fact a summary of an expert's conclusions must serve that summary—

(a) on the court officer and on each party from whom that admission is sought; and
(b) as soon as practicable after the defendant whom it affects pleads not guilty.

(2) A party on whom such a summary is served must—
(a) serve a response stating—
(i) which, if any, of the expert's conclusions are admitted as fact, and
(ii) where a conclusion is not admitted, what are the disputed issues concerning that conclusion; and
(b) serve the response—
(i) on the court officer and on the party who served the summary, and
(ii) as soon as practicable, and in any event not more than 10 business days after service of the summary.

(3) A party who wants to introduce expert evidence otherwise than as admitted fact must—
(a) serve a report by the expert which complies with rule 19.4 (Content of expert's report) on—
(i) the court officer, and
(ii) each other party;
(b) serve the report as soon as practicable, and in any event with any application in support of which that party relies on that evidence;
(c) serve with the report—
(i) notice of anything of which the party serving it is aware which might reasonably be thought capable of undermining the reliability of the expert's opinion, or detracting from the credibility or impartiality of the expert, and
(ii) an explanation of how facts stated in the report are admissible as evidence if that is not explained by the report;
(d) if another party so requires, give that party a copy of, or a reasonable opportunity to inspect—
(i) a record of any examination, measurement, test or experiment on which the expert's findings and opinion are based, or that were carried out in the course of reaching those findings and opinion, and
(ii) anything on which any such examination, measurement, test or experiment was carried out.

(4) Unless the parties otherwise agree or the court directs, a party may not—
(a) introduce expert evidence if that party has not complied with paragraph (3); or
(b) introduce in evidence an expert report if the expert does not give evidence in person.

[Note. A party who accepts another party's expert's conclusions may admit them as fact under section 10 of the Criminal Justice Act 1967.

Under section 81 of the Police and Criminal Evidence Act 1984, and under section 20(3) of the Criminal Procedure and Investigations Act 1996, Criminal Procedure Rules may require the disclosure of expert evidence before it is introduced as part of a party's case and prohibit its introduction without the court's permission, if it was not disclosed as required.

Under section 30 of the Criminal Justice Act 1988, an expert report is admissible in evidence whether or not the person who made it gives oral evidence, but if that person does not give oral evidence then the report is admissible only with the court's permission.

Evidence of facts which are material to the opinions expressed in an expert report, or upon which those opinions are based, may be admissible if (i) they are within the expert witness' own direct knowledge, or (ii) as hearsay evidence within the meaning of section 114 of the Criminal Justice Act 2003: see also rule 19.4(b), (c), (d) and (e). Evidence of examinations etc. on which an expert relies may be admissible under section 127 of the 2003 Act. Part 20 contains rules about the introduction of hearsay evidence under other provisions of that Act.]

19.4. Content of expert's report

Where rule 19.3(3) applies, an expert's report must—

(a) give details of the expert's qualifications, relevant experience and accreditation;
(b) give details of any literature or other information which the expert has relied on in making the report;
(c) contain a statement setting out the substance of all facts given to the expert which are material to the opinions expressed in the report, or upon which those opinions are based;
(d) make clear which of the facts stated in the report are within the expert's own knowledge;
(e) where the expert has based an opinion or inference on a representation of fact or opinion made by another person for the purposes of criminal proceedings (for example, as to the outcome of an examination, measurement, test or experiment)—
   (i) identify the person who made that representation to the expert,
   (ii) give the qualifications, relevant experience and any accreditation of that person, and
   (iii) certify that that person had personal knowledge of the matters stated in that representation;
(f) where there is a range of opinion on the matters dealt with in the report—
   (i) summarise the range of opinion, and
   (ii) give reasons for the expert's own opinion;
(g) if the expert is not able to give an opinion without qualification, state the qualification;
(h) include such information as the court may need to decide whether the expert's opinion is sufficiently reliable to be admissible as evidence;
(i) contain a summary of the conclusions reached;
(j) contain a statement that the expert understands an expert's duty to the court, and has complied and will continue to comply with that duty; and
(k) contain the same declaration of truth as a witness statement.

[Note. Part 16 contains rules about written witness statements. Declarations of truth in witness statements are required by section 9 of the Criminal Justice Act 1967.]

19.5. Expert to be informed of service of report

A party who serves on another party or on the court a report by an expert must, at once, inform that expert of that fact.

19.6. Pre-hearing discussion of expert evidence

(1) This rule applies where more than one party wants to introduce expert evidence.

(2) The court may direct the experts to—
   (a) discuss the expert issues in the proceedings; and
   (b) prepare a statement for the court of the matters on which they agree and disagree, giving their reasons.

(3) Except for that statement, the content of that discussion must not be referred to without the court's permission.

(4) A party may not introduce expert evidence without the court's permission if the expert has not complied with a direction under this rule.

[Note. At a pre-trial hearing, a court may make binding rulings about the admissibility of evidence and about questions of law under section 9 of the Criminal Justice Act 1987; sections 31 and 40 of the Criminal Procedure and Investigations Act 1996; and section 8A of the Magistrates' Courts Act 1980.]

19.7. Court's power to direct that evidence is to be given by a single joint expert

(1) Where more than one defendant wants to introduce expert evidence on an issue at trial, the court may direct that the evidence on that issue is to be given by one expert only.

(2) Where the co-defendants cannot agree who should be the expert, the court may—

(a) select the expert from a list prepared or identified by them; or

(b) direct that the expert be selected in another way.

19.8. Instructions to a single joint expert

(1) Where the court gives a direction under rule 19.7 for a single joint expert to be used, each of the co-defendants may give instructions to the expert.

(2) A co-defendant who gives instructions to the expert must, at the same time, send a copy of the instructions to each other co-defendant.

(3) The court may give directions about—

(a) the payment of the expert's fees and expenses; and

(b) any examination, measurement, test or experiment which the expert wishes to carry out.

(4) The court may, before an expert is instructed, limit the amount that can be paid by way of fees and expenses to the expert.

(5) Unless the court otherwise directs, the instructing co-defendants are jointly and severally liable for the payment of the expert's fees and expenses.

19.9. Application to withhold information from another party

(1) This rule applies where—

(a) a party introduces expert evidence under rule 19.3(3);

(b) the evidence omits information which it otherwise might include because the party introducing it thinks that that information ought not be revealed to another party; and

(c) the party introducing the evidence wants the court to decide whether it would be in the public interest to withhold that information.

(2) The party who wants to introduce the evidence must—

(a) apply for such a decision; and

(b) serve the application on—

(i) the court officer, and

(ii) the other party, but only to the extent that serving it would not reveal what the applicant thinks ought to be withheld.

(3) The application must—

(a) identify the information;

(b) explain why the applicant thinks that it would be in the public interest to withhold it; and

(c) omit from the part of the application that is served on the other party anything that would reveal what the applicant thinks ought to be withheld.

(4) Where the applicant serves only part of the application on the other party, the applicant must—

(a) mark the other part, to show that it is only for the court; and

(b) in that other part, explain why the applicant has withheld it from the other party.

(5) The court may—

(a) direct the applicant to serve on the other party any part of the application which has been withheld; and

(b) determine the application at a hearing or without a hearing.

(6) Any hearing of an application to which this rule applies—

(a) must be in private, unless the court otherwise directs; and
(b) if the court so directs, may be, wholly or in part, in the absence of the party from whom information has been withheld.

(7) At any hearing of an application to which this rule applies—
(a) the general rule is that the court must consider, in the following sequence—
(i) representations first by the applicant and then by the other party, in both parties' presence, and then
(ii) further representations by the applicant, in the absence of the party from whom information has been withheld; but
(b) the court may direct other arrangements for the hearing.

19.10. Court's power to vary requirements under this Part

(1) The court may extend (even after it has expired) a time limit under this Part.
(2) A party who wants an extension of time must—
(a) apply when serving the report, summary or notice for which it is required; and
(b) explain the delay.

PART 20 HEARSAY EVIDENCE

20.1. When this Part applies

This Part applies in a magistrates' court and in the Crown Court where a party wants to introduce hearsay evidence, within the meaning of section 114 of the Criminal Justice Act 2003.

[Note. Under section 114 of the Criminal Justice Act 2003, a statement not made in oral evidence is admissible as evidence of any matter stated if—
(a) a statutory provision makes it admissible;
(b) a rule of law preserved by section 118 makes it admissible;
(c) the parties agree to it being admissible; or
(d) it is in the interests of justice for it to be admissible.

Under section 115 of the Act—
(a) a 'statement' means any representation of fact or opinion, by any means, and includes a representation in pictorial form; and
(b) a 'matter stated' is something stated by someone with the apparent purpose of—
(i) causing another person to believe it, or
(ii) causing another person, or a machine, to act or operate on the basis that the matter is as stated.]

20.2. Notice to introduce hearsay evidence

(1) This rule applies where a party wants to introduce hearsay evidence for admission under any of the following sections of the Criminal Justice Act 2003—
(a) section 114(1)(d) (evidence admissible in the interests of justice);
(b) section 116 (evidence where a witness is unavailable);
(c) section 117(1)(c) (evidence in a statement prepared for the purposes of criminal proceedings); or
(d) section 121 (multiple hearsay).

(2) That party must—
(a) serve notice on—
(i) the court officer, and
(ii) each other party;
(b) in the notice—
(i) identify the evidence that is hearsay,
(ii) set out any facts on which that party relies to make the evidence admissible,

(iii) explain how that party will prove those facts if another party disputes them, and
(iv) explain why the evidence is admissible; and

(c) attach to the notice any statement or other document containing the evidence that has not already been served.

(3) A prosecutor who wants to introduce such evidence must serve the notice not more than—

(a) 20 business days after the defendant pleads not guilty, in a magistrates' court; or
(b) 10 business days after the defendant pleads not guilty, in the Crown Court.

(4) A defendant who wants to introduce such evidence must serve the notice as soon as reasonably practicable.

(5) A party entitled to receive a notice under this rule may waive that entitlement by so informing—

(a) the party who would have served it; and
(b) the court.

[Note. The sections of the Criminal Justice Act 2003 listed in this rule set out the conditions on which hearsay evidence may be admitted under them.

If notice is not given as this rule requires, then under section 132(5) of the 2003 Act—

(a) the evidence is not admissible without the court's permission;
(b) if the court gives permission, it may draw such inferences as appear proper from the failure to give notice; and
(c) the court may take the failure into account in exercising its powers to order costs.

This rule does not require notice of hearsay evidence that is admissible under any of the following sections of the 2003 Act—

(a) section 117 (business and other documents), otherwise than as required by rule 20.2(1)(c);
(b) section 118 (preservation of certain common law categories of admissibility);
(c) section 119 (inconsistent statements);
(d) section 120 (other previous statements of witness); or
(e) section 127 (expert evidence: preparatory work): but see Part 19 for the procedure where a party wants to introduce such evidence.]

20.3. Opposing the introduction of hearsay evidence

(1) This rule applies where a party objects to the introduction of hearsay evidence.

(2) That party must—

(a) apply to the court to determine the objection;
(b) serve the application on—
(i) the court officer, and
(ii) each other party;
(c) serve the application as soon as reasonably practicable, and in any event not more than 10 business days after—
(i) service of notice to introduce the evidence under rule 20.2,
(ii) service of the evidence to which that party objects, if no notice is required by that rule, or
(iii) the defendant pleads not guilty
whichever of those events happens last; and
(d) in the application, explain—
(i) which, if any, facts set out in a notice under rule 20.2 that party disputes,
(ii) why the evidence is not admissible, and
(iii) any other objection to the evidence.

(3) The court—
  (a) may determine an application—
    (i) at a hearing, in public or in private, or
    (ii) without a hearing;
  (b) must not determine the application unless the party who served the notice—
    (i) is present, or
    (ii) has had a reasonable opportunity to respond;
  (c) may adjourn the application; and
  (d) may discharge or vary a determination where it can do so under—
    (i) section 8B of the Magistrates' Courts Act 1980 (ruling at pre-trial hearing in a magistrates' court), or
    (ii) section 9 of the Criminal Justice Act 1987, or section 31 or 40 of the Criminal Procedure and Investigations Act 1996 (ruling at preparatory or other pre-trial hearing in the Crown Court).

20.4. Unopposed hearsay evidence

(1) This rule applies where—
  (a) a party has served notice to introduce hearsay evidence under rule 20.2; and
  (b) no other party has applied to the court to determine an objection to the introduction of the evidence.

(2) The court must treat the evidence as if it were admissible by agreement.

[Note. Under section 132(4) of the Criminal Justice Act 2003, rules may provide that evidence is to be treated as admissible by agreement of the parties if notice to introduce that evidence has not been opposed.]

20.5. Court's power to vary requirements under this Part

(1) The court may—
  (a) shorten or extend (even after it has expired) a time limit under this Part;
  (b) allow an application or notice to be in a different form to one issued under the Practice Direction, or to be made or given orally; and
  (c) dispense with the requirement for notice to introduce hearsay evidence.

(2) A party who wants an extension of time must—
  (a) apply when serving the application or notice for which it is needed; and
  (b) explain the delay.

PART 21 EVIDENCE OF BAD CHARACTER

21.1. When this Part applies

This Part applies in a magistrates' court and in the Crown Court where a party wants to introduce evidence of bad character within the meaning of section 98 of the Criminal Justice Act 2003.

[Note. Under section 98 of the Criminal Justice Act 2003, evidence of a person's bad character means evidence of, or of a disposition towards, misconduct on that person's part, other than evidence that—
  (a) has to do with the alleged facts of the offence; or
  (b) is evidence of misconduct in connection with the investigation or prosecution.

Under section 100(1) of the Criminal Justice Act 2003, evidence of a non-defendant's bad character is admissible if—
  (a) it is important explanatory evidence;
  (b) it has substantial probative value in relation to a matter which—

(i) is a matter in issue in the proceedings, and

(ii) is of substantial importance in the context of the case as a whole; or

(c) all parties to the proceedings agree to the evidence being admissible.

The section explains requirements (a) and (b). Unless the parties agree to the evidence being admissible, it may not be introduced without the court's permission.

Under section 101(1) of the Criminal Justice Act 2003, evidence of a defendant's bad character is admissible if—

(a) all parties to the proceedings agree to the evidence being admissible;

(b) the evidence is introduced by the defendant, or is given in answer to a question asked by the defendant in cross-examination which was intended to elicit that evidence;

(c) it is important explanatory evidence;

(d) it is relevant to an important matter in issue between the defendant and the prosecution;

(e) it has substantial probative value in relation to an important matter in issue between the defendant and a co-defendant;

(f) it is evidence to correct a false impression given by the defendant; or

(g) the defendant has made an attack on another person's character.

Sections 102 to 106 of the Act supplement those requirements. The court must not admit evidence under (d) or (g) if, on an application by the defendant, the court concludes that to do so would be unfair.]

21.2. Content of application or notice

(1) A party who wants to introduce evidence of bad character must—

(a) make an application under rule 21.3, where it is evidence of a non-defendant's bad character; or

(b) give notice under rule 21.4, where it is evidence of a defendant's bad character.

(2) An application or notice must—

(a) set out the facts of the misconduct on which that party relies,

(b) explain how that party will prove those facts (whether by certificate of conviction, other official record, or other evidence), if another party disputes them, and

(c) explain why the evidence is admissible.

[Note. The fact that a person was convicted of an offence may be proved under—

(a) section 73 of the Police and Criminal Evidence Act 1984 (conviction in the United Kingdom); or

(b) section 7 of the Evidence Act 1851 (conviction outside the United Kingdom).

See also sections 117 and 118 of the Criminal Justice Act 2003 (admissibility of evidence contained in business and other documents).

Under section 10 of the Criminal Justice Act 1967, a party may admit a matter of fact.]

21.3. Application to introduce evidence of a non-defendant's bad character

(1) This rule applies where a party wants to introduce evidence of the bad character of a person other than the defendant.

(2) That party must serve an application to do so on—

(a) the court officer; and

(b) each other party.

(3) The applicant must serve the application—

(a) as soon as reasonably practicable; and in any event

(b) not more than 10 business days after the prosecutor discloses material on which the application is based (if the prosecutor is not the applicant).

(4) A party who objects to the introduction of the evidence must—

(a) serve notice on—

(i) the court officer, and
(ii) each other party not more than 10 business days after service of the application; and
(b) in the notice explain, as applicable—
(i) which, if any, facts of the misconduct set out in the application that party disputes,
(ii) what, if any, facts of the misconduct that party admits instead,
(iii) why the evidence is not admissible, and
(iv) any other objection to the application.

(5) The court—
(a) may determine an application—
(i) at a hearing, in public or in private, or
(ii) without a hearing;
(b) must not determine the application unless each party other than the applicant—
(i) is present, or
(ii) has had at least 10 business days in which to serve a notice of objection;
(c) may adjourn the application; and
(d) may discharge or vary a determination where it can do so under—
(i) section 8B of the Magistrates' Courts Act 1980 (ruling at pre-trial hearing in a magistrates' court), or
(ii) section 9 of the Criminal Justice Act 1987, or section 31 or 40 of the Criminal Procedure and Investigations Act 1996 (ruling at preparatory or other pre-trial hearing in the Crown Court).

[Note. See also rule 21.5 (reasons for decisions must be given in public).]

21.4. Notice to introduce evidence of a defendant's bad character

(1) This rule applies where a party wants to introduce evidence of a defendant's bad character.

(2) A prosecutor or co-defendant who wants to introduce such evidence must serve notice on—
(a) the court officer; and
(b) each other party.

(3) A prosecutor must serve any such notice not more than—
(a) 20 business days after the defendant pleads not guilty, in a magistrates' court; or
(b) 10 business days after the defendant pleads not guilty, in the Crown Court.

(4) A co-defendant who wants to introduce such evidence must serve the notice—
(a) as soon as reasonably practicable; and in any event
(b) not more than 10 business days after the prosecutor discloses material on which the notice is based.

(5) A party who objects to the introduction of the evidence identified by such a notice must—
(a) apply to the court to determine the objection;
(b) serve the application on—
(i) the court officer, and
(ii) each other party not more than 10 business days after service of the notice; and
(c) in the application explain, as applicable—
(i) which, if any, facts of the misconduct set out in the notice that party disputes,
(ii) what, if any, facts of the misconduct that party admits instead,
(iii) why the evidence is not admissible,
(iv) why it would be unfair to admit the evidence, and
(v) any other objection to the notice.

(6) The court—
(a) may determine such an application—
(i) at a hearing, in public or in private, or
(ii) without a hearing;
(b) must not determine the application unless the party who served the notice—
(i) is present, or
(ii) has had a reasonable opportunity to respond;
(c) may adjourn the application; and
(d) may discharge or vary a determination where it can do so under—
(i) section 8B of the Magistrates' Courts Act 1980 (ruling at pre-trial hearing in a magistrates' court), or
(ii) section 9 of the Criminal Justice Act 1987, or section 31 or 40 of the Criminal Procedure and Investigations Act 1996 (ruling at preparatory or other pre-trial hearing in the Crown Court).
(7) A party entitled to receive such a notice may waive that entitlement by so informing—
(a) the party who would have served it; and
(b) the court.
(8) A defendant who wants to introduce evidence of his or her own bad character must—
(a) give notice, in writing or orally—
(i) as soon as reasonably practicable, and in any event
(ii) before the evidence is introduced, either by the defendant or in reply to a question asked by the defendant of another party's witness in order to obtain that evidence; and
(b) in the Crown Court, at the same time give notice (in writing, or orally) of any direction about the defendant's character that the defendant wants the court to give the jury under rule 25.14 (Directions to the jury and taking the verdict)

[Note. See also rule 21.5 (reasons for decisions must be given in public).

If notice is not given as this rule requires, then under section 111(4) of the Criminal Justice Act 2003 the court may take the failure into account in exercising its powers to order costs.]

21.5. Reasons for decisions

The court must announce at a hearing in public (but in the absence of the jury, if there is one) the reasons for a decision—
(a) to admit evidence as evidence of bad character, or to refuse to do so; or
(b) to direct an acquittal or a retrial under section 107 of the Criminal Justice Act 2003.

[Note. See section 110 of the Criminal Justice Act 2003.]

21.6. Court's power to vary requirements under this Part

(1) The court may—
(a) shorten or extend (even after it has expired) a time limit under this Part;
(b) allow an application or notice to be in a different form to one issued in the Practice Direction, or to be made or given orally; and
(c) dispense with a requirement for notice to introduce evidence of a defendant's bad character.
(2) A party who wants an extension of time must—
(a) apply when serving the application or notice for which it is needed; and
(b) explain the delay.

PART 22 EVIDENCE OF A COMPLAINANT'S PREVIOUS SEXUAL BEHAVIOUR

22.1. When this Part applies

This Part applies in a magistrates' court and in the Crown Court where—

(a) section 41 of the Youth Justice and Criminal Evidence Act 1999 prohibits the introduction of evidence or cross-examination about any sexual behaviour of the complainant of a sexual offence, and

(b) despite that prohibition, a defendant wants to introduce such evidence or to cross-examine a witness about such behaviour.

[Note. Section 41 of the Youth Justice and Criminal Evidence Act 1999 prohibits evidence or cross-examination about the sexual behaviour of a complainant of a sexual offence, subject to exceptions.

See also—

(a) section 42 of the 1999 Act, which among other things defines 'sexual behaviour' and 'sexual offence';

(b) section 34, which prohibits cross-examination by a defendant in person of the complainant of a sexual offence (Part 23 contains relevant rules).]

22.2. Exercise of court's powers

(1) The court—

(a) must determine an application under rule 22.4 (Application for permission to introduce evidence or cross-examine)—

(i) at a hearing in private, and

(ii) in the absence of the complainant;

(b) must not determine the application unless—

(i) each party other than the applicant is present, or has had at least 10 business days in which to make representations, and

(ii) the court is satisfied that it has been able to take adequate account of the complainant's rights;

(c) may adjourn the application; and

(d) may discharge or vary a determination where it can do so under—

(i) section 8B of the Magistrates' Courts Act 1980 (ruling at pre-trial hearing in a magistrates' court), or

(ii) section 9 of the Criminal Justice Act 1987, or section 31 or 40 of the Criminal Procedure and Investigations Act 1996 (ruling at preparatory or other pre-trial hearing in the Crown Court).

[Note. See also section 43 of the Youth Justice and Criminal Evidence Act 1999, which among other things requires an application under section 41 of the Act to be heard in private and in the absence of the complainant.

At a pre-trial hearing a court may make binding rulings about the admissibility of evidence and about questions of law under sections 31 and 40 of the Criminal Procedure and Investigations Act 1996 and section 8A of the Magistrates' Courts Act 1980.]

22.3. Decisions and reasons

(1) A prosecutor who wants to introduce the evidence of a complainant in respect of whom the court allows the introduction of evidence or cross-examination about any sexual behaviour must—

(a) inform the complainant of the court's decision as soon as reasonably practicable; and

(b) explain to the complainant any arrangements that as a result will be made for him or her to give evidence.

(2) The court must—

(a) promptly determine an application; and

(b) allow the prosecutor sufficient time to comply with the requirements of—

(i) paragraph (1), and

(ii) the code of practice issued under section 32 of the Domestic Violence, Crime and Victims Act 2004 or under section 2 of the Victims and Prisoners Act 2024.

(3) The court must announce at a hearing in public—

(a) the reasons for a decision to allow or refuse an application under rule 22.4; and

(b) if it allows such an application, the extent to which evidence may be introduced or questions asked.

[Note. Under section 43 of the Youth Justice and Criminal Evidence Act 1999—

(a) the reasons for the court's decision on an application must be given in open court; and

(b) the court must state in open court the extent to which evidence may be introduced or questions asked.

Under section 32 of the Domestic Violence, Crime and Victims Act 2004, the Secretary of State for Justice must issue a code of practice as to the services to be provided by specified persons to a victim of criminal conduct. Section 2 of the Victims and Prisoners Act 2024 imposes a corresponding obligation. Under section 2(13) of the 2024 Act, until the first code of practice issued under section 2 is in operation, references in sections 5 to 12 and 32 of that Act to the 'victims' code' are references to the code of practice issued under section 32 of the 2004 Act for the time being in operation.]

22.4. Application for permission to introduce evidence or cross-examine

(1) A defendant who wants to introduce evidence or cross-examine a witness about any sexual behaviour of the complainant must—

(a) serve an application for permission to do so on—

(i) the court officer, and

(ii) each other party; and

(b) serve the application—

(i) as soon as reasonably practicable after becoming aware of the grounds for doing so, and in any event

(ii) not more than 10 business days after the prosecutor discloses material on which the application is based.

(2) The application must—

(a) identify the issue to which the defendant says the complainant's sexual behaviour is relevant;

(b) give particulars of—

(i) any evidence that the defendant wants to introduce, and

(ii) any questions that the defendant wants to ask;

(c) identify the exception to the prohibition in section 41 of the Youth Justice and Criminal Evidence Act 1999 on which the defendant relies; and

(d) give the name and date of birth of any witness whose evidence about the complainant's sexual behaviour the defendant wants to introduce.

22.5. Application containing information withheld from another party

(1) This rule applies where—

(a) an applicant serves an application under rule 22.4 (Application for permission to introduce evidence or cross-examine); and

(b) the application includes information that the applicant thinks ought not be revealed to another party.

(2) The applicant must—

(a) omit that information from the part of the application that is served on that other party;

(b) mark the other part to show that, unless the court otherwise directs, it is only for the court; and

(c) in that other part, explain why the applicant has withheld that information from that other party.

(3) If the court so directs, the hearing of an application to which this rule applies may be, wholly or in part, in the absence of a party from whom information has been withheld.

(4) At the hearing of an application to which this rule applies—

(a) the general rule is that the court must consider, in the following sequence—

(i) representations first by the applicant and then by each other party, in all the parties' presence, and then

(ii) further representations by the applicant, in the absence of a party from whom information has been withheld; but

(b) the court may direct other arrangements for the hearing.

[Note. See section 43(3)(c) of the Youth Justice and Criminal Evidence Act 1999.]

22.6. Representations in response

(1) This rule applies where a party wants to make representations about—

(a) an application under rule 22.4 (Application for permission to introduce evidence or cross-examine); or

(b) a proposed variation or discharge of a decision allowing such an application.

(2) Such a party must—

(a) serve the representations on—

(i) the court officer, and

(ii) each other party; and

(b) do so not more than 10 business days after, as applicable—

(i) service of the application, or

(ii) notice of the proposal to vary or discharge.

(3) Where representations include information that the person making them thinks ought not be revealed to another party, that person must—

(a) omit that information from the representations served on that other party;

(b) mark the information to show that, unless the court otherwise directs, it is only for the court; and

(c) with that information include an explanation of why it has been withheld from that other party.

(4) Representations against an application under rule 22.4 must explain the grounds of objection.

(5) Representations against the variation or discharge of a decision must explain why it should not be varied or discharged.

22.7. Special measures, etc. for a witness

(1) This rule applies where the court allows an application under rule 22.4 (Application for permission to introduce evidence or cross-examine).

(2) Despite the time limits in rule 18.4 (Making an application for a direction or order)—

(a) a party may apply for a special measures direction or for the variation of an existing special measures direction not more than 10 business days after the court's decision; and

(b) the court may shorten the time for opposing that application.

(3) Where the court allows the cross-examination of a witness, the court must give directions for the appropriate treatment and questioning of that witness in accordance with rule 3.8(6) and (7) (setting ground rules for the conduct of questioning).

[Note. Special measures to improve the quality of evidence given by certain witnesses may be directed by the court under section 19 of the Youth Justice and Criminal Evidence Act 1999 and varied under section 20. An application for a special measures direction may be made by a party under Part 18 or the court may make a direction on its own initiative. Rule 18.13(2) sets the usual time limit (10 business days) for opposing a special measures application.]

22.8. Court's power to vary requirements under this Part

The court may shorten or extend (even after it has expired) a time limit under this Part.

PART 23 RESTRICTION ON CROSS-EXAMINATION BY A DEFENDANT

GENERAL RULES

23.1. When this Part applies

This Part applies where—

(a) a defendant may not cross-examine in person a witness because of section 34 or section 35 of the Youth Justice and Criminal Evidence Act 1999 (Complainants in proceedings for sexual offences; Child complainants and other child witnesses); or

(b) the court can prohibit a defendant from cross-examining in person a witness under section 36 of that Act (Direction prohibiting accused from cross-examining particular witness).

[Note. Under section 34 of the Youth Justice and Criminal Evidence Act 1999, no defendant charged with a sexual offence may cross-examine in person a witness who is the complainant, either—

(a) in connection with that offence; or

(b) in connection with any other offence (of whatever nature) with which that defendant is charged in the proceedings.

Under section 35 of the 1999 Act, no defendant charged with an offence listed in that section may cross-examine in person a protected witness, either—

(a) in connection with that offence; or

(b) in connection with any other offence (of whatever nature) with which that defendant is charged in the proceedings.

A 'protected witness' is one who—

(a) either is the complainant or is alleged to have been a witness to the commission of the offence; and

(b) either is a child, within the meaning of section 35, or is due to be cross-examined after giving evidence in chief—

(i) by means of a video recording made when the witness was a child, or

(ii) in any other way when the witness was a child.

Under section 36 of the 1999 Act, where neither section 34 nor section 35 applies the court may give a direction prohibiting the defendant from cross-examining, or further cross-examining, in person a witness, on application by the prosecutor or on the court's own initiative. See also rules 23.3 to 23.7.]

23.2. Appointment of advocate to cross-examine witness

(1) This rule applies where a defendant may not cross-examine in person a witness in consequence of—

(a) the prohibition imposed by section 34 or section 35 of the Youth Justice and Criminal Evidence Act 1999; or

(b) a prohibition imposed by the court under section 36 of the 1999 Act.

(2) The court must, as soon as practicable, explain in terms the defendant can understand (with help, if necessary)—

(a) the prohibition and its effect;

(b) that if the defendant will not be represented by a lawyer with a right of audience in the court for the purposes of the case then the defendant is entitled to arrange for such a lawyer to cross-examine the witness on his or her behalf;

(c) that the defendant must notify the court officer of the identity of any such lawyer, with details of how to contact that person, by no later than a date set by the court; and

(d) that if the defendant does not want to make such arrangements, or if the defendant gives no such notice by that date, then—

(i) the court must decide whether it is necessary in the interests of justice to appoint such a lawyer to cross-examine the witness in the defendant's interests, and

(ii) if the court decides that that is necessary, the court will appoint a lawyer chosen by the court who will not be responsible to the defendant.

(3) Having given those explanations, the court must—

(a) ask whether the defendant wants to arrange for a lawyer to cross-examine the witness, and set a date by when the defendant must notify the court officer of the identity of that lawyer if the answer to that question is 'yes'; and

(b) if the answer to that question is 'no', or if by the date set the defendant has given no such notice—

(i) decide whether it is necessary in the interests of justice for the witness to be cross-examined by an advocate appointed to represent the defendant's interests, and

(ii) if the court decides that that is necessary, give directions for the appointment of such an advocate.

(4) The court may give the explanations and ask the questions required by this rule—

(a) at a hearing, in public or in private; or

(b) without a hearing, by written notice to the defendant.

(5) The court may extend (even after it has expired) the time limit that it sets under paragraph (3)(a)—

(a) on application by the defendant; or

(b) on its own initiative.

(6) Paragraphs (7), (8), (9) and (10) apply where the court appoints an advocate.

(7) The directions that the court gives under paragraph (3)(b)(ii) must provide for the supply to the advocate of a copy of—

(a) all material served by one party on the other, whether before or after the advocate's appointment, to which applies—

(i) Part 8 (Initial details of the prosecution case),

(ii) in the Crown Court, rule 3.19 (service of prosecution evidence in a case sent for trial),

(iii) Part 16 (Written witness statements),

(iv) Part 19 (Expert evidence),

(v) Part 20 (Hearsay evidence),

(vi) Part 21 (Evidence of bad character), or

(vii) Part 22 (Evidence of a complainant's previous sexual behaviour);

(b) any material disclosed, given or served, whether before or after the advocate's appointment, which is—

(i) prosecution material disclosed to the defendant under section 3 (Initial duty of prosecutor to disclose) or section 7A (Continuing duty of prosecutor to disclose) of the Criminal Procedure and Investigations Act 1996,

(ii) a defence statement given by the defendant under section 5 (Compulsory disclosure by accused) or section 6 (Voluntary disclosure by accused) of the 1996 Act,

(iii) a defence witness notice given by the defendant under section 6C of that Act (Notification of intention to call defence witnesses), or
(iv) an application by the defendant under section 8 of that Act (Application by accused for disclosure);

(c) any case management questionnaire prepared for the purposes of the trial or, as the case may be, the appeal; and
(d) all case management directions given by the court for the purposes of the trial or the appeal.

(8) Where the defendant has given a defence statement—
(a) section 8(2) of the Criminal Procedure and Investigations Act 1996 is modified to allow the advocate, as well as the defendant, to apply for an order for prosecution disclosure under that subsection if the advocate has reasonable cause to believe that there is prosecution material concerning the witness which is required by section 7A of the Act to be disclosed to the defendant and has not been; and
(b) rule 15.5 (Defendant's application for prosecution disclosure) applies to an application by the advocate as it does to an application by the defendant.

(9) Before receiving evidence the court must establish, with the active assistance of the parties and of the advocate, and in the absence of any jury in the Crown Court—
(a) what issues will be the subject of the advocate's cross-examination; and
(b) whether the court's permission is required for any proposed question, for example where Part 21 or Part 22 applies.

(10) The appointment terminates at the conclusion of the cross-examination of the witness.

[Note. See section 38 of the Youth Justice and Criminal Evidence Act 1999. Under section 38(8) the references in that section to a 'legal representative' are to a representative who is an advocate within the meaning of rule 2.2.

Under section 38(7) of the 1999 Act, where the court appoints an advocate Criminal Procedure Rules may apply with modifications any of the provisions of Part I of the Criminal Procedure and Investigations Act 1996. A summary of the disclosure requirements of the 1996 Act is at the end of Part 15 (Disclosure). Under section 5 of that Act, in the Crown Court the defendant must give a defence statement. Under section 6, in a magistrates' court the defendant may give such a statement but need not do so. Under section 6C, in the Crown Court and in magistrates' courts the defendant must give a defence witness notice indicating whether he or she intends to call any witnesses (other than him or herself) and, if so, identifying them. Under section 8 a defendant may apply for prosecution disclosure only if the defendant has given a defence statement.]

APPLICATION TO PROHIBIT CROSS-EXAMINATION

23.3. Exercise of court's powers

(1) The court may decide whether to impose or discharge a prohibition against cross-examination under section 36 of the Youth Justice and Criminal Evidence Act 1999—
(a) at a hearing, in public or in private, or without a hearing; and
(b) in a party's absence, if that party—
(i) applied for the prohibition or discharge, or
(ii) has had at least 10 business days in which to make representations.

(2) The court must announce, at a hearing in public before the witness gives evidence, the reasons for a decision—
(a) to impose or discharge such a prohibition; or
(b) to refuse to do so.

[Note. See section 37 of the Youth Justice and Criminal Evidence Act 1999.]

23.4. Application to prohibit cross-examination

(1) This rule applies where under section 36 of the Youth Justice and Criminal Evidence Act 1999 the prosecutor wants the court to prohibit the cross-examination of a witness by a defendant in person.

(2) The prosecutor must—

(a) apply in writing, as soon as reasonably practicable after becoming aware of the grounds for doing so; and

(b) serve the application on—

(i) the court officer,

(ii) the defendant who is the subject of the application, and

(iii) any other defendant, unless the court otherwise directs.

(3) The application must—

(a) report any views that the witness has expressed about whether he or she is content to be cross-examined by the defendant in person;

(b) identify—

(i) the nature of the questions likely to be asked, having regard to the issues in the case,

(ii) any relevant behaviour of the defendant at any stage of the case, generally and in relation to the witness,

(iii) any relationship, of any nature, between the witness and the defendant,

(iv) any other defendant in the case who is subject to such a prohibition in respect of the witness, and

(v) any special measures direction made in respect of the witness, or for which an application has been made;

(c) explain why the quality of evidence given by the witness on cross-examination—

(i) is likely to be diminished if no such prohibition is imposed, and

(ii) would be likely to be improved if it were imposed; and

(d) explain why it would not be contrary to the interests of justice to impose the prohibition.

23.5. Application to discharge prohibition imposed by the court

(1) A party who wants the court to discharge a prohibition against cross-examination which the court imposed under section 36 of the Youth Justice and Criminal Evidence Act 1999 must—

(a) apply in writing, as soon as reasonably practicable after becoming aware of the grounds for doing so; and

(b) serve the application on—

(i) the court officer, and

(ii) each other party.

(2) The applicant must—

(a) explain what material circumstances have changed since the prohibition was imposed; and

(b) ask for a hearing, if the applicant wants one, and explain why it is needed.

[Note. Under section 37 of the Youth Justice and Criminal Evidence Act 1999, the court can discharge a prohibition against cross-examination which it has imposed—

(a) on application, if there has been a material change of circumstances; or

(b) on its own initiative.]

23.6. Application containing information withheld from another party

(1) This rule applies where—

(a) an applicant serves an application for the court to impose a prohibition against cross-examination, or for the discharge of such a prohibition; and

(b) the application includes information that the applicant thinks ought not be revealed to another party.

(2) The applicant must—
(a) omit that information from the part of the application that is served on that other party;
(b) mark the other part to show that, unless the court otherwise directs, it is only for the court; and
(c) in that other part, explain why the applicant has withheld that information from that other party.

(3) Any hearing of an application to which this rule applies—
(a) must be in private, unless the court otherwise directs; and
(b) if the court so directs, may be, wholly or in part, in the absence of a party from whom information has been withheld.

(4) At any hearing of an application to which this rule applies—
(a) the general rule is that the court must consider, in the following sequence—
(i) representations first by the applicant and then by each other party, in all the parties' presence, and then
(ii) further representations by the applicant, in the absence of a party from whom information has been withheld; but
(b) the court may direct other arrangements for the hearing.

[Note. See section 37 of the Youth Justice and Criminal Evidence Act 1999.]

23.7. Representations in response

(1) This rule applies where a party wants to make representations about—
(a) an application under rule 23.4 for a prohibition against cross-examination;
(b) an application under rule 23.5 for the discharge of such a prohibition; or
(c) a prohibition or discharge that the court proposes on its own initiative.

(2) Such a party must—
(a) serve the representations on—
(i) the court officer, and
(ii) each other party;
(b) do so not more than 10 business days after, as applicable—
(i) service of the application, or
(ii) notice of the prohibition or discharge that the court proposes; and
(c) ask for a hearing, if that party wants one, and explain why it is needed.

(3) Representations against a prohibition must explain in what respect the conditions for imposing it are not met.

(4) Representations against the discharge of a prohibition must explain why it should not be discharged.

(5) Where representations include information that the person making them thinks ought not be revealed to another party, that person must—
(a) omit that information from the representations served on that other party;
(b) mark the information to show that, unless the court otherwise directs, it is only for the court; and
(c) with that information include an explanation of why it has been withheld from that other party.

23.8. Court's power to vary requirements

(1) The court may—
(a) shorten or extend (even after it has expired) a time limit under rule 23.4 (Application to prohibit cross-examination), rule 23.5 (Application to discharge prohibition imposed by the court) or rule 23.7 (Representations in response); and
(b) allow an application or representations required by any of those rules to be made in a different form to one set out in the Practice Direction, or to be made orally.

(2) A person who wants an extension of time must—
(a) apply when serving the application or representations for which it is needed; and
(b) explain the delay.

Attorney General's Guidelines on Disclosure for investigators, prosecutors and defence practitioners*

(Effective from 29 May 2024)

Introduction

These Guidelines are issued by the Attorney General for investigators, prosecutors and defence practitioners on the application of the disclosure regime contained in the Criminal Procedure and Investigations Act 1996 ('CPIA') Code of Practice Order 2020.

These Guidelines replace the existing Attorney General's Guidelines on Disclosure issued in 2013 and the Supplementary Guidelines on Digital Material issued in 2013, which is an annex to the general guidelines.

The Guidelines outline the high-level principles which should be followed when the disclosure regime is applied throughout England and Wales. They are not designed to be an unequivocal statement of the law at any one time, nor are they a substitute for a thorough understanding of the relevant legislation, codes of practice, case law and procedure.

Important Principles**

1. Every accused person has a right to a fair trial. This right is a fundamental part of our legal system and is guaranteed by Article 6 of the European Convention on Human Rights (ECHR). The disclosure process secures the right to a fair trial.

2. The statutory framework for criminal investigations and disclosure is contained in the Criminal Procedure and Investigations Act 1996 (the CPIA 1996). The CPIA 1996 is an important part of the system that ensures criminal investigations and trials are conducted in a fair, objective and thorough manner. The roles, responsibilities and terminology used in this document therefore mirror the definitions given in the CPIA 1996 and its Code of Practice.

3. A fair trial does not require consideration of irrelevant material. It does not require irrelevant material to be obtained or reviewed. It should not involve spurious applications or arguments which aim to divert the trial process from examining the real issues before the court.

4. The statutory disclosure regime does not require the prosecutor to make available to the accused either neutral material or material which is adverse to the accused. This material may be listed on the schedule, alerting the accused to its existence, but does not need to be disclosed: prosecutors should not disclose material which they are not required to, as this would overburden the participants in the trial process, divert attention away from the relevant issues and may lead to unjustifiable delays. **Disclosure should be completed in a thinking manner, in light of the issues in the case, and not simply as a schedule completing exercise**. Prosecutors need to think about what the case is about, what the likely issues for trial are going to be and how this affects the reasonable lines of inquiry, what material is relevant, and whether material meets the test for disclosure.

5. There will always be a number of participants in prosecutions and investigations. Communication within the prosecution team is vital to ensure that all disclosure issues are given sufficient attention by the right person. The respective roles of an investigator, the officer in charge of an investigation, disclosure officer, and prosecutor are set out in the CPIA Code.

6. A full log of disclosure decisions and the reasons for those decisions must be kept on file and made available to the prosecution team. Any prosecutor must be able to see and understand previous disclosure decisions before carrying out their continuous review function.

7. The role of the reviewing lawyer is central to ensuring that all members of the prosecution team are aware of their role and their duties. Where prosecution advocates are instructed, they

* **Editor's Note:** The guidelines are reproduced without footnotes.

** **Editor's Note**: Figure omitted.

should be provided with clear written instructions about disclosure and provided with copies of any unused material which has been disclosed to the defence.

8. Investigators and disclosure officers must be fair and objective and must work together with prosecutors to ensure that disclosure obligations are met. Investigators and disclosure officers should be familiar with the CPIA Code of Practice—in particular their obligations to retain and record the relevant material, to review it and to reveal it to the prosecutor (see paragraphs 3–7 of the Code).

9. Investigators and disclosure officers should be deployed on cases which are commensurate with their training, skills and experience. The conduct of an investigation provides the foundation for the entire case, and may even impact on linked cases. The specific strategy and approach to disclosure that will be taken must always be considered at the start of each investigation.

10. Where there are a number of disclosure officers assigned to a case there should be a lead disclosure officer who is the focus for enquiries and whose responsibility it is to ensure that the investigator's disclosure obligations are complied with. Regular case conferences should be held, as required, to ensure that prosecutors are apprised of all relevant developments. Full records, including detailed minutes, should be kept of any such meetings. The parties involved should agree at the outset whose responsibility it will be to record the case conferences.

The balance between the right to a fair trial (Article 6 of the European Convention of Human Rights) and the right to private and family life (Article 8 of the European Convention of Human Rights)

11. Investigators and prosecutors need to be aware of the delicate questions which arise when both the right to a fair trial and the privacy of complainants and witnesses are engaged.

12. Fulfilling disclosure obligations is part of ensuring a fair trial in accordance with Article 6 of the ECHR. To comply with Article 6, during the course of an investigation, the investigator or prosecutor may decide that it is necessary to request and/or process personal or private information from a complainant or witness to pursue a reasonable line of inquiry; this includes, but is not limited to, digital material.

13. When seeking to obtain and review such material, investigators and prosecutors should be aware that these lines of inquiry may engage that individual's Article 8 rights and those rights in respect of other parties within that material. Such material may also include sensitive data. When seeking to satisfy their disclosure obligations in these circumstances, investigators and prosecutors should apply the following principles:

a. Collecting and/or processing personal or private material can only be done when in accordance with the law, strictly necessary, and proportionate.
b. In order to be in accordance with the law and necessary, an investigator must be pursuing a reasonable line of inquiry in seeking to obtain the material. What constitutes a reasonable line of inquiry may be informed by others, including the prosecutor and the defendant. Seeking the personal or private information of a complainant or witness will not be a reasonable line of inquiry in every case—an assessment of reasonableness is required (see below for an example).
c. The assessment of reasonableness must be made on a case-by-case basis and regard may be had to:
   (i) the prospect of obtaining relevant material; and
   (ii) what the perceived relevance of that material is, having regard to the identifiable facts and issues in the individual case;
d. If, by following a reasonable line of inquiry, it becomes necessary to obtain personal or private material, investigators will also need to consider:
   (i) what review is required;
   (ii) how the review of this material should be conducted;
   (iii) what is the least intrusive method which will nonetheless secure relevant material;

   (iv) are particular parameters for searching best suited to the identification of relevant material;
   (v) is provision of the material in its entirety to the investigator strictly necessary; or alternatively, could the material be obtained from other sources, or by the investigator viewing and/or capturing the material in situ? An incremental approach should be taken to the degree of intrusion.

e. The rationale for pursuing the reasonable line of inquiry and the scope of the review it necessitates should be open and transparent. It should be capable of articulation by the investigator making the decision. It should provide the basis for:
   (i) consultation with the prosecutor,
   (ii) engagement with the defence and,
   (iii) the provision of information to the witness about how their material is to be handled.

f. The refusal by a witness to provide private or personal material requires an investigator and prosecutor to consider the information the witness has been provided (and could be provided) with regard to the use of their personal material, the reasons for refusal, and how the trial process could address the absence of the material.

g. Disclosure of such material to the defence is in accordance with the law and necessary if, but only if, the material meets the disclosure test in the CPIA 1996. Personal information which does not meet this test but is contained within the material to be disclosed should be redacted.

h. Where there is a conflict between both of these rights, investigators and prosecutors should bear in mind that the right to a fair trial is an absolute right. Where prosecutors and investigators work within the framework provided by the CPIA, any unavoidable intrusion into privacy rights is likely to be justified, so long as any intrusion is no more than necessary.

For retention of data, see paragraphs 21–25 of Annex A on Digital Material and paragraph 5(a) and (b) of the Code.

Example

There will be cases where there is no requirement for the police to take the devices of a complainant/witness or others at all, and no requirement for any examination to be undertaken.

Examples of this could include sexual offences committed opportunistically against strangers, or historic allegations where there is considered to be no prospect that the complainant's phone will contain any material relevant to the period in which the conduct is said to have occurred and/or the complainant through age or other circumstances did not have access to a phone at that time.

However, decisions will depend on the facts of the case in question. For example, in the case of a sexual offence committed opportunistically against a stranger, a mobile phone could contain first complaint evidence. Investigators should always carefully consider what is relevant for the case in question.

A case might, for example, involve a complainant contacting the police to make an allegation of an offence against a person they had met that same day. The suspect may accept that they met the complainant but deny the allegation. The complainant and suspect communicated on a single medium. The investigator may consider it is a reasonable line of enquiry to view the messages from the day on which the two persons met as, before and after, they are highly likely to be relevant. They may contain material about what was expected or not expected when the complainant and suspect met, the nature of their relationship, and the response after they met, all of which may cast light on the complainant's account and the suspect's account. That is unlikely to require the investigator taking custody of the phone or obtaining a large volume of data. If, by way of example and contrast, the complainant alleged coercive and controlling behaviour over a period of years, including manipulative conduct over various platforms, a larger quantity of data may be relevant and require review and retention by the investigator by different means.

The investigation

14. Consideration of disclosure issues is an integral part of an investigation and is not something that should be considered in isolation.

15. Investigators should approach the investigation with a view to establishing what actually happened. They are to be fair and objective.

16. . . .*

17. Investigators should ensure that all reasonable lines of inquiry are investigated, whether they point towards or away from the suspect. What is 'reasonable' will depend on the context of the case. A fair investigation does not mean an endless investigation. Investigators and disclosure officers must give thought to defining and articulating the limits of the scope of their investigations. When assessing what is reasonable, thought should be given to what is likely to be obtained as a result of the line of inquiry and how it can be obtained. An investigator may seek the advice of the prosecutor when considering which lines of inquiry should be pursued where appropriate.

18. When conducting an investigation, an investigator should always have in mind their obligation to retain and record all relevant material. Material which is presumed to meet the test for disclosure, as set out in the dedicated section of these guidelines, must always be retained and recorded. All relevant material must be retained, whereas non- relevant material does not need to be retained.

Definitions

Relevant Material

Material may be relevant to an investigation if it appears to an investigator, or to the officer in charge of an investigation, or to the disclosure officer, that it has some bearing on any offence under investigation or any person being investigated, or on the surrounding circumstances of the case, unless it is incapable of having any impact on the case.

Reasonable Line of Inquiry

A reasonable line of inquiry is that which points either towards or away from the suspect. What is reasonable will depend on the circumstances of the case and consideration should be had of the prospect of obtaining relevant material, and the perceived relevance of that material.

Disclosure Test

Material that might reasonably be considered capable of undermining the case for the prosecution against the accused, or of assisting the case for the accused.

All definitions correspond to the CPIA and CPIA Code of Practice

19. The decision as to relevance requires an exercise of judgment and, although some material may plainly be relevant or non-relevant, ultimately this requires a decision by the disclosure officer or investigator.

20. Disclosure officers and/or investigators must inspect, view, listen to, or search all relevant material. The disclosure officer must provide a personal declaration that this task has been completed. In some cases a detailed examination of every item of material seized would be disproportionate. In such cases the disclosure officer can apply search techniques using the principles contained in Annex A. Whatever the approach taken by disclosure officers in examining material, it is crucial that disclosure officers record their reasons for a particular approach in writing. Where third party material is under consideration, reference should be made to paragraph 26 et seq. of these Guidelines.

21. Disclosure officers should seek the advice and assistance of prosecutors when in doubt as to their responsibility as early as possible. They must deal expeditiously with requests by the prosecutor for further information on material, which may lead to disclosure.

* **Editor's Note:** Figure omitted.

22. Where prosecutors have reason to believe that the disclosure officer has not inspected, viewed, listened to or searched relevant material, or has not done so sufficiently or has not articulated a reason for doing so, they should raise this issue with the disclosure officer and request that it is addressed. Prosecutors should also assist disclosure officers and investigators in defining the parameters of review and the methodology to be adopted.

23. It may become apparent to an investigator that some material obtained in the course of an investigation, either because it was considered to be potentially relevant, or because it was inextricably linked to material that was relevant, is in fact incapable of impacting on the case. It is not necessary to retain such material. However, the investigator should also exercise considerable caution in reaching that conclusion. The investigator should be particularly mindful of the fact that some investigations continue over some time. Material that is incapable of impact may change over time and it may not be possible to foresee what the issues in the case will be. The advice of the prosecutor may be sought where necessary. Ultimately, however, the decision on whether to retain material is one for the investigator, and should always be based on their assessment of the relevance of the material and the likelihood of it having any impact on the case in future.

24. Prosecutors must be alert to the need to provide advice to and, where necessary, probe actions taken by the investigator to ensure that disclosure obligations are capable of being met. This should include advice on potential further reasonable lines of inquiry. There should be no aspects of an investigation about which prosecutors are unable to ask probing questions.

25. In some investigations it may be appropriate for the officer in charge of the investigation to seek engagement with the defence at the pre-charge stage. This is likely to be where it is possible that such engagement will lead to the defence volunteering additional information which may assist in identifying new lines of inquiry. Annex B sets out the process for any such pre-charge engagement.

Third party material

26. Third party material is material held by a person, organisation, or government department other than the investigator and prosecutor, either within the UK or outside the UK. Third parties are not directly involved in the case in question but may hold information relevant to it.

27. The CPIA addresses material once it has come into the possession of an investigator or prosecutor. These guidelines prescribe the approach to be taken to disclosure of material held by third parties, either when it comes into the possession of the investigator or prosecutor or remains in the possession of the third party.

Principles of accessing third party material

Step 1: Establishing a Reasonable Line of Inquiry

28. The CPIA Code and these guidelines make clear the obligation on the investigator to pursue all reasonable lines of inquiry in relation to any offence under investigation, its surrounding circumstances or any person being investigated. This requires the investigator to pursue all lines of inquiry, whether they point towards or away from the suspect, that may reveal material **relevant** to the investigation or the likely issues at trial. This obligation is the same in respect of material held by third parties within the UK.

29. It is for investigators, in consultation or discussion with prosecutors where appropriate, to identify and pursue all reasonable lines of inquiry. Prosecutors can advise on additional reasonable lines of inquiry and should satisfy themselves that such reasonable lines of inquiry have been pursued.

Step 2: Establishing Relevance

30. Third party material should only be requested in an individual case if it has been identified as relevant to an issue in the case. This will depend on the circumstances of the individual case, including any potential defence, and any other information informing the direction of the case. Access to third party material should never occur as a matter of course. It should never be assumed that because of the nature of an offence that is being investigated that particular types of material will need to be accessed. There will be cases where no investigation of third party

material is necessary at all, and others where detailed scrutiny is needed. There must be a properly identifiable foundation for the inquiry, not mere conjecture or speculation.

31. A written record must be made of any decision to access third party material in the Investigation or Disclosure Management Document as appropriate. This record must also detail the underlying basis or rationale for the decision to access third party material. Disclosure Management Documents should be drafted to include the lines of inquiry pursued relating to third party material. This will assist in demonstrating to the defence and court the steps that have or have not been taken and why.

32. Investigators and prosecutors, when deciding whether third party material should be requested in an individual case, should consider the following, although this list is not exhaustive, and the considerations will vary depending on the circumstances of the case:

i. What relevant information is the material believed to contain?

ii. Why is it believed that the material contains that relevant information? If it is likely that no relevant information will be contained within the material, a request should not be made.

iii. Will the request for the material intrude on a complainant's or witness's privacy?

iv. If the material requested does amount to an invasion of privacy, is it a proportionate and justifiable request to make in the circumstances of the individual case and any known issues? Consider vi. below or whether the information which may result in access amounting to an invasion of privacy can be redacted to remove anything that does not meet the disclosure test.

v. Depending on the stage of the case, does the material need to be obtained or would a request to preserve the material suffice until more information is known?

vi. Is there an alternative way of readily accessing the information such as open-source searches, searches of material obtained from the suspect, or speaking directly to a witness, that does not require a request to a third party?

vii. Consider the scope of the material required, for example are the entirety of an individual's medical records required or would a particular month or year be sufficient? Ensure the request is focused so that only relevant information is being sought.

viii. The process of disclosure and its role in the justice system should be clearly and understandably expressed to the third party. They must be kept appraised of any ongoing disclosure decisions that are made with regard to their material.

Step 3: Balancing Rights

33. If as a result of the duty to pursue all reasonable lines of inquiry, the investigator or prosecutor obtains or receives material from a third party, then it must be dealt with in accordance with the CPIA 1996, (i.e. the prosecutor must disclose material only if it meets the disclosure test, subject to any public interest immunity claim). The person who has an interest in the material (the third party) may make representations to the court concerning public interest immunity (see section 16 of the CPIA 1996).

34. In some cases, third party material may reveal intimate, personal or delicate information. Prosecutors should give close scrutiny to such material and only disclose it where absolutely necessary. Further guidance and best practice on obtaining third party material can be found in the Joint Protocol on Third Party Material and Chapter 5 of the CPS Disclosure Manual. Investigators and prosecutors must also comply with data protection law when accessing third party material which contains personal information; they must consider closely how to balance the right to fair trial and right to privacy as set out at paragraph 11 et seq. For more information, please consult Annex A on Digital Material and Annex D on Redaction.

Material held by Government departments

35. During an investigation or prosecution it may become apparent that a Government department or another Crown body has material that may be relevant to an issue in the case. Investigators or prosecutors should seek access to this material if and only if they have met the principles for accessing third party material as set out above. Any access must be in accordance with those principles.

36. The investigator or prosecutor should inform the Government department or Crown body at the earliest opportunity of the nature of the case and the relevant issues in the case, and ask whether it has any relevant material. They should assist the Government department or Crown body in understanding what may be relevant in the context of the case in question.

37. Crown Servants have a duty to support the administration of justice and should take reasonable steps to identify and consider such material. This extends to revealing to the investigator or prosecutor the extent of the searches conducted and the existence of any information which they believe may be relevant to the issues in the case, to supply them with that information unless it is protected to the issues in the case, and to supply them with that information unless it is protected in law, subject to legal professional privilege or attracts public interest immunity.

38. If access is denied to relevant material, the investigator or prosecutor should consider the reasons given by the Government department or Crown body and what, if any, further steps might be taken to obtain the material. The final decision on further steps rests with the prosecutor.

39. Investigators and prosecutors cannot be regarded to be in constructive possession of material held by Government departments or Crown bodies simply by virtue of their status as Government departments or Crown bodies.

40. The steps taken to identify and obtain relevant material held by a Government department or Crown body should be recorded by the investigator and the prosecutor.

41. Where appropriate, the defence should be informed of the steps taken to obtain material and the results of the line of inquiry.

Other domestic bodies

42. If an investigator, disclosure officer or a prosecutor considers a third party (for example a local authority, social services department, hospital, doctor, school, provider of forensic services, or CCTV operator) has material or information that is relevant to an issue in the case, they should seek access to this material if and only if they have met the principles for accessing third party material as set out above. A third party has no obligation under the CPIA to reveal material to investigators or prosecutors. There is also no duty on the third party to retain material which may be relevant to the investigation and, in some circumstances, the third party may not be aware of the investigation or prosecution.

43. If access to the material is refused and, despite the reasons given for refusal of access, it is still believed that it is reasonable to seek production of the material or information and that the requirements of a witness summons are satisfied (or any other relevant power), then the prosecutor or investigator should apply for the summons causing a representative of the third party to produce the material to court. A witness summons is only available once a case has been charged. If the material is sought pre-charge, investigators and prosecutors should request that the third party preserve the material. This request should be documented.

44. When the third party material in question is personal data, investigators and prosecutors must refer to paragraphs 11–13 of these guidelines to ensure that there is no unjust intrusion of privacy.

45. The defence should be informed of what steps have been taken to obtain material and what the results of the inquiry have been. Disclosure Management Documents should be used in Crown Court cases.

International enquiries

46. The obligations under the CPIA Code to pursue all reasonable lines of inquiry apply to material held overseas.

47. Where it appears that there is material relevant to an issue in the case held overseas, the investigator or prosecutor should seek access to this material if and only if they have met the principles for accessing third party material as set out above. If this standard is met, they must take reasonable steps to obtain it while acting in accordance with the principles. Investigators or

prosecutors may do so either informally or by making use of the powers contained in the Crime (International Co-operation) Act 2003, the Criminal Justice (European Investigation Order) Regulations 2017 and any international conventions.

48. There may be cases where a foreign state or court refuses to make the material available to the investigator or prosecutor. There may be other cases where the foreign state, though willing to show the material to investigators, will not allow the material to be copied or otherwise made available and the courts of the foreign state will not order its provision.

49. It is for these reasons that there is no absolute duty on the prosecutor to disclose relevant material held overseas by entities not subject to the jurisdiction of the courts in England and Wales. However, consideration should be given to whether the type of material believed to be held can be provided to the defence.

50. The obligation on the investigator and prosecutor under the CPIA Code is to take reasonable steps. Where investigators are allowed to examine the files of a foreign state but are not allowed to take copies, take notes or list the documents held, there is no breach by the prosecution in its duty of disclosure by reason of its failure to obtain such material, provided reasonable steps have been taken to try and obtain it. Prosecutors have a margin of consideration as to what steps are appropriate in the particular case, but prosecutors must be alive to their duties and there may be some circumstances where these duties cannot be met. Whether or not a prosecutor has taken reasonable steps is for the court to determine in each case if the matter is raised.

51. Where it is apparent during the investigation that there may be relevant material held overseas then investigators and prosecutors should consider engaging with the defence at the pre-charge stage, applying the principles contained in Annex B, to ensure that all reasonable lines of inquiry are followed.

52. It is important that the position taken in relation to any material held overseas is clearly set out in a document such as a disclosure management document (DMD) so that the court and the defence know what the position is. Further information on DMDs can be found below.

53. In the DMD, investigators and prosecutors must record and explain the situation and set out, insofar as they are permitted by the foreign state, such information as they can and the steps they have taken to obtain it.

54. The defence should be informed of what steps have been taken to obtain material and what the results of the enquiry have been.

Electronic material

55. The exponential increase in the use of technology in society means that many routine investigations are increasingly likely to have to engage with digital material of some form. It is not only in large and complex investigations where there may be large quantities of such material. When dealing with large quantities of digital material prosecutors and investigators should apply the principles contained in Annex A to these guidelines.

56. Where investigations involve a large quantity of digital material it may be impossible for investigators to examine every item of such material individually. Therefore there should be no expectation that this should happen. Investigators and disclosure officers will need to decide how best to pursue a reasonable line of inquiry in relation to the relevant digital material, and ensure that the extent and manner of the examination are appropriate to the issues in the case. In reaching any such decisions, investigators and disclosure officers must bear in mind the overriding obligation to ensure a fair trial of any suspect who is charged and the requirement to provide disclosure in the trial process.

57. Prosecutors and investigators must ensure that any line of inquiry pursued in relation to the digital devices of victims and witnesses are reasonable in the context of the likely issues in the case. Digital devices should not be obtained as a matter of course and the decision to obtain and examine a digital device will be a fact-specific decision to be made in each and every case. Where digital devices are obtained, if it becomes apparent that they do not contain relevant material they should be returned at the earliest opportunity.

58. Prosecutors should be consulted, where appropriate, to agree a strategy for dealing with digital material. This strategy should be set out in a disclosure management document (DMD) and shared with the defence at the appropriate time.

Revelation of material to a prosecutor

59. Prosecutors only have knowledge of the matters which are revealed to them by investigators and disclosure officers. The schedules are the means by which that revelation takes place. Therefore it is crucial that the schedules detail all of the relevant material and that the material is adequately described. This process will also enable defence practitioners to become appraised of relevant material at the appropriate stage of the investigation. More detail on what constitutes relevant material can be found here.

60. Schedules must be completed in a form which not only reveals sufficient information to the prosecutor, but which demonstrates a transparent and thinking approach to the disclosure exercise. The speed with which the schedule is produced should not reduce the quality of the material contained therein.

61. Descriptions on the schedules must be clear and accurate and must contain sufficient detail to enable the prosecutor to make an informed decision on disclosure. Abbreviations and acronyms should be avoided as they risk significant material being overlooked.

62. Investigators and disclosure officers must ensure that material which is presumed to meet the test for disclosure, as set out in paragraph 86 of these guidelines and paragraph 6.6 of the CPIA Code, is placed on the schedules. The requirement to schedule this material is in addition to the requirement to schedule all other relevant unused material.

63. Where relevant unused material has been omitted from the schedule or where material is not described sufficiently, and the prosecutor asks the disclosure officer to rectify the schedule, the disclosure officer must comply with this request in a timely manner.

64. Disclosure officers must bring to the prosecutor's attention any material which is potentially capable of meeting the test for disclosure. This material should be provided to the prosecutor along with the reasons why it is thought to meet the test.

65. Disclosure officers must also draw material to the attention of the prosecutor for consideration where they have doubt as to whether it might reasonably be considered capable of undermining the prosecution case or of assisting the case for the accused.

Revelation of sensitive material

What is sensitive material?

66. Sensitive material is material that, if disclosed, would give rise to a **real** risk of **serious** prejudice to an **important** public interest. Investigators must ensure that all relevant unused sensitive material is retained, reviewed and revealed to the prosecutor. Sensitive material should be revealed to a prosecutor on a separate schedule to the non-sensitive material.

Examples of sensitive material can be found in paragraph 6.14 of the CPIA Code.

Sensitive material as defined by the CPIA Code of Practice is distinct from personal information requiring strict necessity processing under the Data Protection Act 2018, which is sometimes referred to as 'sensitive personal information/data.'

67. When making a decision about the sensitivity of an item, investigators should have regard to the types of material listed in paragraph 6.14 of the CPIA Code. The disclosure officer must ensure that the sensitive material schedule includes the reasons why it is asserted that items on the schedule are considered sensitive.

68. Where a document contains a mix of sensitive and non-sensitive material, the sensitive material must be redacted, with a copy of the redacted document placed on the non-sensitive unused material schedule and the original placed on the sensitive schedule.

69. Investigators must ensure that the descriptions of sensitive unused material are sufficiently clear to enable the prosecutor to make an informed decision as to whether or not the material itself should be viewed, to the extent possible without compromising the confidentiality of the information.

70. Prosecutors must carefully review the sensitive unused material schedule in order to be satisfied that there are no omissions, that the items have been correctly identified as sensitive, and that the items are adequately described. If a prosecutor identifies that a schedule is inadequate, the investigator must provide an adequate schedule as soon as possible. This may involve items being moved from the sensitive unused material schedule to the non-sensitive unused material schedule.

The timing of revelation

71. In order to support prosecutors' assessment of the impact of unused material on any proposed prosecution, it is essential that prosecutors are provided with the schedule of unused material at an early stage, as well as any material which the disclosure officer considers potentially capable of meeting the test for disclosure. This will allow for a thorough review of the case and enable the prosecutor to consider what the disclosure strategy should be.

72. The timing of revelation of material should be in accordance with paragraph 7.1 of the Code. The point at which the case file is submitted to the CPS will depend on the circumstances of the charging decision and on the anticipated plea:

a. Where the police are seeking a charging decision under the Full Code Test from the CPS, and it is anticipated that the defendant will plead not guilty, the unused material schedules should be provided to the prosecutor by the disclosure officer at the same time as seeking this charging decision.
b. Where the police have charged a suspect on the Full Code Test under the arrangements contained in the Director's Guidance on Charging, and a not guilty plea is anticipated, then the unused material schedule should be provided to the prosecutor at the point at which the case file is submitted to the CPS.
c. In all other cases the disclosure officer must provide the schedules as soon as possible after a not guilty plea has either been indicated or entered.

73. There may be instances where an investigator is seeking a charging decision on the Full Code Test and anticipating a not guilty plea, but where it is not feasible to provide the unused material schedules to the prosecutor at the same time as seeking a charging decision. This may be the case where an arrest is not planned, and the suspect cannot be bailed.

74. For large and complex investigations, particularly those conducted by the Serious Fraud Office, it is recognised that the preparation of schedules continues beyond the point of charge due to the quantity and complexity of data to be analysed, and that it may not be feasible or necessary to provide the schedules at the same time that a charging decision is sought.

75. Disclosure officers should apply the criteria contained in the Director's Guidance on Charging when making a decision about a suspect's likely plea and must follow any additional guidance provided by the prosecutor.

The charging decision

76. Prosecutors must ensure that all reasonable lines of inquiry likely to affect the application of the Full Code Test have been pursued before the Test is applied, unless the prosecutor is satisfied that any further evidence or material is unlikely to affect the application of the Full Code Test. The failure to pursue reasonable lines of inquiry may result in the application of the Full Code Test being deferred, or in a decision that the Test cannot be met.

77. If a decision is made to charge a case under the Threshold Test, then prosecutors and investigators need to be proactive in ensuring that any outstanding lines of inquiry are pursued and that the case is kept under continuous review.

Common law disclosure

78. A prosecutor's statutory duty of disclosure applies from the point of a not guilty plea in the magistrates' court and from the point a case is sent to the Crown Court. However, prosecutors must also consider their duties under the common law which apply at all stages of a case, from charge to sentence and post-conviction (see paragraphs 139 and 140) and regardless of anticipated or actual plea.

79. These duties may require the prosecutor to disclose material to the accused outside the statutory scheme in accordance with the interests of justice and fairness. An example of this is where it would assist the accused in the preparation of the defence case, prior to plea and regardless of anticipated plea. This would include material which would assist in the making of a bail application, material which may enable the accused to make an early application to stay the proceedings as an abuse of process, material which may enable the accused to make representations about the trial venue or a lesser charge, or material which would enable an accused to prepare for trial effectively.

Initial disclosure

80. The defence must be provided with copies of, or access to, any prosecution material not previously disclosed, which might reasonably be considered capable of undermining the case for the prosecution against the accused, or of assisting the case for the accused. Paragraphs 101 et seq. of these Guidelines contain guidance as to when initial disclosure should be served.

81. In order for the prosecutor to comply with their duty of initial disclosure they must analyse the case for the prosecution, the defence case, and the likely trial issues. A prosecutor can anticipate the likely issues on the basis of information available (such as any explanation provided by the accused in interview).

82. The prosecutor and defence are both under a duty to engage promptly in order to aid understanding of the defence case and the likely issues for trial at an early stage. This engagement assists in ensuring compliance with the overriding objective of the Criminal Procedure Rules and that any further reasonable lines of inquiry can be identified and pursued. Without engagement from defence at an early stage, the accuracy of disclosure can be compromised. Significant cooperation should be a regular occurrence and all parties should consider the Criminal Practice Direction CPD1, para 1A.1 which includes the statement of Lord Justice Auld that *'a criminal trial is not a game under which a guilty defendant should be provided with a sporting chance. It is a search for truth in accordance with the twin principles that the prosecution must prove its case and that a defendant is not obliged to inculpate himself'.*

83. Prosecutors must review schedules prepared by disclosure officers thoroughly at an early stage and must be alert to the possibility that relevant material may exist which has not been revealed to them or material included which should not have been. If no schedules are provided, if there are apparent omissions from the schedules, or if documents or other items are inadequately described or are unclear, the prosecutor must request properly completed schedules from the investigator. Investigators must comply with any such request. A log of such communications should be kept by the prosecutor.

84. In deciding whether material satisfies the disclosure test, consideration should include:

- a. The use that might be made of it in cross-examination;
- b. Its capacity to support submissions that could lead to:
  - i. The exclusion of evidence;
  - ii. A stay of proceedings, where the material is required to allow a proper application to be made;
  - iii. A court or tribunal finding that any public authority had acted incompatibly with the accused's rights under the European Convention of Human Rights;
- c. Its capacity to suggest an explanation or partial explanation of the accused's actions;
- d. Its capacity to undermine the reliability or credibility of a prosecution witness;
- e. The capacity of the material to have a bearing on scientific or medical evidence in the case.

85. Material relating to the accused's mental or physical health, intellectual capacity, or to any ill treatment which the accused may have suffered when in the investigator's custody is likely to meet the test for disclosure.

Material should not be viewed in isolation as, whilst items taken alone may not be reasonably considered capable of undermining the prosecution case or assisting the case for the accused, several items together can have that effect.

Material which is likely to meet the test for disclosure

86. The following material, which is produced and obtained in the majority of investigations is likely to include information which meets the test for disclosure:

a) records which are derived from tapes or recordings of telephone messages (for example 999 calls) containing descriptions of an alleged offence or offender;
b) any incident logs relating to the allegation;
c) contemporaneous record of the incident such as crime reports and crime report forms, or where not already contained within the crime report:
   - an investigation log;
   - any record or note made by an investigator (including police notebook entries and other handwritten notes) on which they later make a statement or which relates to contact with suspects, victims or witnesses;
   - an account of an incident or information relevant to an incident noted by an investigator in manuscript or electronically;
   - records of actions carried out by officers (such as house-to- house interviews, CCTV or forensic enquiries) noted by a police officer in manuscript or electronically;
   - CCTV footage, or other imagery, of the incident in action;
d) the defendant's custody record or voluntary attendance record;
e) any previous accounts made by a complainant or by any other witnesses;
f) interview records (written records, or audio or video tapes, of interviews with actual or potential witnesses or suspects);
g) any material casting doubt on the reliability of a witness e. g. relevant previous convictions and relevant cautions of any prosecution witnesses and any co-accused.

87. When providing CCTV footage, or other imagery, of the incident in action as material which is likely to meet the test for disclosure, investigators should include all relevant body-worn footage that is not provided as evidence. It may be that the entirety of the footage contains both relevant and irrelevant material. Irrelevant footage should not be provided to prosecutors in the first instance. It may be the footage requires clipping or editing to achieve this. Where multiple body worn cameras capture the same content, it may be that only one set of footage needs be provided. The remainder should be listed clearly on the unused material schedule. This decision must be made on a case-by-case basis, as it may be that similar but distinct footage has been captured, in which case multiple sets of footage should be provided.

88. This list is reflected in paragraph 5.4 and 6.6 of the Code. This material, in addition to all other material which may be relevant to an investigation, must, in the first instance, be **retained** and **listed** on the schedule by the investigator. It is likely that some of this material will need to be redacted (see paragraph 6(c) of the Code and the sensitive material provisions of these guidelines for redaction and revelation of sensitive material.) Before any of this material is provided to the prosecutor, investigators should apply the disclosure test to the material to ascertain if in fact it is disclosable. When providing the material to the prosecutor the investigator should highlight the material they consider is disclosable and why.

Assessment by the Investigator

89. Before any of this material is provided to the prosecutor, investigators should apply the disclosure test to the material to ascertain if in fact it is disclosable. When providing the material to the prosecutor the investigator should highlight the material they consider is disclosable and why.

Assessment by the Prosecutor

90. Once the material has been provided to the prosecutor, as this material is likely to contain information which meets the test for disclosure, prosecutors should start their review of

the material with a presumption that this material should be disclosed to the defence. However, in every instance the disclosure test should be applied in a thinking manner.

91. After applying the disclosure test, a prosecutor must record on the unused material schedule whether each item of this material does or does not meet the test for disclosure and they must record the reason for that decision.

92. This list of material is not intended to cause automatic disclosure – investigators and prosecutors should always apply the disclosure test and consider each list of material carefully in the context of the case in question. Defence should not expect to be provided with this material as of right in every case. The material is always subject to the disclosure test first before any material is provided.

Disclosure management document (DMD)

What is a disclosure management document?

93. A disclosure management document (DMD) outlines the strategy and approach taken in relation to disclosure and should be served to the defence and the court at an early stage. DMDs will require careful preparation and presentation which is tailored to the individual case. The investigator should provide information for use in the DMD and the prosecutor should prepare it.

94. A DMD is a living document which should be amended in light of developments in the case and kept up to date as the case progresses. DMDs are intended to assist the court in case management and will also enable the defence to engage from an early stage with the prosecution's proposed approach to disclosure.

95. DMDs may set out:

a. Where prosecutors and investigators operate in an integrated office, an explanation as to how the disclosure responsibilities have been managed.
b. A brief summary of the prosecution case and a statement outlining how the prosecutor's general approach will comply with the CPIA 1996 regime and these guidelines
c. The prosecutor's understanding of the defence case, including information revealed during interview. The prosecutor may wish to explain their understanding of what is in dispute and what is not in dispute, the lines of inquiry that have been pursued in light of these issues, and specific disclosure decisions that have been taken.
d. An outline of the prosecution's general approach to disclosure, which may include detail relating to:
    i. The lines of inquiry pursued, particularly those which may assist the defence.
    ii. The timescales for disclosure and, where relevant, how the review of unused material has been prioritised.
    iii. The method and extent of examination of digital material, in accordance with the Annex A to these guidelines.
    iv. Any potential video footage.
    v. Any linked investigations, including an explanation of the nexus between investigations and any memoranda of understanding and disclosure agreements between investigators.
    vi. Any third party material, including the steps taken to obtain the material.
    vii. Any international material, including the steps taken to obtain the material.
    viii. Credibility of prosecution witnesses (including professional witnesses).

96. In cases heard in the magistrates' court and the youth court, prosecutors should always consider whether or not a disclosure management document (DMD) would be beneficial. DMDs are most likely to be beneficial in cases with the following features:

a. Substantial or complex third party material;
b. Digital material in which parameters of search, examination or analysis have been set;

c. Cases involving international enquiries;
d. Cases where there are linked operations;
e. Non-recent offending;
f. Cases involving material held or sought by the investigation that is susceptible to a claim of legal professional privilege.

97. DMDs should be prepared in all Crown Court cases.

98. In order for the prosecutor to complete a DMD at an early stage, the investigator should, at the point of or prior to charge, provide written details as to the lines of inquiry that have been pursued.

99. Where a DMD has been prepared, it should be served at the same time as initial disclosure.

100. An example template for a DMD is contained in Annex C.

The timing of initial disclosure

101. In all cases it is essential that the prosecution takes a grip on the case and its disclosure requirements at an early stage. Prosecutors must adopt a considered and appropriately resourced approach to providing initial disclosure. Initial disclosure in this context refers to the period post-charge; more detailed timings for this are set out below.

Cases expected to be tried in the magistrates' courts

102. Where a case is charged on the Full Code Test and a not guilty plea is anticipated, initial disclosure should be served in advance of the first hearing.

103. Where a guilty plea was originally anticipated but a not guilty plea is entered then initial disclosure should be served as soon as possible after a not guilty plea is entered.

104. Where a case is charged on the Threshold Test, initial disclosure should be served as soon as possible after the Full Code Test is applied and in accordance with any order made by the court.

Cases sent to the Crown Court for trial

105. Where it is expected that the accused will maintain a not guilty plea, it is encouraged as a matter of best practice for initial disclosure to be served prior to the Plea and Trial Preparation Hearing (PTPH).

106. It is accepted that it may not be appropriate or possible to serve initial disclosure prior to the PTPH for cases charged on the Threshold Test. Where initial disclosure has not been served at the PTPH it should be served as soon as possible after that hearing and in accordance with any direction made by the court.

107. In cases prosecuted by the Serious Fraud Office, or other similarly large or complex cases, it is accepted that full initial disclosure may not be capable of being served prior to the PTPH. In such cases, best practice is to adopt a phased approach to disclosure, ensuring that robust judicial case management during Further Case Management Hearings, and in line with the Criminal Procedure Rules and Criminal Practice Directions, manages the on-going disclosure process. Utilising an initial DMD at the PTPH which outlines the intended plan for onwards staged disclosure of remaining materials and associated schedules, can be an effective mechanism for this approach and is to adopted where possible.

108. Nothing in these guidelines should undermine the established principles of the Better Case Management Framework.

Case management

109. In order for the statutory disclosure regime to work effectively all parties should ensure compliance with the Criminal Procedure Rules. The rules require the court to actively manage the case by identifying the real issues. Each party is obliged to assist the court with this duty.

110. It is important that prosecutors keep a record of all correspondence which relates to disclosure and keep a record of any disclosure decisions made.

111. Any party who takes the view that another party is not complying with their obligations under the disclosure regime should bring this to the attention of the court as soon as possible.

Magistrates' court

112. Following a not guilty plea being entered in the magistrates' court, the defence must ensure that the trial issues are clearly identified both in court and on the preparation for effective trial form. Prosecutors should ensure that any issues of dispute that are raised are noted on file. The preparation for effective trial form should be carefully reviewed, alongside the DMD (where this exists). Consideration of any issues raised in court or on the form will assist in deciding whether any further material undermines the prosecution case or assists the accused.

Crown Court

113. A focus of the Plea and Trial Preparation Hearing (PTPH) must be on the disclosure strategy. This will involve the defence identifying the likely trial issues, a discussion of any additional lines of inquiry, and scrutiny of the DMD.

114. Prosecutors must ensure that the disclosure strategy and any disclosure decisions taken previously are reviewed in light of any issues raised at the PTPH and on the plea and trial preparation form.

115. Where the defence do not feel that the prosecution have adequately discharged their obligations then this must be brought to the court's attention at an early stage. The defence should be proactive in ensuring that any issue is addressed, and must not delay raising these issues until a late stage in the proceedings. The DMD may be relevant in any challenge raised.

116. Where any party has not complied with their obligations, the court will consider giving any direction appropriate to ensure compliance and progression of the case.

Applications for non-disclosure in the public interest

117. The CPIA 1996 allows prosecutors to apply to the court for an order to withhold material which would otherwise fall to be disclosed if disclosure would give rise to a real risk of serious prejudice to an important public interest. Before making such an application, prosecutors should aim to disclose as much of the material as they properly can (for example, by giving the defence redacted or edited copies or summaries). Neutral material or material damaging to the defendant should not be disclosed and should not be brought to the attention of the court. Only in truly borderline cases should the prosecution seek a judicial ruling on whether material in its possession should be disclosed.

118. Prior to the hearing, the prosecutor and the prosecution advocate must examine all material which is the subject matter of the application and make any necessary enquiries of the investigator. There is an additional duty of candour on the advocate at this hearing, given the defendant will not be present. In order to assist the court, it is best practice for the advocate to prepare a note that is either written in conjunction, or agreed with, the prosecutor and disclosure officer.

119. The investigator must also be frank with the prosecutor about the full extent of the sensitive material. Prior to, or at the hearing, the court must be provided with full and accurate information about the material.

120. The prosecutor and/or investigator should attend such applications. Section 16 of the CPIA 1996 allows a person claiming to have an interest in the sensitive material to apply to the court for the opportunity to be heard at the application.

121. The prosecutor should carefully consider the series of questions contained in paragraph 36 of *R v H and others* [2004] UKHL 3. These are the questions that the court must address before it makes a decision to withhold material. It is essential that these principles are scrupulously adhered to, to ensure that the procedure for examination of material in the absence of the accused is compliant with Article 6 of the ECHR.

122. If the prosecutor concludes that a fair trial cannot take place because material which satisfies the test for disclosure cannot be disclosed and that this cannot be remedied by an application for non-disclosure in the public interest, through altering the presentation of the case or by any other means, then they should not continue with the case.

The defence statement

123. Defence statements are an integral part of the statutory disclosure regime. A defence statement should help to focus the attention of the prosecutor, court and co-defendants on the relevant issues in order to identify material which may meet the test for disclosure. The defence must serve their defence statement in a timely manner, in accordance with any court directions made.

124. There is no requirement for a defence statement to be served in the magistrates' court but it should be noted that if one is not provided the court does not have a power to hear an application for further prosecution disclosure under section 8 of the CPIA 1996.

125. Defence practitioners must ensure that defence statements are drafted in accordance with the requirements in the CPIA 1996. Defence statements must not make general and unspecified allegations in order to seek far reaching disclosure and should not describe the defence in ambiguous or limited terms (such as self-defence, mistaken identity, consent).

126. It is vital that prosecutors consider defence statements thoroughly. Prosecutors should challenge the lack of (in the Crown Court) or inadequate defence statements in writing, copying the document to the court and the defence and seeking directions from the court to require the provision of an adequate defence statement from the defence as soon as possible.

127. Prosecutors must send a copy of the defence statement to the investigator as soon as reasonably practicable after receipt and, at the same time, provide guidance to the disclosure officer about the key issues. The advice should contain guidance on whether any further reasonable lines of inquiry need to be pursued, guidance on what to look for when reviewing the unused material and guidance on what further material may need to be disclosed. On receipt of a defence statement, disclosure officers must re-review retained unused material and draw to the attention of the prosecutor any material which is potentially capable of meeting the test for disclosure and consider whether any further reasonable lines of inquiry need to be pursued. They should address the matters raised in guidance given by the prosecutor.

128. Defence requests for further disclosure should ordinarily only be answered by the prosecution if the request is relevant to, and directed to, an issue identified in the defence statement. If it is not, then a further or amended defence statement should be sought and obtained by the prosecutor before considering the request for further disclosure.

Continuing disclosure

129. The obligation of continuing disclosure is crucial and particular attention must be paid to understanding the significance of developments in the case on the unused material and earlier disclosure decisions. After service of initial disclosure, a prosecutor must keep under review whether or not there is prosecution material which might reasonably be considered capable of undermining the case for the prosecution against the accused, or of assisting the case for the accused, which has not been previously been disclosed. This obligation is a continuous one, and it can be beneficial for it to take place in tranches, particularly in large and/or complex cases.

130. In particular, prosecutors should consider any issues raised by the defence at the first hearing in the magistrates' court or the PTPH in the Crown Court, as well as during any further hearings and after receipt of a defence statement. Any matters raised on the preparation for effective trial form or the PTPH form should also be carefully considered.

Applications for disclosure under Section 8 of the CPIA

131. An application for disclosure can only be made if the defence have provided an **adequate** defence statement.

132. Any application for disclosure must describe the material which is subject to the application and explain why there is reasonable cause to believe that the prosecutor has the material and why it meets the test for disclosure. There must not be any speculative requests for material.

133. Prosecutors must carefully review any application for disclosure and consider whether any items described in the application meet the test for disclosure. This may require the prosecutor asking the disclosure officer for copies of the items or inspecting the items.

The trial

134. Prosecutors must ensure that advocates in court are provided with sufficient instructions regarding the disclosure strategy and any disclosure decisions taken.

135. Prosecution advocates should ensure that all material which ought to be disclosed under the CPIA 1996 is disclosed to the defence. Prosecution advocates must ensure that they are fully informed about disclosure so that they are able to make decisions. Prosecution advocates must consider, in every case, whether they can be satisfied that they are in possession of all relevant documentation and that they have been fully instructed regarding disclosure matters. If the advocate considers that further information or action is required then written advice should be provided setting out the aspects that need clarification or action.

136. All decisions regarding disclosure must be kept under review until the conclusion of the trial, whenever possible in consultation with the reviewing prosecutor. The prosecution advocate must in every case specifically consider whether they can satisfactorily discharge the duty of continuing review on the basis of the material supplied already, or whether it is necessary to reconsider the unused material schedule and/or unused material.

137. Prosecution advocates must not abrogate their responsibility under the CPIA 1996 by disclosing material which does not pass the test for disclosure. This is especially so where it is proposed to disclose material engaging Article 8 rights.

138. There is no basis in practice or law for counsel-to-counsel disclosure. It is of critical importance that, even where prosecution counsel is advising and leading on disclosure, the duty to disclose material that meets the test for disclosure remains with the prosecutor. A record of material disclosed made must be kept, not least in the event of an appeal or a re-trial.

Material relevant to sentence

139. At sentence, the prosecutor should disclose any material which might reasonably be considered capable of ensuring fairness in the sentencing process. This material could include information which might mitigate the seriousness of the offence or the level of the defendant's involvement.

Post-conviction

140. Where, at any stage after the conclusion of the proceedings, material comes to light which might reasonably be considered capable of casting doubt upon the safety of the conviction, the prosecutor should disclose such material.

Confiscation Proceedings

141. The disclosure regime in the CPIA ceases to have effect post-conviction and the continuing duty of disclosure does not apply to confiscation proceedings (see section 7A(1)(b) of the CPIA).

142. Part 2 of the Proceeds of Crime Act 2002 provides the legislative scheme for confiscation in the Crown Court following a conviction. The prosecutor is required to set out relevant matters in accordance with Section 16 of the Proceeds of Crime Act 2002 apply and the disclosure requirements at common law also apply meaning that there may be a requirement to disclose material in the interests of justice and fairness in the proceedings.

. . .*

* **Editor's Note:** The guidelines are followed by 'Annex A—Digital Material'; 'Annex B—Pre-charge engagement'; 'Annex C—Disclosure Management Documents (DMDs) and 'Annex D—Redaction' to which further reference may be made.

Part III

Human Rights—Act and Convention

Human Rights Act 1998

(1998, c. 42)

Introduction

1 The Convention Rights

(1) In this Act 'the Convention rights' means the rights and fundamental freedoms set out in—

(a) Articles 2 to 12 and 14 of the Convention,

(b) Articles 1 to 3 of the First Protocol, and

(c) Article 1 of the Thirteenth Protocol,

as read with Articles 16 to 18 of the Convention.

(2) Those Articles are to have effect for the purposes of this Act subject to any designated derogation or reservation (as to which see sections 14 and 15).

(3) The Articles are set out in Schedule 1.

(4) The Secretary of State may by order make such amendments to this Act as he considers appropriate to reflect the effect, in relation to the United Kingdom, of a protocol.

(5) In subsection (4) 'protocol' means a protocol to the Convention—

(a) which the United Kingdom has ratified; or

(b) which the United Kingdom has signed with a view to ratification.

(6) No amendment may be made by an order under subsection (4) so as to come into force before the protocol concerned is in force in relation to the United Kingdom.

2 Interpretation of Convention rights

(1) A court or tribunal determining a question which has arisen in connection with a Convention right must take into account any—

(a) judgment, decision, declaration or advisory opinion of the European Court of Human Rights,

(b) opinion of the Commission given in a report adopted under Article 31 of the Convention,

(c) decision of the Commission in connection with Article 26 or 27(2) of the Convention, or

(d) decision of the Committee of Ministers taken under Article 46 of the Convention,

whenever made or given, so far as, in the opinion of the court or tribunal, it is relevant to the proceedings in which that question has arisen.

(2) Evidence of any judgment, decision, declaration or opinion of which account may have to be taken under this section is to be given in proceedings before any court or tribunal in such manner as may be provided by rules.

(3) In this section 'rules' means rules of court or, in the case of proceedings before a tribunal, rules made for the purposes of this section—

(a) by the Lord Chancellor or the Secretary of State, in relation to any proceedings outside Scotland;

(b) by the Secretary of State, in relation to proceedings in Scotland; or
(c) by a Northern Ireland department, in relation to proceedings before a tribunal in Northern Ireland—
(i) which deals with transferred matters; and
(ii) for which no rules made under paragraph (a) are in force.

Legislation

3 Interpretation of legislation

(1) So far as it is possible to do so, primary legislation and subordinate legislation must be read and given effect in a way which is compatible with the Convention rights.

(2) This section—
(a) applies to primary legislation and subordinate legislation whenever enacted;
(b) does not affect the validity, continuing operation or enforcement of any incompatible primary legislation; and
(c) does not affect the validity, continuing operation or enforcement of any incompatible subordinate legislation if (disregarding any possibility of revocation) primary legislation prevents removal of the incompatibility.

4 Declaration of incompatibility

(1) Subsection (2) applies in any proceedings in which a court determines whether a provision of primary legislation is compatible with a Convention right.

(2) If the court is satisfied that the provision is incompatible with a Convention right, it may make a declaration of that incompatibility.

(3) Subsection (4) applies in any proceedings in which a court determines whether a provision of subordinate legislation, made in the exercise of a power conferred by primary legislation, is compatible with a Convention right.

(4) If the court is satisfied—
(a) that the provision is incompatible with a Convention right, and
(b) that (disregarding any possibility of revocation) the primary legislation concerned prevents removal of the incompatibility,

it may make a declaration of that incompatibility.

(5) In this section 'court' means—
(a) the Supreme Court;
(b) the Judicial Committee of the Privy Council;
(c) the Court Martial Appeal Court;
(d) in Scotland, the High Court of Justiciary sitting otherwise than as a trial court or the Court of Session;
(e) in England and Wales or Northern Ireland, the High Court or the Court of Appeal;
(f) the Court of Protection, in any matter being dealt with by the President of the Family Division, the Chancellor of the High Court or a puisne judge of the High Court.

(6) A declaration under this section ('a declaration of incompatibility')—
(a) does not affect the validity, continuing operation or enforcement of the provision in respect of which it is given; and
(b) is not binding on the parties to the proceedings in which it is made.

5 Right of Crown to intervene

(1) Where a court is considering whether to make a declaration of incompatibility, the Crown is entitled to notice in accordance with rules of court.

(2) In any case to which subsection (1) applies—
(a) a Minister of the Crown (or a person nominated by him),
(b) a member of the Scottish Executive,
(c) a Northern Ireland Minister,
(d) a Northern Ireland department,

is entitled, on giving notice in accordance with rules of court, to be joined as a party to the proceedings.

(3) Notice under subsection (2) may be given at any time during the proceedings.

(4) A person who has been made a party to criminal proceedings (other than in Scotland) as the result of a notice under subsection (2) may, with leave, appeal to the Supreme Court against any declaration of incompatibility made in the proceedings.

(5) In subsection (4)—

'criminal proceedings' includes all proceedings before the Court Martial Appeal Court; and

'leave' means leave granted by the court making the declaration of incompatibility or by the Supreme Court.

Public authorities

6 Acts of public authorities

(1) It is unlawful for a public authority to act in a way which is incompatible with a Convention right.

(2) Subsection (1) does not apply to an act if—

(a) as the result of one or more provisions of primary legislation, the authority could not have acted differently; or

(b) in the case of one or more provisions of, or made under, primary legislation which cannot be read or given effect in a way which is compatible with the Convention rights, the authority was acting so as to give effect to or enforce those provisions.

(3) In this section 'public authority' includes—

(a) a court or tribunal, and

(b) any person certain of whose functions are functions of a public nature,

but does not include either House of Parliament or a person exercising functions in connection with proceedings in Parliament.

(4) . . .

(5) In relation to a particular act, a person is not a public authority by virtue only of subsection (3)(b) if the nature of the act is private.

(6) 'An act' includes a failure to act but does not include a failure to—

(a) introduce in, or lay before, Parliament a proposal for legislation; or

(b) make any primary legislation or remedial order.

7 Proceedings

(1) A person who claims that a public authority has acted (or proposes to act) in a way which is made unlawful by section 6(1) may—

(a) bring proceedings against the authority under this Act in the appropriate court or tribunal, or

(b) rely on the Convention right or rights concerned in any legal proceedings,

but only if he is (or would be) a victim of the unlawful act.

(2) In subsection (1)(a) 'appropriate court or tribunal' means such court or tribunal as may be determined in accordance with rules; and proceedings against an authority include a counterclaim or similar proceeding.

(3) If the proceedings are brought on an application for judicial review, the applicant is to be taken to have a sufficient interest in relation to the unlawful act only if he is, or would be, a victim of that act.

(4) . . .*

(5) Proceedings under subsection (1)(a) must be brought before the end of—

(a) the period of one year beginning with the date on which the act complained of took place; or

(b) such longer period as the court or tribunal considers equitable having regard to all the circumstances,

but that is subject to any rule imposing a stricter time limit in relation to the procedure in question.

* **Editor's Note:** Applies to Scotland only.

(6) In subsection (1)(b) 'legal proceedings' includes—

(a) proceedings brought by or at the instigation of a public authority; and

(b) an appeal against the decision of a court or tribunal.

(7) For the purposes of this section, a person is a victim of an unlawful act only if he would be a victim for the purposes of Article 34 of the Convention if proceedings were brought in the European Court of Human Rights in respect of that act.

(8) Nothing in this Act creates a criminal offence.

(9) In this section 'rules' means—

(a) in relation to proceedings before a court or tribunal outside Scotland, rules made by the Lord Chancellor or the Secretary of State for the purposes of this section or rules of court,

(b) . . .*

(c) . . .**

and includes provision made by order under section 1 of the Courts and Legal Services Act 1990.

(10) In making rules, regard must be had to section 9.

(11) The Minister who has power to make rules in relation to a particular tribunal may, to the extent he considers it necessary to ensure that the tribunal can provide an appropriate remedy in relation to an act (or proposed act) of a public authority which is (or would be) unlawful as a result of section 6(1), by order add to—

(a) the relief or remedies which the tribunal may grant; or

(b) the grounds on which it may grant any of them.

(12) An order made under subsection (11) may contain such incidental, supplemental, consequential or transitional provision as the Minister making it considers appropriate.

(13) 'The Minister' includes the Northern Ireland department concerned.

7A Limitation: overseas armed forces proceedings

(1) A court or tribunal exercising its discretion under section 7(5)(b) in respect of overseas armed forces proceedings must do so—

(a) in accordance with subsection (2), and

(b) subject to the rule in subsection (4).

(2) The court or tribunal must have particular regard to—

(a) the effect of the delay in bringing proceedings on the cogency of evidence adduced or likely to be adduced by the parties, with particular reference to—

(i) the likely impact of the operational context on the ability of individuals who are (or, at the time of the events to which the proceedings relate, were) members of Her Majesty's forces to remember relevant events or actions fully or accurately, and

(ii) the extent of dependence on the memories of such individuals, taking into account the effect of the operational context on the ability of such individuals to record, or to retain records of, relevant events or actions;

(b) the likely impact of the proceedings on the mental health of any witness or potential witness who is (or, at the time of the events to which the proceedings relate, was) a member of Her Majesty's forces.

(3) In subsection (2) references to 'the operational context' are to the fact that the events to which the proceedings relate took place in the context of overseas operations, and include references to the exceptional demands and stresses to which members of Her Majesty's forces are subject.

(4) The rule referred to in subsection (1)(b) is that overseas armed forces proceedings must be brought before the later of—

(a) the end of the period of 6 years beginning with the date on which the act complained of took place;

(b) the end of the period of 12 months beginning with the date of knowledge.

(5) In subsection (4), the 'date of knowledge' means the date on which the person bringing the proceedings first knew, or first ought to have known, both—

(a) of the act complained of, and

* **Editor's Note:** Applies to Scotland only.

** **Editor's Note:** Applies to Northern Ireland only.

(b) that it was an act of the Ministry of Defence or the Secretary of State for Defence.

(6) 'Overseas armed forces proceedings' means proceedings—

(a) against the Ministry of Defence or the Secretary of State for Defence, and

(b) in connection with overseas operations.

(7) 'Overseas operations' means any operations outside the British Islands, including peace-keeping operations and operations for dealing with terrorism, civil unrest or serious public disorder, in the course of which members of Her Majesty's forces come under attack or face the threat of attack or violent resistance.

(8) In this section the reference to the British Islands includes the territorial sea adjacent to the United Kingdom and the territorial sea adjacent to any of the Channel Islands or the Isle of Man.

(9) In this section 'Her Majesty's forces' has the same meaning as in the Armed Forces Act 2006 (see section 374 of that Act).

8 Judicial remedies

(1) In relation to any act (or proposed act) of a public authority which the court finds is (or would be) unlawful, it may grant such relief or remedy, or make such order, within its powers as it considers just and appropriate.

(2) But damages may be awarded only by a court which has power to award damages, or to order the payment of compensation, in civil proceedings.

(3) No award of damages is to be made unless, taking account of all the circumstances of the case, including—

(a) any other relief or remedy granted, or order made, in relation to the act in question (by that or any other court), and

(b) the consequences of any decision (of that or any other court) in respect of that act,

the court is satisfied that the award is necessary to afford just satisfaction to the person in whose favour it is made.

(4) In determining—

(a) whether to award damages, or

(b) the amount of an award,

the court must take into account the principles applied by the European Court of Human Rights in relation to the award of compensation under Article 41 of the Convention.

(5) A public authority against which damages are awarded is to be treated—

(a) . . .*

(b) for the purposes of the Civil Liability (Contribution) Act 1978 as liable in respect of damage suffered by the person to whom the award is made.

(6) In this section—

'court' includes a tribunal;

'damages' means damages for an unlawful act of a public authority; and

'unlawful' means unlawful under section 6(1).

9 Judicial acts

(1) Proceedings under section 7(1)(a) in respect of a judicial act may be brought only—

(a) by exercising a right of appeal;

(b) on an application . . . for judicial review; or

(c) in such other forum as may be prescribed by rules.

(2) That does not affect any rule of law which prevents a court from being the subject of judicial review.

(3) In proceedings under this Act in respect of a judicial act done in good faith, damages may not be awarded otherwise than—

(a) to compensate a person to the extent required by Article 5(5) of the Convention, or

(b) to compensate a person for a judicial act that is incompatible with Article 6 of the Convention in circumstances where the person is detained and, but for the incompatibility, the person would not have been detained or would not have been detained for so long.

* **Editor's Note:** Applies to Scotland only.

(4) An award of damages permitted by subsection (3) is to be made against the Crown; but no award may be made unless the appropriate person, if not a party to the proceedings, is joined.

(5) In this section—

'appropriate person' means the Minister responsible for the court concerned, or a person or government department nominated by him;

'court' includes a tribunal;

'judge' includes a member of a tribunal, a justice of the peace (or, in Northern Ireland, a lay magistrate) and a clerk or other officer entitled to exercise the jurisdiction of a court;

'judicial act' means a judicial act of a court and includes an act done on the instructions, or on behalf, of a judge; and

'rules' has the same meaning as in section 7(9).

Remedial action

10 Power to take remedial action

(1) This section applies if—

(a) a provision of legislation has been declared under section 4 to be incompatible with a Convention right and, if an appeal lies—

(i) all persons who may appeal have stated in writing that they do not intend to do so;

(ii) the time for bringing an appeal has expired and no appeal has been brought within that time; or

(iii) an appeal brought within that time has been determined or abandoned;

or

(b) it appears to a Minister of the Crown or Her Majesty in Council that, having regard to a finding of the European Court of Human Rights made after the coming into force of this section in proceedings against the United Kingdom, a provision of legislation is incompatible with an obligation of the United Kingdom arising from the Convention.

(2) If a Minister of the Crown considers that there are compelling reasons for proceeding under this section, he may by order make such amendments to the legislation as he considers necessary to remove the incompatibility.

(3) If, in the case of subordinate legislation, a Minister of the Crown considers—

(a) that it is necessary to amend the primary legislation under which the subordinate legislation in question was made, in order to enable the incompatibility to be removed, and

(b) that there are compelling reasons for proceeding under this section,

he may by order make such amendments to the primary legislation as he considers necessary.

(4) This section also applies where the provision in question is in subordinate legislation and has been quashed, or declared invalid, by reason of incompatibility with a Convention right and the Minister proposes to proceed under paragraph 2(b) of Schedule 2.

(5) If the legislation is an Order in Council, the power conferred by subsection (2) or (3) is exercisable by Her Majesty in Council.

(6) In this section 'legislation' does not include a Measure of the Church Assembly or of the General Synod of the Church of England.

(7) Schedule 2 makes further provision about remedial orders.

. . .

21 Interpretation etc.

(1) In this Act—

'amend' includes repeal and apply (with or without modifications);

'the appropriate Minister' means the Minister of the Crown having charge of the appropriate authorised government department (within the meaning of the Crown Proceedings Act 1947);

'the Commission' means the European Commission of Human Rights;

'the Convention' means the Convention for the Protection of Human Rights and Fundamental Freedoms, agreed by the Council of Europe at Rome on 4th November 1950 as it has effect for the time being in relation to the United Kingdom;

'declaration of incompatibility' means a declaration under section 4;

'Minister of the Crown' has the same meaning as in the Ministers of the Crown Act 1975;

'primary legislation' means any—

(a) public general Act;
(b) local and personal Act;
(c) private Act;
(d) Measure of the Church Assembly;
(e) Measure of the General Synod of the Church of England;
(f) Order in Council—
  (i) made in exercise of Her Majesty's Royal Prerogative;
  (ii) . . .*
  (iii) amending an Act of a kind mentioned in paragraph (a), (b) or (c);

and includes an order or other instrument made under primary legislation . . . to the extent to which it operates to bring one or more provisions of that legislation into force or amends any primary legislation;

'the First Protocol' means the protocol to the Convention agreed at Paris on 20th March 1952;

'the Eleventh Protocol' means the protocol to the Convention (restructuring the control machinery established by the Convention) agreed at Strasbourg on 11th May 1994;

'the Thirteenth Protocol' means the protocol to the Convention (concerning the abolition of the death penalty in all circumstances) agreed at Vilnius on 3rd May 2002;

'remedial order' means an order under section 10;

'subordinate legislation' means any—

(a) Order in Council other than one—
  (i) made in exercise of Her Majesty's Royal Prerogative;
  (ii) . . .**
  (iii) amending an Act of a kind mentioned in the definition of primary legislation;
(b) . . .
(ba) . . .
(bb) . . .
(c) . . .
(d) . . .
(e) . . .
(f) order, rules, regulations, scheme, warrant, byelaw or other instrument made under primary legislation (except to the extent to which it operates to bring one or more provisions of that legislation into force or amends any primary legislation);
(g) . . .
(h) . . .

'tribunal' means any tribunal in which legal proceedings may be brought.

(2) The references in paragraphs (b) and (c) of section 2(1) to Articles are to Articles of the Convention as they had effect immediately before the coming into force of the Eleventh Protocol.

(3) The reference in paragraph (d) of section 2(1) to Article 46 includes a reference to Articles 32 and 54 of the Convention as they had effect immediately before the coming into force of the Eleventh Protocol.

(4) The references in section 2(1) to a report or decision of the Commission or a decision of the Committee of Ministers include references to a report or decision made as provided by paragraphs 3, 4 and 6 of Article 5 of the Eleventh Protocol (transitional provisions).

(5) . . .

22 Short title, commencement, application and extent

(1) This Act may be cited as the Human Rights Act 1998.

(2) Section 18, 20 and 21(5) and this section come into force on the passing of this Act.

(3) The other provisions of this Act come into force on such day as the Secretary of State may by order appoint; and different days may be appointed for different purposes.

* **Editor's Note:** Applies to Northern Ireland only.

** **Editor's Note:** Applies to Northern Ireland only.

(4) Paragraph (b) of subsection (1) of section 7 applies to proceedings brought by or at the instigation of a public authority whenever the act in question took place; but otherwise that subsection does not apply to an act taking place before the coming into force of that section.

(4A) Section 7A (limitation: overseas armed forces proceedings) applies to proceedings brought under section 7(1)(a) on or after the date on which section 7A comes into force, whenever the act in question took place.

(5) This Act binds the Crown.

(6) This Act extends to Northern Ireland.

Convention for the Protection of Human Rights and Fundamental Freedoms* (European Convention on Human Rights)

(Rome, 4.11.1950)[1]

The governments signatory hereto, being members of the Council of Europe,

Considering the Universal Declaration of Human Rights proclaimed by the General Assembly of the United Nations on 10th December 1948;

Considering that this declaration aims at securing the universal and effective recognition and observance of the rights therein declared;

Considering that the aim of the Council of Europe is the achievement of greater unity between its members and that one of the methods by which that aim is to be pursued is the maintenance and further realisation of human rights and fundamental freedoms;

Reaffirming their profound belief in those fundamental freedoms which are the foundation of justice and peace in the world and are best maintained on the one hand by an effective political democracy and on the other by a common understanding and observance of the human rights upon which they depend;

Being resolved, as the governments of European countries which are like-minded and have a common heritage of political traditions, ideals, freedom and the rule of law, to take the first steps for the collective enforcement of certain of the rights stated in the Universal Declaration,

Affirming that the High Contracting Parties, in accordance with the principles of subsidiarity, have the primary responsibility to secure the rights and freedoms defined in this Convention and the Protocols thereto, and that in doing so they enjoy a margin of appreciation, subject to the supervisory jurisdiction of the European Court of Human Rights established by this Convention,

Have agreed as follows:

Article 1

Obligation to respect Human Rights

The High Contracting Parties shall secure to everyone within their jurisdiction the rights and freedoms defined in Section 1 of this Convention.

Section I
Rights and Freedoms

Article 2

Right to Life

1. Everyone's right to life shall be protected by law. No one shall be deprived of his life intentionally save in the execution of a sentence of a court following his conviction of a crime for which this penalty is provided by law.

* Reproduced with permission from the Council of Europe.

[1] European Treaty Series, No. 5. Text amended according to the provisions of Protocol No. 3 (ETS No. 45), which entered into force on 21 September 1970, of Protocol No. 5 (ETS No. 55), which entered into force on 20 December 1971, and of Protocol No. 8 (ETS No. 118), which entered into force on 1 January 1990, and comprising also the text of Protocol No. 2 (ETS No. 44) which, in accordance with Article 5, paragraph 3, therefore, has been an integral part of the Convention since its entry into force on 21 September 1970.

2. Deprivation of life shall not be regarded as inflicted in contravention of this article when it results from the use of force which is no more than absolutely necessary:

(a) in defence of any person from unlawful violence;
(b) in order to effect a lawful arrest or to prevent the escape of a person lawfully detained;
(c) in action lawfully taken for the purpose of quelling a riot or insurrection.

Article 3

Prohibition of torture

No one shall be subjected to torture or to inhuman or degrading treatment or punishment.

Article 4

Prohibition of slavery and forced labour

1. No one shall be held in slavery or servitude.
2. No one shall be required to perform forced or compulsory labour.
3. For the purpose of this article the term 'forced or compulsory labour' shall not include:
   (a) any work required to be done in the ordinary course of detention imposed according to the provisions of Article 5 of this Convention or during conditional release from such detention;
   (b) any service of a military character or, in case of conscientious objectors in countries where they are recognised, service exacted instead of compulsory military service;
   (c) any service exacted in case of an emergency or calamity threatening the life or well-being of the community;
   (d) any work or service which forms part of normal civic obligations.

Article 5

Right to liberty and security

1. Everyone has the right to liberty and security of person. No one shall be deprived of his liberty save in the following cases and in accordance with a procedure prescribed by law:

(a) the lawful detention of a person after conviction by a competent court;
(b) the lawful arrest or detention of a person for non-compliance with the lawful order of a court or in order to secure the fulfilment of any obligation prescribed by law;
(c) the lawful arrest or detention of a person effected for the purpose of bringing him before the competent legal authority on reasonable suspicion of having committed an offence or when it is reasonably considered necessary to prevent his committing an offence or fleeing after having done so;
(d) the detention of a minor by lawful order for the purpose of educational supervision or his lawful detention for the purpose of bringing him before the competent legal authority;
(e) the lawful detention of persons for the prevention of the spreading of infectious diseases, of persons of unsound mind, alcoholics or drug addicts or vagrants;
(f) the lawful arrest or detention of a person to prevent his effecting an unauthorised entry into the country or of a person against whom action is being taken with a view to deportation or extradition.

2. Everyone who is arrested shall be informed promptly, in a language which he understands, of the reasons for his arrest and of any charge against him.

3. Everyone arrested or detained in accordance with the provisions of paragraph 1(c) of this article shall be brought promptly before a judge or other officer authorised by law to exercise judicial power and shall be entitled to trial within a reasonable time or to release pending trial. Release may be conditioned by guarantees to appear for trial.

4. Everyone who is deprived of his liberty by arrest or detention shall be entitled to take proceedings by which the lawfulness of his detention shall be decided speedily by a court and his release ordered if the detention is not lawful.

5. Everyone who has been the victim of arrest or detention in contravention of the provisions of this article shall have an enforceable right to compensation.

Article 6

Right to a fair trial

1. In the determination of his civil rights and obligations or of any criminal charge against him, everyone is entitled to a fair and public hearing within a reasonable time by an independent and impartial tribunal established by law. Judgment shall be pronounced publicly but the press and public may be excluded from all or part of the trial in the interests of morals, public order or national security in a democratic society, where the interests of juveniles or the protection of the private life of the parties so require, or to the extent strictly necessary in the opinion of the court in special circumstances where publicity would prejudice the interests of justice.

2. Everyone charged with a criminal offence shall be presumed innocent until proved guilty according to law.

3. Everyone charged with a criminal offence has the following minimum rights;

(a) to be informed promptly, in a language which he understands and in detail, of the nature and cause of the accusation against him;

(b) to have adequate time and facilities for the preparation of his defence;

(c) to defend himself in person or through legal assistance of his own choosing or, if he has not sufficient means to pay for legal assistance, to be given it free when the interests of justice so require;

(d) to examine or have examined witnesses against him and to obtain the attendance and examination of witnesses on his behalf under the same conditions as witnesses against him;

(e) to have the free assistance of an interpreter if he cannot understand or speak the language used in court.

Article 7

No punishment without law

1. No one shall be held guilty of any criminal offence on account of any act or omission which did not constitute a criminal offence under national or international law at the time when it was committed. Nor shall a heavier penalty be imposed than the one that was applicable at the time the criminal offence was committed.

2. This article shall not prejudice the trial and punishment of any person for any act or omission which, at the time when it was committed, was criminal according to the general principles of law recognised by civilised nations.

Article 8

Right to respect for private and family life

1. Everyone has the right to respect for his private and family life, his home and his correspondence.

2. There shall be no interference by a public authority with the exercise of this right except such as is in accordance with the law and is necessary in a democratic society in the interests of national security, public safety or the economic well-being of the country, for the prevention of disorder or crime, for the protection of health or morals, or for the protection of the rights and freedoms of others.

Article 9

Freedom of thought, conscience and religion

1. Everyone has the right to freedom of thought, conscience and religion; this right includes freedom to change his religion or belief and freedom, either alone or in community with others and in public or private, to manifest his religion or belief, in worship, teaching, practice and observance.

2. Freedom to manifest one's religion or beliefs shall be subject only to such limitations as are prescribed by law and are necessary in a democratic society in the interests of public safety, for the protection of public order, health or morals, or for the protection of the rights and freedoms of others.

Article 10

Freedom of expression

1. Everyone has the right to freedom of expression. This right shall include freedom to hold opinions and to receive and impart information and ideas without interference by public authority and regardless of frontiers. This article shall not prevent States from requiring the licensing of broadcasting, television or cinema enterprises.

2. The exercise of these freedoms, since it carries with it duties and responsibilities, may be subject to such formalities, conditions, restrictions or penalties as are prescribed by law and are necessary in a democratic society, in the interests of national security, territorial integrity or public safety, for the prevention of disorder or crime, for the protection of health or morals, for the protection of the reputation of rights of others, for preventing the disclosure of information received in confidence, or for maintaining the authority and impartiality of the judiciary.

Article 11

Freedom of assembly and association

1. Everyone has the right to freedom of peaceful assembly and to freedom of association with others, including the right to form and to join trade unions for the protection of his interests.

2. No restrictions shall be placed on the exercise of these rights other than such as are prescribed by law and are necessary in a democratic society in the interests of national security or public safety, for the prevention of disorder or crime, for the protection of health or morals or for the protection of the rights and freedoms of others. This article shall not prevent the imposition of lawful restrictions on the exercise of these rights by members of the armed forces, of the police or of the administration of the state.

Article 12

Right to marry

Men and women of marriageable age have the right to marry and to found a family, according to the national laws governing the exercise of this right.

Article 13

Right to an effective remedy

Everyone whose rights and freedoms as set forth in this Convention are violated shall have an effective remedy before a national authority notwithstanding that the violation has been committed by persons acting in an official capacity.

Article 14

Prohibition of discrimination

The employment of the rights and freedoms set forth in this Convention shall be secured without discrimination on any ground such as sex, race, colour, language, religion, political or other opinion, national or social origin, association with a national minority, property, birth or other status.

Article 15

Derogation in time of emergency

1. In time of war or other public emergency threatening the life of the nation any High Contracting Party may take measures derogating from its obligations under this Convention to the extent strictly required by the exigencies of the situation, provided that such measures are not inconsistent with its other obligations under international law.

2. No derogation from Article 2, except in respect of deaths resulting from lawful acts of war, or from Articles 3, 4 (paragraph 1) and 7 shall be made under this provision.

3. Any High Contracting Party availing itself of this right of derogation shall keep the Secretary General of the Council of Europe fully informed of the measures which it has taken and the reasons therefor. It shall also inform the Secretary General of the Council of Europe when such measures have ceased to operate and the provisions of the Convention are again being fully executed.

Article 16

Restrictions on political activity of aliens

Nothing in Articles 10, 11 and 14 shall be regarded as preventing the High Contracting Parties from imposing restrictions on the political activity of aliens.

Article 17

Prohibition of abuse of rights

Nothing in this Convention may be interpreted as implying for any State, group or person any right to engage in any activity or perform any act aimed at the destruction of any of the rights and freedoms set forth herein or at their limitation to a greater extent than is provided for in the Convention.

Article 18

Limitation on use of restrictions on rights

The restrictions permitted under this Convention to the said rights and freedoms shall not be applied for any purpose other than those for which they have been prescribed.

. . .

Part IV

Civil Proceedings—Statutes and Rules

Civil Evidence Act 1968

(1968, c. 64)

11 Convictions as evidence in civil proceedings

(1) In any civil proceedings the fact that a person has been convicted of an offence by or before any court in the United Kingdom or of a service offence anywhere shall (subject to subsection (3) below) be admissible in evidence for the purpose of proving, where to do so is relevant to any issue in those proceedings, that he committed that offence, whether he was so convicted upon a plea of guilty or otherwise and whether or not he is a party to the civil proceedings; but no conviction other than a subsisting one shall be admissible in evidence by virtue of this section.

(2) In any civil proceedings in which by virtue of this section a person is proved to have been convicted of an offence by or before any court in the United Kingdom or of a service offence—

(a) he shall be taken to have committed that offence unless the contrary is proved; and

(b) without prejudice to the reception of any other admissible evidence for the purpose of identifying the facts on which the conviction was based, the contents of any document which is admissible as evidence of the conviction, and the contents of the information, complaint, indictment or charge-sheet on which the person in question was convicted, shall be admissible in evidence for that purpose.

(3) Nothing in this section shall prejudice the operation of section 13 of this Act or any other enactment whereby a conviction or a finding of fact in any criminal proceedings is for the purposes of any other proceedings made conclusive evidence of any fact.

(4) Where in any civil proceedings the contents of any document are admissible in evidence by virtue of subsection (2) above, a copy of that document, or of the material part thereof, purporting to be certified or otherwise authenticated by or on behalf of the court or authority having custody of that document shall be admissible in evidence and shall be taken to be a true copy of that document or part unless the contrary is shown.

(5) Nothing in any of the following enactments, that is to say—

(a) section 82 of the Sentencing Code (under which a conviction leading to discharge is to be disregarded except as therein mentioned);

(aa) section 187 of the Armed Forces Act 2006 (which makes similar provision in respect of service convictions);

(b) section 191 of the Criminal Procedure (Scotland) Act 1975 (which makes similar provision in respect of convictions on indictment in Scotland); and

(c) section 8 of the Probation Act (Northern Ireland) 1950 (which corresponds to the said section 12) or any corresponding enactment of the Parliament of Northern Ireland for the time being in force, shall affect the operation of this section; and for the purposes of this section any order made by a court of summary jurisdiction in Scotland under section 383 or section 384 of the said Act of 1975 shall be treated as a conviction.

(7) In this section—

'service offence' has the same meaning as in the Armed Forces Act 2006;

'conviction' includes anything that under section 376(1) and (2) of that Act is to be treated as a conviction, and 'convicted' is to be read accordingly.

12 Findings of adultery and paternity as evidence in civil proceedings

(1) In any civil proceedings—

(a) the fact that a person has been found guilty of adultery in any matrimonial proceedings; and

(b) the fact that a person has been found to be the father of a child in relevant proceedings before any court in England and Wales or Northern Ireland or has been adjudged to be the father of a child in affiliation proceedings before any court in the United Kingdom;

shall (subject to subsection (3) below) be admissible in evidence for the purpose of proving, where to do so is relevant to any issue in those civil proceedings, that he committed the adultery to which the finding relates or, as the case may be, is (or was) the father of that child, whether or not he offered any defence to the allegation of adultery or paternity and whether or not he is a party to the civil proceedings; but no finding or adjudication other than a subsisting one shall be admissible in evidence by virtue of this section.

(2) In any civil proceedings in which by virtue of this section a person is proved to have been found guilty of adultery as mentioned in subsection (1)(a) above or to have been found or adjudged to be the father of a child as mentioned in subsection (1)(b) above—

(a) he shall be taken to have committed the adultery to which the finding relates or, as the case may be, to be (or have been) the father of that child, unless the contrary is proved; and

(b) without prejudice to the reception of any other admissible evidence for the purpose of identifying the facts on which the finding or adjudication was based, the contents of any document which was before the court, or which contains any pronouncement of the court, in the other proceedings in question shall be admissible in evidence for that purpose.

(3) Nothing in this section shall prejudice the operation of any enactment whereby a finding of fact in any matrimonial or affiliation proceedings is for the purposes of any other proceedings made conclusive evidence of any fact.

(4) Subsection (4) of section 11 of this Act shall apply for the purposes of this section as if the reference to subsection (2) were a reference to subsection (2) of this section.

(5) In this section—

'matrimonial proceedings' means any matrimonial cause in the High Court or family court in England and Wales or in the High Court in Northern Ireland, any consistorial action in Scotland, or any appeal arising out of any such cause or action;

'relevant proceedings' means—

(a) . . .;

(b) proceedings under the Children Act 1989;

(c) proceedings which would have been relevant proceedings for the purposes of this section in the form in which it was in force before the passing of the Children Act 1989.

and in this subsection 'consistorial action' does not include an action of aliment only between husband and wife raised in the Court of Session or an action of interim aliment raised in the sheriff court.

13 Conclusiveness of convictions for purposes of defamation actions

(1) In an action for libel or slander in which the question whether the plaintiff did or did not commit a criminal offence is relevant to an issue arising in the action, proof that, at the time when that issue falls to be determined, he stands convicted of that offence shall be conclusive evidence that he committed that offence; and his conviction thereof shall be admissible in evidence accordingly.

(2) In any such action as aforesaid in which by virtue of this section the plaintiff is proved to have been convicted of an offence, the contents of any document which is admissible as evidence of the conviction, and the contents of the information, complaint, indictment or charge-sheet on which he was convicted, shall, without prejudice to the reception of any other admissible evidence for the purpose of identifying the facts on which the conviction was based, be admissible in evidence for the purpose of identifying those facts.

(2A) In the case of an action for libel or slander in which there is more than one plaintiff—

(a) the references in subsections (1) and (2) above to the plaintiff shall be construed as references to any of the plaintiffs, and

(b) proof that any of the plaintiffs stands convicted of an offence shall be conclusive evidence that he committed that offence so far as that fact is relevant to any issue arising in relation to his cause of action or that of any other plaintiff.

(3) For the purposes of this section a person shall be taken to stand convicted of an offence if but only if there subsists against him a conviction of that offence by or before a court in the United Kingdom or (in the case of a service offence) a conviction (anywhere) of that service offence.

(4) Subsections (4) to (7) of section 11 of this Act shall apply for the purposes of this section as they apply for the purposes of that section, but as if in the said subsection (4) the reference to subsection (2) were a reference to subsection (2) of this section.

(5) The foregoing provisions of this section shall apply for the purposes of any action begun after the passing of this Act, whenever the cause of action arose, but shall not apply for the purposes of any action begun before the passing of this Act or any appeal or other proceedings arising out of any such action.

Civil Evidence Act 1972

(1972, c. 30)

3 Admissibility of expert opinion and certain expressions of non-expert opinion

(1) Subject to any rules of court made in pursuance of this Act, where a person is called as a witness in any civil proceedings, his opinion on any relevant matter on which he is qualified to give expert evidence shall be admissible in evidence.

(2) It is hereby declared that where a person is called as a witness in any civil proceedings, a statement of opinion by him on any relevant matter on which he is not qualified to give expert evidence, if made as a way of conveying relevant facts personally perceived by him, is admissible as evidence of what he perceived.

(3) In this section 'relevant matter' includes an issue in the proceedings in question.

Children Act 1989

(1989, c. 41)

96 Evidence given by, or with respect to, children

(1) Subsection (2) applies where a child who is called as a witness in any civil proceedings does not, in the opinion of the court, understand the nature of an oath.

(2) The child's evidence may be heard by the court if, in its opinion—

(a) he understands that it is his duty to speak the truth; and

(b) he has sufficient understanding to justify his evidence being heard.

(3) The Lord Chancellor may, with the concurrence of the Lord Chief Justice, by order make provision for the admissibility of evidence which would otherwise be inadmissible under any rule of law relating to hearsay.

(4) An order under subsection (3) may only be made with respect to—

(a) civil proceedings in general or such civil proceedings, or class of civil proceedings, as may be prescribed; and

(b) evidence in connection with the upbringing, maintenance or welfare of a child.

(5) An order under subsection (3)—

(a) may, in particular, provide for the admissibility of statements which are made orally or in a prescribed form or which are recorded by any prescribed method of recording;

(b) may make different provision for different purposes and in relation to different descriptions of court; and

(c) may make such amendments and repeals in any enactment relating to evidence (other than in this Act) as the Lord Chancellor considers necessary or expedient in consequence of the provision made by the order.

(6) Subsection (5)(b) is without prejudice to section 104(4).

(7) In this section—

'civil proceedings' means civil proceedings, before any tribunal, in relation to which the strict rules of evidence apply, whether as a matter of law or agreement between the parties, and reference to 'the court' shall be construed accordingly;

'prescribed' means prescribed by an order under subsection (3).

98 Self-incrimination

(1) In any proceedings in which a court is hearing an application for an order under Part IV or V, no person shall be excused from—

(a) giving evidence on any matter; or

(b) answering any question put to him in the course of his giving evidence,

on the ground that doing so might incriminate him or his spouse or civil partner of an offence.

(2) A statement or admission made in such proceedings shall not be admissible in evidence against the person making it or his spouse or civil partner in proceedings for an offence other than perjury.

Civil Evidence Act 1995

(1995, c. 38)

Admissibility of hearsay evidence

1 Admissibility of hearsay evidence

(1) In civil proceedings evidence shall not be excluded on the ground that it is hearsay.

(2) In this Act—

(a) 'hearsay' means a statement made otherwise than by a person while giving oral evidence in the proceedings which is tendered as evidence of the matters stated; and

(b) references to hearsay include hearsay of whatever degree.

(3) Nothing in this Act affects the admissibility of evidence admissible apart from this section.

(4) The provisions of sections 2 to 6 (safeguards and supplementary provisions relating to hearsay evidence) do not apply in relation to hearsay evidence admissible apart from this section, notwithstanding that it may also be admissible by virtue of this section.

Safeguards in relation to hearsay evidence

2 Notice of proposal to adduce hearsay evidence

(1) A party proposing to adduce hearsay evidence in civil proceedings shall, subject to the following provisions of this section, give to the other party or parties to the proceedings—

(a) such notice (if any) of that fact, and

(b) on request, such particulars of or relating to the evidence,

as is reasonable and practicable in the circumstances for the purpose of enabling him or them to deal with any matters arising from its being hearsay.

(2) Provision may be made by rules of court—

(a) specifying classes of proceedings or evidence in relation to which subsection (1) does not apply, and

(b) as to the manner in which (including the time within which) the duties imposed by that subsection are to be complied with in the cases where it does apply.

(3) Subsection (1) may also be excluded by agreement of the parties; and compliance with the duty to give notice may in any case be waived by the person to whom notice is required to be given.

(4) A failure to comply with subsection (1), or with rules under subsection (2)(b), does not affect the admissibility of the evidence but may be taken into account by the court—

(a) in considering the exercise of its powers with respect to the course of proceedings and costs, and

(b) as a matter adversely affecting the weight to be given to the evidence in accordance with section 4.

3 Power to call witness for cross-examination on hearsay statement

Rules of court may provide that where a party to civil proceedings adduces hearsay evidence of a statement made by a person and does not call that person as a witness, any other party to the proceedings may, with the leave of the court, call that person as a witness and cross-examine him on the statement as if he had been called by the first-mentioned party and as if the hearsay statement were his evidence in chief.

4 Considerations relevant to weighing of hearsay evidence

(1) In estimating the weight (if any) to be given to hearsay evidence in civil proceedings the court shall have regard to any circumstances from which any inference can reasonably be drawn as to the reliability or otherwise of the evidence.

(2) Regard may be had, in particular, to the following—

(a) whether it would have been reasonable and practicable for the party by whom the evidence was adduced to have produced the maker of the original statement as a witness;

(b) whether the original statement was made contemporaneously with the occurrence or existence of the matters stated;

(c) whether the evidence involves multiple hearsay;

(d) whether any person involved had any motive to conceal or misrepresent matters;

(e) whether the original statement was an edited account, or was made in collaboration with another or for a particular purpose;

(f) whether the circumstances in which the evidence is adduced as hearsay are such as to suggest an attempt to prevent proper evaluation of its weight.

Supplementary provisions as to hearsay evidence

5 Competence and credibility

(1) Hearsay evidence shall not be admitted in civil proceedings if or to the extent that it is shown to consist of, or to be proved by means of, a statement made by a person who at the time he made the statement was not competent as a witness.

For this purpose 'not competent as a witness' means suffering from such mental or physical infirmity, or lack of understanding, as would render a person incompetent as a witness in civil proceedings; but a child shall be treated as competent as a witness if he satisfies the requirements of section 96(2)(a) and (b) of the Children Act 1989 (conditions for reception of unsworn evidence of child).

(2) Where in civil proceedings hearsay evidence is adduced and the maker of the original statement, or of any statement relied upon to prove another statement, is not called as a witness—

(a) evidence which if he had been so called would be admissible for the purpose of attacking or supporting his credibility as a witness is admissible for that purpose in the proceedings; and

(b) evidence tending to prove that, whether before or after he made the statement, he made any other statement inconsistent with it is admissible for the purpose of showing that he had contradicted himself.

Provided that evidence may not be given of any matter of which, if he had been called as a witness and had denied that matter in cross-examination, evidence could not have been adduced by the cross-examining party.

6 Previous statements of witnesses

(1) Subject as follows, the provisions of this Act as to hearsay evidence in civil proceedings apply equally (but with any necessary modifications) in relation to a previous statement made by a person called as a witness in the proceedings.

(2) A party who has called or intends to call a person as a witness in civil proceedings may not in those proceedings adduce evidence of a previous statement made by that person, except—

(a) with the leave of the court, or

(b) for the purpose of rebutting a suggestion that his evidence has been fabricated.

This shall not be construed as preventing a witness statement (that is, a written statement of oral evidence which a party to the proceedings intends to lead) from being adopted by a witness in giving evidence or treated as his evidence.

(3) Where in the case of civil proceedings section 3, 4 or 5 of the Criminal Procedure Act 1865 applies, which make provision as to—

(a) how far a witness may be discredited by the party producing him,

(b) the proof of contradictory statements made by a witness, and

(c) cross-examination as to previous statements in writing,

this Act does not authorise the adducing of evidence of a previous inconsistent or contradictory statement otherwise than in accordance with those sections.

This is without prejudice to any provision made by rules of court under section 3 above (power to call witness for cross-examination on hearsay statement).

(4) Nothing in this Act affects any of the rules of law as to the circumstances in which, where a person called as a witness in civil proceedings is cross-examined on a document used by him to refresh his memory, that document may be made evidence in the proceedings.

(5) Nothing in this section shall be construed as preventing a statement of any description referred to above from being admissible by virtue of section 1 as evidence of the matters stated.

7 Evidence formerly admissible at common law

(1) The common law rule effectively preserved by section 9(1) and (2)(a) of the Civil Evidence Act 1968 (admissibility of admissions adverse to a party) is superseded by the provisions of this Act.

(2) The common law rules effectively preserved by section 9(1) and (2)(b) to (d) of the Civil Evidence Act 1968, that is, any rule of law whereby in civil proceedings—

(a) published works dealing with matters of a public nature (for example, histories, scientific works, dictionaries and maps) are admissible as evidence of facts of a public nature stated in them,

(b) public documents (for example, public registers, and returns made under public authority with respect to matters of public interest) are admissible as evidence of facts stated in them, or

(c) records (for example, the records of certain courts, treaties, Crown grants, pardons and commissions) are admissible as evidence of facts stated in them,

shall continue to have effect.

(3) The common law rules effectively preserved by section 9(3) and (4) of the Civil Evidence Act 1968, that is, any rule of law whereby in civil proceedings—

(a) evidence of a person's reputation is admissible for the purpose of proving his good or bad character, or

(b) evidence of reputation or family tradition is admissible—

(i) for the purpose of proving or disproving pedigree or the existence of a marriage, or

(ii) for the purpose of proving or disproving the existence of any public or general right or of identifying any person or thing, shall continue to have effect in so far as they authorise the court to treat such evidence as proving or disproving that matter.

Where any such rule applies, reputation or family tradition shall be treated for the purposes of this Act as a fact and not as a statement or multiplicity of statements about the matter in question.

(4) The words in which a rule of law mentioned in this section is described are intended only to identify the rule and shall not be construed as altering it in any way.

Other matters

8 Proof of statements contained in documents

(1) Where a statement contained in a document is admissible as evidence in civil proceedings, it may be proved—

(a) by the production of that document, or

(b) whether or not that document is still in existence, by the production of a copy of that document or of the material part of it,

authenticated in such manner as the court may approve.

(2) It is immaterial for this purpose how many removes there are between a copy and the original.

9 Proof of records of business or public authority

(1) A document which is shown to form part of the records of a business or public authority may be received in evidence in civil proceedings without further proof.

(2) A document shall be taken to form part of the records of a business or public authority if there is produced to the court a certificate to that effect signed by an officer of the business or authority to which the records belong.

For this purpose—

(a) a document purporting to be a certificate signed by an officer of a business or public authority shall be deemed to have been duly given by such an officer and signed by him; and

(b) a certificate shall be treated as signed by a person if it purports to bear a facsimile of his signature.

(3) The absence of an entry in the records of a business or public authority may be proved in civil proceedings by affidavit of an officer of the business or authority to which the records belong.

(4) In this section—

'records' means records in whatever form;

'business' includes any activity regularly carried on over a period of time, whether for profit or not, by any body (whether corporate or not) or by an individual;

'officer' includes any person occupying a responsible position in relation to the relevant activities of the business or public authority or in relation to its records; and

'public authority' includes any public or statutory undertaking, any government department and any person holding office under Her Majesty.

(5) The court may, having regard to the circumstances of the case, direct that all or any of the above provisions of this section do not apply in relation to a particular document or record, or description of documents or records.

General

11 Meaning of 'civil proceedings'

In this Act 'civil proceedings' means civil proceedings, before any tribunal, in relation to which the strict rules of evidence apply, whether as a matter of law or by agreement of the parties.

References to 'the court' and 'rules of court' shall be construed accordingly.

12 Provisions as to rules of court

(1) Any power to make rules of court regulating the practice or procedure of the court in relation to civil proceedings includes power to make such provision as may be necessary or expedient for carrying into effect the provisions of this Act.

(2) Any rules of court made for the purposes of this Act as it applies in relation to proceedings in the High Court apply, except in so far as their operation is excluded by agreement, to arbitration proceedings to which this Act applies, subject to such modifications as may be appropriate.

Any question arising as to what modifications are appropriate shall be determined, in default of agreement, by the arbitrator or umpire, as the case may be.

13 Interpretation

In this Act—

'civil proceedings' has the meaning given by section 11 and 'court' and 'rules of court' shall be construed in accordance with that section;

'document' means anything in which information of any description is recorded, and 'copy', in relation to a document, means anything onto which information recorded in the document has been copied, by whatever means and whether directly or indirectly;

'hearsay' shall be construed in accordance with section 1(2);

'oral evidence' includes evidence which, by reason of a defect of speech or hearing, a person called as a witness gives in writing or by signs;

'the original statement', in relation to hearsay evidence, means the underlying statement (if any) by—

(a) in the case of evidence of fact, a person having personal knowledge of the fact, or

(b) in the case of evidence of opinion, the person whose opinion it is; and

'statement' means any representation of fact or opinion, however made.

14 Savings

(1) Nothing in this Act affects the exclusion of evidence on grounds other than that it is hearsay.

This applies whether the evidence falls to be excluded in pursuance of any enactment or rule of law, for failure to comply with rules of court or an order of the court, or otherwise.

(2) Nothing in this Act affects the proof of documents by means other than those specified in section 8 or 9.

(3) Nothing in this Act affects the operation of the following enactments—

(a) section 2 of the Documentary Evidence Act 1868 (mode of proving certain official documents);

(b) section 2 of the Documentary Evidence Act 1882 (documents printed under the superintendence of Stationery Office);

(c) section 1 of the Evidence (Colonial Statutes) Act 1907 (proof of statutes of certain legislatures);

(d) section 1 of the Evidence (Foreign, Dominion and Colonial Documents) Act 1933 (proof and effect of registers and official certificates of certain countries);

(e) section 5 of the Oaths and Evidence (Overseas Authorities and Countries) Act 1963 (provision in respect of public registers of other countries).

16 Short title commencement and extent

(1) This Act may be cited as the Civil Evidence Act 1995.

. . .

(4) This Act extends to England and Wales.

Civil Procedure Rules 1998

(SI 1998, No. 3132 (L. 17))

PART 32 EVIDENCE

32.1 Power of court to control evidence

(1) The court may control the evidence by giving directions as to—

(a) the issues on which it requires evidence;

(b) the nature of the evidence which it requires to decide those issues; and

(c) the way in which the evidence is to be placed before the court.

(2) The court may use its power under this rule to exclude evidence that would otherwise be admissible.

(3) The court may limit cross-examination.

32.2 Evidence of witnesses—general rule

(1) The general rule is that any fact which needs to be proved by the evidence of witnesses is to be proved—

(a) at trial, by their oral evidence given in public; and

(b) at any other hearing, by their evidence in writing.

(2) This is subject—

(a) to any provision to the contrary contained in these Rules or elsewhere; or

(b) to any order of the court.

(3) The court may give directions—

(a) identifying or limiting the issues to which factual evidence may be directed;

(b) identifying the witnesses who may be called or whose evidence may be read; or

(c) limiting the length or format of witness statements.

32.3 Evidence by video link or other means

The court may allow a witness to give evidence through a video link or by other means.

32.4 Requirement to serve witness statements for use at trial

(1) A witness statement is a written statement signed by a person which contains the evidence which that person would be allowed to give orally.

(2) The court will order a party to serve on the other parties any witness statement of the oral evidence which the party serving the statement intends to rely on in relation to any issues of fact to be decided at the trial.

(3) The court may give directions as to—

(a) the order in which witness statements are to be served; and

(b) whether or not the witness statements are to be filed.

32.5 Use at trial of witness statements which have been served

(1) If—

(a) a party has served a witness statement; and

(b) he wishes to rely at trial on the evidence of the witness who made the statement,

he must call the witness to give oral evidence unless the court orders otherwise or he puts the statement in as hearsay evidence.

(Part 33 contains provisions about hearsay evidence)

(2) Where a witness is called to give oral evidence under paragraph (1), his witness statement shall stand as his evidence in chief unless the court orders otherwise.

(3) A witness giving oral evidence at trial may with the permission of the court—

(a) amplify his witness statement; and

(b) give evidence in relation to new matters which have arisen since the witness statement was served on the other parties.

(4) The court will give permission under paragraph (3) only if it considers that there is good reason not to confine the evidence of the witness to the contents of his witness statement.

(5) If a party who has served a witness statement does not—

(a) call the witness to give evidence at trial; or

(b) put the witness statement in as hearsay evidence, any other party may put the witness statement in as hearsay evidence.

32.6 Evidence in proceedings other than at trial

(1) Subject to paragraph (2), the general rule is that evidence at hearings other than the trial is to be by witness statement unless the court, a practice direction or any other enactment requires otherwise.

(2) At hearings other than the trial, a party may rely on the matters set out in—

(a) his statement of case; or

(b) his application notice, if the statement of case or application notice is verified by a statement of truth.

32.7 Order for cross-examination

(1) Where, at a hearing other than the trial, evidence is given in writing, any party may apply to the court for permission to cross-examine the person giving the evidence.

(2) If the court gives permission under paragraph (1) but the person in question does not attend as required by the order, his evidence may not be used unless the court gives permission.

32.8 Form of witness statement

A witness statement must comply with the requirements set out in Practice Direction 32.

(Part 22 requires a witness statement to be verified by a statement of truth)

32.9 Witness summaries

(1) A party who—
- (a) is required to serve a witness statement for use at trial; but
- (b) is unable to obtain one, may apply, without notice, for permission to serve a witness summary instead.

(2) A witness summary is a summary of—
- (a) the evidence, if known, which would otherwise be included in a witness statement; or
- (b) if the evidence is not known, the matters about which the party serving the witness summary proposes to question the witness.

(3) Unless the court orders otherwise, a witness summary must include the name and address of the intended witness.

(4) Unless the court orders otherwise, a witness summary must be served within the period in which a witness statement would have had to be served.

(5) Where a party serves a witness summary, so far as practicable rules 32.4 (requirement to serve witness statements for use at trial), 32.5(3) (amplifying witness statements), and 32.8 (form of witness statement) shall apply to the summary.

32.10 Consequence of failure to serve witness statement or summary

If a witness statement or a witness summary for use at trial is not served in respect of an intended witness within the time specified by the court, then the witness may not be called to give oral evidence unless the court gives permission.

32.11 Cross-examination on a witness statement

Where a witness is called to give evidence at trial, he may be cross-examined on his witness statement whether or not the statement or any part of it was referred to during the witness's evidence in chief.

32.12 Use of witness statements for other purposes

(1) Except as provided by this rule, a witness statement may be used only for the purpose of the proceedings in which it is served.

(2) Paragraph (1) does not apply if and to the extent that—
- (a) the witness gives consent in writing to some other use of it;
- (b) the court gives permission for some other use; or
- (c) the witness statement has been put in evidence at a hearing held in public.

(3) This rule applies to affidavits in the same way as it applies to witness statements.

32.13 Availability of witness statements for inspection

(1) A witness statement which stands as evidence in chief is open to inspection during the course of the trial unless the court otherwise directs.

(2) Any person may ask for a direction that a witness statement is not open to inspection.

(3) The court will not make a direction under paragraph (2) unless it is satisfied that a witness statement should not be open to inspection because of—
- (a) the interests of justice;
- (b) the public interest;
- (c) the nature of any expert medical evidence in the statement;

(d) the nature of any confidential information (including information relating to personal financial matters) in the statement; or

(e) the need to protect the interests of any child or protected party.

(4) The court may exclude from inspection words or passages in the statement.

32.14 False statements

(1) Proceedings for contempt of court may be brought against a person who makes or causes to be made a false statement in a document, prepared in anticipation of or during proceedings and verified by a statement of truth without an honest belief in its truth.

(Part 22 makes provision for statements of truth.)

(Part 81 contains provisions in relation to proceedings for contempt of court.)

32.15 Affidavit evidence

(1) Evidence must be given by affidavit instead of or in addition to a witness statement if this is required by the court, a provision contained in any other rule, a practice direction or any other enactment.

(2) Nothing in these Rules prevents a witness giving evidence by affidavit at a hearing other than the trial if he chooses to do so in a case where paragraph (1) does not apply, but the party putting forward the affidavit may not recover the additional cost of making it from any other party unless the court orders otherwise.

(Rule 32.12 makes provision about the use of affidavits for purposes other than the proceedings in which they are served.)

32.16 Form of affidavit

An affidavit must comply with the requirements set out in Practice Direction 32.

32.17 Affidavit made outside the jurisdiction

A person may make an affidavit outside the jurisdiction in accordance with—

(a) this Part; or

(b) the law of the place where he makes the affidavit.

32.18 Notice to admit facts

(1) A party may serve notice on another party requiring him to admit the facts, or the part of the case of the serving party, specified in the notice.

(2) A notice to admit facts must be served no later than 21 days before the trial.

(3) Where the other party makes any admission in response to the notice, the admission may be used against him only—

(a) in the proceedings in which the notice to admit is served; and

(b) by the party who served the notice.

(4) The court may allow a party to amend or withdraw any admission made by him on such terms as it thinks just.

32.19 Notice to admit or produce documents

(1) A party shall be deemed to admit the authenticity of a document disclosed to him under Part 31 (disclosure and inspection of documents) unless he serves notice that he wishes the document to be proved at trial.

(2) A notice to prove a document must be served—

(a) by the latest date for serving witness statements; or

(b) within 7 days of disclosure of the document,

whichever is later.

32.20 Notarial acts and instruments

A notarial act or instrument may be received in evidence without further proof as duly authenticated in accordance with the requirements of law unless the contrary is proved.

PRACTICE DIRECTION 32

EVIDENCE

EVIDENCE IN GENERAL

1.1

Rule 32.2 sets out how evidence is to be given and facts are to be proved.

1.2

Evidence at a hearing other than the trial should normally be given by witness statement (see paragraph 17 onwards). However a witness may give evidence by affidavit if he wishes to do so (and see paragraph 1.4 below).

1.3

Statements of case (see paragraph 26 onwards) and application notices may also be used as evidence provided that their contents have been verified by a statement of truth.

(For information regarding evidence by deposition see Part 34 and Practice Direction 34A.)

1.4

Affidavits must be used as evidence in the following instances:

(1) where sworn evidence is required by an enactment, rule, order or practice direction, and

(2) in any application for a search order, a freezing injunction, or an order requiring an occupier to permit another to enter his land.

(By rule 81.4(1), unless and to the extent that the court directs otherwise every contempt application must be supported by written evidence given by affidavit or affirmation.).

1.5

If a party believes that sworn evidence is required by a court in another jurisdiction for any purpose connected with the proceedings, he may apply to the court for a direction that evidence shall be given only by affidavit on any pre-trial applications.

1.6

The court may give a direction under rule 32.15 that evidence shall be given by affidavit instead of or in addition to a witness statement or statement of case:

(1) on its own initiative, or

(2) after any party has applied to the court for such a direction.

1.7

An affidavit, where referred to in the Civil Procedure Rules or a practice direction, also means an affirmation unless the context requires otherwise.

AFFIDAVITS

Deponent

2

A deponent is a person who gives evidence by affidavit or affirmation.

Heading

3.1

The affidavit should be headed with the title of the proceedings (see paragraph 4 of Practice Direction 7A and paragraph 5 of Practice Direction 20); where the proceedings are between several parties with the same status it is sufficient to identify the parties as follows:

	Number:
A.B. (and others)	Claimants/Applicants
C.D. (and others)	Defendants/Respondents
	(as appropriate)

3.2
At the top right hand corner of the first page (and on the backsheet) there should be clearly written:

(1) the party on whose behalf it is made,
(2) the initials and surname of the deponent,
(3) the number of the affidavit in relation to that deponent,
(4) the identifying initials and number of each exhibit referred to, and
(5) the date sworn.

Body of affidavit

4.1
The affidavit must, if practicable, be in the deponent's own words, the affidavit should be expressed in the first person and the deponent should:

(1) commence 'I (*full name*) of (*address*) state on oath......',
(2) if giving evidence in his professional, business or other occupational capacity, give the address at which he works in (1) above, the position he holds and the name of his firm or employer,
(3) give his occupation or, if he has none, his description, and
(4) state if he is a party to the proceedings or employed by a party to the proceedings, if it be the case.

4.2
An affidavit must indicate:

(1) which of the statements in it are made from the deponent's own knowledge and which are matters of information or belief, and
(2) the source for any matters of information or belief.

4.3
Where a deponent:

(1) refers to an exhibit or exhibits, he should state 'there is now shown to me marked '...' the (*description of exhibit*)', and
(2) makes more than one affidavit (to which there are exhibits) in the same proceedings, the numbering of the exhibits should run consecutively throughout and not start again with each affidavit.

Jurat

5.1
The jurat of an affidavit is a statement set out at the end of the document which authenticates the affidavit.

5.2
It must:

(1) be signed by all deponents,
(2) be completed and signed by the person before whom the affidavit was sworn whose name and qualification must be printed beneath his signature,
(3) contain the full address of the person before whom the affidavit was sworn, and
(4) follow immediately on from the text and not be put on a separate page.

Format of affidavits

6.1
An affidavit should:

(1) be produced on durable quality A4 paper with a 3.5cm margin,
(2) be fully legible and should normally be typed on one side of the paper only,
(3) where possible, be bound securely in a manner which would not hamper filing, or otherwise each page should be endorsed with the case number and should bear the initials of the deponent and of the person before whom it was sworn,
(4) have the pages numbered consecutively as a separate document (or as one of several documents contained in a file),

(5) be divided into numbered paragraphs,

(6) have all numbers, including dates, expressed in figures, and

(7) give the reference to any document or documents mentioned either in the margin or in bold text in the body of the affidavit.

6.2

It is usually convenient for an affidavit to follow the chronological sequence of events or matters dealt with; each paragraph of an affidavit should as far as possible be confined to a distinct portion of the subject.

Inability of Deponent to read or sign affidavit

7.1

Where an affidavit is sworn by a person who is unable to read or sign it, the person before whom the affidavit is sworn must certify in the jurat that:

(1) he read the affidavit to the deponent,

(2) the deponent appeared to understand it, and

(3) the deponent signed or made his mark, in his presence.

7.2

If that certificate is not included in the jurat, the affidavit may not be used in evidence unless the court is satisfied that it was read to the deponent and that he appeared to understand it. Two versions of the form of jurat with the certificate are set out at Annex 1 to this practice direction.

Alterations to affidavits

8.1

Any alteration to an affidavit must be initialled by both the deponent and the person before whom the affidavit was sworn.

8.2

An affidavit which contains an alteration that has not been initialled may be filed or used in evidence only with the permission of the court.

Who may administer oaths and take affidavits

9.1

Only the following may administer oaths and take affidavits:

(1) A commissioner for oaths;

(2) omitted

(3) other persons specified by statute;

(4) certain officials of the Senior Courts;

(5) a circuit judge or district judge;

(6) any justice of the peace; and

(7) certain officials of any county court appointed by the judge of that court for the purpose.

9.2

An affidavit must be sworn before a person independent of the parties or their representatives.

Filing of affidavits

10.1

If the court directs that an affidavit is to be filed, it must be filed in the court or Division, or Office or Registry of the court or Division where the action in which it was or is to be used, is proceeding or will proceed.

10.2

Where an affidavit is in a foreign language:

(1) the party wishing to rely on it—

(a) must have it translated, and

(b) must file the foreign language affidavit with the court, and

(2) the translator must make and file with the court an affidavit verifying the translation and exhibiting both the translation and a copy of the foreign language affidavit.

EXHIBITS

Manner of exhibiting documents

11.1

A document used in conjunction with an affidavit should be:

(1) produced to and verified by the deponent, and remain separate from the affidavit, and

(2) identified by a declaration of the person before whom the affidavit was sworn.

11.2

The declaration should be headed with the name of the proceedings in the same way as the affidavit.

11.3

The first page of each exhibit should be marked:

(1) as in paragraph 3.2 above, and

(2) with the exhibit mark referred to in the affidavit.

Letters

12.1

Copies of individual letters should be collected together and exhibited in a bundle or bundles. They should be arranged in chronological order with the earliest at the top, and firmly secured.

12.2

When a bundle of correspondence is exhibited, the exhibit should have a front page attached stating that the bundle consists of original letters and copies. They should be arranged and secured as above and numbered consecutively.

Other documents

13.1

Photocopies instead of original documents may be exhibited provided the originals are made available for inspection by the other parties before the hearing and by the judge at the hearing.

13.2

Court documents must not be exhibited (official copies of such documents prove themselves).

13.3

Where an exhibit contains more than one document, a front page should be attached setting out a list of the documents contained in the exhibit; the list should contain the dates of the documents.

Exhibits other than documents

14.1

Items other than documents should be clearly marked with an exhibit number or letter in such a manner that the mark cannot become detached from the exhibit.

14.2

Small items may be placed in a container and the container appropriately marked.

General provisions

15.1

Where an exhibit contains more than one document:

(1) the bundle should not be stapled but should be securely fastened in a way that does not hinder the reading of the documents, and

(2) the pages should be numbered consecutively at bottom centre.

15.2
Every page of an exhibit should be clearly legible; typed copies of illegible documents should be included, paginated with 'a' numbers.

15.3
Where affidavits and exhibits have become numerous, they should be put into separate bundles and the pages numbered consecutively throughout.

15.4
Where on account of their bulk the service of exhibits or copies of exhibits on the other parties would be difficult or impracticable, the directions of the court should be sought as to arrangements for bringing the exhibits to the attention of the other parties and as to their custody pending trial.

Affirmations

16
All provisions in this or any other practice direction relating to affidavits apply to affirmations with the following exceptions:

(1) the deponent should commence 'I (*name*) of (*address*) do solemnly and sincerely affirm . . . . . .', and

(2) in the jurat the word 'sworn' is replaced by the word 'affirmed'.

WITNESS STATEMENTS

Heading

17.1
The witness statement should be headed with the title of the proceedings (see paragraph 4 of Practice Direction 7A and paragraph 5 of Practice Direction 20); where the proceedings are between several parties with the same status it is sufficient to identify the parties as follows:

	Number:
A.B. (and others)	Claimants/Applicants
C.D. (and others)	Defendants/Respondents
	(as appropriate)

17.2
At the top right hand corner of the first page there should be clearly written:

(1) the party on whose behalf it is made,
(2) the initials and surname of the witness,
(3) the number of the statement in relation to that witness,
(4) the identifying initials and number of each exhibit referred to,
(5) the date the statement was made, and
(6) the date of any translation.

Body of witness statement

18.1
The witness statement must, if practicable, be in the intended witness's own words and must in any event be drafted in their own language; the statement should be expressed in the first person and should also state:

(1) the full name of the witness,

(2) his place of residence or, if he is making the statement in his professional, business or other occupational capacity, the address at which he works, the position he holds and the name of his firm or employer,

(3) his occupation, or if he has none, his description,

(4) the fact that he is a party to the proceedings or is the employee of such a party if it be the case and

(5) the process by which it has been prepared, for example, face-to-face, over the telephone, and/or through an interpreter.

18.2

A witness statement must indicate:

(1) which of the statements in it are made from the witness's own knowledge and which are matters of information or belief, and

(2) the source for any matters of information or belief.

18.3

An exhibit used in conjunction with a witness statement should be verified and identified by the witness and remain separate from the witness statement.

18.4

Where a witness refers to an exhibit or exhibits, he should state 'I refer to the (*description of exhibit*) marked "...".

18.5

The provisions of paragraphs 11.3 to 15.4 (exhibits) apply similarly to witness statements as they do to affidavits.

18.6

Where a witness makes more than one witness statement to which there are exhibits, in the same proceedings, the numbering of the exhibits should run consecutively throughout and not start again with each witness statement.

Format of witness statement

19.1

A witness statement should:

(1) be produced on durable quality A4 paper with a 3.5cm margin,

(2) be fully legible and should normally be typed on one side of the paper only,

(3) where possible, be bound securely in a manner which would not hamper filing, or otherwise each page should be endorsed with the case number and should bear the initials of the witness,

(4) have the pages numbered consecutively as a separate statement (or as one of several statements contained in a file),

(5) be divided into numbered paragraphs,

(6) have all numbers, including dates, expressed in figures,

(7) give the reference to any document or documents mentioned either in the margin or in bold text in the body of the statement and

(8) be drafted in the witness's own language.

19.2

It is usually convenient for a witness statement to follow the chronological sequence of the events or matters dealt with, each paragraph of a witness statement should as far as possible be confined to a distinct portion of the subject.

Statement of Truth

20.1

A witness statement is the equivalent of the oral evidence which that witness would, if called, give in evidence; it must include a statement by the intended witness in their own language that they believe the facts in it are true.

20.2

To verify a witness statement the statement of truth is as follows:

'I believe that the facts stated in this witness statement are true. I understand that proceedings for contempt of court may be brought against anyone who makes, or causes to be made, a false statement in a document verified by a statement of truth without an honest belief in its truth.'

20.3

Attention is drawn to rule 32.14 which sets out the consequences of verifying a witness statement containing a false statement without an honest belief in its truth.

(Rule 22.1 (9) sets out the procedure to be followed where the person who should sign a document which is verified by a statement of truth is unable to read or sign the document other than by reason of language alone.)

21

Omitted

Alterations to witness statements

22.1

Any alteration to a witness statement must be initialled by the person making the statement or by the authorised person where appropriate (see paragraph 21).

22.2

A witness statement which contains an alteration that has not been initialled may be used in evidence only with the permission of the court.

Filing of witness statements

23.1

If the court directs that a witness statement is to be filed, it must be filed in the court or Division, or Office or Registry of the court or Division where the action in which it was or is to be used, is proceeding or will proceed.

23.2

Where a witness statement is in a foreign language—

(a) the party wishing to rely on it must —
  (i) have it translated; and
  (ii) file the foreign language witness statement with the court; and
(b) the translator must sign the original statement and must certify that the translation is accurate.

Certificate of court officer

24.1

Where the court has ordered that a witness statement is not to be open to inspection by the public or that words or passages in the statement are not to be open to inspection the court officer will so certify on the statement and make any deletions directed by the court under rule 32.13(4).

Defects in affidavits, witness statements and exhibits

25.1

Where:

(1) an affidavit,
(2) a witness statement, or
(3) an exhibit to either an affidavit or a witness statement,

does not comply with Part 32 or this practice direction in relation to its form, the court may refuse to admit it as evidence and may refuse to allow the costs arising from its preparation.

25.2
Permission to file a defective affidavit or witness statement or to use a defective exhibit may be obtained from a judge in the court where the case is proceeding.

STATEMENTS OF CASE

26.1
A statement of case may be used as evidence in an interim application provided it is verified by a statement of truth.

26.2
To verify a statement of case the statement of truth should be set out as follows:

'[I believe] [the (*party on whose behalf the statement of case is being signed*) believes] that the facts stated in the statement of case are true'.

26.3
Attention is drawn to rule 32.14 which sets out the consequences of verifying a witness statement containing a false statement without an honest belief in its truth.

(For information regarding statements of truth see Part 22 and Practice Direction 22.)

(Practice Directions 7A and 17 provide further information concerning statements of case.)

AGREED BUNDLES FOR HEARINGS

27.1
The court may give directions requiring the parties to use their best endeavours to agree a bundle or bundles of documents for use at any hearing.

27.2
All documents contained in bundles which have been agreed for use at a hearing shall be admissible at that hearing as evidence of their contents, unless—

(1) the court orders otherwise; or
(2) a party gives written notice of objection to the admissibility of particular documents.

27.3
Rule 39.5 provides that unless the court orders otherwise, the claimant must file a trial bundle containing documents required by—

(a) a relevant practice direction; and
(b) any court order.

27.4
Rule 39.5 provides that the claimant must file the trial bundle not more than 7 days and not less than 3 days before the start of the trial.

27.4A
If the trial is to take place in the Family Division, then Practice Direction 27A supplementing the Family Procedure Rules 2010 shall apply to provide what must happen in relation to the trial bundle in place of paragraphs 27.5 to 27.15 below.

27.5
Unless the court orders otherwise, the trial bundle should include a copy of—

(a) the claim form and all statements of case;
(b) a case summary and/or chronology where appropriate;
(c) requests for further information and responses to the requests;
(d) all witness statements to be relied on as evidence;
(e) any witness summaries;
(f) any notices of intention to rely on hearsay evidence under rule 32.2;
(g) any notices of intention to rely on evidence (such as a plan, photograph etc.) under rule 33.6 which is not—

(i) contained in a witness statement, affidavit or experts' report;
(ii) being given orally at trial; and
(iii) hearsay evidence under rule 33.2;

(h) any medical reports and responses to them;
(i) any experts' reports and responses to them;
(j) any order giving directions as to the conduct of the trial; and
(k) any other necessary documents.

27.6

The originals of the documents contained in the trial bundle, together with copies of any other court orders should be available at the trial.

27.7

The preparation and production of the trial bundle, even where it is delegated to another person, is the responsibility of the legal representative who has conduct of the claim on behalf of the claimant. If the claimant is unrepresented, the court may direct that another party must prepare and produce the trial bundle.

27.8

The trial bundle should be paginated (continuously) throughout, and indexed with a description of each document and the page number. Where the total number of pages is more than 100, numbered dividers should be placed at intervals between groups of documents.

27.9

The bundle should normally be contained in a ring binder or lever arch file. Where more than one bundle is supplied, they should be clearly distinguishable, for example, by different colours or letters. If there are numerous bundles, a core bundle should be prepared containing the core documents essential to the proceedings, with references to the supplementary documents in the other bundles.

27.10

For convenience, experts' reports may be contained in a separate bundle and cross referenced in the main bundle.

27.11

If a document to be included in the trial bundle is illegible, a typed copy should be included in the bundle next to it, suitably cross-referenced.

27.12

The contents of the trial bundle should be agreed where possible. The parties should also agree where possible—

(a) that the documents contained in the bundle are authentic even if not disclosed under Part 31; and
(b) that documents in the bundle may be treated as evidence of the facts stated in them even if a notice under the Civil Evidence Act 1995 has not been served.

Where it is not possible to agree the contents of the bundle, a summary of the points on which the parties are unable to agree should be included.

27.13

The party filing the trial bundle should supply identical bundles to all the parties to the proceedings and for the use of the witnesses.

27.14

Unless the court otherwise directs, contemporaneous documents in the trial bundle relied on by the parties or either of them should be assembled as a single unit in chronological order of creation.

27.15

Unless the court otherwise directs, documents in the trial bundle should be copied double-sided.

. . .

VIDEO CONFERENCING

29.1

Guidance on the use of video conferencing in the civil courts is set out at Annex 3 to this practice direction.

A list of the sites which are available for video conferencing can be found on HM Courts and Tribunals Service website.

ANNEX 1

Certificate to be used where a deponent to an affidavit is unable to read or sign it

Sworn at .... this ...... day of .... Before me, I having first read over the contents of this affidavit to the deponent [*if there are exhibits, add* 'and explained the nature and effect of the exhibits referred to in it'] who appeared to understand it and approved its content as accurate, and made his mark on the affidavit in my presence.

Or; (after, *Before me*) the witness to the mark of the deponent having been first sworn that he had read over etc. (*as above*) and that he saw him make his mark on the affidavit. (*Witness must sign*).

Certificate to be used where a deponent to an affirmation is unable to read or sign it

Affirmed at .... this ...... day of .... Before me, I having first read over the contents of this affirmation to the deponent [*if there are exhibits, add* 'and explained the nature and effect of the exhibits referred to in it'] who appeared to understand it and approved its content as accurate, and made his mark on the affirmation in my presence.

Or, (after, *Before me*) the witness to the mark of the deponent having been first sworn that he had read over etc. (*as above*) and that he saw him make his mark on the affirmation. (*Witness must sign*).

ANNEX 2

Omitted

ANNEX 3

VIDEO CONFERENCING GUIDANCE

This guidance is for the use of video conferencing (VCF) in civil proceedings. It is in part based, with permission, upon the protocol of the Federal Court of Australia. It is intended to provide a guide to all persons involved in the use of VCF, although it does not attempt to cover all the practical questions which might arise.

Video conferencing generally

1.

The guidance covers the use of VCF equipment both (a) in a courtroom, whether via equipment which is permanently placed there or via a mobile unit, and (b) in a separate studio or conference room. In either case, the location at which the judge sits is referred to as the 'local site'. The other site or sites to and from which transmission is made are referred to as 'the remote site' and in any particular case any such site may be another courtroom. The guidance applies to cases where VCF is used for the taking of evidence and also to its use for other parts of any legal proceedings (for example, interim applications, case management conferences, pre-trial reviews).

2.

VCF may be a convenient way of dealing with any part of proceedings: it can involve considerable savings in time and cost. Its use for the taking of evidence from overseas witnesses will, in particular, be likely to achieve a material saving of costs, and such savings may also be achieved by its use for taking domestic evidence. It is, however, inevitably not as ideal as having the witness physically present in court. Its convenience should not therefore be allowed to dictate its use. A judgment must be made in every case in which the use of VCF is being considered not only as to whether it will achieve an overall cost saving but as to whether its use will be likely to be beneficial to the efficient, fair and economic disposal of the litigation. In particular, it needs to be recognised that the degree of control a court can exercise over a witness at the remote site is or may be more limited than it can exercise over a witness physically before it.

3.
When used for the taking of evidence, the objective should be to make the VCF session as close as possible to the usual practice in a trial court where evidence is taken in open court. To gain the maximum benefit, several differences have to be taken into account. Some matters, which are taken for granted when evidence is taken in the conventional way, take on a different dimension when it is taken by VCF: for example, the administration of the oath, ensuring that the witness understands who is at the local site and what their various roles are, the raising of any objections to the evidence and the use of documents.

4.
It should not be presumed that all foreign governments are willing to allow their nationals or others within their jurisdiction to be examined before a court in England or Wales by means of VCF. If there is any doubt about this, enquiries should be directed to the Foreign, Commonwealth and Development (Public Facing Services, Taking of Evidence Team) TOE.Enquiries@fcdo.gov.uk with a view to ensuring that the country from which the evidence is to be taken raises no objection to it at diplomatic level. The party who is directed to be responsible for arranging the VCF (see paragraph 8 below) will be required to make all necessary inquiries about this well in advance of the VCF and must be able to inform the court what those inquiries were and of their outcome.

5.
Time zone differences need to be considered when a witness abroad is to be examined in England or Wales by VCF. The convenience of the witness, the parties, their representatives and the court must all be taken into account. The cost of the use of a commercial studio is usually greater outside normal business hours.

6.
Those involved with VCF need to be aware that, even with the most advanced systems currently available, there are the briefest of delays between the receipt of the picture and that of the accompanying sound. If due allowance is not made for this, there will be a tendency to 'speak over' the witness, whose voice will continue to be heard for a millisecond or so after he or she appears on the screen to have finished speaking.

7.
With current technology, picture quality is good, but not as good as a television picture. The quality of the picture is enhanced if those appearing on VCF monitors keep their movements to a minimum.

Preliminary arrangements

8.
The court's permission is required for any part of any proceedings to be dealt with by means of VCF. Before seeking a direction, the applicant should notify the listing officer, diary manager or other appropriate court officer of the intention to seek it, and should enquire as to the availability of court VCF equipment for the day or days of the proposed VCF. The application for a direction should be made to the Master, District Judge or Judge, as may be appropriate. If all parties consent to a direction, permission can be sought by letter, fax or e-mail, although the court may still require an oral hearing. All parties are entitled to be heard on whether or not such a direction should be given and as to its terms. If a witness at a remote site is to give evidence by an interpreter, consideration should be given at this stage as to whether the interpreter should be at the local site or the remote site. If a VCF direction is given, arrangements for the transmission will then need to be made. The court will ordinarily direct that the party seeking permission to use VCF is to be responsible for this. That party is hereafter referred to as 'the VCF arranging party'.

9.
Subject to any order to the contrary, all costs of the transmission, including the costs of hiring equipment and technical personnel to operate it, will initially be the responsibility of, and must be met by, the VCF arranging party. All reasonable efforts should be made to keep the transmission to a minimum and so keep the costs down. All such costs will be considered to be part of the costs of the

proceedings and the court will determine at such subsequent time as is convenient or appropriate who, as between the parties, should be responsible for them and (if appropriate) in what proportions.

10.
The local site will, if practicable, be a courtroom but it may instead be an appropriate studio or conference room. The VCF arranging party must contact the listing officer, diary manager or other appropriate officer of the court which made the VCF direction and make arrangements for the VCF transmission. Details of the remote site, and of the equipment to be used both at the local site (if not being supplied by the court) and the remote site (including the number of ISDN lines and connection speed), together with all necessary contact names and telephone numbers, will have to be provided to the listing officer, diary manager or other court officer. The court will need to be satisfied that any equipment provided by the parties for use at the local site and also that at the remote site is of sufficient quality for a satisfactory transmission. The VCF arranging party must ensure that an appropriate person will be present at the local site to supervise the operation of the VCF throughout the transmission in order to deal with any technical problems. That party must also arrange for a technical assistant to be similarly present at the remote site for like purposes.

11.
It is recommended that the judge, practitioners and witness should arrive at their respective VCF sites about 20 minutes prior to the scheduled commencement of the transmission.

12.
If the local site is not a courtroom, but a conference room or studio, the judge will need to determine who is to sit where. The VCF arranging party must take care to ensure that the number of microphones is adequate for the speakers and that the panning of the camera for the practitioners' table encompasses all legal representatives so that the viewer can see everyone seated there.

13.
The proceedings, wherever they may take place, form part of a trial to which the public is entitled to have access (unless the court has determined that they should be heard in private). If the local site is to be a studio or conference room, the VCF arranging party must ensure that it provides sufficient accommodation to enable a reasonable number of members of the public to attend.

14.
In cases where the local site is a studio or conference room, the VCF arranging party should make arrangements, if practicable, for the royal coat of arms to be placed above the judge's seat.

15.
In cases in which the VCF is to be used for the taking of evidence, the VCF arranging party must arrange for recording equipment to be provided by the court which made the VCF direction so that the evidence can be recorded. An associate will normally be present to operate the recording equipment when the local site is a courtroom. The VCF arranging party should take steps to ensure that an associate is present to do likewise when it is a studio or conference room. The equipment should be set up and tested before the VCF transmission. It will often be a valuable safeguard for the VCF arranging party also to arrange for the provision of recording equipment at the remote site. This will provide a useful back-up if there is any reduction in sound quality during the transmission. A direction from the court for the making of such a back-up recording must, however, be obtained first. This is because the proceedings are court proceedings and, save as directed by the court, no other recording of them must be made. The court will direct what is to happen to the back-up recording.

16.
Some countries may require that any oath or affirmation to be taken by a witness accord with local custom rather than the usual form of oath or affirmation used in England and Wales. The VCF arranging party must make all appropriate prior inquiries and put in place all arrangements necessary to enable the oath or affirmation to be taken in accordance with any local custom. That party must be in a position to inform the court what those inquiries were, what their outcome was and what arrangements have been made. If the oath or affirmation can be administered in the manner

normal in England and Wales, the VCF arranging party must arrange in advance to have the appropriate holy book at the remote site. The associate will normally administer the oath.

17.
Consideration will need to be given in advance to the documents to which the witness is likely to be referred. The parties should endeavour to agree on this. It will usually be most convenient for a bundle of the copy documents to be prepared in advance, which the VCF arranging party should then send to the remote site.

18.
Additional documents are sometimes quite properly introduced during the course of a witness's evidence. To cater for this, the VCF arranging party should ensure that equipment is available to enable documents to be transmitted between sites during the course of the VCF transmission. Consideration should be given to whether to use a document camera. If it is decided to use one, arrangements for its use will need to be established in advance. The panel operator will need to know the number and size of documents or objects if their images are to be sent by document camera. In many cases, a simpler and sufficient alternative will be to ensure that there are fax transmission and reception facilities at the participating sites.

The hearing

19.
The procedure for conducting the transmission will be determined by the judge. He will determine who is to control the cameras. In cases where the VCF is being used for an application in the course of the proceedings, the judge will ordinarily not enter the local site until both sites are on line. Similarly, at the conclusion of the hearing, he will ordinarily leave the local site while both sites are still on line. The following paragraphs apply primarily to cases where the VCF is being used for the taking of the evidence of a witness at a remote site. In all cases, the judge will need to decide whether court dress is appropriate when using VCF facilities. It might be appropriate when transmitting from courtroom to courtroom. It might not be when a commercial facility is being used.

20.
At the beginning of the transmission, the judge will probably wish to introduce himself and the advocates to the witness. He will probably want to know who is at the remote site and will invite the witness to introduce himself and anyone else who is with him. He may wish to give directions as to the seating arrangements at the remote site so that those present are visible at the local site during the taking of the evidence. He will probably wish to explain to the witness the method of taking the oath or of affirming, the manner in which the evidence will be taken, and who will be conducting the examination and cross-examination. He will probably also wish to inform the witness of the matters referred to in paragraphs 6 and 7 above (co-ordination of picture with sound, and picture quality).

21.
The examination of the witness at the remote site should follow as closely as possible the practice adopted when a witness is in the courtroom. During examination, cross-examination and re-examination, the witness must be able to see the legal representative asking the question and also any other person (whether another legal representative or the judge) making any statements in regard to the witness's evidence. It will in practice be most convenient if everyone remains seated throughout the transmission.

PART 33 MISCELLANEOUS RULES ABOUT EVIDENCE

33.1 Introductory

In this Part—

(a) 'hearsay' means a statement made, otherwise than by a person while giving oral evidence in proceedings, which is tendered as evidence of the matters stated; and
(b) references to hearsay include hearsay of whatever degree.

33.2 Notice of intention to rely on hearsay evidence

(1) Where a party intends to rely on hearsay evidence at trial and either—

(a) that evidence is to be given by a witness giving oral evidence; or

(b) that evidence is contained in a witness statement of a person who is not being called to give oral evidence;

that party complies with section 2(1)(a) of the Civil Evidence Act 1995 serving a witness statement on the other parties in accordance with the court's order.

(2) Where paragraph (1)(b) applies, the party intending to rely on the hearsay evidence must, when he serves the witness statement—

(a) inform the other parties that the witness is not being called to give oral evidence; and

(b) give the reason why the witness will not be called.

(3) In all other cases where a party intends to rely on hearsay evidence at trial, that party complies with section 2(1)(a) of the Civil Evidence Act 1995 by serving a notice on the other parties which—

(a) identifies the hearsay evidence;

(b) states that the party serving the notice proposes to rely on the hearsay evidence at trial; and

(c) gives the reason why the witness will not be called.

(4) The party proposing to rely on the hearsay evidence must—

(a) serve the notice no later than the latest date for serving witness statements; and

(b) if the hearsay evidence is to be in a document, supply a copy to any party who requests him to do so.

33.3 Circumstances in which notice of intention to rely on hearsay evidence is not required

Section 2(1) of the Civil Evidence Act 1995 (duty to give notice of intention to rely on hearsay evidence) does not apply—

(a) to evidence at hearings other than trials;

(aa) to an affidavit or witness statement which is to be used at trial but which does not contain hearsay evidence;

(b) to a statement which a party to a probate action wishes to put in evidence and which is alleged to have been made by the person whose estate is the subject of the proceedings; or

(c) where the requirement is excluded by a practice direction.

33.4 Power to call witness for cross-examination on hearsay evidence

(1) Where a party—

(a) proposes to rely on hearsay evidence; and

(b) does not propose to call the person who made the original statement to give oral evidence,

the court may, on the application of any other party, permit that party to call the maker of the statement to be cross-examined on the contents of the statement.

(2) An application for permission to cross-examine under this rule must be made not more than 14 days after the day on which a notice of intention to rely on the hearsay evidence was served on the applicant.

33.5 Credibility

(1) Where a party—

(a) proposes to rely on hearsay evidence; but

(b) does not propose to call the person who made the original statement to give oral evidence; and

(c) another party wishes to call evidence to attack the credibility of the person who made the statement,

the party who so wishes must give notice of his intention to the party who proposes to give the hearsay statement in evidence.

(2) A party must give notice under paragraph (1) not more than 14 days after the day on which a hearsay notice relating to the hearsay evidence was served on him.

33.6 Use of plans, photographs and models as evidence

(1) This rule applies to evidence (such as a plan, photograph or model) which is not—

(a) contained in a witness statement, affidavit or expert's report;

(b) to be given orally at trial; or

(c) evidence of which prior notice must be given under rule 33.2.

(2) This rule includes documents which may be received in evidence without further proof under section 9 of the Civil Evidence Act 1995.

(3) Unless the court orders otherwise the evidence shall not be receivable at a trial unless the party intending to put it in evidence has given notice to the other parties in accordance with this rule.

(4) Where the party intends to use the evidence as evidence of any fact then, except where paragraph (6) applies, he must give notice not later than the latest date for serving witness statements.

(5) He must give notice at least 21 days before the hearing at which he proposes to put in the evidence, if—

(a) there are not to be witness statements; or

(b) he intends to put in the evidence solely in order to disprove an allegation made in a witness statement.

(6) Where the evidence forms part of expert evidence, he must give notice when the expert's report is served on the other party.

(7) Where the evidence is being produced to the court for any reason other than as part of factual or expert evidence, he must give notice at least 21 days before the hearing at which he proposes to put in the evidence.

(8) Where a party has given notice that he intends to put in the evidence, he must give every other party an opportunity to inspect it and to agree to its admission without further proof.

33.7 Evidence of finding on question of foreign law

(1) This rule sets out the procedure which must be followed by a party who intends to put in evidence a finding on a question of foreign law by virtue of section 4(2) of the Civil Evidence Act 1972.

(2) He must give any other party notice of his intention.

(3) He must give the notice—

(a) if there are to be witness statements, not later than the latest date for serving them; or

(b) otherwise, not less than 21 days before the hearing at which he proposes to put the finding in evidence.

(4) The notice must—

(a) specify the question on which the finding was made; and

(b) enclose a copy of a document where it is reported or recorded.

33.8 Evidence of consent of trustee to act

A document purporting to contain the written consent of a person to act as trustee and to bear his signature verified by some other person is evidence of such consent.

33.9 Human Rights

(1) This rule applies where a claim is—

(a) for a remedy under section 7 of the Human Rights Act 1998 in respect of a judicial act which is alleged to have infringed the claimant's Article 5 Convention rights; and

(b) based on a finding by a court or tribunal that the claimant's Convention rights have been infringed.

(2) The court hearing the claim—

(a) may proceed on the basis of the finding of that other court or tribunal that there has been an infringement but it is not required to do so, and

(b) may reach its own conclusion in the light of that finding and of the evidence heard by that other court or tribunal.

PART 34 WITNESSES, DEPOSITIONS AND EVIDENCE FOR FOREIGN COURTS

I WITNESSES AND DEPOSITIONS

34.1 Scope of this Section

(1) This Section of this Part provides—

(a) for the circumstances in which a person may be required to attend court to give evidence or to produce a document; and

(b) for a party to obtain evidence before a hearing to be used at the hearing.

(2) In this Section, reference to a hearing includes a reference to the trial.

34.2 Witness summonses

(1) A witness summons is a document issued by the court requiring a witness to—

(a) attend court to give evidence; or

(b) produce documents to the court.

(2) A witness summons must be in the relevant practice form.

(3) There must be a separate witness summons for each witness.

(4) A witness summons may require a witness to produce documents to the court either—

(a) on the date fixed for a hearing; or

(b) on such date as the court may direct.

(5) The only documents that a summons under this rule can require a person to produce before a hearing are documents which that person could be required to produce at the hearing.

34.3 Issue of a witness summons

(1) A witness summons is issued on the date entered on the summons by the court.

(2) A party must obtain permission from the court where he wishes to—

(a) have a summons issued less than 7 days before the date of the trial;

(b) have a summons issued for a witness to attend court to give evidence or to produce documents on any date except the date fixed for the trial; or

(c) have a summons issued for a witness to attend court to give evidence or to produce documents at any hearing except the trial.

(3) A witness summons must be issued by—

(a) the court where the case is proceeding; or

(b) the court where the hearing in question will be held.

(4) The court may set aside or vary a witness summons issued under this rule.

34.4 Witness summons in aid of inferior court or of tribunal

(1) The court may issue a witness summons in aid of an inferior court or of a tribunal.

(2) The court which issued the witness summons under this rule may set it aside.

(3) In this rule, 'inferior court or tribunal' means any court or tribunal that does not have power to issue a witness summons in relation to proceedings before it.

34.5 Time for serving a witness summons

(1) The general rule is that a witness summons is binding if it is served at least 7 days before the date on which the witness is required to attend before the court or tribunal.

(2) The court may direct that a witness summons shall be binding although it will be served less than 7 days before the date on which the witness is required to attend before the court or tribunal.

(3) A witness summons which is—

(a) served in accordance with this rule; and

(b) requires the witness to attend court to give evidence,

is binding until the conclusion of the hearing at which the attendance of the witness is required.

34.6 Who is to serve a witness summons

(1) A witness summons is to be served by the court unless the party on whose behalf it is issued indicates in writing, when he asks the court to issue the summons, that he wishes to serve it himself.

(2) Where the court is to serve the witness summons, the party on whose behalf it is issued must deposit, in the court office, the money to be paid or offered to the witness under rule 34.7.

34.7 Right of witness to travelling expenses and compensation for loss of time

At the time of service of a witness summons the witness must be offered or paid—

(a) a sum reasonably sufficient to cover his expenses in travelling to and from the court; and

(b) such sum by way of compensation for loss of time as may be specified in Practice Direction 34A.

34.7A Fines imposed under section 55 of the County Courts Act 1984

If a person has failed to comply with an order under section 55 of the County Courts Act 1984 but can demonstrate any reason why they should not be (or should not have been) fined for failure to comply with the order, the court may direct that that person give evidence by witness statement, affidavit or otherwise.

(Part 70 contains general rules about fines imposed under the County Courts Act 1984.)

34.8 Evidence by deposition

(1) A party may apply for an order for a person to be examined before the hearing takes place.

(2) A person from whom evidence is to be obtained following an order under this rule is referred to as a 'deponent' and the evidence is referred to as a 'deposition'.

(3) An order under this rule shall be for a deponent to be examined on oath before—

(a) a judge;

(b) an examiner of the court; or

(c) such other person as the court appoints.

(Rule 34.15 makes provision for the appointment of examiners of the court)

(4) The order may require the production of any document which the court considers is necessary for the purposes of the examination.

(5) The order must state the date, time and place of the examination.

(6) At the time of service of the order the deponent must be offered or paid—

(a) a sum reasonably sufficient to cover his expenses in travelling to and from the place of examination; and

(b) such sum by way of compensation for loss of time as may be specified in Practice Direction 34A.

(7) Where the court makes an order for a deposition to be taken, it may also order the party who obtained the order to serve a witness statement or witness summary in relation to the evidence to be given by the person to be examined.

(Part 32 contains the general rules about witness statements and witness summaries)

34.9 Conduct of examination

(1) Subject to any directions contained in the order for examination, the examination must be conducted in the same way as if the witness were giving evidence at a trial.

(2) If all the parties are present, the examiner may conduct the examination of a person not named in the order for examination if all the parties and the person to be examined consent.

(3) The examiner may conduct the examination in private if he considers it appropriate to do so.

(4) The examiner must ensure that the evidence given by the witness is recorded in full.

(5) The examiner must send a copy of the deposition—

(a) to the person who obtained the order for the examination of the witness; and

(b) to the court where the case is proceeding.

(6) The party who obtained the order must send each of the other parties a copy of the deposition which he receives from the examiner.

34.10 Enforcing attendance of witness

(1) If a person served with an order to attend before an examiner—

(a) fails to attend; or

(b) refuses to be sworn for the purpose of the examination or to answer any lawful question or produce any document at the examination,

a certificate of his failure or refusal, signed by the examiner, must be filed by the party requiring the deposition.

(2) On the certificate being filed, the party requiring the deposition may apply to the court for an order requiring that person to attend or to be sworn or to answer any question or produce any document, as the case may be.

(3) An application for an order under this rule may be made without notice.

(4) The court may order the person against whom an order is made under this rule to pay any costs resulting from his failure or refusal.

34.11 Use of deposition at a hearing

(1) A deposition ordered under rule 34.8 may be given in evidence at a hearing unless the court orders otherwise.

(2) A party intending to put in evidence a deposition at a hearing must serve notice of his intention to do so on every other party.

(3) He must serve the notice at least 21 days before the day fixed for the hearing.

(4) The court may require a deponent to attend the hearing and give evidence orally.

(5) Where a deposition is given in evidence at trial, it shall be treated as if it were a witness statement for the purposes of rule 32.13 (availability of witness statements for inspection).

34.12 Restrictions on subsequent use of deposition taken for the purpose of any hearing except the trial

(1) Where the court orders a party to be examined about his or any other assets for the purpose of any hearing except the trial, the deposition may be used only for the purpose of the proceedings in which the order was made.

(2) However, it may be used for some other purpose—

(a) by the party who was examined;

(b) if the party who was examined agrees; or

(c) if the court gives permission.

34.13 Where a person to be examined is out of the jurisdiction—letter of request

(1) This rule applies where a party wishes to take a deposition from a person who is—

(a) out of the jurisdiction;

(1A) The High Court may order the issue of a letter of request to the judicial authorities of the country in which the proposed deponent is.

(2) A letter of request is a request to a judicial authority to take the evidence of that person, or arrange for it to be taken.

(3) The High Court may make an order under this rule in relation to county court and tribunal proceedings.

(4) If the government of a country allows a person appointed by the High Court to examine a person in that country, the High Court may make an order appointing a special examiner for that purpose.

(5) A person may be examined under this rule on oath or affirmation or in accordance with any procedure permitted in the country in which the examination is to take place.

(6) If the High Court makes an order for the issue of a letter of request, the party who sought the order must file with the Foreign Process Section of the Central Office of the High Court in the Royal Courts of Justice—

(a) the following documents and, except where paragraph (7) applies, a translation of them—

(i) a draft letter of request;

(ii) a statement of the issues relevant to the proceedings;

(iii) a list of questions or the subject matter of questions to be put to the person to be examined; and

(b) an undertaking to be responsible for the Secretary of State's expenses.

(7) There is no need to file a translation if—

(a) English is one of the official languages of the country where the examination is to take place; or

(b) a practice direction has specified that country as a country where no translation is necessary.

34.13A Letter of request—Proceeds of Crime Act 2002

(1) This rule applies where a party to existing or contemplated proceedings in—

(a) the High Court; or

(b) a magistrates' court,

under Part 5 of the Proceeds of Crime Act 2002 (civil recovery of the proceeds etc. of unlawful conduct) wishes to take a deposition from a person who is out of the jurisdiction.

(2) The High Court may, on the application of such a party, order the issue of a letter of request to the judicial authorities of the country in which the proposed deponent is.

(3) Paragraphs (4) to (7) of rule 34.13 shall apply irrespective of where the proposed deponent is.

34.14 Fees and expenses of examiner of the court

(1) An examiner of the court may charge a fee for the examination.

(2) He need not send the deposition to the court unless the fee is paid.

(3) The examiner's fees and expenses must be paid by the party who obtained the order for examination.

(4) If the fees and expenses due to an examiner are not paid within a reasonable time, he may report that fact to the court.

(5) The court may order the party who obtained the order for examination to deposit in the court office a specified sum in respect of the examiner's fees and, where it does so, the examiner will not be asked to act until the sum has been deposited.

(6) An order under this rule does not affect any decision as to the party who is ultimately to bear the costs of the examination.

34.15 Examiners of the court

(1) The Lord Chancellor shall appoint persons to be examiners of the court.

(2) The persons appointed shall be barristers or solicitor-advocates who have been practising for a period of not less than three years.

(3) The Lord Chancellor may revoke an appointment at any time.

II EVIDENCE FOR FOREIGN COURTS

34.16 Scope and interpretation

(1) This Section applies to an application for an order under the 1975 Act for evidence to be obtained.

(2) In this Section—

(a) 'the 1975 Act' means the Evidence (Proceedings in Other Jurisdictions) Act 1975;

(b) 'the Hague Evidence Convention' means the Hague Convention of 18 March 1970 on the Taking of Evidence Abroad in Civil or Commercial Matters

34.17 Application for order

(1) An application for an order under the 1975 Act for evidence to be obtained must be made to the High Court and may be made without notice.

(2) The application may be made either—

(a) by an application notice under Part 23, which must be—

(i) supported by written evidence; and

(ii) accompanied by the request as a result of which the application is made, and where appropriate, a translation of the request into English; or

(b) where—
(i) the requesting state is a party to the Hague Evidence Convention, by a Letter of Request using the Model Form published by the Permanent Bureau of the Hague Conference on Private International Law (which is annexed to Practice Direction 34A); or
(ii) the requesting state is not a party to the Hague Evidence Convention, by a Letter of Request submitted via the Foreign and Commonwealth Office.

34.18 Examination

(1) The court may order an examination to be taken before—
(a) any fit and proper person nominated by the person applying for the order;
(b) an examiner of the court; or
(c) any other person whom the court considers suitable.
(2) Unless the court orders otherwise—
(a) the examination will be taken as provided by rule 34.9; and
(b) rule 34.10 applies.
(3) The court may make an order under rule 34.14 for payment of the fees and expenses of the examination.

34.19 Dealing with deposition

(1) The examiner must send the deposition of the witness to the Senior Master unless the court orders otherwise.
(2) The Senior Master will—
(a) give a certificate sealed with the seal of the Senior Courts for use out of the jurisdiction identifying the following documents—
(i) the request;
(ii) the order of the court for examination; and
(iii) the deposition of the witness; and
(b) send the certificate and the documents referred to in paragraph (a) to—
(i) the Secretary of State; or
(ii) where the request was sent to the Senior Master by another person in accordance with a Civil Procedure Convention, to that other person,
for transmission to the court or tribunal requesting the examination.

34.20 Claim to privilege

(1) This rule applies where—
(a) a witness claims to be exempt from giving evidence on the ground specified in section 3(1)(b) of the 1975 Act; and
(b) That claim is not supported or conceded as referred to in section 3(2) of that Act.
(2) The examiner may require the witness to give the evidence which he claims to be exempt from giving.
(3) Where the examiner does not require the witness to give that evidence, the court may order the witness to do so.
(4) An application for an order under paragraph (3) may be made by the person who obtained the order under section 2 of the 1975 Act.
(5) Where such evidence is taken—
(a) it must be contained in a document separate from the remainder of the deposition;
(b) the examiner will send to the Senior Master—
(i) the deposition; and
(ii) a signed statement setting out the claim to be exempt and the ground on which it was made;
(6) On receipt of the statement referred to in paragraph (5)(b)(ii), the Senior Master will—

(a) retain the document containing the part of the witness's evidence to which the claim to be exempt relates; and
(b) send the statement and a request to determine that claim to the foreign court or tribunal together with the documents referred to in rule 34.17.

(7) The Senior Master will—
(a) if the claim to be exempt is rejected by the foreign court or tribunal, send the document referred to in paragraph (5)(a) to that court or tribunal;
(b) if the claim is upheld, send the document to the witness; and
(c) in either case, notify the witness and person who obtained the order under section 2 of the foreign court or tribunal's decision.

34.21 Order under 1975 Act as applied by Patents Act 1977

Where an order is made for the examination of witnesses under section 1 of the 1975 Act as applied by section 92 of the Patents Act 1977 the court may permit an officer of the European Patent Office to—
(a) attend the examination and examine the witnesses; or
(b) request the court or the examiner before whom the examination takes place to put specified questions to them.

PRACTICE DIRECTION 34A

DEPOSITIONS AND COURT ATTENDANCE BY WITNESSES

This Practice Direction supplements CPR Part 34

WITNESS SUMMONSES

Issue of witness summons

1.1

A witness summons may require a witness to:
(1) attend court to give evidence,
(2) produce documents to the court, or
(3) both,

on either a date fixed for the hearing or such date as the court may direct.

1.2

Two copies of the witness summons should be filed with the court for sealing, one of which will be retained on the court file.

1.3

A mistake in the name or address of a person named in a witness summons may be corrected if the summons has not been served.

1.4

The corrected summons must be re-sealed by the court and marked 'Amended and Re-Sealed'.

Witness summons issued in aid of an inferior court or tribunal

2.1

A witness summons may be issued in the High Court or the County Court in aid of a court or tribunal which does not have the power to issue a witness summons in relation to the proceedings before it.

2.2

A witness summons referred to in paragraph 2.1 may be set aside by the court which issued it.

2.3

An application to set aside a witness summons referred to in paragraph 2.1 will be heard:

(1) in the High Court by a Master at the Royal Courts of Justice or by a District Judge in a District Registry, and

(2) in the County Court by a District Judge.

2.4

Unless the court otherwise directs, the applicant must give at least 2 days' notice to the party who issued the witness summons of the application, which will normally be dealt with at a hearing.

Travelling expenses and compensation for loss of time

3.1

When a witness is served with a witness summons they must be offered a sum to cover his travelling expenses to and from the court and compensation for their loss of time.

3.2

If the witness summons is to be served by the court, the party issuing the summons must deposit with the court:

(1) a sum sufficient to pay for the witness's expenses in travelling to the court and in returning to his home or place of work, and

(2) a sum in respect of the period during which earnings or benefit are lost, or such lesser sum as it may be proved that the witness will lose as a result of his attendance at court in answer to the witness summons.

3.3

The sum referred to in 3.2(2) is to be based on the sums payable to witnesses attending the Crown Court.

3.4

Where the party issuing the witness summons wishes to serve it, they must:

(1) notify the court in writing that they wish to do so, and

(2) at the time of service offer the witness the sums mentioned in paragraph 3.2 above.

DEPOSITIONS

To be taken in England and Wales for use as evidence in proceedings in courts in England and Wales

4.1

A party may apply for an order for a person to be examined on oath before:

(1) a judge,

(2) an examiner of the court, or

(3) such other person as the court may appoint.

4.2

The party who obtains an order for the examination of a deponent before an examiner of the court must:

(1) apply to the Foreign Process Section at the Royal Courts of Justice for the allocation of an examiner; alternatively engage a person who satisfies the criteria in CPR 34.8 (3) (a) or (c);

(2) when allocated, provide the examiner with copies of all documents in the proceedings necessary to inform the examiner of the issues, and

(3) pay the deponent a sum to cover their travelling expenses to and from the examination and compensation for their loss of time.

4.3

In ensuring that the deponent's evidence is recorded in full, the court or the examiner may permit it to be recorded by audio or video, but the deposition must always be recorded in writing by them or by a competent shorthand writer or stenographer.

4.4

If the deposition is not recorded word for word, it must contain, as nearly as may be, the statement of the deponent; the examiner may record word for word any particular questions and answers which appear to them to have special importance.

4.5

If a deponent objects to answering any question or where any objection is taken to any question, the examiner must:

(1) record in the deposition or a document attached to it—

(a) the question,

(b) the nature of and grounds for the objection, and

(c) any answer given, and

(2) give their opinion as to the validity of the objection and must record it in the deposition or a document attached to it.

The court will decide as to the validity of the objection and any question of costs arising from it.

4.6

Documents and exhibits must:

(1) have an identifying number or letter marked on them by the examiner, and

(2) be preserved by the party or their legal representative who obtained the order for the examination, or as the court or the examiner may direct.

4.7

The examiner may put any question to the deponent as to:

(1) the meaning of any of his answers, or

(2) any matter arising in the course of the examination.

4.8

Where a deponent:

(1) fails to attend the examination, or

(2) refuses to:

(a) be sworn, or

(b) answer any lawful question, or

(c) produce any document,

the examiner will sign a certificate of such failure or refusal and may include in their certificate any comment as to the conduct of the deponent or of any person attending the examination.

4.9

The party who obtained the order for the examination must file the certificate with the court and may apply for an order that the deponent attend for examination or as may be. The application may be made without notice.

4.10

The court will make such order on the application as it thinks fit including an order for the deponent to pay any costs resulting from their failure or refusal.

4.11

A deponent who wilfully refuses to obey an order made against them under Part 34 may be proceeded against for contempt of court.

4.12

A deposition must:

(1) be signed by the examiner,

(2) have any amendments to it initialled by the examiner and the deponent,

(3) be endorsed by the examiner with—

(a) a statement of the time occupied by the examination, and
(b) a record of any refusal by the deponent to sign the deposition and of their reasons for not doing so, and

(4) be sent by the examiner to the court where the proceedings are taking place for filing on the court file.

4.13
Rule 34.14 deals with the fees and expenses of an examiner.

Depositions to be taken abroad for use as evidence in proceedings before courts in England and Wales

5.1
Where a party wishes to take a deposition from a person outside the jurisdiction, the High Court may order the issue of a letter of request to the judicial authorities of the country in which the proposed deponent is.

5.2
An application for an order referred to in paragraph 5.1 should be made by application notice in accordance with Part 23.

5.3
The documents which a party applying for an order for the issue of a letter of request must file with their application notice are set out in rule 34.13(6). They are as follows:

(1) a draft letter of request in the form set out in Annex A to this practice direction,
(2) a statement of the issues relevant to the proceedings,
(3) a list of questions or the subject matter of questions to be put to the proposed deponent,
(4) a translation of the documents in (1), (2) and (3) above, unless the proposed deponent is in a country of which English is an official language, and
(5) an undertaking to be responsible for the expenses of the Secretary of State (see Form PF78: Solicitor's Undertaking as to Expenses (rule 34.13(6)(b))

In addition to the documents listed above the party applying for the order must file a draft order.

5.4
The above documents should be filed with the Foreign Process Section of the Royal Courts of Justice.

5.5
The application will be dealt with by the Senior Master of the King's Bench Division of the High Court who will, if appropriate, sign the letter of request.

5.6
Attention is drawn to the provisions of rule 23.10 (application to vary or discharge an order made without notice).

5.7
If parties are in doubt as to whether a translation under paragraph 5.3(4) above is required, they should seek guidance from the Foreign Process Section.

5.8
A special examiner appointed under rule 34.13(4) may be the British Consul or the Consul-General or his deputy in the country where the evidence is to be taken if:

(1) there is in respect of that country a Civil Procedure Convention providing for the taking of evidence in that country for the assistance of proceedings in the High Court or other court in this country, or
(2) with the consent of the Secretary of State.

5.9
The provisions of paragraphs 4.1 to 4.12 above apply to the depositions referred to in this paragraph.

Depositions to be taken in England and Wales for use as evidence in proceedings before courts abroad pursuant to letters of request

6.1
Section II of Part 34 relating to obtaining evidence for foreign courts applies to letters of request and should be read in conjunction with this part of the practice direction.

6.2
The Evidence (Proceedings in Other Jurisdictions) Act 1975 applies to these depositions.

6.3
An application under rule 34.17 must be filed with the Foreign Process Section at the Royal Courts of Justice and include or exhibit—

(1) a statement of the issues relevant to the proceedings;

(2) a list of questions or the subject matter of questions to be put to the proposed deponent;

(3) a translation of the documents in (1) and (2) into English, if necessary; and

(4) where the application is made by an application notice under Part 23 in accordance with rule 34.17(2)(a), a draft order.

6.4
(1) The Senior Master will send to the Treasury Solicitor any request—

- (a) forwarded by the Secretary of State with a recommendation that effect should be given to the request without requiring an application to be made; or
- (b) received by him in pursuance of a Civil Procedure Convention providing for the taking of evidence of any person in England and Wales to assist a court or tribunal in a foreign country where no person is named in the document as the applicant.

(2) In relation to such a request, the Treasury Solicitor may, with the consent of the Treasury—

- (a) apply for an order under the 1975 Act; and
- (b) take such other steps as are necessary to give effect to the request.

6.5
The order for the deponent to attend and be examined together with the evidence upon which the order was made must be served on the deponent.

6.6
Attention is drawn to the provisions of rule 23.10 (application to vary or discharge an order made without notice).

6.7
Arrangements for the examination to take place at a specified time and place before an examiner of the court or such other person as the court may appoint shall be made by the applicant for the order and approved by the Senior Master.

6.8
The provisions of paragraph 4.2 to 4.12 apply to the depositions referred to in this paragraph, except that the examiner must send the deposition to the Senior Master.

(For further information about evidence see Part 32 and Practice Direction 32.)

Annex A Draft Letter of Request (where the Taking of Evidence Regulation does not apply)

To the Competent Judicial Authority of [name of court] in [country]

I [*name*] Senior Master of the King's Bench Division of the Senior Courts of England and Wales respectfully request the assistance of your court with regard to the following matters.

1
A claim is now pending in the Division of the High Court of Justice in England and Wales entitled as follows [*set out full title and claim number*] in which [*name*] of [*address*] is the claimant and [*name*] of [*address*] is the defendant.

2
The names and addresses of the representatives or agents of [*set out names and addresses of* representatives of the parties].

3
The claim by the claimant is for:-

(a) [*set out the nature of the claim*]
(b) [*the relief sought, and*]
(c) [*a summary of the facts.*]

4
It is necessary for the purposes of justice and for the due determination of the matters in dispute between the parties that you cause the following witnesses, who are resident within your jurisdiction, to be examined. The names and addresses of the witnesses are as follows:

5
The witnesses should be examined on oath or if that is not possible within your laws or is impossible of performance by reason of the internal practice and procedure of your court or by reason of practical difficulties, they should be examined in accordance with whatever procedure your laws provide for in these matters.

6
Either/
The witnesses should be examined in accordance with the list of questions annexed hereto.
Or/
The witnesses should be examined regarding [set out full details of evidence sought]
N.B. Where the witness is required to produce documents, these should be clearly identified.

7
I would ask that you cause me, or the agents of the parties (if appointed), to be informed of the date and place where the examination is to take place.

8
Finally, I request that you will cause the evidence of the said witnesses to be reduced into writing and all documents produced on such examinations to be duly marked for identification and that you will further be pleased to authenticate such examinations by the seal of your court or in such other way as is in accordance with your procedure and return the written evidence and documents produced to me addressed as follows:

Senior Master of the King's Bench Division
Royal Courts of Justice
Strand
London WC2A 2LL
England
Dated
Signed
Senior Master of the King's Bench Division

PART 35 EXPERTS AND ASSESSORS

35.1 Duty to restrict expert evidence

Expert evidence shall be restricted to that which is reasonably required to resolve the proceedings.

35.2 Interpretation and definitions

(1) A reference to an 'expert' in this Part is a reference to a person who has been instructed to give or prepare expert evidence for the purpose of proceedings.

(2) 'Single joint expert' means an expert instructed to prepare a report for the court on behalf of two or more of the parties (including the claimant) to the proceedings.

35.3 Experts—overriding duty to the court

(1) It is the duty of experts to help the court on matters within their expertise.

(2) This duty overrides any obligation to the person from whom experts have received instructions or by whom they are paid.

35.4 Court's power to restrict expert evidence

(1) No party may call an expert or put in evidence an expert's report without the court's permission.

(2) When parties apply for permission they must provide an estimate of the costs of the proposed expert evidence and identify—

- (a) the field in which expert evidence is required and the issues which the expert evidence will address; and
- (b) where practicable, the name of the proposed expert.

(3) If permission is granted it shall be in relation only to the expert named or the field identified under paragraph (2). The order granting permission may specify the issues which the expert evidence should address.

(3A) Where a claim has been allocated to the small claims track or the fast track, if permission is given for expert evidence, it will normally be given for evidence from only one expert on a particular issue.

(3B) In a soft tissue injury claim, permission—

- (a) may normally only be given for one expert medical report;
- (b) may not be given initially unless the medical report is a fixed cost medical report. Where the claimant seeks permission to obtain a further medical report, if the report is from a medical expert in any of the following disciplines—
  - (i) Consultant Orthopaedic Surgeon;
  - (ii) Consultant in Accident and Emergency Medicine;
  - (iii) General Practitioner registered with the General Medical Council; or
  - (iv) Physiotherapist registered with the Health and Care Professions Council,

the report must be a fixed cost medical report.

(3C) In a claim for a whiplash injury, whether or not it is part of a claim for other injuries—

- (a) permission—
  - (i) may normally only be given for one expert medical report in respect of the claim for the whiplash injury; and
  - (ii) may not be given initially unless the medical report is a fixed cost medical report; and
- (b) where the claimant seeks permission to obtain a further medical report in respect of the claim for the whiplash injury only, the report must be a fixed cost medical report if the report is from a medical expert in any of the following disciplines—
  - (i) Consultant Orthopaedic Surgeon;
  - (ii) Consultant in Accident and Emergency Medicine;
  - (iii) General Practitioner registered with the General Medical Council; or
  - (iv) Physiotherapist registered with the Health and Care Professions Council.

(3D) Where, in respect of a claim for a whiplash injury, the claimant lives outside England and Wales, but chooses to be examined in England or Wales, paragraph (3C) applies.

(3E) Where the claimant obtains a medical report in respect of a more serious injury suffered on the same occasion as the whiplash injury, the claimant may be given permission to use that report instead of a fixed cost medical report under paragraph (3C) provided that—

(a) the report is from a doctor who is listed on the General Medical Council's Specialist Register; and

(b) the report provides evidence of the whiplash injury.

(3F) Unless paragraph (3D) applies, where, in respect of a claim for a whiplash injury—

(a) the claimant lives outside England and Wales;

(b) permission is given for a medical report,

the medical report (or, if there is more than one report, the first report) must be obtained from a person who is recognised by the country in which they practise as—

(i) being a medical expert; and

(ii) having the required medical qualifications for the purposes of diagnosis and prognosis of a whiplash injury.

(3G) In this rule—

(a) in respect of a soft tissue injury claim, 'fixed cost medical report' and 'soft tissue injury claim' have the meanings ascribed to them by paragraph 1.1(10A) and (16A), respectively, of the Pre-Action Protocol for Low Value Personal Injury Claims in Road Traffic Accidents; and

(b) in respect of a claim for a whiplash injury, 'fixed cost medical report' and 'whiplash injury' have the meanings ascribed to them by paragraph 1.2(17) and (38), respectively, of the Pre-Action Protocol for Personal Injury Claims Below the Small Claims Limit in Road Traffic Accidents

(4) The court may limit the amount of a party's expert's fees and expenses that may be recovered from any other party.

35.5 General requirement for expert evidence to be given in a written report

(1) Expert evidence is to be given in a written report unless the court directs otherwise.

(2) If a claim is on the small claims track or the fast track, the court will not direct an expert to attend a hearing unless it is necessary to do so in the interests of justice.

35.6 Written questions to experts

(1) A party may put written questions about an expert's report (which must be proportionate) to—

(a) an expert instructed by another party; or

(b) a single joint expert appointed under rule 35.7.

(2) Written questions under paragraph (1)—

(a) may be put once only;

(b) must be put within 28 days of service of the expert's report; and

(c) must be for the purpose only of clarification of the report,

unless in any case—

(i) the court gives permission; or

(ii) the other party agrees.

(3) An expert's answers to questions put in accordance with paragraph (1) shall be treated as part of the expert's report.

(4) Where—

(a) a party has put a written question to an expert instructed by another party; and

(b) the expert does not answer that question,

the court may make one or both of the following orders in relation to the party who instructed the expert—

(i) that the party may not rely on the evidence of that expert; or

(ii) that the party may not recover the fees and expenses of that expert from any other party.

35.7 Court's power to direct that evidence is to be given by a single joint expert

(1) Where two or more parties wish to submit expert evidence on a particular issue, the court may direct that the evidence on that issue is to be given by a single joint expert.

(2) Where the parties who wish to submit the evidence ('the relevant parties') cannot agree who should be the single joint expert, the court may—

(a) select the expert from a list prepared or identified by the relevant parties; or

(b) direct that the expert be selected in such other manner as the court may direct.

35.8 Instructions to a single joint expert

(1) Where the court gives a direction under rule 35.7 for a single joint expert to be used, any relevant party may give instructions to the expert.

(2) When a party gives instructions to the expert that party must, at the same time, send a copy to the other relevant parties.

(3) The court may give directions about—

(a) the payment of the expert's fees and expenses; and

(b) any inspection, examination or experiments which the expert wishes to carry out.

(4) The court may, before an expert is instructed—

(a) limit the amount that can be paid by way of fees and expenses to the expert; and

(b) direct that some or all of the relevant parties pay that amount into court.

(5) Unless the court otherwise directs, the relevant parties are jointly and severally liable for the payment of the expert's fees and expenses.

35.9 Power of court to direct a party to provide information

Where a party has access to information which is not reasonably available to another party, the court may direct the party who has access to the information to—

(a) prepare and file a document recording the information; and

(b) serve a copy of that document on the other party.

35.10 Contents of report

(1) An expert's report must comply with the requirements set out in Practice Direction 35.

(2) At the end of an expert's report there must be a statement that the expert understands and has complied with their duty to the court.

(3) The expert's report must state the substance of all material instructions, whether written or oral, on the basis of which the report was written.

(4) The instructions referred to in paragraph (3) shall not be privileged against disclosure but the court will not, in relation to those instructions—

(a) order disclosure of any specific document; or

(b) permit any questioning in court, other than by the party who instructed the expert,

unless it is satisfied that there are reasonable grounds to consider the statement of instructions given under paragraph (3) to be inaccurate or incomplete.

35.11 Use by one party of expert's report disclosed by another

Where a party has disclosed an expert's report, any party may use that expert's report as evidence at the trial.

35.12 Discussions between experts

(1) The court may, at any stage, direct a discussion between experts for the purpose of requiring the experts to—

(a) identify and discuss the expert issues in the proceedings; and

(b) where possible, reach an agreed opinion on those issues.

(2) The court may specify the issues which the experts must discuss.

(3) The court may direct that following a discussion between the experts they must prepare a statement for the court setting out those issues on which—

(a) they agree; and

(b) they disagree, with a summary of their reasons for disagreeing.

(4) The content of the discussion between the experts shall not be referred to at the trial unless the parties agree.

(5) Where experts reach agreement on an issue during their discussions, the agreement shall not bind the parties unless the parties expressly agree to be bound by the agreement.

35.13 Consequence of failure to disclose expert's report

A party who fails to disclose an expert's report may not use the report at the trial or call the expert to give evidence orally unless the court gives permission.

35.14 Expert's right to ask court for directions

(1) Experts may file written requests for directions for the purpose of assisting them in carrying out their functions.

(2) Experts must, unless the court orders otherwise, provide copies of the proposed requests for directions under paragraph (1)—

(a) to the party instructing them, at least 7 days before they file the requests; and

(b) to all other parties, at least 4 days before they file them.

(3) The court, when it gives directions, may also direct that a party be served with a copy of the directions.

35.15 Assessors

(1) This rule applies where the court appoints one or more persons under section 70 of the Senior Courts Act 1981 or section 63 of the County Courts Act 1984 as an assessor.

(2) An assessor will assist the court in dealing with a matter in which the assessor has skill and experience.

(3) An assessor will take such part in the proceedings as the court may direct and in particular the court may direct an assessor to—

(a) prepare a report for the court on any matter at issue in the proceedings; and

(b) attend the whole or any part of the trial to advise the court on any such matter.

(4) If an assessor prepares a report for the court before the trial has begun—

(a) the court will send a copy to each of the parties; and

(b) the parties may use it at trial.

(5) The remuneration to be paid to an assessor is to be determined by the court and will form part of the costs of the proceedings.

(6) The court may order any party to deposit in the court office a specified sum in respect of an assessor's fees and, where it does so, the assessor will not be asked to act until the sum has been deposited.

(7) Paragraphs (5) and (6) do not apply where the remuneration of the assessor is to be paid out of money provided by Parliament.

PRACTICE DIRECTION 35

EXPERTS AND ASSESSORS

This Practice Direction supplements CPR Part 35

Introduction

1

Part 35 is intended to limit the use of oral expert evidence to that which is reasonably required. In addition, where possible, matters requiring expert evidence should be dealt with by only one expert. Experts and those instructing them are expected to have regard to the guidance contained in the Guidance for the Instruction of Experts in Civil Claims 2014 at www.judiciary.gov.uk. (Further guidance on experts is contained in Annex C to the Practice Direction (Pre-Action Conduct)).

Expert Evidence—General Requirements

2.1

Expert evidence should be the independent product of the expert uninfluenced by the pressures of litigation.

2.2

Experts should assist the court by providing objective, unbiased opinions on matters within their expertise, and should not assume the role of an advocate.

2.3

Experts should consider all material facts, including those which might detract from their opinions.

2.4

Experts should make it clear—

(a) when a question or issue falls outside their expertise; and

(b) when they are not able to reach a definite opinion, for example because they have insufficient information.

2.5

If, after producing a report, an expert's view changes on any material matter, such change of view should be communicated to all the parties without delay, and when appropriate to the court.

2.6

(1) In a soft tissue injury claim, where permission is given for a fixed cost medical report, the first report must be obtained from an accredited medical expert selected via the MedCo Portal (website at: www.medco.org.uk).

(1A) In a claim for a whiplash injury, whether or not it is part of a claim for other injuries—

(a) where in respect of the claim for a whiplash injury, permission is given for a fixed cost medical report, the first report must be obtained from an accredited medical expert selected via the MedCo Portal;

(b) where the claimant lives outside England and Wales, but chooses to be examined for the purposes of a medical report in England or Wales, paragraph (a) applies;

(c) where the claimant obtains a medical report in respect of a more serious injury suffered on the same occasion as the whiplash injury, where permission is given, the claimant may use that report instead of a fixed costs medical report under paragraph (a) provided that—

(i) the report is from a doctor who is listed on the General Medical Council's Specialist Register; and

(ii) the report provides evidence of the whiplash injury; and

(d) unless paragraph (b) applies, in any other case where the claimant lives outside England and Wales, the medical report in respect of the claim for the whiplash injury (or, if there is more than one report, the first report) must be from a person who is recognised by the country in which they practise as—

(i) being a medical expert; and

(ii) having the required qualifications for the purposes of diagnosis and prognosis of a whiplash injury.

(2) The cost of obtaining a further report from an expert not listed in rule 35.4(3C)(a) to (d) or (3C)(b)(i) to (iv) is not subject to rules 45.62(2)(b), but the use of that expert and the cost must be justified.

(3) In this paragraph—

(a) in respect of a soft tissue injury claim, 'accredited medical expert', 'fixed cost medical report', 'MedCo', and 'soft tissue injury claim' have the same meaning as in paragraph 1.1(A1), (10A), (12A) and (16A), respectively, of the Pre-Action Protocol for Low Value Personal Injury Claims in Road Traffic Accidents; and

(b) in respect of a claim for a whiplash injury, 'fixed cost medical report', 'accredited medical expert', 'MedCo', and 'whiplash injury' have the same meaning as in paragraph 1.2(1), (17), (19) and (38) of the Pre-Action Protocol for Personal Injury Claims Below the Small Claims Limit in Road Traffic Accidents.

Form and Content of an Expert's Report

3.1

An expert's report should be addressed to the court and not to the party from whom the expert has received instructions.

3.2

An expert's report must:

(1) give details of the expert's qualifications;

(2) give details of any literature or other material which has been relied on in making the report;

(3) contain a statement setting out the substance of all facts and instructions which are material to the opinions expressed in the report or upon which those opinions are based;

(4) make clear which of the facts stated in the report are within the expert's own knowledge;

(5) say who carried out any examination, measurement, test or experiment which the expert has used for the report, give the qualifications of that person, and say whether or not the test or experiment has been carried out under the expert's supervision;

(6) where there is a range of opinion on the matters dealt with in the report—

(a) summarise the range of opinions; and

(b) give reasons for the expert's own opinion;

(7) contain a summary of the conclusions reached;

(8) if the expert is not able to give an opinion without qualification, state the qualification; and

(9) contain a statement that the expert—

(a) understands their duty to the court, and has complied with that duty; and

(b) is aware of the requirements of Part 35, this practice direction and the Guidance for Instruction of Experts in Civil Claims 2014.

3.3

An expert's report must be verified by a statement of truth in the following form—

I confirm that I have made clear which facts and matters referred to in this report are within my own knowledge and which are not. Those that are within my own knowledge I confirm to be true. The opinions I have expressed represent my true and complete professional opinions on the matters to which they refer.

I understand that proceedings for contempt of court may be brought against anyone who makes, or causes to be made, a false statement in a document verified by a statement of truth without an honest belief in its truth.

(Part 22 deals with statements of truth. Rule 32.14 sets out the consequences of verifying a document containing a false statement without an honest belief in its truth.)

Information

4

Under rule 35.9 the court may direct a party with access to information, which is not reasonably available to another party to serve on that other party a document, which records the information. The document served must include sufficient details of all the facts, tests, experiments and assumptions which underlie any part of the information to enable the party on whom it is served to make, or to obtain, a proper interpretation of the information and an assessment of its significance.

Instructions

5

Cross-examination of experts on the contents of their instructions will not be allowed unless the court permits it (or unless the party who gave the instructions consents). Before it gives permission the court must be satisfied that there are reasonable grounds to consider that the statement in the report of the substance of the instructions is inaccurate or incomplete. If the court is so satisfied, it will allow the cross-examination where it appears to be in the interests of justice.

Questions to Experts

6.1

Where a party sends a written question or questions under rule 35.6 direct to an expert, a copy of the questions must, at the same time, be sent to the other party or parties.

6.2

The party or parties instructing the expert must pay any fees charged by that expert for answering questions put under rule 35.6. This does not affect any decision of the court as to the party who is ultimately to bear the expert's fees.

Single joint expert

7

When considering whether to give permission for the parties to rely on expert evidence and whether that evidence should be from a single joint expert the court will take into account all the circumstances in particular, whether:

(a) it is proportionate to have separate experts for each party on a particular issue with reference to—
  (i) the amount in dispute;
  (ii) the importance to the parties; and
  (iii) the complexity of the issue;
(b) the instruction of a single joint expert is likely to assist the parties and the court to resolve the issue more speedily and in a more cost-effective way than separately instructed experts;
(c) expert evidence is to be given on the issue of liability, causation or quantum;
(d) the expert evidence falls within a substantially established area of knowledge which is unlikely to be in dispute or there is likely to be a range of expert opinion;
(e) a party has already instructed an expert on the issue in question and whether or not that was done in compliance with any practice direction or relevant pre-action protocol;
(f) questions put in accordance with rule 35.6 are likely to remove the need for the other party to instruct an expert if one party has already instructed an expert;
(g) questions put to a single joint expert may not conclusively deal with all issues that may require testing prior to trial;
(h) a conference may be required with the legal representatives, experts and other witnesses which may make instruction of a single joint expert impractical; and
(i) a claim to privilege makes the instruction of any expert as a single joint expert inappropriate.

Orders

8

Where an order requires an act to be done by an expert, or otherwise affects an expert, the party instructing that expert must serve a copy of the order on the expert. The claimant must serve the order on a single joint expert.

Discussions between experts

9.1

Unless directed by the court discussions between experts are not mandatory. Parties must consider, with their experts, at an early stage, whether there is likely to be any useful purpose in holding an experts' discussion and if so when.

9.2

The purpose of discussions between experts is not for experts to settle cases but to agree and narrow issues and in particular to identify:

(i) the extent of the agreement between them;
(ii) the points of and short reasons for any disagreement;

(iii) action, if any, which may be taken to resolve any outstanding points of disagreement; and
(iv) any further material issues not raised and the extent to which these issues are agreed.

9.3
Where the experts are to meet, the parties must discuss and if possible agree whether an agenda is necessary, and if so attempt to agree one that helps the experts to focus on the issues which need to be discussed. The agenda must not be in the form of leading questions or hostile in tone.

9.4
Unless ordered by the court, or agreed by all parties, and the experts, neither the parties nor their legal representatives may attend experts discussions.

9.5
If the legal representatives do attend—
(i) they should not normally intervene in the discussion, except to answer questions put to them by the experts or to advise on the law; and
(ii) the experts may if they so wish hold part of their discussions in the absence of the legal representatives.

9.6
A statement must be prepared by the experts dealing with paragraphs 9.2(i)–(iv) above. Individual copies of the statements must be signed by the experts at the conclusion of the discussion, or as soon thereafter as practicable, and in any event within 7 days. Copies of the statements must be provided to the parties no later than 14 days after signing.

9.7
Experts must give their own opinions to assist the court and do not require the authority of the parties to sign a joint statement.

9.8
If an expert significantly alters an opinion, the joint statement must include a note or addendum by that expert explaining the change of opinion.

Assessors

10.1
An assessor may be appointed to assist the court under rule 35.15. Not less than 21 days before making any such appointment, the court will notify each party in writing of the name of the proposed assessor, of the matter in respect of which the assistance of the assessor will be sought and of the qualifications of the assessor to give that assistance.

10.2
Where any person has been proposed for appointment as an assessor, any party may object to that person either personally or in respect of that person's qualification.

10.3
Any such objection must be made in writing and filed with the court within 7 days of receipt of the notification referred to in paragraph 10.1 and will be taken into account by the court in deciding whether or not to make the appointment.

10.4
Copies of any report prepared by the assessor will be sent to each of the parties but the assessor will not give oral evidence or be open to cross-examination or questioning.

Concurrent expert evidence

11.1
At any stage in the proceedings the court may direct that some or all of the evidence of experts from like disciplines shall be given concurrently. The procedure set out in paragraph 11.4 shall apply in respect of any part of the evidence which is to be given concurrently.

11.2
To the extent that the expert evidence is not to be given concurrently, the court may direct the evidence to be given in any appropriate manner. This may include a direction for the experts from like disciplines to give their evidence and be cross-examined on an issue-by-issue basis, so that each party calls its expert or experts to give evidence in relation to a particular issue, followed by the other parties calling their expert or experts to give evidence in relation to that issue (and so on for each of the expert issues which are to be addressed in this manner).

11.3
The court may set an agenda for the taking of expert evidence concurrently or on an issue-by-issue basis, or may direct that the parties agree such an agenda subject to the approval of the court. In either case, the agenda should be based upon the areas of disagreement identified in the experts' joint statements made pursuant to rule 35.12.

11.4
Where expert evidence is to be given concurrently, then (after the relevant experts have each taken the oath or affirmed) in relation to each issue on the agenda, and subject to the judge's discretion to modify the procedure—

(1) the judge will initiate the discussion by asking the experts, in turn, for their views in relation to the issues on the agenda. Once an expert has expressed a view the judge may ask questions about it. At one or more appropriate stages when questioning a particular expert, the judge may invite the other expert to comment or to ask that expert's own questions of the first expert;

(2) after the process set out in (1) has been completed for any issue (or all issues), the judge will invite the parties' representatives to ask questions of the experts. Such questioning should be directed towards:

- (a) testing the correctness of an expert's view;
- (b) seeking clarification of an expert's view; or
- (c) eliciting evidence on any issue (or on any aspect of an issue) which has been omitted from consideration during the process set out in (1); and

(3) after the process set out in (2) has been completed in relation to any issue (or all issues), the judge may summarise the experts' different positions on the issue and ask them to confirm or correct that summary.

Index